John Singer Sargent

Portraits of the 1890s

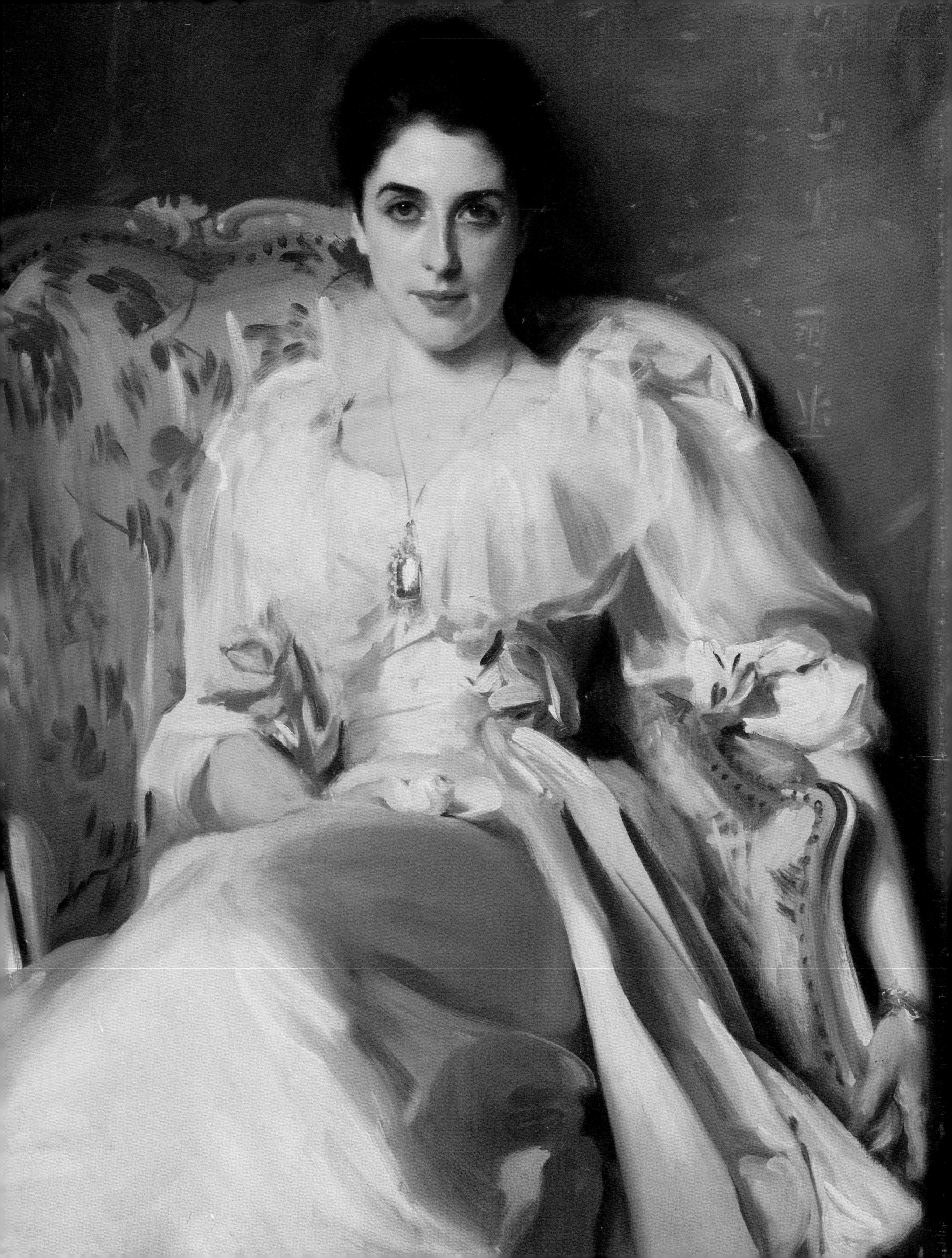

JOHN SINGER SARGENT

PORTRAITS OF THE 1890s

COMPLETE PAINTINGS VOLUME II

Richard Ormond

Elaine Kilmurray

Published for
The Paul Mellon Centre for Studies in British Art
by Yale University Press New Haven and London

Library of Congress Control Number: 2002110823

ISBN 0 300 09067 6

Designed by Kate Gallimore
Typeset in Bembo by SNP Best-set Typesetter
Printed in Singapore

The catalogue raisonné project has received substantial financial support from

The Coe Kerr Gallery, New York, 1980–92

Adelson Galleries, New York, since 1994

Illustration on page ii:
detail of no. 286, *Lady Agnew of Lochnaw.*

Illustration on page vi:
detail of no. 318, *Helen Sears.*

Illustration on page xxvi:
detail of no. 368, *Lady Elcho, Mrs Adeane and Mrs Tennant* or *The Wyndham Sisters.*

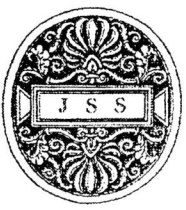

The Complete Paintings of John Singer Sargent

is a project supported by Adelson Galleries, Inc., New York, in collaboration with

Warren Adelson and Elizabeth Oustinoff

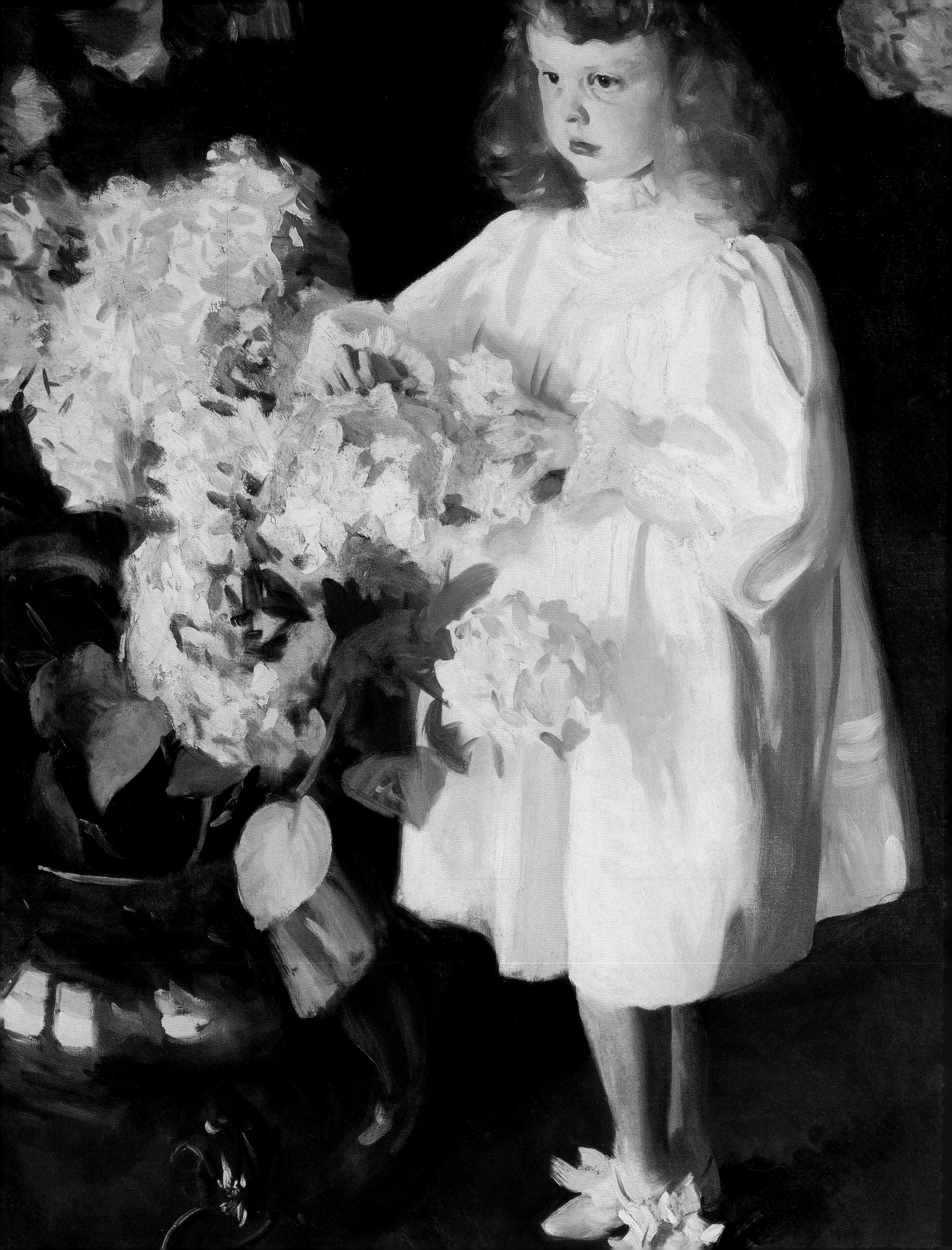

CONTENTS

PREFACE

This second volume of the catalogue raisonné, detailing the portraits of John Singer Sargent from 1890 to 1900, is published four years after the first volume covering his early portraits. My co-author and I had hoped that there would be a shorter interval between the two, but the vastly greater size and scale of the second and third volumes has made the task of finalizing the text a daunting one. My own role in this has been minimal, and the burden of incorporating new research and of checking the thousands of references has fallen entirely on Elaine Kilmurray. She is the guiding spirit of this volume and, though I wrote some early entries, the wealth of new material is largely due to her research, which has continued up to the present time.

Volume four of the catalogue, figure subjects and landscapes 1874–89, is already well under way, and should be completed in the not too distant future. It has been facilitated by my appointment as the Samuel H. Kress Professor at the Center for Advanced Study in the Visual Arts at the National Gallery of Art in Washington, D.C. I am deeply grateful to the trustees of the Kress Foundation and to the director and trustees of the National Gallery of Art for the research opportunities offered by this appointment. Two more volumes on the later figure subjects and landscapes will follow, together with a volume on the murals by Mary Crawford Volk.

The history of the catalogue raisonné project, going back to 1947 when David McKibbin first began the task of collating Sargent's work, is told in the preface to the previous volume. I must, however, once more give credit to the immense support, scholarly, technical, moral and financial, we have received from Warren Adelson. Without him, there would be no database, no catalogue and no publication. In honour of his contribution and commitment, we dedicate this volume to him. We are also deeply indebted to Elizabeth Oustinoff, a director of Adelson Galleries, who is another of our partners and fellow scholars. She runs the Sargent database in New York, and she has been a tower of strength, advice and support throughout the project. We acknowledge elsewhere the invaluable administrative and research help we have received from Cynthia Bird and Richard H. Finnegan of Adelson Galleries.

John Nicoll our publisher, who so successfully launched volume one of the catalogue, has inspired our confidence and contributed significantly to the way in which the material is presented. Kate Gallimore has once again edited and designed the book, thus giving unity and a sense of continuity to the series. The elegance and clarity of volume one has been much remarked on. Finally we must thank Brian Allen and The Paul Mellon Centre for Studies in British Art for continuing to support the project financially.

Richard Ormond   *Washington, D.C.*

We begin our acknowledgments as we ended them in volume one of the catalogue raisonné with our profound thanks to Warren Adelson whose vision, dedication and commitment transformed the project from an idea to a reality. We extend our warmest thanks to our colleagues and friends at Adelson Galleries: Elizabeth Oustinoff, ever our first point of contact, has supervised research in America with an intelligent eye and efficient hand and her practical and moral support have been invaluable; Richard Finnegan's cultured approach and forensic detective work has illuminated many a dark corner, and his knowledge of the American art world and its history has rendered some particularly difficult provenances more cogent and precise; Cynthia Bird has assembled a daunting range of photography and organized issues of rights and reproductions in America with calm assurance and commendable professionalism. For her early work on the manuscript we would like to thank Carol Flechner. Our thanks also to Jan Adelson, and to Fran Bird, Chris Blythe, Tom Burr, Pamela Ivinski, Andrea Maltese, Susan Mason, Caroline Owens, and Richard Reilly.

We continue to be indebted to our colleagues in institutions with significant collections of Sargent's work. We would, in particular, like to thank Malcolm Rogers, Erica Hirshler, Carol Troyen and Sue Welsh Reed at the Museum of Fine Arts, Boston; Barbara Dayer Gallati at the Brooklyn Museum of Art; Miriam Stewart and Kerry Schauber, Drawing Department, Fogg Art Museum, Cambridge, Massachusetts; David Fraser Jenkins at the Tate Gallery, London, and Nicolai Cikovsky Jr and D. Dodge Thompson at the National Gallery of Art, Washington, D.C.

We thank Barbara Weinberg and Stephanie Herdrich at the Metropolitan Museum of Art, New York, for their help with the paintings in the museum's collection and particularly for their input into the material for *Mrs Hugh Hammersley* (no. 284), which resulted in a redrafted entry. We are grateful to George T. M. Shackelford for his help in identifying the painting by Monet mentioned in *Lady with a Blue Veil* (no. 261). We would like to express our gratitude to Conall Macfarlane of Christie's, London, for his invaluable advice on furniture and accessories and to Jacob Simon of the National Portrait Gallery, London, for sharing with us his work on Sargent's frames, a subject we intend to pursue in later volumes.

We are fortunate in our fellow Sargent scholars and we acknowledge our great debt to them, notably Trevor Fairbrother, Marc Simpson and Mary Crawford Volk. We watch with pleasure a new generation of Sargent scholars at work, among them Leigh Culver, Jane Dini, Stephanie Herdrich, Lacey Jordan and Susan Sidlauskas, and read with admiration work of commentators such as Kathleen Adler, Elizabeth Prettejohn and Sally Promey.

We reserve special thanks for the long-suffering members of the Ormond family, whose generosity and support have never failed us, for John and Judy Fox, Ben Harrison and the late Sally Harrison, whose familial loyalty and interest have been a constant, and for those private collectors who have tolerated our endless enquiries and intrusions with goodwill and forbearance.

We would also like to thank the following for their help with particular queries: Lady Abdy; Louise Ambler; Nicole Anselona; Andrea Barnwell; Julian Barrow; Thomas J. Barry; Bernard Barryte; Judith Barter, Art Institute of Chicago; Elizabeth Barthleman; Kurt Bell; Laurie Benson, National Gallery of Victoria, Melbourne; Diana Berry; Louise Tharaud Brasher; Susanne Brendel-Pandich; Douglas Brown; Julius Bryant; Anne Buddle; Christopher Burke, Quesada/Burke; Alice Carter; Edward Cazalet; Dottore Marco Chiarini; Lady Aline Cholmondeley; the Marquess of Cholmondeley; Margie Christian; Dottore Arabella Cifani; Sarah Cloud, Worcester Art Museum, Massachusetts; Steven Comen; Helen Cooper, Yale University Art Gallery; Lord Crathorne; Prudence Cuming Associates, London; Wallace Dailey, curator of the Theodore Roosevelt Collection, Houghton Library, Harvard University; Caroline Dakers; April Dance, Artists' General Benevolent Institution, London; Oliver Davis, Roya College of Music, London; Owen R. Davison; Peter Day; Ian A. C. Dejardin; the late Sir John Dilke; Mary Adair Dockery, Evergreen House, Johns Hopkins University, Baltimore; Richard Dorment; Peter Drummey, Massachusetts Historical Society, Boston; Odile Duff; Mildred Eisele; Barbara Emery; the late Sir Brinsley Ford; Peter Funnell, curator, Nineteenth-Century Collection, National Portrait Gallery, London; Mary E. Garofalo, the Alan Mason Chesney Medical Archives, the Johns Hopkins Medical Institutions, Baltimore; Lori M. Garst; Juliette Gawade; Laura Genninger; Hilliard Goldfarb; Veronica Franklin Gould; Edward Griffiths; David F. Guertin Jr; Jonathan Harding; Gregory Hedberg; Raymond Hemmlinger, the Hampden-Booth Theatre Library, New York; the late Major J. H. Hirsch; Helen Lefkowitz Horowitz; Mrs C. D. Howard-Johnson; James H. Hutson;

William Hutton; Francina Irwin; Mrs E. M. James; Donna Seldin Janis; Richard H. Jefferies, the Watts Gallery, Compton, Surrey; Lacey Jordan; Elvine R. King; James H. Kirkman; Mary-Jo Kline; John Hay and Rockefeller Libraries, Brown University; Hans P. Kraus Jr; Geneviève Lacambre and Dominique Lobstein, Musée d'Orsay, Paris; Mrs George Lewis; lan F. Locke; James Lomax; Mrs G. S. McElroy; Patrick McMahon; J. Robert Maguire; Colin Manson, Advocates Library, Parliament House, Edinburgh; R. Russell Maylone; Melissa de Medeiros, M. Knoedler & Co., New York; David Meschutt; Lucia T. Miller; Dottore Franco Monetti; Christopher Monkhouse; Margaret S. Moore; Eileen Moran, Wellgate Library, Local Studies Department, Dundee; Tim Moreton, National Portrait Gallery, London; Anne F. Morris; Janice Murray, Dundee Arts and Heritage, MacManus Galleries, Dundee; Richard Mortimer, Keeper of the Muniments, Westminster Abbey, London; Steven Nash, M. H. de Young Memorial Museum, San Francisco; Sarah Newton, National Maritime Museum, Greenwich; Francis Nichols; Charles Noble, formerly of the Royal Collection and now Deputy Keeper, Devonshire Collection, Chatsworth; Stephen Nonack; the late Stanley Olson; Yvonne Holmes Packer; David R. Paton; the late Mrs F. Winifred Pedley; Phoebe Peebles; Lady Penn; Hanna Pennock; Mary Louise Pixley; Stephen D. Pratt; Hayden Russell Proud, South African National Gallery, Cape Town; Lord Pym; Lord Rathcreedan; Dr Wolfgang Rebetzky; Claudie Ressort; Jacqueline Ridge; Joseph Rishel; Ellen Roberts; Meg Robertson; Julia Rayer Rolfe; Helene A. Rundell; Charles Saumarez Smith; Mary Saunders, Harvard Club of New York City; Gail Sefarty; Anna B. Selfridge; Nancy Rivard Shaw; Susan Sinclair; Sir Reresby Sitwell; Anna Southall; Theodore E. Stebbins Jr; Robert G. Stewart; Susan E. Strickler; Major-General Sir John Swinton; Michael Tollemache; Juliette Tomlinson; Michael Tree; Julian Treuhertz; Patricia Curtis Vigano; Julia Waley; R. K. Watson; the Earl of Wemyss and March; Arnold Whitridge; the late Daniel Wildenstein; Victoria Williams; John Wilson; Carol Wojtowicz; Angus Wrenn; Michael Wynne; Kai Kin Yung; Elaine Zair; Judith Zilczer; Dr Jurgen Zimmer, Kunst Bibliotheque, Berlin.

We would like to thank the staff of the following libraries and institutions for responding to our enquiries and for making material available to us: Archives of American Art in New York and Washington, D.C.; Archives of the Musée du Louvre, Paris; Bibliothèque Nationale, Paris; Bodleian Library, Oxford; the Library of the Boston Athenaeum; British Library, London and the Newspaper Library, Colindale; Fine Arts Department, Boston Public Library; University Library, Cambridge; Special Collections, the Millar Library, Colby College, Waterville, Maine; Conway Library, Courtauld Institute of Art, London; Fogg Art Museum, Cambridge, Massachusetts; Frick Art Reference Library, New York; Houghton Library and Pusey Library, Harvard University, Cambridge, Massachusetts; archives of the Isabella Stewart Gardner Museum, Boston; Library of Congress, Washington, D.C.; London Library; Massachusetts Historical Society, Boston; National Portrait Gallery, London; New-York Historical Society; New York Public Library; Music Division, New York Public Library for the Performing Arts; Pierpont Morgan Library, New York; the library of the Royal Academy, London; the Tate Gallery archive; National Art Library, Victoria and Albert Museum, London; Witt Library, London; Bienecke Library, Yale University, New Haven.

We acknowledge the help of the following individuals or organizations who have helped us to trace paintings whose whereabouts were unknown: Berry-Hill Galleries, New York; Charles O'Brien, Bonhams & Brooks, London; Butterfield & Butterfield, San Francisco; Jay Cantor; Andrew L. Schoelkopf and Paul Provost of Christie's, New York; Rachel Hidderley of Christie's, London; Peter H. Davidson, New York; Peyton Skipwith and Andrew Macintosh Patrick, The Fine Art Society, London; Hirschl & Adler Galleries, New York; Meredith Long & Company, Houston, Texas; Peter Nahum; James Rawlin, Phillips, London; Galerie Schmit, Paris; Max Schweitzer, New York; Perry Rathbone and Dara Mitchell, Sotheby's, New York; Ira Spanierman, New York; Richard M. Thune, New York; Vose Galleries, Boston.

We appreciate the public spiritedness of those museums who have waived or abridged the usual rights and reproduction fees thus enabling us to reproduce works from their collections in colour in the catalogue.

At Yale University Press, we thank John Nicoll and Kate Gallimore for coping magnificently with the demanding detail of the material which comprises the present volume, and for their patience in waiting for it to be delivered to them.

It is usual on these occasions to express gratitude to one's family, and our thanks here are more than nominal. Our families, Leonée, Augustus and Marcus Ormond and Emma Griffin, and Christopher, Eleanor, Antonia and Benedict Calnan, have contributed to the present volume in a variety of guises, as scholars, researchers or photographers, couriers, photocopy operators or general factotums, and they have been graceful in accepting all the time the catalogue has taken us away from them.

ERRATUM   Sargent's visit to Bologna with Vernon Lee took place in 1873, *not* 1872. Vernon Lee misremembered the date, which was followed by her biographer, Peter Gunn, and by us in our chronology in the first printing of volume one of the catalogue raisonné (*Early Portraits*, p. xii). The primary source are letters from Fitzwilliam Sargent to George Bemis 26 September [1873] and 29 October [1873] (MHS). Neither has a year date, but both can be securely dated to 1873 on internal evidence. We are grateful to Stephanie Herdrich for drawing the discrepancy to our attention and for the 26 September reference. Stanley Olson recorded the Bologna visit correctly as 1873 in his biography (Olson 1986, p. 27) and in his chronology in Hills *et al.* 1986, p. 277. The visit is recalled in a letter from Vernon Lee to Sargent of 4 September 1874 (Private Collection), see Ormond, *Colby Library Quarterly*, 1970, pp. 158–9, 160.

1890

Sargent and his younger sister Violet had sailed to New York on 4 December 1889. Violet went on to Boston, where she was a guest of Mr and Mrs Charles Fairchild.

January: New York: Sargent stays at the Clarendon Hotel on Fourth Avenue and Twentieth Street. His friend James Carroll Beckwith makes arrangements for him to use Dora Wheeler Keith's studio at 115 East Twenty-third Street. Other friends Frank and Lily Millet are nearby on Twenty-third Street.

15 January: working on a portrait of Richard McCurdy (no. 240).[1] Paints a number of portraits: the actor Edwin Booth (no. 232) for The Players, New York, and portraits of George Washington Vanderbilt, Beatrice Goelet and Homer Saint-Gaudens and his mother, the latter in exchange for a portrait relief of Violet by Augustus Saint-Gaudens (nos 247, 239 and 243).

27 January–8 February: exhibits *A Summer Morning* (*A Morning Walk*) at the midwinter exhibition of the St Botolph Club in Boston.

Towards the end of the month, makes a brief visit to Boston for about ten days, where he probably paints a sketch of Edwin Booth (no. 233).

13–15 February: *A Summer Morning* (*A Morning Walk*) and *Paul Helleu Sketching with his Wife* (*An Out-of-Doors Study*) (*Early Portraits*, no. 230) are exhibited at the Union League Club, New York.

17 February: Beckwith and Sargent go to Koster, Bial & Co., a music hall or saloon on Fourteenth Street, where they hear what Beckwith described as 'an awful performance' closed by Carmencita's dancing 'such a Spanish dance I have never seen before'.[2]

21 February: Sargent and Beckwith go to the opera and a party.[3]

27 February: Sargent, Beckwith, Frank Millet and others attend a performance of *The Gondoliers*. After the theatre they go to Beckwith's studio. Carmencita arrives at midnight and 'danced superbly until near 3 o'clock'. Augustus Saint-Gaudens is one of the guests.[4]

1 March: after dinner, Beckwith, Sargent and party go to see Carmencita again at Koster, Bial & Co.

16 March: Beckwith visits Sargent's studio and finds Carmencita posing. He writes that she is now asking $100 for a performance, adding '[Sargent's] work is so stunning that it makes me blue'.[5]

27 March: Sargent and Beckwith attend a performance of *The Heir at Law*, with Joseph Jefferson as Dr Pangloss.[6] It is a very lively and sociable period. Visits the theatre and concerts with Dennis Miller Bunker (see *Early Portraits*, no. 204), who writes that he and Sargent 'recite French poetry until 12 o'clock'.[7] Bunker describes Sargent as 'busy all the time – at white heat always, rushing from one place to another'.[8]

22 April: Edwin Austin Abbey's wedding to Mary Gertrude Mead. Sargent acts as usher.

24 April: Sargent and Isabella Stewart Gardner (see *Early Portraits*, no. 206) host a party at William Merritt Chase's studio on Tenth Street at which Carmencita dances.[9]

6 May: Sargent and Beckwith dine at Mr and Mrs Thomas Lincoln Manson Jr's (see no. 241).[10]

7 May: Sargent dines with Charles Follen McKim, Stanford White, Edwin Austin Abbey and Augustus Saint-Gaudens at The Players, New York. They discuss a mural commission for the new Boston Public Library designed by the architectural firm McKim, Mead & White. Sargent shows an 'interest in the direction of Spanish literature [which] was a most natural one'.[11]

14 May: Sargent and Abbey and his wife, Mary, travel to Boston by private railway car. They attend a baseball game in the afternoon, visit the Boston Public Library and dine with the trustees. Sargent is offered a commission to decorate the Special Collections Hall on the top floor and Abbey the frieze of the Book

Delivery Room on the floor beneath, but no contracts are signed.[12]

May: Sargent exhibits seven works at the Society of American Artists spring annual exhibition in New York: *La Carmencita* (no. 234), *A Morning Walk* (Private Collection), and portraits of George W. Vanderbilt (no. 247), Alice Vanderbilt Shepard, Caspar Goodrich, Georg Henschel and Flora Priestley (*Early Portraits*, nos 209, 195, 180, 225). *La Carmencita* is exhibited in the place of honour. It is a landmark exhibition – the most significant number of Sargent's paintings shown in New York to date – and it attracts significant critical attention.

London: exhibits portraits of Mrs Benjamin Kissam and Clementina Anstruther-Thomson at the Royal Academy and studies of Mrs Comyns Carr and Ightham Mote at the New Gallery (*Early Portraits*, nos 210, 216, 222 and 231).

Paris: exhibits *Ellen Terry as Lady Macbeth* and an unidentified portrait (possibly *Princesse Louis de Scey-Montbéliard*) at the Société nationale des beaux-arts (see *Early Portraits*, nos 183, 186).

3 June: Sargent arrives in Worcester, Massachusetts; he stays at the Worcester Club on Elm Street.

June–early July: Worcester, painting portraits of Mrs Edward Davis and her son Livingston (no. 250); *c.* 4 July, Mrs Francis Henshaw Dewey Jr (no. 251) at 114 Main Street and Mrs Alexander Hamilton Bullock (no. 252) at 48 Elm Street.

July/early August: stays with the Fairchilds at Nahant, the summer colony south of Boston, paints Henry Cabot Lodge (no. 264).[13]

August (dates unspecified): Narragansett, Rhode Island and Cohasset, Massachusetts.

11 August: returns to Worcester to paint a portrait of Katharine Pratt (no. 253), stays with her parents, Mr and Mrs Frederick Pratt, at 53 West Street. By 16 August, Sargent has begun a second portrait of Katharine Pratt (no. 254).

19 August: leaves Worcester.

September: Buzzards Bay,[14] Cape Cod, Massachusetts, where he paints a portrait of Joseph Jefferson (no. 273).

Later in September: Manchester-on-Sea, Massachusetts; he gives his address as c/o Mrs James T. Fields.

Possibly pays a visit to Niagara with the Fairchilds.[15]

October: the mural commission for the Boston Public Library is confirmed (the contract is not signed until January 1893).

2 October: Bunker's wedding at Emmanuel Church in Boston. Sargent and Violet are among the guests, Charles Martin Loeffler (see no. 444) is best man. Lucia Fairchild's diary entry for that day: '[Sargent] said he would not be here [Boston] for a week or ten days yet, as he had not begun Mr Peabody [no. 267], and had not finished Mrs Loring [no. 265]. Had to go back to Manchester for the night on account of a dinner'.[16]

4 November: New York: Sargent has a farewell lunch with the Bunkers and the Beckwiths. Sails for Liverpool the following day. Beckwith writes in his diary 'I think he will come back soon' (it will be the spring of 1895 before he returns).[17]

At some point prior to his departure, the trustees of the Boston Public Library write to inform him that he may proceed with his mural work for the library as discussed in May.[18]

November–December: Sargent exhibits his portraits of Lawrence Barrett (no. 272) and Joseph Jefferson in the role of Dr Pangloss (no. 273) and Mrs Edward Davis and her son at the National Academy of Design, New York, and is awarded a Gold Medal for his portrait of Homer Saint-Gaudens and his mother (no. 243) at the Philadelphia Art Club exhibition.

28 December: Dennis Miller Bunker dies in Boston, probably as a result of meningitis.

At some point during the year there is a plan for Sargent to paint Mrs George Meyer (no portrait is recorded).[19]

By the end of the year, he and Violet have joined their mother and their sister, Emily, in Marseilles, travelling from there to Egypt.

1891

January: Alexandria then Cairo, where Sargent takes a studio. He travels in Upper Egypt: Luxor, Thebes, Asswān and Philae.

In England, Edwin Austin Abbey takes a twenty-one-year lease on Morgan Hall, Fairford, Gloucestershire. He builds a studio in the grounds, which provides a spacious working space. Sargent later described it to Paul Helleu as somewhere 'où une toile de deux metres a l'air d'un timbre post'.[20]

March: Cairo: Sargent paints a full-length nude of an Egyptian girl (*Nude Egyptian Girl*, Art Institute of Chicago) in his rented studio. He travels to El Fayoum.

April: Greece: travels with a dragoman to Olympia and Delphi; Constantinople, Turkey. His experiences inspire a change of subject for the Boston Public Library murals – it will become *The History of Religion*.[21]

April/May: his portrait of Beatrice Goelet (no. 239) is hung in the place of honour at the Society of American Artists annual exhibition in New York. An article expressing the opinions of several of his fellow artists on the painting is published in *Harper's Weekly*.[22]

London: *La Carmencita* and a portrait of Mrs Thomas Lincoln Manson Jr at the Royal Academy (nos 234, 241) and 'A Portrait' (*Elsie Palmer*, see *Early Portraits*, no. 187) at the New Gallery.

Paris: Homer Saint-Gaudens and his mother exhibited at the Société nationale des beaux-arts as 'Portrait de jeune garçon'.

Early summer: travels back across Europe with his mother and sisters. According to Charteris, they travel via Vienna and are in San Remo at the Villa Ormond in July.[23] Sargent, however, appears to have been in Paris by the end of June.[24] A telegram to Mrs Fairchild (postmarked 25 June 1891) suggests that he may have visited Giverny briefly. In Paris, his family takes an apartment at 4, rue de Presbourg, opposite the Arc de Triomphe. Vernon Lee stays with them. Sargent accompanies Lucia Fairchild on a visit to the Louvre. He expresses his admiration for Ingres, Veronese, Rembrandt, Giorgione, Titian, Raphael and Botticelli, and talks to her about drawings by Ingres, Leonardo da Vinci and Raphael. He talks about the ceiling *Gloria Mariae Medicis*, on which he worked with Carolus-Duran in 1877.[25]

17 August: attends the wedding of his sister Violet to (Louis) Francis Ormond in Paris. He is still in Paris on 21 August.[26] Borrows the studio of his friend Albert de Belleroche (see *Early Portraits*, nos 96–100) and paints a portrait of the Honorable Thomas Brackett Reed (no. 277).

September: London: Mrs Sargent leases a flat in Chelsea, at 10 Carlyle Mansions (conveniently close to Tite Street), for herself and Emily. Nevertheless, she and Emily spend the best part of the following year travelling (Nice, Italy, Barcelona), and it will be two years before they move in.

October: Camille Pissarro's sons visit Sargent in London with an introduction from Octave Mirabeau.[27]

Autumn/Winter: Morgan Hall, Fairford, where Sargent works on his Boston murals. Lucia Fairchild visits. At some point towards the end of the year he is involved in a fracas with a local farmer, across whose wheat field he has inadvertently ridden. There is an unpleasant scene and dispute, Sir George Lewis (see no. 335) acts for him and Sargent pays the farmer damages of £50.[28]

He is in discussion with Mr and Mrs Hugh Hammersley about painting a portrait of Mrs Hammersley. Writing to Mrs Hammersley, he gives an indication of his prices: 'In case your idea of my prices is based on Mrs Playfair, Mrs Harrison, Miss Vickers [*Early Portraits*, nos 175, 142 and possibly no. 132] or other portraits done here two or more years ago, I must inform you that I have raised my prices since then, to: head 200 Guineas / 3/4 length 400 / full length 500'.[29]

He is elected Associate of the National Academy of Design, New York.

1892

January–June: London and Fairford: portraits and murals.

6 March: Sargent writes to Charles Fairchild: 'I am amazed to see myself the possessor of that respectable thing an income.'[30]

To Mrs Fairchild, he describes his progress on the murals: 'It is getting on very slowly as it need must, and requires more brain work than is good for a would be impressionist'.[31]

May: London: begins painting a portrait of Mrs Hugh Hammersley (no. 284). After visiting the Royal Academy (where he has not exhibited) and New Gallery exhibitions, he dines at the Café Royal and burns his thigh when the matches in his pocket catch fire.[32]

May: Paris: *La Carmencita* and the study of a nude Egyptian girl, painted the previous spring in Cairo, are exhibited at the Société nationale des beaux-arts.

16 June: Lady Agnew of Lochnaw has the first sitting for her portrait (see no. 286).

July: *La Carmencita* is purchased by the French government for 1,200 francs and hung in the Palais du Luxembourg.

August: Spain, to visit his mother, Emily and Violet, who has just given birth to her first child, Marguerite.

September: visits Amsterdam.

Autumn/Winter: Morgan Hall, Fairford.

November: exhibits portraits of Helen Dunham (no. 279) and Flora Priestley (*Early Portraits*, no. 225), and *Paul Helleu Sketching with his Wife* at the New English Art Club, London.

30 November: Charles Follen McKim and Samuel Abbott sail for Europe.

December: Paris: meets Mrs Gardner and sees Vermeer's *The Concert* (*c.* 1658–60), which Mrs Gardner has bought at the auction of Théophile Thoré's estate on 5 December in Paris.

Sargent and the Gardners dine with Whistler. The following day he introduces Whistler to McKim and Abbott: they discuss the possibility of Whistler's contributing to the Boston mural schemes.[33] McKim is unable to secure the necessary funds for Whistler's involvement and nothing comes of the proposed commission.

Luigi and Nicola d'Inverno come to Fairford to model. Nicola will become Sargent's valet and studio assistant.

December: an exhibition of water-colours by Hercules Brabazon Brabazon is held at the Goupil Gallery, London; Sargent writes the preface to the accompanying catalogue.

Sargent exhibits a portrait (probably his half-length study of the musician Georg Henschel, *Early Portraits*, no. 180) at the Internationale Kunstausstellung, Glasplast, Munich.

1893

18 January: Sargent signs the formal contract for the Boston Public Library murals. He is to complete the work by 30 December 1897, is given responsibility for the north and south ends of the Special Collections Hall, and will received $15,000 for the commission (his work on the project is by now well underway).

He works at Morgan Hall. Models come from London, among them Angelo Colarossi and Nicola d'Inverno, to pose for Abbey and for Sargent's *Frieze of the Prophets*.

Spring: the World's Columbian Exposition (the World's Fair) takes place in Chicago – McKim,

Mead & White are the architects. Frank Millet, who was director of decorations of the White City, the Beaux-Arts ideal model city, which was at the heart of the exhibition, had asked Sargent to paint a tympanum. Sargent is unable to comply at such short (two months) notice.[34] In the event, he contributes eight portraits and his *Nude Egyptian Girl* to the American section and is awarded a medal.

May: *Lady Agnew of Lochnaw* is exhibited at the Royal Academy and *Mrs Hugh Hammersley* at the New Gallery. Vernon Lee writes: 'As to Mr Sargent, London is at his feet. Mrs Hammersley & Mrs Lewis are at the New Gallery, Lady Agnew at the Academy. There can be no two opinions this year. He has had a cracking success.'[35]

June: painting a portrait of Elizabeth Chanler (no. 287).

July: has begun a portrait of Mrs Mahlon Day Sands (no. 289).

Autumn/Winter: Morgan Hall: completes the lunette of *The Children of Israel Beneath the Yoke of their Oppressors*, except for the bas-relief additions.

1894

January: he is elected an Associate of the Royal Academy.[36] Completes the vaulting section with *Pagan Deities* and begins *Frieze of the Prophets*.

February: the portrait of Mrs Mahlon Day Sands, begun the previous summer, is finished.

May: *Miss Chanler* (no. 287) and *Lunette and Portion of the Ceiling* (the first section of the Boston Library decorations) are shown at the Royal Academy.

Paris: Mrs Hugh Hammersley is shown at the Société nationale des beaux-arts.

Consults Frederick MacMonnies in Paris about technical aspects of the applied reliefs for the Boston decorations.

9 May: sees Lord Ribblesdale at an Artists' General Benevolent Institution dinner in London (see no. 421).

Meets his future biographer Evan Charteris at a party given by Mrs Henry White (see *Early Portraits*, nos 105 and 106) at Loseley Park, Surrey.

May: Paris: sees Whistler's portrait of Comte Robert de Montesquiou at the Salon.

Summer: paints a kit-cat portrait of Coventry Patmore (no. 302). He is also painting the *Frieze of the Prophets*; uses Patmore's profile for the head of Ezekiel.

June/July: London: portrait sittings, including Mrs Graham Robertson, W. Graham Robertson and Ada Rehan (nos 305, 306 and 308). In an undated letter to Ralph Curtis, he writes: 'For the moment I am going to do some portraits here, among others Miss Rehan who is very paintable.'[37]

October: *Lady Agnew of Lochnaw* and *Ellen Terry as Lady Macbeth* are exhibited in the Fair Women

exhibition at the Grafton Galleries.

November: exhibits nine portraits at a loan exhibition at the National Academy of Design, New York (*Loan Exhibition: Portraits of Women for the Benefit of St John's Guild and the Orthopaedic Hospital*).

Autumn/Winter: Morgan Hall.

1895

January: working hard at completing the *Frieze of the Prophets*.

March: London: finishes his portrait of Ada Rehan.

Boston: exhibits five portraits at a loan exhibition at Copley Hall (*Loan Collection of Portraits of Women for the Benefit of the Boston Children's Aid Society and the Sunnyside Day Nursery*).

4 April: Sargent hosts a party at his studio, at which Carmencita dances. Lady Agnew is a guest.[38]

6 April: sails for Boston.

12 April: arrives in Boston for the installation of the first section of the library murals, the 'Pagan end' at the north end of the Special Collections Hall (*Pagan Gods, Israelites Oppressed* and *Frieze of the Prophets*).

25 April: Sargent's and Abbey's murals are unveiled. McKim, Mead & White hold a grand reception for Sargent and Abbey at the Boston Public Library.[39] The party, a lavish private event in a public building with over two hundred guests, is criticized in the Boston press: Samuel Abbott resigns as president of the library trustees. The murals are admired: Sargent writes to Mrs Curtis: 'The Bostonians like them I am glad to say, to the extent of entertaining the idea of giving me a further order for more walls of the same hall. So I shall be at it for years.'[40] A subscription of $15,000 is organized by Edward Robinson to pay for the next phase of the mural project and Sargent is formally asked to continue.

During his visit to Boston, he paints portraits of Helen Sears and Gardiner Greene Hammond (nos 317, 318).

May: five portraits, including *W. Graham Robertson* and *Coventry Patmore* (nos 306, 302), exhibited at the Royal Academy; *Miss Ada Rehan* (no. 308) at the New Gallery.

15 May: travels from New York to Biltmore, George W. Vanderbilt's estate, in Asheville, North Carolina, to paint portraits of the architect of Biltmore, Richard Morris Hunt, and its landscape designer, Frederick Law Olmsted (nos 319, 320).

22 June: sails from New York to Spain on SS *Werra*. He meets Dr and Mrs William White on board (see nos 458, 557); George Santayana, instructor in philosophy at Harvard University, is a fellow traveller.[41] They dock in Gibraltar on 1 July. Sargent meets his mother, who has been ill with peritonitis, and Emily; finds his mother better than expected and travels on immediately to Tangier with the Whites.[42]

Dr White writes: 'Sargent, who knows Algiers

and Egypt and northern Africa thoroughly, says there is nothing so savage and picturesque and thoroughly Oriental to be seen anywhere else; and so far as Algiers and Egypt go they don't compare with this. It is his second visit here [the first was in January 1880] and yet he is enthusiastic about it.'[43]

The Whites travel with Sargent to Ronda – he goes on to Granada. Mrs Sargent and Emily go to Aix-les-Bains. The Whites rejoin him. Sargent paints in the Alhambra and the cathedral.[44]

c. 10 July: Sargent and the Whites go their separate ways. Sargent goes on to Gaudix.[45]

26–31 July: Madrid: Sargent registers as a copyist at the Prado to study El Greco, Titian and Tintoretto.[46] Returns to London and portrait work.

October: Visitor at the Royal Academy Schools, London.

5 December: the expansion of the Boston mural project is formalized: a fund set up by private subscription from citizens of Boston and others has secured the money.[47]

During the autumn, Mrs Sargent and Emily are established in Carlyle Mansions. Philip Wilson Steer introduces Sargent to Henry Tonks. Sargent ceases to work at Morgan Hall and takes a twenty-one-year lease on two studios on Fulham Road.

October–December: exhibits five portraits at a loan exhibition at the National Academy of Design, New York (*Loan Exhibition of Portraits for the Benefit of St John's Guild and the Orthopaedic Hospital*).

Exhibition of Spanish Art, New Gallery, London: Sargent lends several objects including *Saint Martin and the Beggar*, then attributed to El Greco, but now given to his son, Jorge Manuel.

At around this time, Sargent expresses admiration for Whistler's *Harmony in Blue and Gold: The Peacock Room* (1876–7), designed for the London home of F. R. Leyland; and Sargent hopes that it might be installed as a committee room at the Boston Public Library, or possibly in one of Mrs Gardner's houses.[48]

1896

January: he lends his Fulham Road studio to Paul Helleu and then to Whistler.

February: receives a commission from the Metropolitan Museum of Art, New York, to paint Henry G. Marquand (no. 343)

1 March: portrait of Mrs Walter Rathbone Bacon is finished (no. 326)

March: exhibits a portrait of Helen Sears (no. 318) at the Society of American Artists, New York; a head and shoulders study of Gordon Greene Hammond (no. 317) at the National Academy of Design, New York; and six portraits at Copley Hall, Boston (*Loan Collection of Portraits for the Benefit of the Associated Charities and the North End Union*).

April: sittings for *Mrs George Swinton* (no. 327).

May: visits Sir John and Lady Horner at Mells Park in Somerset (see nos 371, 372).

May: exhibits five portraits in London at the Royal Academy, and *Countess Clary Aldringen* (no. 325) at the New Gallery. In Paris, exhibits his portrait of W. Graham Robertson at the Société nationale des beaux-arts.

3 June: Sargent is one of the guests at a dinner hosted by John Hay (see no. 440) in London.[49]

July: appointments for sittings for the portrait of Henry G. Marquand are made, but Marquand is too ill to attend.[50]

Summer: sittings for *Mrs Carl Meyer and her Children* (no. 324).

December: Visitor, Royal Academy Schools, London.

1897

Elected to the Royal Academy, London, as a full member (he was an Associate in 1894).

January–February: he goes to Italy to do research for the Boston Public Library murals. He visits Sicily, and makes studies in the cathedral at Palermo. Moves north to Rome: Harry Brewster arranges for him to visit the Borgia Apartment in the Vatican, where he sees Pinturicchio's decorations.

Late February: Florence.[51]

March: London: his portrait of Mrs George Swinton is finished.

He is elected a full member of the National Academy of Design, New York.

April: visits Dr and Mrs William Playfair (see *Early Portraits*, nos 175, 176) on the Isle of Schona, Loch Moidart, Scotland.

May: *Mrs Carl Meyer and her Children* and *The Honourable Laura Lister* at the Royal Academy, *Mrs George Swinton* and *Study by Lamplight of Mrs George Batten Singing* at the New Gallery. Two portraits and *Nude Egyptian Girl* at the Venice biennale.

June: sittings for the portrait of Mr and Mrs I. N. Phelps Stokes (no. 337). His portrait of Asher Wertheimer, the first in an important series of portraits of the Wertheimer family, is almost finished (no. 347).[52]

Sargent intends to send his portrait of Thomas Francis Bayard (no. 342) to the Royal Academy as his diploma picture, but is dissatisfied with it and mentions the possibility of presenting a portrait of Lawrence Alma-Tadema, who had agreed to sit to him. No portrait of Alma-Tadema appears to have been painted. Sargent deposits a portrait of Johannes Wolff (no. 341) as a temporary measure.

July: sittings for Henry G. Marquand's portrait.

October: Visitor, Royal Academy Schools, London.

December: Arthur Cohen sits for his portrait (no. 344).

Sargent's portrait of Coventry Patmore (no. 302) is presented to the National Portrait Gallery, London, by his widow.

He is made an Officier of the French Légion d'honneur.

1898

January–February: paints portraits of Mrs Charles Hunter (no. 363) and Lord Watson (no. 351).

February: begins portrait of Francis Cranmer Penrose (no. 350).

March: paints Miss Jane Evans (no. 365).

March–April: exhibits three portraits and two subject pictures at the Society of American Artists, New York.

Spring: exhibits at the Vienna Secession (*Jubeljahr Kunst-Ausstellung*).

May: exhibits eight portraits, including his portraits of Asher Wertheimer (no. 347) and Mrs Asher Wertheimer (no. 348) at the Royal Academy and four at the New Gallery. Serves as chairman of the hanging committee of the Royal Academy.[53]

May: Venice: stays at the Palazzo Barbaro, where he paints *An Interior in Venice* (no. 367). He mentions his forthcoming plans, which include a trip to Milan where he hopes to meet up with Ralph Curtis and his wife. Visits Bologna, Bergamo and Ravenna, where he paints the mosaics in Sant'Apollinare. Writing from Ravenna to thank Mrs Daniel Curtis for her hospitality, he notes: 'The Barbaro is a sort of Fontaine de Jouvence, for it sends one back twenty years, besides making the present seem remarkably all right.'[54]

June: London: his time is consumed by portrait sittings. Increases his fee to 1,000 guineas for a full-length. Writes to Mrs George Swinton [4 July 1898]: 'I am up to my ears in previous orders [for portraits] and must keep at least six months for my decorations.'[55]

July: Senator Calvin Brice sits for his portrait (no. 346).

October: working on *The Dogma of Redemption* and crucifix for the Boston Public Library. Consults Augustus Saint-Gaudens about his crucifix for the Christian section of the Boston Public Library murals.

December: exhibits four portraits at the winter exhibition of the National Academy of Design, New York.

Visitor, Royal Academy Schools, London.

1899

15 February: begins work on his group portrait of the three Wyndham sisters (no. 368) in the Wyndham house in Belgrave Square.

20 February–13 March: his second one-man exhibition is held in Boston, this time at Copley Hall (Boston Art Student's Association). The exhibition includes fifty-three oils, sixteen drawings and forty-one sketches. Sargent does not attend, but he contributes works from his own collection.

Owing to a mistake by the Press Association, an erroneous account of Sargent's death appears in newspapers on both sides of the Atlantic. The deceased artist was Frederick Sargent (no relation). He sends a telegram to Mrs Gardner: 'Alive and Kicking, Sargent'.[56]

March: two portraits and a sketch for Astarte at the Society of American Artists, New York.

April: Paris: consults Augustus Saint-Gaudens about the design and casting of the crucifix in *The Dogma of the Redemption*.[57]

May: four portraits and a design for a mural decoration at the Royal Academy. *Colonel Ian Hamilton* (no. 352) at the New Gallery.

Devotes much of the summer to his mural work.

June: Mells Park, Somerset, where he paints two studies of Cicely Horner (nos 371, 372).

July: paints M. Carey Thomas in his London studio (no. 373).

August: visits the Swintons who are staying at Calwick Abbey, and the Sitwells at Renishaw in Derbyshire. On leaving Renishaw, he travels to Gisburne Park in Yorkshire and executes a portrait drawing of Lord Ribblesdale's young son, Charles Lister (see no. 421). The drawing is dated 'Aug. 30th 1899'.

September: meets Edith Wharton.

November: serves on the council of the Royal Academy.

December: Visitor, Royal Academy Schools, London. *An Interior in Venice* is submitted and accepted as his official Royal Academy diploma picture.

Sargent is approached by Cardinal Vaughn to contribute designs for a mosaic decoration for a chapel in Westminster Cathedral. Cardinal Vaughn is acting on the recommendation of the cathedral's architect, John Francis Bentley. Sargent declines the invitation.[58]

1. James Carroll Beckwith's diary (15 January 1890): 'Went to McCurdy's office [Mutual Life Assurance Company of New York] and lunched there with him, Sargent and Walton, a fine lunch. We stopped some time to see John work on his big portrait of Mr McC and then came home.' Beckwith's diary is in the National Academy (formerly National Academy of Design), New York, and on microfilm in the Archives of American Art.
2. Beckwith's diary (17 February 1890).
3. Beckwith's diary (21 February 1890).
4. Beckwith's diary (27 February 1890): 'Carmencita came at 12 a dozen men I had spoken to came in. I had a guitarist & mandolinist. She danced superbly until near 3 o'clock when Sargent took her home. I have never had a more novel fête than tonight.'
5. Beckwith's diary (16 March 1890).
6. Beckwith's diary (27 March 1890).
7. Dennis Miller Bunker to Eleanor Hardy, n.d. [early 1890], Dennis Miller Bunker Papers, Private Collection, quoted Boston 1994, p. 176.
8. Dennis Miller Bunker to Eleanor Hardy, n.d. [early 1890], Dennis Miller Bunker Papers, Private Collection, quoted Boston 1994, p. 73.
9. For Sargent's undated letter to William Merritt Chase asking to borrow Chase's studio for the party, see AAA roll N 69 137, frames 463–6.
10. Beckwith's diary (6 May 1890).
11. Letter from Charles Follen McKim to Mr [Samuel Appleton Browne] Abbott, president of the board of trustees, Boston Public Library, Charteris 1927, pp. 104–6. See also Moore 1929, p. 73.
12. See Moore 1929, pp. 74–5.
13. F. S. Pratt to his wife, 14 July 1890: 'Mr Sargent asked permission to put off Kitty's picture [no. 253] till next week. He met Mrs Lodge in Boston yesterday or Saturday, and if he can do it this week he is to paint Mr L's portrait. Congressman Lodge is a man worth painting so I granted permission to Mr Sargent. It is wonderful how rapidly he works'. Strickler 1982–3, p. 25.
14. JSS to Frank Millet, the letter is headed Buzzards Bay, 1 September [1890]: 'I have been doing one portrait after the other at Nahant, Worcester, Beverley farms and am now doing Joseph Jefferson here. Have just done Barrett. Have been a great deal with the Fairchilds.' Private Collection.
15. 'I am off to join the Fairchilds at Niagra [sic] for a day or two, and afterwards this [Manchester] will again be my address for a while c/o Mrs James T. Fields'. Undated [mid-late September 1890] letter from JSS to Lawrence Barrett, Private Collection.
16. Lucia Fairchild Fuller's papers are in the collection of Dartmouth College, Hanover, New Hampshire (and on microfilm at the AAA, reel 3825, frames 1–266).
17. 'Sargent lunched with us. He sails for Europe tomorrow but I think he will come back soon'. Beckwith's diary (4 November 1890).
18. JSS wrote to Ralph Curtis from Tite Street (18 November [1890]): 'I was informed by the Trustees that I might proceed with the work and could not find out what had occurred to settle the matter. Did she [Mrs Gardner] intervene?' Boston Athenaeum, Sargent Papers, box 1, folder 11.
19. JSS to Mrs Charles Fairchild, 'Masconomo' [Manchester] [1890]: 'Whether I return here or not is problematic, as Mrs Meyer is so ill that they think her portrait must be postponed. They may send the canvas to your care, if they don't keep it for a future occasion, and I beg you to house it if they do so, on the lower piazza where I painted Gordon [see no.

260] and forgive its size.' Boston Athenaeum, Sargent Papers, box 1, folder 16. Mrs Meyer is almost certainly Marian Alice Appleton, who had married George von Lengerke Meyer (1858–1918) on 25 June 1885, the same day that McKim married her sister Julia Amory Appleton. Meyer was a member of the Boston city government when McKim was building the public library. He was later ambassador to Italy (1900–5), to Russia (1905–7), postmaster-general in the Roosevelt cabinet and secretary of the navy in the Taft cabinet.
20. 'where a two-metres-square canvas looks like a postage stamp'. JSS to Paul Helleu [undated], Madame Howard-Johnston.
21. He writes to Mrs Gardner [undated, probably c. 14 April 1890] from Bursa in Turkey: 'The consequence of going up the Nile is, as might have been foreseen, that I must do an Old Testament thing for the Boston Library . . . I saw things in Egypt that I hope will come in[to] play.' ISGM archive.
22. 'What the artists think of Sargent's Beatrice', Harper's Weekly, 35 (9 May 1891), pp. 346–7.
23. See Charteris 1927, p. 115.
24. In un undated letter to Mrs Gardner (probably c. 14 April 1890), he writes: 'The consequence of going up the Nile is, as might have been foreseen, that I must do an Old Testament thing for the Boston Library, besides the other one [Spanish literature], & I saw things in Egypt that I hope will come in play. While I was out here it seemed best to see Greece and Turkey, so I gave up Spain for another year . . . In a couple of weeks I will be in Paris.' ISGM archive.
25. 'Diary of visit to the Louvre with John S. Sargent written by Lucia Fairchild in 1891 when she was an art student of 18', I, II, III (DCL).
    Sargent and Lucia Fairchild's exchange about the ceiling: 'He took me to see the room of Ingres drawings – We passed through one with a ceiling by Duran, which he said he had worked a great deal on. "Oh yes", said he, "a man having a big thing to do like that gets tired of it – All his pupils I rather think had a hand in it". "Which did you do?" I asked. "There", said he, "do you see that old man in armor? I did him. And the dark fellow to his right – that's Carolus himself – That used to be me that he is talking to – that old fellow in profile with a white beard, but Carolus must have changed it since" (ibid. III). For a reproduction of the ceiling, see Early Portraits, figs 4 and 5.
26. JSS wrote to Augustus Saint-Gaudens from Paris, 21 August [1891], Saint-Gaudens Collection, DCL, see no. 243.
27. Camille Pissarro replied to a letter from his son Lucien about the visit (6 October 1891): 'What you say about Sargent doesn't surprise me. Monet had told me that he is very kind. As for his painting, that, of course, we can't approve of; he is not an enthusiast but rather an adroit performer, and it is not for his painting that Mirbeau wanted you to meet him.' John Rewald ed., Camille Pissarro. Letters to His Son Lucien, London, 1980, p. 183.
28. For an account of the episode, see Charteris 1927, pp. 119–20 and Olson 1986, pp. 176–7.
    Sargent's letter to Henry James [28 February 1892] recounting the episode and its legal consequences is in the Houghton Library, Harvard University.
29. JSS to Mrs Hugh Hammersley, n.d. (MMA).
30. JSS to Charles Fairchild, 6 March 1892, on receipt of a statement of his financial accounts: 'I am amazed to see myself the possessor of that respect-

able thing an income . . . I shall do two or three portraits this spring and may have a little money to send you to add to my nugget.' Boston Athenaeum, Sargent Papers, box 1, folder 15.
31. JSS to Mrs Fairchild, 6 March [1892], Boston Athenaeum, Sargent Papers, box 1, folder 15.
32. See Charteris 1927, p. 137.
33. JSS wrote to Whistler [undated, December 1892] that McKim and Abbott were anxious to secure his involvement in the library decorations and were hopeful of obtaining funds: 'They feel that the room for you to do is the very holy of holies. If you have not taken the idea en grippe I feel sure that something might result from a meeting with these two excellent fellows, so I propose that we dine together at Foyots on Saturday . . . I am running over to Paris for a day or two, and mainly for this.' Glasgow University Library. The commission for Whistler to contribute to the library murals never materialized.
34. Sargent told Frederick Law Olmsted's son about Millet's cabled request to him at Biltmore in 1895, see Olmsted's letter to Chester Aldrich, 13 June 1895, Library of Congress, Washington, D.C.
35. Undated letter from VL to Clementina Anstruther-Thomson, CC.
36. Sargent replied to a letter of congratulation from Ralph Curtis: 'Thanks for your flourish of trumpets and waving of caps – If one lives in London, as I seem to be doing vaguely, I suppose it counts for something to be an A.R.A. It remains to be proved; but I shall watch for the symptoms with interest. I have had no end of letters of congratulation from Academicians which would point to the fact of my having more of an affinity with old fogies than I expected. Today I have called on about 20 of them, such is the tradition and it is a curious revelation to find the man whose name and work one has hated and railed at for years, is a man of the world and altogether delightful – for instance [James] Sant, whom one considered the Antichrist.' Charteris 1927, p. 141.
37. JSS to Ralph Curtis [undated, May 1894], Boston Athenaeum.
38. Monkswell 1944, p. 265.
39. For a first-hand account, see T. R. Sullivan, Passages from the Journal of Thomas Russell Sullivan, 1891–1903, New York, 1917, pp. 133–4.
40. JSS to Mrs Curtis, 7 May 1895, Boston Athenaeum.
41. The date of departure from Dr White's diary. He goes on to note: 'Probably the most distinguished man among the passengers is Sargent, the artist, but I have seen very little of him. He spends most of his time playing chess.' Journal of 1895, Dr James William White Papers, University Archives, University of Pennsylvania.
42. Dr White's diary, 2 July [1895]: 'We were delighted as we reached the steamer's side to get a hail from Sargent who had found his mother so much better that he had decided to go at once to Tangier.' Ibid.
43. Ibid.
44. Dr White's diary, 7 July 1895, ibid.
45. Dr White's diary, 10 July 1895, ibid. Dr White writes: 'We then said "Goodbye" to Sargent with real reluctance. He has been a most charming companion, not only because he has helped us to see and appreciate artistic subjects but also for the reason that he is a jolly good fellow and would be first-rate company if he didn't know a Raphael from a Fortuny.'
46. Libro de Registro: Los copistas (1887–1895),

Archivos del Prado, Museo del Prado, Madrid.

47. For details of the contract, see Boston Public Library (Rare Books and Manuscripts), MS Bos Li BI 8 a. I.

48. JSS to Mrs Gardner, 29 August [1895 or possibly 1897?]: 'How can you let the Peacock Room belong to anybody else! I don't know what is going to be done about it, whether it will be entirely removed or not – it ought to be kept together, but the shutters alone would be a treasure.' ISGM archive. The Peacock Room was acquired by Charles L. Freer in 1904 and bequeathed by him to the Freer Gallery of Art, Washington, D.C., 1919.

49. Henry Adams wrote to Elizabeth Cameron, 3 June 1896: 'Hay had his feast on Monday . . . as men, figured Bret Harte, Harry James, Sargent, Cowles, Sydney Buxton and the youth Geoffrey.' Quoted Monteiro 1965, p. 180.

50. Marquand neglected to inform Sargent that he would be unable to keep his appointments. Sargent wrote to him on 25 July: 'So many plans hinged on our engagement from the 24th, that you cannot believe how opportune a cablegram received two weeks ago would have been.' Quoted Burke 1980, p. 252.

51. Sargent's letter to Mrs George Swinton, 26 February 1897, was sent from Florence. Private Collection.

52. See Stokes 1941, p. 118.

53. 'Mr Sargent, it is reported, is chairman of the Hanging Committee of the Royal Academy this year. This is the first time, I believe, that an American has been so honored by that conservative body.' Montague Marks 'The London Letter', *Art Amateur*, 38 (May 1898), p. 129.

54. JSS to Mrs Curtis, 27 [May 1898], Boston Athenaeum, Sargent Papers, box 1, folder 11.

55. JSS to Mrs George Swinton, [4 July 1898], Private Collection.

56. Telegram, ISGM archive. For a typical notice and retraction, see 'Death of Mr Sargent, R. A.: An Unexpected Event', *Pall Mall Gazette*, LXVIII (13 April 1899) and 'Occasional Notes', *Pall Mall Gazette*, LXVIII (14 April 1899). Sargent's friends responded before the retraction was published. Captain and Mrs Swinton, for example, called at Tite Street. Sargent's housekeeper, Carr, wrote on their visiting card: 'Mr Sargent is alive and well, gone out to a Dinner Party Yours respectfully Carr' (Private Collection). Sargent sent his own card to the Swintons with the message: 'thanks for sympathy and beautiful wreath' (Private Collection). A representative from the *New York Sun* (14 April 1899) interviewed Sargent, who was entertained and bemused by the report, particularly as it stated that he had died at the residence of his son at Parsons Green, Fulham. For an account of the episode, see Mount 1955 and 1969 eds, p. 227. Frederick Sargent was best known as a portrait draughtsman: a collection of his pencil drawings is in the National Portrait Gallery, London.

57. Augustus Saint-Gaudens, 12 April 1899: 'Sargent has been here [Paris] recently, and I saw a good deal of him during his visit.' Saint Gaudens 1913, vol. 2, p. 194.

58. See Winefride de L'Hôpital, *Westminster Cathedral and its Architect*, New York, 1919, pp. 28–9.

CATALOGUE SECTIONS

The portraits have been grouped into two chronological sections. Each section is preceded by an introduction, which is intended to provide a context for the group of works in question and to highlight points of thematic interest, stylistic development and critical reception. The sections and the introductions present a personal view of the phases of Sargent's portraiture.

The portraits are presented in chronological order where possible. Within individual years, they are arranged chronologically, where precise information about date is available. The compilers have used some discretion in grouping together portraits of family members, or placing together works with close stylistic affinities. Where none of these points pertain, the portraits proceed alphabetically by sitter's name within a particular year.

CATALOGUE NUMBERS

These are sequential and relate to the master dossier for each picture in the catalogue raisonné archive. For catalogue entries for portraits after no. 381 referred to in this volume, see *The Late Portraits* (to be published 2003). Such portraits are referred to by number only, without the volume title.

TITLES

Portraits are given the title under which they were first exhibited (where relevant) or by which they are best known. Alternative titles are given in parentheses. The title used for a portrait which did not appear in a contemporary exhibition or publication indicates the sitter's name at the time the portrait was painted. Those sitters whose names have been subject to change (usually peers or women) are designated by the name by which they were known at the time that their portrait was painted. Alternate names and titles are given in the short biography for each sitter and in the index. In the Exhibitions section for each picture, titles of paintings are only indicated where they differ significantly from the title at first exhibition.

DATING

Serious problems of dating in this volume are relatively few. A large proportion of works have an inscribed date on the canvas, and a number of works which are not so dated can be securely dated by reference to contemporary documentation. It is usually assumed that exhibited portraits without inscribed dates were painted near to the time of first exhibition. Details concerning dating are discussed, where relevant, in the text of individual entries.

MEDIUM, SUPPORT AND SIZES

Pictures are on the whole designated as oil on canvas or water-colour on paper, without further analysis of materials and support used by the artist. Sizes are normally those of the stretcher, board or sheet of paper and are given first in inches then in centimetres (height before width).

SIGNATURES AND INSCRIPTIONS

A high proportion of portraits in this volume are signed, and a considerable number are dated. It is normally assumed that signature and date were added at the time of completion, but this is not always the case and, where inscribed portraits are concerned, there may be a gap of time between completion and gift.

Sargent's mature signature is 'John S. Sargent' and variants, at this stage in his career, are rare. Inscriptions on the reverse of pictures have only been noted if they are in the artist's hand or if they have a particular relevance.

COMMENTARY

Every effort has been made to document each portrait securely, to provide a biography of the sitter, to explain the context in which the portrait was created, with the aid of contemporary biographical sources and critical reviews, and to discuss any other issues bearing on its history and significance.

APPARATUS

The traditional apparatus of a catalogue raisonné has been retained, with basic data, sections on provenance, exhibition history and literary references. Every effort has been made to include references to contemporary and primary sources, but the catalogue cannot claim to be comprehensive in its listing either of exhibition or bibliographic references. Passing references to, or illustrations of, a particular work in a publication are not included.

PROVENANCE

Every effort has been made to trace the history of ownership of each work through research, auction catalogues and dealers' records, and with reference to exhibition catalogues, published accounts and family information. However, dealers' records are frequently unavailable, family tradition can be unreliable and detective work is sometimes unproductive. In consequence, gaps and uncertainties remain in the provenance sections of certain works. Such lacunae and questions are indicated by 'possibly' or 'probably' at a particular juncture or by a note that the history is uncertain at a particular point. Occasionally, a phrase such as 'by family descent' is used where more precise information is unavailable.

M. Knoedler & Co. handled a significant corpus of Sargent's work over a long period of time: Knoedler stock numbers are indicated in the provenance section of relevant works.

DOCUMENTARY SOURCES

Many of Sargent's commissioned portraits are well documented in terms of contemporary manuscript sources and references, and in early exhibition histories. Sargent himself kept no sitters' book or records of his work.

BIBLIOGRAPHIC REFERENCES

The earliest catalogue of Sargent's work, with descriptions and quotations from critics, was published by W. H. Downes in his monograph of 1925. Evan Charteris and Charles Mount both included checklists of portraits in oils in their respective biographies of 1927 and 1955. David McKibbin's checklist of portraits in all media was published as an appendix to the exhibition catalogue of *Sargent's Boston*, 1956. Other important source materials include the catalogues of the three major retrospective exhibitions which followed the artist's death, in Boston, New York and London and the catalogue of the sale of his work at Christie's in 1925 and subsequent exhibition catalogues from the 1950s onwards.

Bibliographic and exhibition references are cited in abbreviated form in the relevant sections of the catalogue entries. The corresponding full citations are provided in Bibliography Cited in Abbreviated Form and Exhibitions Cited in Abbreviated Form (pp. 194–202).

There are two editions of the catalogue *Memorial Exhibition of the Works of the Late John Singer Sargent*, held at the Museum of Fine Arts, Boston (3 November–27 December 1925). The second edition of the catalogue, published in January 1926, incorporates some late additions to the exhibition into its chronological listing of works shown, which results in differences in numeration. In the Exhibitions section, the number listed in the first edition catalogue is listed, and the number in the revised edition of the catalogue is given afterwards in parentheses. The two editions of the catalogue are listed separately in the individual Literature sections.

The three editions of Charles Merrill Mount's biography and checklist are kept together in the individual Literature sections. Mount's catalogue number for each picture (which is occasionally revised from edition to edition) is indicated in each case.

The catalogue for the exhibition held at the Museum of Fine Arts, Boston, *Sargent's Boston*, is listed as 'Boston 1956', but the checklist of Sargent's portraits contained in the catalogue is so important that it is listed separately as 'McKibbin 1956'.

In the Literature section for each picture, references are listed chronologically, but, within an individual year, reviews are listed alphabetically by journal title.

TRANSLATIONS

The original language of the lengthier quoted material is given in the notes.

ACCESSORIES

This section provides an inventory of the furniture and objects which can be identified as belonging to the artist and which appear in his portraits. The accessories have, where possible, been identified with pieces sold after the artist's death, in current private collections, or shown in reproductions of the artist's studio. The accessories are numbered, described, identified with the portraits in which they appear and, where pos-sible, illustrated; cross-references to the relevant accessories are given in the individual portrait entries. Items belonging to the artist's sitters or friends, which are used in particular portraits, are described in the relevant entries.

TECHNICAL ANALYSIS

No sustained analysis of Sargent's technique has yet been undertaken, although some preliminary work has been carried out by conservators at the Tate Gallery, London, and the Fogg Art Museum, Cambridge, Massachusetts. In the absence of reliable scientific data, the catalogue compilers have restricted their commentary to general points on technique and condition.

FRAMES

The study of frames in Sargent's oeuvre is relatively new. There are occasional references to frames in the text of this volume, but a sustained study will be undertaken and published in subsequent volumes of the catalogue raisonné.

NEW MATERIAL

Inevitably, as we continue to work on Sargent, new material comes to light. In order to proceed with publication, a cut-off date of 1 April 2002 has been imposed.

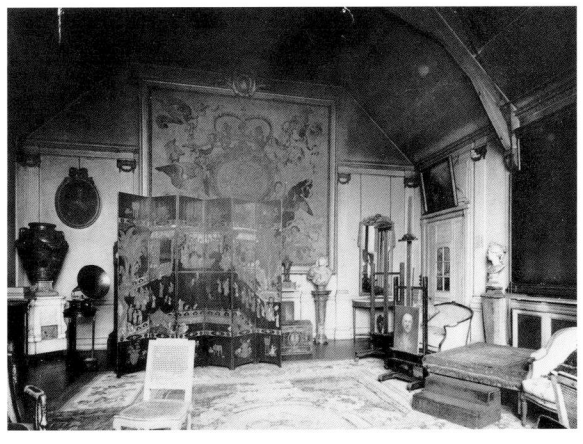

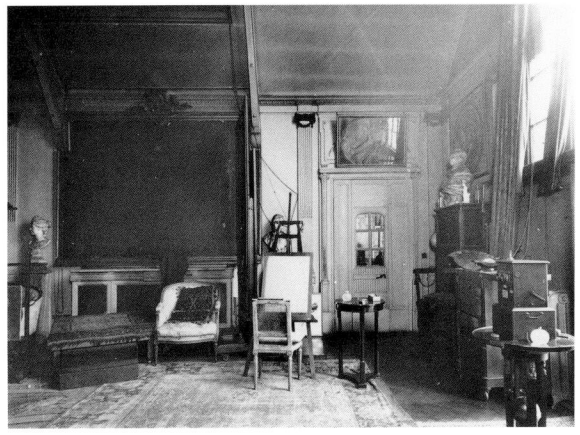

fig. 15 (top, left) Photograph of the studio at 31 Tite Street, *c.* 1922, west wall. Private Collection. Visible are a bergère chair (see no. 2), canapé (no. 3), cane chair (no. 7), pilasters (no. 18), majolica vase (no. 23), lacquer screen (no. 25), Gobelin tapestry (no. 32) and carpets (no. 35).

fig. 16 (top, right) Photograph of the studio at 31 Tite Street, *c.* 1922, north wall. Private Collection Visible are a bergère chair (see no. 2), canapé (no. 3), cane chair (no. 7), circular table (far right, no. 14), pilasters (no. 18) and carpets (no. 35).

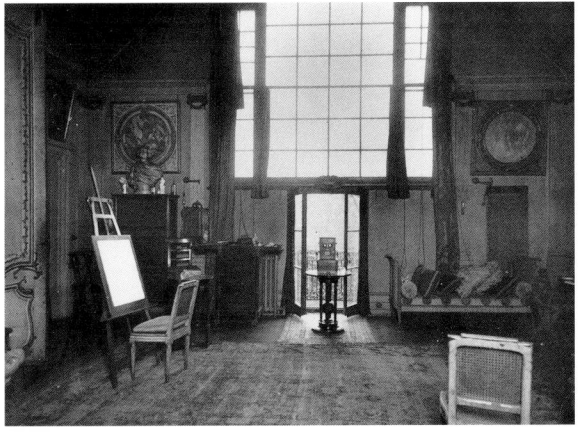

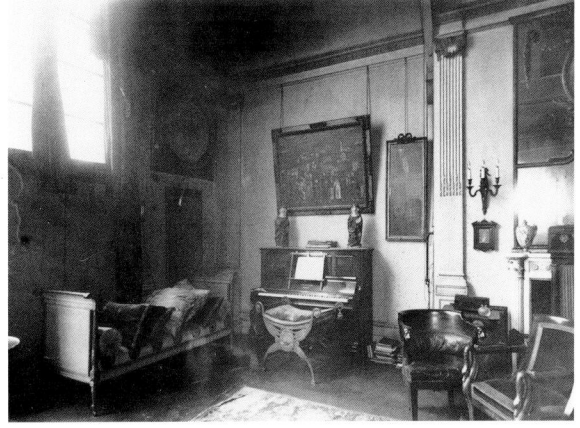

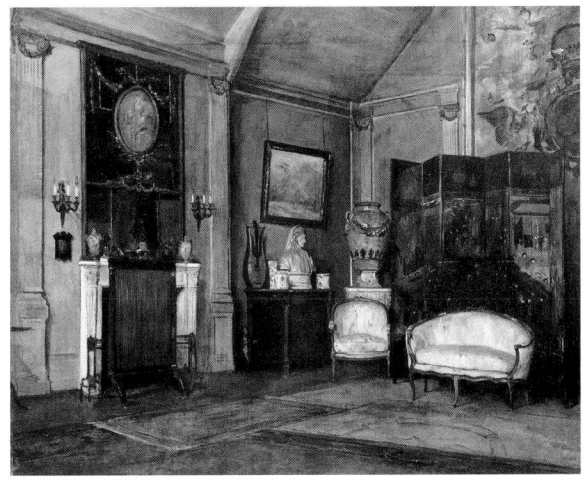

fig. 17 (above, left) Photograph of the studio at 31 Tite Street, *c.* 1922, east wall. Private Collection. Visible are the day bed (no. 4), cane chair (no. 7), circular table (no. 14), boiserie panel (far left, no. 17), pilasters (no. 18), plaster bust (no. 26) and carpet (no. 35)

fig. 18 (above, right) Photograph of the studio at 31 Tite Street, *c.* 1922, south wall. Private Collection. Visible are the day-bed (no. 4), fauteuil (no. 5), fauteuil de bureau (no. 6), X-shaped iron seat (no. 12), Bechstein piano (no. 16), pilasters (no. 18), fire-place (no. 19) and carpet (no. 35).

fig. 19 (far left) Oil painting of Sargent's studio at 31 Tite Street by Susie Zileri, *c.* 1922. Oil on canvas, approximately 22 18. Fogg Art Museum, Cambridge, Massachusetts. Visible are a bergère chair (no. 2), canapé (no. 3), pilasters (no. 18), fire-place (no. 19), majolica vase (no. 23), lacquer screen (no. 25), bust of a cleric (no. 27), Gobelins tapestry (no. 32), and carpets (no. 35).

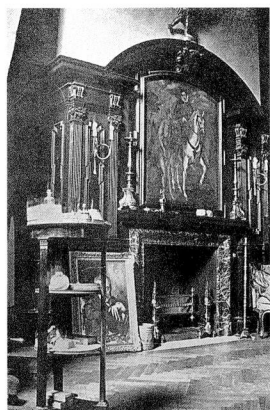

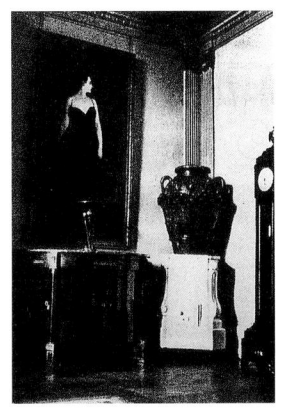

fig. 20 (far left) Photograph of the studio at 33 Tite Street. Note the panelling (no. 20).

fig. 21 (left) Photograph of a corner of Sargent's studio.

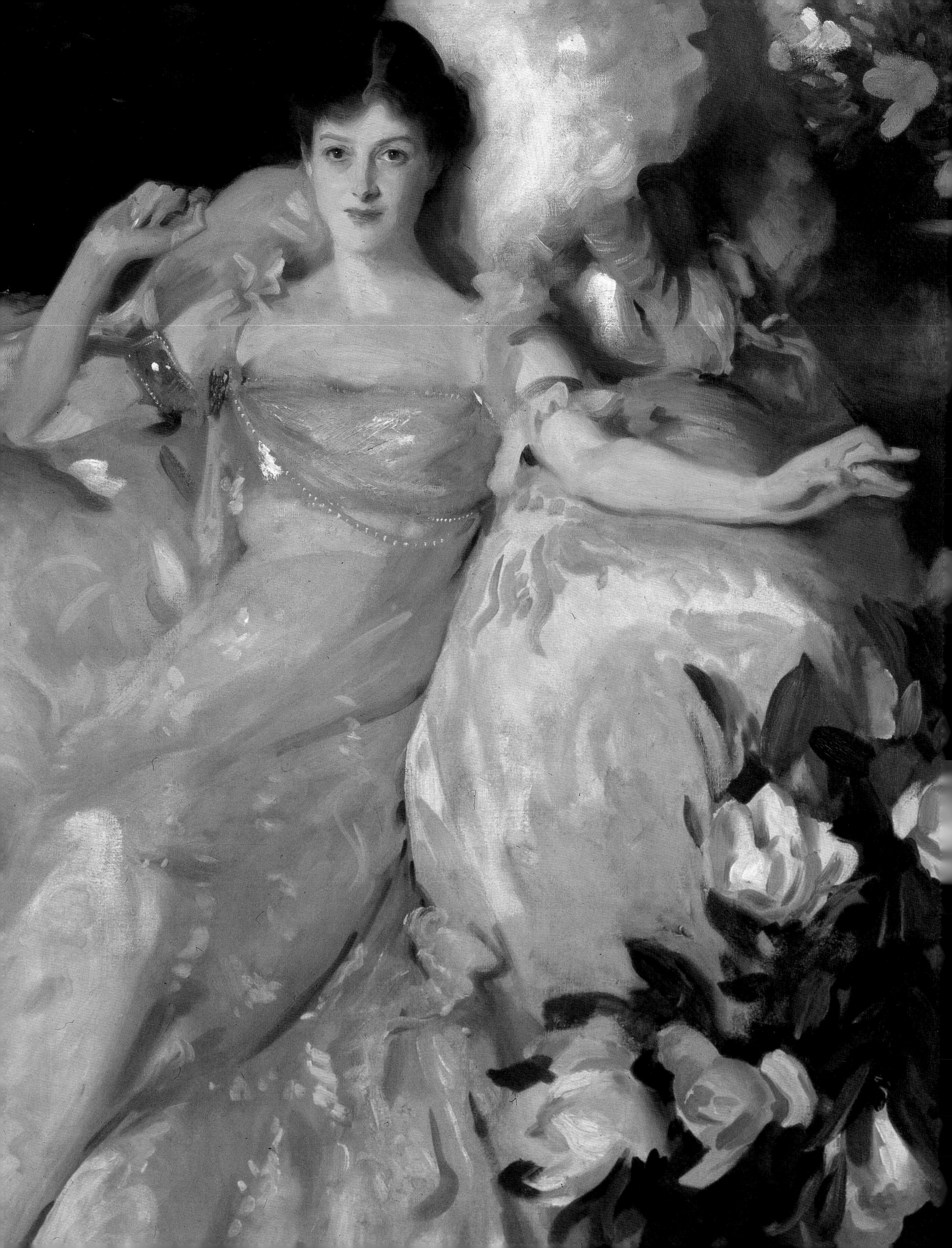

Sargent and British Portraiture

Sargent's success as a portraitist coincided with a renaissance in the art of portraiture in Britain. In the mid-nineteenth century, there were few portrait painters of distinction, and the romantic style of Sir Thomas Lawrence and his contemporaries had become enervated. There were exceptions, the stylish Sir Francis Grant, for example, the veteran George Richmond, and the suave international court painter Franz Xaver Winterhalter, but they were nearing the end of their professional careers. Younger talents like Richard Buckner and James Sant started promisingly but failed to stay the course.[1] In any case, the 1850s were the age of the subject picture, of early Pre-Raphaelite masterpieces, of history paintings like Frederic Leighton's *Cimabue's Celebrated Madonna is Carried in Procession through the Streets of Florence* (Royal Collection), and of genre scenes such as W. P. Frith's *The Derby Day* (Tate Gallery, London). Portraiture was left behind in the artistic ferment. People continued to be painted and reviewers dutifully recorded the latest crop of portraits at the annual Royal Academy exhibitions, but public attention was focused elsewhere on narrative painting and landscape. Interestingly, it was the avant-garde who rescued portraiture from artistic oblivion and gave it fresh life.

In the 1850s, George Frederic Watts, an allegorical painter with dreams of creating a vast cycle on the theme of 'The House of Life', painted a highly original series of full length portraits of female sitters. He had already begun to paint his famous contemporaries for a 'House of Fame', which he would eventually give to the nation. His portraits of fashionable women are quite different in style to those heroic and timeless images. They are painted in the conventions of grand-manner portraiture, they consciously draw on the iconography of eighteenth-century British portrait painters like Sir Joshua Reynolds and Thomas Gainsborough, and they reflect the worldly aspects of Watts's art as well as his idealizing tendencies. With portraits like *Mrs Nassau Senior* (1858, Wightwick Manor, Wolverhampton), *Mrs Louis Huth* (1858, National Gallery of Ireland, Dublin) and *Lady Margaret Beaumont and her Daughter* (fig. 22), Watts would, at a stroke, revolutionize portraiture in Britain.[2] The young aesthetic painters of the 1860s took up the gauntlet he had thrown down. Frederic Leighton's romantic portrait of May Sartoris (fig. 23) has become one of the icons of Victorian art – the soulful, poetic image of a young girl in a black riding habit slashed with red, painted against a ravishing view of the English countryside.

Watts and Leighton were only occasional portrait painters. It was Leighton's friend, the American artist James McNeill Whistler, who would put the aesthetic portrait on the map. His early picture, *At the Piano* (1858, Taft Museum, Cincinnati), is consciously decorative and poetic, with its harmonious arrangement of figures and accessories and its mood of musical reverie. It was to be followed a decade later by such cardinal works as *Arrangement in Grey and Black: Portrait of the Painter's Mother* (1871, Musée d'Orsay, Paris), *Arrangement in Grey and Black, No. 2: Portrait of Thomas Carlyle* (fig. 24), and *Harmony in Grey and Green: Miss Cicely Alexander* (1872–3, Tate Gallery, London). In these portraits, Whistler preserved a balance between form and composition, on the one hand, and, on the other colour and the penetrating interpretation of individual character. The artist exhibited the portrait of his mother at the Royal Academy, London, but the other two works appeared in a special Whistler exhibition at the Flemish Gallery in Pall Mall, London, in 1874. It was not until the founding of the Grosvenor Gallery in London in 1877 that Whistler, like other outsiders of his generation, found a congenial place in which to exhibit his work.

Another influential portraitist of his generation, an artist of a very different stamp, was the Pre-Raphaelite painter John Everett Millais.[3] His early works, including *Isabella* (1848–9, Walker Art Gallery, Liverpool) and *Ophelia* (1851–2, Tate Gallery, London), are meticulously detailed, brilliant in colour and execution, and intensely poetic in conception. They remain among the greatest masterpieces of British art. In the later 1850s, Millais's style broadened, and he came briefly under the sway of aestheticism before turning to the popular historical subjects and genre works with which he made his name. From the late 1860s onwards, Millais added to his reputation and income by painting portraits. He was both responding to market forces and exploiting his natural talent for the figure. His robust, painterly style, strong brand of realism and selective borrowings from the old masters established him as the foremost portrait painter of his generation. To the fashionable elegance of *Clarissa Bischoffsheim* (fig. 25) and *Hearts Are Trumps* (1872, Tate Gallery, London), with their air of opulence and richness, he joined the simplicity and gravity of his portraits

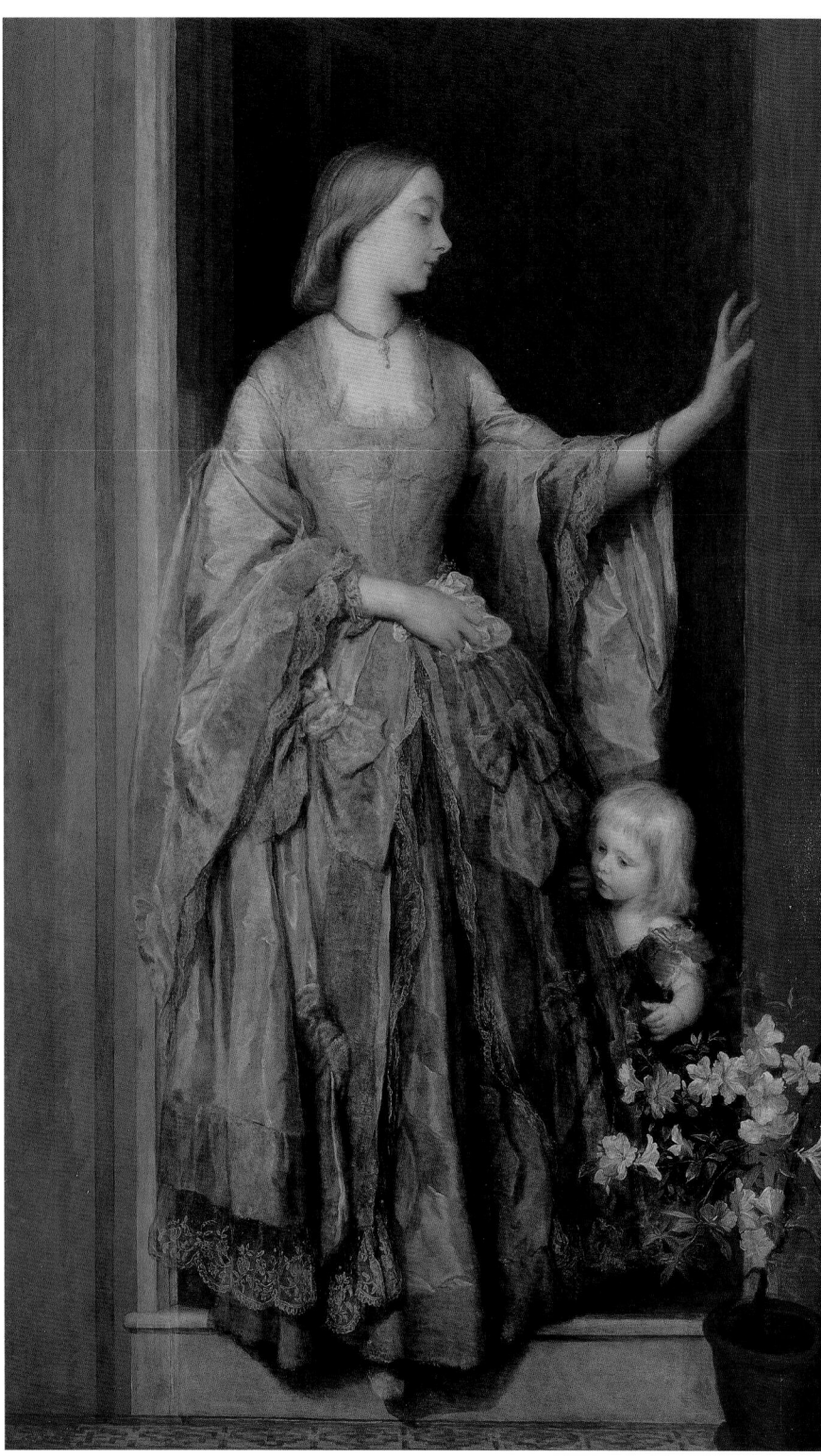

fig. 22 G. F. Watts, *Lady Margaret Beaumont and her Daughter*, 1862. Oil on panel, 76 × 45 ½ (193 × 115.6). Private Collection.

in the 1880s.[4] Frank Holl, for example, whose picture *Newgate – Committed for Trial* (Royal Holloway College, Egham, Surrey) was one of the sensations at the 1878 Royal Academy, had practically abandoned subject painting for portraiture by the time of his early death in 1888 at the age of forty-three. The relentless demands of sitters on a sensitive temperament are said to have hastened his end. Holl deserves greater recognition for the originality of his portraits, with their dramatic chiaroscuro, dark tones and painterly fluency, inspired by Rembrandt and the Dutch school (see fig. 26).

Holl's friend, Luke Fildes, followed the same path – early success as a subject painter, followed by portraiture. A much admired portrait of his wife at the Royal Academy of 1877 (Walker Art Gallery, Liverpool) opened up a new career that culminated in his state portraits of Edward VII and Queen Alexandra (Royal Collection). The Bavarian-born Herkomer also became a full-time portraitist, noted for his powerful images of men of action like Kitchener of Khartoum (National Portrait Gallery, London). He was not alone in finding portrait painting a lucrative alternative to other forms of art. The neoclassical portraits of Sir Edward Poynter, the artfully arranged works by Sir William Quiller Orchardson, the opulent and colourful pictures by Sir William Blake Richmond, and the frothy creations of Sir Frank Dicksee attest to the depth and strength of contemporary portrait painting in Britain. Several of Sargent's avant-garde contemporaries were also making their mark as portraitists in the 1890s, including fellow New English Art Club colleagues Philip Wilson Steer and Sir George Clausen, the brilliant Glasgow school 'boys' Sir John Lavery and Sir James Guthrie, and Sargent's special protégé Charles Wellington Furse.

It says much for the liberation of British art in the 1890s that an artist of such foreign antecedents as Sargent should have been absorbed by the establishment and relabelled as the premier British portraitist of his generation. Sargent's views of his fellow portraitists are unrecorded, but with the exception of Whistler and those younger artists who shared his views, they are unlikely to have been very flattering. His artistic allegiances were overwhelmingly cosmopolitan and international, yet he accepted his role as doyen of British portraiture without demur. The Royal Academy was the venue to which he sent his best work and where he looked for judgement on his performance. He was a loyal supporter of the institution itself and of the values that it represented, and he took his duties as an academician seriously. True that he painted a number of American sitters and that he had accepted a commission for mural decorations from the Boston Public Library, but to the British he was unquestionably one of their own. They saw him as the living embodiment of that great portrait tradition that stretched back to Sir Joshua Reynolds and Thomas Gainsborough and, before them, to Sir Peter Lely and Sir Anthony Van

of statesmen, among them William Ewart Gladstone and Benjamin Disraeli (1879 and 1881, respectively, both in the National Portrait Gallery, London).

Millais, like Whistler, was a pioneer in the revival of portrait painting; but where he led, others were soon to follow. A new generation of social realists came to the fore who had made their mark in the 1870s with disturbing images of social deprivation and poverty, many of them published as black-and-white illustrations in the *Graphic*. The leaders of the new school – Frank Holl, Sir Luke Fildes and Sir Hubert Herkomer – all became established painters and built up flourishing portrait practices

Dyck. Sargent saw it in the same way, adopting an iconography as time passed that was steeped in the British tradition of portraiture.

SARGENT AND SOCIETY

GREAT BRITAIN

Sargent's success as a portraitist in London in the 1890s can be linked directly to the changing nature of British society. The landed aristocracy, which had formed the governing élite for centuries, was in serious decline from the 1880s onwards, its influence eroded by political reform, falling agricultural rents and land values, the increasing professionalism of the modern state, and the rise of a new plutocracy. The vast fortunes being made in trade, industry and banking during the last quarter of the twentieth century dwarfed the fortunes of all but the very greatest territorial grandees.

> Between 1809 and 1879, some 88 per cent of British millionaires had been landowners, but between 1880 and 1914, the figure dropped to only 33 per cent, and it fell still further thereafter. And the advent of such wealth – often Jewish, often foreign, often American – engendered a real and justified sense of patrician anxiety. Quite rightly, they saw their economic supremacy threatened by this new form of wealth, which was in greater amounts, was in more liquid form, was less vulnerable to political exactions, and carried with it fewer obligations.[5]

The new plutocrats adopted many of the attributes of the landed families they were gradually supplanting. They entered Parliament, they sought and were granted titles, they acquired country seats and large London houses, they collected works of art, they intermarried with the old aristocracy, they lived and entertained in a grand style and with conspicuous expenditure. A number of these new tycoons were recent immigrants, financiers from Frankfurt and Hamburg, diamond kings from South Africa, sheep millionaires from Australia; some were homegrown businessmen and industrialists with fortunes from tea, railways, iron and steel, chemicals, and newspapers. Collectively they represented the growth and power of a global economy, in which Britain was a key player but by no means the only one. David Cannadine has written of British landowners: 'Their economic circumstances were much less determined by the state of the harvest in Barset or by the health of their bank account in London, than by the price of wheat in Chicago and by financial dealings on the New York stock exchange.'[6]

The lavish scale on which the upper classes lived suggests a stability that was more apparent than real. Thoughtful aristocratic leaders lamented the declining influence of their class, and among aristocrats generally there was a sense of foreboding of the old order passing. Reviewing changes in society, the veteran Lady Dorothy Nevill wrote: 'Birth to-day, is of small account, whilst wealth wields an unquestioned sway. It would indeed seem that society – aristocratic society that is – might have made a better bargain if it had exercised a greater amount of discrimination and reserve, while extending a welcome to millionaires shrewd enough to despise those whose ends they easily divined.'[7] In the country at large, there was much popular agitation against the landed interest as well as the rise of socialist societies and trade unions, strikes and demonstrations, and other signs of popular unrest. Land reform, the Irish question, the position of the House of Lords, votes for women, social legislation, education, free trade

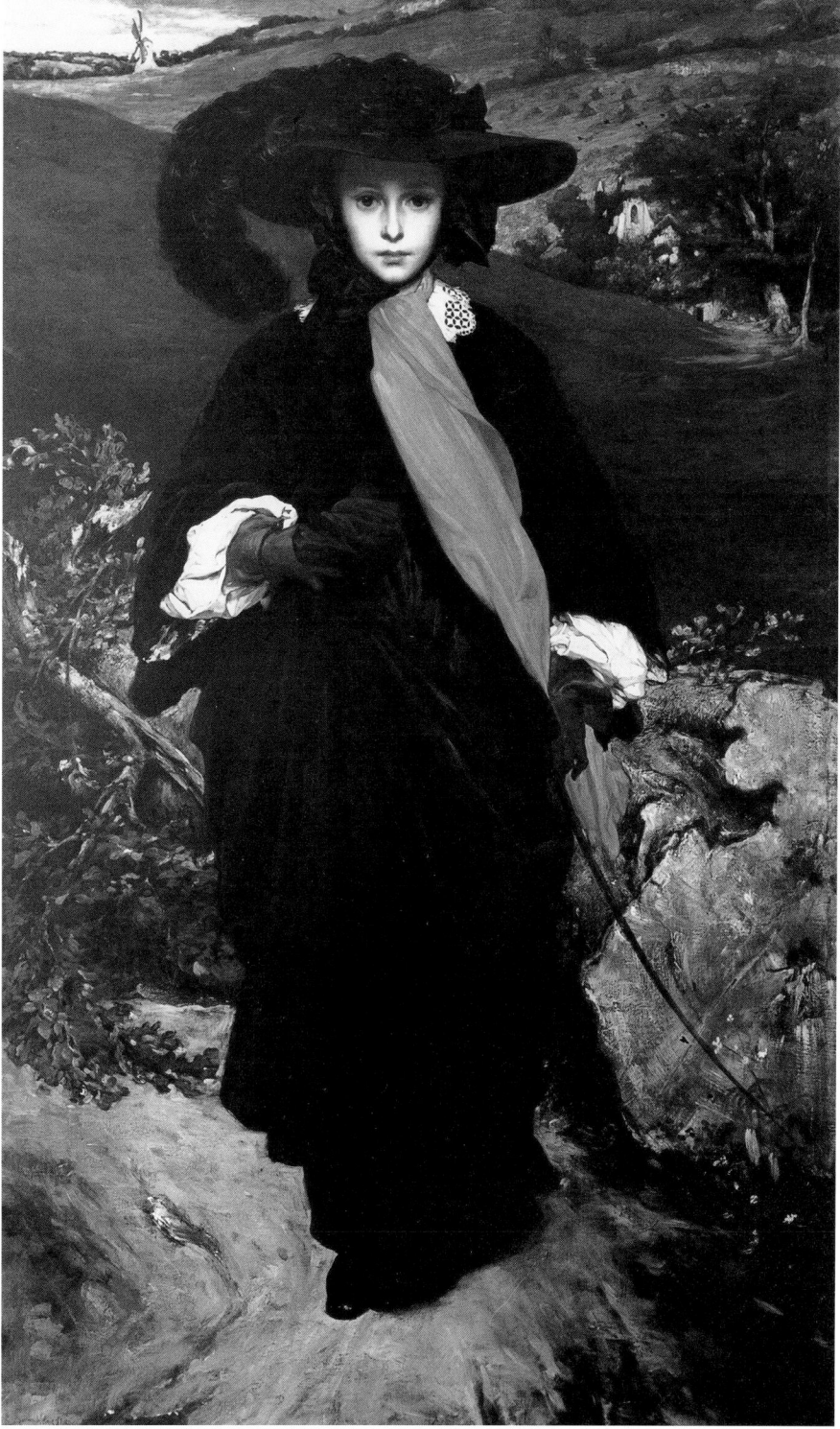

fig. 23 Frederic Leighton, *May Sartoris*, *c.* 1860. Oil on canvas, 59 ⅞ × 35 ½ (152.1 × 90.2). Kimbell Art Museum, Fort Worth, Texas.

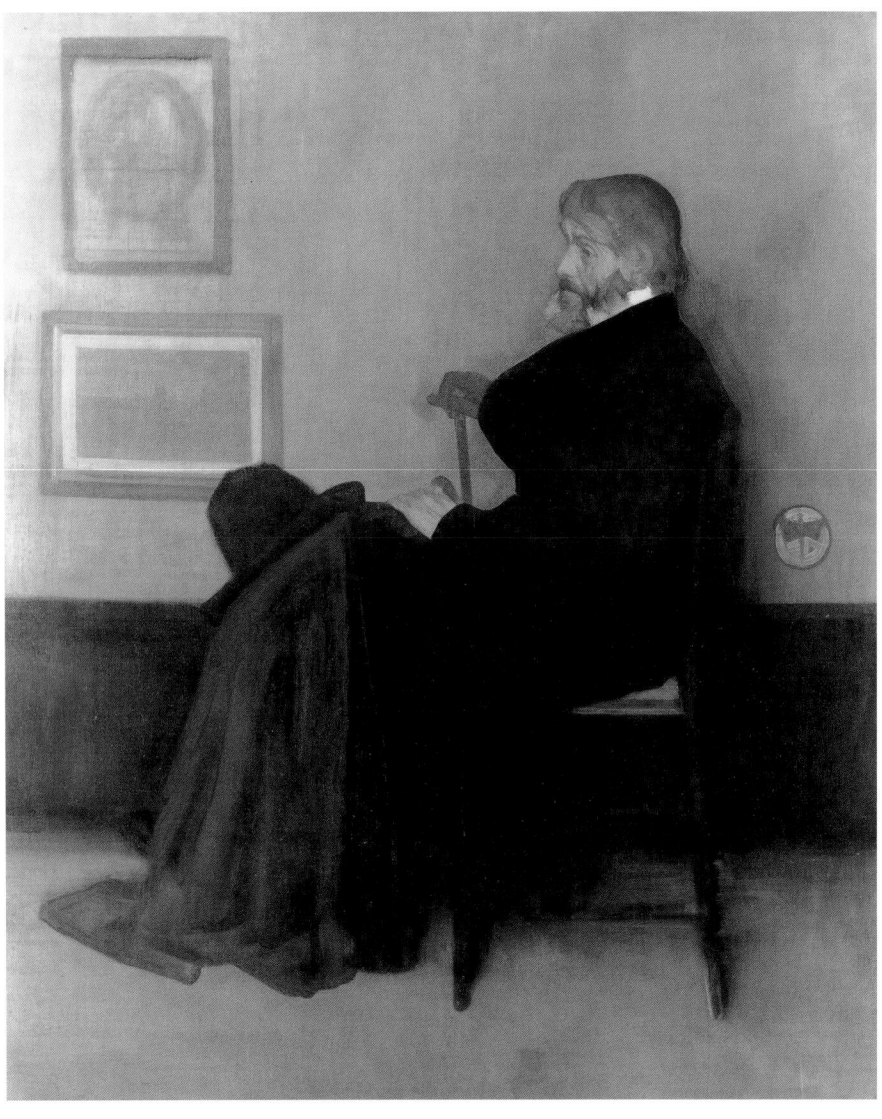

exuded confidence and self-importance whatever they may have lacked in distinguished ancestry. Their portraits by Sargent sat easily in the period interiors they created to prove their taste and display their wealth. The artist captured the hedonism, the extravagance, the vitality and the cultural pretensions of this thrusting new class. It is summed up in portraits like *Mrs Hugh Hammersley*, *Mrs Carl Meyer and her Children*, and *Mrs Charles Hunter* (nos 284, 324, 363). No one would mistake Mrs Meyer for an aristocrat of the old school. She is too full of herself, too expansive, fulsome and energetic. Everything about her, from her ropes of pearls to the gleaming gilt of the Louis Quinze furniture and panelling bespeaks the opulence of new money. You have only to compare her with the aloof beauty and restrained sensitivity of the Wyndham sisters (no. 368), members of that exclusive group of aesthetes, 'the Souls',[10] to appreciate at a glance their high breeding, studied nonchalance and good form. Sargent does not make moral judgements on his sitters, he may have been happier in the company of Mrs Meyer than in that of the Wyndham sisters, but he records social distinctions with an unerring eye.

Late nineteenth-century society was not only transformed by the wealth of the new capitalists, but also by the expansion of the professional classes. The development of trained expertise, allied to selection by merit, led to the rise of professional hierarchies, able to extend their power and influence by persuading the rest of society that their services were indispensable. Ultimately, as Harold Perkin has shown, the professional class

fig. 24 James McNeill Whistler, *Arrangement in Grey and Black, No.2: Portrait of Thomas Carlyle*, 1872–3. Oil on canvas, 67 ⅜ × 56 ½ (171.1 × 143.5). Glasgow Museum and Art Gallery.

and imperial preference, these were the fiercely debated issues of the day. This was not as settled an age as the mid-Victorian era had been, but one of radical changes, with all its attendant uncertainties and anxieties.

Many of Sargent's sitters in the 1890s were members of the new plutocracy, who were transforming traditional upper-class society.[8] Together with American millionaires, they created a boom in the market for the work of English portrait painters of the eighteenth century, whose popularity and prices soared during the last quarter of the nineteenth century. Robert Jensen writes: 'The same class of client who bought Romneys were as likely to purchase Sargent and it was probably no coincidence that most of the leading painters of the *juste milieu* including Whistler, Sargent, Liebermann, Boldini and Zorn (to cite only a few) were all notable portraitists, painting the aristocracy and the nouveau riche from London and Paris to New York and Chicago.'[9]

It is not difficult to see why Sargent should have appealed to this new type of patron. The artist endowed them with social prestige, power and glamour – they were sanctioned by the sweep of his brush. They were the new grandees who

fig. .25 Sir John Everett Millais, *Mrs Bischoffsheim*, 1873. Oil on canvas, 51 ½ × 35 ½ (130.8 × 90.2). Tate Gallery, London.

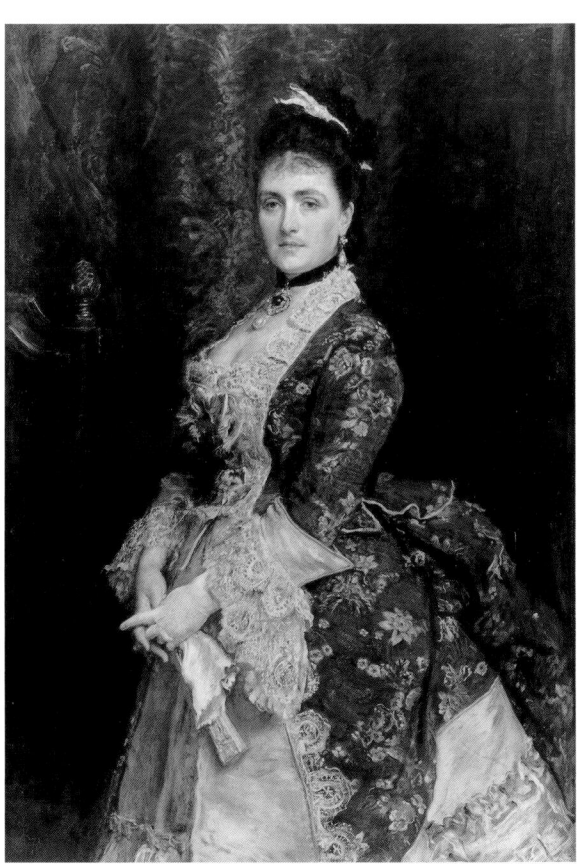

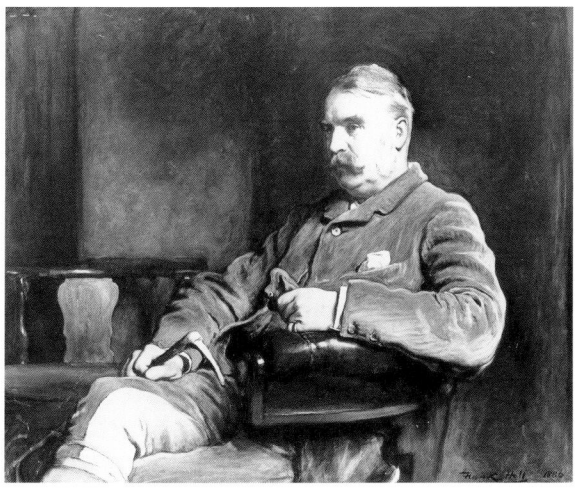

came 'to infiltrate all the major institutions of the modern state and modern society, from the executive government and parliament to the private capitalist corporations, and eventually to take them over.'[11] It is the members of the more established professions rather than the new breed of managers and civil servants who feature in Sargent's portraiture. He painted lawyers and politicians in some numbers and an occasional military man and academic. A significant proportion of these portraits were official or presentation commissions and represented the decisions of committees rather than the choice of individuals. The presence among Sargent's 'professional' sitters of several outstanding women, among them Jane Evans and Octavia Hill (nos 365 and 366), is another sign of changing times. They are not represented with fashionable dress and accessories, but as serious career women dedicated to their work.

Sargent's portraits of professional men extol their status in obvious ways. They are often represented in official roles or uniforms in accordance with traditional iconography. There is also imagery conditioned by the setting in which they were to hang. That of Lord Chief Justice Russell in Lincoln's Inn (no. 375) joined a large and distinguished collection of legal worthies stretching back to Tudor times. Sargent represents Russell conventionally in his robes of office, as a weighty representative of the law. We can judge Sargent's response to the human personality much more clearly in the informal study of Russell which he painted for the family (no. 376). Another famous jurist painted by the artist was Lord Watson (no. 351), again for a very public place, the Parliament House in Edinburgh. Here Sargent avoided obvious pomp and circumstance, depicting Watson not on the bench, but as if in the privacy of his chambers. In a subtle and reflective characterization, Sargent captures the sitter's authority and intellectual force.

The only soldier painted at this period was Colonel Ian Hamilton (no. 352), a man whom Sargent knew and admired. The subtly rendered features, seen in profile, the clutching hands and the refined silhouette reveal a sensitive and complex personality that transcends the stereotype of the military hero. Sargent exploits the frogging of the uniform, the soldier's sash, medals and sword, and the elegant, undulating outline of the greatcoat, to create a striking design expressive of military style and discipline. But the uniform does not swamp the man, and we can detect a questioning, uncertain air in the way Hamilton holds himself and gazes into space.

Politicians have no robes or symbols of office, and in conventional morning coats they are not easily distinguished from professional men and businessmen. It is through context and inference that we detect their office. The way in which Joseph Chamberlain stands (no. 333), one hand on a pile of documents, suggests that he is at the point of addressing an audience, perhaps at the dispatch box of the House of Commons.

Fashionable society at the turn of the century was not only opening itself up to financiers and politicians, but also to artists and writers, musicians and actors. In his portraits of such people, Sargent includes explicit references to their professional status and explores the sources of their creativity. The architect Francis Penrose (no. 350) has a look of beatific inspiration, hands clasped in front in an attitude of contemplation, a folder of plans beside him. Mrs George Batten (no. 340) throws back her head, closes her eyes and gives voice to an unheard aria. In the case of writers it is the sheer force of characterization that makes us aware that we are in the presence of genius. The far-away gaze and flowing locks of the elderly Coventry Patmore (no. 302) embody the poet at a moment of vision. The young writer and artist W. Graham Robertson (no. 306) is characterized as an exquisite aesthete, draped in a long close-fitting coat and sporting a jade-topped cane. In such pictures, Sargent recorded exceptionally gifted personalities, whose outlook and interests he shared, and created some of his most telling images in the process.

In contrast to the entrepreneurs and figures in the arts, this British nobility was slow to respond to Sargent's advance. He remained too risqué for them during the 1890s. The artist had painted the Honourable Laura Lister, daughter of Lord Ribblesdale (no. 323) in 1896, and two notable European noblewomen, Countess Clary Aldringen and Princess Demidoff (nos 325, 328) in the same year, but it was only in the wake of the success of *The Wyndham Sisters* (no. 368) that British aristocrats began to beat a path to his door.

AMERICA

The social scene in America was very different to that in Britain. The country was vast, expanding economically at a prodigious rate, and transforming itself into a world power. A *laissez-faire* approach to regulation, a huge but protected domestic market, cheap sources of energy and rapid technological innovation led to mass production on an unprecedented scale. The fall in

fig. 26 Frank Holl, *Sir W. S. Gilbert*, 1886. Oil on canvas, 39 ½ × 49 ½ (100.3 × 125.7). National Portrait Gallery, London.

production costs in turn stimulated demand. Fierce competition – which included price wars, manipulation of the stock market and aggressive take-overs – enabled successful capitalists to build up huge business empires: John D. Rockefeller in oil, Andrew Carnegie and Henry Frick in steel, J. P. Morgan and Cornelius Vanderbilt in railways and Alfred du Pont in chemicals. There was a reaction against the forces of big business, anti-trust and monopoly legislation was enacted; pro-agrarian, progressive movements were founded, and union agitation reached a crescendo in the 1890s. But the rationalization and incorporation of major industries brought obvious benefits to the nation in terms of wealth creation and efficiency, and the expanding economy was never seriously threatened by restrictive regulation. America was the land of opportunity and democratic freedoms, where everyone could dream of becoming a millionaire through their own efforts, and where progress was driven by market forces. American tycoons amassed fortunes that dwarfed those of their European counterparts. They also exerted immense influence in policy and affairs of state, though few of them entered the political arena. Men like Rockefeller and Morgan had a vision and a philosophy, which they promoted using their powerful position in society. Ruthless in their pursuit of business objectives, they sought to transform the nature of American society, to encourage integrity, enterprise and self-reliance, and to preach the benefits of efficiency and technology. They were also notable philanthropists who used their wealth to endow foundations, religious charities and places of learning. Although the old families of New York, so eloquently recorded in the novels of Edith Wharton, might regard themselves as superior to new money by right of lineage, taste and culture, they could continue to set the tone and the rules of social intercourse, but they were powerless to exclude newcomers or to dictate the terms on which they were allowed in. The situation was a little different in Boston, where a group of long-established families continued to hold sway. Elsewhere in the country, 'society' was in a rapid state of transition.

Those who made money expended their fortunes on a prodigious scale. The row of huge mansions that line Belmont Avenue in the Rhode Island resort of Newport testify to the extravagance of the American super rich. They employed the best architects for their houses, using the most expensive materials money could buy, and they filled them with rare works of art and opulent accessories. This was the age when American millionaires acquired major European art treasures and created some of the greatest art collections ever assembled. Among them are the Isabella Stewart Gardner Museum in Boston, the Cloisters and the Frick Collection in New York City, and the Huntington Library and Art Gallery in Pasadena. The super rich chose Sargent as their portraitist in the same way as they chose their furniture and houses because he represented the best that Europe had to offer. And he, in turn, endowed these magnates, their wives and their daughters with the aura of beauty, sophisticated taste and fashionable elegance.

Sargent's mural work for the Boston Public Library brought him to America in 1895, and, as in 1890, he was inundated with comissions. On either side of 1895, a steady stream of American patrons beat a path to the door of his Tite Street studio to be recorded for posterity. Among them were members of the leading families of American big business and banking: Astor (finance), Leiter (corn), Marquand (finance) and Vanderbilt (railways). Sargent also painted several 'Boston Brahmins', representatives of the old moneyed families of New England's capital; these included Brooks, Hammond, Loring, Peabody and Sears. Here he was on home ground, in the company of congenial people whose values and outlook he shared.

The character of Sargent's portraiture is intrinsically cosmopolitan. Like his patrons, he belonged to an international set which felt equally at home in London, Paris and New York. Whether British or American, his sitters exude the same aura of fashionability; French-style furniture and accessories surround them; they wear the same *haute-couture* dresses and formal morning coats; they have the self-confidence of those who take wealth and privilege for granted; they recognize their own kind across national boundaries and treat the world as their oyster. Sargent's success lay in his ability to capture the aspirations of this turn of the century 'jet set' and to portray them as glamorous international figures.

Sargent was, however, too acute an observer to blur all national distinctions. It may be difficult to distinguish Florence Twombly (no. 245) from her British contemporaries – Mrs Hugh Hammersley (no. 284), for example. She is every bit as elegant and refined as her rival, and the palatial interior in which she poses could just as easily be European as American. Nevertheless, in Sargent's American portraits there is sometimes a sharper line of jaw, a more assured self-confidence, a straighter carriage and a greater sense of ease. As early as 1903, the poet and critic Alice Meynell noted this phenomenon: 'When Mr Sargent paints an American – the portrait of Mr Roosevelt, for example – the eye has the look of America, the national habit is in the figure and head... In like manner, Mr Sargent paints an Englishwoman with all the accents, all the negatives, all the slight things that are partly elegant and partly dowdy.'[12] Though posed in similar dresses and sitting in French bergère chairs, Lady Agnew (no. 286) and Mrs Joshua Montgomery Sears (no. 370) are intrinsically different, the one languorous, laid back and soulful, the other all energy and alert intelligence.

Not all Sargent's female sitters are presented as creatures of fashion and culture. In a break with normal practice, he chose to present Edith Phelps Stokes as a new type of woman in the double portrait with her husband, Isaac (no. 337). Dressed for outdoors, in long skirt and jacket and carrying a boater, she is the image of liberated womanhood – strong, self-confident, independent and in command of her own destiny. The shadowy figure of her husband in the background serves to point up her own vitality and resolution. Something of this same elasticity and freedom of spirit informs the portraits of other young American women. For all her billowing shawls and statuesque gown, painted in emulation of Sir Joshua Reynolds and Sir Thomas Lawrence, Daisy Leiter (no. 358), soon to marry into the British aristocracy, remains a fresh and spontaneous presence. She is, it can be argued, unmistakably American.

In his portraits of the tycoons themselves, Sargent was most successful with those whom he admired for reasons other than their wealth. George Washington Vanderbilt (no. 247) appears book in hand as a bibliophile and aesthete – everything about the portrait proclaims it. Henry G. Marquand (no. 343) had been the person who gave Sargent his first chance in America by commissioning the portrait of his wife in 1887 (see *Early Portraits*, no. 192). He was chairman of the Metropolitan Museum of Art's board of trustees, a great patron of contemporary art, as well as a highly successful banker. Sargent's portrait of this rugged and powerful old man is couched in terms of intellectual energy and vision. Marquand supports his head with his hand in a traditional pose symbolizing thoughtfulness and introspection. The majority of politicians were pygmies by comparison with the entrepreneurs, and the issues facing them were parochial compared with the magnitude of economic expansion. This was not an era of great political events or constitutional crises, and there was little to test the mettle of American leadership. The Spanish-American War of 1898, which led to the liberation of Cuba and the acquisition of Puerto Rico and other territories by the United States, replaced one form of imperialism with another. That apart, politics were dominated by domestic issues, where Republican protectionists regularly changed places with progressive Democrats, and the pendulum of public opinion swung this way and that.

Sargent was to paint a significant number of the American political establishment, including two distinguished presidents. His 1890 portrait of the prominent Boston senator Henry Cabot Lodge (no. 264), establishes the format he was to repeat in later political portraits. Lodge is depicted three-quarter length, in a dark suit, the thumb of one hand stuck in his pocket, the other fingering his watch chain. His inward look of thoughtfulness is enhanced by the dramatic underlighting. Trevor Fairbrother links the essential theatricality of the image to that of the contemporary portrait of the actor Edwin Booth (no.

232).[13] Both sitters are in some sense on-stage, though neither is in character. The formidable southern senator Calvin Brice (no. 346) is shown in a pose similar to Lodge's, though the former is dressed more formally in frock-coat and bow-tie. He radiates charisma, from his well-groomed hair, gleaming beard and level gaze to his easy, self-confident stance and the negligent way in which he holds his pince-nez by its cord, as if about to swing it. The inclusion in the background of a peacock panel from one of Sargent's Chinese lacquer screens is a witty touch which Sargent uses to throw character into relief.

The professions are as well represented in Sargent's American portraiture as they are in his English. Here the sitters are distinguished by a conscious weightiness of intellect and dignity of setting. M. Carey Thomas (no. 371), the president of Bryn Mawr College in Pennsylvania, sits swathed in dark impressive robes, her eyes gazing fearlessly out, her left hand grasping the end of a Renaissance-style chair arm. She is the embodiment of intellectual force and moral probity

The professions for which Sargent felt most sympathy were inevitably those of the theatre and the arts. In 1890, he painted three famous American actors – Edwin Booth, Lawrence Barrett and Joseph Jefferson (nos 232, 233, 272, 273, 274). The full-length portrait of Booth, which hangs in The Players in New York, is a strange and eerie evocation of the actor and his craft, an off-stage characterization that is yet intensely dramatic. The same is true of the portrait of the American actress Ada Rehan (no. 308), who might at first glance pass for an expansive society hostess. The strut of the figure, the huge feather fan and the opulent setting, however, betray the character of a performer.

In painting figures from the arts, Sargent invariably makes explicit reference to their profession. The architect and the designer respectively of the great Vanderbilt estate at Biltmore in North Carolina, Richard Morris Hunt and Frederick Law Olmsted (nos 319, 320), both inhabit the spaces they created in a tribute to their artistry. Sargent posed Olmstead against a backdrop of rhododendron, mountain laurel and dogwood, in a woodland area on the northern side of the estate. Surrounded by so much foliage he takes on the character of a benign Jack-`o-the-Green. Hunt, by contrast, stands like a grandee beside a red marble well-head in the courtyard of the château he had designed, his greatcoat thrown stylishly over one shoulder.

CHILDREN

One aspect of Sargent's portraiture that deserves special mention is his portraits of children. Children feature not only on their own, but as family members in the group portraits that Sargent painted at regular intervals after 1890. Like Van Dyck before him, Sargent had a special affinity

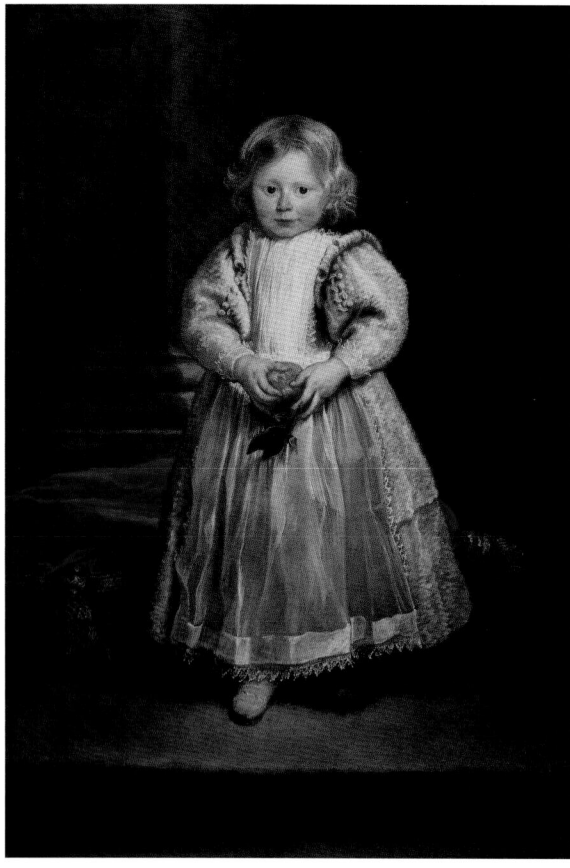

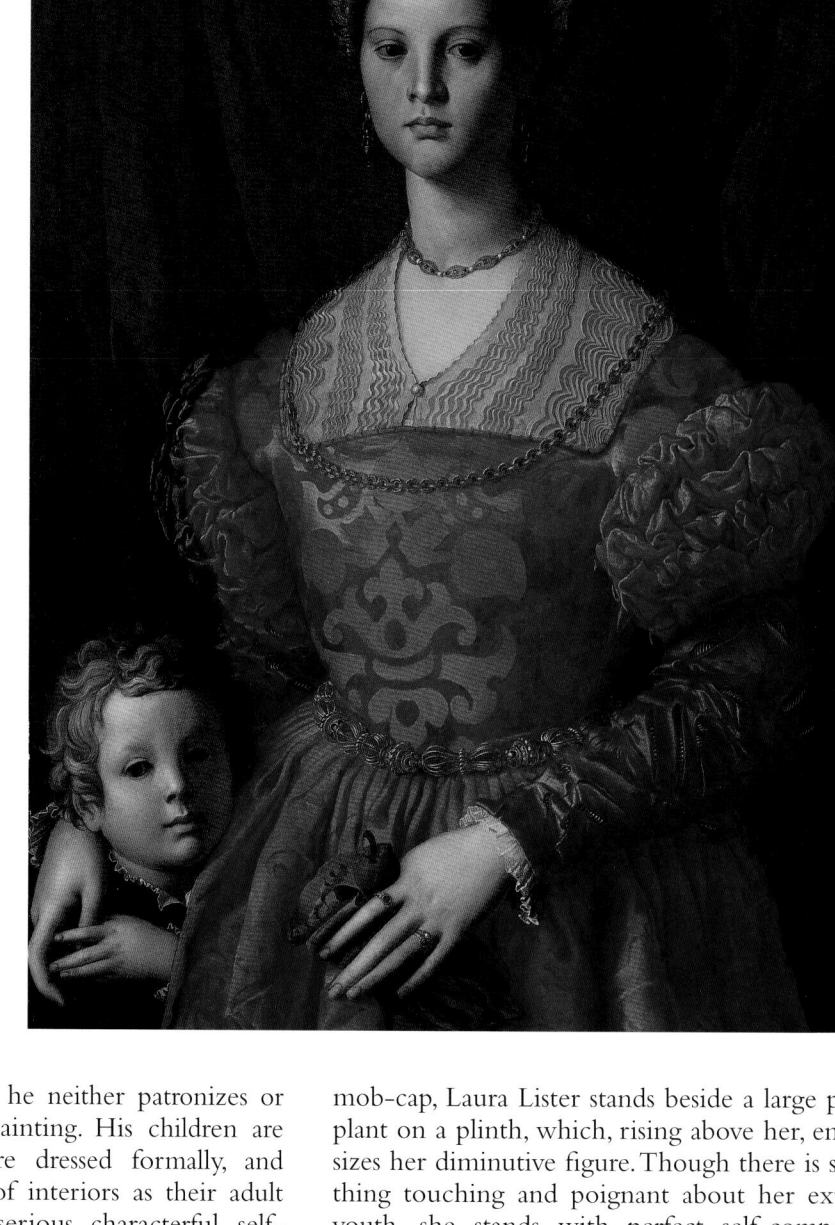

fig. 27 (above)
Sir Anthony Van Dyck,
*Clelia Cattaneo, Daughter
of Marchesa Elena
Grimaldi*, 1623. Oil on
canvas, 48 ⅛ × 33 ⅛
(122.2 × 84.1). National
Gallery of Art,
Washington, D.C.,
Widener Collection
1942.9.94.

fig. 28 (right) Agnolo
Bronzino, *A Young
Woman and her Little
Boy*, c. 1540. Oil on
panel, 39 ⅛ × 29 ⅞ (99.5
× 76). National Gallery
of Art, Washington, D.C.,
Widener Collection,
1942.9.6.

with the young, whom he neither patronizes or sentimentalizes in his painting. His children are evidently high-born, are dressed formally, and inhabit the same kind of interiors as their adult counterparts. They are serious, characterful, self-contained, self-confident, individualistic and full of life. The series of full-length portraits of children opens in 1890 with *Beatrice Goelet* (no. 239), one of Sargent's masterpieces. Holding her hands together in a gesture of greeting, the little girl exhibits a self-possession rare in such a young child. Dressed like an infanta in a striped gown of pink and green, with a necklace of pearls and a pink bow in her hair, she holds the centre of the stage with Van Dyckian gravity, while the pet parrot in its bird-cage symbolizes the world of wealth and privilege from which she comes (see fig. 27).

Later portraits in the same vein include those of the Honourable Laura Lister, Helen Sears and the Honourable Victoria Stanley (nos 323, 318, 369). The first of these is, like the portrait of Beatrice Goelet, reminiscent of the old masters in presentation. In full-length formal gown and

mob-cap, Laura Lister stands beside a large potted plant on a plinth, which, rising above her, emphasizes her diminutive figure. Though there is something touching and poignant about her extreme youth, she stands with perfect self-composure, confronting us without guile or self-consciousness, just as she is. The portrait of the American Helen Sears is quite different in mood and character. Here, the little girl in white, surrounded by large pots of hydrangeas, is less formal and more abstract. She is reminiscent of those Impressionist pictures of the 1880s which show little girls in white surrounded by flowers. The mood of the picture is poetic, suggesting the transience of youth and beauty in the close juxtaposition of flowers and figure, and in the dark receding space behind them.

The same Velázquez-inspired use of space sets off the flamboyant figure of the Honourable Victoria Stanley. Energy and vitality are evident in every line of her lithe figure, in the alert, expressive features, in the slightly parted legs and gleaming shoes, in the crisp white folds of the dress, set off by the red jacket and flamboyant feathered bonnet, and in the circular patterns of the Aubusson carpet. The presence of the crop, though she is not dressed for riding, is a reminder of the country pursuits beloved by the British upper classes. The Honourable Victoria Stanley proclaims her aristocratic rank through the inborn sense of superiority she exhibits. She is not a little princess in the old-fashioned style of Beatrice Goelet, but a thoroughly modern young girl.

In double portraits and groups, Sargent's children are never simply ciphers or appendages. They exhibit just as much individuality as they do in single portraits, and their relationship to adults is subtle and unforced. Invariably children are portrayed with their mother, if only one parent is present. Homer Saint-Gaudens listening to his mother reading is the real subject of the double portrait of mother and son (no. 243). Livingston Davis, wearing a sailor suit, shares star billing with his mother, putting a protective arm around her waist, while she passes her arm around his shoulders to grasp his other hand in a pose which may derive from Agnolo Bronzino's *A Young Woman and her Little Boy*, c. 1540 (fig. 28) (no. 250). Mrs Meyer's children are relegated to walk-on parts, peering out shyly from behind the sofa that she fills so amply, but they are essential to the design and to the psychology of the elaborate family group (no. 324).

NOTES TO THE INTRODUCTION

1. Richard Buckner (1812–83), fashionable portraitist, partly based in Rome. James Sant (1820–1916), prolific and successful portraitist and subject painter.
2. The significance of Watts's full-length portraits of women was discussed by Barbara Bryant in a lecture at Kenwood House, London, in 1999.
3. See Peter Funnell and others, *Millais: Portraits*, National Portrait Gallery, London, 1999.
4. For a recent discussion of the work of Frank Holl, Sir Luke Fildes, and Sir Hubert Herkomer, see Paula Gillett, *The Victorian Painter's World*, London, 1990, pp. 101–32.
5. David Cannadine, *The Decline and Fall of the British Aristocracy*, New Haven and London, 1990, p. 91.
6. Ibid. p. 90.
7. Lady Dorothy Nevill, *Under Five Reigns*, ed. R. Nevill, London, 1910, pp. 140–1.
8. Several of Sargent's sitters appear in Joe Mordaunt Crook, *The Rise of the Nouveaux Riches*, London, 1999.
9. Robert Jensen, *Marketing Modernism in Fin-de-Siècle Europe*, Princeton, 1994, p. 147.
10. Patrician, high-minded, intellectual and artistic, 'the Souls' were an Edwardian social and cultural élite. Sargent painted a number of individuals either prominent in, or associated with the coterie. For an account of the milieu and for biographical information about the principal figures, their relationships and activities, see Abdy and Gere 1983.
11. Harold Perkin, *The Rise of Professional Society*, London and New York, 1998, p. xii.
12. Meynell 1903, n.p.; Meynell Manson 1927, n.p.
13. Fairbrother 1986, pp. 158–9.

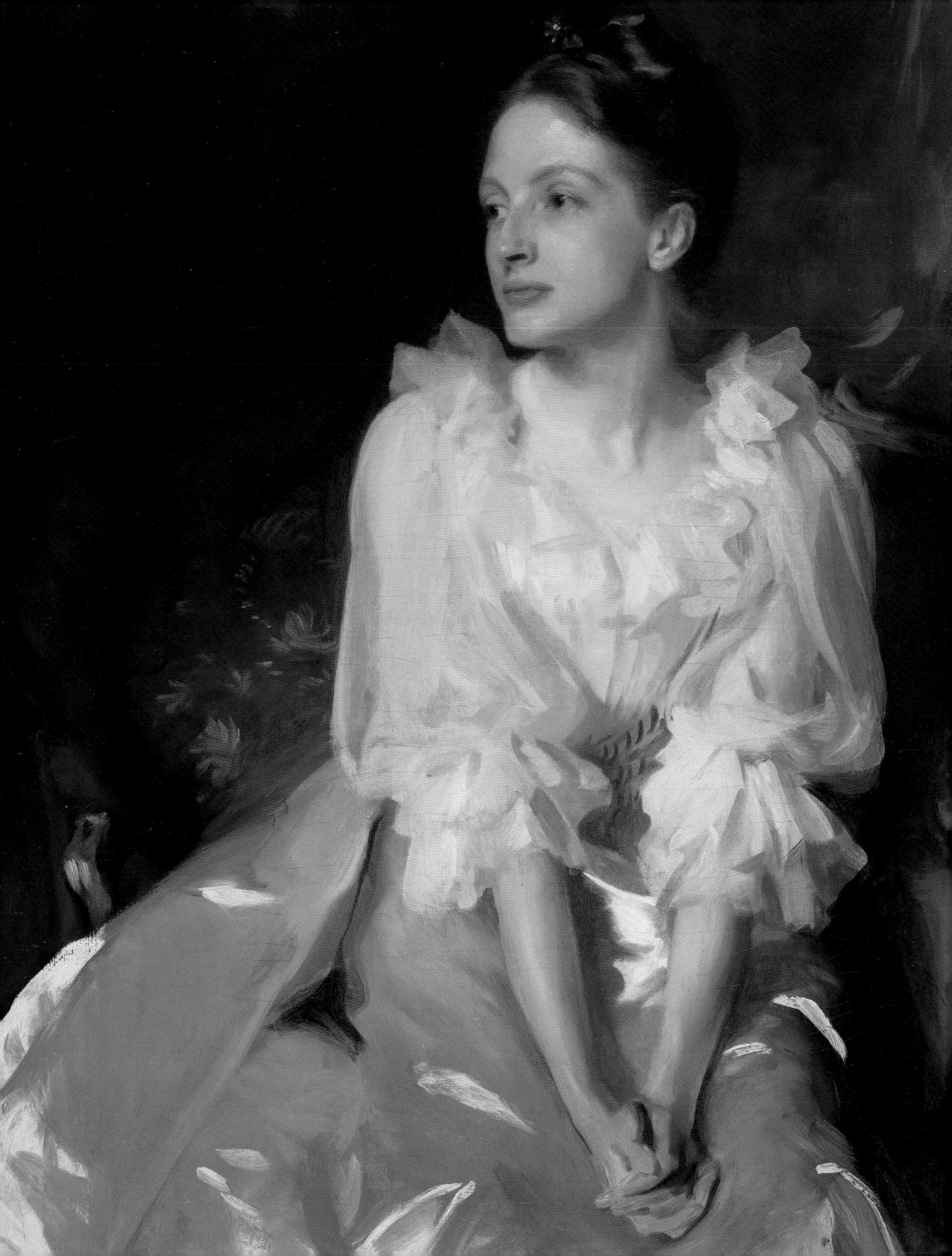

PORTRAITS

1890–3

The year 1890 marked a watershed for Sargent. In the mid-1880s, his career as a portrait painter faltered. He had moved from Paris to London, but his professional prospects did not seem promising and he considered abandoning painting altogether.[1] In the absence of portrait commissions, he painted in the English countryside, experimenting with landscapes and figure studies, placing his brushstrokes more discretely, working in a brighter palette and developing a broader facture. In 1887 he had two breakthroughs: at the Royal Academy, his twilight study of two girls lighting Chinese lanterns, *Carnation, Lily, Lily, Rose* (Tate Gallery, London) both appealed to late Victorian taste and opened eyes to a new style of painting; and his first professional visit to America later in the year resulted in an unexpected rush of commissions. There was a decisive shift, too, in his personal life: his father had died in 1889 and the young Sargent assumed responsibility for his mother and two unmarried sisters.

The decade opened with a significant American interlude. Sargent spent a full ten months in America in 1890, arriving late in December 1889 and sailing back to England early the following November. It was a prolific season and, with regard to patronage, reputation and future direction, a defining one. Dennis Miller Bunker's estimation that Sargent painted 'a hundred portraits' during this period is an exaggeration, but he certainly executed more than forty (twenty-five of them commissioned), which would have required at least a hundred sittings.[2] It is not surprising that Bunker should have described him as 'busy all the time – at white heat always, rushing from one place to another'.[3] Sargent's phenomenal energy was about to be channelled into a new American enterprise. The grand, decorative scheme for the Boston Public Library, which was initiated in 1890, provided him with a sweeping and sustaining artistic and intellectual challenge, and it brought about a radical change in the rhythm of his professional life. From the early 1890s, he was constantly negotiating and juggling the pressures of a burgeoning portrait practice with the logistical, mechanical and administrative demands of a large public undertaking. The significance that the murals assumed in

Sargent's life should not be underestimated. He had been brought up in the French academic tradition, which placed mural art in public places at the pinnacle of the aesthetic hierarchy. There could, in consequence, be no nobler cause than that of beautifying the public monuments of a great city like Boston, and he set about the task of designing allegorical subjects for large spaces with a high sense of mission.

Theatre and theatricality were natural subjects for Sargent, and his portraits of actors and actresses stand out as a distinct group, attesting to his dramatic instincts and his passion for the stage. In 1889, he had painted a portrait of Sir Henry Irving and his famous study of Ellen Terry as Lady Macbeth (*Early Portraits*, nos 181 and 183), and several portraits of that year are decidedly theatrical in character, like those of Clementina Anstruther-Thomson and Flora Priestley (*Early Portraits*, nos 216 and 225). Now, in 1890, Sargent turned to the American theatre, exploring the role of the actor on and off stage and that borderline between fantasy and reality where so many of his finest works had originated. Edwin Booth is one of those wiry, intense creatures to whom Sargent responded pictorially, and the full-length of him (no. 232) might be taken as that of a man in character, so powerfully is his lean figure and air of expectancy projected against the gigantic fireplace. More intense still is the charged image of Booth set down in an oil sketch at a single sitting (no. 233). It is impossible here to disentangle the man from the role-player, able to strike a pose or adopt an attitude at a moment's notice. The same ambiguity is implicit in the sketch of the comedian Joseph Jefferson (no. 274), whose face, dazzled by light, emerges from the shadows like an elfin apparition. The portrait of him in his famous role as Dr Pangloss (no. 273) is paradoxically less startling because it conforms to a more familiar type of theatrical portraiture.

The directness of Sargent's pictorial imagination creates an art of pure appearance with performance and spectacle at its core, and the most sensational of Sargent's theatrical portraits of the 1890s is a full-length of the cultish Spanish dancer, *La Carmencita* (no. 234). An oil study (no.

Detail of no. 279, Helen Dunham.

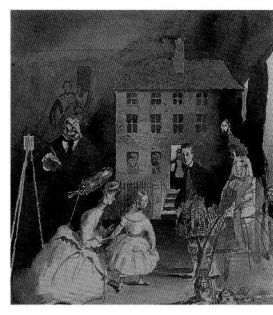

fig. 29 Henry Tonks, caricature of Velázquez's *Las Meninas*. Watercolour on paper, 10 ½ × 9 ½ (26.7 × 24.1), Private Collection.

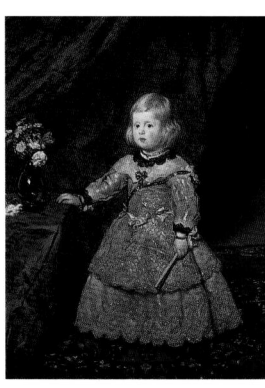

fig. 30 Diego Rodriguez de Silva y Velázquez, *Infanta Margarita*, c. 1653. Oil on canvas, 50 ⅝ × 39 ⅜ (128. 5 × 100). Kunsthistorisches Museum, Vienna.

237) suggests that he may have considered a dancing scene, a latter-day *El Jaleo*, 1882 (Isabella Stewart Gardner Museum, Boston), but he subsequently modified this to a static, standing figure, which expressed a sense of implicit movement and captured the dancer's force of personality and showmanship. The final version resembles a blown-up sketch rather than a finished portrait, so freely and confidently is it painted. In this respect, Sargent's compositional and painterly impulses work as one: the expressive visibility of his brushstrokes on the paint surface confirms his interest in the purely pictorial motif.

Sargent exhibited a range of work in several American cities in 1890.[4] His *A Morning Walk* and *St Martin's Summer* (both now in private collections) had disquieted English critics when they were shown at the New English Art Club in 1889, but American critics responded with more openness to the *frisson* of the French avant-garde when the same works were among a group of paintings shown in various combinations in Boston, New York, Chicago and Philadelphia in 1890.[5] Sargent sent seven paintings to the Society of American Artists exhibition in New York in the spring of 1890, but only two were recent American works: *La Carmencita* (no. 237), and a three-quarter length of George Washington Vanderbilt (no. 247). *La Carmencita* was hung in the place of honour at the head of the main gallery and attracted the lion's share of critical attention: it would also be shown in London, at the Royal Academy, in 1891, and in Paris, at the Société national des beaux-arts, the following year. There were those who disapproved of the painting's ragged energy and bizarrerie, and there were some complaints about a perceived hastiness of execution and inelegance of drawing, but the distortions which troubled certain critics may have served an artist whose purpose was not verisimilitude, but an impressionistic rendering of a remarkable performer.

When Sargent's portraits hung on the walls of galleries in London, Paris, New York, Boston, Chicago or Philadelphia, what seemed to distinguish them from works by other artists was the illusion that they presented of life being lived, as if the membrane between real life and created art had been utterly thinned. At the Royal Academy in 1891, the *Times* critic wrote of *La Carmencita*:

> What one gets from it is in the first place an extraordinary sense of vitality: this, one is half-inclined to say, is not a picture, it is the living being itself, and when the music strikes up she will be bound away in the dance. For beauty, that is another matter; the painter has not gone in search of it in the first instance – he has preoccupied himself with life, in the hope that beauty would emerge with it.

This critic discerned the same life force in *Mrs Thomas Lincoln Manson Jr* (no. 241), but used more physiologically precise language to describe it: 'life, too, the actual breath, and, still more, the actual working of nerve and brain'.[6] *Mrs Hugh Hammersley* (no. 284) communicated an exciting and heightened realism: 'not beauty exactly, but life, reality, an actual and captivating animation',[7] but, in an extended piece in praise of the portrait, George Moore pointed to its sense of the captured moment as a limitation, defining it as 'a picture of the hour; it fixes the idea of the moment and reminds one somewhat of a *première* at the Vaudeville with Sarah [Bernhardt] in a new part. Everyone is on the *qui vive*. The *salle* is alive with murmurs of approbation. It is the joy of the passing hour, the delirium of the sensual present'.[8]

If the vitality and immediacy of Sargent's images marked him out to his contemporaries and signalled his modernity, his portraiture frequently succeeds by the way in which it fuses a modern sensibility with the art of the past, dovetailing the contemporary and the traditional. As early as 1882, Vernon Lee was describing *Lady with the Rose* (*Early Portraits*, no. 55) as 'simply superb & like an old master'[9] and, throughout Sargent's career, the critical discourse reverberates with references both to the influence of the old masters in his work and to Sargent himself as a modern old master. Sargent was steeped in the old master tradition, but his dual touchstones, Velázquez and Hals, were entirely in tune with the enthusiasms of the progressives among his contemporaries. By the mid-1870s, Velázquez – Manet's 'peintre des peintres'[10] – had become a talismanic figure for young artists, fully assimilated into the atelier, and even the academic, canon, and the sophisticated painterly expertise of Frans Hals was the model for 'les enfants volontaires du quai Malquais'.[11] It was Velázquez whose spirit critics most frequently discerned in Sargent's work.[12] It became a commonplace of critical discourse to nominate Sargent the 'new Velázquez', and when Henry Tonks posed Sargent as the figure of Velázquez in his caricature of *Las Meninas*, he was giving visual expression to an idea that had been well canvassed in the press (see fig. 29).[13]

The presence of Velázquez in Sargent's art is palpable, but it has proved difficult to define precisely. There are few borrowings in terms of pose and composition, and the prevailing influence is a diffuse one, a subtle response to Velázquez's painterly realism and tonal asceticism, the elegance and gravity with which his art is infused, the luminous effects of his brushwork, an ambiguous appreciation of space and a sense of form less fixed and defined. In turning again and again to Velázquez in his portraiture, one senses that Sargent was transfixed by the master's power to evoke pictorially the mystery of individual personality and that, by working and reworking Velázquez, he might discover the secrets of his formal grace.[14] When *La Carmencita* was exhibited, many critics (notably those in London) thrilled to the timbre of the characterization, to the interfusion of old master gravity and piquant modernity which seemed to define Sargent's distinctive idiom. One commentator called upon the seventeenth-century Spanish painter in one breath and a contemporary French poet in the next to illustrate his point:

> The execution, if slight, has the masterly breadth obtained by a long study of Velasquez, in imitation of whom the sloping floor is depicted as a grey space without defined limits. 'La Carmencita' is undoubtedly a creation sprung from the artificial soil of the expiring century, a veritable 'Fleur du Mal', such as would have delighted Baudelaire himself; but it would be impossible to give more spontaneous or more passionate expression to a conception which, in its mingled strangeness and naturalistic truth, expresses the very poetry of modern realism.[15]

The critical response to the portraits at the Society of American Artists exhibition was mixed, but the tautness, economy of suggestion and quickness of touch of the paintings meant that the name of Velázquez was frequently invoked. One critic had recourse to oriental terms of reference, describing the handling as 'miraculously clever . . . [suggesting] what a Japanese Velasquez might do'.[16] The 'rediscovery' of Velázquez in the late nineteenth century was closely connected to developments in and discussions about modern art and contemporary writers and artists responded to those qualities in Velázquez that chimed with their own preoccupations. It is natural that critics should have identified the painterly freedom of Sargent's brushwork with what Claude Phillips described as the 'swift magic proper to Velasquez, his [Sargent's] avowed prototype'.[17]

Contemporary enthusiasm for Velázquez was tantamount to hero-worship, but Sargent's painterly responses to the master's work are bold rather than deferential. In the spring of 1891, he contributed a full-length study of a little girl in seventeenth-century dress to the Society of American Artists exhibition, where it succeeded *La Carmencita* in occupying the place of honour. His *Beatrice Goelet* (no. 239) might be described as a homage to Velázquez, a refined commentary on the seventeenth-century motif of the infanta and its various nineteenth-century translations, though one reviewer saw in it not homage, but a blatant, even impertinent, throwing down of the artistic gauntlet: 'the audacity of the direct challenge to a comparison with Velasquez'.[18] With her fair hair, solemn expression and childish dignity, Sargent's Beatrice alludes to Velázquez's series of single portraits of the Infanta Margarita (the first child of Philip IV and his queen, Mariana) (fig. 30), and to her representation in *Las Meninas*.[19] Sargent, however, chose a perspective quite different to Velázquez's frontality. Looking down on Beatrice's diminutive figure, which seems surrounded by air, the spectator experiences both the integrity and the vulnerability of her presence: the isolation inherent in a royal role transferred to a princess of the New World.

Sargent's *Beatrice Goelet* is a highly sophisticated painting. It is rich with historical associations, but they do not swamp the little girl. Standing in witty juxtaposition to her parrot's cage, which overtops her, she transcends the popular Victorian genre of little girls dressed as Infantas.[20] She is presented as a fictionalized character, recalling Henry James's description of Madame Merle's daughter Pansy in *Portrait of a Lady*: 'She had the style of a little princess; if you couldn't see it you had no eye. It was not modern, it was not conscious, it would produce no impression in Broadway; the small, serious damsel in her stiff little dress, only looked like an Infanta of Velazquez.'[21] In choosing a parrot as Beatrice's chief accessory, Sargent could not but be conscious of the literary and artistic references associated with it and, in particular, of two celebrated nineteenth-century paintings in which a parrot is portrayed as a female companion and where the relationship of woman and bird is allusive and ambiguous: Courbet's *Woman with a Parrot*, exhibited at the Salon in 1866, and Manet's rejoinder, *Woman with a Parrot* (fig. 31).[22] In each painting the bird has a different identity, but both are free: Sargent's bird is the only one that is caged. In this respect he is tapping into the Baroque tradition, in which the caged bird denotes fettered innocence, a motif expressed in Goya's *Don Manuel Osorio Manrique de Zuñiga* (fig. 32).[23] It does not seem fanciful to see Sargent's portrait as an image of childhood constrained by decorum or by exiguous social demands.

The Spanish influence, reflected in bold contrasts of dark and light and a subdued palette, can be seen in the portrait of another child, the young son of Augustus Saint-Gaudens, listening to a story told by his mother who is half-hidden behind him (no. 243). This is a mysterious and ambiguous work, lying on the border between narrative and portraiture (he is looking at us but is absorbed in listening to her).[24] The fact that it was painted as a gift from one artist to another may explain its unconventional and sketch-like character. *Mrs Edward Davis and her Son, Livingston* (no. 250) is a much more formal study of mother and son, but painted in the same severe Velázquez style – blacks and whites, a neutral background and no accessories. Comparison with the exuberant portrait of *Mrs Hamilton McKown Twombly* (no. 245) demonstrates the wide range of styles that Sargent could embrace to suit the personality of a particular sitter and the circumstances of each commission, the first spartan and subfusc, the second extravagantly Baroque and ostentatious. The atmosphere and associations of the two portraits are markedly different, but, in each, the essential recording of personality and the sense of real people in a modern world transcend the elements of fashion and accessory.[25]

These two pictures represent the high point of Sargent's formal portraiture from his 1890 campaign. He painted other fashionable women in a more modest way, including the three-quarter

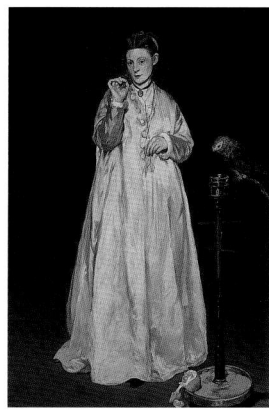

fig. 31 Edouard Manet, *Woman with a Parrot*, 1866. Oil on canvas, 72 ⅞ × 50 ⅝ (185 × 128). Metropolitan Museum of Art, New York.

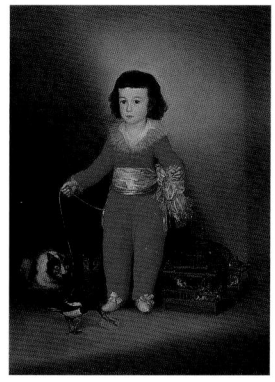

fig. 32 Francisco Goya y Lucientes, *Don Manuel Osorio Manrique de Zuñiga*, c. 1788. Oil on canvas, 50 × 39 ¾ (127 × 101). Metropolitan Museum of Art, New York.

lengths of Grace Woodhouse, Mrs Peter Chardon Brooks, her daughter Eleanor Brooks and Mrs Augustus Loring (nos 249, 257, 258, 265). Among his male sitters, there is a fascinating study in contrasts between the three-quarter-length portraits of George Washington Vanderbilt and Henry Cabot Lodge (nos 247, 264), the first thoughtful and nervously contorted, almost sinister, the other an energetic and self-confident public figure. Sargent's painting style shifts in response to each sitter: improvised impressionistic handling in the case of Lodge, smooth and stylized in that of Vanderbilt. Sargent's list of 1890s sitters includes many great names in American public life and business. He was becoming the portraitist of choice for New York's high society, for Boston's Brahmins, merchant princes and philanthropists, and for the wives of creators of new money in centres like Worcester, Massachusetts.[26] Sargent's American sitters were attracted by the sense of European glamour which surrounded him and which they hoped a portrait by his hand would confer on them.[27] In 1890, as in the earlier visit of 1887–8, an American élite was eager to secure his services and ready to pay high prices for the privilege of sitting to him. This was very different from the situation in England, where commissions were still relatively scarce and usually resulted from personal recommendation through his network of friends.

In spite of the pressure from portrait work, Sargent found time to paint sketches of his friends in a quite different style, and the spirit of Fladbury was revived in studies like those of Katharine Pratt seated before bowls of hydrangeas and Gordon Fairchild curled up in a wicker armchair (nos 253, 260). There is a sense of vibrant creative energy at work in these sketches executed in the intervals between painting formal portraits, which represent a return to the impressionist experiments of the 1880s. At this stage, Sargent's career seems to be characterized by its discontinuity, its pattern a series of intense but discrete episodes rather than the seamless line a retrospective intelligence might be tempted to trace. After the 'white heat' activity of his American visit, 1891 was effectively a portrait-free year. He spent eight months travelling in Egypt and Europe, pursuing ideas for the themes and imagery for the Boston Public Library mural project and fulfilling family commitments.[28] While he reconstituted himself as an academic artist and quarried materials on the story of religion in those countries where it had originated, his portrait practice stuttered along: he appears to have painted two portraits in 1891, four in 1892 and five in 1893. It is impossible to know what effects the roller-coaster ride of successes and reverses of the early years had on Sargent's attitude to his art, but a small group of works does pose an intriguing question. Perhaps it is a matter of chance, an accident of survival, that there are more oil studies for portraits of this period than for any other – *Elsie Palmer* (*Early Portraits*, nos 188, 189),

Mrs Thomas Lincoln Manson Jr (no. 242), *Mrs Hugh Hammersley* (no. 285), *Mrs Mahlon Day Sands* (no. 290) – or perhaps the number suggests that, after several campaigns devoted to landscape experiment, Sargent was returning to first principles and grappling afresh with the technical demands of portrait composition.[29]

The trajectory from avant-garde to establishment has seductive narrative appeal, but it is misleadingly simple. In 1891, when he had been exhibiting in London for a decade, Sargent was still regarded as a young pretender. In a review of the Royal Academy exhibition that year, the *Pall Mall Gazette* noted:

On this occasion, as for some years lately, much of the best work in the Academy is contributed by the outsiders. Of course, the first place will be accorded by artists to Mr J. S. Sargent. They do not like his work at the Academy, and he achieved only one vote at the last election for Associateship, but they have always hung him, because he came from Paris with a great reputation. The papers say that he is 'eccentric', a term which is applied indiscriminately to any artist who does not year after year turn out exactly the same sort of picture with the regularity of a machine.[30]

He was still very much a painter's painter, his edgy style and innovatory compositions continued to arouse suspicion and unease. The magisterial sweep, in terms of critical and public acceptance, was yet to come. The change hinged on one pivotal season.[31] During the spring of 1892, Sargent painted two beautiful, cultivated women, one the wife of a Scottish baronet, the second the wife of a London banker. Both women are seated, but the portraits are a study in contrasts: *Lady Agnew of Lochnaw* (no. 286) the epitome of stylish repose and *Mrs Hugh Hammersley* (no. 284) an exercise in nervy refinement; attitudes of passivity and action that characterize many female portraits of the 1890s. When the portraits were exhibited the following spring at the Royal Academy and the New Gallery respectively, contemporary audiences experienced a shiver of excitement. There were a few dissenting voices, but many critics were transported, writing in language rich with the vocabulary of sensation and abandon. *Mrs Hugh Hammersley* inspired George Moore to write about 'the delirium of the sensual present' and another reviewer described 'the sense of debauch that one returns to riot in the grand bravura . . . One is whirled away by the breadth of mind which covers a whole view in the majestic sweep and recreates the vision through the vivacious play of a touch as rapid as lightening.'[32]

The season was also tinged with irony. Carolus-Duran's portrait of Madame Pulitzer, 'a lady in old-rose majenta velvet', featured prominently in the Society of Portrait Painters exhibition. Several critics pointed to the similarity with *Mrs Hugh Hammersley*, and wondered at Duran's portrait as a possible source of influence on that of his protégé, but the judgement on the relative merits of the paintings was unequivocal: 'we venture to think that the pupil has both out-dared and out-painted the master'.[33] Over a decade of concentrated experiment, Sargent had developed a form of bravura realism crossed with impressionism, painting with an eye for the realities of light and colour in powerful and succulent brushstrokes so that his sitters were presented as real people. His vision and technique was introducing something new to the English portrait tradition and was beginning to stamp an exciting authority on the English art world.

EK

NOTES

1. Sir Edmund Gosse gave the following testimony to Sargent's biographer Evan Charteris: 'In this juncture [the periods spent in Broadway, Worcestershire, in 1885 and 1886], it will perhaps be believed with difficulty that he talked of giving up art altogether. I remember his telling me this in one of our walks, and the astonishment it caused me. Sargent was so exclusively an artist that one could think of no other occupation. "But then," I cried, "whatever will you do?" "Oh", he answered, 'I shall go into business." "What kind of business?" I asked in bewilderment. "Oh, I don't know!" with a vague wave of the hand, "or go in for music, don't you know?"' Charteris 1927, p. 76. For Sargent's portraits of Gosse, see *Early Portraits*, nos 167 and 168.

2. Undated letter [late summer 1890] from Sargent's friend, the Boston artist Dennis Miller Bunker, to Isabella Stewart Gardner, who was in Venice, ISGM archive. For Sargent's portrait of Bunker, see *Early Portraits*, no. 204.

3. Dennis Miller Bunker to Eleanor Hardy, undated [early 1890], Dennis Miller Bunker and Eleanor Hardy Papers, Private Collection; quoted Hirshler 1994, p. 73.

4. Trevor Fairbrother's groundbreaking Ph.D. thesis (published as *John Singer Sargent and America*, New York and London, 1986) is an invaluable analysis of Sargent's relationship with America in terms of patronage, exhibition strategy, stylistic development and critical discourse, and we are indebted to him for numerous references and research routes. Fairbrother's thesis is cited as Fairbrother 1986 and Sargent's 1890 visit is discussed pp. 142–207.

5. Sargent exhibited the following works in America in 1890:

Boston, St Botolph Club, *Midwinter Exhibition*, 27 January–8 February:
27 Georg Henschel
61 A Summer Morning [A Morning Walk]

New York, Union League Club, *Pictures by American Figure Painters together with an Exhibition of Persian and Indian Art*, 13–15 February:
35 Summer Morning [A Morning Walk]
36 An Out-of-Doors Study [Paul Helleu Sketching with his Wife]

New York, Society of American Artists, *Twelfth Annual Exhibition*, 28 April–24 May:
153 La Carmencita
154 Portrait [either Alice Vanderbilt Shepard or George Washington Vanderbilt]
155 Portrait [either Alice Vanderbilt Shepard or George Washington Vanderbilt]
156 Portrait of Georg Henschel
157 Master Caspar Goodrich
158 Summer Morning [A Morning Walk]
159 Study [Flora Priestley]

Chicago, Art Institute of Chicago, *Third Annual Exhibition of American Paintings and Sculpture*, 9 June–30 July:
151 La Carmencita
152 A Summer Morning [A Morning Walk]
153 Study [Flora Priestley]

Philadelphia, Art Club of Philadelphia, *Second Special Exhibition*, 3 November–7 December:
63 Plein Air Study [either St Martin's Summer or Paul Helleu Sketching with his Wife]
65 Portrait – Son of Mr Saint-Gaudens
67 Plein Air Study [either St Martin's Summer or Paul Helleu Sketching with his Wife]

New York, National Academy of Design, *Ninth Annual Autumn Exhibition*, 24 November–20 December:
83 Portrait of Mr Lawrence Barrett
92 Portrait of Mr Jos. Jefferson in the Part of Dr Pangloss
252 Portrait of Mrs E. L. Davis and Her Son

Boston, St Botolph Club, *Exhibition*, 29 December 1890–17 January 1891:
22 Portrait

6. 'The Royal Academy. (First Notice)', *The Times* (2 May 1891), p. 14.

7. 'The New Gallery. Second Notice', *Saturday Review*, LXXV (10 June 1893), p. 627.

8. G[eorge] M[oore], 'A Portrait in the New Gallery', *Speaker* (6 May 1893), p. 513. The vitality of the characterization aroused widespread admiration.

9. VL to her mother, 8 June 1882; quoted in *Vernon Lee's Letters* 1937, p. 84.

10. The phrase occurs in a letter from Manet to Henri Fantin-Latour (3 September 1865): 'Que je vous regrette ici, et quelle joie c'eut été pour vous de voir ce Velasquez qui à lui tout seul vaut le voyage; les peintres de toutes les écoles qui l'entourent au musée de Madrid et qui y sont très bien ici représentés semblent tous déchiquetés. C'est le peintre des peintres; il ne m'a pas étonné mais m'a ravi' Juliet Wilson-Bareau, *Edouard Manet, Voyage en Espagne*, Paris, 1988.

11. 'the willing [possibly meaning servile, unthinking, deferential] pupils of the Quai Malquais [the Ecole des beaux-arts]', Georges Rivière, 'L'Exposition des impressionistes', *L'Impressioniste*, I (6 April 1877), p. 3.

12. For a survey and discussion of critical allusions to Velázquez in Sargent's early work, see Simpson 1998, pp. 3–12.

13. *Las Meninas* and the shifts between painting and reality with which it plays, has been a potent inspiration and metaphor for artists with sensibilities as different as William Merritt Chase and Picasso. Sargent's copy of *Las Meninas*, painted during his visit to Spain in 1879, is notable for its fluid, impressionistic handling; it is about one-third the size of the original (see *Early Portraits*, fig. 7). Sargent clearly valued his copy, exhibiting it at the Whitechapel Art Gallery in 1908. For a contemporary review of the exhibition, see Laurence Binyon, 'In Bond Street and Whitechapel', *Saturday Review*, CV (11 April 1908), p. 463.

14. Sargent painted a number of copies of works by Velázquez in addition to *Las Meninas*: *Las Hilanderas* (Albert Beit Foundation, Russborough, Republic of Ireland), *Aesop* (Ackland Art Museum, University of North Carolina), the head of Apollo from the *Forge of Vulcan* (Albert Beit Foundation), the buffoon of Philip IV (Altman & Co., Inc., New York), the Infanta Margarita (untraced), two of Prince Baltasar Carlos (private collections), and Don Antonio, 'El Inglés' (then attributed to Velázquez; Hispanic Society of America, New York). The copies are loosely brushed painterly translations rather than literal transcriptions. For a lucid exposition of Sargent's technique with particular reference to Velázquez, see Fairbrother 2000, pp. 46–51.

15. 'Fine Art. The Royal Academy. II', *Academy*, XXXIX (16 May 1891), p. 471.

16. 'The Society of American Artists', *Critic*, 16 (3 May 1890), p. 225. For a series of quotations from contemporary reviews of the Society of American Artists exhibition, see Fairbrother 1986, pp. 160–1.

17. Claude Phillips is responding to the technical freedom of *Lady Agnew of Lochnaw*: 'Mr Sargent's brush has here, as elsewhere, much of the swift magic proper to Velasquez, his avowed prototype, but on the present occasion he has a little, without suppressing, tempered its virtuosity', 'The Royal Academy. II', *Academy*, XLIII (13 May 1893), p. 421.

For an example of the association between Velázquez and Impressionism in the nineteenth-century critical debate, see D. S. MacColl's review of R. A. M. Stevenson's seminal book on the seventeenth-century master, *Art of Velazquez* (1895), 'Art. A Book on Impressionism', *Spectator* (28 September 1895), pp. 933–4.

18. 'My Note Book. The Society of American Artists', *Art Amateur*, 25 (June 1891), p. 5.

19. None of Velázquez's portraits of the Infanta Margarita is dated. The three single portraits of her are in the Kunsthistorisches Museum, Vienna. The first portrait, in which she wears a salmon pink gown covered in silk brocade is usually dated 1653; the second, in which she wears her hair longer and looser and is dressed in ivory silk, *c.* 1656, and the third, in which she wears dark blue satin and a diagonal gold chain, 1659. The Infanta Margarita is the central figure in *Las Meninas*, 1656–7 (Museo del Prado, Madrid).

Sargent executed a copy of a portrait of the Infanta Margarita, but the work is untraced and it is not known whether the copy was of one of the three paintings now in Vienna, or that of the Infanta in the Louvre (a painting attributed at the time to Velázquez, but now given to his workshop).

Sargent's copy was in his studio sale, Christie's, London, 27 July 1925, lot 235, 'The Infanta Margaret, after Velazquez'. For the Louvre portrait, see José Lopez-Rey, *Velázquez: A Catalogue Raisonné of His Oeuvre*, London, 1963, no. 398. The Louvre painting exerted a powerful pull on contemporary artists (Manet and Degas, for example, both did etchings after it). For Manet's etching after the painting, see Jean Harris, *Edouard Manet: Graphic Works*, New York, 1970, no. 14; for Degas's etching (in reverse), see Sue Welsh Reed and Barbara Stern Shapiro, *The Painter as Printmaker*, New York and Boston, 1984, no. 16. It is an article of Impressionist apocrypha that Manet and Degas met for the first time in the Louvre when Degas was engaged on this etching, and that Manet expressed his surprise at Degas's working directly onto the copper plate. See Loys Delteil, *Le Peintre-Graveur illustré*, 31 vols, Paris, 1906–26, vol. 17, no. 12.

20. The image of the Spanish infanta, as filtered through the paintings of Velázquez, had become an established literary and artistic conceit and an icon

for nineteenth-century artists. Painterly reinterpretations range from John Everett Millais's vivid *A Souvenir of Velasquez* (1868, Royal Academy of Arts, London), to William Merritt Chase's copy of the Infanta Margarita (*c.* 1881, Private Collection) and a later portrait of his daughter, *An Infanta, A Souvenir of Velasquez* (1899, Private Collection), to the jejune *Portrait of Peggy Guggenheim* by Franz von Lenbach (*c.* 1903, Solomon R. Guggenheim Foundation).

21. Henry James, *The Portrait of a Lady* (Penguin edition), p. 369.

22. Courbet's *Woman with a Parrot*, exhibited at the Salon in 1866, is an erotic portrayal of a nude woman lying outstretched in a boudoir, her pose sensual and abandoned, her expression one of transported rapture, her left hand extended, reaching for a parrot who descends with outspread wings. Manet's *Woman with a Parrot*, painted in 1866, is a subtle and enigmatic portrayal of a woman almost completely concealed in her pink peignoir, the bird sitting independently on its perch. Renoir's more conventional study of a woman with a parrot depicts the bird as a tame plaything in the setting of a claustrophobic bourgeois salon (1871, Solomon R. Guggenheim Museum, New York).

23. Parrots are variously seen as symbols of the soul, of air, of touch and, traditionally, the parrot as imitator of the human voice is seen to be more responsive to women and children. Sargent would have been aware of Gustave Flaubert's tender tale *Un coeur simple* (1876), one of the *Trois Contes* published in 1877. A servant woman, Félicité, develops a close relationship with a parrot, Loulou, who comes to represent the various people she has loved; when the parrot dies, she has it stuffed and its little effigy assumes mystical importance for her. *Trois Contes* was the last of Flaubert's works to be published before his death in 1880, and the only one of his works to meet with unqualified critical and popular success.

24. The subject matter of *La Carmencita* invited a range of Hispanic allusions, as had that of *El Jaleo* eight years earlier. Its powerful sense of the grotesque suggested Goya as an inspiration. Claude Phillips, for example, wrote: 'If the critics of the genial painter say that the influence of Velasquez over him is strong as ever, and that superimposed on it comes in this instance that of Goya in his *Caprichos*, we shall be unable to contradict them', 'The Royal Academy and the New Gallery', *Art Journal* (1891), p. 198.

25. The portrait of Mrs Twombly was one of five works by Sargent exhibited at the Society of American artists exhibition in December 1892. At least one critic responded powerfully to its opulent mood: 'In this neighborhood also were to be seen again Mr Sargent's two wonderful little Venetian scenes [*Street in Venice*, National Gallery of Art, Washington, D.C. and *Venetian Bead Stringers*, Albright-Knox Art Gallery, Buffalo, New York], with their abundant and very telling blacks and which contrasted so strongly with his showy portrait of a lady, superbly upholstered, opposite the entrance', 'Art Gossip', *Art Interchange*, XXX, (February 1893), p. 39.

26. In New York, the Vanderbilts (nos 244, 245, 246, 247), the Marquands (nos 278, 343) and the Goelets (no. 239). See also *Early Portraits*, nos 9, 10, 192, 208, 209, 210, 211. In Boston, Henry Cabot Lodge, the Brooks family, the Peabodys, Lorings and Fields (nos 264, 256, 257, 258 and 259, 267, 265, 266 and 262). In Worcester, the Davis, Dewey and Bullock families (nos 250, 251, 252).

27. Writing in 1904, Charles Caffin was sceptical about the insecurity of his compatriots and their desire for instant social and cultural caché: 'I wonder if American fashionable people would be so eager to be painted by Sargent, if he had always maintained his studio in New York? . . . For I understand that it is *de règle* with our "swell set" to purchase everything, as far as possible, that is of foreign manufacture' Charles H. Caffin, 'Some American Portrait Painters', *Critic*, 44 (January 1904), p. 31.

28. Sargent travelled to Egypt with his mother and sisters and spent part of the year with them. His younger sister Violet married (Louis) Francis Ormond in Paris on 17 August 1891. By the end of the year, his mother and Emily were, nominally at least, settled in London; Mrs Sargent signed the lease on a flat in 10 Carlyle Mansions in September.

29. To place this group within the context of Sargent's early career, there are, from the late 1870s and early 1880s, two surviving oil studies for Sargent's portrait of Carolus-Duran (*Early Portraits*, nos 22 and 23 respectively) and a study for *Madame Edouard Pailleron* (Appendix, no. 616).

30. 'The Royal Academy', *Pall Mall Gazette*, LII (2 May 1891), p. 3. The perception of Sargent as a radical artist was widespread in the early 1890s. When he was elected an Associate of the Royal Academy in 1894, the *New York Times* wrote: 'The Royal Academy has been passing over painters of the orthodox Academic routine to elect revolutionaries like John S. Sargent . . . In their present fit they may be quite capable of electing even J. M. Whistler if they did not feel certain he would laugh at them' (21 January 1894). A few years later, D. S. MacColl referred to Sargent as an 'outsider' in a passage discussing the radicalness of the Glasgow School, a group of artists not yet assimilated by the Royal Academy: 'The Academy will, no doubt, upon this capitulate, and attempt to secure Messrs Guthrie and Lavery, as they secured Mr Sargent when he became too dangerous an outsider. He too enjoyed the hospitality of the New English while Burlington House regarded him with grudging distaste. It was a critical moment for the Academy while the brilliant American hesitated whether to accept or refuse', 'The Academy', *Saturday Review*, LXXXV (7 May 1898), p. 616.

31. There is an ironic echo of that other critical season, 1884, when Sargent exhibited two markedly different portraits, the provocatively dark *Madame Pierre Gautreau* at the Salon and *Mrs Henry White*, the American winter queen, at the Royal Academy. In 1893, however, the critical sensation was an entirely positive one.

32. 'The New Gallery', *Pall Mall Gazette*, LVI (1 May 1893), p. 2.

33. 'The Society of Portrait Painters', *Black and White*, V (20 May 1893), p. 601.

232 *Edwin Booth*

1890
Oil on canvas, 87½ × 61¾ (222.3 × 156.8)
Inscribed, upper left: *John S. Sargent*
Private Collection

Edwin Booth (1833–1893) was the fourth son of actor Junius Brutus Booth and his wife, Mary Anne (*née* Holmes). He first made his appearance on the American stage at the Boston Museum in 1849 but only slowly established his reputation after periods of near privation. He excelled in roles that complemented his lofty and melancholy personality, like Hamlet and Richelieu. His lavish productions at Booth's Theatre in New York from 1869–1874 set a new standard of theatrical production and dramatic interpretation. Though bankrupted in 1874, he continued to act with distinction in Europe and America until his retirement in 1891. His private life was marred by a succession of misfortunes, including the assassination by his brother, John Wilkes Booth, of Abraham Lincoln.

In 1888, Booth founded The Players as a club for actors and people interested in the theatre; he purchased a house at 16 Gramercy Park, New York, which became its permanent premises. As a token of their regard, the club members, in turn, decided to commission a portrait of their founder; the chief donor appears to have been E. C. Benedict. The decision to select Sargent may have been by the architect Stanford White, a founding member of the club, who had remodelled 16 Gramercy Park for Booth and was a close friend.

The portrait was begun early in January 1890 at the studio Sargent had taken on East Twenty-third Street. Booth wrote to a friend on 2 January:

> Just as I had packed my bag, and was about starting for the station at two, Sargent the artist called, to say that he had word from the art committee to paint my portrait for the club. You know, I told you if it was decided he should paint it, I would stay for as many sittings as I could give him from now till Saturday. I wired you at once. I will start by the 3 o'clock train Saturday. Of course, this is the only opportunity to have so distinguished an artist at me; consequently I yield to the annoyance of posing. (Grossman 1894, p. 103)

Later he wrote from Philadelphia on 12 February: 'I wrote you before I left New York, and sent you a present in a letter. In it I also told you of the successful result of Sargent's work, but I did not tell you that at intervals, while I rested, he would sit at the piano and play "Racoksy" (is that the name and the spell of it?) and other Hungarian airs' (Grossman 1894, pp. 103–4).

The painting of the portrait did not pass without hitches. After the second sitting, Booth records telling his friend T. B. Aldrich, who had advised him to sandpaper his soul before the ordeal: '"I am disappointed in the picture, for if it is a true portrayal of myself, why, that as I don't feel as I look." Aldrich's advice was urgent, since the picture was for succeeding generations of the club, it was only justice to the artist that he should be told. Upon this cue I spoke. Mr Sargent, apparently unconscious of my words, painted on for a few minutes and then said, "Look now, and see if you like it any better." The face on the canvas was entirely painted out, and with ready alacrity a new picture was begun.' (Aldrich 1891, p. 266). Henry Harper went with Lawrence Hutton to Sargent's New York studio, to see the unfinished picture (date unrecorded):

> The portrait of Booth struck us as exceedingly life-like, and we so reported to the Club. Imagine our surprise when we were told the next day that Sargent had scraped the entire work off the canvas because the pose did not entirely suit him; but I suppose that it is conscientious work of this order which has made him the greatest portrait painter of our time. (Harper 1912, p. 466)

Harper later had the picture engraved for his magazine, *Harper's New Monthly* (February 1891), and commissioned a much-quoted sonnet from T. B. Aldrich to accompany it:

> A master's hand
> Has set the master-player here,
> In the fair temple that he planned
> Not for himself. To us most dear
> This image of him! 'It was thus
> He looked; such pallor touched his cheek;
> With that same grace he greeted us –
> Nay, 'tis the man, could it but speak!'

Sargent saw a proof of the *Harper's* reproduction, which he called miserable, telling Mrs Fairchild that he had strongly recommended the magazine to use the sketch in preference ('Thursday', [26 June?] [1890], Boston Athenaeum, Sargent Papers, box 1, folder 15).

Sargent's portrait of Booth was much admired at the time, and it remains one of his finest, if now underestimated, portraits. Booth is shown in a heroic attitude, legs apart, standing before the Renaissance-style white-marble mantelpiece in the Great Hall of the club with a proprietary air. The fire-irons are still there, and so is the brass mask of Comedy and Tragedy, and the brass inscription:

> Goode Frende for Frendships sake forbeare
> To utter what is gossip here
> In social chat lest unawares
> Thy tonge offend thy fellow plaiers

Though seemingly casual and relaxed, Booth's pose is full of nervous force and energy; even the crinkly folds of the trousers convey a sense of agitated movement. Sargent had earlier used the motif of thumbs in pockets for his portrait of Cecil Harrison (*Early Portraits*, no. 178), but it was

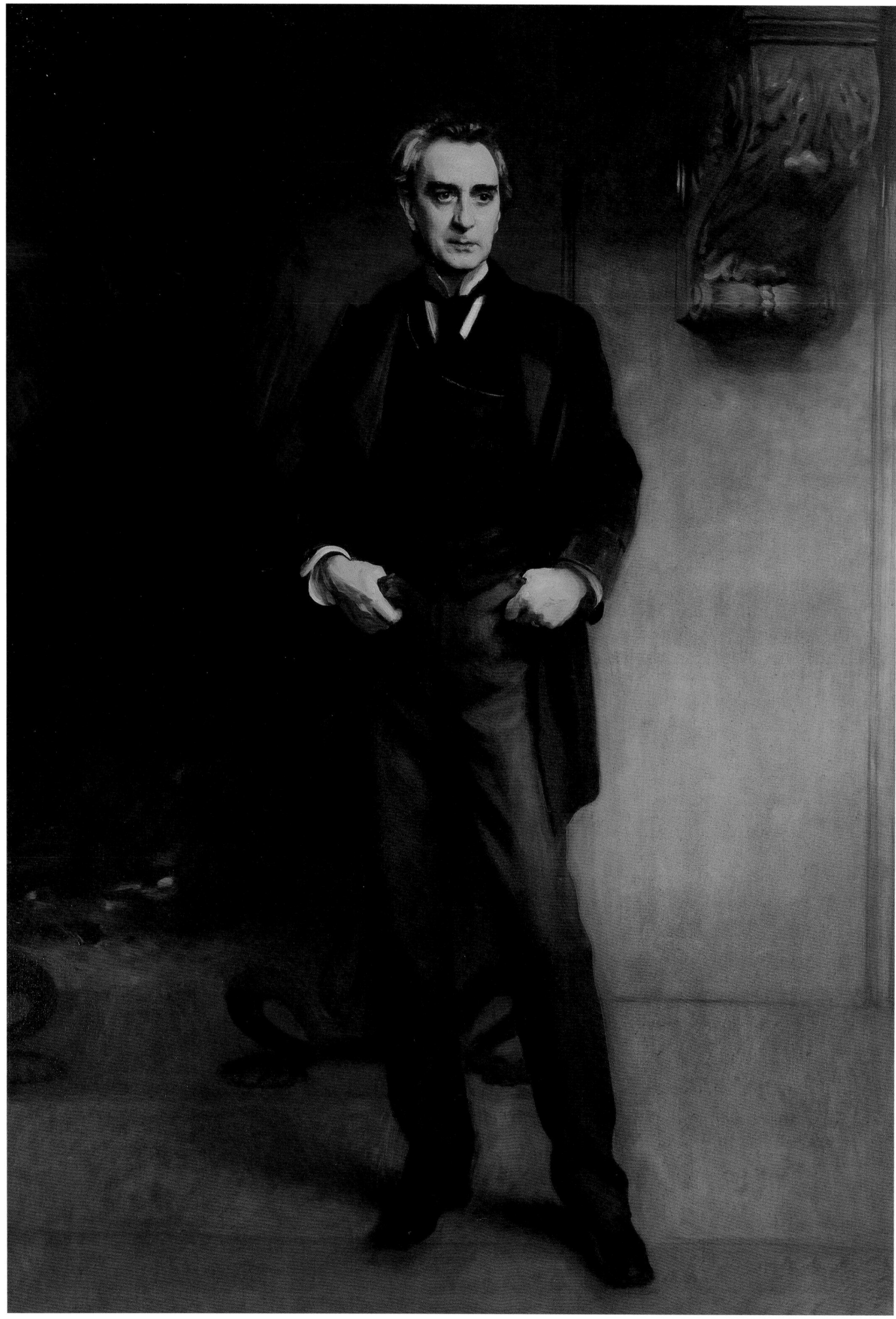

evidently characteristic of Booth, both on stage and off. While not a representation of Booth in character, Sargent's portrait comes close to being a theatrical portrait with its charged, dramatic overtones. Booth himself wrote to a friend in April 1890:

I was surprised to find myself standing in the very attitude when I asked Sargent if it was usual with me, and I find my hands in the same position even on the stage – in Hamlet, very frequently. By actual measurements the dimensions are correct; but the picture, being placed so high upon the wall, I suppose, appears as you describe it. Bispham and all who saw it in the studio liked it, but I could not decide positively how it impressed me. (Grossman 1894, p. 111)

Henry Cabot Lodge saw the picture when he visited The Players in May 1890. Writing to his mother, he called it 'a really noble portrait, one of the best pieces of modern work I have ever seen' (10 May 1890, MHS, microfilm roll PN 171). Sargent would also paint a portrait of Lodge that summer (no. 264).

Later in 1890, Booth himself commissioned Sargent to paint two portraits for the club: *Lawrence Barrett* (no. 272) and *Joseph Jefferson* (no. 273). All three portraits hung in the club's reading room, that of Booth inset in panelling above the fireplace in the centre. For a contemporary account of the club, see Brander Mathews, 'The Players', *Century Magazine*, 43 (November 1891), pp. 28–34. A reproduction of a drawing of the reading room on page 29 shows the lower part of the portrait *in situ*. For photographs of the room showing the portrait *in situ*, see figs. 33, 34.

233 *Edwin Booth*

1890
Oil on canvas, 24 × 20 (61 × 50.7)
Inscribed, upper left: *John S. Sargent*
Private Collection

On 27 January 1890, the *Boston Evening Transcript* noted that Sargent was working on a portrait of the actor Edwin Booth in the city. Booth was in Boston for a short theatrical run with Madame Modjeska, and Sargent was there to collect his sister Violet from the Fairchilds. It is extremely unlikely that Sargent would have transported the large canvas on which he was painting the formal portrait of Booth from his New York studio, especially for such a short period – he was in Boston for a scant ten days – and the newspaper report almost certainly refers to the present work. The sketch does not relate directly to the full-length (no. 232): the image of the actor is wilder and much less composed in the sketch, suggesting an impromptu, off-guard view. When the portrait was included in a loan collection of portraits exhibited at Copley Hall, Boston, in the spring of 1896, it

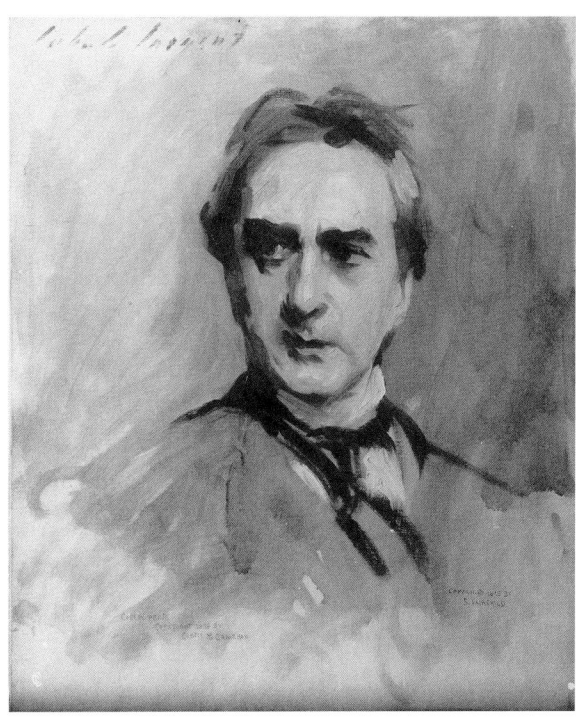

was described in the catalogue as 'painted in three-quarters of an hour', and the speed of execution is evident in the loose, improvised brushstrokes. Sargent gave the sketch to Sally Fairchild (see no. 261). Writing to her mother, Mrs Charles Fairchild (undated, inscribed 'Thursday' [1890]), Sargent criticized the proof of the illustration of the large portrait of Booth in *Harper's*: 'I daresay they will publish it all the same but I have strongly recommended them to do the sketch in preference – I hope it was not much bother expressing it' (Boston Athenaeum, Sargent Papers, box 1, folder 15). In the event, *Harper's* went ahead with printing the full-length picture, as planned.

The sketch was published as a 'Copley Print' by Curtis and Cameron of Boston in 1898; it is inscribed 'COPYRIGHT 1898 BY / S. FAIRCHILD'.

234 *La Carmencita*

1890
Oil on canvas, 91⅝ × 55⅞ (232 × 142)
Inscribed, upper left: *John S. Sargent*
Musée d'Orsay, Paris

La Carmencita was a Spanish dancer who became something of a cult in America and England in the 1890s. She was born Carmen Dauset (or Dausset) in Almería, Spain, in 1868 and made her first appearance, in Spain, at the Cervantes Theatre in 1880. In a letter of 28 February 1890 to Helen Dunham (see no. 279), John Jay Chapman described seeing her dance as 'the most wonderful dancing I shall ever see. She was like the daughter of Herodias . . . She sang at the same time that she danced. She is about twenty and like a young panther' (De Wolfe Howe 1937, p. 83). For a biography,

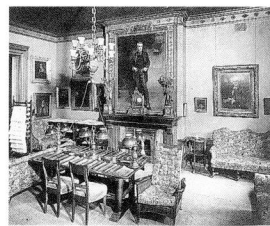

fig. 33 Photograph of the Reading Room at The Players, New York, 1907. The Players, New York.

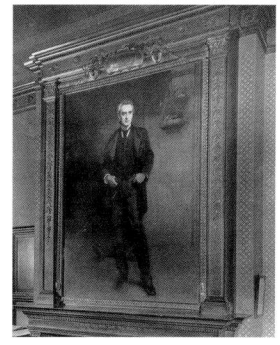

fig. 34 Photograph of the portrait of Edwin Booth hanging in The Players, New York. Catalogue raisonné archive.

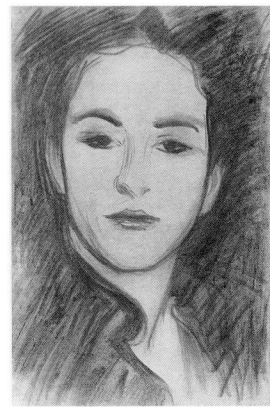

fig. 35 *La Carmencita*.
Charcoal on paper, 11 ½
× 8 (29.2 × 20.3). Fogg
Art Museum, Harvard
University Art
Museums. Bequest of
Grenville L. Winthrop
1943. 581.

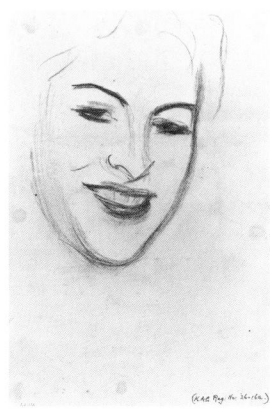

fig. 36 *La Carmencita*.
Pencil, 11 ½ × 8
(29.2 × 20.3). Glasgow
Museums. Art Gallery
and Museum,
Kelvingrove.
PR.1926.16a.

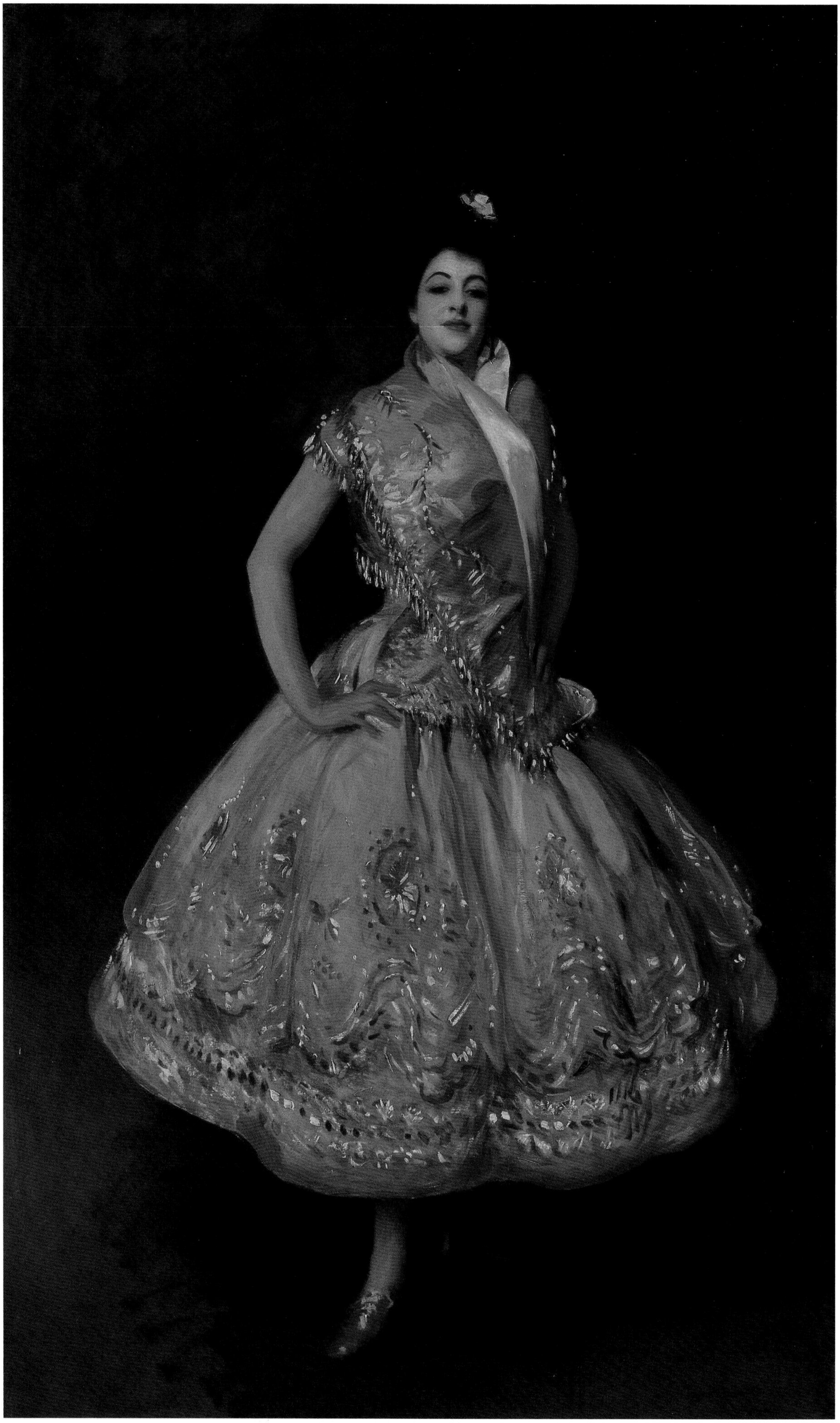

see J. Ramirez, *Carmencita, the Pearl of Seville*, New York, 1890.

It is quite possible that Sargent's acquaintance with La Carmencita dates from the Exposition universelle in Paris in 1889, but the first record of his seeing her dance is in New York in the early months of 1890. He and his old friend from Paris, James Carroll Beckwith, saw her perform at Koster, Bial & Co., a saloon or music hall on Fourteenth Street, on 17 February, and Beckwith held a party on 27 February at which she danced. Beckwith wrote in his diary: 'Carmencita came at 12 a dozen men I had spoken to came in. I had a guitarist & mandolinist. She danced superbly until near 3 o'clock when Sargent took her home. I have never had a more novel fête than tonight' (NA). Beckwith also records going with Sargent to see her perform at Koster, Bial & Co. on 1 March. On 16 March Beckwith visited Sargent's studio and found Carmencita posing, and he was present at the party, which Sargent gave with Isabella Stewart Gardner at William Merritt Chase's Tenth Street studio on 24 April, when Carmencita again danced. Sargent's three undated letters to Mrs Gardner about preparations for the party are in the archives of the Isabella Stewart Gardner Museum, Boston. In one of them, he writes: 'You must come to the studio on Tuesday at any time and see the figure I am doing of the bewilderingly superb creature.'

The artist's relationship with Carmencita can only be surmised, and from available accounts she was a demanding and trying sitter. Sargent is said to have spent a small fortune 'on bracelets and things' in order to placate her. The story of the bracelets may have another explanation, for Sally Fairchild (see no. 261), who was present at one of the parties, told David McKibbin that the ladies present were so carried away by the excitement of the occasion, they threw bracelets and other pieces of jewellery at the dancer's feet, which Sargent had later to buy back. Carmencita's intense physicality was shocking to some sensibilities. *Town Topics*, for example, wrote: 'On stage, the torsal shivers and upheavals indulged in by Carmencita might be allowed to pass for art, but in the privacy of a richly furnished room, with innocent eyes to view her, nothing but the fatal earthiness of the woman's performances could make any impression' (*Town Topics*, 3 April 1890, p. 2, quoted in Fairbrother 1986, p. 162). The energy and abandon of her dancing can be inferred from the series of photographs reproduced in Fairbrother 1982, p. 30, figs 5a, b, c, d. Four pencil drawings of a dancing figure in a sketchbook given by the artist to Mrs Gardner in 1919 (ISGM archive), and two further studies are probably studies of Carmencita dancing (see Adelson and Oustinoff 1992, p. 471, n. 14 and figs 39–44).

Sargent was excited by Carmencita's uninhibited performance, her wild looks, and by everything she represented of Spain and Spanish culture. Lucia Fairchild's diary entry for 2 October 1890 notes 'when Violet stopped he talked to Mrs H[igginson] awhile about Carmencita (whom of course he admires beyond anything) and brought down his photographs to show her' (Private Collection). Carmencita appealed to Sargent both as model and performer and this portrait of her was, like *Madame X* (*Early Portraits*, no. 114), an uncommissioned work. An exotic creature, her dark sensual looks relate closely to his preferred pictorial types – from the Capri model Rosina Ferrara to his friend Flora Priestley (see *Early Portraits*, nos 225–8) and Ena and Betty Wertheimer (see nos 397, 479, 485, 553, 565). Sargent's interest in painting actresses is particularly powerful at this time. In 1889, he painted Ellen Terry as Lady Macbeth (*Early Portraits*, no. 183) in a highly dramatic pose and later sketched the head of Eleanora Duse (no. 298). W. Graham Robertson relates how Sargent 'only narrowly escaped asking to paint' Sarah Bernhardt, when the latter accompanied Robertson to his sittings (Robertson 1931, p. 241). Her rival, Ada Rehan, was painted by Sargent in 1894–5 (no. 308). In Sargent's work, there is a recurrent strain of women dancing, from Rosina dancing a tarantella on a rooftop in 1878 (Warner Collection of Gulf States Corporation, Tuscaloosa, Alabama and Private Collection) to *El Jaleo* in 1882 (Isabella Stewart Gardner Museum, Boston) and his series of Javanese dancing girls in 1889. Carmencita's dramatic silhouette is clearly indebted to Edouard Manet's *Lola de Valence* (1862, Musée d'Orsay, Paris).

Carmencita's face is rendered *à la japonais*, as in several studies of women of this period (for example, Alice Vanderbilt Shepard and Flora Priestley: see *Early Portraits*, nos 209, 225). The effect of the white mask-like features is stylized and enigmatic, hinting at a powerful, detached, even cruel presence. The sense of theatre is unapologetic; the figure seems to have been frozen in mid-movement, having stepped out from a dark background into bold lighting, the line of the silhouette calculated for maximum dramatic effect. Parts of the picture, like the prominent right arm, appear barely finished. Writing to Paul Helleu, (5 June [1890]), Sargent himself described it as 'une grande figure, malheureusement très pochade' (a big picture, unfortunately very sketchy) (Private Collection).

The portrait was shown at the Society of American Artists in May 1890, taking the place of honour at the head of the main gallery. It was called 'amazingly clever' but criticized for 'too much haste and "trop d'esprit"' (*Art Amateur*, June 1890, p. 3). In Chicago, it received a prize of $250 awarded by the Art Institute. In an undated letter to his wife, Eleanor, Sargent's friend Dennis Miller Bunker described it as 'very stunning' (quoted Boston 1994, p. 176).

The portrait was sent back to London shortly before Sargent's return. Sargent wrote to Louisa Loring (see no. 266) from 33 Tite Street on 27

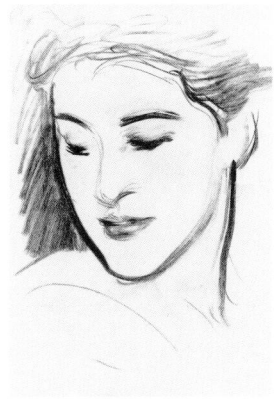

fig. 37 *La Carmencita*. Pencil, dimensions unknown. Untraced.

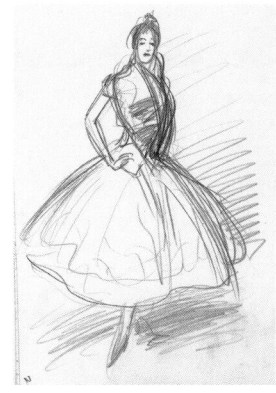

fig. 38 *La Carmencita*. Pencil, 6 ⅞ × 4 ⅜ (17.5 × 11.1). Yale University Art Gallery, sketchbook 1937.4083, p. 2.

November 1890: 'By the way you must put your photo of Carmencita in a black frame, for I suspect the picture of having gone to the bottom of the sea. It left New York before I did and has not yet turned up. In a few days it will be high time to consider her lost and to regret not having given her to you instead of the photo' (AAA). Henry James wrote to Mrs Curtis (18 December 1890): 'Sargent is de retour, with heaps of American gold, but unfortunately with only one picture (the rest are *là bas*, like the little Bopeep tails,) an admirable full-length of a yellow-satin Spanish dancer, fièrement campée, who is making the rain & the fine weather of New York' (Horne 1999, p. 234). James wrote again (10 January [1891]): 'Sargent spent a month here on his way from New York to Cairo, where he now is, & had a wonderfully brilliant full length portrait of a yellow satin Spanish dancer to show' (DCL).

When the portrait appeared at the Royal Academy in 1891, it caused a sensation, provoking lively comment both for and against it. Several critics saw in it 'something of that halo of decay which gives a lurid fascination to the creations of Baudelaire' (*Art Journal*, 1891, p. 198); 'the handsome face frankly exhibits the white and red of the theatre; the lips have that painted scarlet so attractive to the modern French poets; the lean arm and hand – for one only is seen – is full of life; and the little Andalusian feet, though in perfect repose, literally bite the ground . . . a creation sprung from the artificial soil of the expiring century, a veritable "Fleur du Mal", such as would have delighted Baudelaire himself.' (*Academy*, 16 May 1891, p. 471) It was criticized for vulgarity, acclaimed for its spontaneity and unity of impression: 'As she stands there, with her whitened face, her blackened brows and lashes and her parted lips, one yellow-shod foot extended ready for the dance, she is a very incarnation – at once fascinating and repulsive. The picture kills everything on the wall, and surpasses for strength almost every modern picture I have ever seen' (*Magazine of Art*, 1891, p. 254). Claude Phillips described it as 'the picture of the year . . . intensely modern, intensely realistic in treatment' (*Art Journal*, 1891, p. 198). The *Art Amateur* spoke of its 'barbaric splendour' and the characterization as 'a deliberate and offensive libel, to serve a painter's purpose' (*Art Amateur*, July 1891, p. 24).

The picture made a similar impact in Paris, when it was shown at the Société nationale des beaux-arts in 1892, and was purchased by the French government for 1,200 francs. Two letters from Sargent, of 4 and 26 July 1892, to the director of the Société nationale des beaux-arts, and other documents relating to its purchase are in the Archives nationales, Paris (dossier F21 2149). In later years Sargent expressed regret that this should be the painting that represented him at the Luxembourg, telling Julie Heyneman: 'After all, it is little more than a sketch' (Charteris 1927, p. 113). Theodore Robinson, who saw the portrait in Paris, noted in his diary (23 May 1892): 'I thought his Carmencita

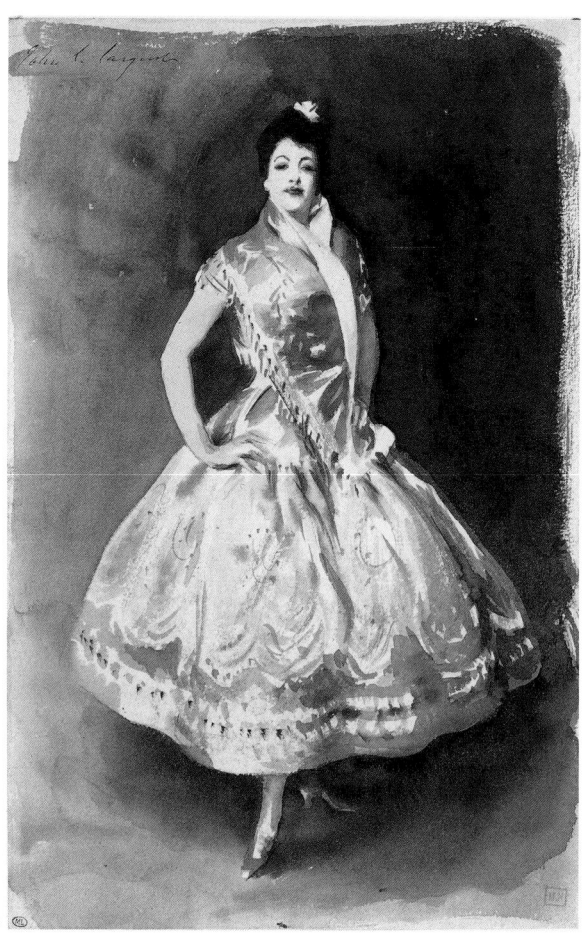

235

looked badly' (FARL). George Meredith wrote to Mrs Seymour Trower (6 October 1892), who had sent him a photograph of the painting: 'Carmencita has come, to challenge, provoke, enchant me. Such a type she is, that I touch her and live the life with her, drinking agonies of jealousy, until she loses power to pose – fattens into sedativeness. But thanks to Sargent, it will be long before that happens' (Cline 1970, vol. II, p. 1104).

In one of several letters from Sargent to Miss [Violet] Maxse (8 March 1895), which were at Winifred Myers, London, 1969, and are presently untraced, the artist wrote: 'I went to see the Carmencita last night and for my part it seems to me all right for jeunes filles . . . a great falling off in the style of her dance which is getting less Spanish, and her figure is gone.' He held a private party in his studio on 4 April 1895, at which Carmencita danced; among the guests were Lady Agnew, Lady Monkswell and W. G. Robertson. For contemporary accounts of the evening and impressions of Carmencita, see Monkswell 1944, pp. 265–6 and Robertson 1931, pp. 244–6.

Related drawings are as follows: grisaille sketch (no. 235); pencil study of the full-length figure, Museum of Fine Arts, Boston, no. 48.1112; head, full face (fig. 35); slight sketch of head, laughing (fig. 36); and head, looking down, formerly Grand Central Art Galleries, New York (fig. 37), and full-length (fig. 38).

Carmencita was much photographed, and a full-length oil portrait of her by William Merritt Chase is in the Metropolitan Museum of Art, New York.

Sargent later lent the yellow silk dress embroidered with lace and silver in which Carmencita posed to his friend Sybil Sassoon (see nos 566, 603), possibly for a fancy-dress ball. He mentions the dress in two undated letters to Miss Sassoon, and a note on one of the letters, presumably in her hand, reads: 'He gave me the lovely yellow Carmencita dress & I have it still' (Private Collection).

235 *La Carmencita*

1890–2
Pen and ink wash, 13⁹⁄₁₆ × 8⁷⁄₈ (34.5 × 22.6)
Inscribed, upper left: *John S. Sargent*
Musée du Louvre, Paris, Département des arts graphiques

The artist presented this wash drawing of Carmencita to the Musée du Luxembourg in 1892, the year in which his oil portrait of her was exhibited at the Société nationale des beaux-arts and then bought by the French state (see no. 234). The drawing is presumably a copy after the oil, to which it is closely related.

Sargent wrote to the 'Directeur des Beaux-Arts' (26 July 1892): 'Conformément aux instructions confermées dans votre lettre du 2 [?] Juin, j'ai l'honneur de vous addresser par ce même courrier un croquis de mon tableau le "Carmencita" et d'une photographie non collée'[1] (Archives nationales, dossier F21 2149).

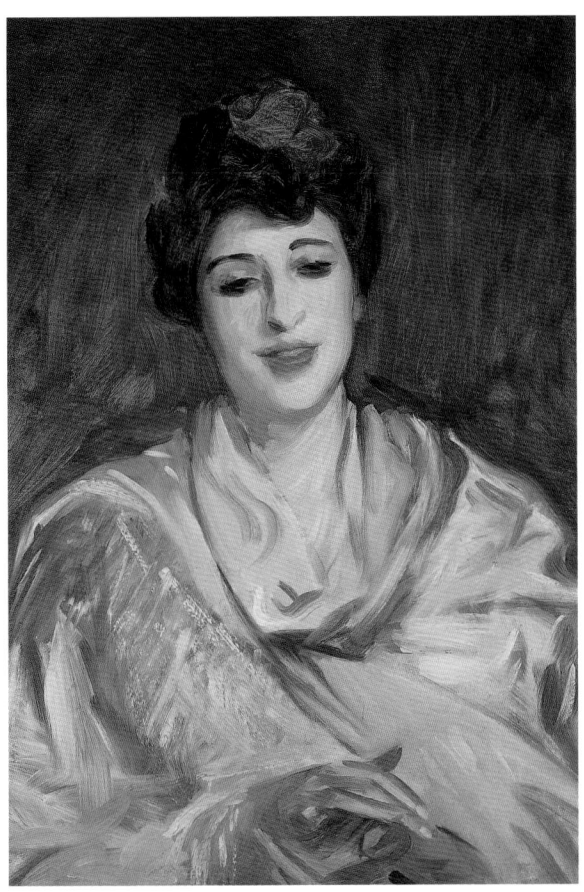

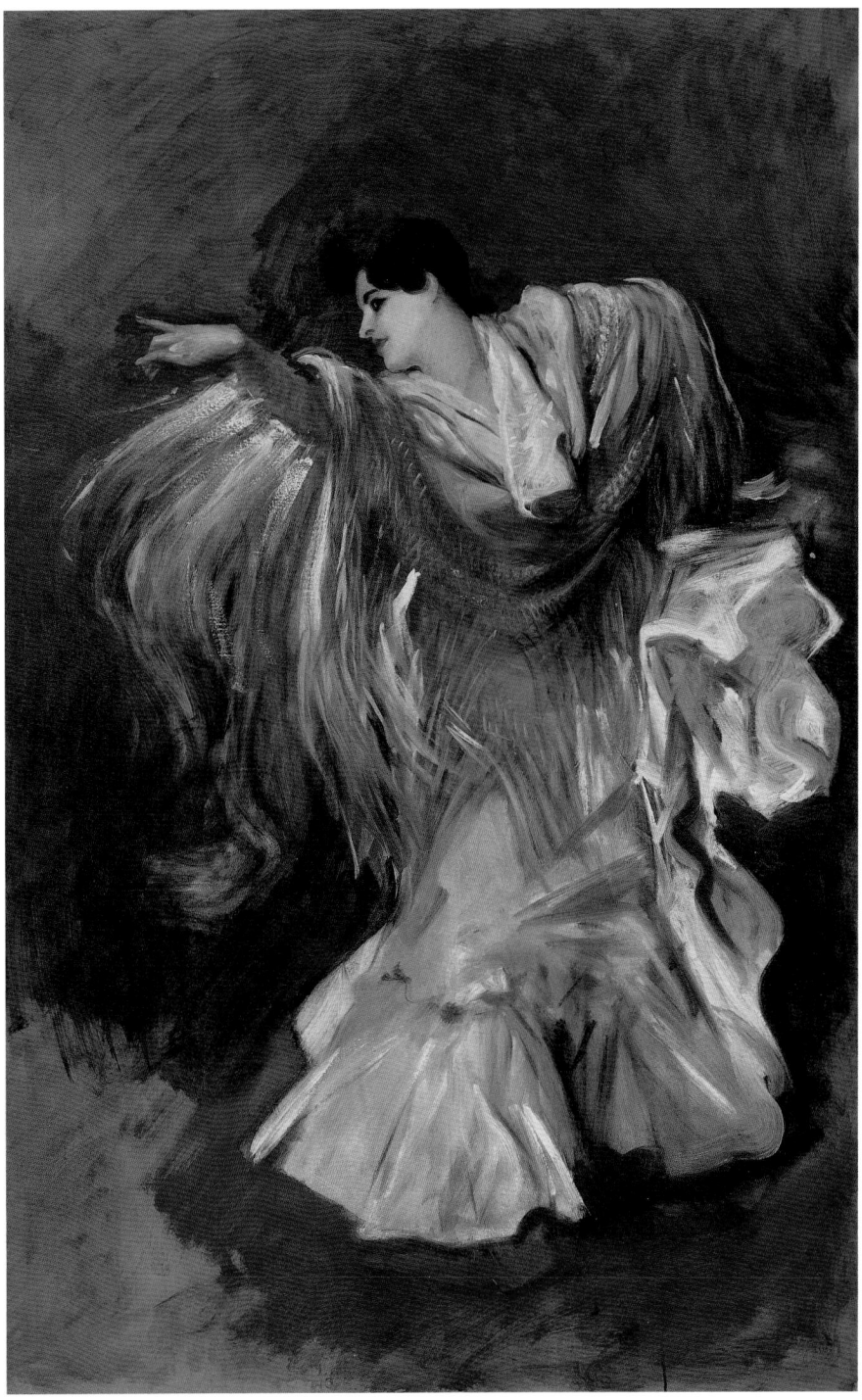

237

236 *La Carmencita*

1890
Oil on canvas, 28³⁄₄ × 19³⁄₄ (73 × 50.2)
Mr and Mrs Harry Spiro

This sketch is described in the Boston 1899 exhibition catalogue as a study of Carmencita singing (Boston 1899, p. 17). Her lips are parted and she is in the act of clapping her hands. Although her head is tilted down rather than up and she wears a red rose in her hair rather than a yellow one, there is a close similarity between the treatment of the features in this sketch and that in the full-length portrait (no. 234). The figure is draped in a loose white shawl and appears more oriental in type

1. In accordance with the instructions given in your letter of 2 [?] June, I am pleased to enclose herewith a sketch of my painting 'Carmencita' and an unmounted photograph.

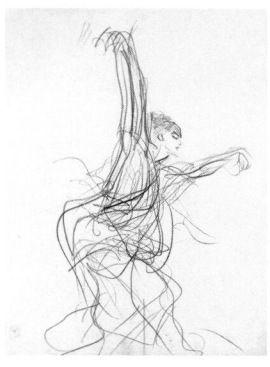

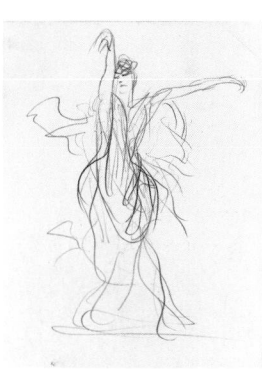

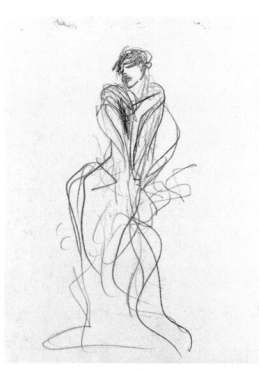

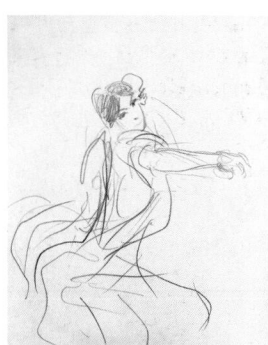

figs 39-42 Single folded sheet with four sketches of a dancing figure, 22 ¾ × 9 (57.8 × 22.9); each drawing 11 ⅜ × 9 (28.9 × 22.9). Sargent sketchbook, Isabella Stewart Gardner Museum, Boston.

than she does in the larger work, perhaps because of the flatter modelling of the features.

The sketch appears to have been in Carmencita's possession at one time and may have been a gift to her from the artist, though it must have been returned to him since it was included in his studio sale of 1925. The sketch which the artist A. S. Hartrick described seeing in Carmencita's apartment some time after her New York debut appears to be this work:

> What happened next is not so clear, but I believe Sullivan, Charles Sheldon, the American War Correspondent of *Black and White*, and myself joined the company at Stuart's rooms after the dinner, and the next thing I distinctly recall is that we went to Carmencita's lodgings to see the sketch which Sargent had given her in memory of her debut in New York . . . On an easel beyond the folding doors was the painting of 'Carmencita' which we had come to see – a charming sketch from her at her best some years before – apparently singing to the playing of a guitar – which was her husband's job – and keeping time by clapping her hands. (Hartrick 1939, p. 127)

The sketch is in the *Sargent Trust List* [1927], 'Pictures. Framed. no. 4'.

237 *La Carmencita*

1890
Oil on canvas, 54 × 35 (137.2 × 88.9)
Private Collection

Carmencita is wearing the same dress and shawl as in no. 236 and has the same flower in her hair. She is represented impressionistically in the act of dancing, her skirt and shawl swirling with movement, the profile pose and the bent-back gesture of the wrist referring back to the figure in *El Jaleo*, 1882 (Isabella Stewart Gardner Museum, Boston). In contrast to the drama of the arrested moment caught in no. 234, this oil study expresses what a contemporary columnist described as 'the torsal shivers and upheavals' of Carmencita's dancing (quoted in Fairbrother 1986, p. 162).

The rediscovery of this picture supports the suggestion made by Warren Adelson and Elizabeth Oustinoff that four sketches of dancing figures (on two sheets, recto and verso) inserted into an album of studies for El Jaleo, which Sargent gave to Mrs Gardner in 1919 (figs 39–42) are studies of Carmencita dancing (see Adelson and Oustinoff 1992, p. 471 n. 14). These sketches and two further related studies on loose sheets in the Fogg Art Museum, Cambridge, Massachusetts, which depict similar dancing forms (figs 43, 44), have previously been associated with El Jaleo (see Washington 1992, pp. 172–5, nos 28 a–d, 29 and 30). The oil and the six pencil studies show Carmencita in action and express the flamboyance and posturing

of her dancing, with its histrionic writhings and exaggerated contortions. It may be that the difficulty in giving convincing pictorial form to such an energetic style of dancing led Sargent to opt for the static image of no. 234.

The present picture was exhibited in the Annual Exhibition of American Paintings and Sculpture at the Art Institute of Chicago in the winter of 1911 as 'Sketch of Carmencita dancing', but is otherwise unrecorded in Sargent literature.

238 *Dr Carroll Dunham*

c. 1890
Dimensions and medium unknown
Apparently destroyed (no image)

The portrait of Dr Carroll Dunham of Irvington, New York, was commissioned by Louis McCagg, a friend of the sitter, who also owned Sargent's *Spanish Gypsy Dancer* and *Venetian Courtyard*. Little is known about the painting, and no image of it survives. The date is given as 1889–90 in the catalogue of Sargent's one-man show held at Copley Hall, Boston, in 1899 (see Boston 1899, p. 8). David McKibbin notes that, in a copy of the 1899 Boston catalogue owned by Mabel Gage, it was described as a head-and-shoulders portrait, very florid and very strong (McKibbin papers). According to McKibbin, the colouring of the portrait was considered offensive, and the picture was destroyed by the family at an unspecified date (McKibbin papers).

The picture was exhibited in 1898 at the Society of American Artists exhibition in New York, and in 1899 it was shown both in Sargent's one-man show in Boston and at the Pennsylvania Academy of the Fine Arts; on each occasion, it was one of three paintings catalogued as owned by Louis McCagg. In a letter of 1926 on file at the Frick Art Reference Library, Mrs McCagg states that she no longer owned the picture.

The only related visual record is a caricature – an extraordinary collage of paint, chains, cotton, glass eye and lobster claws – by an unknown artist, which was shown at a Society of American Fakirs exhibition in New York as 'Poor-Trait of Dr C. D. Lobster, 1898'. The Society of Fakirs was a group of students at the Art Students League of New York who executed and exhibited caricatures of works submitted to the Society of American Artists' annual exhibitions. The original caricature is in the collection of the Art Students League, New York. For an illustration of the caricature, see Pisano and Weber 1993, no. 37A.

1890
Oil on canvas, 64 × 34 (162.6 × 86.3)
Inscribed, lower right: *John S. Sargent 1890*;
upper right: *BEATRICE*
Private Collection

Beatrice Goelet (1885–1902) was the daughter of Robert Goelet and his wife, Harriet Louise Warren, whom Sargent had painted in 1877 (see *Early Portraits*, nos 9, 10). Goelet inherited large tracts of property in Manhattan and managed them with such skill that he left an estate valued at twenty-five to forty million dollars. He was a major patron of the architectural firm McKim, Mead & White; they designed a huge, shingle-style house, Ochre Point at Newport, Rhode Island (1882–4), for him, and between 1885 and 1889 six commercial buildings and a family mausoleum. This association may have influenced the commission: Sargent had begun to negotiate plans for the Boston Public Library murals with Charles McKim at about the time the portrait was painted.

In an interview, the painter Dora Wheeler Keith (24 January 1937) said that Sargent rented her studio on Twenty-third Street and that he 'painted the little Gillette [*sic*] girl there, and he painted Carmencita there' (AAA). The parrot in its birdcage, overtopping the little girl reprises the compositional device of the huge vases in *The Daughters of Edward D. Boit* (*Early Portraits*, no. 56). The painting was widely and eloquently praised when it was exhibited at the Society of American Artists exhibition. The critics pointed to its antique echoes and to the spirit of Velázquez in particular. The *Art Amateur* nominated it

> beyond all dispute the best picture in the gallery, and the best work which the painter has yet done, and one which the New or the Old World will find it very hard to beat. The brilliant reality of this piquantly solemn babe is marvellous, and the audacity of the direct challenge to a comparison with Velasquez, conveyed in the simple arrangement of the little figure against the dark background and the color-scheme of silver grays and dull pinks and purples, is vindicated by the excellence of the result. The apparently reckless ease of the handling has never for a moment been permitted to generate into carelessness. (*Art Amateur*, June 1891, p. 5)

The critic for the *Art Interchange* wrote: 'In this scheme he has been aided and abetted by his sitter, a very charming little blonde maid of very few summers indeed, and he has posed her in infantile serenity in front of his canvas, draped her in a full-skirted stiff Venetian gown, put a rakish little toquet on top of her curls, and set a cockatoo in a gilded cage up behind her to support her' (*Art Interchange*, May 1891, p. 145). M. G. van

Rensselaer noted that Sargent 'did not "costume" the child for the sake of pictorial effect. The dress is one she was in the habit of wearing, and the bird is her own particular pet' (*Century Magazine*, March 1892, p. 798).

Five artists – William Merritt Chase, Julian Alden Weir, Kenyon Cox, John White Alexander and Francis David Millet – contributed their opinions of the picture to an article 'What the Artists Think of Sargent's "Beatrice"' in *Harper's Weekly* (9 May 1891). Chase noted that Sargent had created 'a great picture' rather than 'a mere portrait of a charming little girl' (p. 346), and Julian Alden Weir wrote: 'Sargent has painted his impression of the subject as he saw it, and not as he thought it ought to be, therefore it is distinctly an impression of nature and not a mere imitation of nature. In this regard the picture recalls Velázquez' (pp. 346–7). A rare dissenting note came from Theodore Robinson who, in his diary (7 December 1895) records seeing the portrait at the National Academy of Design: 'Sargent is disappointing – even the little Goelet girl seems to me poor in color' (FARL).

The portrait explicitly recalls old master paintings in composition. The little girl is dressed and posed like an infanta, recalling both Velázquez's *Las Meninas*, which Sargent had copied in 1879 (Private Collection), and his studies of the Infanta Margarita (see fig. 30). Sargent would also have been aware of the significance of the parrot as a leitmotif in nineteenth-century literature, for example in Gustave Flaubert's tale *Un coeur simple* (1876) and in two seminal and controversial works of art: Courbet's *Woman with a Parrot* (1866, Metropolitan Museum of Art, New York) and Manet's *Woman with a Parrot*, painted in response and in the same year. Manet's *Woman with a Parrot* had been presented to the Metropolitan Museum of Art by Erwin Davis in 1889.

American artist Thomas Wilmer Dewing had been commissioned to paint a full-length portrait of Beatrice's older brother, Robert Walton Goelet, in 1886 (Private Collection). Dewing's picture employs a consciously aesthetic design; but in placing his figure against a spare background and in deploying subtle pink and grey tonalities, he is making reference to Velázquez, and in his choice of costume of velvet suit and lace collar he is recalling both Velázquez and Van Dyck. Dewing inscribed the sitter's name and the date of the picture's execution in gilt capitals across the top of his canvas, and the self-consciously antique gilded lettering in the present work – an inscription unique in Sargent's *oeuvre* – may have been conceived to harmonize with that in Dewing's portrait.

For Sargent's letter to Mariana Griswold van Rensselaer, in which the 'Goelet baby' is mentioned, see Charteris 1927, pp. 109–10. For a caricature of the portrait by the artist, drawn on a menu, with the vertical inscription MEHITABLE, see fig. 45.

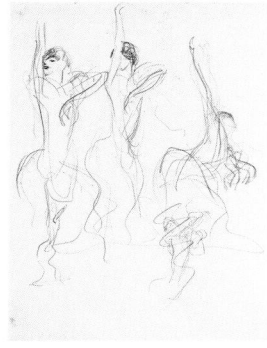

fig. 43 Sketches of dancers performing. Pencil, 11 ⅜ × 9 (28.9 × 22.9). Fogg Art Museum, Harvard University Art Museums. Gift of Mrs Francis Ormond 1937.8.118.

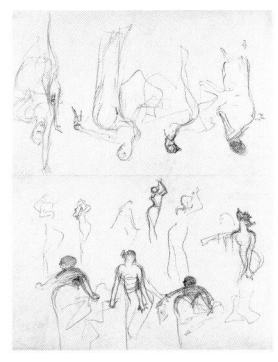

fig. 44 Sketches of dancers performing. Pencil, 18 × 14 ? (45.7 × 36.8). Fogg Art Museum, Harvard University Art Museums. Gift of Mrs Francis Ormond 1937.8.1 v.

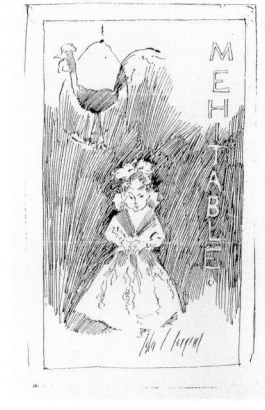

fig. 45 Caricature of the portrait of Beatrice Goelet. Archives of American Art, Washington, D.C.

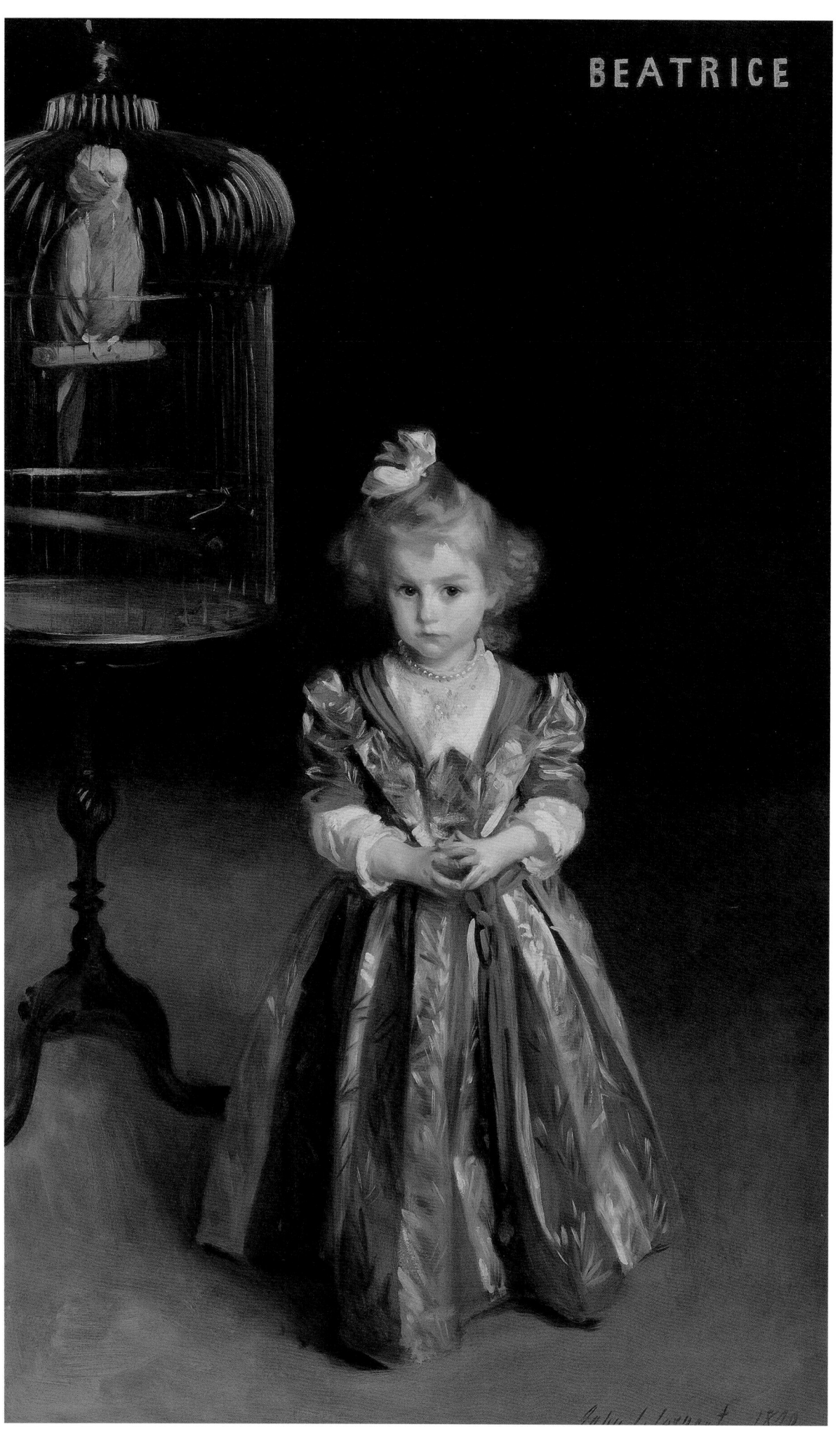

BEATRICE

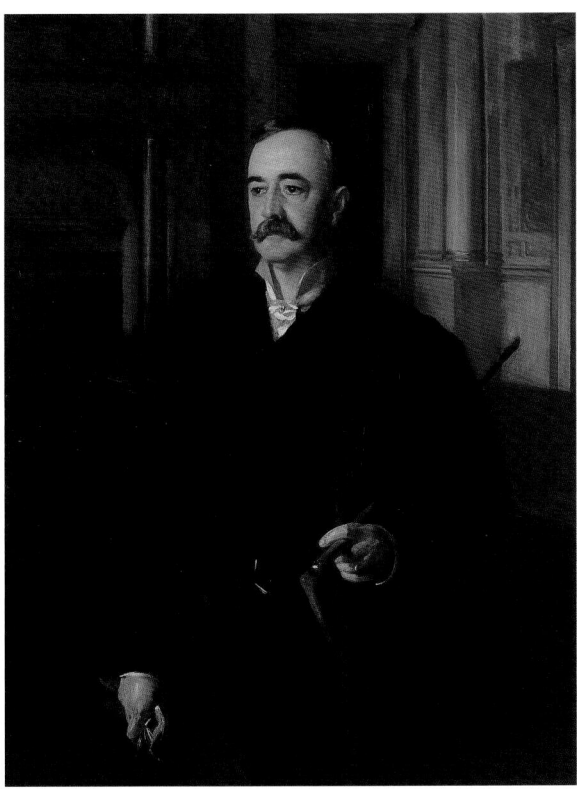

date, though it occurs in portraits after 1900. McCurdy is painted in morning suit, high collar, tie-pin and fob and overcoat, with gloves in his right hand and a cane in his left; there is a blankness, even sadness, in his rigid and unfeeling expression.

The separate piece of canvas bearing the signature and date suggests that the portrait was probably originally full length.

240   *Richard Aldrich McCurdy*

1890
Oil on canvas, 51 × 38¾ (129.5 × 98.5)
Inscribed (on a separate piece of canvas now fixed to the stretcher): *John S. Sargent 1890*
Charles Hosmer Morse Museum of American Art, Winter Park, Florida

Richard Aldrich McCurdy (1835–1916), of Morristown, New Jersey, was the son of Robert H. McCurdy and Gertrude Lee. A lawyer by training, he became president of the Mutual Life Insurance Company of New York in 1885 and a director of several major corporations. He was forced to retire in the wake of the insurance scandals of 1905, and, though his reputation was later vindicated, he never returned to business.

Sargent's portrait of McCurdy was commissioned by the Mutual Life Insurance Company for $3,000 in December 1889. The commission had originally been promised by McCurdy to Sargent's friend James Carroll Beckwith, who had painted McCurdy's wife and daughter in 1879, and who was not a little mortified to find himself supplanted (see his diary entries for 18 and 21 December 1889, NA; quoted in Fairbrother 1986, p. 155). On 15 January 1890, Beckwith records going to McCurdy's office for lunch: 'We stopped some time to see John work on his big portrait of McC and then came home.' This suggests that the portrait was painted at the offices of the Mutual Life Insurance Company, and the imposing setting may be a record of them. The use of a spacious architectural background, with fireplace, pilasters and painted decorations, is rare in Sargent's portraiture of this

241   *Mrs Thomas Lincoln Manson Jr*

1890
Oil on canvas, 56 × 44¼ (142.4 × 112.4)
Honolulu Academy of Fine Arts

Mrs Thomas Lincoln Manson Jr, *née* Mary Groot. The Mansons were mentioned in an undated [1890] letter to Mrs Gardner as being among those whom Sargent wished to invite to the evening party at which Carmencita was to dance (ISGM archive).

According to Mount, when Sargent was in New York, he stayed with the Mansons at their house, 325 Madison Avenue (Mount 1955, 1969 eds, p. 186). It has not been possible to confirm this, but it may be that the portrait was painted as a gesture of gratitude for the Mansons' hospitality.

Mrs Manson is shown in an evening gown of brown striped silk, shot with green and persimmon echoing an eighteenth-century design. The fitted bodice is trimmed with red at the neck, and the flounces of the elbow-length sleeves are lined with red. She is seated on an elegant gilt-edged Neoclassical sofa.

The portrait was exhibited at the Royal Academy in London in 1891, where it was overshadowed by the more flamboyant *La Carmencita* (no. 234). The *Academy* wrote that it was 'necessarily more ordinary than the preceding fantasy in portraiture, has much piquancy and elegance, marred to a certain extent, however, by the painty quality of the flesh in the neck and arms' (*Academy*, 16 May 1891, p. 471). Another critic described it as

> remarkable . . . This is an elegant but thin and starved-looking lady of an American type, dressed in a satin shot with scarlet and sapgreen, a lunette of diamonds in her hair, and the mouth curiously drawn. It is to be conjectured that this is one of Mr Sargent's brilliant 'caricatures', although it is excessively clever, and beautifully painted. The refined and bony hands are miracles of technical skill. But to like to see one's beloved relatives through Mr Sargent's spectacles must be an acquired taste. (*Saturday Review*, 13 June 1891, p. 715)

For a preliminary oil sketch for the portrait, see no. 242.

242 *Mrs Thomas Lincoln Manson Jr*

1890
Oil on canvas, 16¾ × 13¹³⁄₁₆ (42.5 × 35.1)
High Museum of Art, Atlanta, Georgia

This preliminary study for no. 241 is one of several preparatory oil sketches that Sargent made in the early 1890s (see nos 285, 307). Its early history is unknown, but it was exhibited at Cronyn and Lowndes Gallery, New York, in 1933 (see 'In all Mediums: Paintings, Concrete and Abstract', *New York Herald Tribune*, 24 December 1933, p. 10), and presumably purchased, as a sketch of Mrs Dwyer (a misappellation of Mrs Dyer; see *Early Portraits*, no. 57). It has been suggested that, in the finished portrait (no. 241), Sargent painted a head over the original head (Kiliaen Van Rensselaer to McKibbin, 11 February 1947, McKibbin papers), but there are no pentimenti visible, and the position of the head in this preliminary study is similar to that in the finished picture. The pose differs only in the position of the right arm, which is bent upwards in this sketch and is held loosely downwards in no. 241.

243 *Homer Saint-Gaudens and his Mother*

1890
Oil on canvas, 59¾ × 56 (151.8 × 142.2)
Carnegie Institute, Pittsburgh.
Patrons Art Fund

Homer Saint-Gaudens (1880–1953), son of the celebrated American sculptor Augustus Saint-Gaudens, is shown here with his mother, Augusta (1848–1926). Sargent had met Augustus Saint-Gaudens in Paris in the late 1870s, when Saint-Gaudens had a studio at 49, rue Notre Dame des Champs and they remained friends throughout their lives; both were engaged in decorations for the Boston Public Library, Sargent consulting Saint-Gaudens about the crucifix for the Christian portion of the decorations in 1898. Homer Saint-Gaudens was director of the Fine Arts Department, Carnegie Institute from 1923 until 1949.

It was during Sargent's visit to America with his sister Violet, from December 1889 until the following November, that initial negotiations, to which Saint-Gaudens was party, began with the architectural firm McKim, Mead & White for Sargent to contribute murals for the Boston Public Library. In February 1890, Saint-Gaudens was one of the guests at a party which Sargent held in William Merritt Chase's studio in the Tenth Street Studio Building in New York in honour of La Carmencita (see no. 234). Saint-Gaudens expressed a desire to execute a portrait of Violet in exchange for one by Sargent of Saint-Gaudens's ten-year-old son, Homer. In 1890, in

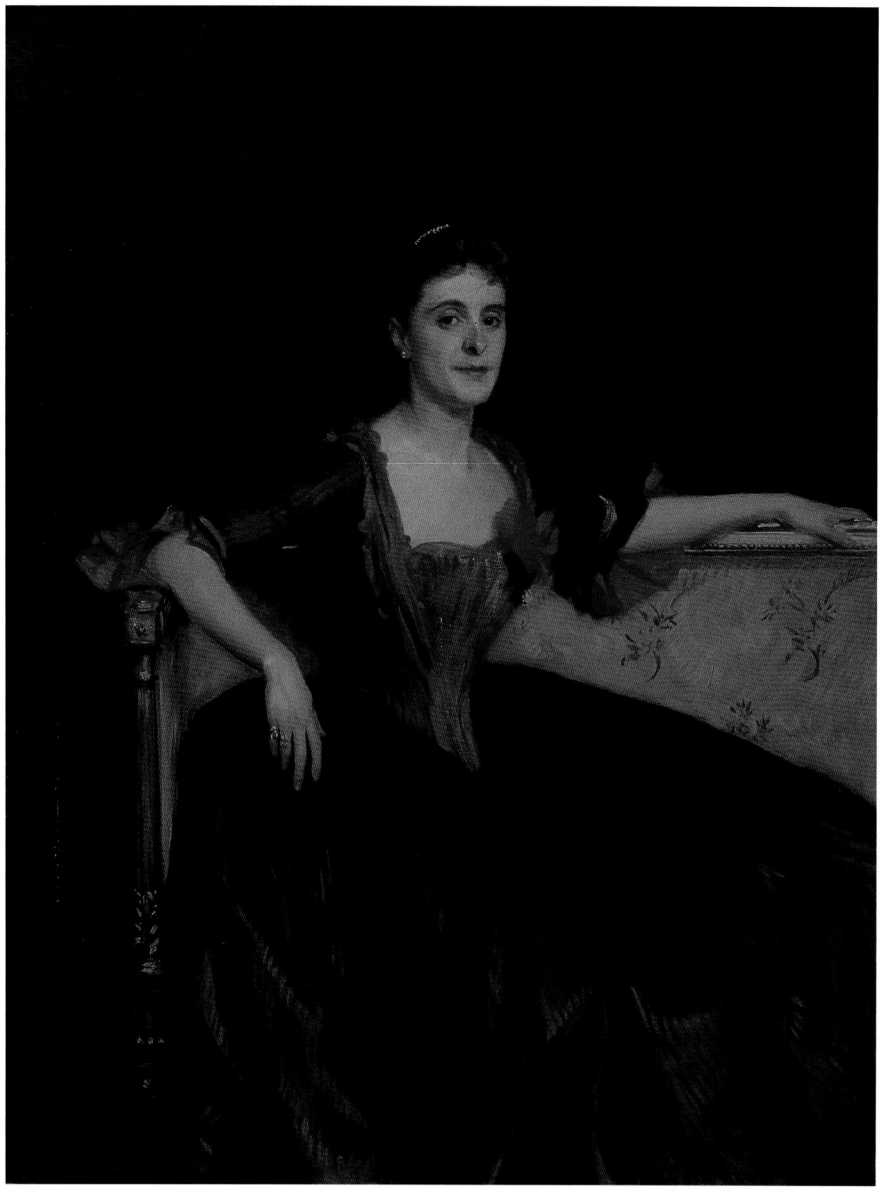

242

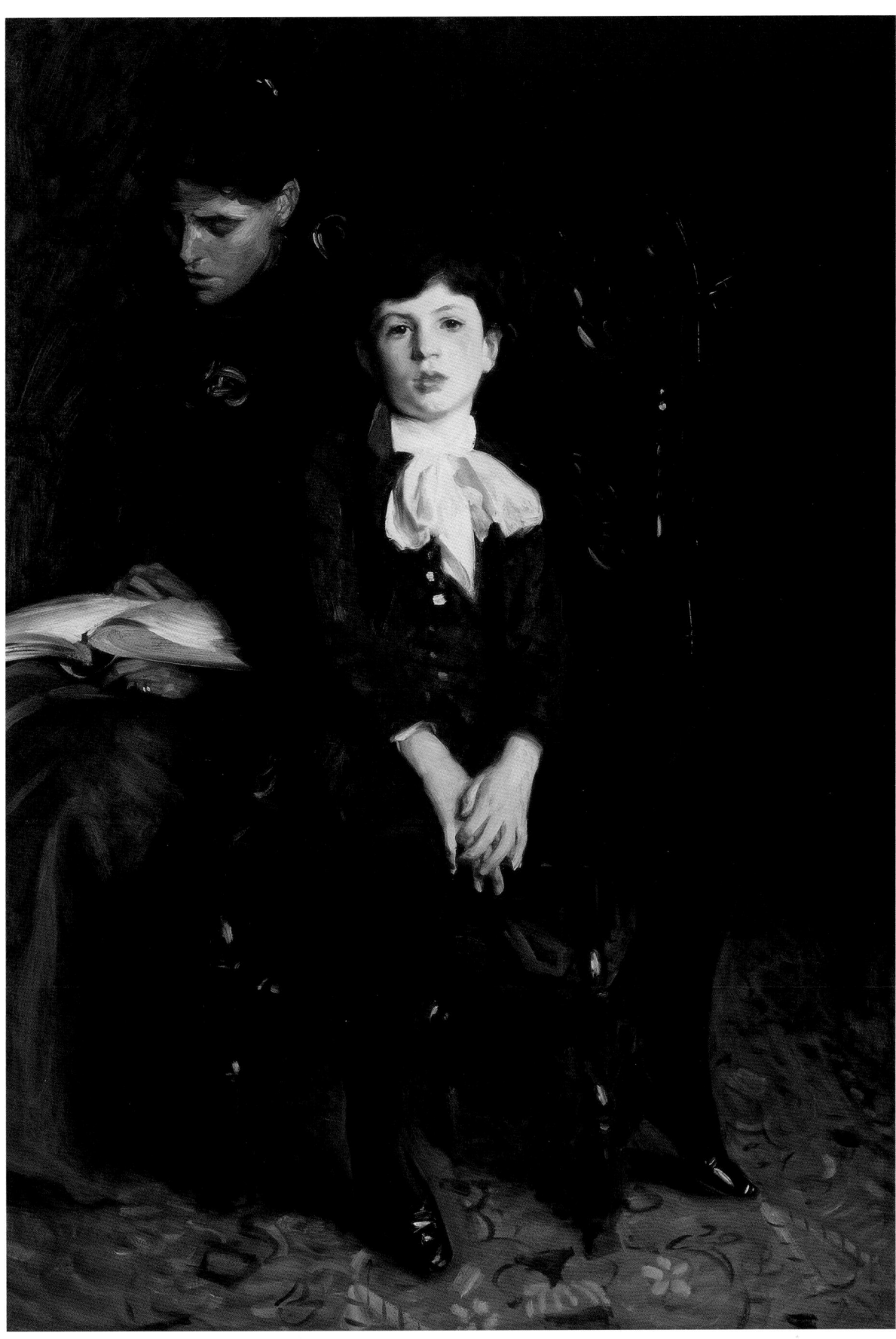

his studio in Cornish, New Hampshire, when Saint-Gaudens was working on a bas-relief of Violet playing the guitar, Sargent painted Saint-Gaudens's son, Homer in the New York studio he had borrowed on Twenty-third Street and Lexington Avenue. (For the story of the friendship and the circumstances of the exchange of portraits, see Donald Miller, 'Inspired Friendship: Sargent and Saint-Gaudens', *Carnegie Magazine*, 53, April 1979, pp. 4–11.) Sargent wrote to Saint-Gaudens about the form the portrait of Violet was to take, expressing a preference for a *ronde-bosse* (a sculpture 'in the round' – as opposed to relief) rather than a bas-relief: 'Pardon my silly interference. I am surprised at myself behaving just like the worst bourgeois, and you can have your revenge on me about your boy. I like his head very much by the way' (undated letter from Sargent to Saint-Gaudens, Saint-Gaudens Collection, DCL). The cast of the bronze relief of Violet Sargent given to her brother is in the National Museum of American Art, Washington, D.C., presented by her daughter Mrs Hugo Pitman; a marble version was presented to the Saint-Gaudens Museum by her son Jean-Louis Ormond.

The portrait blends an emotional edginess with a quasi-historical charm. Homer Saint-Gaudens is represented wearing a black velvet 'Little Lord Fauntleroy' suit, seated in a Charles II revival carved wooden chair, but this traditionalism is off-set by an oblique, casual pose. In his account of the sittings, Homer Saint-Gaudens wrote that he was excessively restless, and, while his mother read him the story of the sea battle between the *Constitution* and the *Guerrière* from *The Blue Jackets of 1812* to calm him, Sargent sketched in her figure (Saint-Gaudens 1941, p. 40). When the portrait was exhibited at the Philadelphia Art Club Exhibition in 1890, it received the gold medal for painting: Saint-Gaudens was awarded the gold medal for sculpture for his bust of General W. T. Sherman. When it was shown in Paris in 1891 at the Société nationale des beaux-arts, the *Art Journal's* critic wrote: 'In addition to his unvarying qualities of strength and vitality, [it] reveals to an unusual degree those of sympathy and of an easy, nonchalant grace' ('The Salons', *Art Journal*, 1891, p. 248).

Sargent wrote to Augustus Saint-Gaudens (21 August [1891]), from Paris thanking him for allowing the portrait to be exhibited there and chiding him for the arrangements, which Sargent felt had not fully been at his (Sargent's) expense (Saint-Gaudens Collection, DCL). In the same letter, he requested two copies of the bas-relief of Violet – one for himself, a second for Violet's mother-in-law, Mrs Louis Ormond (Violet had married Francis Ormond in Paris on 17 August): the latter is the marble now in the Saint-Gaudens Museum. In a letter to Mrs Saint-Gaudens (4 May 1909), Sargent confirms that the portrait was painted in 1890 (Carnegie Institute archives, Pittsburgh). A letter from Sargent to Walter Clark (25 January [1924]) with regard to the portrait's being included in the 1924 exhibition at the Grand Central Art Galleries is in the GCAG archive.

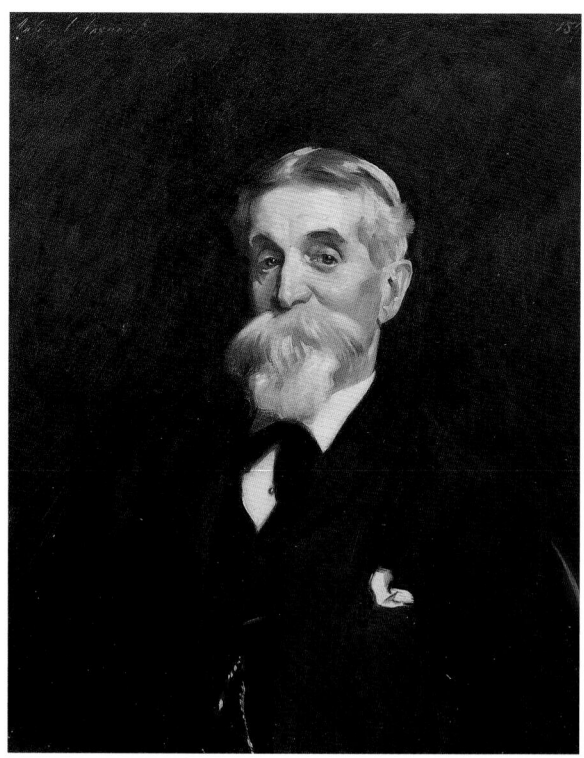

244 *Benjamin P. Kissam*

c. 1890
Oil on canvas, 32 × 26 (81.2 × 66.1)
Inscribed, upper left: *John S. Sargent*; upper right: *1890*
Private Collection

Benjamin Kissam (1818–1891), son of Reverend Samuel Kissam and Margaret Hamilton Adams, was a prominent New York banker, whose wife Sargent had painted in 1888 (see *Early Portraits*, no. 210).

The story of how the portrait came to be signed is told by the sitter's son-in-law, Arthur Train in an account published in *Atlantic Monthly*. The artist was lunching with Train in 1921 and, seeing the portrait of Kissam on the walls, failed to recognize it as his own work. 'Then, taking a glass from his pocket, he went over the canvas in detail. "Well", we heard him mutter after a few moments, "it *looks* like me!" Then in a tone of half-credulous amusement, "It *is* me!"' (*Atlantic Monthly*, 1929, pp. 663–4). The conclusive point was the green line around the handkerchief; the artist's astigmatism made him see green or red lines around white objects. Having accepted the portrait as his, the artist forthwith signed and dated it.

Train says the picture was painted in five sittings in London. If he is right about location, then the date must indeed have been added subsequently since Sargent was absent from London for almost all of 1890. On the other hand, several of the Vanderbilt commissions were done in New York in 1890, and it is logical to assume that Kissam might have been done then (his sister, Maria Louisa, was Mrs William Henry Vanderbilt). The style of the picture accords with a date in or around 1890; Charteris's dating of 1875 (see Charteris 1927, pp. 39, 257) is clearly wrong. The portrait is well described by Train:

> It is a brilliant full-face portrait of a slight, pink and white old gentleman with soft white hair and beard and flowing white moustache. He wears a dark-coloured business suit that merges into a background of indefinite bronze-green. An impression of punctilious neatness is conveyed by the turn-down collar, the soft bow tie, the pearl stud, and the white handkerchief which protrudes from the pocket of the sack coat. The face is highly intelligent, the expression at once whimsical, shrewd, immensely tolerant, but the slanting blue eyes are a little sad and world-weary. Keen but kindly, they follow one everywhere. (*Atlantic Monthly*, 1929, pp. 663–4)

Sargent also painted Kissam's sister, Maria Louisa (Mrs W. H. Vanderbilt); see *Early Portraits*, no. 211.

245 *Mrs Hamilton McKown Twombly*

1890
Oil on canvas, 90⅛ × 56½ (229 × 143.5)
Inscribed, upper right: *John S. Sargent 1890*
Columbia University, City of New York

Mrs Hamilton McKown Twombly, *née* Florence Adele Vanderbilt (*c.* 1854–1952), was the daughter of William Henry Vanderbilt and Maria Louisa (*née* Kissam) and the younger sister of Margaret Louise Vanderbilt (Mrs Elliott Fitch Shepard), whom Sargent had painted in 1888 (see *Early Portraits*, no. 208). She married Hamilton McKown Twombly in 1877.

Mrs Twombly is painted in a lavish and elegant interior – presumably her New York town house, 684 Fifth Avenue – surrounded by eighteenth-century *objets de luxe*. She is seated on a white Louis Seize footstool with a pink and green tapestry design and curved gilt supports; behind her is a framed tapestry with three figures – one crouching, the second sprinkling petals, the third playing a cymbal. On the curved wall behind her is a panelling of boiserie design ending in a pilaster; a red Baroque drape hangs at the far left and there is a figured strawberry-pink Aubusson carpet on the floor. She is wearing a white satin evening gown picked out with sequins and decorated with bows, a train swept around to her right.

Painted to hang in the Red Room of Mrs Twombly's Fifth Avenue house, the portrait is now displayed in the Twombly-Burden Room in the Low Memorial Library at Columbia University. It was presented to the university by the sitter's daughter, Mrs W. A. M. Burden, and the latter's sons, William A. M. Burden and Shirley C. Burden, as a memorial to Mrs Twombly.

Emily Sargent gave a chalk sketch for the portrait to Mrs Theodore Luling (*née* Grace

Dunham), who in turn gave it to the Ashmolean Museum, Oxford (fig. 46). The seated pose in the sketch is directly frontal, differing from the slightly twisted pose of the oil portrait. Also, the sitter's right hand is held up with an open fan, whereas in the oil it is held down with a closed fan.

246 *Cornelius Vanderbilt*

1890
Oil on canvas, approximately 30 × 23 (76.2 × 58.4)
Untraced (no image)

Cornelius ('Corneil') Vanderbilt II (1843–1899) of The Breakers, Newport, Rhode Island, was the eldest child of William Henry Vanderbilt and the grandson of 'Commodore' Cornelius Vanderbilt, who established the great railroad fortune. Cornelius II began his working life as a clerk in the New York Shoe and Leather Bank before working and learning his way into the family business so that, on his father's death, he assumed joint control with his brother William Kissam Vanderbilt. A serious minded and religious man, Cornelius devoted himself and a large part of his personal fortune to charities and church affairs. He was married to Alice Claypoole Gwynne with whom he had seven children.

In his later years, the American painter Frank Duveneck told his daughter-in-law Josephine that Vanderbilt had originally approached the English artist Sir John Everett Millais with the commission on a visit to the latter's London studio (at which Duveneck was present), and that Millais had recommended Sargent in his stead. Duveneck's comment that Sargent's American success began with his portrait of 'the elder Vanderbilt' also seems to refer to the present work (see Duveneck 1970, p. 147).

McKibbin and Mount both date the portrait 1895. However, the portrait was exhibited in 1891 at the National Academy of Design exhibition, and it is highly probable that it was painted during Sargent's extended visit to America in 1890, when the artist also painted Cornelius Vanderbilt's youngest brother, George Washington Vanderbilt (no. 247). Reviewing the National Academy exhibition, the critic for the *Art Amateur* wrote: 'Mr Sargent sends . . . a head of Cornelius Vanderbilt, very fresh in color and ultra realistic to the verge of vulgarity' (*Art Amateur*, May 1891, p. 142).

The family were apparently unhappy with the painting. Louis Auchincloss, a chronicler of the 'gilded age' in America, noted in his biography of the Vanderbilts: 'Cornelius's daughter Gladys (Countess Széchényi) [see no. 508] would never let anyone so much as glimpse a Sargent portrait of her father which she had inherited because she deemed it an unflattering resemblance' (Auchincloss 1989, p. 38). The compilers have seen neither the original nor a photograph. The measurements are taken from the checklists of Mount

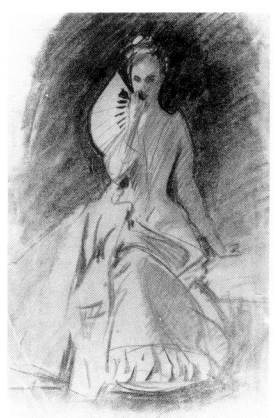

fig. 46 Sketch of *Mrs Hamilton McKown Twombly*. Chalk, 18 ¹¹⁄₁₆ × 11 ¹³⁄₁₆ (47.4 × 30). Ashmolean Museum, Oxford.

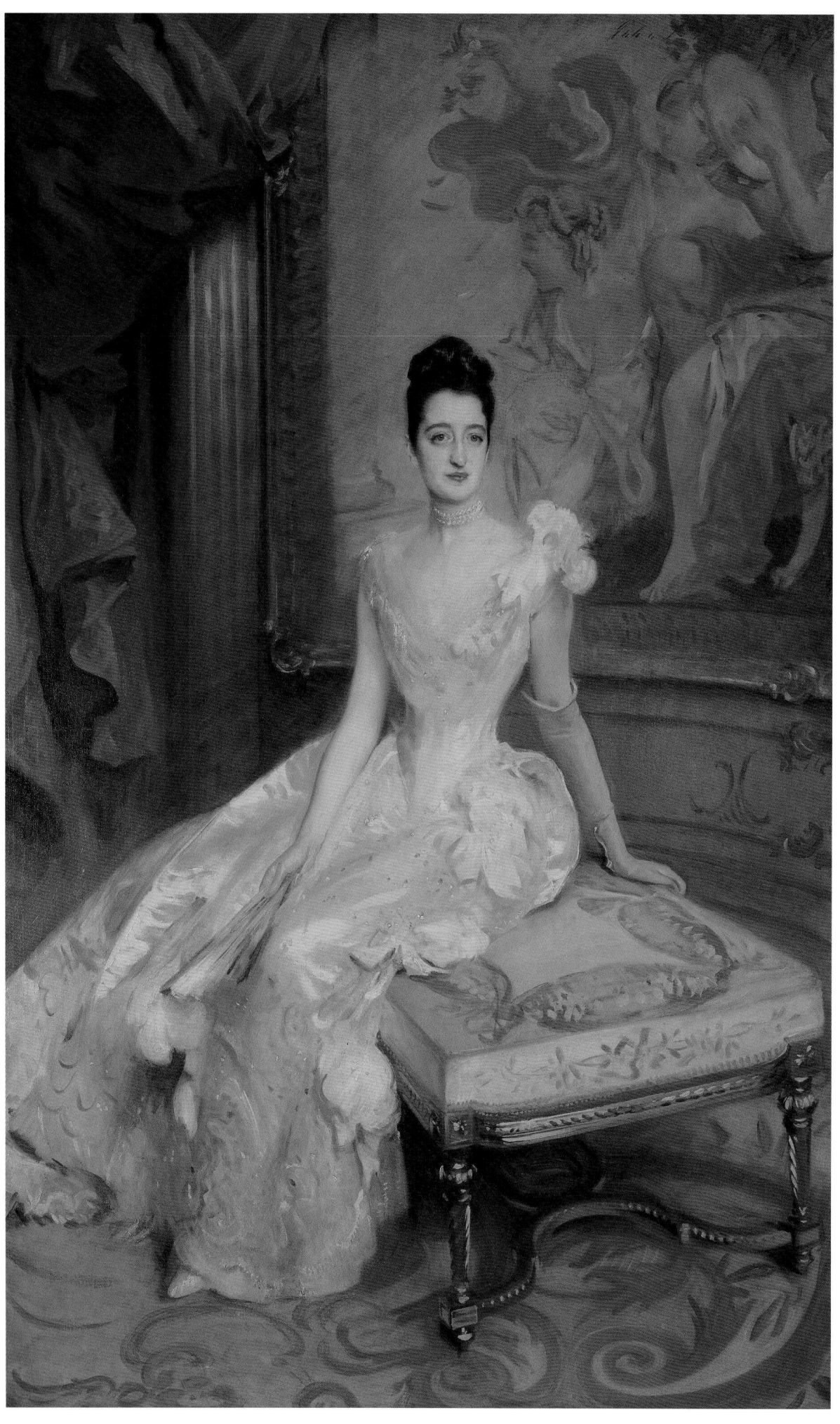

and McKibbin. Mount in his checklist and McKibbin on his index card for the picture (McKibbin papers) both indicate that the work is signed and dated.

A portrait of Cornelius Vanderbilt by Frank Holl (1888) is in a private collection.

247 *George Washington Vanderbilt*

1890
Oil on canvas, 42 × 26½ (106.6 × 67.3)
Inscribed, upper left: *John S. Sargent*; upper right: *1890*
The Biltmore Company, Biltmore House, Asheville, North Carolina

George Washington Vanderbilt III (1862–1914), was the youngest of the eight children of William Henry Vanderbilt and his wife, Maria Louisa Kissam. His father left him $20 million in 1885 and, on his mother's death in 1896, he inherited his parents' New York house (640 Fifth Avenue) and their art collection. Temperamentally shy and serious, he had cultivated tastes and became a celebrated bibliophile, reading in eight languages and building up a personal library of some 23,000 volumes. His niece Consuelo (see no. 486) remarked that his bookish manner and intellectual interests made him singular among his generation of Vanderbilts: 'With his dark hair and eyes, he might have been a Spaniard. He had a narrow sensitive face, and artistic and literary tastes' (Balsan 1953, p. 3). He was generous with his wealth; he had a small library built at 251 West Thirteenth Street, which he gave to the city (it is now incorporated into the New York Public Library), and he donated land for the campus of Teachers College in New York. His great passion was Biltmore, the quasi-French château which he had built in the midst of 125,000 acres of the North Carolina mountains and which remains the largest private house in America. In 1898, he married Edith Stuyvesant Dresser, a direct descendant of Peter Stuyvesant, governor of Dutch colonial New Netherland in the mid-1860s; their only child, Cornelia, was born in 1900.

George Vanderbilt had commissioned Sargent to paint his mother in 1888 (see *Early Portraits*, no. 211). The present work was presumably painted in New York in the early months of 1890. It was one of seven works that Sargent showed at the Society of American Artists exhibition held at the Fifth Avenue Art Galleries, New York, at the end of April 1890, the first time such a significant group of his works had been seen in the city and the occasion of sustained, if varied, critical comment. Sargent places Vanderbilt's slender frame in a slight *contrapposto*, leaning against the top of a marble mantlepiece in a gesture of mannered elegance. The *Art Interchange* noted that Sargent had responded to Vanderbilt's saturnine looks, describing the portrait as 'an oriental-looking young gentleman with a

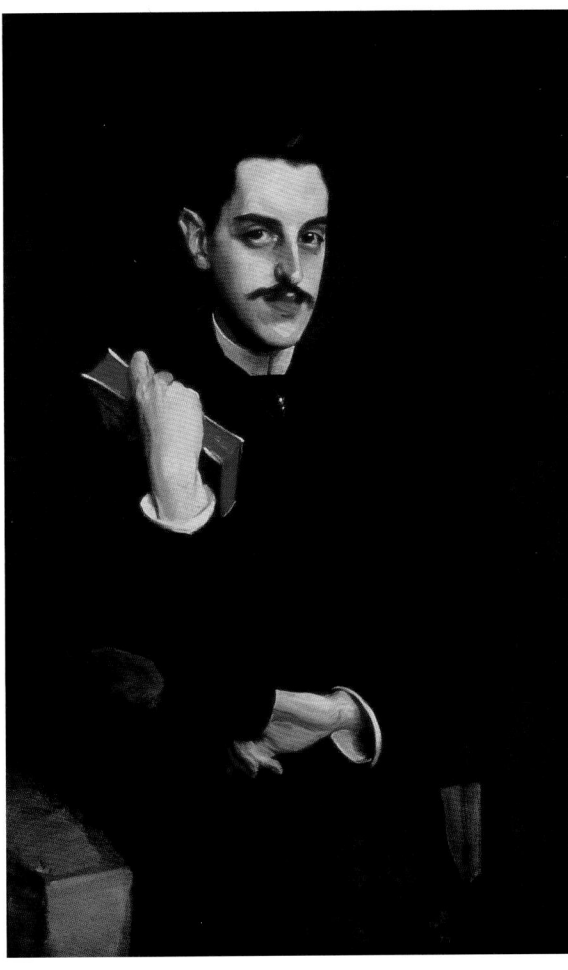

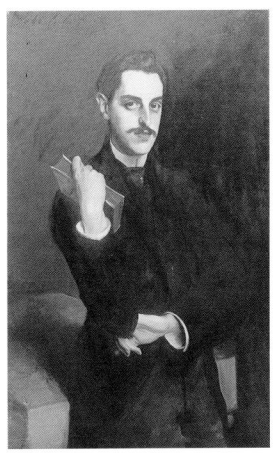

fig. 47 Photograph of Sargent's portrait of George Vanderbilt (catalogue raisonné archive).

very red-edged book held close to his face' (*Art Interchange*, 24 May 1890, p. 176). Critics praised the vitality of colour repeated in the vivid mouth and the page edges, but the *New York Daily Tribune* noted that 'Mr Sargent's devotion to color is not accompanied necessarily by neglect of structural truth' (*New York Daily Tribune*, 26 April 1890, p. 7). It was, however, the freedom of facture that most startled an American audience unused to such painterly fluidity: 'an amazing piece of brushwork, but viewed as a portrait, dashed in with such brutality that it falls little short of caricature' (*Art Amateur*, 23, June 1890, p. 3) and 'the handling is miraculously clever, and suggests what a Japanese Velasquez might do' (*Critic*, 16, 3 May 1890, p. 225).

The portrait has frequently been misdated 1895, the year when Sargent was at Biltmore fulfilling Vanderbilt's commission to paint portraits of the estate's architect Richard Morris Hunt, and landscape designer, Frederick Law Olmsted (nos 317, 318). The date '1890' on the upper right of the canvas has been eroded and is indistinct, but it is visible in an early archival photograph (see fig. 47).

James McNeill Whistler painted a sensitive, etiolated full-length of Vanderbilt (1897–1903, National Gallery of Art, Washington, D.C.) and a portrait of his wife (1902, the Biltmore Company, Biltmore House, Asheville, North Carolina). A portrait of Mrs Vanderbilt by Giovanni Boldini (1911) is also at Biltmore.

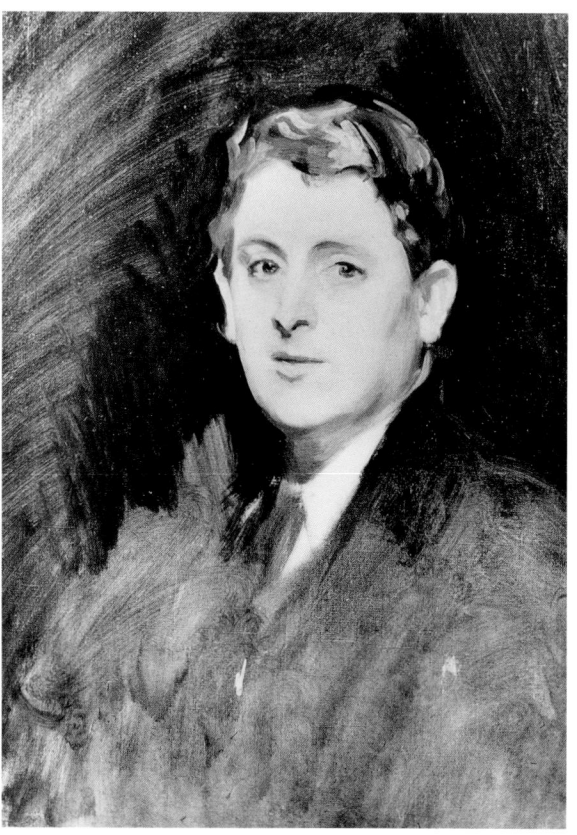

248 *Julian Alden Weir*

1890
Oil on canvas, 25½ × 21½ (64.8 × 54.6)
Untraced

The well-known American painter Julian Alden Weir (1852–1919) was born into a family of artists; his father was Robert W. Weir and his elder brother, John Ferguson Weir, was director of Yale University School of Fine Arts. Julian Alden Weir studied in New York, at the National Academy of Design, and in Paris, where he was a near contemporary of Sargent's, with Jean-Léon Gérôme (1873–7). He painted both portraits and genre as well as some remarkably delicate floral still lifes and, in the late 1880s, developed a looser, higher-keyed impressionist style, which infused his poetic landscapes. He was a founder of the Society of American Artists in 1877, becoming its president in 1882, and was one of the founders of the progressive independent group the Ten American Artists in 1898. His correspondence is in the Archives of American Art.

McKibbin's index card for this unfinished sketch indicates that it was painted in New York on 8 April 1890 (McKibbin papers).

249 *Grace Woodhouse*

1890
Oil on canvas, 64⅛ × 37 (162.9 × 94)
Inscribed, upper left: *John S. Sargent*; upper right: *1890*
National Gallery of Art, Washington, D.C. Gift of Olga Roosevelt Graves

Grace Guernsey Woodhouse (1867–1894) was the daughter of Colonel Lorenzo Woodhouse, a Civil War veteran and a partner in Marshall Field of Chicago, and his wife, Emma Douglas Arrowsmith. The family lived in New York and Chicago. Grace married Robert Barnwell Roosevelt Jr, a nephew of Theodore Roosevelt, on 7 April 1890, and they had one child. She died at her summer home on Shelter Island apparently of blood poisoning, a complication of tonsillitis, some four years later. The picture was painted shortly before her marriage, almost certainly in New York.

The portrait was exhibited at the National Academy of Design's annual exhibition in the spring of 1891. The critic for *Art Amateur* described it as 'a hurriedly painted [portrait] of a pretty young debutante in pink, the crimson bulb of the orchids in her hands furnishing the high note of the composition. The lady seems worthy of more considerate treatment. So charming a subject might at least have been spared the mortification of the flesh – note the leaden-hued, unfinished right arm' ('"The Academy" Exhibition', *Art Amateur*, 24, May 1891, pp. 142, 145).

The museum's old accession number for the painting is 1660.

250 *Mrs Edward Davis and her Son, Livingston*

1890
Oil on canvas, 86⅛ × 48¼ (218.8 × 122.6)
Inscribed, lower right: *John S. Sargent*
Los Angeles Museum of Art. Frances and Armand Hammer Purchase Fund

Mrs Edward Davis, *née* Maria Louisa Robbins (d. 1916), was the daughter of the Reverend Chandler Robbins of Boston and his wife, Mary Frothingham. Her husband, Edward L. Davis, was connected with the Washburn Iron Company. He served as mayor of Worcester and as a Massachusetts senator, and both he and his wife were prominent members of Worcester society. Livingston (1882–1932) was their only son.

This was one of Sargent's Worcester commissions, a triumph of his 1890 visit. Sargent, staying at the Worcester Club in July 1890, painted no less than five portraits. He posed Mrs Davis and her son against the deep shadow of their carriage-house door. Frederick Pratt noted in his diary jottings: 'Saw him [Sargent] in E. L. Davis stable when

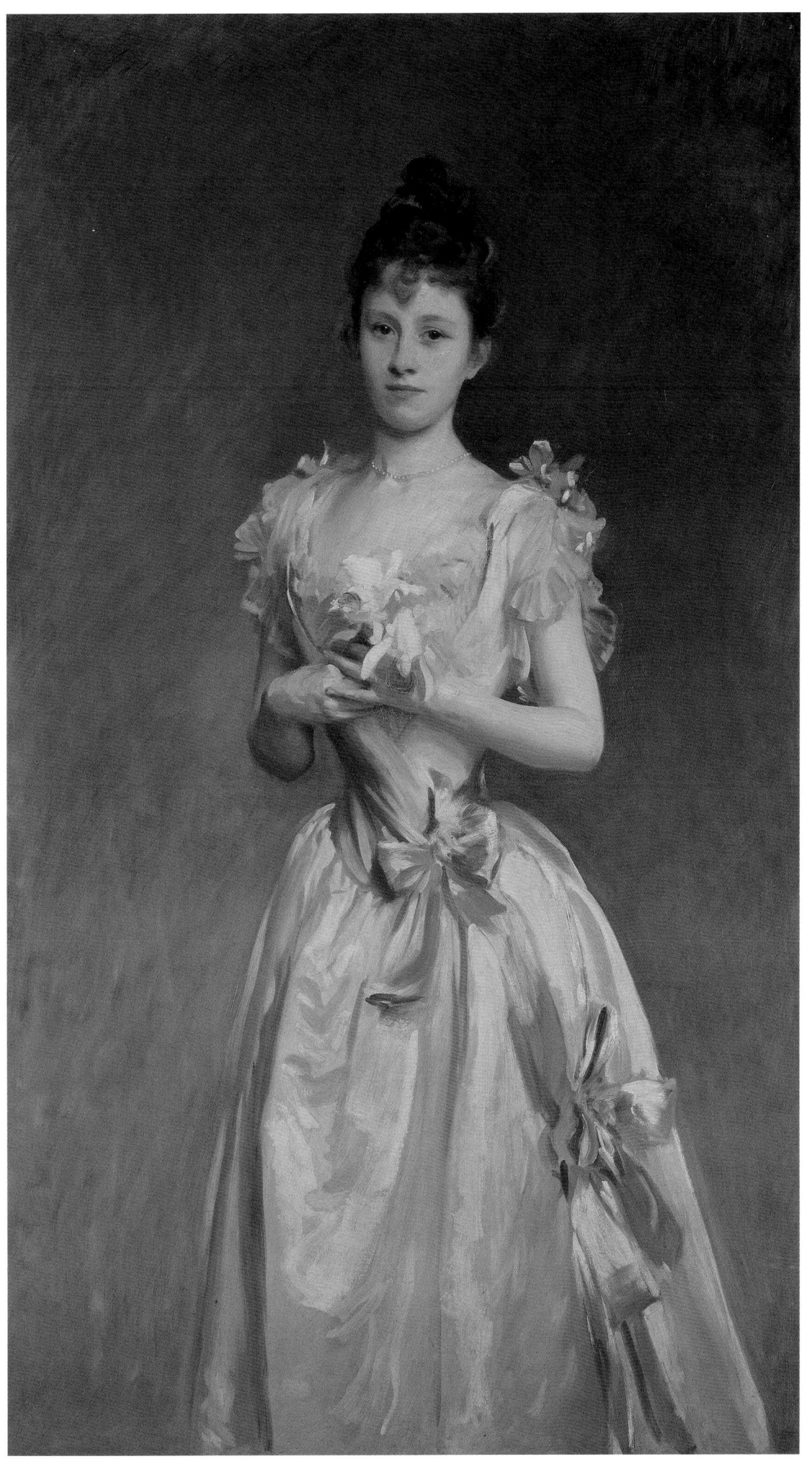

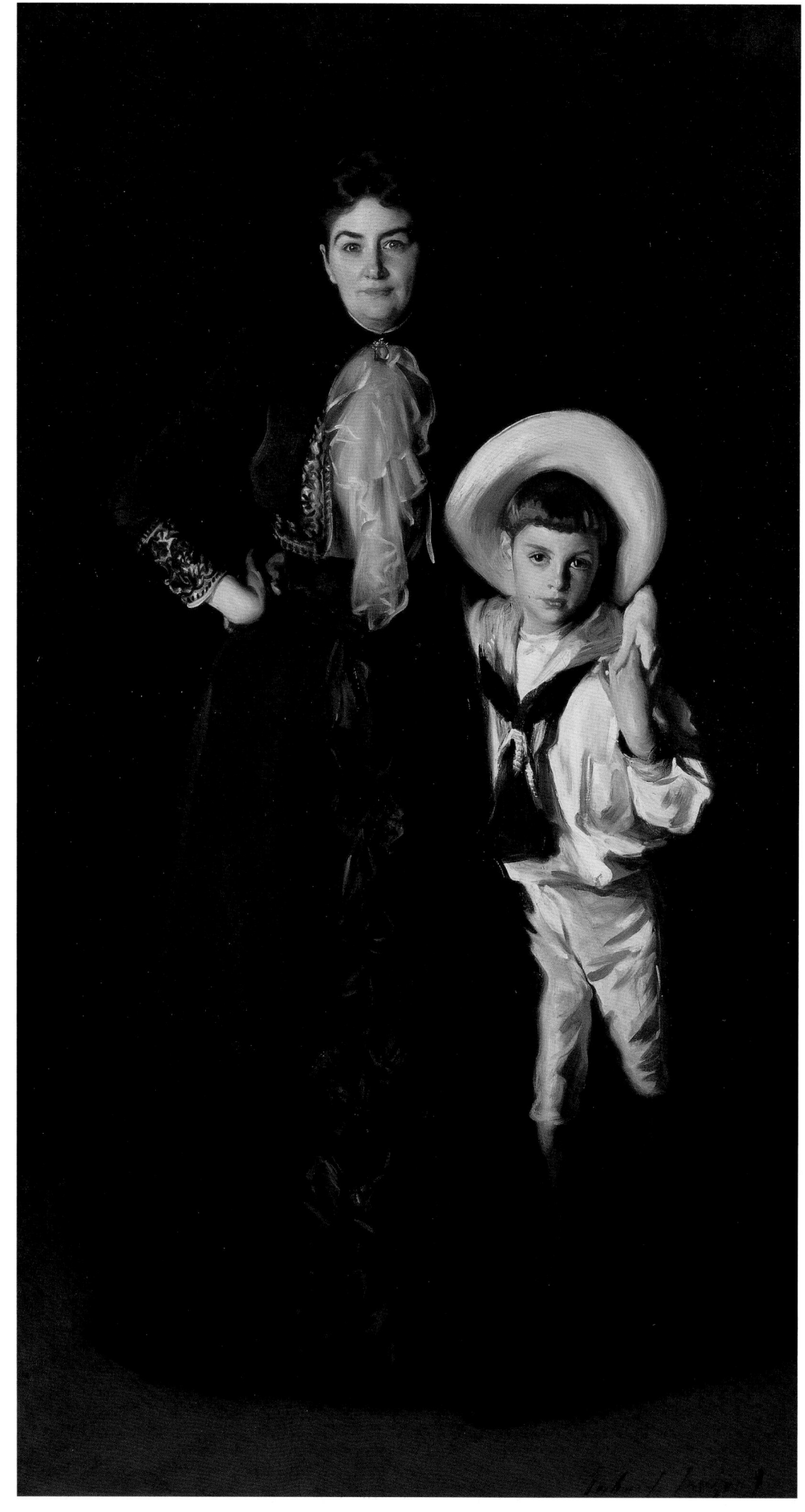

he was painting Mrs D. and Livingston' (Stephen Pratt).

Mrs Davis wears a straight black skirt decorated down the front with bows, a tight sash round her waist, an embroidered Spanish-style bolero or waistcoat, a black satin jacket with embroidered cuffs and a white fichu secured by a cameo brooch at her neck. Her right arm is bent at the wrist and resting on her hip. Her son is in a white sailor suit and large brimmed hat, his right arm around his mother's waist.

There is something theatrical about the pose of Mrs Davis, the face dramatically lit from below, the hairline and eyebrows accentuated. The portrait exhibits some of the exotic elements to be found in, for example, *Flora Priestley* (see *Early Portraits*, no. 225). The motif of the wrist on the hip occurs, too, in the much earlier portrait of the *Lady with the Rose* (see *Early Portraits*, no. 55), and both pictures find a common source in Velázquez. Mother and son have their arms about each other in a rhythmic pose, but the independence of the figures is emphasize by the strong chromatic contrasts in their costumes. The portrait was widely exhibited in America, contributing positively to his rising reputation there.

In a letter of 10 December [1923], Sargent wrote to Walter Clark concerning the Grand Central Art Galleries exhibition:

I happened to meet at a concert Mr Livingston Davis of 48 Beacon Street Boston. He is the now grown up small boy in that full length portrait that you asked me about of a lady in black, standing with her son – I asked him whether he would lend the picture and he seemed disposed to do so, but he wanted more particulars than I at that moment had time to give him. Would you write to him and furnish him with them? (GCAG archives).

The frame is an original Stanford White frame, similar to that on no. 258.

251 *Mrs Francis Henshaw Dewey*

1890
Oil on canvas, 36 × 29⅛ (91.5 × 74)
Inscribed, upper left: *John S. Sargent 1890*
Worcester Art Museum, Worcester, Massachusetts

Mrs Francis Henshaw Dewey, née Lizzie Davis Bliss (1856–1950), was the daughter of Harrison Bliss of Worcester. In 1878, she married Francis Henshaw Dewey II, a lawyer and banker in Worcester who was later elected mayor. They had two children. Like her husband, Mrs Dewey was noted for her public spirit, founding the Worcester Girls' Club and serving as president of the Women's Alliance. She was vice-president of the Worcester Employment Society and a director of the home for aged women.

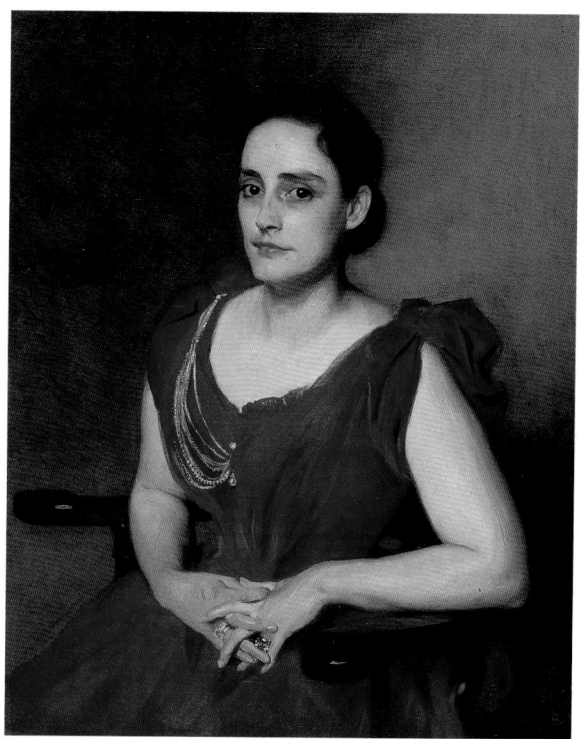

The commission almost certainly came through Frederick Pratt (see nos 253, 254). The artist, who was in Worcester in July 1890 painting several portraits, apparently painted Mrs Dewey on the fourth of that month (McKibbin papers). Two letters from Sargent to Dewey are extant (Worcester Art Museum archives). In the first, headed 'at Mr Pratt's Worcester' and dated 12 August [1890], the artist writes:

I have just returned to Worcester after a much longer absence than I had planned, and I find both your letters in Mr Pratt's keeping. Many thanks for the cheque and for the kind invitation to Narragansett. I am sorry I did not receive it in time to go or at any rate to write. I hope that Mrs Dewey and the children are well. My compliment to the apple of my eye and tell Mrs Dewey that I will send a photo of myself as soon as I get one.

The second letter, postmarked 13 October 1890, is written from Manchester, Massachusetts:

There would be a great deal to be said about the subject of your letter but I daresay it would merely confirm us in our different points of view. I am sorry that the portrait of Mrs Dewey does not give universal satisfaction but am not very much surprised at its sharing the fate of most portraits of very handsome ladies, and I cannot try experiments with a picture completed to the best of my lights and ability. Please give my kindest regards to Mrs Dewey. I will ask Mr Pratt to send her a photo that his son took of me.

McKibbin notes the price for the portrait as $5,000, but this must be a misprint for $500 (McKibbin papers).

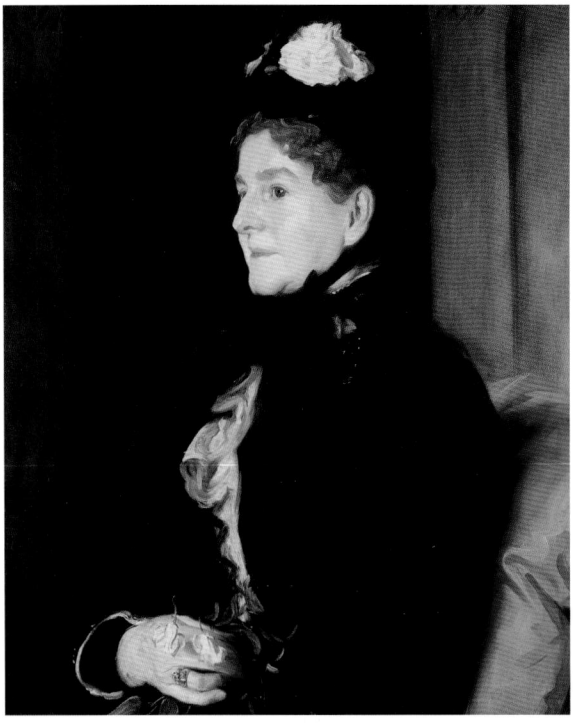

Mrs Dewey is painted seated in a colonial-style chair, wearing a red sleeveless dress with a silver-and-pearl necklace pinned to the shoulder of her gown, diamond rings on the index finger of both hands.

252　*Mrs Alexander Hamilton Bullock*

1890
Oil on canvas, 31 × 26 (76.2 × 63.5)
Inscribed, upper left: *John S. Sargent*; upper right: *1890*
Worcester Art Museum, Worcester, Massachusetts

Mrs Alexander Hamilton Bullock, née Elvira Hazard (1824–1894), was the daughter of Colonel A. G. Hazard of Enfield, Connecticut, founder of the Hazard Gunpowder Manufacturing Company. In 1844, she married A. H. Bullock, a lawyer and insurance agent who was twice mayor of Worcester and Governor of Massachusetts; they had one son and two daughters. The history of the Hazard family records that she was generous and sympathetic: 'For the last few years of her life she was an invalid, and was obliged to retire from society, but she never allowed her suffering to interfere with her Charities' (*The Hazard Family*, n.d., privately printed, p. 227).

The portrait was one of several Worcester commissions, apparently arranged through Mrs Davis (see no. 250). Mrs Bullock was at this time living with her son, Augustus, at 48 Elm Street (her husband had died in 1882), only several doors from the Davis family. A notice in the *Worcester Daily Spy* (21 June 1890) reads: 'He [Sargent] will also before leaving Worcester be given sittings by Mrs Alexander H. Bullock and Mrs Francis H. Dewey, Jr.' In the Worcester Art Society 1891 exhibition

catalogue, the lender is listed as Mrs Bullock's son, and it was he who presumably commissioned it.

According to Chandler Bullock, 'She had just come out of her garden behind the house with a flower in her hand when Sargent called at the house and first saw her. So he insisted on painting her with that particular flower in her hand as the portrait shows.' (letter to McKibbin, 31 October 1947, McKibbin papers.) She is painted sitting upright against a red cushion with a brown curtain in the background, wearing a dark cape, the front partially open to reveal the white flounces of a dress or blouse underneath and a black bonnet decorated with flounces and tied under the chin with a large bow. She has gold and diamond rings on her right hand and is holding a bunch of edelweiss.

253　*Katharine Pratt*

1890
Oil on canvas, 40 × 30⅛ (101.6 × 76.5)
Worcester Art Museum, Worcester, Massachusetts.
Gift of William I. Clark

Katharine Chase Pratt (1875–1942) was the daughter of Frederick Sumner Pratt, a member of Sumner Pratt & Co. of Worcester, Massachusetts, agents for cotton and woollen machinery, and his wife, Sarah Hilliard. She married a doctor, Alfred L. Shapleigh, and went with him to China as a missionary. Following the death of two of her sons and her husband in 1905 from the effects of smallpox, she carried on alone with what her nephew calls 'a remarkable quality of peace and helpfulness' (Stephen Pratt to compilers, 16 November 1982).

Sargent had met Frederick Pratt in June 1890, when he came to Worcester to paint Mrs Davis (no. 250). Pratt was a collector and connoisseur of painting, one of the corporators of the Worcester Art Museum and its acting director in 1908 and 1917, as well as an amateur water-colourist, and he and Sargent became friends. In August, Sargent returned to Worcester for a nine-day stay with Pratt and painted two portraits of his daughter. Pratt's brief memories of Sargent's two 1890 visits (Collection Stephen Pratt) record some of the sketches that he did, including an oil of roses and a water-colour of fir trees.

Pratt remained in touch with Sargent and occasionally visited him in Boston and London. It was through this connection that the Worcester Art Museum acquired the portrait *The Countess of Warwick and her Son* (no. 484) and an important group of Vizcaya water-colours. In 1921, Sargent recommended the purchase of an *Odalisque* by Ingres from the collection of his friend Sir Philip Sassoon; this was not acquired.

This first portrait of Katharine Pratt was painted on Sargent's return visit to Worcester in August 1890. The idea of painting her against hydrangeas had occurred to him earlier in June. He had made a sketch of hydrangeas on that occasion at Lange's greenhouse (untraced) and had subsequently arranged to have some flowers sent to Pratt's house; importing flowers for his pictures was nothing new. Pratt noted in his memories of Sargent's visit in June: 'His walk to Lange's to prevent his sending Hydrangea plant to my house after putting off his visit and sketch of Kitty' (Collection Stephen Pratt). Sargent had promised to return later to paint Kitty. On 14 July, Pratt told his wife, who was holidaying with the children, that the artist had postponed his visit for a week. On 8 August, he wrote again: 'I have finally heard from Mr. Sargent who promises to come on Monday next in the evening. So Kitty need not come until then. I am afraid it will be difficult to get any *blue* Hydrangea now, but I shall search for some.' Later Pratt noted in his diary: 'Our dining together after Hydrangea plants. His letter of thanks to lady who loaned the plant' (both quoted by Strickler 1982–3, pp. 24–5).

Sargent's hydrangea portrait of Katharine never progressed beyond a sketch; the features especially are very broadly indicated. Perhaps he became dissatisfied with the idea, or found it too difficult to carry through. He seems to have painted the more formal and finished portrait of Katharine (no. 254) after the hydrangea picture, which suggests that it was done as a substitute to satisfy the demands of likeness. The sitter wears the same muslin dress in both portraits.

The location of the portrait is established by an inscription on the back of a reduced copy by Pratt himself (32 × 24 in, Collection Mrs Elizabeth Pratt Cheely): 'Copied from John S. Sargent's portrait sketch of Katharine Chase Pratt. Original was painted August 1890 in veranda of house, 53 West Street, Worcester, Mass. Copied by F. S. Pratt. Original measured 30 × 40 inches'.

The girl is seated in a garden chair documented in Pratt family photographs of the late 1880s, and the line visible to the right of her head appears to indicate the corner of the house. The warm, reflective lighting (dabs of pink in the face, mauves, greens and greys in the dress) is characteristic of a partially outdoor setting. The flowing lines of the dress, with frilly collar, tight sash at the waist, billowing sleeves and flounced hem, create a strong diagonal movement, balanced by the clumps of hydrangeas on either side. Decorative, aesthetic design and tender mood combine here, as they do in the studies of young girls in white painted at Broadway, to suggest youthful innocence and beauty, see, for example *Teresa Gosse* (*Early Portraits* no. 161) and *Carnation, Lily, Lily, Rose* (Tate Gallery, London). The abstracted and wistful mood is complemented by the luxuriant colour of the flowers and the indolent summery atmosphere.

The exhibition history of this portrait and that of no. 254 are difficult to disentangle and to establish securely. We have used 'probably' to indicate

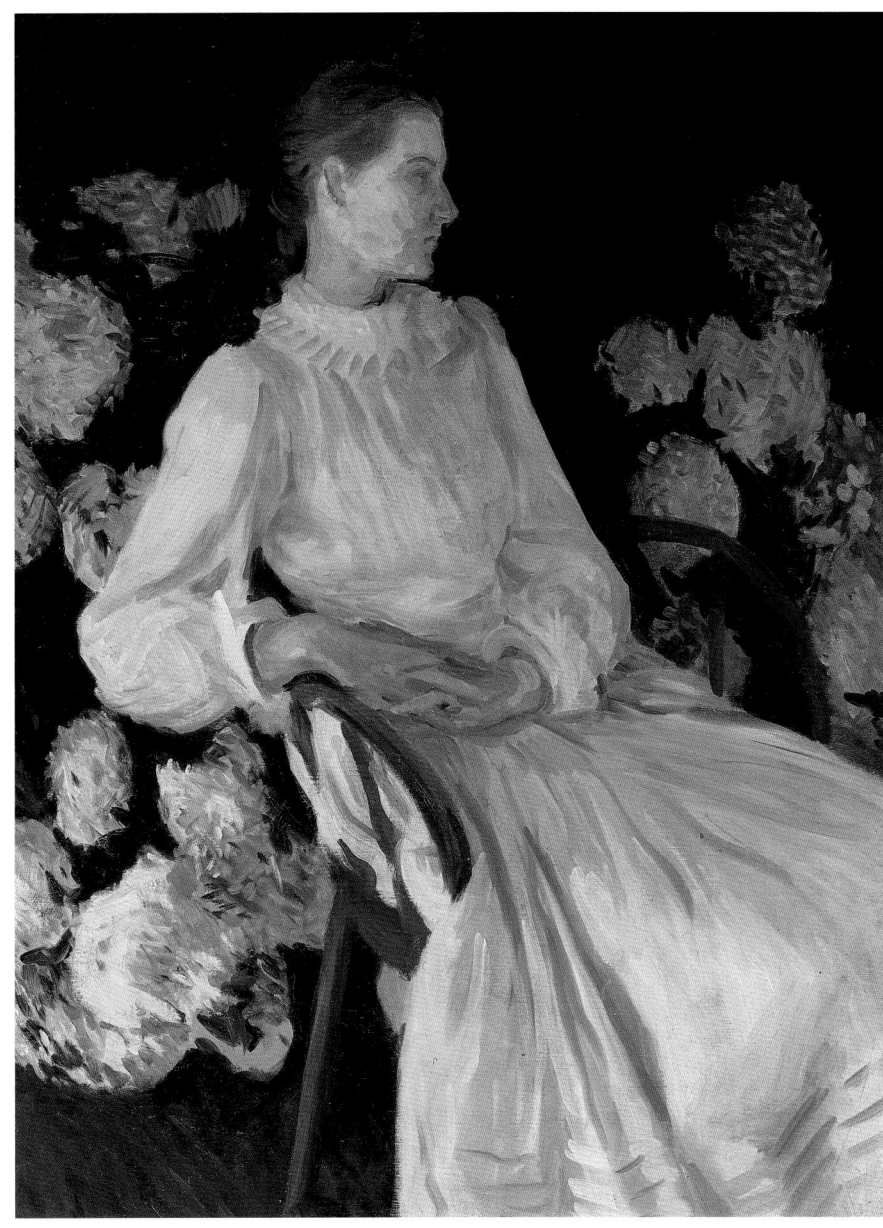

253

where we are uncertain about which of the two pictures is the one shown in a particular exhibition.

254 *Katharine Pratt*

1890
Oil on canvas, 40⅜ × 30⅛ (102.6 × 76.5)
The Peters Corporation, Santa Fe, New Mexico

By 16 August, Sargent had begun a second portrait of Kitty. Frederick Pratt noted to his wife: 'The picture (new one) is beautiful. S. did not try to have a good likeness in the first one'. This portrait of Katharine was painted after the hydrangea picture (no. 253), probably to provide Sargent's host with a more satisfactory likeness of his daughter. Frederick Pratt noted in his diary: 'Visit to Green Hill after finishing K's portrait. His drawing on the banks of pond sketching the swan (pencil). Watching the spiders under bridge.' (Collection Stephen Pratt).

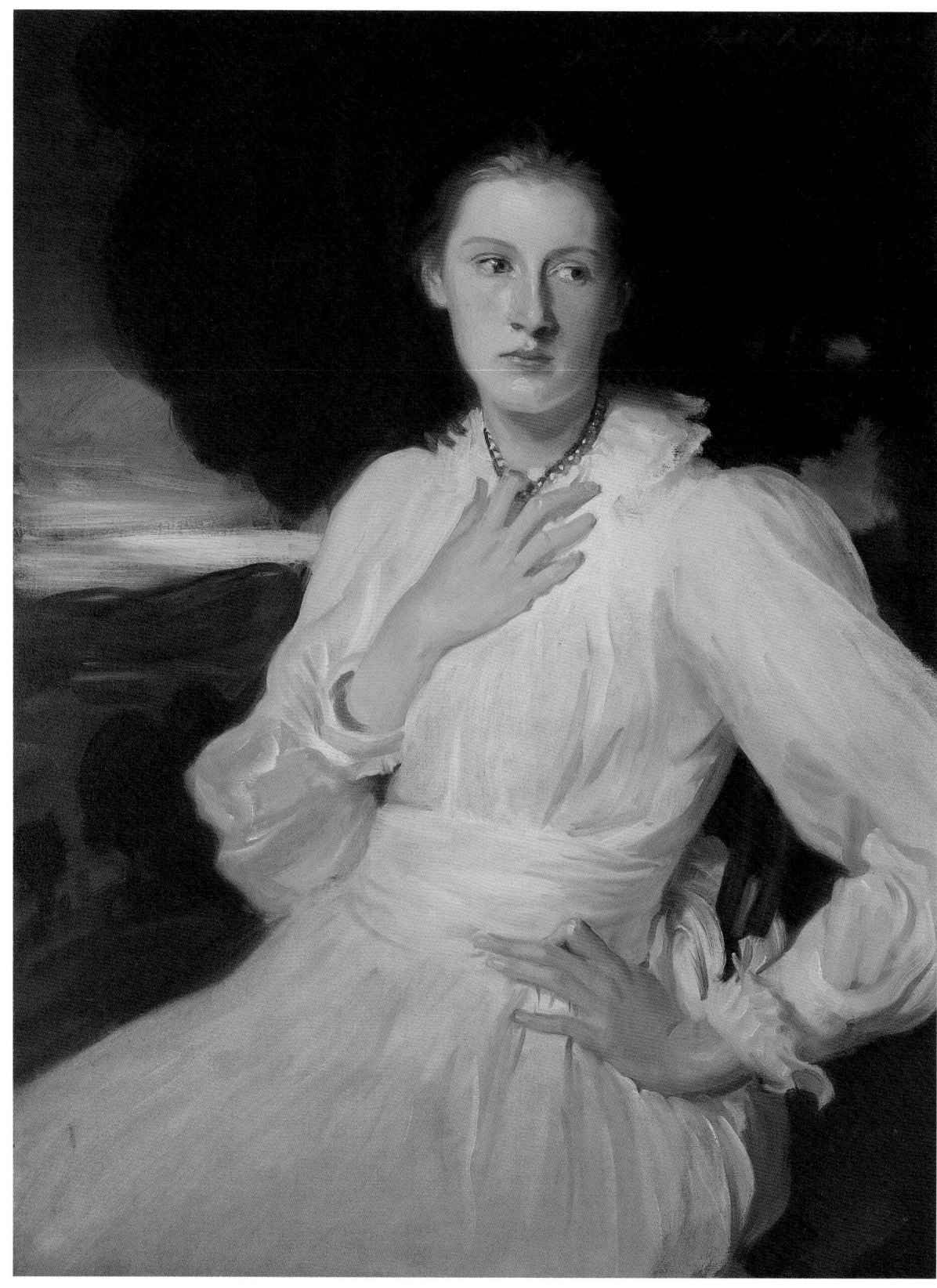

Katharine wears the same white muslin dress as in the hydrangea picture, with pleated collar and cuffs and tight sash tied in a bow behind. She is seated on a simple wooden chair, one hand on her hip (a favourite Sargent device), the other fingering a necklace of amber beads. The landscape, with its dark framing tree and distant view of hills and sky, has the appearance of a conventional backdrop. The associations here, perhaps consciously, are with the romantic portrait tradition of Thomas Lawrence and John Hoppner.

Sargent later referred to the picture as 'insignificant' when discussing loans for the 1924 New York exhibition (Sargent to Walter Clark, 13 February 1924, GCAG archives).

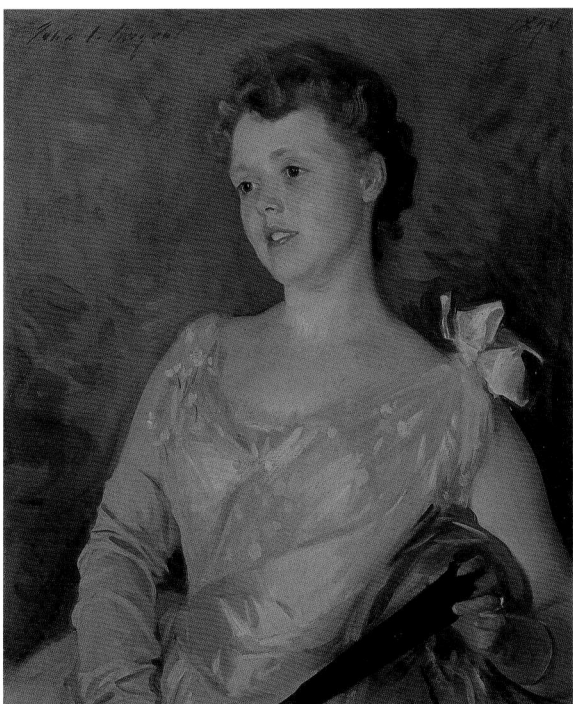

255 *Florence Addicks*

1890
Oil on canvas, 30 × 25 (76.2 × 63.5)
Inscribed, upper left: *John S. Sargent*; upper right:
1890
The Toledo Museum of Art, Ohio. Gift of Arthur J.
Secor

Florence Addicks (1866–1945) was the daughter
of John Edward O'Sullivan Addicks and his
first wife, Laura Watson Butcher. O'Sullivan was
a businessman and politician, a pioneer in the
production of illuminating gas, a director of
New Amalgamated Copper Company, and a US
senator; Mrs Addicks's grandfather, Washington
Butcher, had been a director of the Pennsylvania
Railroad Company, and president of the American
Steamship Company. Florence herself was a student in the English department of the University
of Pennsylvania and a member of the Pennsylvania
Society of Daughters of the American Revolution
and the Colonial Dames of America.

The portrait was painted at Nahant,
Massachusetts, where Sargent passed part of the
summer of 1890 with the Fairchilds. Miss Addicks
is painted in a cream silk evening gown with a
bow on the left shoulder. She is wearing a long silk
glove on her right arm, a bracelet on her left arm
and a ring on her index finger; she appears to have
a cape or wrap under her left arm and is holding a
closed fan.

256 *Peter Chardon Brooks*

1890
Oil on canvas, 27 × 23½ (68.6 × 59.7)
Inscribed, upper left: *John S. Sargent*; upper right:
1890
Private Collection

Peter Chardon Brooks (1831–1920) was a member
of a long-established family of New England
merchants whose father, Peter Chardon Brooks,
was reputedly Boston's first millionaire, having
made his fortune in marine insurance. Brooks senior was a prominent art collector; the younger
Brooks began his own distinguished career as a
collector by purchasing works by Jean-François
Millet and the Barbizon school, later developing a
taste for contemporary paintings by Jean-Charles
Cazin, Joachin Sorolla and especially Claude
Monet.

According to the Copley Hall, Boston, 1899,
catalogue, the portrait was painted at the Brooks
house in West Medford, Massachusetts, in October
1890. An entry in Lucia Fairchild's diary for 2
October 1890, may refer to the present work:
'Monday half way through dinner, he [Sargent]
arrived to stay with us, & paint the Brooks
portrait' (DCL). On 25 September 1890, Foxcroft
Cole had bought three paintings by Monet for
Brooks from Durand-Ruel in Paris, and Sargent
saw them at the Brooks' house at a later date. In an
undated note to Mrs Brooks headed 'Saturday',
Sargent wrote: 'Your kind note gives me great
pleasure. I am glad that you and Mr Brooks should
think the sketch [perhaps the present work, or
the portrait of their daughter, no. 259] worthy of
such warm thanks. Please tell Mr Brooks that I
enjoyed seeing the pictures this morning very
much. Monet always delights me and these are

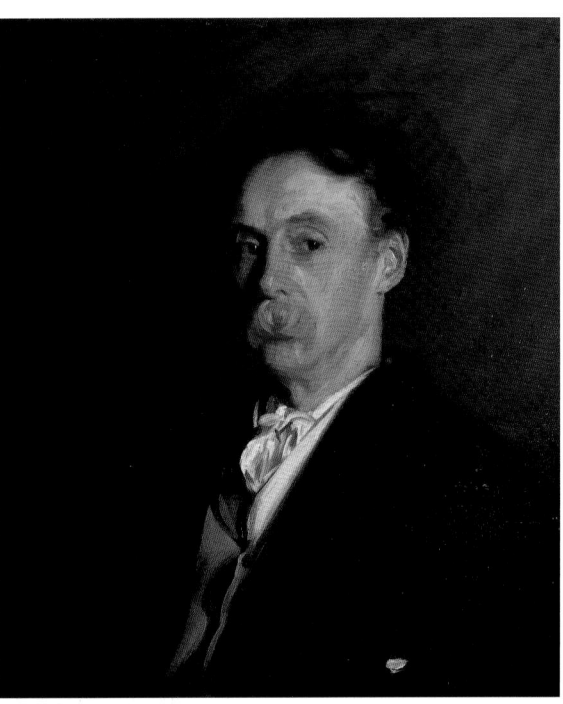

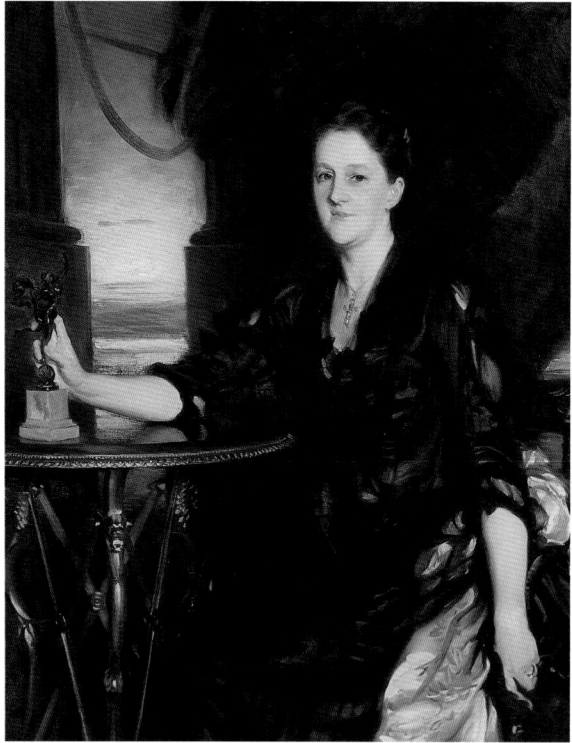

very good examples of him, and I think the Corot is a very fine one and the Hunts!' (MHS).

During his visit to West Medford, Sargent painted a landscape sketch of a pond and trees (Private Collection), which he gave to Brooks's daughter, Eleanor (see nos 258, 259).

257 Mrs Peter Chardon Brooks

1890
Oil on canvas, 49¾ × 40⅛ (126.5 × 102)
Inscribed, upper right: *John S. Sargent 1890*
Peabody Essex Museum, Salem, Massachusetts

Mrs Peter Chardon Brooks, *née* Sarah Lawrence (1845–1915), was the daughter of Amos Adams Lawrence and Sarah Elizabeth Appleton, both from prominent Boston Brahmin families. She married Peter Chardon Brooks (see no. 256) in 1866, and had several children by him, including Eleanor, whom Sargent also painted at this time (nos 258, 259).

Mrs Brooks, wearing a black gown, is seated stiffly in a low-backed chair, resting her arm on a Gueridon table while fingering with her right hand a small bronze statuette of a winged Victory. The composition is closed off at the back by the traditional props of pillars and drapes. The format of the portrait is something of a novelty in Sargent's work and foreshadows his designs of post-1900. Mount attributes the use of this design to the influence of John Singleton Copley's American portraits, which Sargent could have seen in New England in considerable numbers; but Mount is not accurate in saying that this was the first time the artist had employed pillars and drapes (Mount 1955, 1969 eds, p. 183). The portrait of

Mrs Hamilton McKown Twombly (no. 245), for example, shows them in the context of a grandiose Baroque design, which is in marked contrast to the simpler, more sober treatment of this New England matron.

This portrait, like that of the sitter's husband and possibly one of those of her daughter was painted in West Medford, Massachusetts, in October 1890.

There are two mentions of sittings for the portrait in Lucia Fairchild's diary entry for 2 October 1890: 'Then he went off to arrange with Mrs Brooks, who is to be taken out of turn after all'; and 'Today, Friday, it was dreadfully dark, and at first he didn't think he would go out to Mrs Brooks. Then he decided that after all as he could neither go tomorrow or the day after he had better, as "If I skipped three days in a row it would make rather a long gap, wouldn't it? And besides I should feel so dreadfully lazy and shabby." He is painting her in Mig's Topaz necklace [Mig was a family nickname for Elizabeth Fairchild, the writer's mother, whom Sargent had painted in 1887; see *Early Portraits*, no. 200] which, he says, he "tried all over her person, & finally is painting on her neck".' (DCL). A subsequent story about his seeing a snake while 'going through the woods to Mrs Brooks' is recounted.

258 Eleanor Brooks

1890
Oil on canvas, 61 × 31 (154.9 × 78.8)
Inscribed, upper right: *John S. Sargent 1890*
Private Collection

Eleanor Brooks (1867–1961) was the daughter of Peter Brooks and his wife, Sarah Lawrence (see nos 256 and 257). She married R. M. Saltonstall of Boston in 1891, the year after this portrait was painted.

Both Downes and Mount state that this portrait was painted in West Medford, Massachusetts, in October 1890. In an undated letter (inscribed 'Thursday'), Sargent wrote to Mrs Fairchild from 'Mosconomo' (Manchester), Massachusetts: 'Miss Brooks' portrait will be done on Saturday & I will be off to Worcester' (Boston Athenaeum, Sargent Papers, box 1, folder 15). The reference to Worcester suggests that one of the portraits of Miss Brooks might have been painted earlier in the summer: Sargent is known to have been in Worcester from early June to early July and from 11 to 19 August. The letter might refer to the sketch head of Miss Brooks (no. 259), rather than to this larger and more finished work.

She is painted in pink morning dress and straw garden hat with greenish tinge, standing with her left hand on her hip, holding a closed white lace parasol in her right hand. The parasol rests on an exotic hexagonal stool or box decorated with a painted oriental floral design. The theme of young women in white or light-coloured gowns was one

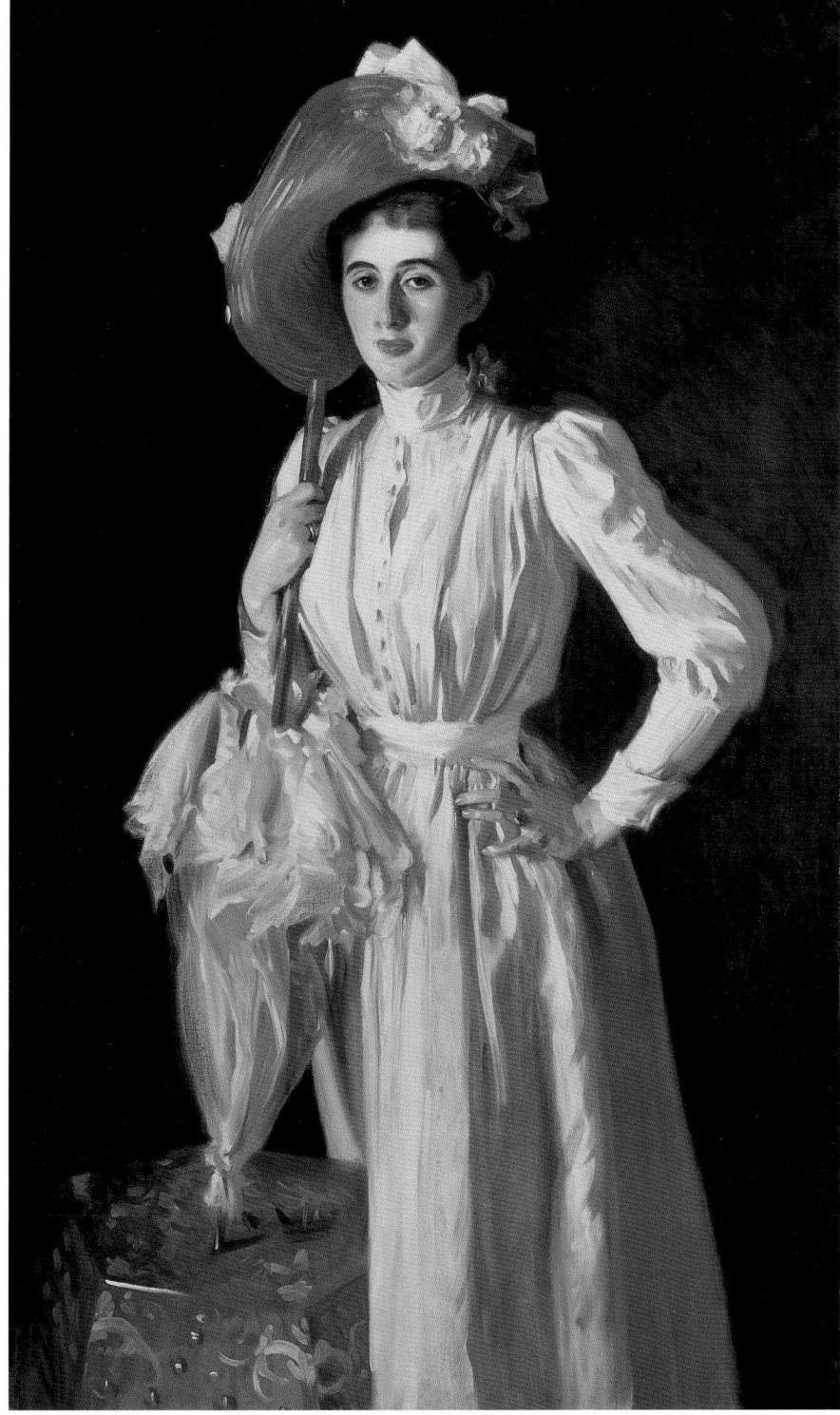

258

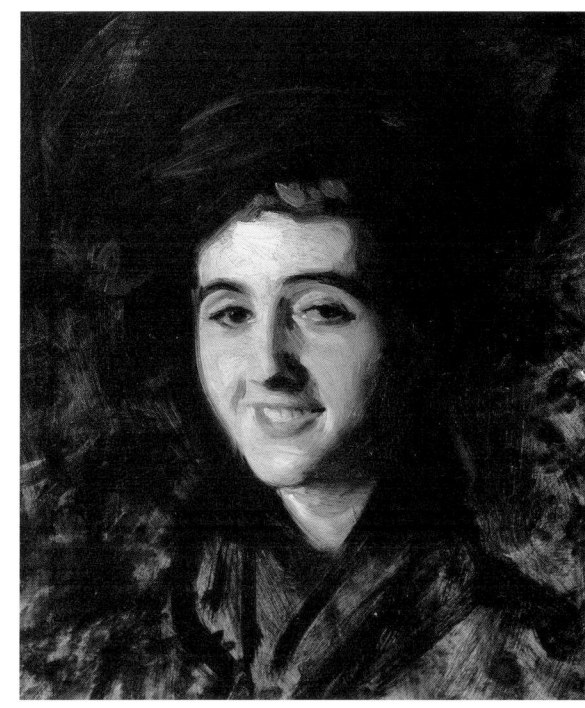

259

that preoccupied Sargent during this period. In contrast to the portraits of older women, who are invariably depicted in evening gowns, Eleanor is, in her simple dress, a fresh and youthful figure, standing out from the dark background, appearing to have just come in or to be on the point of going out, and evoking the spirit of a summer's day. Yet the figure is as carefully posed and as coolly distant as the artist's more ostensibly formal portraits of women.

The frame is an original Stanford White frame, similar to those on nos 250 and 272.

259 *Eleanor Brooks*

1890
Oil on panel, 19½ × 16½ (49.5 × 41.9)
Peabody Essex Museum, Salem, Massachusetts.
Gift of Mrs Leverett Saltonstall

This is a portrait sketch of Eleanor Brooks (see no. 258) painted, according to a note on McKibbin's index card for the picture, in forty-five minutes (McKibbin papers); McKibbin's information probably came from the family. It may have been painted in the summer of 1890 (see no. 258), or at West Medford in October at the same time as the portraits of her parents (nos 256, 257).

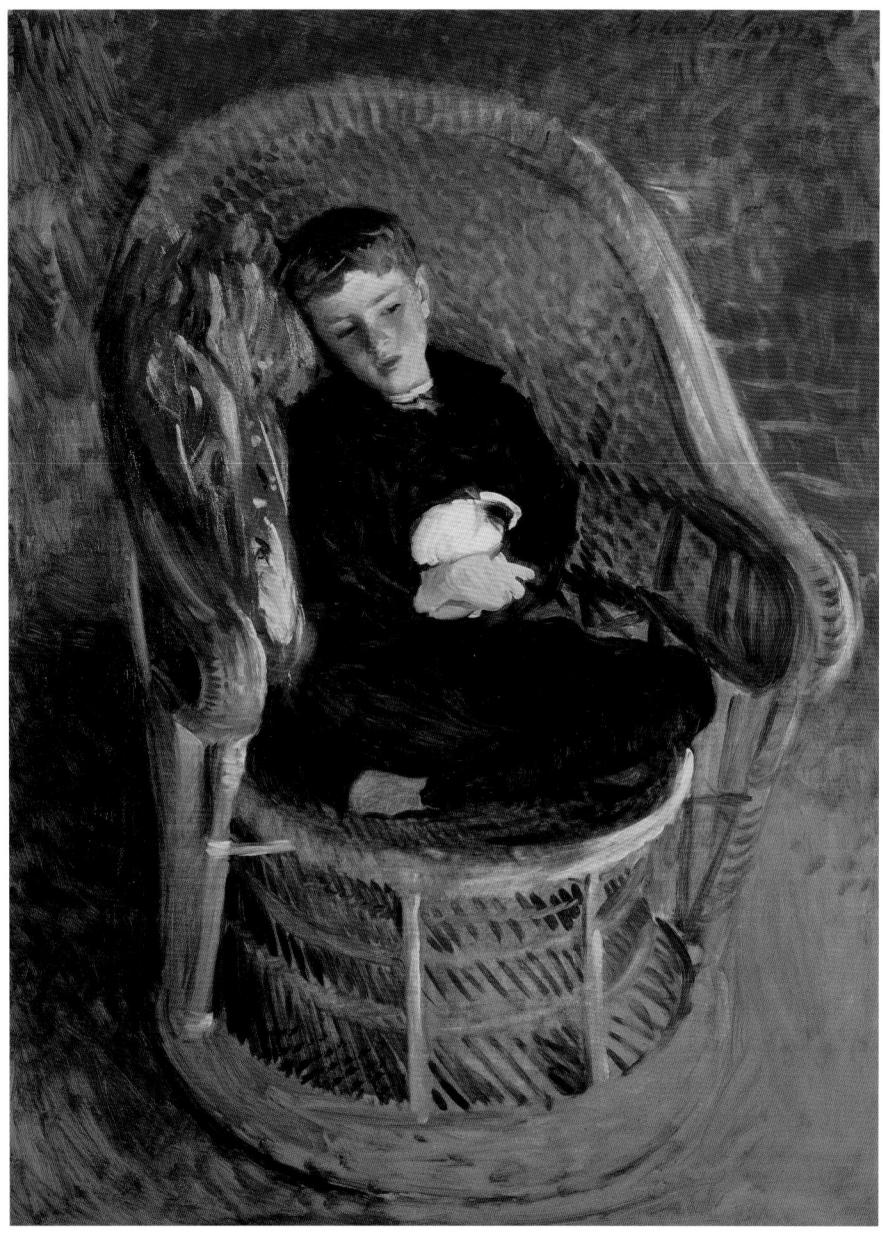

atmosphere of friends, Sargent often painted in his tenderest and most experimental vein. There is a beguiling charm about the little boy, legs crossed, holding a pet guinea pig and leaning sleepily against a red-and-white cushion and dwarfed by the curves of a wicker garden chair. Grass and foliage are summarily indicated, and there is a red-brick wall behind. This is essentially a *plein-air* sketch rather than a portrait, and its treatment reflects the rapidity of its execution. Only the head is carried to any degree of finish.

Referring to the portrait in a letter of 1890 to Mrs Fairchild, the artist wrote: 'Whether I return here [Manchester, Massachusetts] or not is problematic, as Mrs Meyer is so ill that they think her portrait must be postponed. They may send the canvas to your care, if they don't keep it for a future occasion, and I beg you to house it if they must do so, on the lower piazza where I painted Gordon, and forgive its size' (Boston Athenaeum, Sargent Papers, box 1, folder 16).

A photograph of the artist and Gordon lying in the grass at Nahant is in Mary Hale's scrapbooks (Boston Athenaeum).

261 *Lady with a Blue Veil (Sally Fairchild)*

1890
Oil on canvas, 30 × 25¼ (76.2 × 64.1)
Private Collection

Sally ('Sattie') Fairchild (1869–1960) was the daughter of Charles Fairchild of Boston and his wife, Elizabeth (see *Early Portraits*, no. 200), whom Sargent had painted twice by 1887 (see *Early Portraits*, nos 202, 203). She was the first woman

260 *Gordon Fairchild*

1890
Oil on canvas, 53½ × 39⅜ (135.9 × 100)
Inscribed, upper right: *to Mrs Fairchild John S. Sargent*
Private Collection

Gordon Fairchild (1882–1932) was the youngest of the eight children of Sargent's close friend and patron Charles Fairchild of Boston. He taught at St Paul's School, Concord.

Sargent had painted members of the Fairchild family on his first professional visit to the United States in 1887, including an earlier half-length of Gordon (see *Early Portraits*, no. 201). The second portrait of Gordon was painted during the early summer of 1890 at Nahant, near Boston, while Sargent was staying with the Fairchilds, and was given to his hostess. Sargent wrote to his friend Frank Millet from Buzzards Bay on 1 September [1890] that he had 'been a great deal with the Fairchilds' (Private Collection). In the relaxed

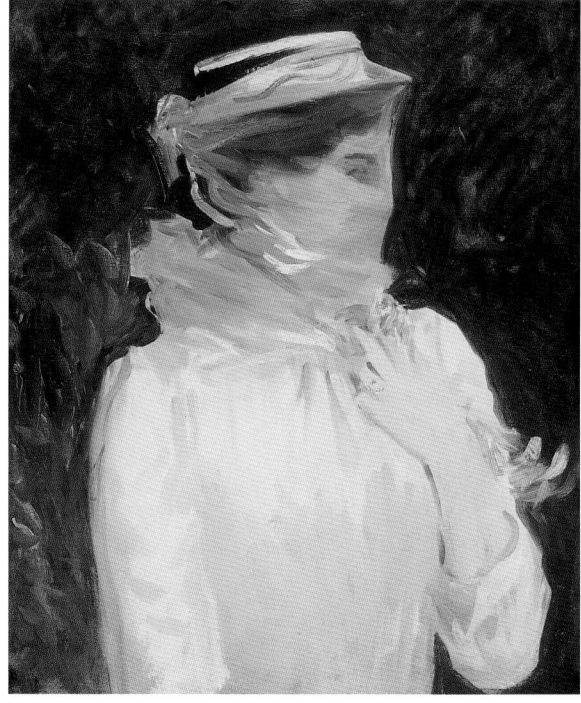

allowed to attend lectures at Harvard, listening from behind a screen to William James's lectures on psychology. She became a close friend of the artist's sister Violet, meeting her first at Fladbury in 1889. Sargent wrote to Mrs Gardner about his proposed visit to America from London (1 November 1889): 'I must come over and see and will sail next month on the 4th. I will also do some portraits and bring over a young sister [Violet] who is going to stay with the Fairchilds with whom she struck up a great friendship a year ago' (ISGM archive).

This outdoor sketch of Sally Fairchild was painted at Nahant near Boston, where Sargent spent part of the summer of 1890. It is mentioned in Lucia Fairchild's diary entry for 2 October 1890:

> This morning he finished the Blue Veil of Satty, & did another sketch . . . he, sketching Satty this morning, said he should like to do her just the way the sky of the Monet at Dolls [the Boston dealer Doll and Richards on Tremont Street] was done – 'very good for one, that', he said – and then went on saying how in painting portraits especially 'one got into a sort of way – like handwriting, you know – capital letters and that sort of thing. It's very good for one to get quite away from it once in a while – etc.' Later he mentioned Whistler as being remarkably free from 'anything like that' (DCL).

The painting by Monet to which Sargent was referring is almost certainly *Antibes Seen from the Plateau Notre-Dame* of 1888 (Museum of Fine Arts, Boston); it is the only pre-1890 painting with a recorded Doll and Richards provenance (see Wildenstein III, no. 1172).

There is a reference to a portrait of Miss Fairchild in the diary of Theodore Robinson (28 February 1893): 'And a curious row with Mr Fairchild. He painted Miss Sallie [or Sattie] which the father wanted to buy and on Sargent objecting, he likewise objected, whereupon Sargent destroyed the canvas' (FARL). This may refer to yet another picture of Sally (now destroyed), or, if the story of the canvas being destroyed is erroneous, it may refer to this picture, which remained in Sargent's possession until his death. It was a late addition to the studio sale and is not included in the printed catalogue. A pencil annotation 'lot 149A Girl veiled with sailor hat poor unfinished' in a catalogue raisonné archive copy of the sale catalogue identifies the late lot 149A as the present work.

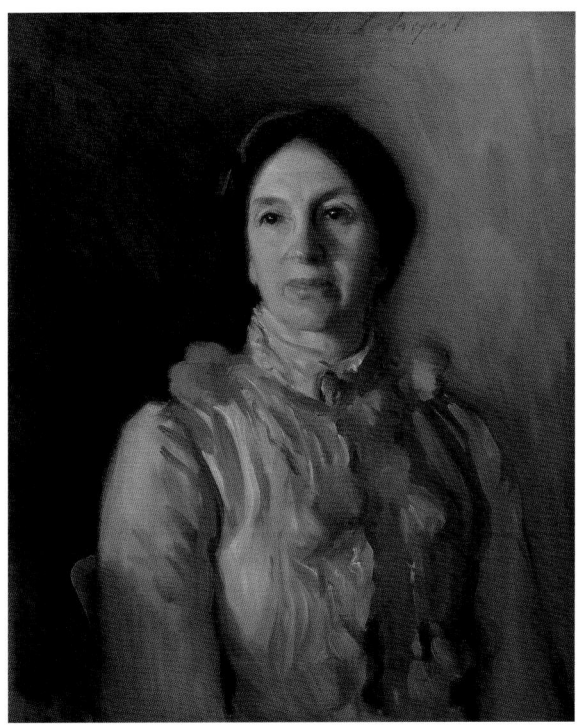

262   *Mrs James Thomas Fields*

1890
Oil on canvas, 30 × 25 (76.2 × 63.5)
Inscribed, upper left: *to Mrs Fields*; upper right:
John S. Sargent
Boston Athenaeum, Massachusetts

Mrs James Thomas Fields, *née* Ann West Adams (1834–1915), was the daughter of Dr Zabdiel Boylston Adams of Boston and his wife Sarah May Holland, and the second wife of author and publisher James T. Fields. Fields was the editor of *Atlantic Monthly*, 1861–71, and their house became a centre of social and literary life in Boston. The confidante of many famous writers, Mrs Fields was a distinguished author in her own right, publishing volumes of essays, poems, biography and reminiscences.

Sargent gave his address in September and October 1890 as c/o Mrs Fields Manchester. In a letter to Mrs Fairchild postmarked 8 October 1890, he wrote: 'Mrs Fields has a cold, which kept her to her room yesterday, rather a matter of precaution than anything else. We both mean to go up to town for Saturday's concert' (DCL). It is probable that the portrait was painted during this period, perhaps to thank Mrs Fields for her hospitality.

Mrs Fields, in cream dress decorated with furbelows, is depicted with an intense expression, her eyes raised towards the light; her pose is similar to that in other Sargent portraits of literary figures.

A drawing of Mrs Fields by Sargent is in a private collection. This may be the drawing referred to by Martin Birnbaum in his memoir: 'On one of those flying visits from Maine he stopped in Manchester long enough to make a drawing of his feeble old friend Mrs Field [*sic*], the publisher's

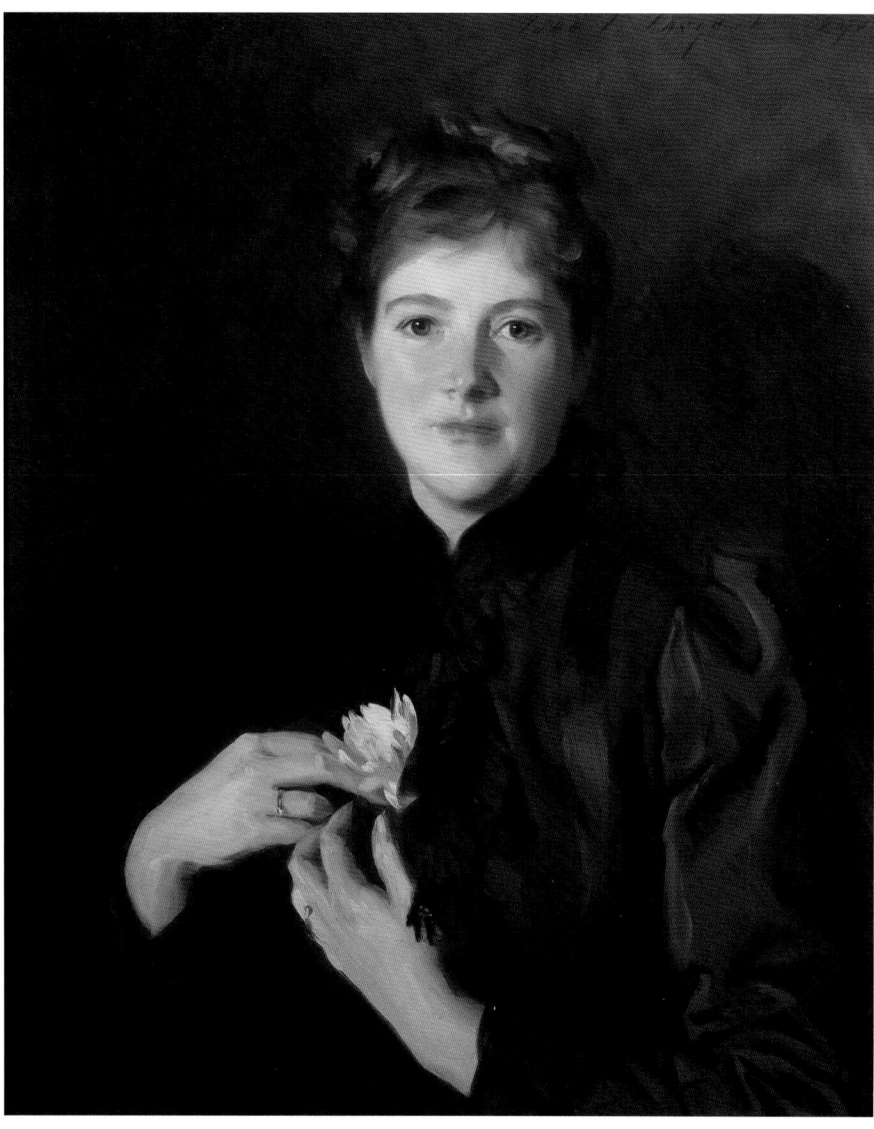

established Boston merchant family – his father, Augustus Hemenway had opened up trade with South America and his mother, Mary, was an indefatigable and progressive educationalist and liberal. In the late 1890s, Mrs Hemenway junior was one of the founders of the Massachusetts Audubon Society, which pledged itself against the fashion of women wearing egret feathers in their hats. In later life, she was regarded as one of the doyennes of Boston society. Her husband was one of the trustees of the fund established to raise money to meet payment for the artist's second contract for the Boston Public Library murals in 1895 (see Promey 1999, pp. 15, 189, 191, 335 n. 39).

Information about the portrait was provided by the sitter's granddaughter, Elvine, in a memorandum (catalogue raisonné archive). According to her account, Hemenway requested his wife to arrange with Sargent to paint a member of the family, shortly before he left on a fishing trip. He didn't mind who the subject was, but wanted a work by Sargent. The family owned a property in Milton, north of Boston, and the artist was nearby at Nahant. At Mrs Hemenway's suggestion, Sargent began a portrait of her eldest child, Gussie, then aged eight, but he proved too 'wiggly'. After doing a sketch of her daughter, Hope, Sargent intimated to Mrs Hemenway that it was she whom he would really like to paint. She was surprised at the suggestion, being in an advanced state of pregnancy (her daughter Hetty was born in December 1890), but agreed. Sargent had four morning sittings. 'When the head seemed finished, he asked her to put her hands in some interesting way, and as they were trying various positions he saw a vase of white flowers in the room and gave her one to hold.' Sargent talked while at work, to hold Mrs Hemenway's attention, and 'called for wine rather a lot'. Hemenway, who owned pictures by Winslow Homer and Childe Hassam, and gave a Corot landscape and two Fortuny prints to the Museum of Fine Arts, Boston, was a connoisseur and admired the picture, but other members of the family preferred an earlier and more sentimental portrait of the same subject. The gesture of the hands with the flower has the same tenderness of motif of an earlier portrait, *Mrs Wilton Phipps* (*Early Portraits*, no. 138).

When the portrait was shown at a loan exhibition of Sargent's work at the Museum of Fine Arts, Boston, in 1916, W. H. Downes wrote:

> the brilliant, vital, vivid and animated portrait of Mrs Hemenway, also dated 1890 . . . is especially remarkable for the rich, glowing, transparent flesh tones, so handsomely contrasted with the fine tone of the black dress. The expression is that of a splendidly alive, normal, wholesome personality, whose wide-open eyes look out with boldness, courage and confidence upon a world that is well worth living in. (*Boston Evening Transcript*, 10 May 1916, Part Two, p. 12).

widow, about whom Henry James wrote one of his happiest essays' (Birnbaum 1941, p. 26). Ten letters from Sargent to Mrs Fields are in the Department of Manuscripts, The Huntington Library, Art Collections and Botanical Gardens, San Marino, California.

For biographical information about Mrs Fields, see Mark Antony De Wolfe Howe, *Memories of a Hostess: A Chronicle of Eminent Friendships*, Boston, 1922, and Nathan Huggins, *Protestants against Poverty: Boston's Charities 1870–1900*, Westport, Connecticut, 1971, pp. 162–94. For a photograph of Mrs Fields at home, 37 Charles Street, see Boston 1986, fig. 4.

263   *Mrs Augustus Hemenway*

1890
Oil on canvas, 30½ × 25¼ (77.5 × 64.2)
Inscribed, upper right: *John S. Sargent 1890*
Private Collection

Mrs Augustus Hemenway, *née* Harriet Dexter Lawrence (1858–1960), was the daughter of Amos Lawrence and Sarah Appleton. In 1881, she married Augustus Hemenway, who came from an

1890
Oil on canvas, 50 × 34 (127 × 86.5)
Inscribed, upper left: *John S. Sargent*; upper right:
1890
National Portrait Gallery, Washington, D.C.

Henry Cabot Lodge (1850–1924) was a powerful and distinguished American statesman. An ardent Republican, he was elected to the US House of Representatives in 1886. He later served in the Senate for many years and was chairman of the influential Foreign Relations Committee. He married Anna Cabot Mills Davis in 1871. His contemporaries saw him as an embodiment of old Boston values and tradition, a man convinced of his own place in society and armed with an unassailable sense of his abilities and superiority.

At the time Sargent painted Lodge he was a Massachusetts congressman and a man marked out for future eminence. Lodge had seen Sargent's portrait of Edwin Booth (no. 232) at The Players club in New York in May 1890 and had written to his mother on 10 May 'A really noble portrait, one of the best pieces of modern work I have ever seen' (Microfilm Roll PN 171, MHS).

This picture was painted in August 1890 at Nahant, the summer colony south of Boston, where Lodge had a house and where Sargent was staying with the Fairchilds. It is said to have been painted in Lodge's house overlooking the sea. F. S. Pratt wrote to his wife, 14 July 1890: 'Mr Sargent asked permission to put off Kitty's picture [no. 253] till next week. He met Mrs Lodge in Boston yesterday or Saturday, and if he can do it this week he is to paint Mr L's portrait.

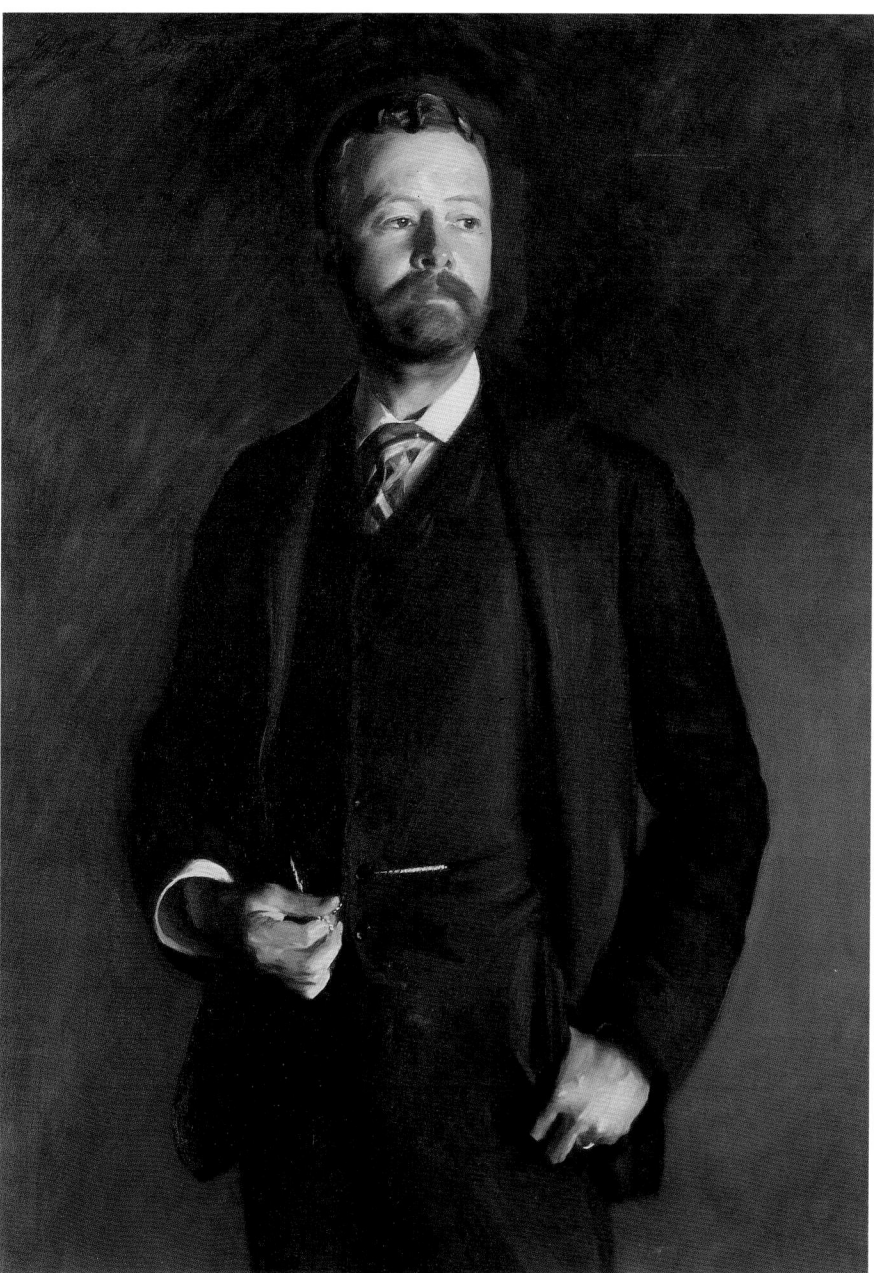

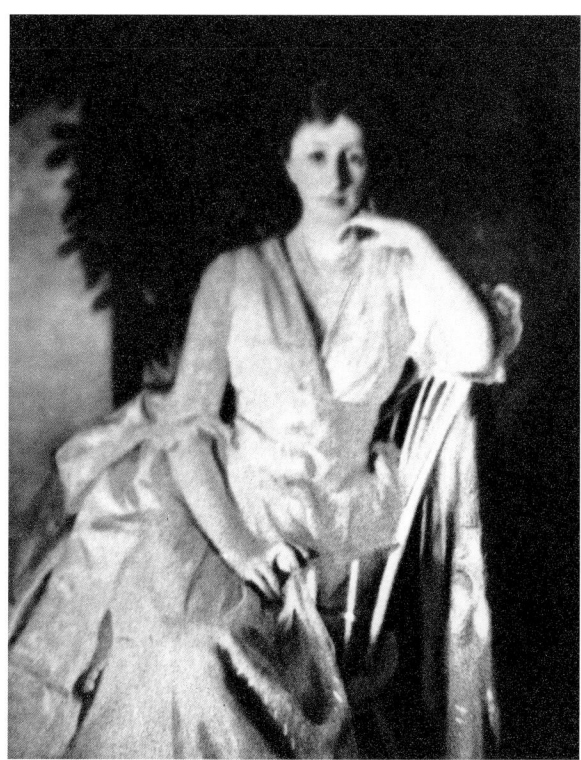

Congressman Lodge is a man worth painting so I granted permission to Mr Sargent. It is wonderful how rapidly he works' (Strickler 1982–3, p. 25). While not a formal essay in political portraiture, in the manner of his later portraits of Balfour and Roosevelt (nos 439, 550), Sargent nevertheless characterizes Lodge as a figure of authority and substance.

265 *Mrs Augustus Peabody Loring*

1890
Oil on canvas, 50 × 40 (127 × 101.6)
Apparently destroyed by fire

Mrs Augustus Peabody Loring (1860–1937), *née* Ellen Gardner, was the daughter of George Augustus Gardner and Eliza Endicott Peabody of Salem. She married Augustus Peabody Loring in 1884.

The catalogue for Sargent's one-man show at the Copley Society, Boston, in 1899 records that the portrait was painted in September 1890. Lucia Fairchild's diary entry for 2 October 1890 notes: 'About the Mrs Mason portrait [possibly no. 241] he [Sargent] said, "Apparently this old gentleman, who has always hated everything that I have done, has seen my portrait of Mrs Loring, and now likes that"' (Private Collection). The portrait was apparently lost in a fire and is known only from an archival photograph and from Downes's description: 'Three-quarters length; life-size. The lady is in white, and she is sitting on a white chair out of doors. Her oval face wears a fatigued and disturbed expression. The coloring of this piece is pure and luminous; the flesh tones are especially fine. Autumn foliage in the background' (Downes 1925 and 1926 eds, p. 159). Downes described it at greater length in his review of an exhibition of Sargent's work held at the Museum of Fine Arts, Boston, in 1916:

> In this canvas the lady is represented sitting on a white verandah chair, with a landscape background. The figure is three-quarters length, facing full-front and wearing a white summer dress. Several strings of small pearls are worn about her neck. The reddening autumn foliage of a vine is seen back of the head. The left elbow rests on the back of the chair and the left hand lightly supports the head, coming against the cheek. The right arm lies along the lap, and the hand lightly grasps in two fingers the arm of the chair. The fine fresh complexion, blue eyes, light brown hair, and the pure oval of the face are rendered with delicacy and sympathy, and the crisp white draperies are beautifully brushed in. But it is to be remarked that the light in which the figure was painted is not the light of outdoors. (*Boston Evening Transcript*, 10 May 1916, Part Two, p. 12)

In the review, Downes refers to the picture as 'Mrs William Caleb Loring', but it is clear from his description that he means the present painting. He also notes that it is dated 1890.

The portrait had previously been exhibited in the 1891 Society of American Artists exhibition (when it moved to Boston and Philadelphia), where one critic noted that the white gown was painted with 'superb mastery' (*Boston Evening Transcript*, 4 June 1891, p. 6).

It is one of a series of studies of women, which Sargent painted in 1890, showing a broad impressionist handling, for example, his three-quarter-length of Eleanor Brooks (no. 258) and his informal characterizations of Katharine Pratt (nos 253, 254). Sargent painted an informal sketch of Mrs Loring's sister-in-law, Louisa, also dressed in white, in the same year (no. 266) and a portrait of her brother-in-law, Judge William Caleb Loring, in 1903 (no. 449).

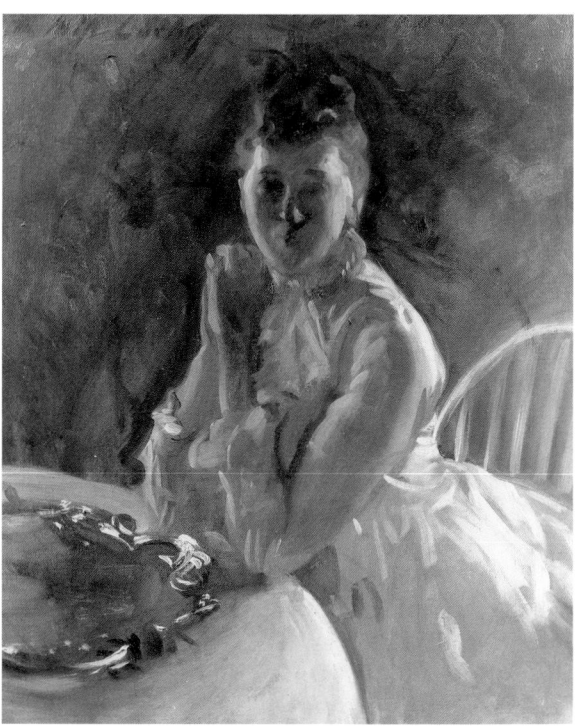

266 *Louisa Loring*

1890
Oil on canvas, 32 × 25 (81.2 × 63.5)
Inscribed, across top: *to Miss Loring John S. Sargent*
[*?1890*]
Private Collection

Louisa Putnam Loring (1854–1924), the daughter of Caleb William Loring of Boston and his wife Elizabeth Smith Peabody, was a friend of the artist and especially of his sister Emily. She was beautiful but consumptive, and she relied on the strength and support of her elder sister Katharine. When well, she enjoyed society, music and domestic life: after their mother's death, she and Katharine ran the household for her father and two brothers, William Caleb and Augustus Peabody Loring. She put her experience of illness to good Bostonian use, founding a sanatorium in Aitken, South Carolina (the scene of one of her rest cures), and serving as a director of the Beverly Hospital, secretary of the Essex County Chapter of the Red Cross, and founder of the Anti-Tuberculosis Society in Beverly.

McKibbin, presumably relying on information from the family, notes that the sketch was painted in twenty minutes (McKibbin papers). Miss Loring is dressed in white, seated in a white Windsor chair, her elbows resting on a table with a silver tray in front of her. It is summarily painted and relates to several informal studies of young women of a similar date (see nos 253,254, 261).

An undated drawing of Louisa under an umbrella is in a private collection, and a watercolour of her with her sister Katharine (no. 574) was destroyed by fire in 1969. In a letter to 'Miss Loring' (8 July, no year date), which might be addressed either to her or her sister, Sargent apologizes for not discussing her brother Caleb's portrait properly (AAA). This might refer to the oil Sargent painted of her brother William Caleb Loring in 1903 (no. 449).

267 *George Peabody*

1890
Oil on canvas, 33½ × 26 (85.1 × 66)
Inscribed, upper right: *John S. Sargent*; upper left: *1890*
Private Collection

Colonel George Peabody (1804–1892) was the son of Captain Joseph Peabody, who was an East India Merchant from Salem, and the founder of one of New England's great shipping dynasties. He married Clarissa (Clara) Endicott in 1827. Sargent painted three generations of the family: his daughter, Ellen, Mrs William Crowninshield Endicott, in 1901 (no. 400), and her daughter, Mrs Joseph Chamberlain, in 1902 (no. 417), and son, William Crowninshield Endicott Jr, in 1907 (no. 544).

The picture was apparently painted at the Peabody house, 29 Washington Square in Salem. Lucia Fairchild's diary entry for 2 October 1890 notes: '[Sargent] said he would not be here for a week or ten days yet, as he had not begun Mr Peabody, and had not finished Mrs Loring [no. 265]' (DCL). A few days later, Sargent wrote to Mrs Fairchild (letter postmarked 8 October 1890) from Manchester, Massachusetts: 'Mr Peabody is half done' (DCL). Lucia Fairchild's diary also records Sargent's account of painting Peabody:

He talked a good deal more about his time over Mr Peabody. 'A very fine looking old man – &

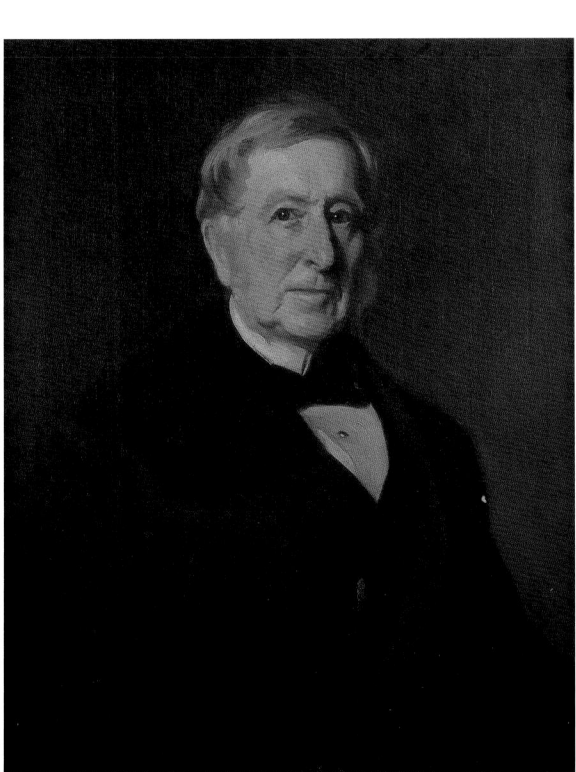

very lively – yes, & charming, I should say – & tells killingly funny stories. But portrait painting, don't you know, is very close quarters – a dangerous thing – no, I must say I had a very disagreeable time of it'. He told us that there was an old family servant who had been with them 86 years, ever since she was a baby, who stayed with them at first when he painted & took all manner of liberties. 'When I was beginning to draw in the hair,' he said, 'which waved in a fine irregular way from his forehead (making a gesture or two with his hands) what should the old creature do but rush up & brush it all down smooth with her hands. And the same way with everything' – going on to say how the coat had fine big folds (pulling his own up to illustrate) & how as soon as he commenced drawing it in again this old woman rushed up & pulled it all down straight. He told us also about Mr Peabody that one day in a rest he had gone up to the painting, said he did not like something about it & with his finger rubbed it out. The next day, seeing him go up in the same way, with an out-stretched finger Sargent had exclaimed 'Oh *Please* don't touch it!' 'Certainly not', said Mr P. drawing himself up, 'Certainly *not*, I should never *think* of such a thing!' etc. etc. growing more and more stiff every moment (DCL).

268 *Royal Elisha Robbins*

1890
Oil on canvas, 30¼ × 24¼ (76.9 × 61.6)
Inscribed, upper left: *John S. Sargent*; upper right: *1890*
Private Collection

Royal Elisha Robbins (1824–1902), the son of a Congregational clergyman and writer, was an entrepreneur. In 1841, he worked for an export marketing company in England owned by an uncle and established his own company in New York in 1846. With a partner he acquired a watch-making company in Waltham, Massachusetts, in 1857 and presided over both periods of expansion and modernization and of difficulty and instability. He married Mary Elizabeth Horton and had three children by her.

Robbins had been seriously ill the year before this portrait was painted. The catalogue of the memorial exhibition held at the Museum of Fine Arts, Boston, in 1925 gives the date, erroneously, as 1887 (see Boston 1925, p. 14), and this has been followed by some subsequent sources.

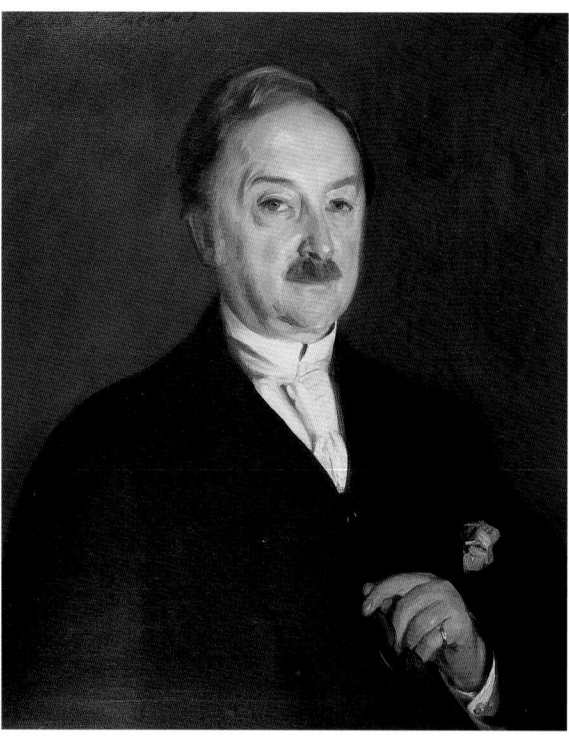

269 *Violet Sargent*

1890
Oil on canvas, 19¾ × 15¾ (50.1 × 40)
Isabella Stewart Gardner Museum, Boston,
Massachusetts

According to Sargent's cousin, Mary Hale (Mrs
Richard W. Hale), this rapidly executed and barely
finished sketch of Sargent's sister Violet was
painted *en plein air* at Nahant, Massachusetts, in
1890 (letter from Mrs Hale to the director of
the Isabella Stewart Gardner Museum, Boston, 6
November 1929, ISGM archive). Violet travelled

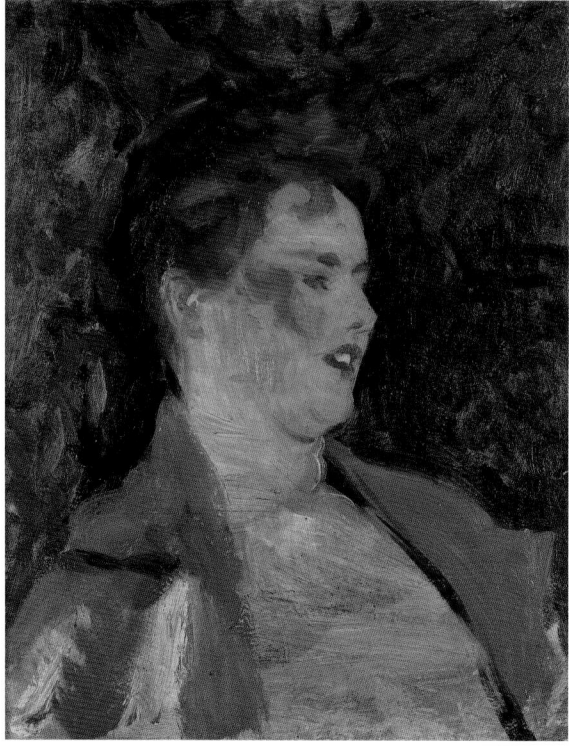

with Sargent to America in December 1889 and
she went to stay with the Fairchilds at Nahant;
Sally Fairchild and Violet were much of an age and
became close friends. The painting was owned by
Sally's sister, Lucia, who was herself an artist and
studied with Sargent's friend, the artist Dennis
Miller Bunker, at the Cowles School, Boston.
Bunker had, apparently, been charmed by Violet
when he had met her in England, at Calcot, in
1888. He wrote to Mrs Gardner on 25 June 1888:
'The youngest Miss Sargent is awfully pretty –
charming. What if I should fall in love with her?'
(ISGM archive). However, late in 1889, he wrote,
less gallantly, to Eleanor Hardy, whom he would
marry some months later: 'How do you like Violet
Sargent? She used to be very pretty in a kind of
pudding way' (Dennis Miller Bunker Papers,
1882–1943, AAA, roll 2773). Violet is represented
sitting reading by a stream, in Sargent's outdoor
study of Bunker painting at Calcot in 1888 (Terra
Museum of American Art, Chicago).

Mrs Gardner bought the picture from Lucia
Fairchild. A cheque stub records the purchase:
'$500.00/Jan. 8. 1895/Eleanor Platt/For Lucia's
Sargent'. Eleanor Platt, née Hardy, was Bunker's
widow; Bunker died in 1890, and she married
Charles Platt in 1893 (ISGM archive).

270 *Violet Sargent*

c. 1890–1
Water-colour on paper, 13¾ × 9½ (34.9 × 24.1)
Private Collection

An undated water-colour study of the artist's
younger sister, Violet, understood, in family tradition, to have been painted when she was aged
twenty or twenty-one. Sargent and Violet travelled
and spent short periods of time together between
the end of 1889, when they sailed to America,
and August 1891, when Violet married Francis
Ormond in Paris, and a date within these parame-
ters is plausible for the present water-colour. Violet
is dressed in a brown coat with a fur collar and the
suggestion of leg-of-mutton sleeves, a high-necked
dress or blouse and a soft, dark hat. The costume
supports a date of *c.* 1890–1, since leg-of-mutton,
or gigot, sleeves were becoming fashionable again
in the early 1890s.

271 *Self-Portrait*

c. 1890
Oil on panel, 7¼ × 5 (18.4 × 12.6)
Private Collection

A self-portrait caricature, painted on a wooden
cigar-box lid, probably in 1890, when Sargent visited the Lorings. Sargent did an outdoor sketch of
Louisa Loring, to whom he gave this caricature of
himself, during this visit (see no. 266).

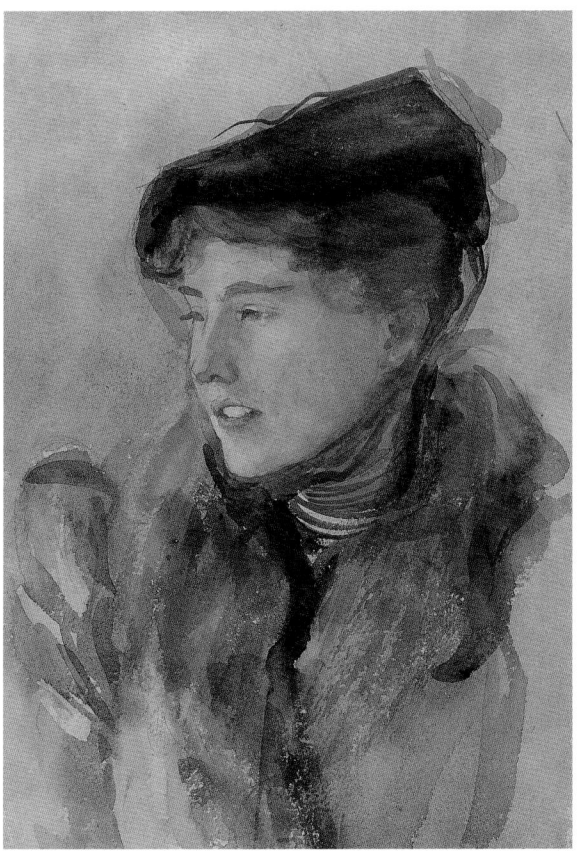

The loop which forms the nose and eyebrows is similar to a motif that Sargent occasionally used as an autograph doodle in his personal correspondence.

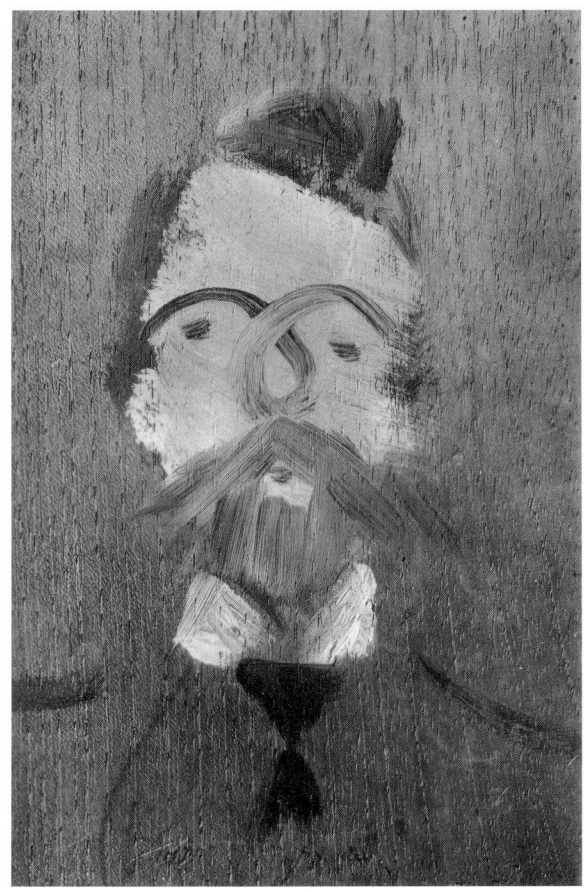

1890
Oil on canvas, 30 × 25 (76.2 × 63.5)
Inscribed, upper left: *John S. Sargent 1890*
Hampden-Booth Theatre Library at The Players, New York

Lawrence Barrett (1838–1891) was the son of Thomas Barrett, an Irishman living in New Jersey. Lawrence Barrett began his association with the theatre at the age of fourteen and went on to a long and distinguished career as a leading actor. His style was painstaking and deliberate, suggesting considerable mental resources. The part for which he became most famous was Cassius in Shakespeare's *Julius Caesar*. For the last four and a half years of his life, he went into partnership with Edwin Booth, an old friend and colleague, and they appeared together in a large number of productions.

Sargent had met Barrett as early as 1884, when the artist was a guest at a party held for Barrett in London by their mutual friends Edwin Austin Abbey and Alfred Parsons (see Lucas 1921, vol. 1, p. 139, and Charteris 1927, p. 58). The portrait of Barrett was commissioned by Booth, whom Sargent had painted in January 1890 (see nos 232, 233), to grace the new premises of The Players in New York. It was painted between late June and the end of August 1890 at Cohasset, a summer colony south of Boston, where the actor had a house and where the artist also had friends. In an undated letter to Mrs Fairchild (inscribed 'Thursday' [1890]), Sargent wrote: 'Please thank Fairchild for his kind note and ask him to let me know at Worcester Club whether Barrett would want me to paint him at the end of next week – I might go then' (Boston Athenaeum, Sargent Papers, box 1, folder 16). Sargent wrote to his

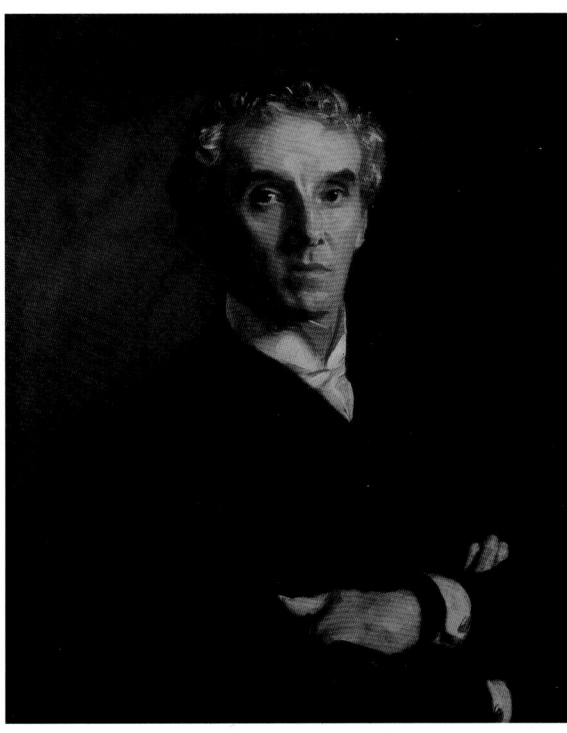

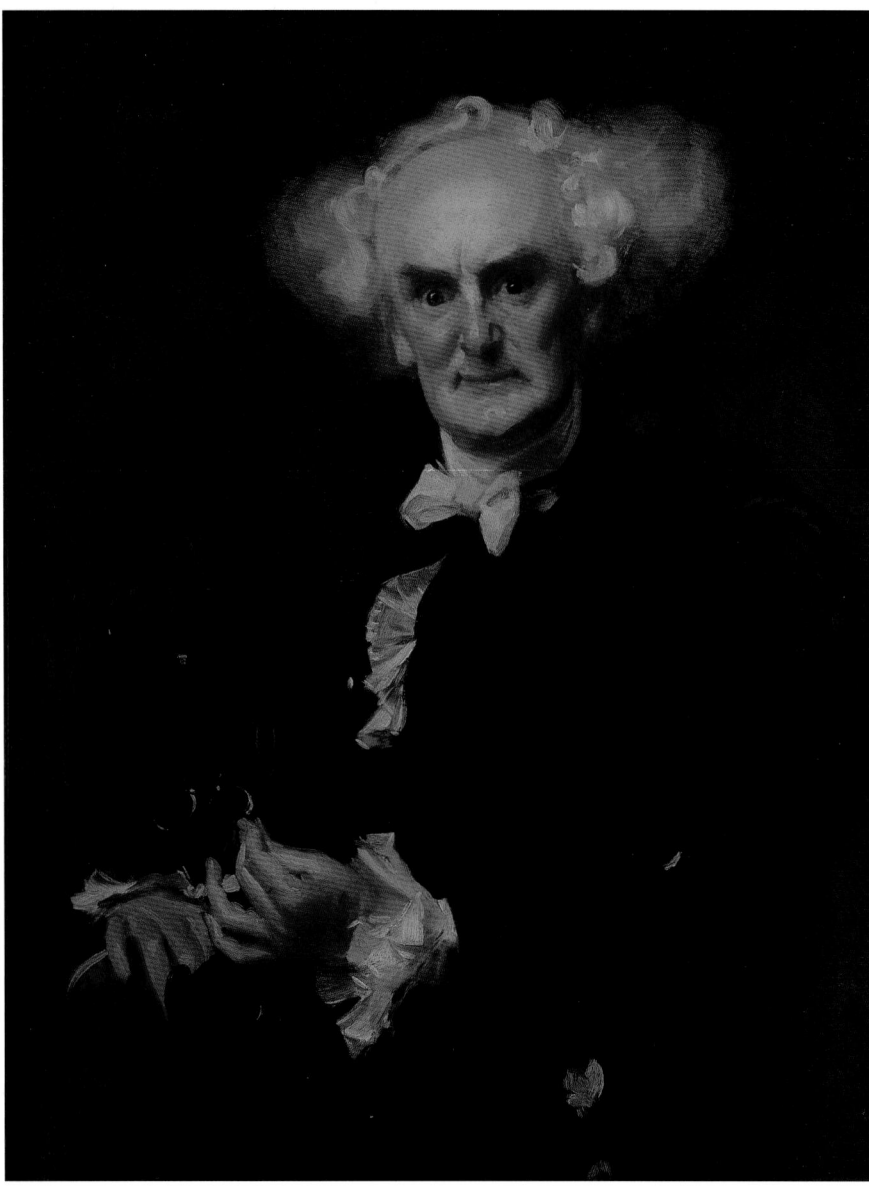

artist at first denied its existence and then wrote to Walter Clark (11 January 1924): 'I don't remember painting Mr Lawrence Barrett and I don't believe it is a good one.' (GCAG archives) There is a reference in the McKibbin papers to a letter from Sargent to Barrett concerning the exhibition of the picture, presumably in 1890 (untraced).

The portrait of Barrett flanked that of Booth in the reading room of The Players, balanced by Sargent's portrait of Joseph Jefferson (no. 273) on the far side.

273 *Joseph Jefferson*

1890
Oil on canvas, 36 × 28½ (91.4 × 72.4)
Inscribed, upper right: *John S. Sargent 1890*
Hampden-Booth Theatre Library at The Players, New York

Joseph Jefferson (1829–1905) was born into a long-established acting family. After a hard, eventful apprenticeship he made his name as a comic actor in New York in the late 1850s. His first success was as Dr Pangloss in *The Heir at Law*, an eighteenth-century comedy by the English playwright George Colman, which he first performed in August 1857. He was still playing the role in 1890, when Sargent went to see him in company with James Carroll Beckwith and it is in this role that Sargent depicts the actor (Beckwith diary, 27 March 1890, NA). Other roles for which Jefferson was famous include the lead in *Rip Van Winkle* and Bob Acres in *The Rivals*; but he was renowned for his versatility, and his acting experience, spanning a period of more than seventy years, was prodigious. He succeeded Booth as president of The Players in 1893, and as the head of his profession. He was greatly loved both as an actor and as a person.

The portrait, commissioned by Edwin Booth and Lawrence Barrett for The Players, New York, appears to have been painted in the late summer of 1890. Sargent wrote to his friend Frank Millet from Buzzards Bay on 1 September [1890]: 'I have been doing one portrait after the other at Nahant, Worcester, Beverly Farms and am now doing Joseph Jefferson here. Have just done Barrett.' (Private Collection). Though Sargent painted many theatrical personalities during this period, his portrait of Jefferson is a rare depiction of an actor in character. It represents his response to a genre that has a long history in England and America: pictures of comic actors were a speciality of artists like George Clint and Samuel de Wilde earlier in the century (see Geoffrey Ashton, Kalman A. Burnim and Andrew Wiltin, *Pictures in the Garrick Club*, London, 1997). Jefferson's sparkling and naturalistic performance seems to have moved Sargent to express something of the manic energy of Jefferson's characterization. The rich impasto and swooping brushwork define Sargent's painterly delight in his subject.

friend Frank Millet from Buzzards Bay on 1 September [1890]: 'I have been doing one portrait after the other at Nahant, Worcester, Beverly Farms and am now doing Joseph Jefferson here. Have just done Barrett. Have been a great deal with the Fairchilds' (Private Collection).

Writing to Barrett (16 September [1890] c/o Mrs James T. Fields, Manchester-on-Sea, see no. 262), Sargent asked: 'Would you allow me to exhibit your portrait in the autumn exhibition at the Academy in New York which is coming off pretty soon? I have not yet found out the date' (AAA, roll D10). He is referring to the annual autumn exhibition at the National Academy of Design; the portrait was included in the exhibition. An undated, later letter to Barrett reads 'Please send your portrait to Wilmarts, the gilders 53 East 131st Street. Mr Jefferson's is probably already on its way to New York and I will have them both sent to the exhibition. Many thanks for your kind permission. I am writing to the framemakers to head off the frame in case it is not already sent to you' (AAA, roll D10).

When asked about the picture during the organization of the 1924 New York exhibition, the

Art Interchange, reviewing the National Academy of Design exhibition, commended the portraits of Lawrence Barrett (no. 272) and of Jefferson for 'the alertness, the life and fire of the regard, and the charm of the rich colour' ('Art Notes', *Art Interchange*, 25, 20 December 1890, p. 201). Though badly hung, the reviewer declared that 'they take their revenge on the injudicious hanging committee who put them there [the small north gallery], by dulling every other canvas in the gallery'. *Art Amateur*, however, found that the stage make-up and wig created a bizarre effect and saw the characterization as an example of Sargent's exposing the 'mask' of his sitters, his way of 'conveying by some touch about the eyes or mouth the fact that it is a mask, and does not quite suit the wearer' ('The Academy of Design', *Art Amateur*, 24, January 1891, p. 31).

In a letter to Barrett (16 September [1890]), Sargent asks him if he would consider lending the portrait (presumably to the National Academy of Design exhibition): 'Mr Jefferson & I both would like it' (AAA, microfilm roll D10).

There are several photographs and theatrical prints of Jefferson in the role of Pangloss.

For a 1907 photograph of the reading room in The Players showing the portrait *in situ*, see fig. 33.

274 *Joseph Jefferson*

1890
Oil on canvas, 18½ × 15 (47 × 38)
Inscribed, upper right: *J. S. S.*
Private Collection

Painted by the artist for himself, at the same time as the more formal study of Jefferson in character (no. 273), this sketch remained with Sargent throughout his life. It shows the actor informally dressed, with an intense, impish expression in a characterization of great verve and spirit. When it was exhibited at the New English Art Club in 1893, a critic commented on its 'breathless dexterity' (*Magazine of Art*, 1893, p. xxx). Sargent appears to have been pleased with the sketch, loaning it to a significant number of contemporary exhibitions. Martin Birnbaum recalls a conversation with Sargent in his sitting-room in the Copley-Plaza Hotel, Boston in 1922, during which the artist showed him 'an early portrait of the actor Joseph Jefferson, which he still liked' (Birnbaum 1941, p. 33).

The sketch is mentioned in a letter to Walter Clark (15 December [1924]), in connection with the proposed exhibition at the Grand Central Art Galleries, as being one of two portraits (the other was *Reconnoitering*, Pitti Palace, Florence) 'no longer in Newport, but in the Boston Museum where they can stay until you need them' (GCAG archives).

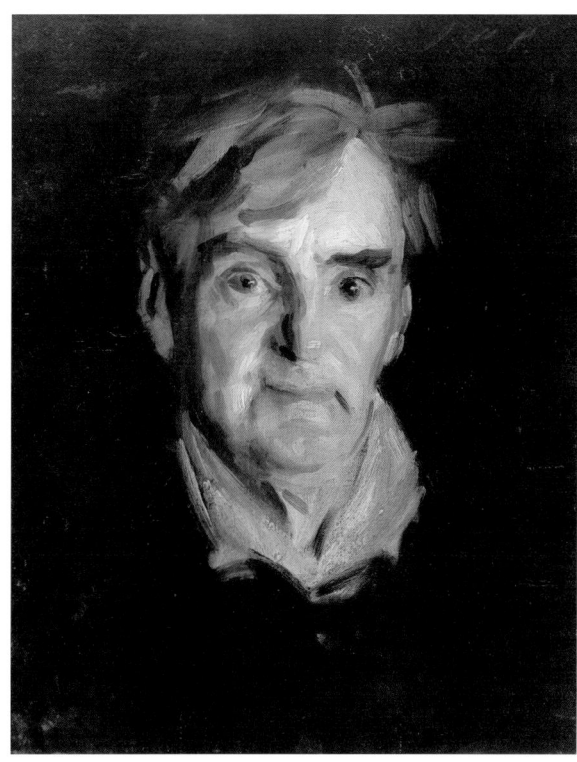

275 *Mrs Leslie Cotton*

c. 1890–3
Pastel on paper, 24½ × 19¾ (62.2 × 50.2)
Inscribed, across top: *to Mrs Cotton John S. Sargent*
Untraced

Marietta ('Pansy') Benedict (1868–1947) was the daughter of Samuel T. and Julia J. Benedict of New York. She married Leslie Cotton (date unknown) and had one son. She studied art in Paris under Carolus-Duran and Jean Henner and exhibited portraits and figure studies at the Royal Academy and elsewhere (1891–1911). Well known on the

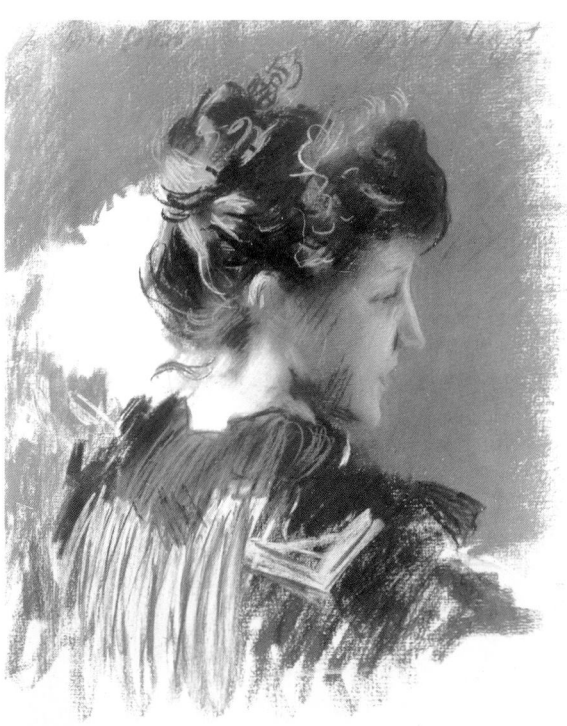

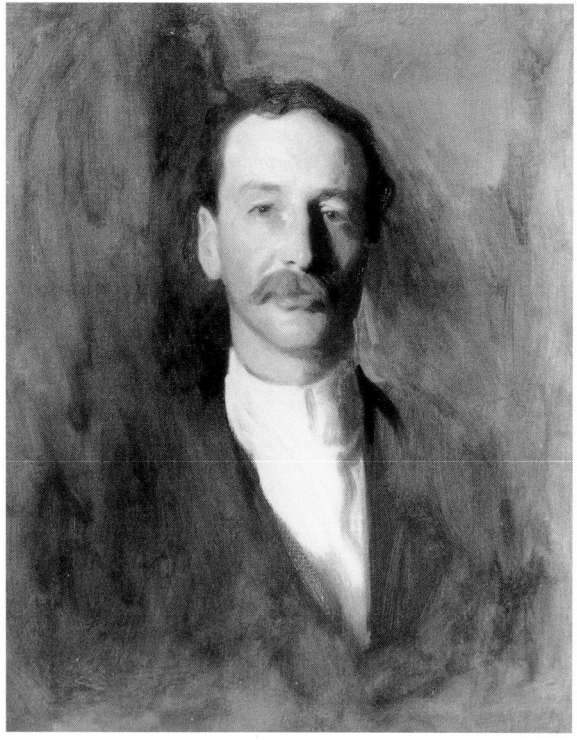

the favour of accepting it as an earnest of my good intentions' (MHS). In an undated letter headed 'Fenway Court Wednesday', Sargent wrote to Mrs Prince:

> I am distressed at disappointing you but I fore-see that it will be utterly impossible for me to carry out my ancient promise before I leave Boston which must be next week. I am strug-gling with two portraits one of them only just begun and my days are numbered. Of course yours would practically mean a new portrait for I remember that it was either half obliterated or in a bad way. I must beg you to excuse me but I do so with real regret (MHS).

This letter probably also dates from 1903, when Sargent was staying at Fenway Court as Mrs Gardner's guest. The correspondence implies that the portrait was painted prior to 1903. It would be difficult to date a broadly painted sketch securely on stylistic grounds, but it is probable that it was painted in America and might belong to Sargent's visits of 1890 or 1895, when Dr Prince would have been thirty-six or forty-one respectively.

international art circuit, she painted such celebri-ties as Lady Cunard (1905). William Merritt Chase's famous full-length portrait of her, *Lady in Black* (1888), is in the Metropolitan Museum of Art, New York. She was also painted by Anders Zorn in 1901.

This rare pastel by Sargent represents her in *pro-fil perdu*, her hair done up in a bun and loosely frizzed at the front; she wears a gown or blouse with a finely pleated organza bodice. Her hair and costume suggest a date of *c.* 1890–3, and the pastel may well have been drawn during Sargent's pro-longed visit to America in 1890.

276 Dr Morton Prince

1890 or 1895?
Oil on canvas, 30 × 25 (76.2 × 63.5)
Tufts University, Medford, Massachusetts

Morton Prince (1854–1929) was a Vienna-trained physician and neurologist, who specialized in the pathology of mental disorders. He studied at Harvard, had a medical practice in Boston, and wrote a number of important psychological studies, including *The Dissociation of a Personality* (1906) and *The Unconscious* (1914). He taught at Tufts University (1902–12) and Harvard (1926–8), and founded and directed the Harvard Psycho-logical Clinic (1927). He married Fannie Lithgow Payson in 1885.

The portrait is not previously recorded in Sargent literature and little is known about the circumstances in which it was painted. There are two letters from Sargent to Mrs Prince. In a letter headed 'Saturday' (the envelope is postmarked 20 April 1903), Sargent wrote to Mrs Prince: 'Of course the old sketch is yours if you will do me

277 Honorable Thomas Brackett Reed

1891
Oil on canvas, 32 × 26 (81.2 × 66)
Inscribed, upper left: *John S. Sargent*; upper right: *1891*
House of Representatives, Washington, D.C.

Honorable Thomas Brackett Reed (1839–1902), lawyer and Speaker of the House of Representa-tives, was born in Portland, Maine, the son of Thomas Brackett, a sailor and watchman, and his wife, Mathilda (*née* Mitchell). He was attorney-gen-

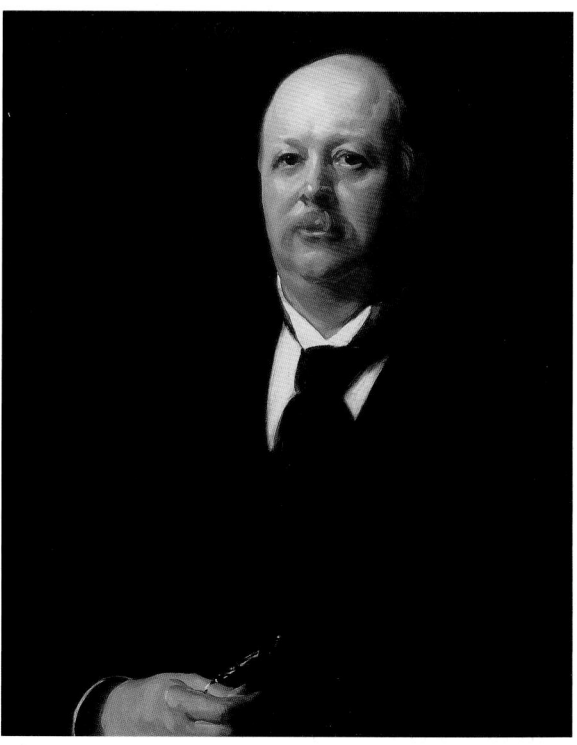

eral of Maine in 1870 and the Republican member of the House of Representatives in 1876. Elected Speaker of the House in 1889, he carried through major procedural reforms, notably the 'Reed Rules', which simplified and rationalized the procedural system of the House, reducing the possibility of obstruction and contrived delays. As a result, the Fifty-first Congress pressed through the most substantial legislative programme since the Civil War. A distinguished debater, he was re-nowned for his invective, sarcastic wit and relentless and piercing cross-examining. His epigrams and aphorisms have survived as part of the American political tradition. He married Mrs Susan P. Jones in 1870.

The initiative for this portrait of Reed seems to have come from Henry Cabot Lodge, a Republican colleague in Congress whom Sargent had painted in 1890 (no. 264). All three men were in Paris in the summer of 1891, Sargent for the wedding of his sister Violet. He borrowed the studio of his old friend Albert de Belleroche to carry out the commission (see Belleroche 1926, p. 44). On a 33 Tite Street address card headed '1 rue Tronchet', Sargent asked Belleroche: 'Could I paint a man's portrait in your studio? Let me know quick' (Private Collection), and, in an undated letter, also headed 1, rue Tronchet and sent to Belleroche at 30, rue de Bruxelles, he wrote: 'My sitter will come in the morning and [we?] will begin tomorrow Thursday at 10. Will you tell the concierge that a canvass will come & that I may work & my name' (Private Collection). He did not find the work easy, confiding to Charles Fairchild, the original intermediary between himself and Lodge:

> I found him awfully hard and this is the result of a second attempt different in view and character from the first which I destroyed. His exterior does not somehow correspond with his spirit and what is a painter to do? I am afraid you and your friends will be disappointed and that I could have made a better picture with a less remarkable man. He has been delightful. (letter from Charles Fairchild to Henry C. Lodge, 29 July 1891, quoting Sargent, from the *Lodge Papers*, Robinson 1930, p. 296)

Sargent wrote to Augustus Saint-Gaudens from Paris, 21 August [1891]: 'Mr Reed's portrait was a difficult job, and I don't believe his friends will think it successful. I didn't find much character in the place where his face ought to be. Perhaps a full length nude would have been the thing to do. What I have done is insignificant, and I beg all your pardons' (Saint-Gaudens Papers, DCL).

The portrait was not generally liked by Reed's friends. One critic wrote: 'He is supposed to be in the act of counting a quorum but in fact has just been inveigled into biting a green persimmon, a distinctly rebel and Democratic fruit, tabooed, unclean and anathema maranatha to all loyal Republicans born north of the fortieth parallel' (*Washington Post*, 17 September 1893, quoted in

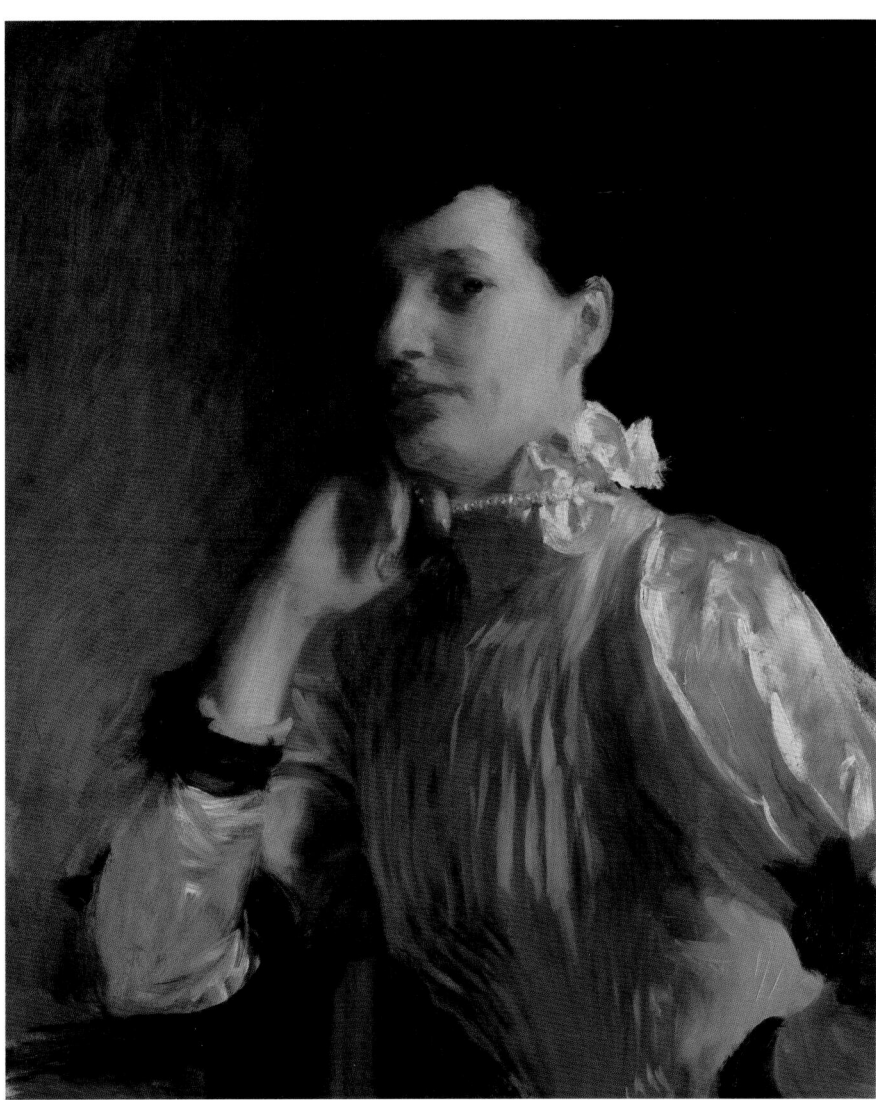

Robinson, p. 296). Reed himself was unmoved by the criticism. While admitting that it was less good-looking than the original, he felt that it was a notable work of art. In a diary entry for 19 December 1895, Asher Hind records his spirited defence of the picture: 'He [Reed] believes it to be the best work of art in the lobby and a fair resemblance' (Manuscripts Division, Library of Congress, Washington, D.C.).

278 *Mabel Marquand, Mrs Henry Galbraith Ward*

probably *c.* 1891–3
Oil on canvas, 27 × 22 (68.6 × 55.9)
Inscribed, upper left: *John S. Sargent*; upper right:
Mrs Ward
Metropolitan Museum of Art, New York

Mabel Marquand (1860–1896) was one of the three daughters of Henry Gurdon Marquand, industrialist and patron of the arts. She married Henry Galbraith Ward, a New York lawyer, in 1891. Their two sons Galbraith and Marquand, were both killed during the First World War.

The date of the portrait has not been certainly established. Sargent painted the sitter's mother, Mrs

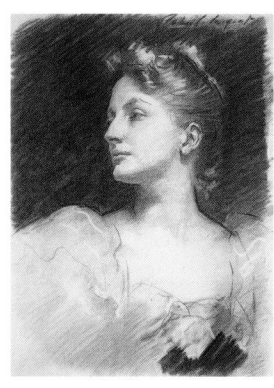

fig. 48 *Helen Dunham.* Charcoal, 24 × 18 ? (61 × 47). Private Collection.

H. G. Marquand, in 1887 (see *Early Portraits*, no. 192) and family tradition has it that this portrait of her daughter was painted at around this time in Newport, where the Marquand family had a country estate, Linden Gate. However, the picture's inscription, 'Mrs Ward', would suggest a date after the sitter's marriage on 13 August 1891, and the fact that the portrait was exhibited twice in 1894, which might imply that it was a recent work, lends support to a later date. The artist knew the family well, painting Marquand himself in 1897 (no. 343) and it is possible that the picture was painted earlier than 1894 and the inscription added at a later date (three letters from McKibbin, 9 July 1897, 10 October 1966 and 9 February 1976, discussing the dating problems are in the MMA archives). The personal inscription suggests that the portrait was not a commissioned work.

The sitter is painted wearing a high-necked, pin-tucked blouse or dress, fingering a string of pearls around her neck. Theodore Robinson was greatly impressed by the work when he saw it at the National Academy of Design, noting in his diary (28 December 1894):

> Sargent's portrait of Mrs H. Galbraith Ward fascinates me – it almost breathes, and a charming type of woman. The body exists under the gown, and a wonderfully caught momentary movement of a woman. Toying with a string of pearls. He is head and shoulders above most painters and the extraordinary drawing and grasp of character, vitality of his people, makes one overlook things that would be blemishes in another, or tendency to brownness in backgrounds and a certain crudity in shadows (FARL).

C. H. Caffin wrote that the picture represented 'one of his [Sargent's] moods of almost brutal frankness' (*Harper's Weekly*, 12 November 1898, p. 1102). McKibbin quotes a letter from the sitter's sister-in-law, Mrs Allan Marquand, in which she mentions that 'no-one . . . liked it as it was not at all characteristic of her' (9 July 1947, MMA archives). With reference to the selection of pictures for the exhibition to be held at the Grand Central Art Galleries, New York, in 1924, Sargent wrote to Walter Clark: 'I don't object to Mrs Marquand – address unknown – nor to a sketch of a daughter of Mrs, now dead' (GCAG archives).

279 *Helen Dunham*

1892
Oil on canvas, 48 × 32 (121.5 × 81.3)
Inscribed, upper right: *John S. Sargent. '92*
David H. Koch

Sargent's relationship with the Dunham family remains difficult to chart, though it was clearly an important one. The bare biographical bones are that James H. Dunham of 29 Washington Square,

New York, married Harriet Winston Lathrop (b. 1834) in 1863 and had six daughters: Harriet Lathrop, Lillian Howland, Helen Bliss, Elizabeth Howland, Catherine Skinner and Grace Louise. Helen, the third daughter, was born in 1868. She married Theodore Holmes-Spicer, an ophthalmic surgeon at St Bartholomew's and Moorfields hospitals in London in 1910. James Dunham died in 1879, when Grace, his youngest child, was three years old.

Sargent painted two of the daughters, Helen and Harriet (Etta) (see no. 321) and executed drawings of three of them, Etta, Helen and Grace. The Dunhams were cultured and intellectual – one admirer called them 'the New York blues, the most admirable of all the sexes' (Carter 1947, p. 325, n. 4) – and they often seem to be referred to collectively. The name 'Miss Dunham' crops up in a number of contemporary letters and accounts written by Sargent's friends, but it is not always possible to establish which of the Dunham daughters is being specified by individual authors. A Miss Dunham, godmother of Dorothy Barnard, is mentioned as early as 1885, visiting the household at Broadway in Worcestershire (Lucia Millet's letters, 24 August 1885, Private Collection). The majority of references, however, are from the 1890s, and a shared enthusiasm for music and theatre appears to have underpinned the friendship between the Dunhams and the artist. In an undated letter to Mrs Gardner [spring 1892], Sargent lists Miss Dunham among the guests he would invite to the party they were hosting to watch Carmencita dance (ISGM archive). The Chapmans, who were at the party, were also mutual friends (see no. 287). There are various references to Helen Dunham in Kit Anstruther-Thomson's letters to Vernon Lee, which mention other Sargent sitters, Lady Agnew and Eleonora Duse (CC). In undated letters [1893] Kit Anstruther-Thomson wrote to Vernon Lee 'I haven't seen him [Sargent] yet. We shall meet at the Duse's play. Miss Dunham says the Duse is very sauvage & won't known anyone'; and 'I saw her [La Duse] in Feodora [*sic*] with Helen Dunham & Mr Sargent'. In an undated letter [1892?], Sargent wrote to Carlo Placci 'Miss Helen Dunham has gone to Brighton for a month. She is coming up for the Padereswki [Ignacy Paderewski, 1860–1941, Polish pianist, composer and statesman] concert' (Biblioteca Marucelliana, Florence).

The artist Theodore Robinson mentions the Dunhams and the portrait of Helen on several occasions in his diaries. On 30 December 1892, he notes: 'Miss Helen Dunham, just returned, has had her portrait painted by Sargent and says it is one of his best. She was enthusiastic over his recent portraits, and the Boston Library works as well' (FARL). Robinson dined with the Dunhams on 26 January 1893 and again on 15 February, when he asked his fellow guest, the pianist Ignacy Paderewski, how he liked Miss Dunham's portrait. Paderewski replied '"Pas de tout, c'est un portrait

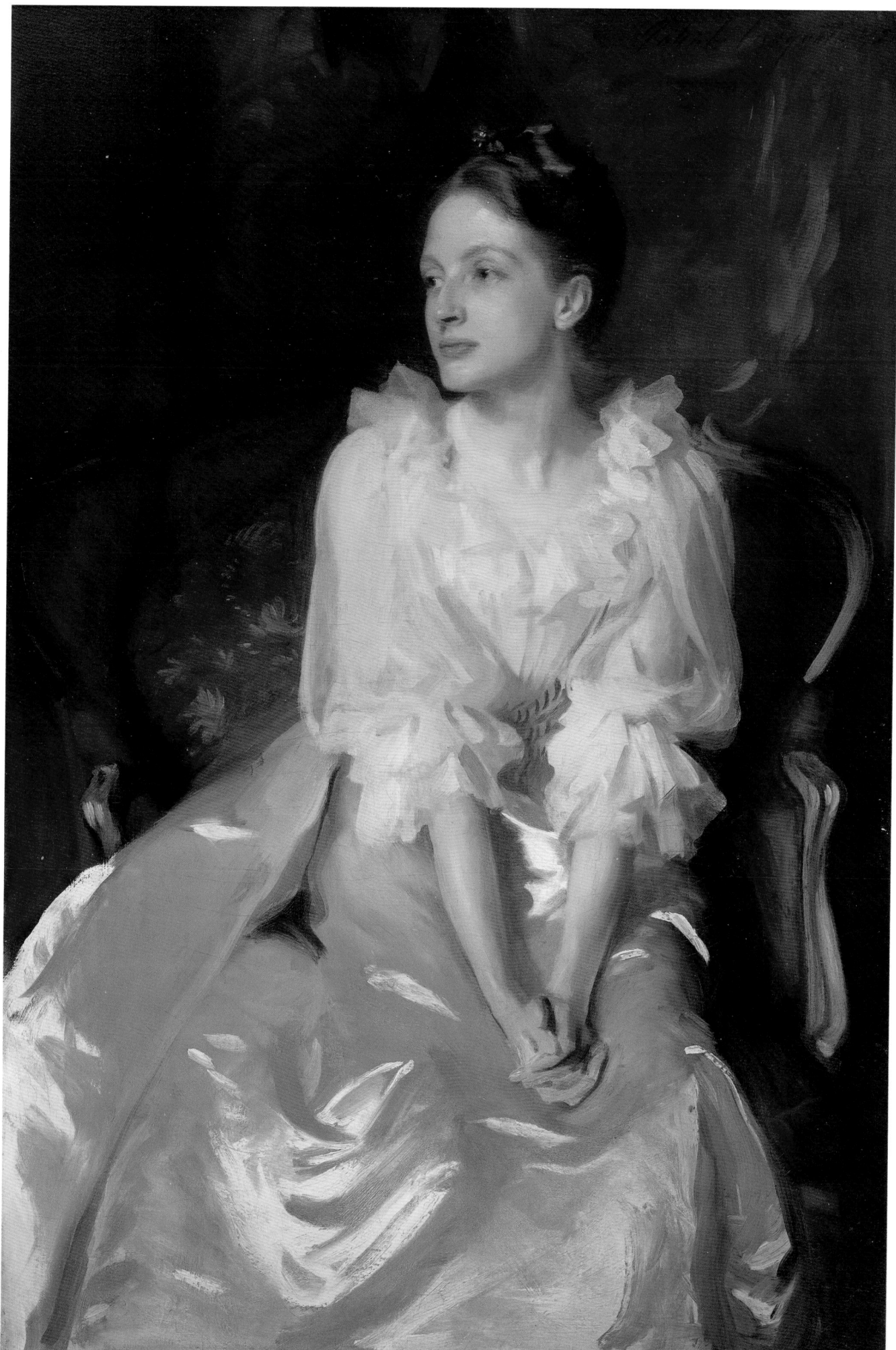

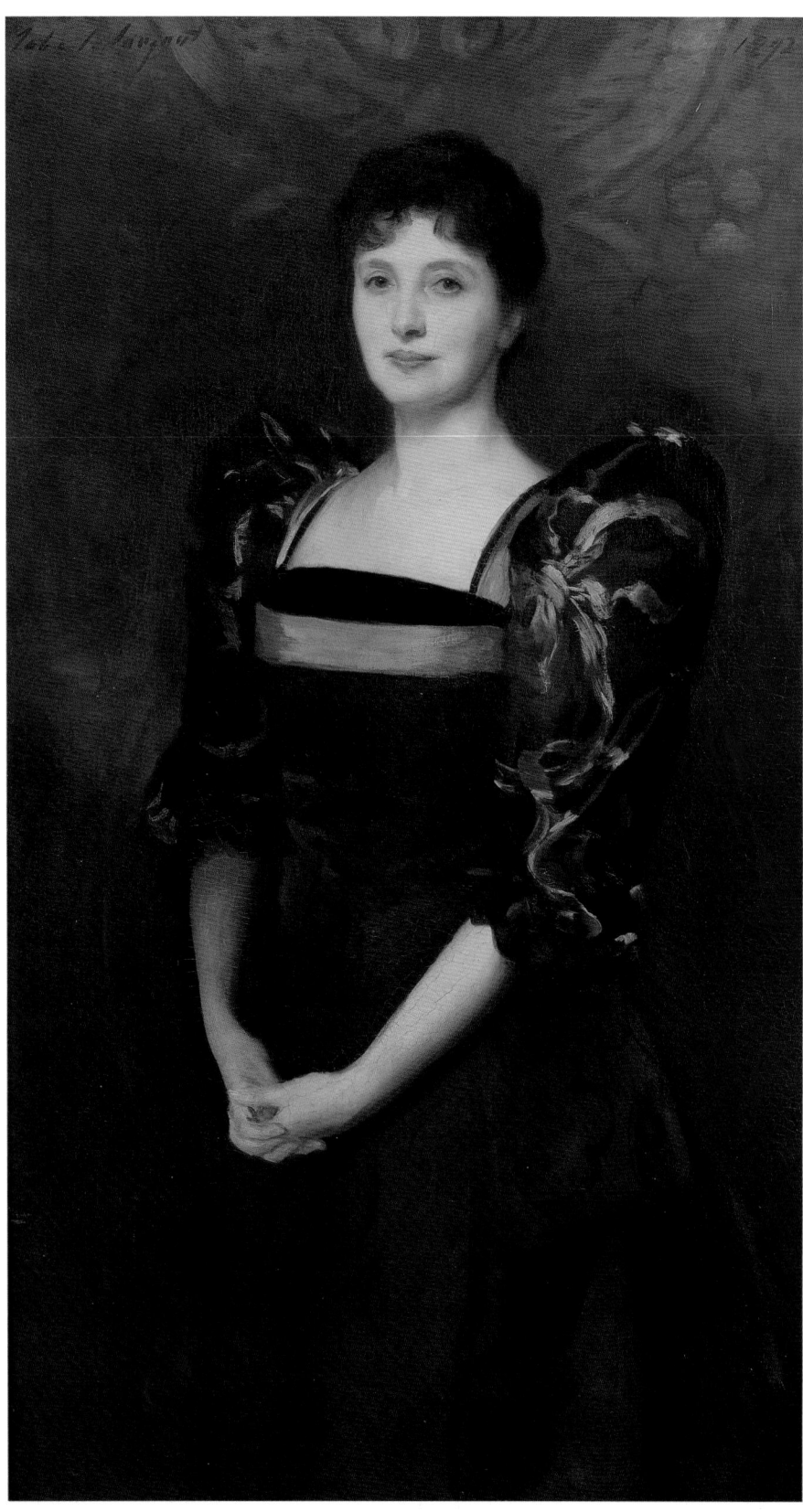

Sargent's portrait of Mrs Gardner herself (see *Early Portraits*, no. 206) (see Fairbrother 1986, p. 136 n. 28).

The Dunhams were friends of Gertrude Agnew and her husband, (Andrew) Noel – they gave Lady Agnew a jewelled enamelled brooch on the occasion of her wedding in October 1889 (see Edinburgh 1997, p. 15) – and it may be that it was through them that the Agnews were introduced to Sargent. It is recorded in Noel Agnew's diary that the Dunhams were dinner guests of the Agnews on 10 and 11 July 1891 and that on the second occasion Sargent accompanied them (see Edinburgh 1997, p. 17).

It is not known exactly when the portrait of Helen was painted, but it was exhibited in London, at the New English Art Club winter exhibition in the autumn of 1892. D. S. MacColl, writing in the *Spectator* (26 November 1892, p. 770), remarked on the portrait's realism and its structural verity but compared it unfavourably with an earlier three-quarter-length portrait of Flora Priestley (see *Early Portraits*, no. 225). In America it was shown at the World's Fair in Chicago in 1893, in New York at the National Academy of Design in 1895 and again at the Society of American Artists in 1897, and in Boston in Sargent's one-man show at Copley Hall in 1899.

The portrait was the subject of caricature at the Society of American Fakirs Exhibition, which was held at the Art Students League in New York in 1897. For an installation photograph of the show, see Ronald G. Pisano and Bruce Weber, *Parodies of the American Masters: Rediscovering the Society of American Fakirs, 1891–1914*, New York, 1993 (exhibition catalogue), fig. A, where two paintings parodying the picture are visible.

McKibbin lists two drawings of Helen Dunham in his checklist (see McKibbin 1956, p. 93). The compilers have only seen the drawing illustrated here (fig. 48).

280 *Mrs George Lewis*

1892
Oil on canvas, 53½ × 30½ (136 × 77.5)
Inscribed, upper left: *John S. Sargent*; upper right: *1892*
Private Collection

saignant" [raw, bleeding] pointing to the fingers where were Sargent's usual crude red tones' (FARL). On 30 March 1894, Robinson also notes that he had met Cecilia Beaux, who praised the way Sargent emphasized Helen Dunham's thin arms and hands instead of concealing them (FARL). The French writer Paul Bourget and his wife, Minnie saw the portrait in London in May 1894, and Mrs Bourget wrote to Mrs Gardner that it was a 'good' portrait but that she preferred

Mrs George Lewis, *née* Elizabeth Eberstadt (1843–1931), was the daughter of Ferdinand Eberstadt of Mannheim, Germany. In 1867, she married the successful solicitor George Lewis, who was later created a baronet, and they had one son and two daughters. She was sensitive and creative by temperament, and she and her husband entertained many literary, artistic and musical celebrities at their house in Portland Place. In her obituary, Max Beerbohm wrote: 'good looks, good plays, good pictures and, above all, good music were for her no mere topics of conversation, but vital needs of her nature' (*The Times*, 14 September 1931, p. 17). Graham Robertson described her as 'a strange woman . . . with a wonderful gift of sympathy and understanding' (Preston 1953 p. 75).

Towards the end of 1891 and in the spring of the following year, Sargent was involved in a dispute with a local farmer near Fairford, Gloucestershire, where he was working on the first phase of his Boston Public Library murals with Edwin Abbey, and sought the services of George Lewis (for accounts of this episode, see Charteris 1927, pp. 119–20; Mount 1969, pp. 194–6; Olson 1986, pp. 176–7). The portrait of Mrs Lewis is said to have been painted in gratitude for the settlement of the case, though it was more likely a commission. Sargent's friendship with the Lewis family lasted for the rest of his life, and he was a frequent guest at their parties. He painted George Lewis in 1896 (no. 335), and his daughter Katherine in 1906 (no. 519), as well as executing charcoal portraits of other members of the family. Though Sargent later reported to the sitter's daughter, Mrs Burney, that Mrs Lewis had 'sat like a rock and then left without looking at the damned thing' (McKibbin papers, from an unidentified source), the portrait clearly pleased both artist and sitter. She is represented in a black and gold embroidered evening dress, in a composition – decorative brocade background and the figure's rhythmically looped hands – that is strongly reminiscent of Sargent's portrait of Isabella Stewart Gardner (*Early Portraits*, no. 206). The red and gold hanging, probably Italian or French in origin, has not been identified.

The portrait was overshadowed at the exhibitions of 1893 by two of Sargent's most memorable creations, the portraits of Mrs Hugh Hammersley and Lady Agnew (nos 284, 286), but was praised for being 'attractive in technique, and at once agreeable and unflinching in its record of the model' (*Magazine of Art*, 1893, p. 290).

Clementina Anstruther-Thomson mentions the portrait in an undated letter [1893] to Vernon Lee 'As to Mr. Sargent, London is at his feet. Mrs Hammersley & Mrs Lewis are at the New Gallery, Lady Agnew at the Academy. There can be no two opinions this year. He has had a cracking success' (CC). Sargent's letters to Mrs Lewis are in the Department of Western Manuscripts, Bodleian Library, Oxford

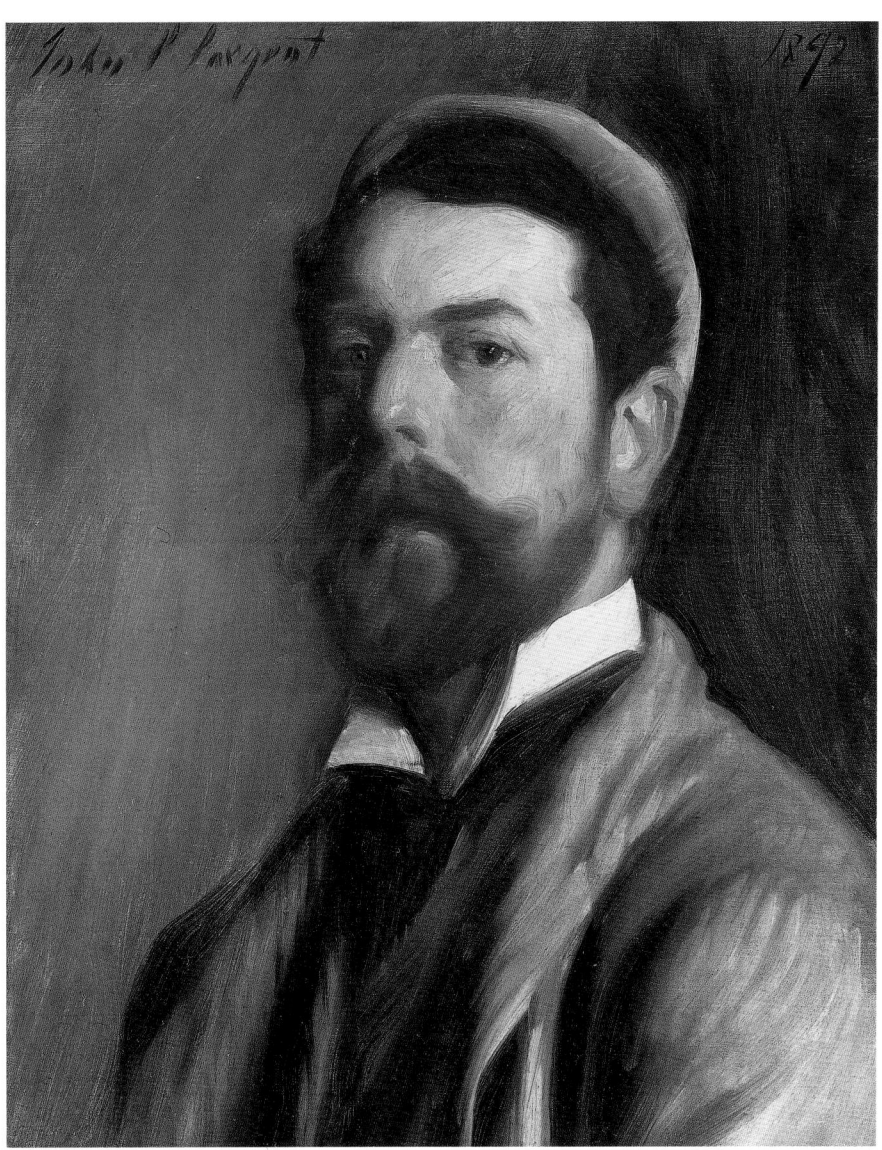

281   *Self-Portrait*

1892
Oil on canvas, 21 × 17 (53.3 × 43.2)
Inscribed, upper left: *John S. Sargent*; upper right: *1892*
National Academy, New York

Sargent's three self-portraits were painted for specific locations and do not represent a natural predilection for self-portraiture. The first of 1886 (see *Early Portraits*, no. 169) was painted for the Macdonald Collection of artists' self-portraits; this, the second, for the National Academy of Design (now the National Academy), New York, and the third, of 1906, for the Uffizi Gallery in Florence (no. 523). All three are head-and-shoulders portraits, painted three-quarter face with the light falling from the right. Sargent wears a tie, wing collar, coat and waistcoat in all three, and in the present work he also wears a cap. There is no particular intensity of expression or quality of self-revelation in the self-portraits. Sargent looks at himself, as at others, with the same trained and observant eye.

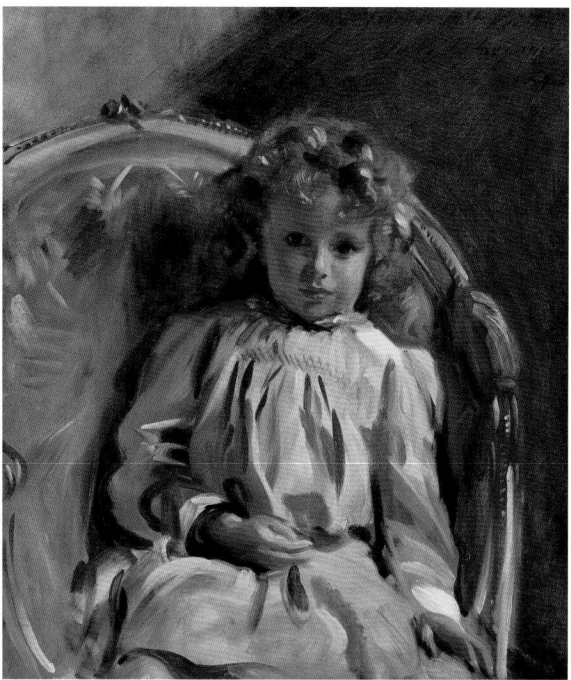

The portrait fulfilled the regulations for Sargent's acceptance as a member of the National Academy of Design in New York. A shipping document in the National Academy archive from Davis Turner & Co. (15 April 1892) notes that customs refused to clear the portrait, which had arrived on the SS *Aurania*, unless its value was shown. A copy of the freight invoice is also in the National Academy archive. The council minutes of 9 May 1892 note that the portrait was presented, that Sargent's membership was proposed and seconded, and that he was 'declared duly qualified as an associate'.

282 *Master Skene Keith*

1892
Oil on canvas, 30 × 26 (76.2 × 66.0)
Inscribed, upper right: *to my friend Mrs Keith /*
John S. Sargent / 1892
Private Collection

Master Skene Keith (1888–1966) was the son of Dr Thomas Skene Keith and his wife Laetitia Parsons. Dr Keith was one of a family of celebrated surgeons, whilst his wife was a relative of the artist Alfred Parsons, a prominent member of the Broadway set and one of Sargent's closest friends.

The little boy is painted in a nursery smock secured by a sash at the waist and is seated tucked into the corner of a large bergère armchair of the type much favoured by the artist for his female portraits (see Accessories, p. xxii, no. 2b).

283 *John Alfred Parsons Millet*

1892
Oil on canvas, 36¼ × 24⅛ (92.1 × 61.3)
Inscribed, across top: *to my friend*
Mrs Millet John S. Sargent / 1892
Richard Manoogian

John Alfred Parsons Millet (1888–1976) was the youngest child of the American painter Frank Millet and his wife, Lily (see *Early Portraits*, no. 165), fellow members of the Broadway colony and among the artist's closest friends. J. A. P. Millet was named after his two godfathers, Sargent and another painter friend, Alfred Parsons. He was educated at Marlborough College, England, and at Harvard University, and began to practise medicine in 1914. In the 1920s he turned to psychiatry and became a distinguished psychiatrist and psychoanalyst, with a private practice in New York and positions with several universities and medical foundations. He married, first, Alice Murrell, in 1913, and Carmen de Gonzalo Manice, in 1941.

Soon after 'Jack' Millet's birth Sargent made two drawings of his godson (one is in the Fitzwilliam Museum, Cambridge, no. 2569, and a second is in a private collection) and continued to take an interest in him. The occasion for this oil is not recorded, but it may have been painted either at Russell House, Broadway, where the Millets continued to reside, or at Morgan Hall, Fairford, where Sargent shared a studio with Edwin Abbey.

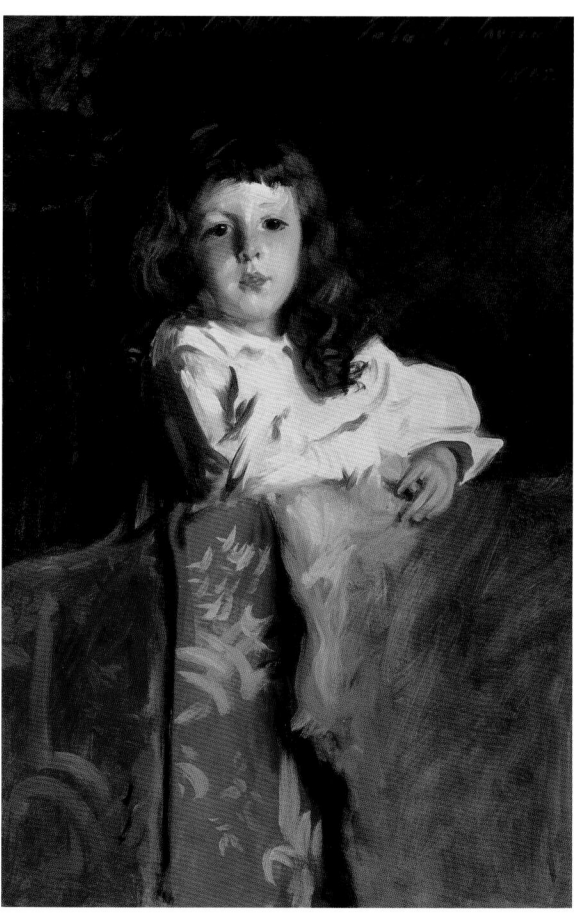

The composition is novel and daring. The four-year-old boy, with his Lord Fauntleroy curls and white nursery smock, is shown looking over the back of a sofa or couch. The lower part of his body is hidden, but he appears to be kneeling on the seat. Nearly half the space is occupied by fabric draped over the sofa, a richly figured dark red cloth of oriental design with a floral motif picked out, and finally a brown fur rug. The corner of an upright desk or cabinet with what looks like a piece of decoration or sculpture on top is dimly visible on the left behind the little boy. The soft lighting from below, throwing deep shadows, suggests lamplight and an evening scene.

284 *Mrs Hugh Hammersley*

1892
Oil on canvas, 81 × 45¼ (205.7 × 114.9)
Inscribed, lower right: *John S. Sargent*
Metropolitan Museum of Art, New York. Gift of
Mr and Mrs Douglass Campbell, in memory of
Mrs Richard E. Danielson

Mrs Hammersley, *née* Mary Frances Grant (1863–1911), was the daughter of a Scotsman, Owen Grant, a clerk in the House of Lords, and his wife, Adelaide Higginson. In 1889, she married Hugh Greenwood Hammersley at St George's, Hanover Square, in London. He was a partner in Cox's bank, which was later absorbed by Lloyd's. They had one child, Eve Mary, who died aged ten of a congenital heart disease. Beautiful, vivacious and entertaining, Mrs Hammersley held court at Admiral's House, Hampstead. In his biography of Philip Wilson Steer, D. S. MacColl quotes Violet Hammersley's reminiscences of the group of artists and writers who regularly frequented her sister-in-law's Sunday afternoons: 'Steer, Tonks and Ronald Gray formed the nucleus, for they seldom missed a Sunday, but Augustus John, Sargent, the William Rothensteins and MacColls, Max Beerbohm and Sickert were of the company' (MacColl 1945, p. 104). Letters from Mrs Hammersley to several of these figures, as well as to Henry James and Charles Furse, were sold at Sotheby's, London, 8 July 1969. Her appreciation of contemporary art was perceptive and well informed, and she actively promoted the careers of those painters who were her friends. W. R. Sickert, for example, would write: 'Your very effectual interest in my work has made my life much easier and more agreeable lately. If I do as much and as well as I intend to do, you will have had a considerable hand in setting me up debout' (Sotheby's, London, 8 July 1969, lot 758). Sargent described her to Dr J. William White as 'awfully pretty' (White's journal entry for 13 September 1895, Dr James William White Papers, University Archives, University of Pennsylvania).

A sequence of sixty-one letters and fourteen letter cards (mostly undated) from Sargent to Mrs Hammersley (MMA, Department of American Paintings and Sculpture) record the development of their professional relationship into an apparently close personal friendship over the course of at least two decades (from 1891 to at least 1906). The letters provide insight into the portrait process, from initial responses about Sargent's availability and prices to the scheduling of sittings. Ensuing letters discuss loans of the completed portrait and various social invitations and engagements. Several letters concern commissions elicited for Paul Helleu, including a pastel portrait of Mrs Hammersley's daughter (untraced).

In a long memorandum of 30 March 1893, addressed from the Hammersley's country house, Greenwood, in Weybridge, Surrey, Mrs Hammersley wrote about sitting to Sargent and about the circumstances of the commission:

I have just collected the lengthy correspondence about my picture & numbered Mr Sargents letters. I think they may be of interest to the future owners of his fine portrait & the following facts about myself may amuse my little Eve shd she live to be an old woman & sit opposite her Mothers picture. [In parentheses is then written: 'Eve Mary Hammersley died 24. May. 1902']. There had been many hitches about my portrait – The choice of painters I may mention lying between [John] Pettie [1839–93] and Sargent. My husband easily decided however that the latter painted women best – I was ill (I very often am!) and Mr S. was away so that it was near a year before the painting was fairly begun. i.e. in May [originally 'June', corrected to 'May'] 1892. Sargent gave it his *best* work and his best energy (and they are both great) I sat thro' May and June [originally 'June and July', corrected to 'May and June'] about 4 sometimes 5 days a week from 2 to 5 or 6 in the afternoon. Some days he wld work the whole time without ceasing, as one possessed, whilst others were spent playing the piano, which he did charmingly! The picture is to go to one of the Summer Exhibitions. I shall collect any criticism on it that may appear in the papers in the mean time the few artists who have seen it are very much pleased with what they consider 'the best thing Sargent has done yet' – Alma Tadema being particularly complimentary about it – My dear Hugh is charmed with the picture both as to work & likeness. The only criticism to be made on the latter is that my hair is not nearly so dark as Mr Sargent saw it! and that (without being vain, may I say) that no one says the portrait is 'pretty eno'' – Sargent never painted a *pretty* head!!!

In a postscript, Mrs Hammersley described herself: 'I am 5 foot 7 inches "in my stockings" – and I weigh eight stone. I am very thin. I am supposed to have very small hands and feet. tho' I wish my feet were as tiny as my dear Grandmother Higginson's. I shall save the shoes painted in the picture to keep with these letters' (MMA).

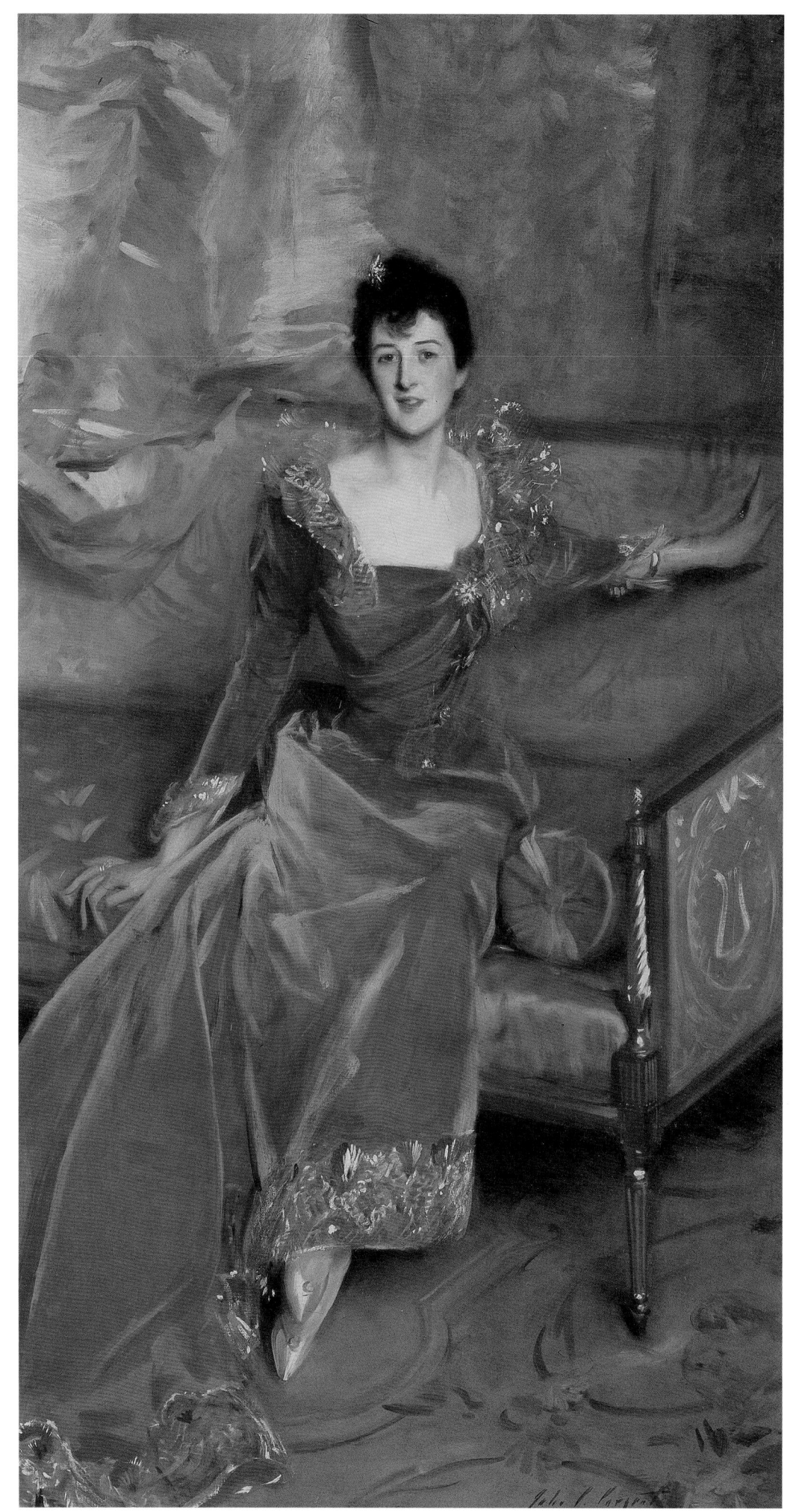

In the earliest of Sargent's letters to Mrs Hammersley, probably dating from the spring or summer of 1891, he informed her of his rates: 'In case your idea of my prices is based on Mrs Playfair, Mrs Harrison, Miss Vickers [see *Early Portraits*, nos 175, 142, and possibly no 132], or other portraits done here two or more years ago, I must inform you that I have raised my prices since then, to: head 200 Guineas / 3/4 length 400 / full length 500. In case you are already acquainted with this scale and do not mind waiting till the winter or spring I shall be delighted to put myself at your disposition' (MMA).

The process of painting the portrait, which lasted from May into June 1892, does not appear to have been untroubled. 'I have begun the routine of portrait painting with anxious relatives hanging on my brush', Sargent wrote to Edwin Abbey in an undated letter: 'Mrs Hammersley has a mother and I am handicapped by a vexatious accident (I have no luck)' (Charteris 1927, p. 137). The 'accident' Sargent referred to had occurred when he was dining at the Café Royal and a box of matches ignited in his trouser pocket, scorching his thigh. Sargent later told his student Julia Heyneman that he had done no less than sixteen heads of Mrs Hammersley: 'He held that it was impossible for a painter to try to repaint a head where the under-structure was wrong, as for a sculptor to remould the features of a head that had not been under-stood in the mass.' (Charteris 1927, p. 184). Despite these difficulties, when the painting was completed (and paid for in full) by 2 July 1892, Sargent wrote to the sitter's husband. 'Both you & Mrs Hammersley have done everything to help the picture along and I am most grateful to you. Our sittings have been a great pleasure and I am not half pleased that the picture is done' (MMA).

Several letters refer to the subsequent history of the picture and indicate that Sargent initially hoped to exhibit the painting at World's Columbian Exposition in Chicago in 1893. He wrote to Mrs Hammersley, probably in 1892: 'Tell me would you really lend me your portrait for Chicago? Or is it too large an order. Next year Chicago must be my principal show [illegible], and I would very much like to subjugate them with the sight of your countenance. But if you think it too painful I will try someone else' (MMA). Mrs Hammersley ultimately refused Sargent's request, and Sargent wrote, 'I will send for the portrait this week, and it shall wait in my studio for Chicago? No, for the New Gallery.' Later letters discuss the possibility of exhibiting the portrait in Birmingham, Manchester, Boston and Venice.

In contrast to the relaxed portrait of Lady Agnew, exhibited in the same year, that of Mrs Hammersley is all nervous energy and life. Kit Anstruther-Thomson wrote to Vernon Lee in the spring of 1893 about Sargent's pictures in the exhibition: 'As to Mr Sargent London is at his feet. Mrs Hammersley & Mrs Lewis are at the New Gallery, Lady Agnew at the Academy. There are no two opinions this year. He has had a cracking success. Mrs Hammersley has just sat down on that peach coloured sofa for *one* minute – she will be up again fidgeting about the room the next moment, but *meanwhile* Mr Sargent has painted her!! frivolous & empty headed & charmingly dressed like some alert springing flower' (CC). *The Times* took up the same point: 'The very head literally vibrates with life; never has the spirit of conversation been more actually and vividly embodied' (*The Times*, 1 May 1893, p. 10). An exchange between the painters G. F. Watts and Frederic Leighton about the painting's energy, recorded in Mrs Watts's diary (25 June 1893), is also telling:

> Signor [the name by which Watts was known in his own circle] had many morning visitors. Sir Frederick [*sic*] began the number. I did not see him but Signor told me they had discussed Sargent's portrait of Mrs Hammersley 'Ah', he said holding up his hands with pleasure 'the vitality of it is wonderful'. Signor said 'not so wonderful as it is in Partridge's[1] work – in such humorous sketches it is in place, in a portrait it is something to be always before one & should be more or less monumental in character – that one quality is a fault' (Watts Gallery, Compton, Surrey).

The critics on the whole were complimentary. The *Athenaeum* praised the 'brilliancy and harmony of its colours in high, which are most craftily disposed to harmonize with the luminous and yet solidly painted carnations of the lady' (*Athenaeum*, no. 3419, 6 May 1893, p. 578). The *Spectator* called it 'a speaking face, a living figure, a brilliant picture' (*Spectator*, 70, 6 May 1893, p. 606), while *The Times* wrote that once seen 'it is the least possible to forget'. The portrait caused nearly as great a sensation as that of Lady Agnew, shocking Sargent's detractors as much as his admirers for its vivacity and cleverness – what a critic for the *Art Journal* described as its 'modern spirit' (*Art Journal*, January 1894, p. 2). When conservative critics compared the portraits of Lady Agnew and Mrs Hammersley they generally favoured the former. Following Sargent's election as an Associate of the Royal Academy in January 1894, the *Sunday Times* concluded that *Lady Agnew* had 'made the election . . . practicable. It supplied that evidence of solidity and seriousness of purpose, that understanding of the graver simplicities of effect which the startling work [*Mrs Hugh Hammersley*] at the New [Gallery] did not quite afford' (*Sunday Times*, 14 January 1894, p. 8).

In a letter to John Hay (see no. 440) of 18 October 1893, Henry Adams used a somewhat forced comparison between the portrait and the architecture he had observed in Chicago, where he had recently been to visit the World's Fair, to make a stinging social attack:

1. Sir Bernard Partridge (1861–1945) cartoonist, portrayed many of the figures of the period, among them George Bernard Shaw and James McNeill Whistler. Many of his cartoons were illustrated in *Punch*.

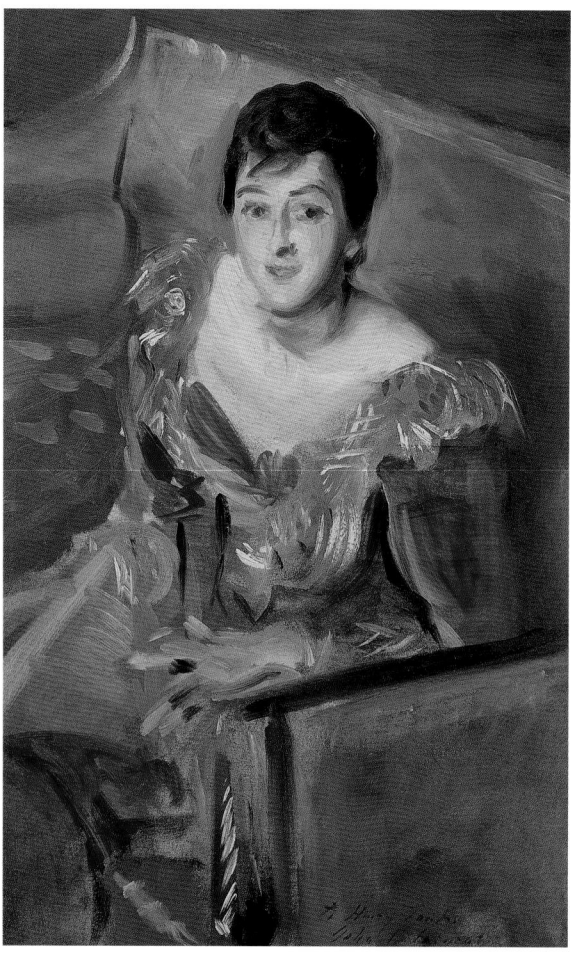

to tell you of it. She was a lovely & charming woman, & I think it is a very beautiful portrait (MMA).

Deering paid 'over sixty thousand dollars' for the portraits of Mrs Hammersley and Madame Paul Escudier (see *Early Portraits*, no. 53) in 1923. Sargent wrote to him on 18 November 1923: 'I am glad to hear that you have bought "Mrs Hugh Hammersley" and I hope you will like her and her really charming Louis XV frame' (W. D. Scott and R. B. Harshe, *Charles Deering. An Appreciation*, Boston, 1929, pp. 39–40).

285 Mrs Hugh Hammersley

c. 1892–3
Oil on canvas, 33 × 21 (83.8 × 53.3)
Inscribed, lower right: *to Henry Tonks/John S. Sargent*
New Britain Museum of American Art, Connecticut. Bequest of Mrs C. Buchanan. The Charles and Elizabeth Buchanan Collection

This vivid sketch of Mrs Hammersley shows her dressed in the same costume and seated on the same sofa as in the finished, full-length portrait. However, the viewpoint is quite different: we look down on the sitter, who appears surprised, caught off-guard and altogether more youthful. It is likely that this was an independent sketch rather than a preliminary study for the larger portrait. Sargent probably gave the sketch to Tonks sometime later than its execution, perhaps after the sitter's early death. Like Sargent, Tonks was a *habitué* of Mrs Hammersley's salon in Hampstead and a close friend. Like Sargent, he painted a large portrait of Mrs Hammersley seated on a sofa and dressed in white (untraced).

286 Lady Agnew of Lochnaw

1892
Oil on canvas, 49½ × 39½ (125.7 × 100.3)
Inscribed, upper left: *John S. Sargent*
National Gallery of Scotland, Edinburgh. Purchased 1925, with funds from the Cowan Smith Bequest

Lady Agnew of Lochnaw, *née* Gertrude Vernon (1865–1932), was the daughter of the Honourable Gowran Charles Vernon, the Recorder of Lincoln, and his wife Caroline (*née* Fazakerly), and granddaughter of the first Baron Lyvedon. In 1889, she married the barrister and politician Sir (Andrew) Noel Agnew of Lochnaw, ninth baronet, who was some fifteen years her senior; and she became Lady Agnew of Lochnaw three years later, when her husband inherited the baronetcy on his father's death. Lady Agnew lived principally in London and at her family farm in Hertfordshire. Sir Noel's landowning responsibilities at his estate, Lochnaw, in Wigtownshire, and his political commitments in

Do you remember Sargent's portrait of Mrs Hamersly [*sic*] in London this summer? Was it a defiance or an insult to our society, or a rendering in good faith of our civilisation, or a conscious snub to French and English art, or an unconscious revelation of the artist's despair of reconciliation with the female of the gold-bug? I say the female, because the male has been the butt of the artist for centuries. Well! The Chicago architecture is precisely an architectural Mrs Hamersly. I like to look at it as an appeal to the human animal, the superstitious and ignorant savage within us that has instincts and no reason, against the world as money has made it (Adams 1988, vol. IV, pp. 134–5).

Compelled by financial reverses to sell the portrait, Hugh Hammersley sent the painting to the Annual Exhibition at the Carnegie Institute, Pittsburgh, in 1923 in search of a buyer. In a letter dated 17 July 1923, Emily Sargent wrote to Charles Deering, who apparently wished to purchase a significant portrait by his longtime friend:

> John dined with me last night, & said to tell you that the only thing of his which may still be available that he knows of is now at the Carnegie Institute, Pittsburgh. It is a beautiful portrait of Mrs Hugh Hammersley, who died some years ago. Her husband lost most of his money in a swindling failure last year, & now wants to sell this picture. It may already be bought, for ought John knows, but he told me

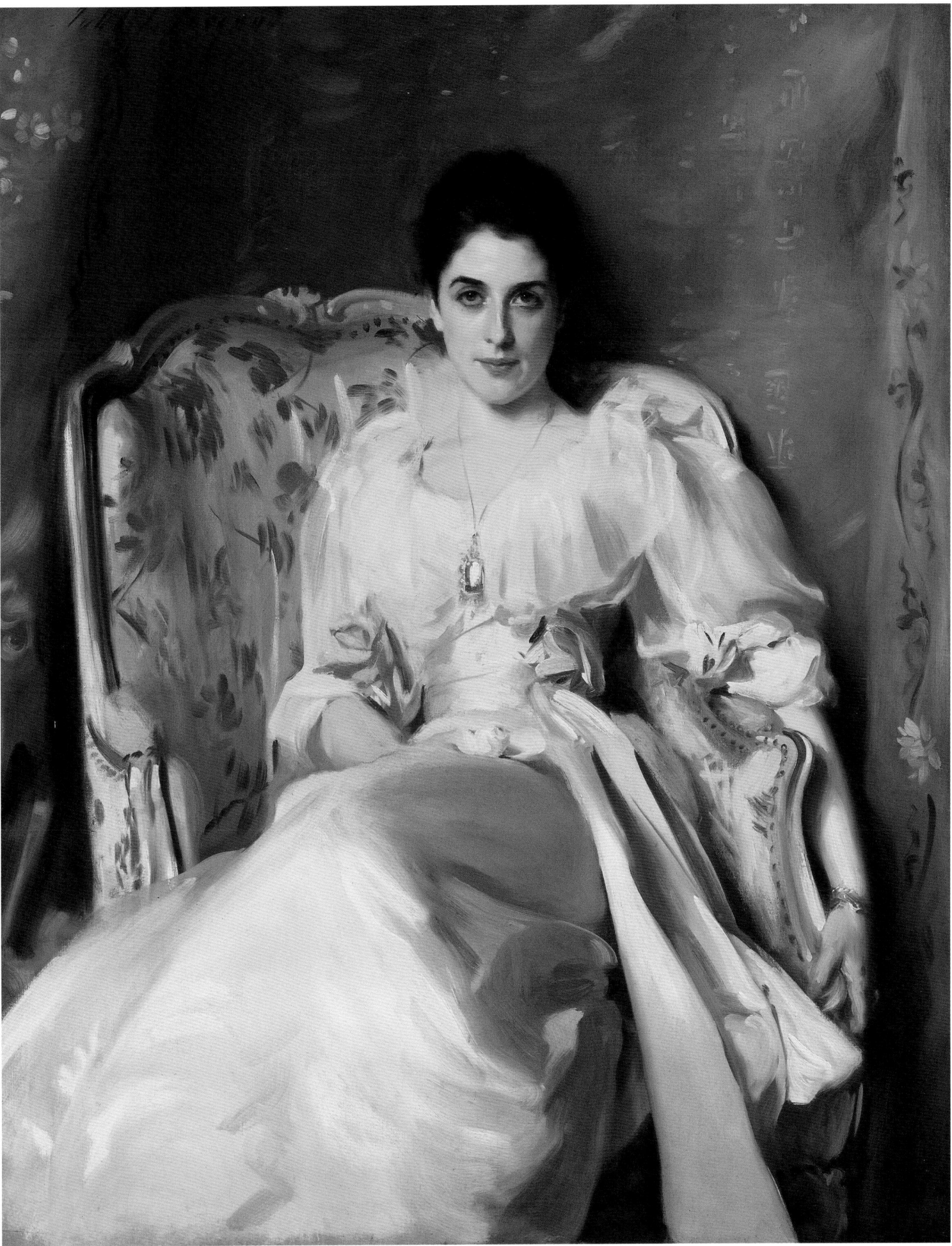

Scotland, meant that the couple maintained somewhat independent lives. A celebrated beauty, she held society parties at her London houses, 16 Eaton Square and later, 10 Smith Square. Lady Monkswell described her as 'pretty Lady Agnew' (Monkswell 1944, p. 240) when she saw her in 1894 and, in April of the following year, sat next to her at a party given by Sargent in his studio, where the guests watched Carmencita dance (Monkswell 1944, p. 265). Lady Agnew's health was never robust and she died of pernicious anaemia, in 1932 after a long illness. For a detailed biographical account see Julia Rayer Rolfe, 'Sargent and Lady Agnew', in Edinburgh 1997, pp. 14–33.

It was probably through the Dunhams, American friends of the Agnews, that the introduction to Sargent and, indirectly, the commission, came about. The chronology of events and relationships is not clear. It is recorded in Sir Noel Agnew's diary that, on 10 and 11 July 1891, the Dunhams came to dine with the Agnews and that, on the second occasion, they were accompanied by Sargent (Agnew of Lochnaw archives, GD 154/ 859-75, Scottish Record Office, Edinburgh). Sargent's portrait of Helen Dunham (no. 279) was exhibited at the New English Art Club in the winter of 1892, and he may have been working on it at this time. It is, however, possible that the Agnews had met Sargent at an earlier date.

Lady Agnew's constitution was extremely delicate and she suffered from periodic nervous exhaustion or neurasthenia. A halting recovery from a severe case of influenza in 1890 had left her particularly weak and fatigued, and she was still convalescent when she first sat to Sargent on 16 June 1892, which may account for the air of lassitude and extreme relaxation in her pose. Her husband's diary (Agnew of Lochnaw archives, GD 154/859-75, Scottish Record Office, Edinburgh) provides the only account of the sittings:

8 June 1892: 'Sargent came to see Gerty in several gowns with a view to a picture.'
9 June 1892: 'Called on Sargent in his studio about a picture of Gerty.'
16 June 1892, after the first sitting: Sir Noel called the picture 'a very pretty arrangement'.
18 June 1892, the second sitting. Sir Noel went to collect his wife from the studio, noting 'picture promising well'.
21 June 1892, the third sitting, after which Sir Noel travelled to Scotland to attend to political obligations.

The remaining sittings are undocumented, but, according to Sargent, the picture was completed in six sittings. Writing to the actress Ada Rehan, who sat to him in 1894 (no. 308), Sargent said: 'Some of my best results have happened to be obtained with few sittings (Lady Agnew was done in six sittings)' (Folger Shakespeare Library, Washington, D.C.).

Sargent wrote to Sir Noel about a frame for the picture:

I am very sorry to have been out when you came to see the picture, and fear that I have been guilty of having forgotten our engagement – I have no sittings today and lots of things to attend to, and it escaped me that you might come – My housekeeper tells me that you like the picture. I hope that it is the case – Today I saw an old frame which I think might suit the picture. It will be sent to the studio tomorrow, so if you could call in and see it during the next few days and give your opinion about it. It is expensive, I think £20, and unless the picture should look remarkably well in it, hardly worth the money. I have been so busy that I have not had a minute to reply to Lady Agnew's very kind note. – Please give her my warmest thanks and hopes that Coombe [Coombe End, a country house that the Agnews rented for the summer months of 1892] will do her lots of good. I hope to be able to run down to see you both there soon. ([1893], Agnew of Lochnaw archives, GD154/756/3/2, Scottish Record Office, Edinburgh, quoted Edinburgh 1997, p. 24)

It is not known whether the French style rococo frame in which the portrait has always hung is the one referred to in Sargent's letter.

When the portrait was exhibited at the Royal Academy in May 1893, Sir Noel wrote that 'Gerty's picture . . . was well hung', while noting that others thought it 'abominably badly hung in a corner of the first room'. It was, in any event, a triumph. In an undated letter [1893], Clementina Anstruther-Thomson wrote to Vernon Lee: 'As to Mr Sargent, London is at his feet. Mrs Hammersley & Mrs Lewis are at the New Gallery, Lady Agnew at the Academy. There can be no two opinions this year. He has had a cracking success' (CC). In a letter of 16 July 1893, Vernon Lee wrote to her mother: 'There is a talk of my going early in September [to Lochnaw] with Helen Dunham to her friend Lady Agnew, a very pretty woman whom John Sargent has just made into a society celebrity by a very ravishing portrait' (Vernon Lee's Letters 1937, p. 352).

Critical acclaim for the portrait was virtually unconditional. It was 'not only a triumph of technique but the finest example of portraiture, in the literal sense of the word, that has been seen here for a long time. While Mr Sargent has abandoned none of his subtlety, he has abandoned his mannerisms, and has been content to make a beautiful picture of a charming subject, under conditions of repose' (The Times, 29 April 1893, p. 13). The painting seemed strikingly modern in its synthesis of realistic portrayal, brilliant, impressionist response to light, exquisite tonal harmonies, and broad, liquid paint handling. The artist R. A. M. Stevenson identified the levels at which the portrait surprised and satisfied contemporary sensibilities: 'as a portrait, a decorative pattern, or a piece of well-engineered impressionistic painting, it tops everything in the Academy' (Art Journal, 1893, p. 242). He also analysed its bold and innovatory technical achievement:

He has shirked no difficulty in the problem before him of modelling the actual form and nuancing the real colour as light models and shades it. He has sought refuge in no cheaper solvent of tonality, whether brown, blue or gold . . . His brushwork boldly challenges you by presenting a definite tone for every inch of surface . . . he never permits some pleasantly warmed juice to veil his view of air, colour and form . . . These colours are sharp as nature, this combination of blues and violets with its acid flavour, as of wild fruit, somehow resolve like a tantalizing discord into a harmony subtler, and fuller, than those built on some obvious base of fundamental brown or yellow. (*Art Journal*, 1893, pp. 242–3)

The composition is consciously aesthetic and decorative in arrangement and in its use of costume, accessories and palette. Lady Agnew is wearing a gown of pearl-white silk with a broad mauve sash; she is holding a white flower – a rose, magnolia or camellia – and her only jewellery is a pendant, a broadly indicated stone or centre-piece in a turquoise and pearl setting, and a gold bangle on the left arm. She is seated to one side of a floral-covered Louis Quinze-style bergère (see Accessories, p. xxii, no. 2 a), with a turquoise silk (probably a late eighteenth- or early nineteenth-century Chinese hanging, with decorative calligraphy and floral motif), hanging in the background. It is probably the same silk as that in *Mrs George Gribble*, 1888 (see *Early Portraits*, no. 179), and *Mrs Charles Thursby* of 1897–8 (no. 360), and may be the same as that seen in a photograph of Sargent seated in his Paris studio (*Early Portraits*, fig. 31). Lady Agnew's graceful poise is beguiling and the characterization enigmatic; her quietly challenging gaze is compelling, and there is the suggestion of something withheld and inviting in her quizzical half-smile.

Sargent was elected an Associate of the Royal Academy in January 1894, and a *Sunday Times* critic wrote: 'The famous picture of Mrs [*sic*] Agnew which appeared on the line at the Academy in 1893 may be said to have made the election of Tuesday practicable. It supplied that evidence of solidity and seriousness of purpose, that understanding of the graver simplicities of effect which the startling work [*Mrs Hugh Hammersley*] at the New [Gallery] did not quite afford, and which was certainly not the "note" of the Carmencita [no. 234]' ('Art and Artists', *Sunday Times*, 14 January 1894, p. 8).

Two letters from Lady Agnew (28 July 1924 and 18 June 1925) to James Caw, director of the National Gallery of Scotland, about the sale of the painting are in the National Gallery of Scotland Archives, Edinburgh.

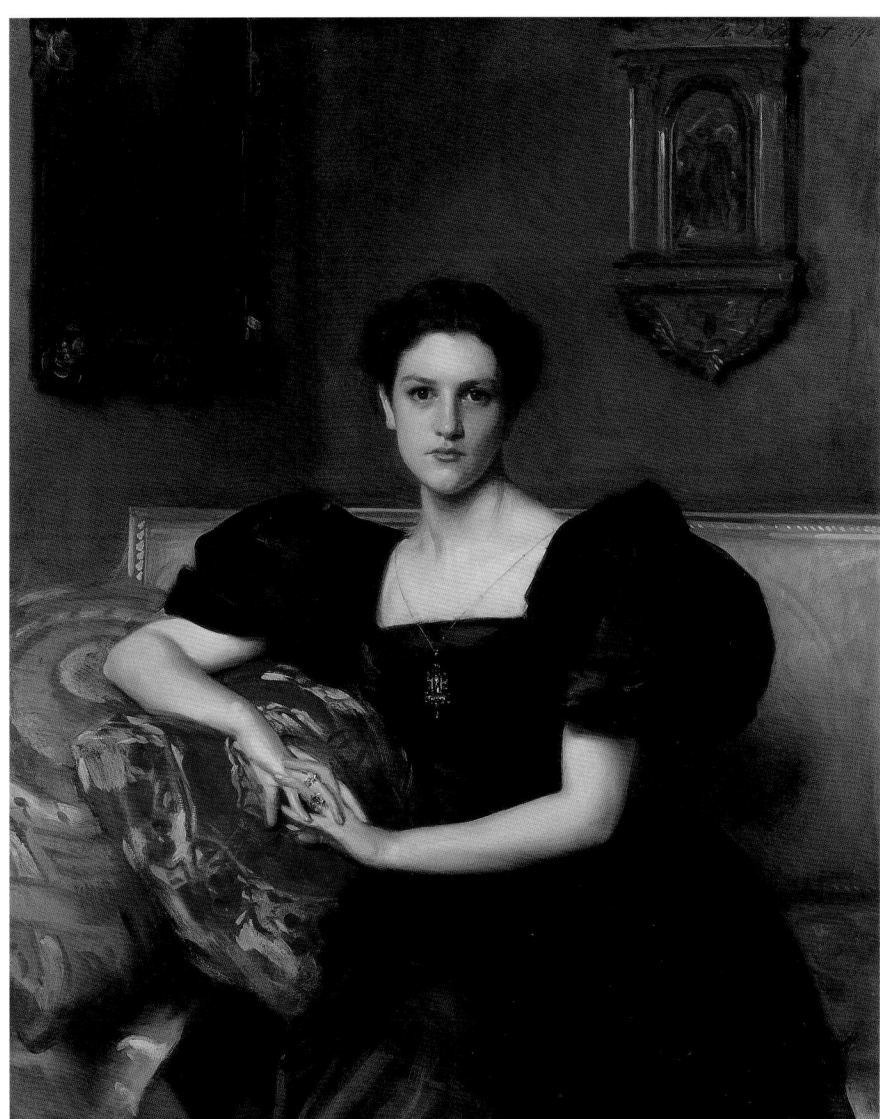

A mezzotint after the painting was engraved by Henry Macbeth-Raeburn in 1926 (see Edinburgh 1997, p. 92, ill.).

287 *Elizabeth Chanler*

1893
Oil on canvas, 49³⁄₈ × 40¹⁄₂ (125.4 × 102.9)
Inscribed, upper right: *John S. Sargent 1893*
National Museum of American Art, Washington, D.C.
Gift of Chanler A. Chapman

Elizabeth Chanler (1866–1937) daughter of John Winthrop Chanler, a Democratic congressman from New York, and his wife, Margaret (*née* Ward), a descendant of John Jacob Astor. She was the eldest of a family of three sisters and five brothers, all of them distinguished by intelligence and talent. Plagued by ill-health from childhood and naturally serious and withdrawn by temperament, she showed great resources of character in caring for the family after her mother's early death. In 1898, she married, as his second wife, the eminent critic and essayist John Jay Chapman, whose sisters Sargent had painted as long ago as

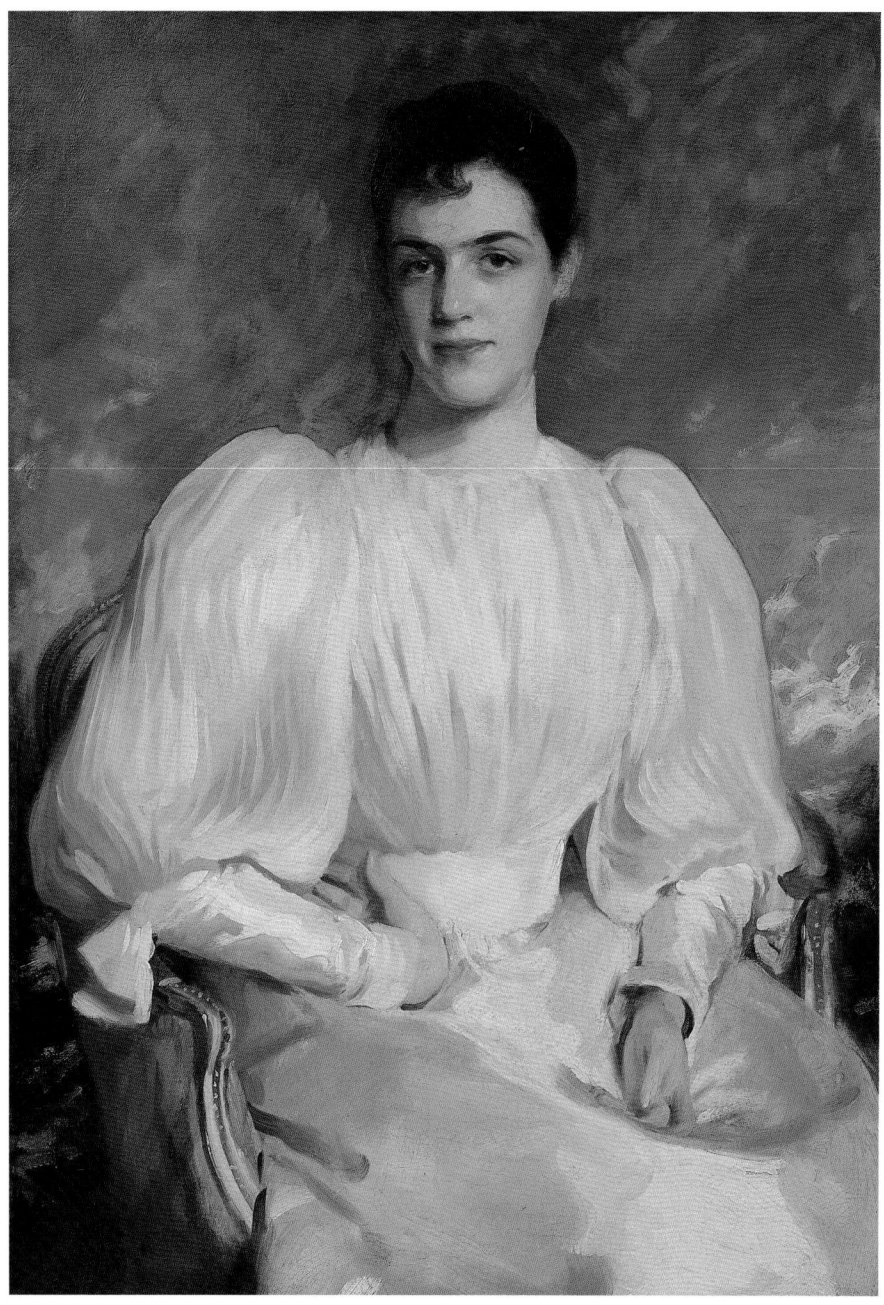

He paints people now while they are talking hard it is wonderful' (CC).

The picture is consciously in the style of the old masters, taking its cue from Velázquez. The black satin evening gown, with puffed leg-of-mutton sleeves and square-cut neck, is picturesquely old-fashioned, and its effect is reinforced by the use of antique accessories, the Renaissance pendant of red and green enamel she wears at her breast, the red and gold figured brocade cushions against which she leans, and the two pictures on the wall behind. The picture on the left appears to be the lower half of Sargent's copy of two figures from the *Regentesses of the Old Men's Almhouse* by Frans Hals (Birmingham Museum of Art, Alabama). On the right, a religious scene in a carved Florentine frame, perhaps the Italian school *Virgin and Child with an Angel Holding a Cross*, which was in the artist's sale, 1925, lot 294 (the frame, subsequently used for the *Study of a Bust at Lille*, is in a private collection). The Louis Seize-style settee appears in other portraits of this time (see Accessories, p. xxii, no. 1).

At the Royal Academy, the portrait aroused mixed reactions. The *Magazine of Art* praised its subtlety, *The Times* (5 May 1894, p. 16) admired the 'expression of intense intellectual interest' and the 'vigorous energy' but noted that the drawing of the arms was careless and the accessories not happy; the *Spectator* (12 May 1894, p. 652) wrote that Sargent's vision seemed 'to have lost its edge a little, and the execution accordingly its magic', while Claude Phillips, reporting for the *Academy* (2 June 1894, p. 460), regarded it as a 'portrait without a physiognomy'. Writing in his diary about the National Academy of Design exhibition of 1894, Theodore Robinson commented: 'I was disappointed in Sargent's Margaret [*sic*] Chanler, it seems to me common in color, and poorly, hastily conceived and carried out' (FARL).

1881 (see *Early Portraits* nos 33, 34). The Chapmans, Chanlers and Dunhams formed part of a close-knit circle in New York, all of them well known to the artist. Elizabeth Chanler is said to have bought *A Street in Venice* (National Gallery of Art, Washington, D.C.) from the St Botolph Club exhibition in 1888 and presented it as a gift to the architect Stanford White.

The portrait was painted in London in June 1893, where Elizabeth was staying for the marriage of her brother Robert, to Julia Chamberlain. It was commissioned by her sister Margaret (letter from her to McKibbin, 15 August 1956, McKibbin papers). Writing to Charles Fairchild on 1 June 1893, Sargent asked him to tell Sattie (Fairchild's daughter Sally) that 'I am painting her friend Bessie Chanler' (Boston Athenaeum, Sargent Papers, box 1, folder 15). Kit Anstruther-Thomson, who visited Sargent's studio at this time, wrote in a letter of June 1893 to Vernon Lee that he was 'painting a Miss Chandler [*sic*] it is beautiful,

288 *Elsie Wagg*

c. 1893
Oil on canvas, 39½ × 27½ (100.4 × 69.8)
Inscribed, twice (upper and lower left): *John S. Sargent*
Private Collection

Elsie Wagg (1876–1949) was the daughter of Arthur Wagg, a director of the merchant bankers Herbert Wagg & Co. Ltd of London, and his wife Mathilde Merton. The youngest of five children, she never married, devoting herself to public work. She was honorary secretary of the East Sussex County Nursing Association, and the originator of the National Gardens Scheme, a charity founded in 1927 to raise money for district nursing services.

The circumstances of the commission are unknown. The date of the portrait is given in the 1926 Royal Academy catalogue, probably correctly.

According to the sitter's brother A. R. Wagg (to McKibbin, 18 March 1947, McKibbin papers), when Sargent saw the portrait again after a lapse of years, 'he did not like either the frame or the background. With great kindness, therefore, he presented us with a new frame, and also painted in a new background.'

The sitter wears a cream-coloured gown, with fitted muslin bodice, high neck and leg-of-mutton sleeves; the skirt is of a heavier satin. Her hair is close-cropped, and she is seated in a low bergère chair, her right wrist bent and resting on the hip. The bergère chair is of the kind much employed by Sargent throughout the nineties, though this is a smaller and more compact chair than those he generally employed (see Accessories, p. xxii, no. 2d). The bent wrist on the hip can be paralleled in several portraits of this period, for example *Flora Priestley* and *Mrs Edward Davis and her Son Livingston* (see *Early Portraits*, no. 225, and no. 250). The background, intended to represent a generalized skyscape of blues and whites, seems unrelated to the figure; it is not surprising to discover that it was an afterthought.

In 1914 Sargent executed a charcoal of the sitter's mother, Mrs Arthur Wagg.

289 *Mrs Mahlon Day Sands*

1893–4
Oil on canvas, 50 × 35½ (127 × 90.2)
Inscribed, upper left: *John S. Sargent*
Private Collection

Mrs Mahlon Day Sands, *née* Mary Hartpeace (1854–1896) was the eldest daughter of the Reverend Alanson Hartpeace and his wife, Martha Morton. In 1872, at the age of eighteen, she married a wealthy New York businessman Mahlon Sands, then recently widowed. In 1874, they moved to London and Mrs Sands's dazzling beauty immediately made an impact on society. She and her husband became part of the Prince of Wales's set and moved easily in the highest circles. Their eldest child, Ethel Sands, became an artist and collector of distinction. Mahlon Sands died in a riding accident in 1888, his widow continued to live in London, where she had many notable friends including W. E. Gladstone and Henry James.

It was through James that Mrs Sands and the artist were introduced, and the progress of the portrait is well documented in Mrs Sands's correspondence with both men (Private Collection). In an undated letter to Mrs Sands, James wrote, offering what he called 'a bushel of good advice . . . of the policy of self surrender to the artist' (Edel 1980, p. 456). Sargent was fastidious about the choice of gown, wanting something with 'the style of body of a year or two ago. I liked the colour of the one you wore last night immensely but I have in my mind the recollection of what you let me do

a sketch of you in, a few years ago'. In the letters, there is an undercurrent of dissatisfaction with the portrait, and talk of a second attempt: 'If our new one is half as good as it ought to be perhaps with one accord we will join hands and dance round a bonfire of the old one – but in the meantime we will spare its life, and perhaps take it up again if my artistic conscience feels differently to what it does now.' Sargent decided to keep faith with the original picture: 'On seeing the portrait again I am bound to say that I like it better than my recollection of it – and I think I see my way to carrying it through to our mutual satisfaction.' When James saw it, he thought it 'almost uncannily, like you, with admirable eyes and a most characteristic regard . . . wonderfully fair and pearly', though he expressed reservations about the painting of the face, which he felt needed 'simplifying a little', and about the position of the right arm, which seemed 'a little meaningless'.

In July 1893, Mrs Sands wrote to her daughter Ethel:

> You will be glad to hear that I had another and most satisfactory sitting with the portrait, and the change of chair, (the blue one has been introduced and made larger), is an immense improvement. The hands have been moved a little (still hold a fan!) and the general effect and lines are very good, and I must say that Mr Sargent is right and the present pose and composition as a whole is really finer than the sketch. There is more dignity in it. I felt I must have one more sitting and reach a solution which has been done and we both leave it in peace. It will be quite a clear path now to the end.

There must, however, have been further sittings because it was not until February 1894 that Sargent was able to write: 'The portrait is practically finished and I shall not need any more sittings.'

The oil sketch (no. 290) shows Mrs Sands seated in a chair, but this was exchanged in the finished picture for the Louis Seize sofa (see Accessories, p. xxii, no. 1). Mrs Sands rests her right arm on a large red velvet cushion with a bolster below it. She is dressed in a creamy satin evening gown fringed with lace, and wears a diamond crescent in her hair, reminiscent of that worn by Madame Pierre Gautreau (*Early Portraits*, no. 114), a pearl necklace and three loops of pearls across her bosom secured by a diamond brooch. The French eighteenth-century panelling in the background is different from the doors which Sargent habitually used as studio props (see Accessories, p. xxiii, no. 17).

Sargent was reluctant to exhibit the picture at the Royal Academy 'I haven't been an Academician long enough to show anything so correct', and 'I really dread the verdict of your friends and admirers who will be certain to find it lacking, as I do, in charm, especially in the horrid surroundings of an exhibition.' The correspondence is quoted at

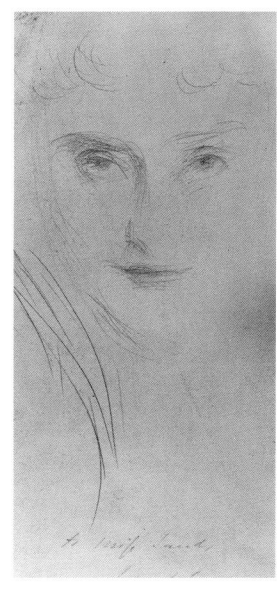

fig. 49 *Mrs Mahlon Day Sands*. Pencil on paper, 7 ½ × 3 ½ (19 × 9). Private Collection.

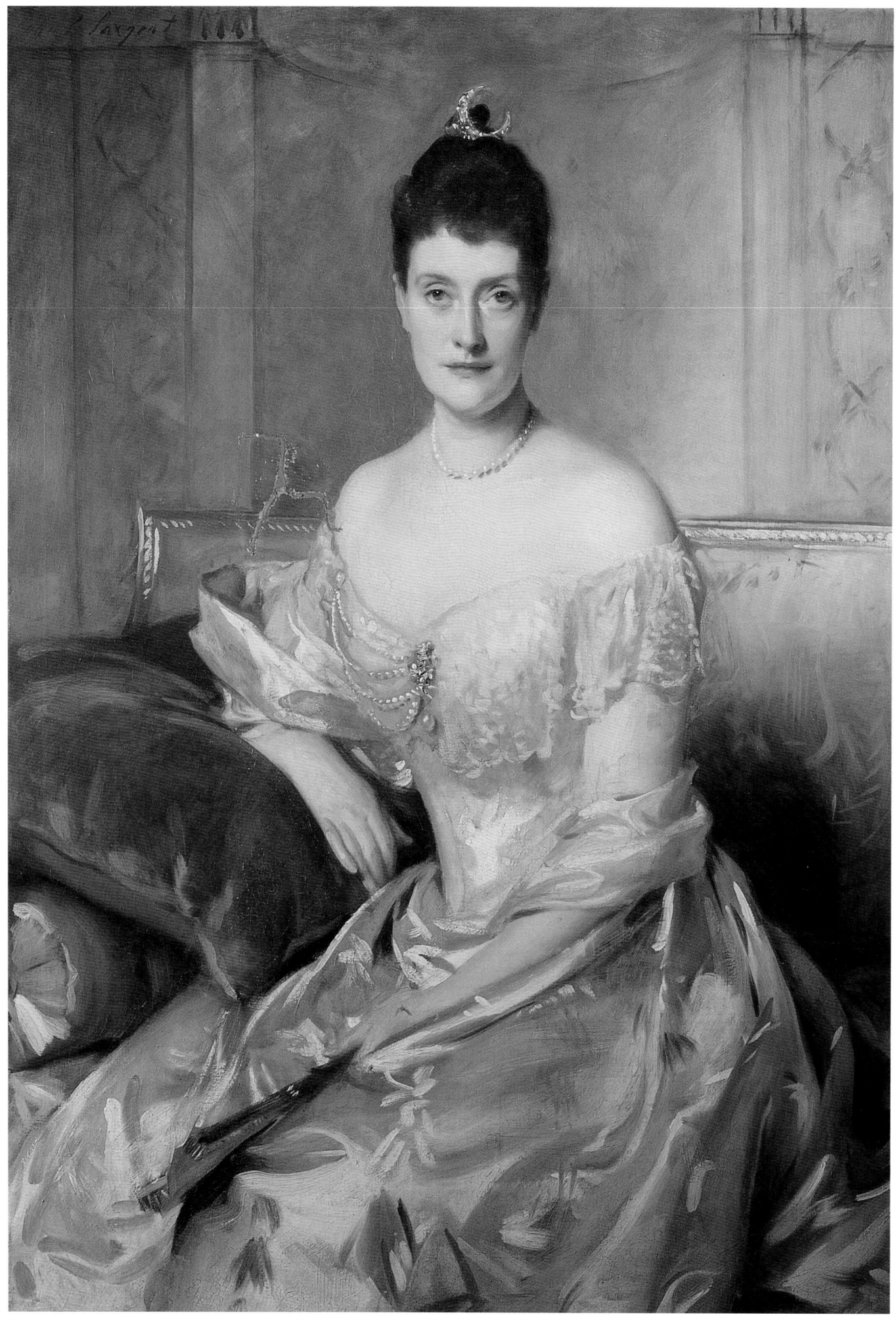

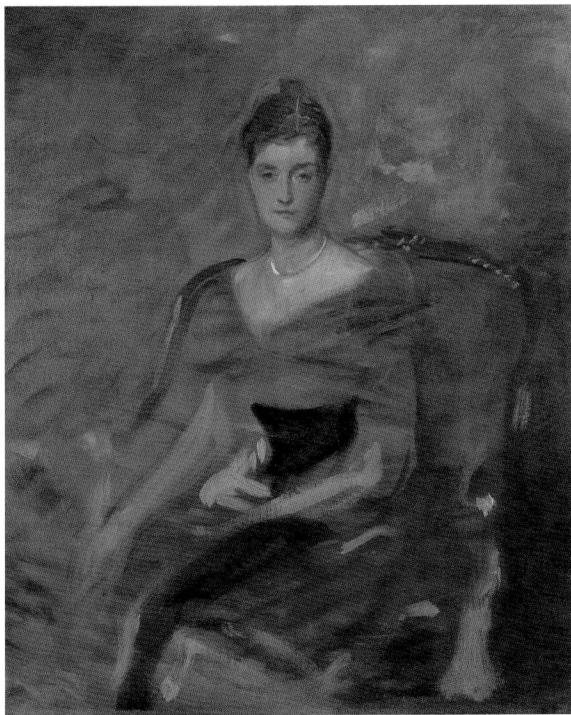

greater length in Wendy Baron, *Miss Ethel Sands and Her Circle*, London, 1977, pp. 24–6.

Two pencil studies of the sitter, listed as in the collection of her daughter, were in the Sargent memorial exhibition in London in 1926 (nos 232 and 237). One of these is presumably the small pencil sketch (fig. 49) inscribed 'to Miss Sands / John S. Sargent', which was sold Christie's, London, 12 June 1970, lot 19. McKibbin dates this drawing *c.* 1886, Paris, though it might arguably be of a similar date to the present oil. McKibbin also lists a drawing of *c.* 1883, Paris, 'in a green Alexandra bonnet' (untraced), which the compilers have not seen.

290 *Mrs Mahlon Day Sands*

c. 1893
Oil on canvas, 30 × 25 (76.2 × 63.5)
Inscribed, upper right: *to Mrs Sands / John S. Sargent*; upper left (in pencil): *Tuesday*
Bernard Osher

This preliminary oil sketch for no. 289 shows Mrs Sands seated in one of Sargent's French bergère chairs (see Accessories, p. xxii, no. 2b). The set of the head is similar to that in the finished work, but the costume, with its black sash and gauzy shawl, is quite different.

291 *Louis Alexander Fagan*

1893
Oil on canvas, 30¼ × 25¼ (77 × 64.2)
Inscribed, across top: *to my friend Fagan John S. Sargent 1893*
Private Collection

Louis Alexander Fagan (1846–1903) was born in Naples, the son of the English representative at the Court of the Two Sicilies. He was an etcher and became keeper of prints at the British Museum, and he wrote a biography of Sir Anthony Panizzi in 1880. He married Frances Purves in 1887. For an obituary and a list of his published works, see *Magazine of Art*, 1, new series (1903), pp. 311–12.

The informal study is reminiscent of Sargent's earlier portraits of fellow artists, for example those of Charles Giron and Jacques-Emile Blanche (see *Early Portraits*, nos 148, 155). Little is known about the friendship between the two men, though Fagan was a friend of Vernon Lee's brother Eugene (see *Vernon Lee's Letters* 1937, p. 121), which is one possible connection. The early history of the painting is also unclear. A label visible in a reproduction

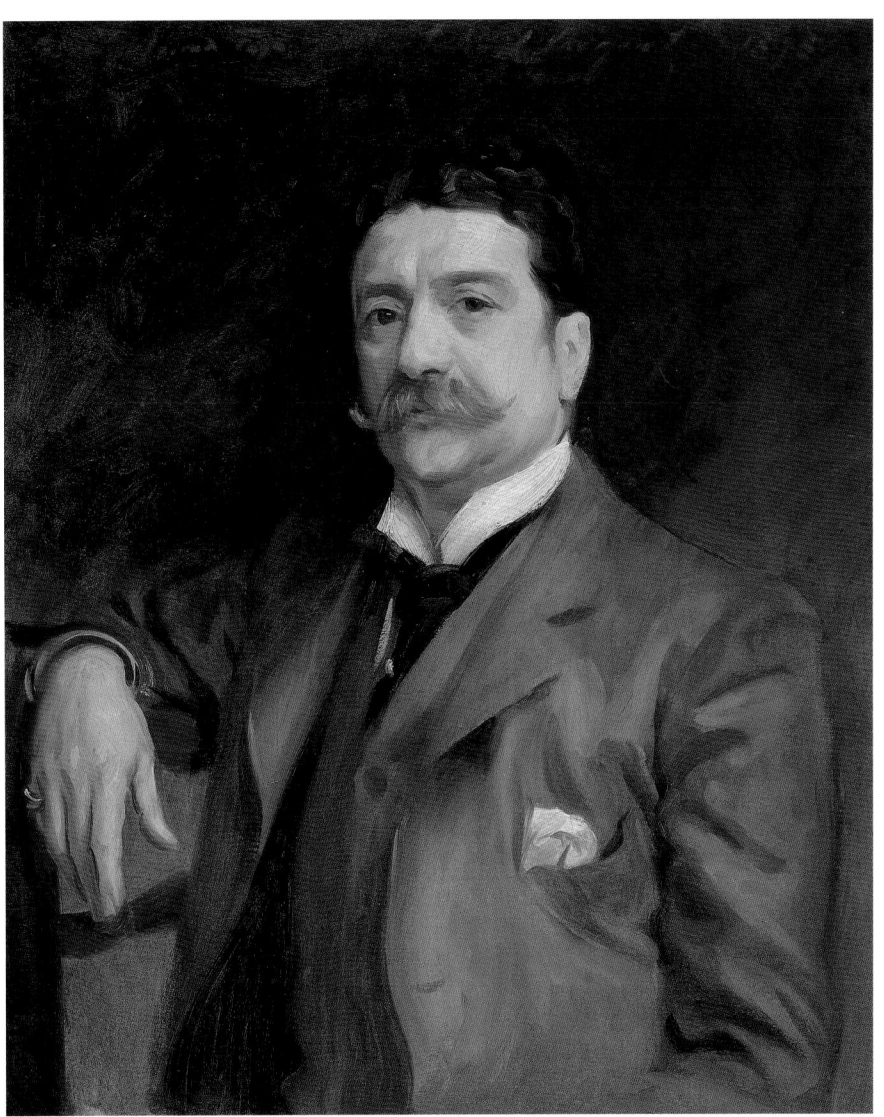

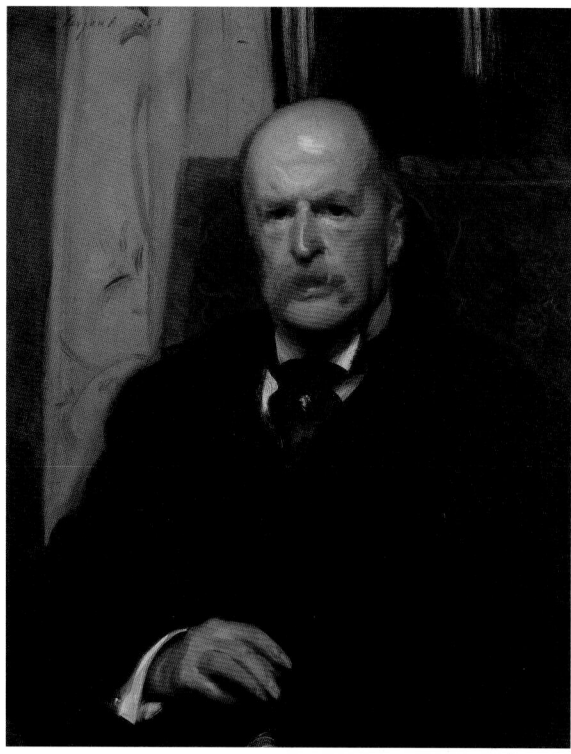

in the *Magazine of Art* (April 1903) reads 'Presented by John S. Sargent ARA 1894', which suggests that Sargent presented the picture to an institution, possibly a London club (Fagan was a popular figure at the Arts Club and at the Reform Club in London). The painting resurfaced at a London auction in 1966, but its location in the intervening period is uncertain.

Julius Weitzner found a second canvas, an unfinished landscape scene with two figures, on the same stretcher. According to McKibbin's notes, an old note on the stretcher reads 'in Fladbury 1893' (McKibbin papers), but any visit Sargent may have made to Fladbury in 1893 is unconfirmed at present.

292 Henry Augustus Cram

1893
Oil on canvas, 30 × 25¼ (76.2 × 64.1)
Inscribed, upper left: *John S. Sargent 1893*
Private Collection

Henry Augustus Cram (1815–1894), who was educated at Harvard, later became a member of the New York Bar. He married Katherine Sergeant in 1849. He is painted seated in a seventeenth-century-style armchair (see Accessories, p. xxii, no. 10), with a figured curtain or hanging behind and two vertical reeded strips of woodwork, possibly representing a frame.

Sargent painted the sitter's granddaughter Charlotte Winthrop Cram in 1900 (no. 391).

293 Mrs Frederick Mead

1893
Oil on canvas, 33⅜ × 24 (84.8 × 61)
Inscribed, across top: *to Mrs Abbey from her friend John S. Sargent 1893*
Yale University Art Gallery, New Haven, Connecticut. Edwin Austin Abbey Memorial Collection

Mrs Frederick Mead (1822–1897), *née* Mary Eliza Scribner, was the daughter of Samuel and Julia Ambler Scribner. In 1842, she married Frederick Mead of the tea merchants Frederick Mead & Co. Their daughter, Mary Gertrude, married Sargent's friend, the artist Edwin Abbey, in 1890. In the early 1890s, Mrs Mead lived at Morgan Hall, Fairford, with her daughter and son-in-law, at the time when the latter and Sargent were working on the murals for the Boston Public Library.

Sargent painted a second oil portrait of Mrs Mead (no. 294) and a water-colour (no. 295). He inscribed an oil study of a calf as a gift to her: 'to Mrs Mead with a Merry Xmas John S. Sargent' (Yale University Art Gallery, 1937.4156).

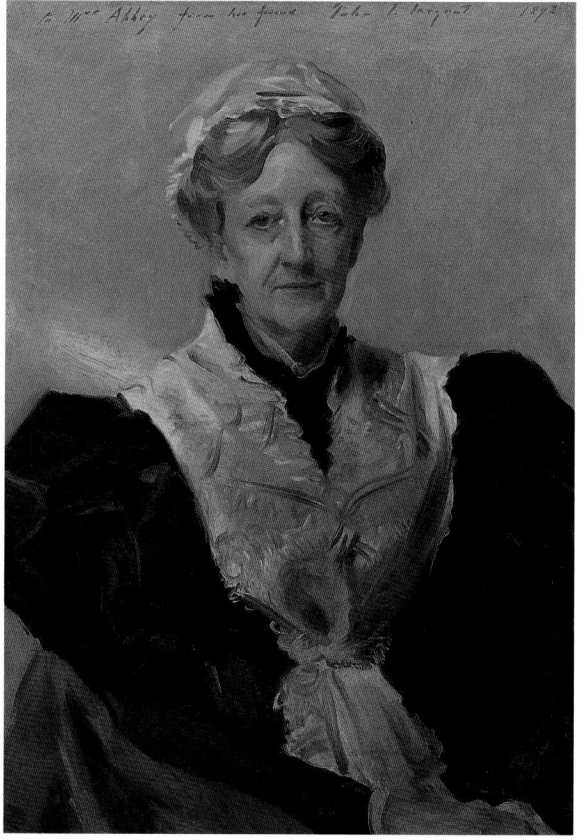

294 *Mrs Frederick Mead*

c. 1893
Oil on canvas, 26¾ × 20⅜ (67.9 × 51.8)
Inscribed, upper right: *John S. Sargent*
Yale University Art Gallery, New Haven,
Connecticut. Edwin Austin Abbey Memorial
Collection

A second portrait of Mrs Mead, probably similar in
date to no. 293.

295 *Mrs Frederick Mead*

c. 1893
Pencil and black ink wash on paper, 14 × 10
(35.5 × 25.2)
Inscribed, across the top: *to Mrs Abbey from her friend
/ John S. Sargent*
Yale University Art Gallery, New Haven,
Connecticut. Edwin Austin Abbey Memorial
Collection

Mrs Mead is seated. She wears a dark dress and
muslin cap, and holds a fan. This wash drawing was
no. 324 in the Abbey estate.

296 *Hercules Brabazon Brabazon*

c. 1893–5
Oil on canvas, 28⅞ × 17 (73.3 × 43.2)
Inscribed, upper left: *to Mr Brabazon*; upper right:
John S. Sargent
National Portrait Gallery, London

Hercules Brabazon Brabazon, *né* Hercules Brabazon
Sharpe (1821–1906), was the son of Hercules
Sharpe from Black Halls, County Durham, and Ann
Brabazon, from County Mayo, Ireland. He was born
in Paris, educated at Harrow and Trinity College,
Cambridge, and studied painting in Rome. He
inherited estates in Ireland in 1847, becoming
Hercules Brabazon Brabazon, and Oaklands estate
in Sussex in 1858, where he settled. He travelled
widely and became a prolific water-colourist. He
first exhibited publicly at the New English Art Club
in 1891 and was at once recognized as a master of
the medium.

Brabazon, who had pursued water-colour
painting as a largely private pastime, was over-
whelmed by the extent of his triumph when, at
the insistence of his friends, he first opened his
portfolios to the public. This retiring, cultivated
country gentleman became an artistic celebrity
almost overnight. There was no greater admirer of
his brilliant, impressionistic water-colour landscapes than Sargent, who first met him around
1886–7 (Charteris 1927, p. 224) and who wrote
the introduction to his first one-man show at the
Goupil Gallery, London, in 1892: 'Each sketch is a

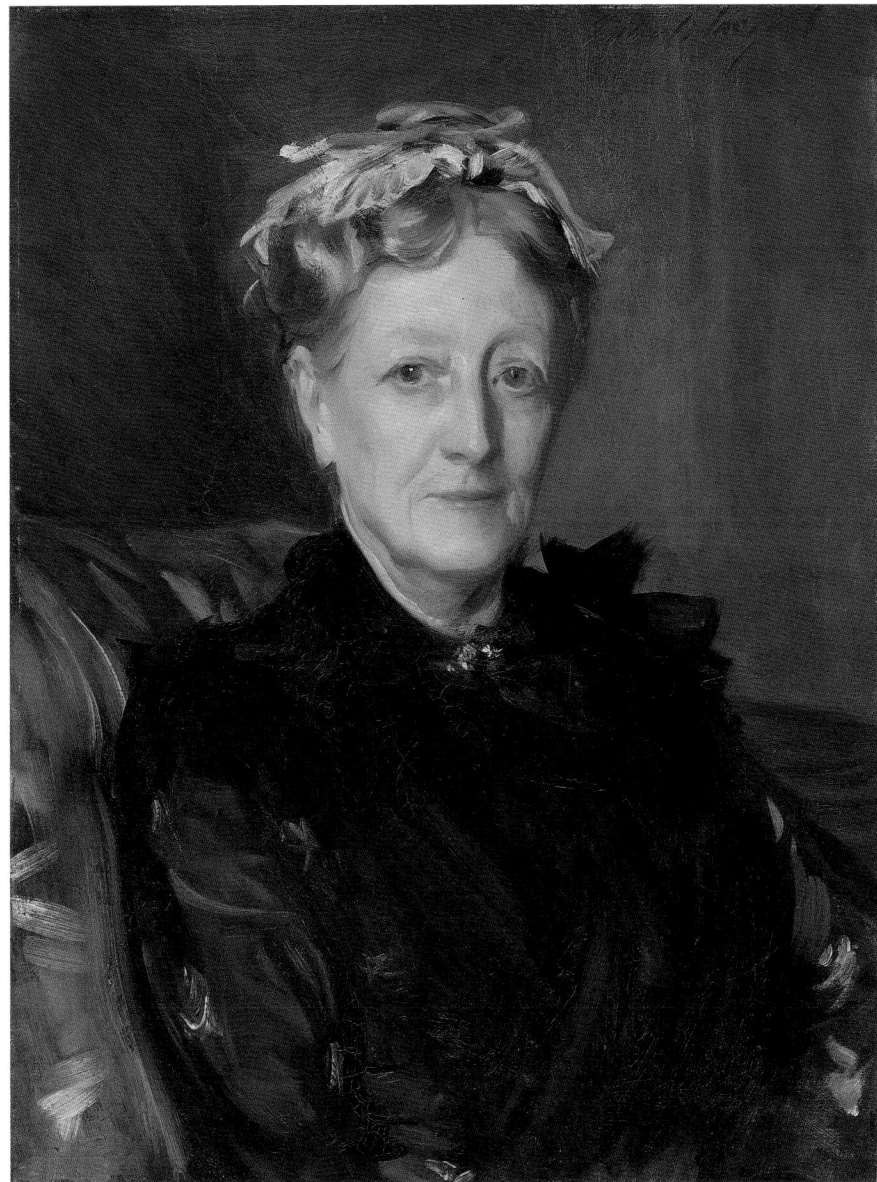

294

295

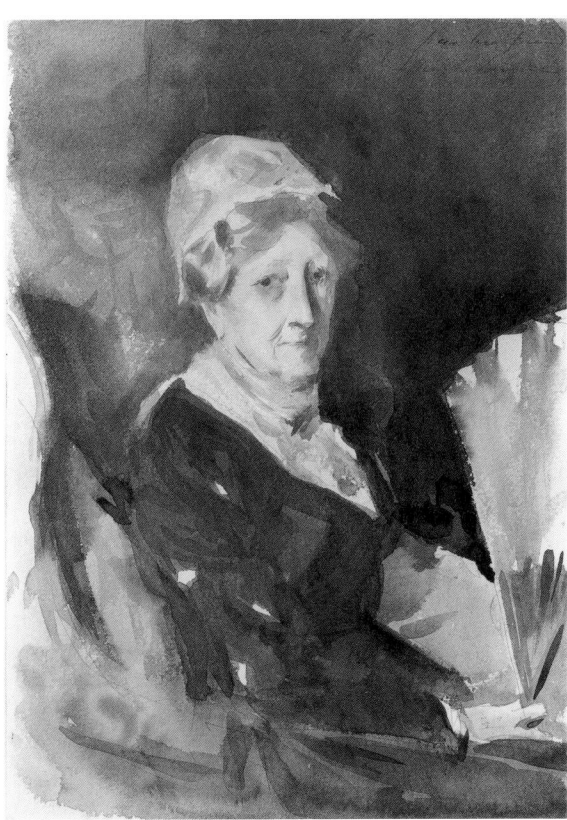

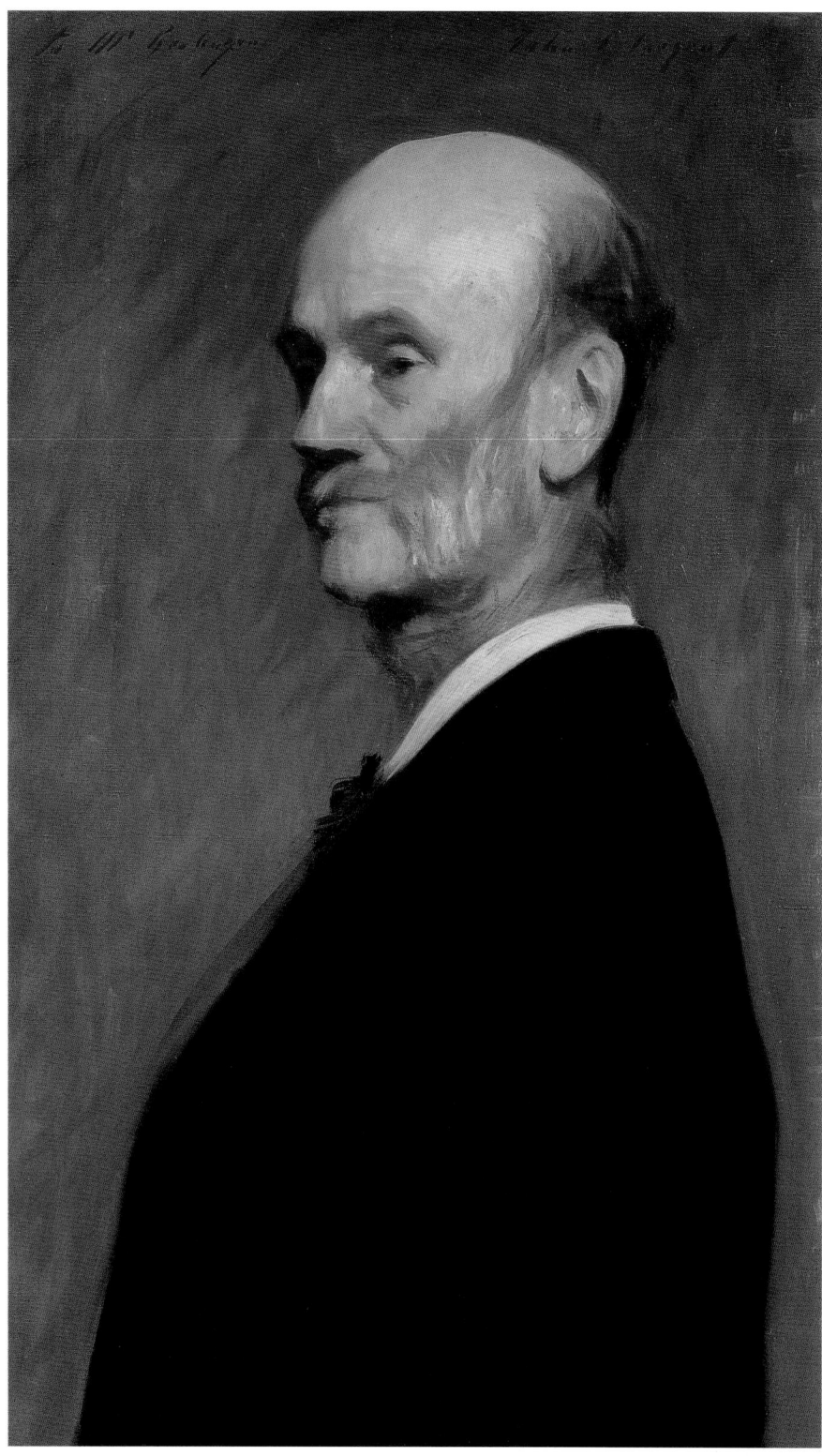

296

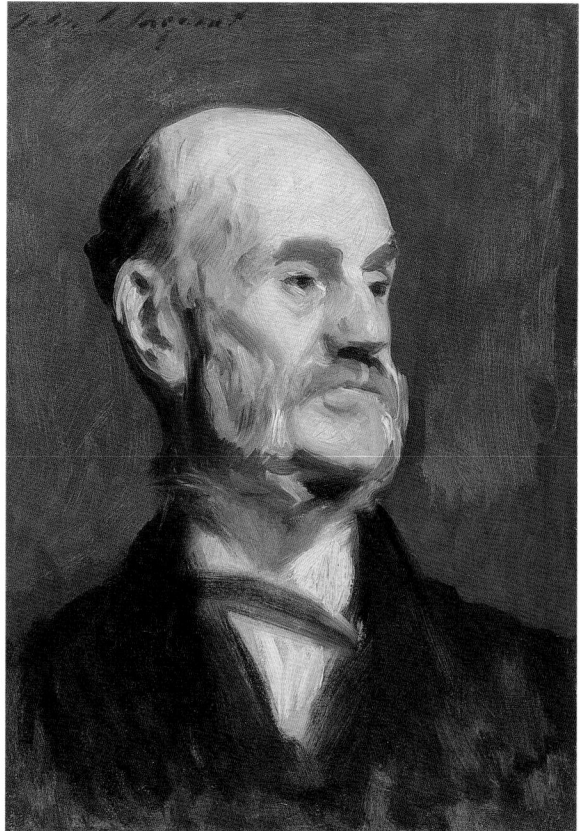

may have been influenced by that of his friend.

Charteris and McKibbin date the two oil portraits of Brabazon to 1900, Mount to 1893. In style and format, they can be compared to the portraits of Coventry Patmore (nos 302, 303), and the early 1890s seems the more plausible date. The colour of the background fabric is similar in effect to that shown in the portrait of Lady Agnew (no. 286).

297 *Hercules Brabazon Brabazon*

c. 1893–5
Oil on canvas, 22¼ × 16 (56.5 × 40.6)
Inscribed, upper left: *John S. Sargent*
National Museum of Wales, Cardiff

A second spirited sketch of Brabazon, painted at about the same period as no. 296. A drawing of very similar format but showing the head more full-face (untraced) is illustrated in C. Lewis Hind, *Hercules Brabazon Brabazon 1821–1906: His Art and Life*, London, 1912, frontispiece. A second drawing is in the Metropolitan Museum of Art, New York (fig. 50).

A water-colour of Sargent by Brabazon, inscribed 'Sore gent', is in a private collection.

new delight of harmony, and the harmonies are innumerable and unexpected, taken from Nature or rather imposed by her. Immediate sensations flower again in Mr. Brabazon's drawings, with a swiftness that makes one for the time forget that there has been a medium.' The manuscript draft of Sargent's note in the Goupil Gallery catalogue and the letters from him to Brabazon about the exhibition were with the Albany Gallery, London, 1968. Sargent encouraged everyone to buy Brabazon's work (he bought many himself) and remained a close friend of the artist until the latter's death. His own style as a water-colourist

If critical recognition was intermittant and success elusive in the mid-1880s, the mid-1890s, in contrast, ushered in a decade of unremitting work. Sargent no longer had the time to experiment, or to undertake new work on his own behalf, as had been the case while he was still struggling to gain recognition. He was running a full-time, professional portrait practice. There was a short visit to America in the spring of 1895, and occasional field trips to Europe in pursuit of material for the Boston Public Library murals, but little else to relieve his intense schedule of work. In 1897 he complained to a friend that he was painting three sitters a day 'with scarcely an interval between each sitting'.[1]

During the six years from 1894 to 1899, Sargent painted approximately seventy-five portraits, or an average of twelve a year. If one discounts the first two years, when phase one of the Boston murals was in course of completion and installation, the average number rises to fourteen. Of these portraits over seventy per cent were either groups, full-lengths or three-quarter-lengths. Female portraits outnumber those of men by twenty per cent, with a much higher predominance of female full-lengths and three-quarter-lengths.

Sargent's sitters represent a wide cross-section of English and American society. For George Vanderbilt he painted full-length portraits of the architect and the designer who had created for him the great mansion and gardens of the Biltmore estate in North Carolina, Richard Morris Hunt and Frederick Law Olmstead (nos 319, 320). Together with the flamboyant full-length of Mrs Walter Bacon (no. 326) they joined an existing gallery of Sargent portraits at Biltmore, making Vanderbilt his most important patron of the 1890s. Another American patron, Mrs Whitin, commissioned the full-length portrait of the distinguished actress, Ada Rehan (no. 308). Among singers and musicians, one can single out the dazzling full-length portrait of Mrs George Swinton (no. 327) and the much smaller portrait of Mrs George Batten (no. 340), who is shown in the act of singing, head thrown back, eyes closed. The portrait of the elderly English poet Coventry Patmore (no. 302) was a commission, but that of the artist

and aesthete W. Graham Robertson (no. 306) was painted at the artist's request.

The majority of Sargent's male portraits were drawn from the worlds of business, politics and the law. A significant number painted later in the decade were official commissions painted for a sponsoring organization, like those of Francis Cranmer Penrose (no. 350) for the Royal Institute of British Architects in London, of which he was president; Sir Thomas Sutherland (no. 349) for the P.&O. Steamship Company, of which he was chairman; Lord Watson (no. 351) for the Faculty of Advocates in Edinburgh; Sir David Richmond (no. 378) for the Corporation of Glasgow, of which he was Lord Provost, and James Coolidge Carter and Joseph Choate (nos 380, 381) for the Harvard Club, New York, for which both served as president.

The two most distinguished statesmen to sit to Sargent at this period were the English MP Joseph Chamberlain (no. 333) and the American senator Calvin Brice (no. 346). Other notable figures in public life include the Lord Chief Justice of England, Lord Russell of Killowen (nos 375–7); the successful soldier Colonel Ian Hamilton (nos 352, 353); the British armaments manufacturer Colonel T. E. Vickers (no. 334); the American banker and philanthropist Henry G. Marquand (no. 343); the American ambassador to Britain Thomas Francis Bayard (no. 342), later secretary of state; the London lawyers Sir George Lewis and Arthur Cohen (nos 335, 344); and the Bond Street art dealer Asher Wertheimer (no. 347). The portraits of the last named sitter and that of his wife (no. 348) herald the great sequence of Wertheimer portraits, which constitute the largest single act of Sargent patronage.

Sargent's female sitters reflect a similarly wide spectrum of social types and occupations. There are foreign grandees, including Countess Clary Aldringen and Princess Demidoff (nos 325, 328), but as yet relatively few representatives of the British aristocracy: the Honourable Laura Lister in 1896 (no. 323) and the three Wyndham sisters and the Honourable Victoria Stanley (nos 368, 369) at the end of the decade. There are wives of bankers and businessmen, among them Mrs Carl Meyer,

Detail of no. 324, *Mrs Carl Meyer and her Children.*

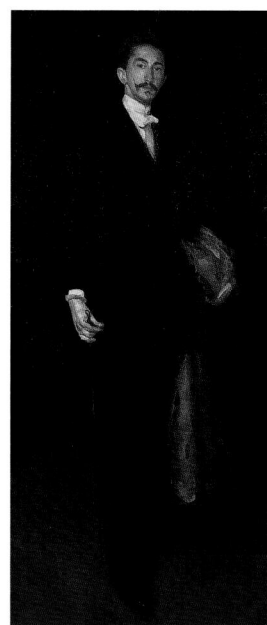

fig. 51 James Abbott McNeill Whistler, *Arrangement in Black and Gold: Comte Robert de Montesquiou-Fezensac*, 1891-2. Oil on canvas, 82 ⅛ × 36 ⅛ (208.6 × 91.8). Frick Collection, New York.

Mrs Charles Huntington, Lady Faudel-Philips and Mrs Charles Hunter (nos 324, 361, 362, 363); American heiresses, Mrs I. N. Phelps Stokes, Pauline Astor and Daisy Leiter (nos 337, 357, 358), and the wives of artist and musical friends like Mrs William Wyllie, Mrs Colin Hunter and Mrs William Shakespeare (nos 313, 330, 331), whose portraits were presented to them as gifts. Sargent's sitters also include a number of women distinguished in their own right, including pioneers of women's rights. Mrs Ernest Franklin (no. 356), for example, was a social liberal, active in a number of progressive causes, and Mrs Joshua Montgomery Sears (no. 370) was a notable artist and photographer, but their portraits can barely be differentiated from those of other fashionable Sargent sitters, whereas Jane Evans, the last Eton dame, Octavia Hill, founder of the English National Trust, and M. Carey Thomas, principal of Bryn Mawr College, Pennsylvania (nos 365, 366, 373), are represented as working women in an altogether more solemn and austere style. These last three portraits were all commissions arranged by friends and admirers of the sitters.

Inevitably, given the number of commissions he received, Sargent could no longer afford the luxury of treating each one as a wholly new challenge. He relies on a fairly limited repertoire of formats and poses, costumes and accessories, which he reworks and reinvents. What is remarkable in his great portraits is the way in which he transcends these conventions to get to the heart of a life and a personality. We see the person rather than the work of art. Where so many English portraitists became dull through repetition, Sargent's virtuosity as a painter, his ability to look at the world with a keen and fresh eye, and to startle the viewer by the unfamiliar juxtaposition of elements, gives his work a vitality and edge. The touch is sure, the paint is applied in broad and exciting brushstrokes, the spaces gleam with real light and colour.

The full-length, standing female figure remains a dominant portrait type throughout the 1890s and beyond. Sargent's sitters are often dressed in sweeping white evening gowns, and posed before studio accessories which are intended to proclaim their wealth and importance. The portrait of Ada Rehan may be regarded as the source of the type, a statuesque and majestic figure in an off-the-shoulder ball gown, holding a feather fan, and placed before a seventeenth-century Flemish tapestry, which is, in contrast to her figure, full of action and movement. The same tapestry appears in the background of Countess Clary Aldringen (no. 325), though it is separated from the sitter by the broad seat of a Louis Seize sofa (another familiar studio prop). This acts as a foil to her pencil-thin figure in a white gown, with the train draped across the sofa, a composition that echoes the 1883 portrait of Mrs Henry White (*Early Portraits*, no. 105). Mrs George Swinton is posed against the French eighteenth-century boiserie

panel in Sargent's studio, with her hand on the back of a small French armchair. Like Ada Rehan and the countess, she is dressed in a magnificent white gown, with a spreading train and silvery satin cape, passages of which read as a painterly discourse on the qualities of different white fabrics.

Later in the decade, Sargent poses some of his sitters out of doors, for example Pauline Astor and Daisy Leiter (nos 357, 358). They are light and youthful figures in similar white gowns and situated with similar elegance and poise. The backgrounds are painted backcloths rather than real landscapes, in obvious imitation of eighteenth-century English portraits. Mrs Phelps Stokes, with her husband sequestered in shadows behind her (no. 337), stands out in vivid contrast to the glamorous display of the society set. This is a spirited young woman, patrician and poised, whose crisp, flowing, black and white outfit betoken the independence and resourcefulness of the modern American woman, the 'Gibson Girl' of contemporary illustrations.[2] Not only is the imagery of the picture startlingly original, but Sargent paints it in a style that emphasizes texture and outline in a powerfully economical and controlled manner.

There are variations on the full-length standing format. Mrs Frederick Roller (no. 311) is dressed in black, and is no less commanding or fashionable than her 'sisters' in white, and the sensuous curves of the background panelling, which serve to frame the lines of her figure, also provide the key to her sophisticated taste. Mrs Charles Huntington (no. 361) is an enigmatic figure in a Velázquez-inspired composition that emphasizes half-lights and shadows. She stands in a severe black gown, relieved by a frilly white jabot at the neck, with her hand on the back of a high-backed seventeenth-century style armchair.

The three-quarter-length portraits of standing women are closely allied to the full-lengths in terms of composition. The sitters are dressed in evening gowns, mostly in white, and posed before the same range of accessories: the boiserie panelling, a floral hanging, the Chinese lacquer screen, a French Empire table, a Louis Quinze bureau and a Bechstein piano. Fans or costume accessories provide occupation for hands. The portraits in this formal style include *Mrs Ernest Hills, Princess Demidoff, Catherine Vlasto, Mrs Charles Anstruther-Thomson* and *Mrs Asher Wertheimer* (nos 312, 328, 339, 355, 348).

From *Mrs Hugh Hammersley* and *Lady Agnew of Lochnaw* via *Mrs Carl Meyer and her Children* to *Lady Elcho, Mrs Adeane and Mrs Tennant* (*The Wyndham Sisters*) one can trace the evolution of that most characteristic of Sargent designs: the seated portrait. The sitters are either, like Lady Agnew of Lochnaw, relaxed and passive, encased in their round bergère chairs, or like, Mrs Hugh Hammersley and Mrs Charles Thursby, nervously perched on the edge of their seats as if about to spring up. The portrait group of Mrs Carl Meyer and her children forms a bridge between these opposing principles. The steeply foreshortened perspective, which makes Mrs Meyer appear to be on the point of sliding out of the space, provides the dynamic, while the sitter's dress, spreading out to fill the lower part of the picture, is decorative and expansive, stabilizing the composition.

The step from *Mrs Carl Meyer and her Children* to *Lady Elcho, Mrs Adeane and Mrs Tennant* is not an enormous one artistically, but it represents a significant leap in terms of social class and tone. The three sitters, reclining luxuriously against huge cushions in a colour scheme of white on white, are rarified creatures of sensitivity and refinement; beautiful and untouchable, self-confident and aloof, they are as much objects of beauty as the furnishings and accessories around them. The large shadowy space above them serves to enhance their air of grandeur and high breeding. In spite of its appearance of luxurious and passive indolence, the composition has a strong diagonal thrust from left to right, and the contrast between the rich ensemble of silks and satins and flowers below and the empty space above is deliberately dramatic. This is Sargent at his most daring, creating a sense of theatre from the relationship, or lack of it, between the three women, and the mysterious world they inhabit.

Lady Elcho, Mrs Adeane and Mrs Tennant is the high point of the seated portrait, but, among other examples, is the group of portraits distinguished by the use of the bergère armchair in the relaxed style of *Lady Agnew of Lochnaw*, including *Mrs Ian Hamilton*, *Mrs Harold Wilson* and *Mrs Ernest Franklin* (nos 329, 338, 356). The bergère armchair is sometimes substituted by a squarer form of chair better suited to the character of challenging personalities as diverse as the Lord Mayor's consort, Lady Faudel-Phillips, and M. Carey Thomas, the university principal (nos 362, 373).

While portrait formats play a part in Sargent's production, his most original works transcend traditional formulae. He was compelled to purify and refine, highlighting and sometimes exaggerating his sitters' salient features, apostrophizing a range of social and psychological types. In a rare insight into his motivation, he confided to Daisy Warwick (see no. 484): 'I must have a type to paint . . . a type that expresses a phase of humanity'.[3] It is this quality that distinguishes a portrait such as that of Asher Wertheimer, which A. C. R. Carter described as best displaying 'the painter's possibilities of reproducing his subject on canvas, with all those subtleties of insight and suggestion – doublures, as it were, of character and of personality . . . It is his wont to catch his sitter unawares and to fix, in the spirit of the most certain impressionism, that unconscious and fleeting attitude or expression which is the living index to character'.[4]

Sargent's art continues to derive both inspiration and pictorial energy from an engagement with the art of the old masters. It is ironic that a number of works which seem to express something particular

about the character of the age in which they were painted are those most enriched by visual and intellectual echoes to the art and decorative imprint of the past. Sargent's characterization of W. Graham Robertson resonated with contemporary audiences in terms of Aestheticism, the figure of the dandy and the cult of Oscar Wilde, and has come to symbolize a certain world-weary, underslept, *fin-de-siècle* aesthete. Wilde's novel *The Portrait of Dorian Gray*, which charts the moral degeneration of a beautiful young man mirrored in the physical deterioration of his full-length portrait, was published in 1890. Four years later, Robert Hichens's novel, *The Green Carnation*, parodied the Aesthetic movement; one of the main characters, Reggie Hastings, is a fair haired boy, remarkable for his 'white weariness of face' and 'pale gilt hair and blue eyes, and a face in which the shadows of fleeting expressions, come and go, and a mouth like the mouth of Narcissus'.[5] Sargent had certainly read *Dorian Gray* and was probably aware of Hichens's work but, in depicting a figure of graceful assurance tinged with vulnerability, he was also haunted by the past, and by the austere outlines of Velázquez and Goya,[6] which continued to exert their powerful pictorial appeal. There is a superficial simlarity to Whistler's contemporary study of Comte Robert de Montesquiou, but Sargent's finely silhouetted young man, grave and beautiful, holding a cane with a poodle at his feet, is a specific echo of Francisco de Goya's portrait of his young son Javier de Goya (figs 51, 52).[7]

Sargent's dialogue with the art of the past might be a guide to reading the extravaganza that is *Mrs Carl Meyer and her Children*. The portrait is sometimes seen as a brilliant display of the material excess and conspicuous taste of the newly rich,[8] but it might be interpreted as a characterization of artifice and romantic bravado, glittering with references to images of previous eras of luxury, to *le style Pompadour* and to Winterhalter's Second Empire. This is an art of caprice and high artificiality, inspired by rococo and the spirit of Tiepolo.[9] Highly theatrical and overtly stage managed, it delights in astonishing the spectator with its playfully decorative excess, its extravagant piling up of sensual effects, its improbable perspective and composition constructed in reckless diagonals. It is also an art where wit and irony come into play, whispering that it wouldn't do to take all this too seriously. *Poudré*, flounced, beribboned and pearl-adorned, Mrs Meyer is herself cast as a *objet de luxe*, perhaps specifically as François Boucher's *Madame de Pompadour* (fig. 53),[10] that synonym for artistic patronage and lavish consumption, sitting on her sofa, with her book cast aside, her tiny, beautifully shod feet peeping out from under the peach cloud of her skirt. The visual allusions, the triangular sweep of the gown so similar to that of Boucher's marquise, and the sofa with its Beauvais tapestry design – a quotation of the decorative work by Boucher, which Madame de Pompadour commissioned –

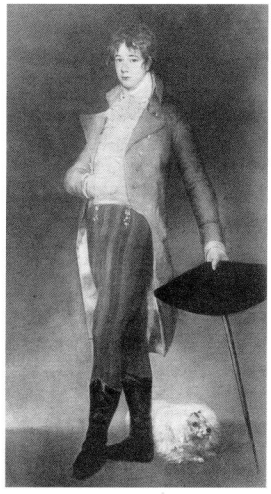

fig. 52 Francisco Goya y Lucientes, *Portrait of Xavier Goya*, 1805. Oil on canvas, dimensions unknown. Private Collection.

fig. 53 François Boucher, *Portrait of Madame de Pompadour*, 1756. Oil on canvas, 79 ⅛ × 61 ¹³⁄₁₆ (201 × 157). Alte Pinakothek, Munich.

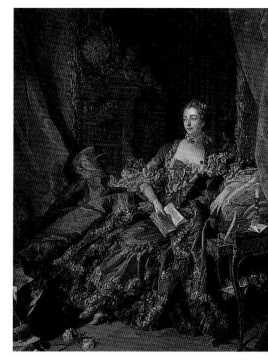

seem too assertively specific to be coincidental. Yet, for all the gaiety of collusion, the sophisticated dalliance with social pretension, there is a dark Sargentesque undertow: one wonders what are we to make of the children, compressed into the upper picture space and kept at a very literal arm's length from her mother?

Sargent's mature style is painterly and rhythmic producing sweeping forms and strong contours, but the expansiveness and opulence of his images carry with them an edge of anxiety and disquiet. He achieves this sense of strain by deviating from and sometimes inverting traditional portrait rules, using spatial dislocations, distortions of perspective and scale, oblique and tilting poses, devices which create tensions across the surface of the canvas. It is an anti-classical, perhaps a Mannerist, impulse, which Sargent exploits to dramatize an absolutely modern sensibility, a contemporary mode of being. It was this edginess or nerviness of Sargent's style – what Vernon Lee had described as 'crispation de nerfs'[11] – that so caught the anxieties and uncertainties of the age that it led Max Beerbohm to nominate him the 'supreme interpreter' of this 'restless, nervous age – an age on edge'.[12]

By the mid-1890s, public acceptance was unequivocal. The critics were bowled over by the inventiveness and boldness of Sargent's compositions, their visual intelligence and technical verve. When *Mrs Carl Meyer and her Children* hung on the walls of the Royal Academy in 1897, Henry James, who had chronicled Sargent's early career in such lapidary style, wrote that it was

a picture of a knock-down insolence of talent and truth of characterization, a wonderful rendering of life, of manners, of aspects, of types, of textures, of everything . . . he expresses himself as no one else scarce begins to do so in the language of the art he practices. The complete acquisition of this language seems to so few, as it happens, a needful precaution! Beside him, at any rate, his competitors appear to stammer; and his accent is not to be caught, his process, thank heaven, not to be analyzed.[13]

Portraiture sounds the major chord in Sargent's working life in the 1890s, but two works painted on either side of the century's end strike an interesting note. In 1899, he chose to deposit a small but dazzling conversation piece, *An Interior in Venice* (no. 367), as his diploma work at the Royal Academy (the scene of so many of his portrait triumphs) and, in 1901, he executed an ambitious, out-of-doors portrait study of Alexander Mc-Culloch (no. 394), young son of the collector George McCulloch. Both works are on the edge of traditional portraiture and they may point to a shift in Sargent's artistic centre of gravity.[14]

EK

NOTES

1. JSS to Julie Heyneman, 15 March 1897, Heyneman Papers, Bancroft Library, University of California, Los Angeles.

2. The 'Gibson Girl', an ideal of young American womanhood, was the creation of Charles Dana Gibson (1867–1944), who established a reputation as an illustrator of fashionable life and aristocratic social ideals.

3. 'I must have a type to paint . . . a type that expresses a phase of humanity. I cannot do a face simply because it happens to belong to somebody who has money to spend.' Frances, Countess of Warwick, *Afterthoughts*, London, Toronto, Melbourne and Sydney, 1931, p. 175.

4. A. C. R. Carter, 'The Royal Academy, 1898', *Art Journal* (1898), pp. 177–8. The portrait of Wertheimer was one of eight (the maximum allowed for an academician) exhibited at the academy in 1898. Carter wrote that Sargent had thereby 'created a standard against himself'. He also noted: 'Mr Sargent's development of style is now a law unto itself, and among the art revenges of time is the public acceptance of this autocracy.'

5. [Robert Hichens], *The Green Carnation*, 1894, pp. 1–3, 33. The short novel about a friendship between a poet, Esmé Amarinth, and an aristocrat, Lord Reggie Hastings, is a thinly veiled fictional account of Oscar Wilde's relationship with Lord Alfred Douglas. Published anonymously, it was highly popular and successful, but was withdrawn from circulation at the time of Wilde's trial and was republished in England only after both Wilde's and Douglas's deaths.

6. The influence of Goya has been noted most powerfully in *El Jaleo*. See Mary Crawford Volk's discussion in Washington 1992, pp. 41–4, 61–2. An element of perceived *grotesquerie* in *La Carmencita* also suggested comparison with Goya.

   Only one copy after Goya by Sargent is recorded. A small panel after Goya's study in an arch at San Antonio was in the Sargent memorial exhibition at the Royal Academy in 1926 (no. 515). McKibbin identified it as a study of part of a transept arch at San Antonio de la Florida in Madrid, featuring two angels. It was a work on panel, which suggests an early date; it was probably painted during Sargent's visit to Spain in 1879. Sargent did, however, own books of Goya's aquatints and etchings, and he expressed his enthusiasm for his painting in letters to Vernon Lee and George Washington Vanderbilt, see Washington 1992, pp. 41–2.

7. The author has seen neither the painting nor a colour reproduction. For the physical description I am indebted to A[ureliano] de Beruete y Moret, *Goya pintor de retratos*, Madrid [second edition], 1919, p. 53, ill. lámina 15: 'Y, por último, antes de terminar con este capítulo el estudio de la producción de Goya en su nota gris, debe quedar mencionado el retrato de *l'homme gris*, muy nombrado en París, aun cuando no muy conocido. Este hombre gris no es otro que el hijo de Goya (no el nieto, como alguien equivocadamente ha dicho), representado en este retrato, admirable por su fineza, vestido de gris, sobre fondo gris, con chaleco y corbata blancos y guantes amarillos. Son lo mejor de la obra la cabeza y los trozos blancos. El perro allí representado es lo más flojo, aun cuando resulta bonito como nota de color. Consérvase este retrato en propiedad de M. Ferdinand Bischoffsheim (París).'

   'And finally, before we finish this chapter devoted to Goya's work in grey, we must mention the portrait of the man in grey, a picture very famous in Paris, but little known elsewhere. The man in grey depicted in this portrait is none other than Goya's son (not his grandson, as has been mistakenly said); it displays a remarkably fine treatment of grey clothes on a grey background, with white waistcoat and cravat and yellow gloves. The handling of the head and the white patches are the best part of the work. The dog is the lightest touch and creates a fine colour note. The portrait is in the collection of M. Ferdinand Bischoffsheim, Paris.'

   I have been unable to establish from Goya literature at which date the portrait passed from Javier Goya or his family to collections in Paris. It is, however, highly plausible that Sargent saw the picture either in Madrid or Paris.

8. It is an eloquent commentary on perceptions of *Mrs Carl Meyer and her Children* that it was chosen as the cover illustration for J. Mordaunt Crook's splendid analysis of Victorian and Edwardian taste, *The Rise of the Nouveaux Riches*, London, 1999.

9. Sargent owned a pen and ink drawing by G. B. Tiepolo of *The Martyrdom of St Catherine* (pen and ink and sepia, $9\frac{1}{2} \times 8\frac{1}{2}$ in. The artist's sale, Christie's, London, 24 and 27 July 1925, lot 271), and a set of four works by Domenico Tiepolo, lot 317 in the artist's sale: *Christ Healing the Sick, David and Bathsheba, The Finding of Moses* and *Susannah and the Elders* – a set of four, 20×18 in. The works are presently untraced and the status of the attributions unconfirmed.

10. Madame de Pompadour, *née* Jeanne-Antoinette Poisson (1721–64), Louis XV's mistress. Boucher decorated a number of rooms in her many houses and she bought his two large pictures depicting the rising and setting of the sun (Wallace Collection, London) from the 1753 Salon as tapestry designs for her château at Bellevue (her favourite house situated on the River Seine between Sèvres and Meudon).

11. 'Crispation de nerfs': twitching nerves. Vernon Lee is writing about *The Misses Vickers* (*Early Portraits*, no. 129), at the Paris salon, 'I fear John is getting rather into the way of painting people too *tense*. They look as though they were in a state of *crispation de nerfs*.' VL to her mother, 25 June 1885, *Vernon Lee's Letters* 1937, p. 171.

12. The critical literature is rich with references to the 'nerviness' of Sargent's style. R. A. M. Stevenson, for example, was held spellbound by Sargent's 'clear, well cut nervously drawn portrait' of Colonel Ian Hamilton, 'The Art Season. Mr Sargent and Others', *Academy* (6 May 1899), p. 510. Rudolf Dircks described Sargent as 'a sophisticated child of his time [who] dazzles, delights, bewilders'. Dircks went on to complain that his 'restless brilliancy may be a sufficient achievement in itself, but it is not quite calculated to charm . . . But Mr Sargent obviously has no desire to remain simple. He does not seek abstractions; he prefers the complexities, the surface *agitée*; he does not object to the *commandes* of a particularly vital and materialistic present' 'Royal Academy Exhibition, 1907', *Art Journal* (1907), p. 196.

    Beerbohm contrasts modern restlessness with the pictorial serenity of earlier portraitists: 'If you look at the portraits painted in the eighteenth century, or in the first half of the nineteenth, you will see a type of humanity which would be impossible today. Gainsborough, Sir Joshua, Sir Thomas, Mr Watts in his youth, show to us a galaxy of solid gentlemen and gracious ladies. That rich solidity, that quiet grace, were the inalienable products of a life not yet bedevilled into a scurry by the progress of applied science.' In contrast, the ladies and gentlemen of his own day are 'caught and fixed there for a brilliant instant in the midst of their overwork and overplay, swished on there in a manner that accords so brilliantly well to its matter – a manner that is, moreover, itself a justly contemptuous criticism, profound in its very superficiality', 'A Gallery of Significant Pictures', *Saturday Review* (18 April 1903), p. 484. A few years later (19 June 1909), Beerbohm was inspired by *The Hermit* (Metropolitan Museum of Art, New York), which was in the New English Art Club summer exhibition of 1909, to parody Sargent's nervy compositions as 'the restlessness of great ladies on priceless sofas': 'As in the art of life, so in pictorial art, a yearning for the simple life has begun to manifest itself. Mr Sargent, who has excelled in depicting the restlessness of great ladies on priceless sofas, is said to have decided that he can do it no more. There is one view at this moment, as an earnest of his resolve, a portrait by him of a naked hermit in a desert; a hermit at rest (so Mr Sargent would have us think) *planté là* and meaning to stay so, undisturbed even by the urban complexity and velocity of Sargentine technique.' Max Beerbohm, 'A Play and an Actress', *Last Theatres: 1904–1910*, London, 1970, p. 471. For Louis de Fourcaud's analysis of the tenseness and melancholy of the age in the context of the Salon of 1881, see Marc Simpson, *Uncanny Spectacle: The Public Career of the Young John Singer Sargent*, New Haven and London, 1997 (exhibition catalogue), p. 131.

13. James 1956, p. 257.

14. *An Interior in Venice* replaced a fine, if conventional, three-quarter-length portrait, *Johannes Wolff* (no. 341).

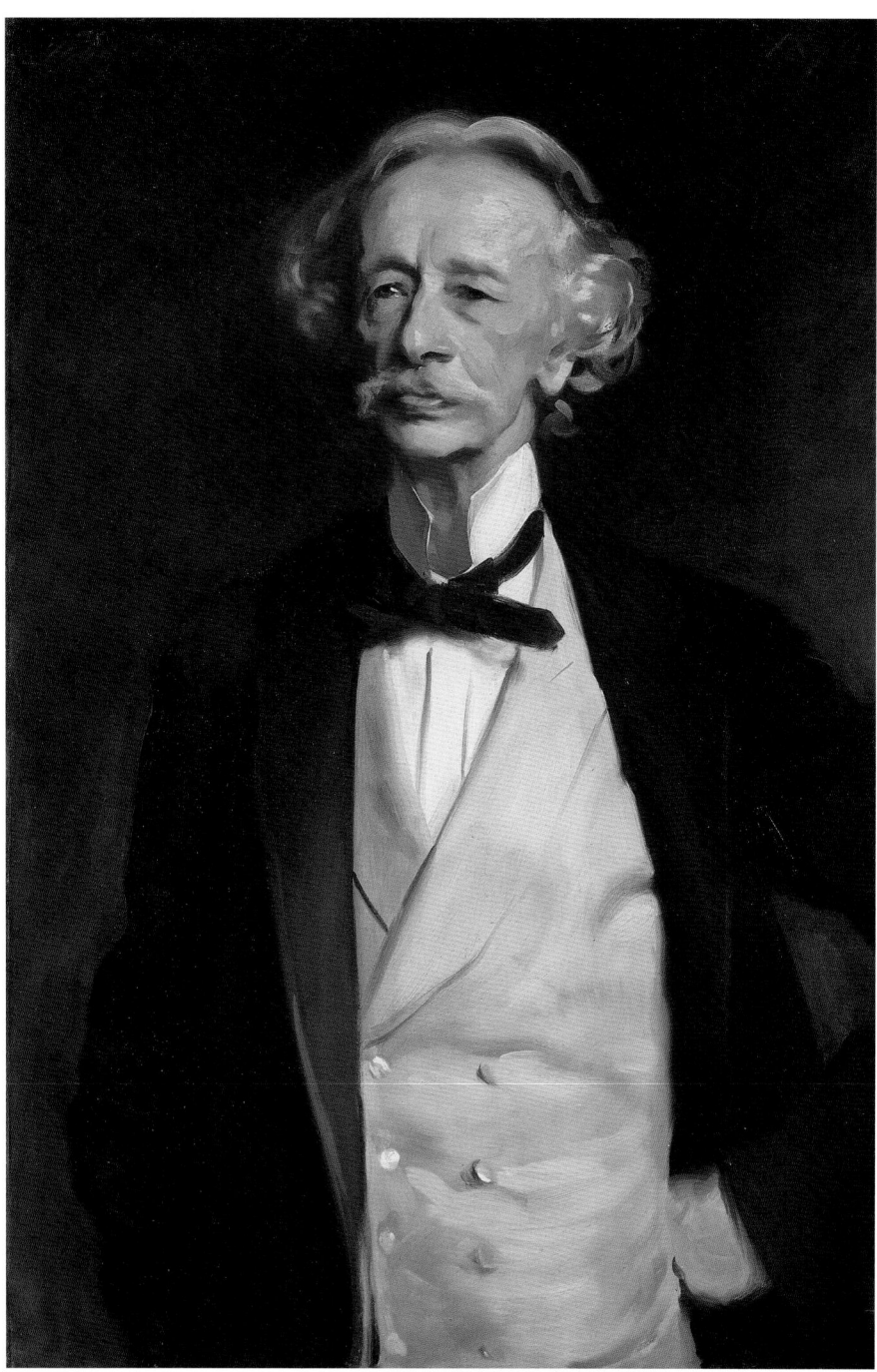

302   *Coventry Patmore*

1894
Oil on canvas, 36 × 24 (91.5 × 61)
Inscribed, upper left: *John S. Sargent*; upper right:
1894
National Portrait Gallery, London

Coventry Kersey Dighton Patmore (1823–1896), the eminent Victorian poet, friend of Ruskin and Tennyson, and advocate of the Pre-Raphaelite brotherhood, is most famous for his long poem *The Angel in the House* (1854–62), a celebration and idealization of married love. He converted to Catholicism in 1864, and much of his later writing is meditative and religious in tone. Patmore's friend, the writer Edmund Gosse, described Patmore's physical appearance: 'Three things were particularly noticeable in the head of Coventry Patmore – the vast convex brows, arched with vision; the bright, shrewd, blueish-grey eyes, the outer fold of one eyelid permanently and humourously drooping and the wilful, sensuous mouth' (Patmore 1949, p. 6).

Edmund Gosse, whom Sargent had painted in 1886 (see *Early Portraits*, nos 167, 168), encouraged Patmore to sit to Sargent, who had expressed a desire to paint him. Sargent's letter to Gosse (10 May 1894), thanking him for Patmore's address is in the Gosse papers, Brotherton Library, Leeds. Patmore wrote to Gosse on 9 May 1894 that 'to be thus *invited* to sit to him for my picture is among the most signal honours I have ever received'. He wrote in eloquent praise of Sargent's talent, saying that he was 'the greatest, not only of living English portrait painters, but of *all* English portrait painters' (Champneys 1900, vol. 2, p. 260). The sittings took place in the summer of 1894. Writing to his wife, Patmore commented: 'The portrait is fearfully like. It is quite ferocious at present', and again, 'He is doing his work *con amore*, and will not leave it off until he has done his best. He has wonderfully softened the expression but he says it is still "too aggressive".' Patmore's wife had been alarmed to hear that her husband was being painted smoking a cigarette; he assured her that it had been taken out and that 'the ferocity likewise has disappeared' (Patmore 1949, p. 208). Patmore wrote to Gosse on 7 September, to inform him that the portrait was finished (Champneys 1900, vol. 2, p. 260), declaring that 'it will be simply, as a work of art, *the* picture of the Academy'.

Patmore's family and friends were impressed by the forcefulness of the characterization. According to Gosse, the poet was 'not always thus ragged and vulturine, not always such a miraculous portent of gnarled mandible and shaken plummage' (Charteris 1927, p. 153). The poet's son, F. J. Patmore, indicated that Sargent had provoked his father to indignation by a well chosen political argument, and to Basil Champneys it seemed 'to incline towards caricature, and to present a somewhat truculent character, alert and active, rather than reflective, thus missing the aspect of "seer" which, in later years, had alone seemed characteristic of him'. Champneys suggestion that if the portrait had been extended downwards Patmore might have been represented with a whip, like a Southern planter about to thrash his slaves, met with the peremptory reply: 'Is that not what I have been doing all my life?' Critical response to the portrait was extremely favourable; the reviews of the 1895 Royal Academy exhibition praised the intensity of characterization and the controlled technical skill. The *Magazine of Art* called it 'the most electrifying portrait in the Academy' (*Magazine of Art*, 1895, p. 281). For the *Academy*, Claude Phillips remarked that it would be difficult 'to imagine anything done with a more Hals-like certainty and breadth, with a more incisive strength and concision, with a greater felicity in the expression of physical character' (*Academy*, 11

May 1895, p. 407). Lady Gregory might be referring either to this or to no. 303, when she noted in her diary entry for 3 May 1895: 'To Academy Private View . . . of the pictures I was struck by Sargent's portrait of Coventry Patmore' (Pethica 1996, p. 71). For a caricature published in *Punch's* review of the Academy show, see fig. 54.

The portrait was used as the frontispiece to Patmore's book of poems *Pathos and Delight*. Sargent wrote at the time expressing pride that his portrait should 'be found worthy' to act as frontispiece to Patmore's poems, recommending that only the head and shoulders be used, and suggesting some slight adjustments to the print (letter of 23 August [1894], sold Christie's, London, 5 May 1982, lot 138).

For information about the frame, see Simon 1996, p. 182.

A copy of the portrait by R. G. Eves was in Eves's studio sale, Phillips, London, 30 October 1973, lot 852.

303 *Coventry Patmore*

1894
Oil on canvas, 20½ × 15½ (52 × 39.4)
Apparently inscribed, upper left: *J.S. Sargent* [?]
Untraced

A more relaxed characterization of Coventry Patmore than the formal kit-cat portrait (no. 302). Painted for the sitter's wife, it was sold soon after her death when it entered the collection of the

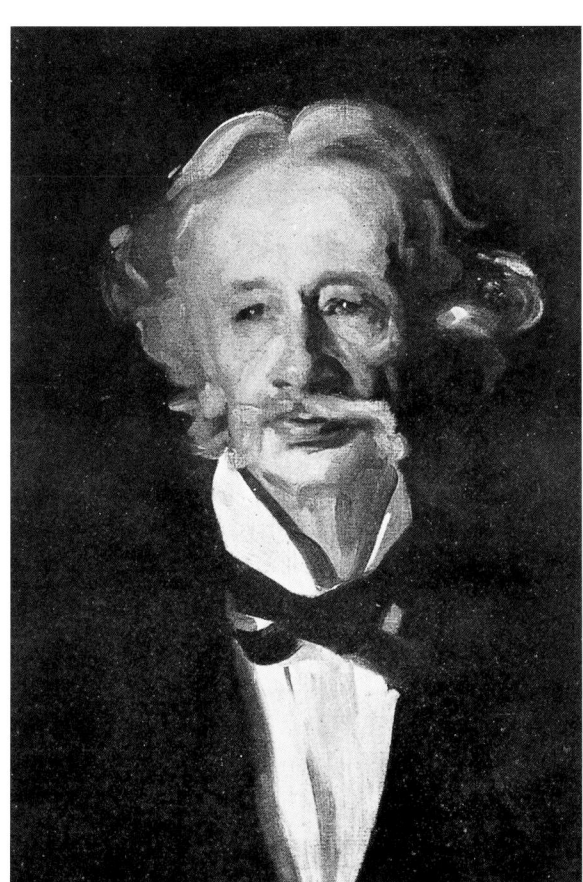

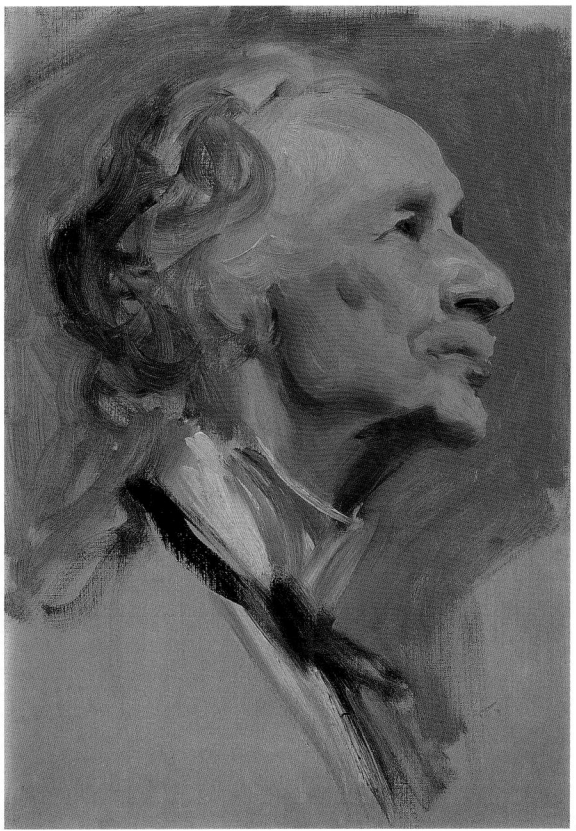

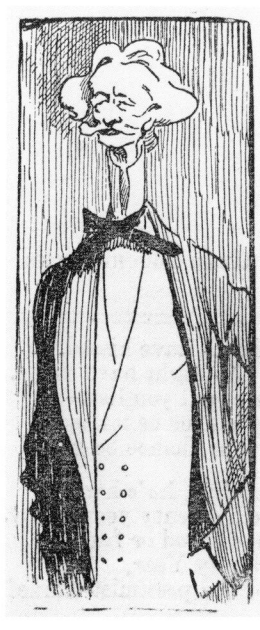

fig. 54 Caricature of Sargent's portrait of Coventry Patmore, 'Couldn't be Padmore?' *Punch*, CVIII (11 May 304 1895), p. 220.

well-known Japanese collector of Impressionist painting, Matsukata. It was listed as no. 1349 in Matsukata's inventory but is presently untraced. Charteris lists five portraits of Patmore and McKibbin four; only three are reliably recorded at present.

This sketch was exhibited at the Royal Academy with the more formal portrait, and some critics felt that it did not suffer in comparison. The reviewer for the *Saturday Review* wrote that the formal portrait

> is unquestionably the most able piece of painting in the present exhibition; and it is not, perhaps, until we come to look at the sketch for this picture, which hangs in another room, that we fully realise how this element of cleverness coming in, just destroys the fineness of the picture, both as a piece of painting and as a portrait. The sketch would be difficult to overpraise. More subtle in form and colour, and less assertive in manner than the finished picture, it is an admirable likeness, and an astonishingly accomplished piece of work'. (*Saturday Review*, 11 May 1895, pp. 617–18)

Lady Gregory might be referring either to this or to no. 302, when she noted in her diary entry for 3 May 1895: 'To Academy Private View . . . of the pictures I was struck by Sargent's portrait of Coventry Patmore' (Pethica 1996, p. 71).

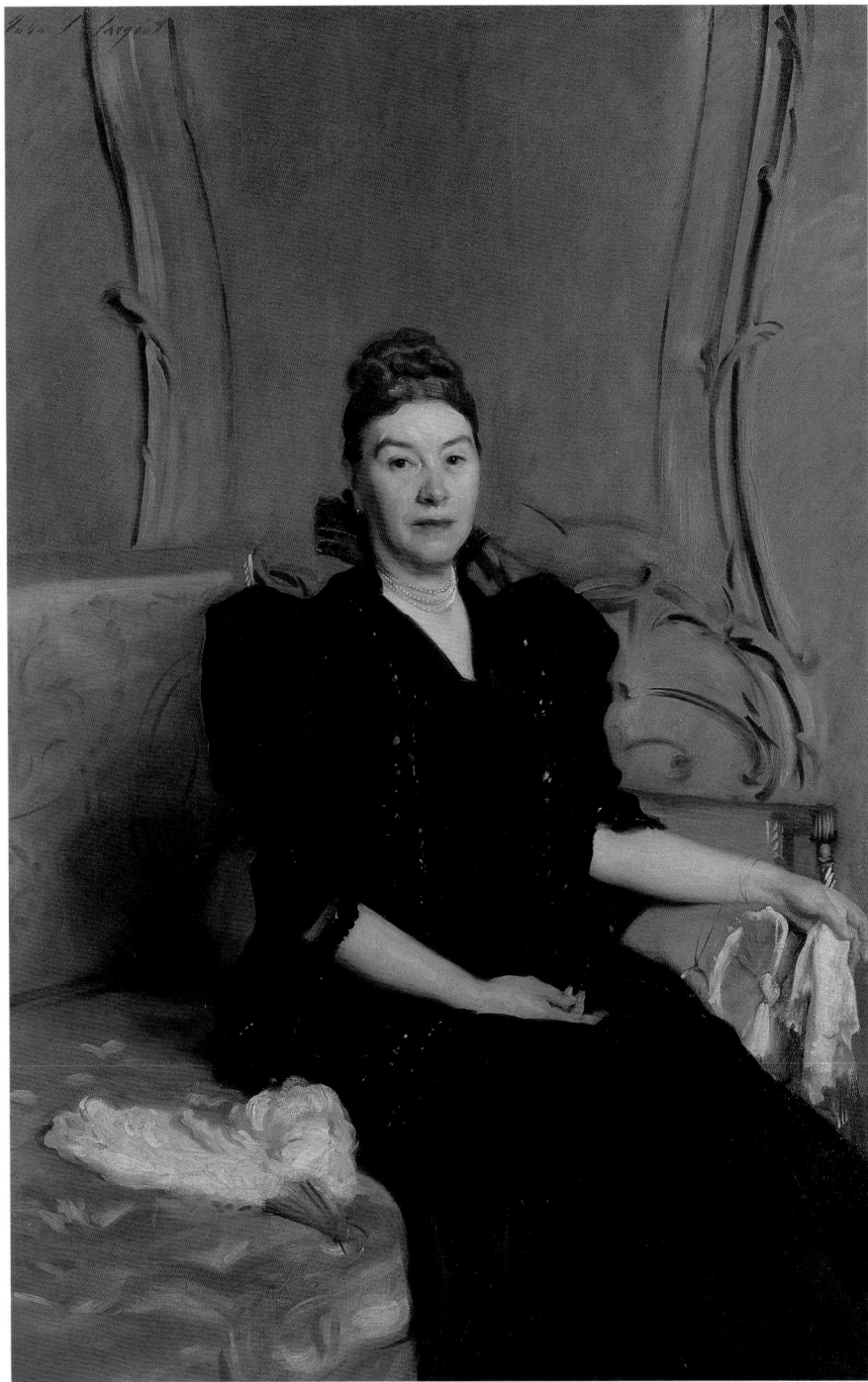

304 *Coventry Patmore*

1894
Oil on canvas, 18½ × 13 (47 × 33)
Inscribed, by the artist on an old label on the back:
*[sk]etch of Mr Coventry Patmore / for prophet- / to be
returned to London*
Private Collection

Painted at the same time as the formal portrait of
Coventry Patmore (no. 302), it was used as a study
for the head of the prophet Ezekiel for the Frieze
of Prophets in Sargent's mural decorations for the
Boston Public Library. In the finished mural, the
prophet is shown swathed in a white robe, his head
hooded and slightly more three-quarter face, but
his features are otherwise recognizable from the
sketch.

The sketch is in the *Sargent Trust List*, 'Pictures.
Framed. no. 17'.

305 *Mrs Graham Moore Robertson*

1894
Oil on canvas, 63 × 40 (160 × 101.5)
Inscribed, upper left: *John S. Sargent*
Watts Gallery, Compton, Surrey

Marion Greatorex (d. 1907) was the daughter of
businessman Jeremiah Greatorex and his wife, *née*
Walford. One of twelve children, she was brought
up first at Springfield, Upper Clapham, in the
Wye Valley on the Welsh borders, and later at
Cleveland Square, Bayswater, in London. In the
1860s, she married Graham Moore Robertson, a
Scotsman from Banff, who had spent twenty years
in India. Their only child, W. Graham Robertson,
has left an affectionate picture of his mother, to
whom he was devoted, in his book of reminiscences, *Time Was* (1931).

Graham Robertson appears to have approached
Sargent to paint his mother in 1893. In an undated
letter headed 'Monday', Sargent wrote: 'You know
I suppose that my stay in London is at an end and
that I would not be able to do another portrait
before next year. I shall however take advantage of
my first free afternoon to call upon your mother.
In case you would like to know my prices they are
200 guineas for a head, 400 for ¾ length and 500
for full-length' (WR 513, Department of
Manuscripts, The Huntington Library, Art Collections, and Botanical Gardens, San Marino,
California).

Robertson describes the painting of his
mother's portrait in *Time Was* though he does not
explain his choice of artist:

> This was Sargent's great period, when he was
> not so over-tasked with commissions and was
> able to concentrate upon the work in hand. I
> had long wanted a portrait of my mother and
> was lucky in persuading him to undertake it,
> though it was perhaps not a complete success.
> My mother was a bad sitter, she was shy and
> very loath, as she expressed it, to 'sit still and be
> stared at' . . . Still the portrait was a fine piece of
> work and a brilliant, superficial likeness.
> (Robertson 1931, pp. 233–4)

The sittings took place in the early summer of
1894, while Sargent was also engaged upon a full-
length portrait of the actress Ada Rehan. Both sitters were shy and reluctant, and 'found a certain
comfort in the other's discomfort; they were com-
rades in misfortune and even shared certain studio
"properties", Sargent borrowing from my mother
her white feather fan for Ada to hold outspread'
(Robertson 1931, p. 234). The same fan of white
ostrich feathers appears in one of the two portraits
of Mrs Ernest Hills (no. 312). In a letter to Graham
Robertson, postmarked 30 July 1894, Sargent

writes: 'A thousand thanks to your mother for the fan' (WR 517, Department of Manuscripts, The Huntington Library, Art Collections and Botanical Gardens, San Marino, California). Robertson, who came to the studio to support his mother, became a friend of the artist and, as a pictorial type, attracted his interest. The result was the portrait of Graham Robertson himself (no. 306), undertaken at Sargent's request.

Mrs Robertson is shown in her portrait wearing a black silk dress with a high collar, and a long pendant necklace of black jet of at least three strands hanging from her neck. She holds a lace handkerchief in her left hand. She is seated in the Louis Seize-style settee and posed against a piece of eighteenth-century French panelling, possibly derived from one of the Louis Quinze-style doors in Sargent's studio (see Accessories, pp. xxii, xxiii, nos 1, 17).

A portrait of Mrs Robertson by Arthur Melville (1900), and an earlier one by Graves (c. 1870), are also in the Watts Gallery.

306   *W. Graham Robertson*

1894
Oil on canvas, 90¾ × 46¾ (230.5 × 118.7)
Inscribed, lower right: *John S. Sargent 1894*
Tate Gallery, London. Gift of the sitter

(Walford) Graham Robertson (1866–1948) was a painter, illustrator, theatre designer, poet and collector. He studied painting under the artist Albert Moore, but was closer in spirit to the Pre-Raphaelitism of Rossetti and Burne-Jones. His children's books with their delicate, whimsical illustrations, were particularly successful. He wrote a number of plays, but only two, *Pinkie and the Fairies* (1908) and *The Fountain of Youth*, were produced in London. Handsome and charming, he cultivated the friendship of many celebrities in the world of literature, art and the theatre. His book of reminiscences, *Time Was*, includes witty stories and vignettes of them which constitute a cameo of the age. His own considerable art collection embraced a large holding of works by William Blake (see Kerrison Preston, *The Blake Collection of W. Graham Robertson*, London, 1952) and several Victorian masterpieces, including *Choosing* by G. F. Watts (National Portrait Gallery, London). For a contemporary account, see M. H. Spielmann, 'Our Rising Artists: Mr W. Robertson', *Magazine of Art*, 24 (1900), pp. 74–81.

The unusual genesis of the portrait is described by Robertson with aplomb. In 1894, he had commissioned Sargent to paint his mother, Mrs Graham Moore Robertson (no. 305). The actress Ada Rehan was sitting for her portrait at the same time (no. 308), and it was through her that Sargent communicated his desire to paint the young man. Having summoned him by letter, Ada Rehan explained the mystery:

'Well, he's very anxious to paint you.'
'Me?'
'Yes. He wants you to sit to him.'
'Wants *me*. But good gracious, why?'
'I don't know,' said Ada, a little tactlessly. 'He says you are so paintable: that the lines of your long overcoat and – and the dog – and – I can't quite remember *what* he said, but he was tremendously enthusiastic'. (Robertson 1931, p. 235)

The coat is a 'Chesterfield' overcoat, so named after the sixth earl of Chesterfield, long and formal and with a velvet collar. Lord Ribblesdale, whom Sargent painted several years later in a not dissimilarly attenuated pose, wears an identical overcoat in his portrait. It is a matter of record that Sargent was first struck by the pictorial possibilities of painting Ribblesdale in the summer of 1894, and it is probable that there is more substance than coincidence in the compositional similarities between the two works (see no. 421).

There are seven letters from the artist to Graham Robertson in the Huntington Library, Art Collections, and Botanical Gardens, several of which deal with arrangements for sittings. In a letter headed 'Tuesday' (the envelope is postmarked 5 June 1894), Sargent wrote: 'I believe I am not to do the lovely American [Miss Ada Rehan, see no. 308] after all, so will you sit on Thursday afternoon or if this does not suit you Friday afternoon? Your mother will let me know tomorrow. Your background has sunk in in spots and looks horrible. Could you bring Mouton next time'. In a letter (postmark 21 July 1894), Sargent mentions arrangements concerning a frame either for this picture or for no. 305.

Robertson's ageing poodle, Mouton, of the St Jean de Luz breed, had already made an impression in the studio, when he went with his master to Mrs Robertson's sittings: 'The comic relief of the sittings was supplied by my dog, Mouton, who, well stricken in years and almost toothless, claimed rather unusual privileges and was always allowed one bite by Sargent, whom he unaccountably disliked, before work began. "He has bitten me now", Sargent would remark mildly, "so we can go ahead"' (Robertson 1931, p. 234). So, when Sargent came to paint Robertson in the summer of 1894, Mouton was included, a fluffy foil to the smooth young man, artlessly arrayed with coat and cane. Robertson found that as 'an amateur model, I was easily entrapped into a trying pose, turning as if to walk away, with a general twist of the whole body and all the weight on one foot' (Robertson 1931, p. 236). He also found it difficult to explain why a very thin young man in a very tight coat should have struck the artist as a subject worthy of treatment, 'but he [Sargent] evidently had the finished picture in his mind from the first and started it almost exactly upon its final lines'. When his sitter objected to wearing an overcoat during the hot summer weather, Sargent ex-claimed ' "But the coat is the picture. . . . You

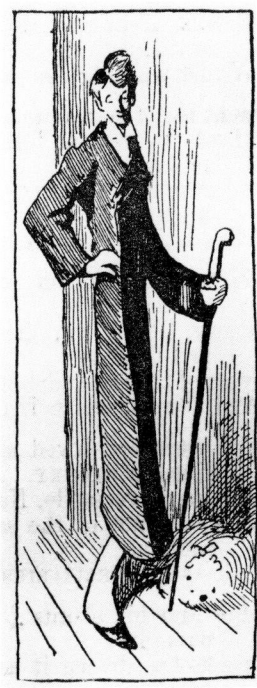

fig. 55 Caricature of Sargent's portrait of W. Graham Robertson, '"How long! How long!" Portrait of a blasé youth. Even his cane is jade-d', *Punch*, CVIII (11 May 1895), p. 220.

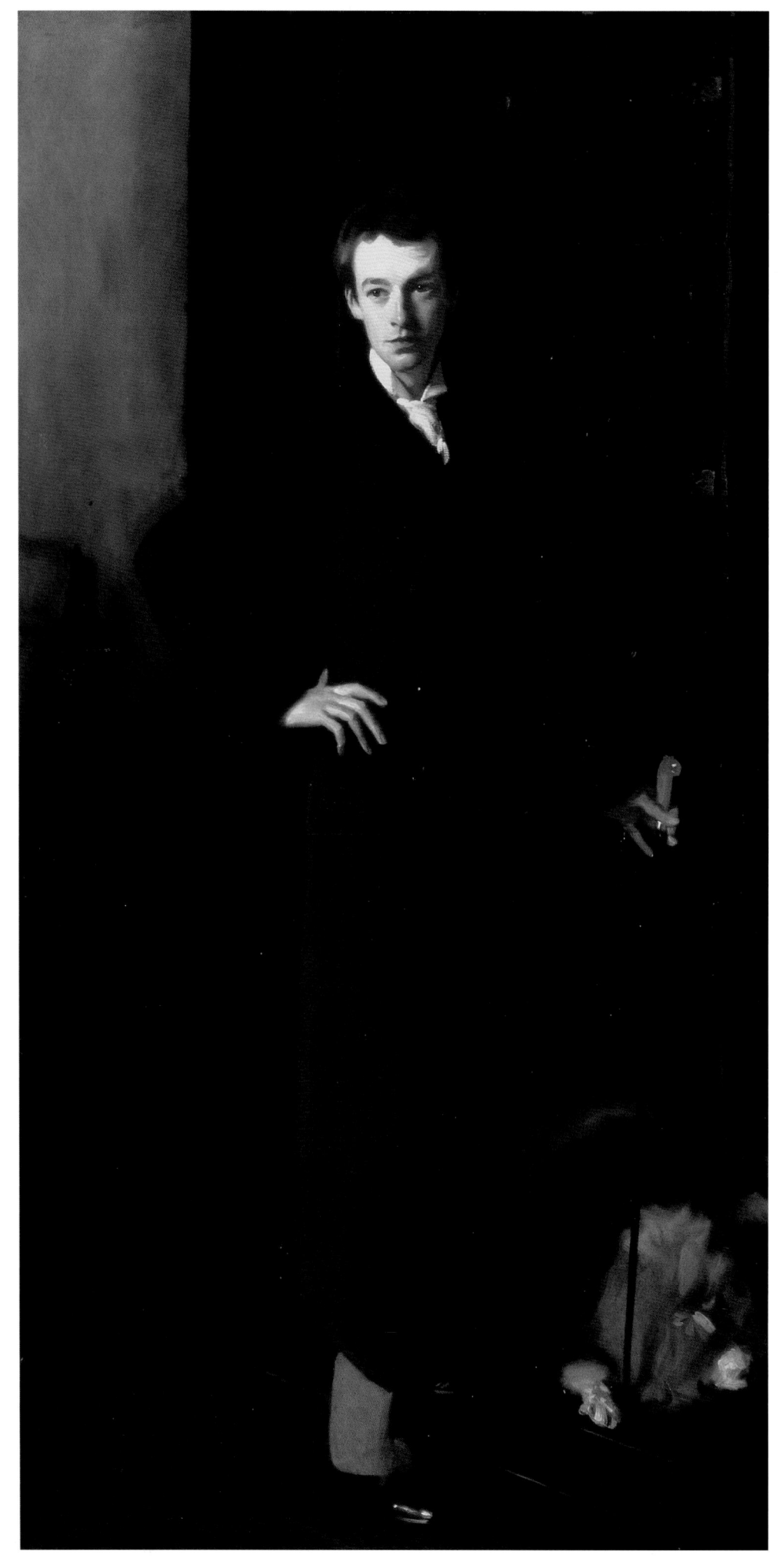

must wear it" "Then I can't wear anything else", I cried in despair, and with the sacrifice of most of my wardrobe I became thinner and thinner, much to the satisfaction of the artist, who used to pull and drag the unfortunate coat more and more closely round me until it might have been draping a lamp-post' (Robertson 1931, p. 238). When Kit Anstruther-Thomson saw the portrait in Paris in 1896 at the Société nationale des beaux-arts, she was struck by the perpendicular emphasis of the composition. She wrote to Vernon Lee: 'Sargent's man and poodle look superb. The picture is slightly pathetic owing to the elusive character the lines give it. No horizontals' (undated letter, CC).

Sittings, interrupted by a trip which Sargent made to Paris, were resumed in the autumn. Even before the portrait was finished, its fame had begun to grow, and luminaries like Henry James came to pass judgement. Sargent himself was worried that people would accuse him of having copied Whistler's portrait of Comte Robert de Montesquiou (fig. 51), which he saw exhibited in Paris. Critics did make the comparison, but without suggesting possible plagiarism. For the *Academy*, Claude Phillips commented that 'of imitation, there can, of course, be no question between artists of this calibre' and went on to describe the essential qualities of Sargent's picture:

> There is an alertness, a momentariness in the arrested action of the slender figure, an expression of nerve force, as distinguished from muscularity, which makes of the portrait, apart from its purely pictorial qualities, a perfect expression of the thoroughly modern individuality placed before us. The only fault that even hyper criticism can find with the execution is that the intense, yet cold, light is concentrated almost too strongly upon the finely modelled head. (*Academy*, 11 May 1895, p. 407)

Phillips was one of a number of critics for whom the portrait seemed to define a particular contemporary 'type', dandy, aesthete or *fin-de-siècle* decadent. For example, the American Agnes Farley Millar described Robertson as 'the ideal dandy of this present year of grace' (*Independent*, 9 July 1896, p. 931); and, in his 1927 biography of Sargent, Evan Charteris called the portrait 'a symbol of the nineties. The picture speaks of the 'Beardsley period, of the "Yellow Book", of the aspiration to startle and the cultivation of civilised detachment . . . He has painted an individual, but he has defined a period, a type, an attitude of mind; he has put on record a date' (Charteris 1927, p. 154). In later life, Robertson objected to what he described as 'the Charteris version of my "legend"', declaring that he had not been part of the Wilde set, 'these dreary "clever" young men of the "Oscar" period', whom he regarded as 'highly obnoxious' (see Preston 1953, p. 455). The attenuated figure was the subject of a *Punch* caricature (fig. 55).

For a detailed discussion of the portrait in the context of the Aesthetic movement and the cult of

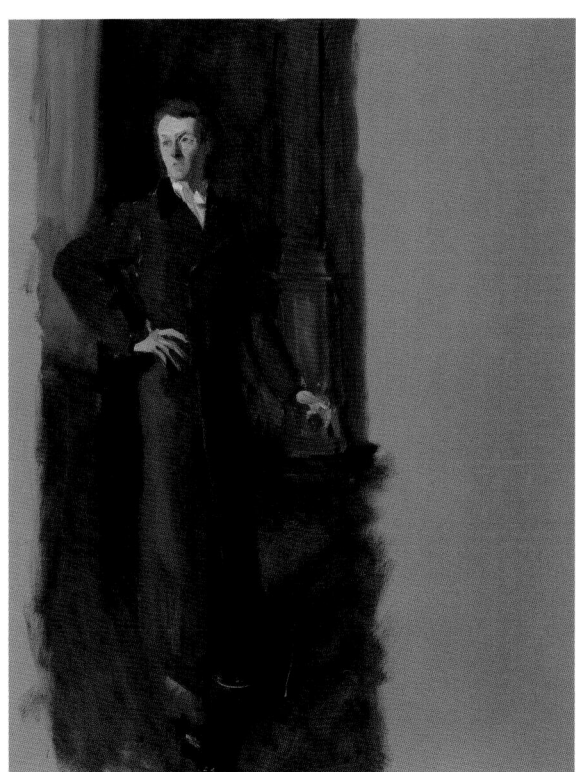

307

Oscar Wilde, see Lacey Taylor Jordan, 'John Singer Sargent's Images of Artists in an International Context' (Ph.D. diss. Emory University, 1999). We are indebted to Dr Jordan for a number of review references cited in the Literature section for this picture.

In a letter dated 12 January [1914], Sargent, acting as president of an American committee for the Panama Pacific exhibition to be held in San Francisco in 1915, wrote to Graham Robertson to request the loan of the present portrait and of Whistler's *Valparaiso* (*Crepuscule in Flesh Colour and Green: Valparaiso*, 1866, Tate Gallery, London), which Robertson owned. Neither work was included in the exhibition. Of the portrait of Robertson, Sargent wrote: 'If you are up to date enough to think my portrait of you an awful bore – would you enjoy having that out of your sight for practically a year?' (WR 519, The Huntington Library, Art Collections, and Botanical Gardens, San Marino, California).

The critic for the *Saturday Review*, when he saw the portrait at the Royal Academy, had cavilled at Sargent's 'inability to make the spectator forget the mere medium of the paint' (*Saturday Review*, 11 May 1895, p. 618). Recent conservation work by Jacqueline Ridge of the Tate Gallery has recovered a picture surface of remarkable lucidity and tonal coolness. It has also provided technical verification that Sargent emphasized the narrow silhouette of the figure progressively as he developed the design (see Ridge and Townsend 1998, p. 26, and Jacqueline Ridge, 'Preparing for the Sargent Exhibition', *Tate: The Art Magazine*, Summer 1998, pp. v–vi).

A preliminary oil sketch (no. 307) for the portrait was discovered on the same stretcher as *Mrs William Russell Cooke* (no. 314) during cleaning *c.* 1960.

307　*W. Graham Robertson*

c. 1894
Oil on canvas, 36 × 28 (91.5 × 71.2)
Private Collection

An experimental sketch for the full-length portrait of W. Graham Robertson (no. 306). It agrees closely with the finished work, but the dog which featured in the finished portrait is absent here. The background comprises a section of panelling with pilaster, probably based on the panelling in the studio at 33 Tite Street, instead of the Japanese screen in the finished picture. The head is less directly frontal; and the walking cane is only indicated by a single line scratched through the paint.

308　*Ada Rehan*

1894
Oil on canvas, 93 × 50⅛ (236.2 × 127.3)
Inscribed, lower left: *John S. Sargent*
Metropolitan Museum of Art, New York. Bequest of Catharine Lasell Whitin, in memory of Ada Rehan

Ada Rehan (1860–1916) was born Delia Crehan in Limerick, Ireland. Her two older sisters had both become actresses, and she made her debut at sixteen with Mrs John Drew's stock company at the Arch Street Theatre in Philadelphia, where a printer misbilled her as 'Ada C. Rehan'. The name stuck, and she became famous in theatres on both sides of the Atlantic. In 1879, Rehan began a partnership with Augustin Daly and his company which was to last for some twenty years, and saw the creation of her great dramatic and comedic performances, perhaps most notably her Katharine in *The Taming of the Shrew*. She was working with Daly in London from 27 June 1893 to 7 May 1894, and she seems to have been introduced to Sargent at some point during the winter. The commission to paint her came from Catharine Lasell Whitin of Whitinsville, Massachusetts, who greatly admired her. Three letters from Sargent to Miss Rehan and one to Mrs Whitin are in the Folger Shakespeare Library, Washington, D.C. The text of four letters from Sargent to Mrs Whitin is published in H. W. Williams, 'Four Letters by J. S. Sargent Concerning His Portrait of Ada Rehan', *Art in America*, 29 (July 1941), pp. 173–4.

According to Mrs Whitin's daughter, Mrs E. K. Swift, her mother met Sargent at a dinner party in December 1893, and the proposed portrait was discussed then (letter of 7 January 1941, MMA, Department of American Art archives). The commission had certainly been given by January of the following year because Sargent wrote in reply to Mrs Whitin on 27 January:

> I am glad that you incline to a portrait *not* in character, as both she and I feel the same way. This is all that we could decide at the time, but

when I go up to town again she is coming to my studio with several dresses to choose from, and there in the proper light, I will be able to come to conclusion about the treatment of the picture. I think it ought to be full length in spite of the fact that it will have to stand on the ground or very nearly. The price that I asked you for painting Miss Rehan ($2,500) is below my usual price and you would do me a favor by not mentioning it, as I have several orders to fulfill in America at a higher figure. I think the whole impression, and the upper part of Miss Rehan's face is very fine, and I hope I shall satisfy your ambition for the portrait. We expect to accomplish it in the months of March and April. (H. W. Williams, 'Four Letters by J. S. Sargent Concerning His Portrait of Ada Rehan', *Art in America*, 29, July 1941, p. 173)

The progress of the painting was beset by delays: Miss Rehan was involved in rehearsals for *Twelfth Night* and Sargent was engaged on the Boston Public Library murals and on portraits for exhibitions. Work did not begin until April. Miss Rehan was reluctant to sit because she had been ill and was suffering from the demands of a heavy theatrical season, but Sargent wrote to persuade her:

> I am very sorry to hear you have been ill and feel unequal to the task of sitting which is a great disappointment. In case there was a chance of making you change your mind I should argue, with more truth than seems likely, that a great many people find it rather a rest than otherwise, and also that some of my best results have happened to be obtained with few sittings. From now to the 6th of May might be ample time for me if fortune favours (Lady Agnew was done in six sittings), but I always admit beforehand that it may take me much longer – Will you give me a chance? or at any rate will you come to my studio with a dress or two, and let me see if really you look the worse for your long season of work. The public does not seem to think so! and I don't believe I shall. (undated letter headed 'Wednesday', Folger Shakespeare Library, Washington, D.C.)

In an undated letter, Sargent explained his plans to Ralph Curtis: 'For the moment I am going to do some portraits here, among others Miss Rehan who is very paintable' (Boston Athenaeum, Sargent Papers, box 1, folder 3). He wrote to Miss Rehan on 7 April from Morgan Hall to arrange a sitting:

> Today my pictures have left here for the Academy and I am at liberty to resume portrait work – I have not been to town since I called on you and have been so pressed for time with my Boston decorations which I have been doing down here that I have not had a minute for our proposed dress rehearsal. If you are in town may we have it next week any day after Monday? I have had a second letter from Mrs

c. 1894
Oil on canvas, 61½ × 40¼ (156.2 × 102.2)
Inscribed, upper left: *John S. Sargent*
National Gallery of Scotland, Edinburgh. Bequest of
Mrs Ernest Hills

Mrs Ernest Hills, *née* Constance Melanie Wynne-Roberts (d. 1932), was the daughter of Evan Wynne-Roberts of The Knowle, Surrey, a barrister and Justice of the Peace. She married Frank Ernest Hills, son of chemicals magnate Frank Clarke Hills of Redleaf, Penshurst, Kent, in 1887. Redleaf had been the home of the famous shipbuilder, collector and horticulturalist William Wells in the early part of the nineteenth century, but from 1870 Frank Clarke Hills remodelled it in the style of Louis Quinze. H. G. Wells, the writer (no relation of William Wells), wrote scathingly about the decor and the 'trail of the Bond Street showroom over it all' (*Tono-Bungay*, 1909, 1912, p. 76). The house has since been demolished. For information about Redleaf, see *The Times* (29 July 1892), p. 6; for a photograph of the drawing-room, see Mordaunt Crook, 1999, pl. 61. In a letter to Mr Preston of Bradford Art Gallery (29 May 1936), the sitter's sister described her as 'a *great* musician, & lover of all that is artistic. Redleaf was the home of everything that was lovely in art. Mrs Ernest Hills had a wonderful character, & only saw the beautiful, & good in life, & so was a *very* happy nature. You will see in her face what I mean' (Bradford Art Galleries and Museums archive).

Mrs Hills is dressed in a black satin evening gown and matching cape with broad panels of white lace. She holds the fan of white ostrich feathers that appears in the contemporary portraits of Mrs Graham Robertson and Ada Rehan (nos 305, 308), and rests it on the French bergère chair made famous by the portrait of Lady Agnew (no. 286) (See Accessories, p. xxii, no. 2a). Behind her is a Chinese silk hanging with delicate floral motifs, possibly the one hanging in a photograph of Sargent's Paris studio, 41, boulevard Berthier by Auguste Giraudon *c.* 1884 (see *Early Portraits* fig. 31). The black dress and sombre mood may reflect mourning for the recent death of the sitter's husband.

When the portrait was exhibited at the Royal Academy in 1895, the *Art Journal* considered that, like the portraits of Graham Robertson and Coventry Patmore, Sargent had 'painted, by the simplest means, an eloquent likeness of the sitter, without bravura or dash, and in a quiet, very refined harmony' (*Art Journal*, 1895, p. 179), while the *Athenaeum* noted that it evinced 'more courage than refinement on the part of the painter' (*Athenaeum*, 22 June 1895, p. 811).

Sargent painted a later portrait of Mrs Hills, *c.* 1906–9 (no. 509), a portrait of her brother-in-law, Sir George Fowke, in 1921 (no. 602), and

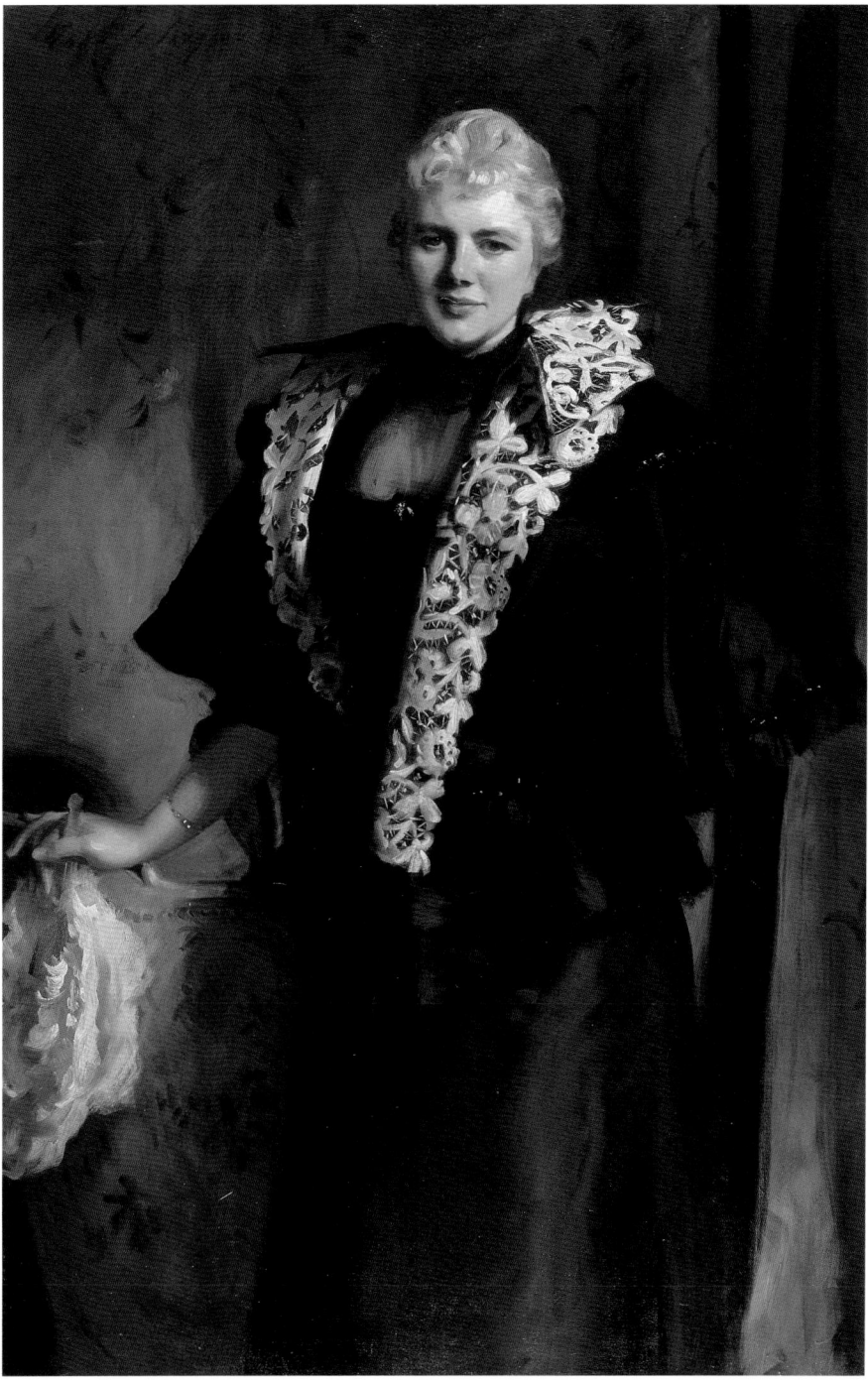

312

drawings of both Sir George and Lady Fowke in 1912 (Manchester City Art Gallery).

313 *Mrs William Lionel Wyllie*

c. 1895
Oil on canvas, 29 × 24½ (73.6 × 62.2)
Inscribed, across top: *to my friend*
Wyllie John S. Sargent
Destroyed during the Second World War.

Mrs William Lionel Wyllie, *née* Marian Amy Carew (1860–1937), met the marine artist William Lionel Wyllie when she was a child of ten, and they married nine years later in Berne in 1879. An accomplished sailor herself, she devoted herself

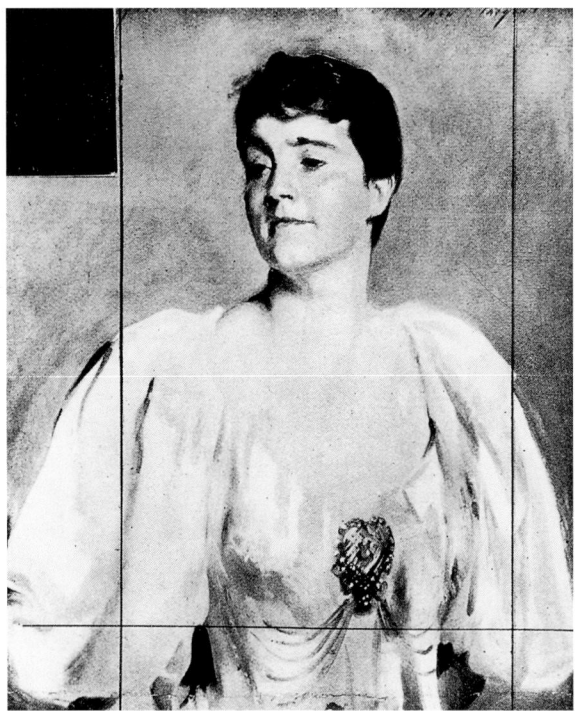

actively to his work: she wrote a catalogue for an exhibition of his work held in 1894 at Dowdeswell's Gallery, Bond Street, and, with her husband, *London to the Nore* (1905), and *Norway and its Fjords* (1907), which include illustrations by him. *We Were One. A Life of W. L. Wyllie* (1935), written by his widow after his death, is a biography and an account of his career and their life together.

Sargent's friendship with Wyllie and the circumstances surrounding the painting of this portrait are undocumented. In a letter to Edwin Russell, a friend from his student days (10 September [1885]), Sargent wrote: 'By this time I know lots of English painters and have some good friends among them. Wyllie, Abbey, Parsons' (Tate Gallery archives). In a letter to McKibbin (30 September 1948) the sitter's daughter, Kathleen, wrote: 'I have several sketches of my mother made by Sargent while he was painting her portrait . . . one of the head only' (McKibbin papers). Destruction of the portrait was confirmed by the sitter's son, Harold Wyllie, in a letter to McKibbin of 5 October 1948 (McKibbin papers).

Sargent owned W. L. Wyllie's *Sea Birds*; it was sold at the artist's sale, Christie's, London, 27 July 1925, lot 320.

314   *Mrs William Russell Cooke*

1895
Oil on canvas, 35 × 27 (89 × 68.6)
Inscribed, upper left: *John S. Sargent*
Private Collection

Mrs William Russell Cooke, *née* Margaret Mary ('Maye') Smith (1856–1914), was the daughter of Thomas Eustace Smith, a wealthy Tyneside ship repairer and politician, and his flamboyant wife, Eustacia, noted socialites and patrons of the arts (see Timothy Wilcox, 'The Aesthete Expunged: The Career and Collection of T. Eustace Smith, MP', *Journal of the History of Collections*, 5, no. 1, 1993, pp. 43–57). Mrs Russell Cooke was the sister of Mrs Robert Harrison, whom Sargent had painted in 1886 (see *Early Portraits*, no. 142), and of Mrs Crawford, both central figures in the celebrated Sir Charles Dilke divorce scandal. She married first the politician Ashton Wentworth Dilke in 1876, and secondly William Russell Cooke, a partner in the prominent London firm of solicitors Russell Cooke (now Russell Cooke, Potter & Chapman) in 1891.

Sargent had drawn Mrs Russell Cooke in 1887 (Private Collection) soon after painting the portrait of her sister Mrs Harrison. The occasion for the later oil portrait is not known. The sitter is portrayed in a black dress trimmed with jet, and with a wide, Jacobean-style stand-up lace collar; she wears a dramatic three-drop-pendant on a gold chain, a gold bracelet and a ring on the wedding finger of her left hand. A dull crimson fabric with a design picked out in gold forms the background. When the portrait was exhibited at the Royal Academy in 1895, Claude Phillips wrote that it had 'a tremendous power of self-assertion, which go[es] far to dwarf and extinguish its neighbours. It has the almost brutal frankness in treatment of Frans Hals, but not his buoyancy or his contagious optimism' (*Academy*, 11 May 1895, p. 408*)*.

During cleaning, a second canvas with a portrait sketch of Graham Robertson (no. 307) was discovered underneath the present picture, attached to the same stretcher.

315   *Madame Flora Reyntiens*

c. 1895
Oil on canvas, 29 × 19¼ (73.7 × 48.9)
Inscribed, upper left: *à* [or *to?*] *Me Reyntiens*;
upper right: *John S. Sargent*.
Private Collection

Madame Reyntiens was born in Brussels at some time in the 1860s, the second daughter of Nicholas Reyntiens, then reputed to be the wealthiest commoner in Belgium. She was married very young to Sergei Kharikoff, from a prominent and flamboyant

Moscow family. The marriage was a disaster, and, a judicial separation from her husband arranged, Flora moved to London with her baby son, where she had a celebrated musical salon. She was a friend of Giuseppe Verdi, Francesco Paolo Tosti, and Jules Massenet, the latter dedicating a song to her at the opening of his opera, *Manon*, at the Théatre de la Monnaie, Brussels; she was herself a talented musician and singer.

The portrait is previously unrecorded in Sargent literature. The canvas was slightly reduced at both sides and shaped at the top to fit an elaborate gilt rococo frame chosen by the sitter. The original inscription thus partly obscured, Sargent signed and inscribed the work a second time in red. Part of the original inscription, '*rgent*', in black, is visible at the upper left of the canvas. Madame Reyntiens is portrayed wearing a grey-green coat with leg-of-mutton sleeves and a dramatic black plumed hat.

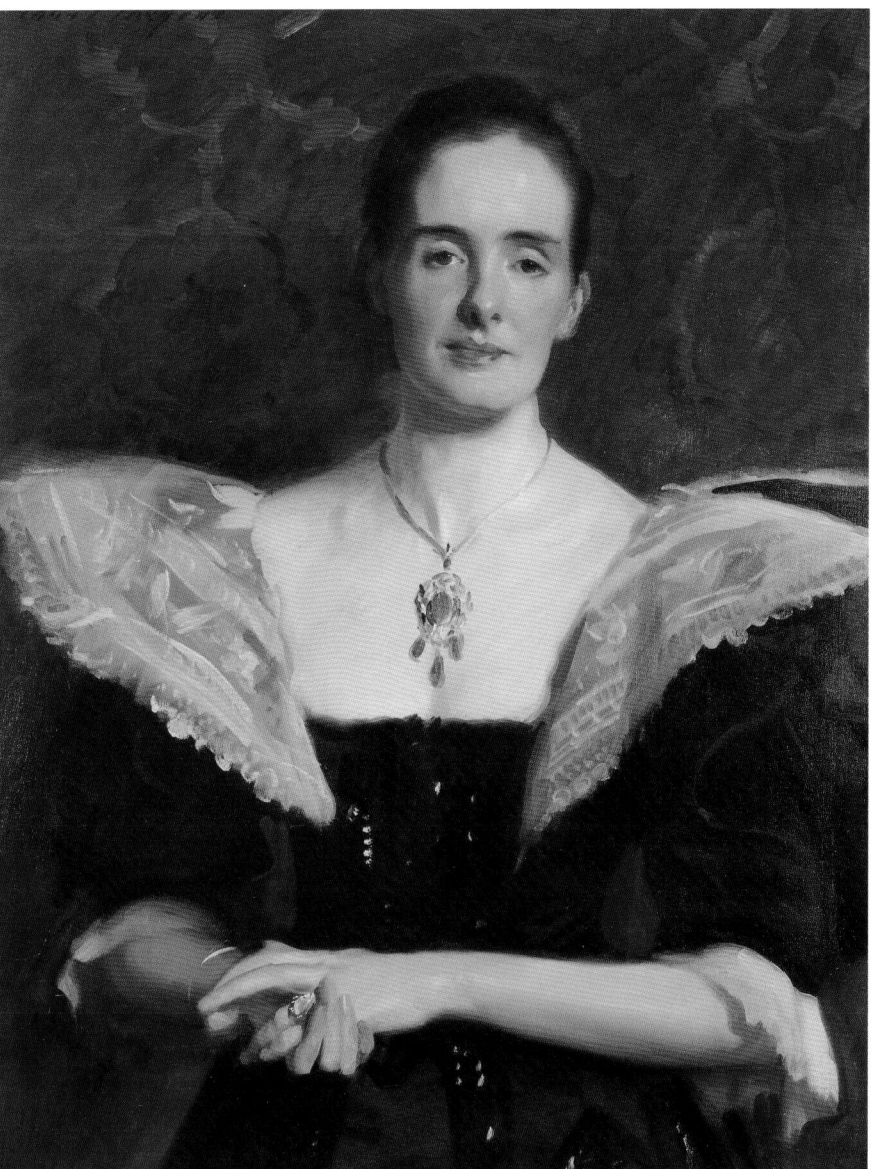

314

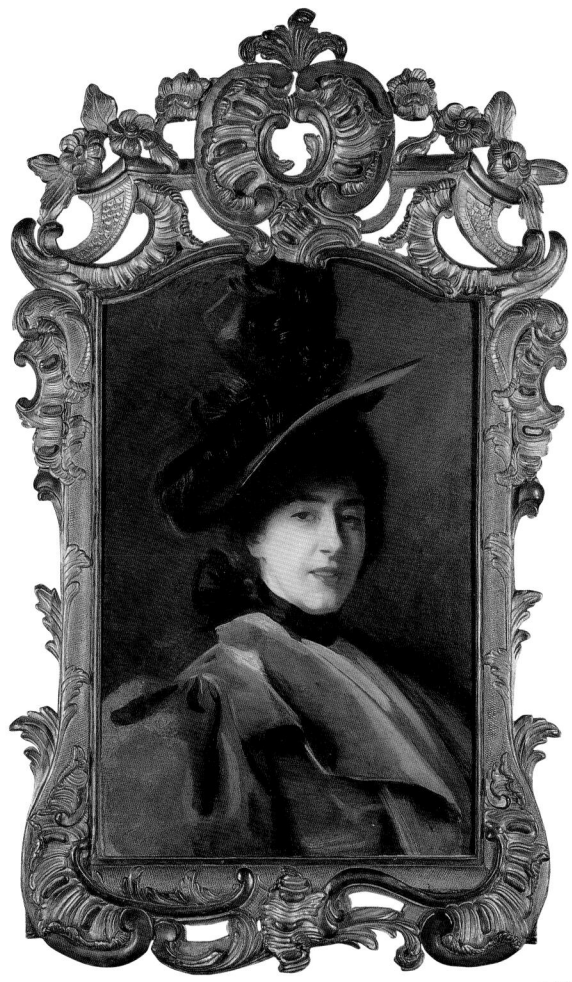

315

316 *Frances Winifred Hill or Expectancy*

c. 1895
Oil on canvas, 39½ × 33½ (100.4 × 85)
Inscribed, upper left: *John S. Sargent*
Private Collection

Frances Winifred Hill, later Mrs Pedley (1891–1991), was the granddaughter of John Maddocks, manager and later chairman of the Bradford Manufacturing Company and a director of the woollen firm Titus Salt & Co. of Saltaire, near Bradford. He was an enthusiastic collector of contemporary painting, especially of the Newlyn School, and he knew many artists. His portrait by H. H. La Thangue hangs at Cartwright Hall, Bradford; two articles on his collection by Butler Wood were published in the *Magazine of Art* (1891), pp. 298–306, and pp. 337–44. In 1902, he moved to a large house in London, Heath Royal, Putney Hill, and, as a result of rash speculations, the collection was sold from there.

Mrs Pedley remembered sitting for the portrait at the age of four or five:

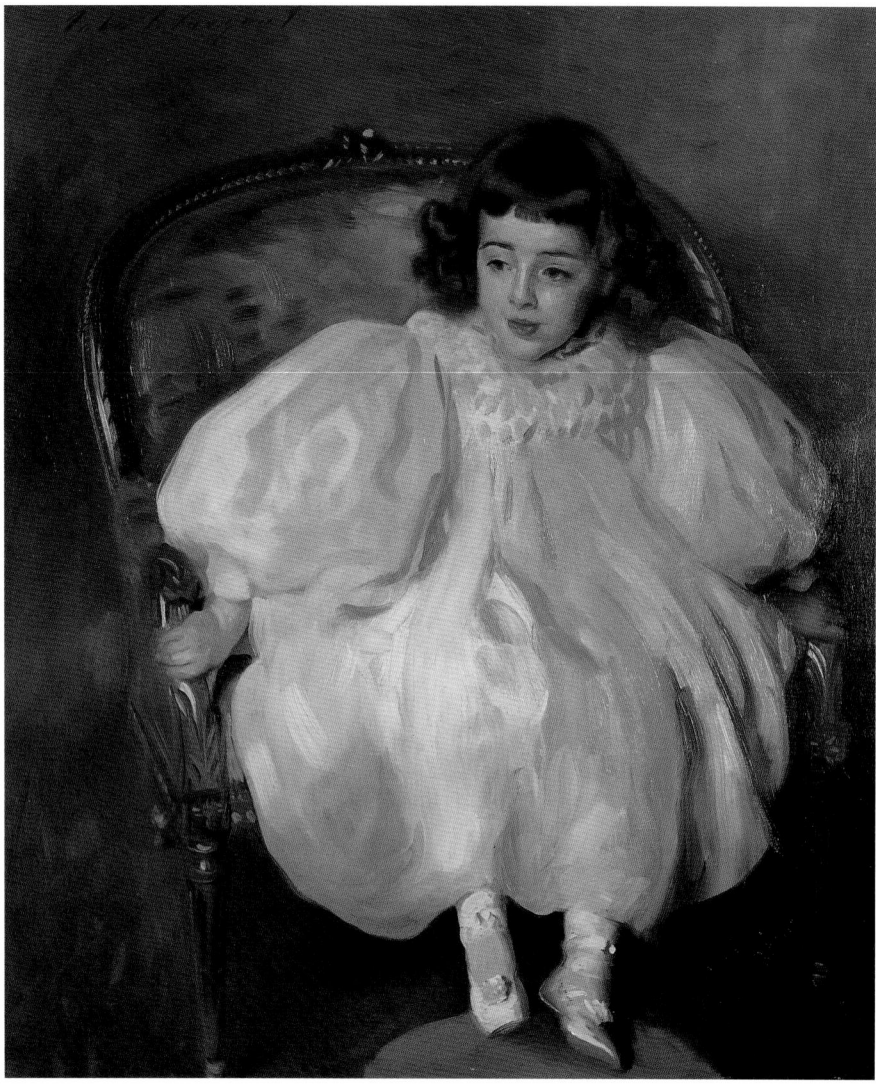

his son, who lived in The Hague, by J. William Middendorf, the then American ambassador to Holland. Following its sale in 1910, the portrait was undocumented until its reappearance on the art market in 1972 (Sotheby Parke-Bernet, New York, April 19–20, 1972, lot 55A).

317 *Gardiner Greene Hammond Jr*

1895
Oil on canvas, 28 × 22 (71 × 55.9)
Inscribed, upper right: *John S. Sargent 1895*
Private Collection

Gardiner Greene Hammond Jr (1859–1921) was the son of Gardiner Greene Hammond of Boston and Elizabeth Crowninshield Mifflin. He married, first, Esther Lathrop Fiske in 1893 (divorced 1912), and, secondly, Mrs Jean Lang in 1916. He managed his first wife's holdings, much of it in Boston real estate.

Sargent had painted Hammond's cousin Lady Playfair in 1884 (see *Early Portraits*, nos 137, 145), and it was through this connection that he came to paint the Hammonds. According to a letter from Hammond's daughter-in-law, Frances Hammond Helm, to Thomas C. Howe, director of the California Palace of the Legion of Honor (4 November 1959): 'There was an exchange of letters in which prices were discussed with some degree of acerbity. By the time Sargent was ready to do them – when he came to Boston to install the Prophets – Mrs Hammond was *enceinte*, as they said in those days, and she was painted upon his next visit to Boston in 1903' (see no. 447) (California Palace of the Legion of Honor, San Francisco).

She remembers coming to London with her mother for about a week; her mother had bought a new dress specially for the portrait, but Sargent disliked it and they were dispatched to Liberty's to get a new one. Sargent was extremely kind and would lift her onto the dais into her child's chair. He bribed her to be good by giving her oranges, and, on one occasion, by being allowed to play with near-empty tubes of paint . . . she remembers his brown beard and him using an easel beside her as he painted in a vigorous manner. She thought he had made a charcoal sketch of her first. (memorandum of a conversation with James Lomax, 4 September 1979, and a letter to the compilers of October 1982)

The chair in which she sits is one of the familiar French bergère chairs to which the artist was so attached (see Accessories, p. xxii, no. 2b). Her feet are propped up on a velvet covered footstool.

The title *Expectancy*, given to the picture in the Maddocks sale catalogue (Christie's, London, 30 April 1910), was probably the invention of the owner or the saleroom. The picture was bought in 1910 by Alexander Teixeira de Mattos, journalist, translator, and brother of the sculptor Henri Teixeira de Mattos, and it was in turn bought from

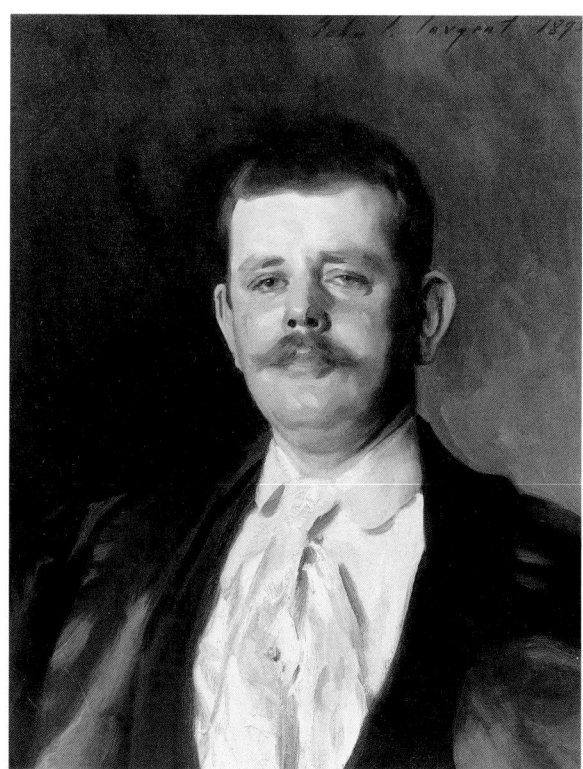

When the portrait was exhibited at the National Academy of Design in 1896, *Art Amateur* commented on the 'broadly painted and characteristic head' (*Art Amateur*, May 1896, p. 129), and the *New York Times* noted that it stood out 'with great distinction, being vigorously painted, modeled with simplicity, certainty of constructive knowledge, and a realization of form and mass' (*New York Times*, 27 March 1896, p. 5).

In 1898, Mary Cassatt was commissioned to execute pastel portraits of three of the Hammond children, apparently on Sargent's recommendation (see Sweet 1966, p. 150 and Mathews 1994, p. 247). For the pastels, see Adelyn Dohme Breeskin, *Mary Cassatt: A Catalogue Raisonné of the Oils, Pastels, Watercolors, and Drawings*, Washington, 1970, nos 292–5.

318 *Helen Sears*

1895
Oil on canvas, 65⅞ × 36 (167.3 × 91.4)
Inscribed, upper right: *John S. Sargent 1895*
Museum of Fine Arts, Boston, Massachusetts. Gift of Mrs J. D. Cameron Bradley

Helen Sears (1889–1966), was the daughter of Joshua Montgomery Sears and Sarah Choate Sears of Boston. She married J. D. Cameron Bradley in 1913 and lived in Southboro, near Boston. Her parents were friends and patrons of Mary Cassatt, Edgar Degas and John La Farge. A full-length frontal portrait of the sitter, painted by Abbott H. Thayer in 1891–2, is in the Toledo Museum of Art, Ohio (no. 58.26). Sargent painted Mrs Montgomery Sears in 1899 (no. 370).

Sargent's portrait of Helen Sears is one of four (see also nos 317, 319 and 320) painted during his visit to America in 1895 (the Copley Hall, Boston, exhibition catalogue notes erroneously that it was painted in 'May 1894'), and the only portrait of a child. She is shown dressed all in white in a silk smock dress and silk shoes tied with ribbons. She stands on a red carpet, a blue and yellow drape behind her; a large copper urn filled with white hydrangeas is to the left and there are blooms of blue hydrangeas to the left and right. Her solemn stance and the flowers overtopping her recall the composition of Sargent's 1890 portrait of Beatrice Goelet (no. 239). The flowers and the white dress also suggest a pictorial reference to *Carnation, Lily, Lily, Rose*, 1885–6 (Tate Gallery, London). The sitter's mother, Sarah Choate Sears, was a considerable artist and photographer. She photographed her young daughter in the same white dress and shoes that she wears in Sargent's portrait. When she sent the photograph to Sargent, he wrote in reply (7 August 1895): 'Many thanks for sending me the photographs. The new one of Helen has a wonderfully fine expression and makes me feel like returning to Boston and putting my umbrella through my portrait. But how can an unfortunate painter hope to rival a photograph by a mother? Absolute truth combined with absolute feeling' (quoted Hirshler 2001, p. 59). For Mrs Sears's photograph of Helen see Hirshler 2001, fig. 31.

When the portrait was shown at the Society of American Artists exhibition in New York in 1896, the critic for the *New York Times* wrote: 'The work is dexterous, of course, and is painted with great breadth and no little force. Nevertheless, it is not entirely successful, the feet being awkwardly arranged and the pose by no means happy' (*New York Times*, 28 March 1896, p. 5).

In a letter to Walter Clark (26 January 1924) about pictures for the Grand Central Art Galleries exhibition of 1924, Sargent wrote 'Mrs Bradley is all right' (GCAG archives).

319 *Richard Morris Hunt*

1895
Oil on canvas, 100 × 55 (254 × 139.7)
Inscribed, lower right: *John S. Sargent 1895*
The Biltmore Company, Biltmore House, Asheville, North Carolina

Richard Morris Hunt (1827–1895) was the most eminent American architect of his generation. He was the son of Jonathan Hunt, a wealthy New England lawyer and congressman, and his wife, Jane Maria Leavitt Hunt, and brother of the painter William Morris Hunt. He married Catharine Clinton Howland in 1861, and they had five children. He designed numerous public monuments including the pedestal for the Statue of Liberty. His long association with the Vanderbilts resulted in Saint Mark's Chapel and Rectory, Islip, New York, the Vanderbilt Mausoleum, and several splendid houses.

Biltmore House, George Vanderbilt's summer residence in North Carolina, represented the culmination of Hunt's professional relationship with the Vanderbilts. The house of 255 rooms was envisaged as a French château, romantic and late Gothic in style. The 125,000 acres of grounds were designed by Frederick Law Olmsted (see no. 320), with whom Hunt had previously collaborated for the Vanderbilt Mausoleum at the Moravian Cemetery on Staten Island. George Vanderbilt commissioned Sargent to paint portraits of both Hunt and Olmsted to hang in the house as a tribute to them. Hunt was painted in the paved courtyard of the entrance pavilion, the lower part of the grand staircase, designed after the spiral staircase at the Château de Blois, in the background.

Sargent was in Boston in April 1895 for the installation of his decorations for the Boston Public Library. A banquet in honour of Edwin Austin Abbey and Sargent was held on 25 April and, in her diary, Catharine Hunt records her husband's attending. On 15 May, Richard and Catharine Hunt met Sargent in New York, and

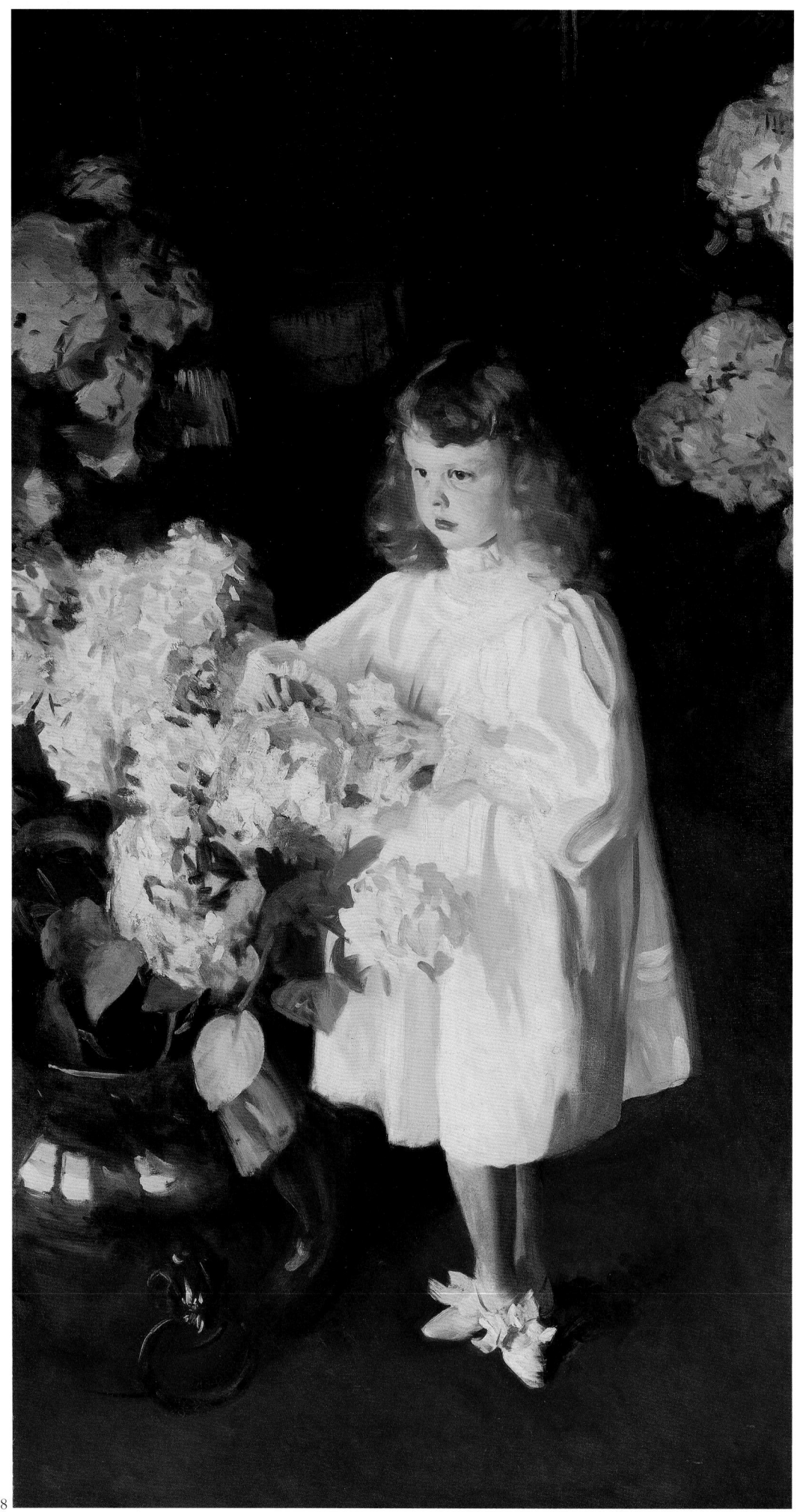

they travelled with him to Biltmore as Vanderbilt's guests in his private railway car. Mrs Hunt recalls that: 'There was much good talk about future work and I remember Mr Sargent saying that he could not finish the decorations in the Boston Public Library without another long and exhaustive visit to Sicily' (Diary of Catharine Clinton Howland Hunt, 1 August 1895, pp. 296–7, American Architectural Archives).

Sargent wrote to Mrs Montgomery Sears in Boston about the constraints that the expectations of his sitters' wives imposed on him: 'My campaign here announces itself ominously, – both wives prove to me that I must imagine thus [that] their husbands look at all like what they look at present – totally different really, and the backgrounds, a stately garden for one and a venerable place [or palace] for the other are at present red earth stuck with specimen vegetables and scaffoldings covered with niggers' (quoted in Olson 1986, p. 192). Mrs Hunt was disappointed that the portrait showed her husband looking ill and exhausted rather than as in his creative prime:

> He chose, as a background to Richard's portrait a place where a well curb stands, just outside the spiral staircase where Richard posed sometimes but oftener in one of the rooms of the Château, where a large fire could be kept burning, as the spring days were still chill. With the extraordinary inner perception or sub-consciousness, which marks so much of Mr. Sargent's work, he seems to have divined, apparently without knowing it himself, how much more ill Richard was than we realized, although all of this visit there seemed to be no more cause for anxiety than usual. The portrait represents a man thin and worn from suffering, and, though it has a certain likeness, the fire, the vigor and the personality are all wanting . . . The memory of it haunted me, and, although Mr. Sargent offered to do a replica of the head for me whenever I should ask him to, I have never had the desire to possess it. (Diary of Catharine Clinton Howland Hunt, 1 August 1895, p. 297)

Hunt's lawyer and friend Joseph Choate, whom Sargent painted in 1899 (no. 381), saw the portrait at Biltmore several years after it was painted and wrote to his wife (30 December 1901) that it was 'a ghastly thing, exhibiting in most glaring way the dreadful disease of which he was dying' (Martin 1920, p. 206).

Hunt died on 31 July 1895. George Vanderbilt ordered all work on Biltmore to be halted until after his funeral and he commissioned a memorial stained glass window for the church of All Souls in Biltmore Village. The window shows Solomon and Hiram of Tyre looking at a parchment design of the unfinished temple behind them.

F. L. Olmsted Jr mentions the portrait with that of his father in a letter to his mother, 30 June 1895: 'As to the final look of the portraits they were quite successful. Mr Hunt's however seems to me much less successful as a picture' (copy book no. 5, pp. 115–20, Frederick Law Olmsted Collection, Library of Congress, Washington, D.C.).

320 *Frederick Law Olmsted*

1895
Oil on canvas, 100 × 55 (254 × 139.7)
Inscribed, lower right: *John S. Sargent*
The Biltmore Company, Biltmore House, Asheville, North Carolina

The celebrated landscape architect Frederick Law Olmsted (1822–1903) was born in Hartford, Connecticut, the son of a wealthy merchant, John Olmsted, and his wife, Charlotte Law (Hull). After a walking tour in England, he wrote *Walks and Talks of an American Farmer in England* (1852); he virtually created a new profession and was a source of inspiration for American foresters. Devoted to the concept of parks for the public, he left a legacy of twenty parks, including Central Park and Prospect Park in New York. He married Mary Olmsted, the widow of his brother John, in 1859 and had two children and three stepchildren.

George Vanderbilt commissioned Sargent to paint portraits of both Olmsted and Hunt, the joint creators of Biltmore. Olmsted designed the formal gardens, planned the farmlands and established the beginnings of scientific forest management of the arboretum and forest. Olmsted was seventy-three at the time the portrait was painted; he had a weak constitution which had been undermined by overwork and exhaustion, and he had begun to show signs of failing memory and bewilderment. In her biography of Olmsted, Laura Wood Roper, whose account of the portrait sittings is drawn from conversations with his son, Frederick, and from his letters, notes that the family was concerned that Sargent might expose Olmsted's weakness on canvas (Roper 1973, pp. 467–68). Olmsted's letters form part of the Frederick Law Olmsted Collection, Library of Congress, Washington, D.C.

Work on the portrait began at Biltmore in the middle of May. Mrs Hunt mentions Olmsted's being at Biltmore when she and her husband arrived there on 15 May (diary of Catharine Clinton Howland Hunt, 1 August 1895, p. 296, American Architectural Archives). Using a backdrop of rhododendron, mountain laurel (*Kalmia*), and dogwood, all native foliage of the mountains of North Carolina, Sargent posed Olmsted against the northerly side of the woodland to the east of the approach road about half a mile from the house. The artist encountered difficulties with the light; he worked on the head outside and completed it in an improvised studio which had been set up in an unfinished west room of the main house, creating congenial lighting by blacking out all openings except one, to the north-west. Olmsted became frustrated by the delays which

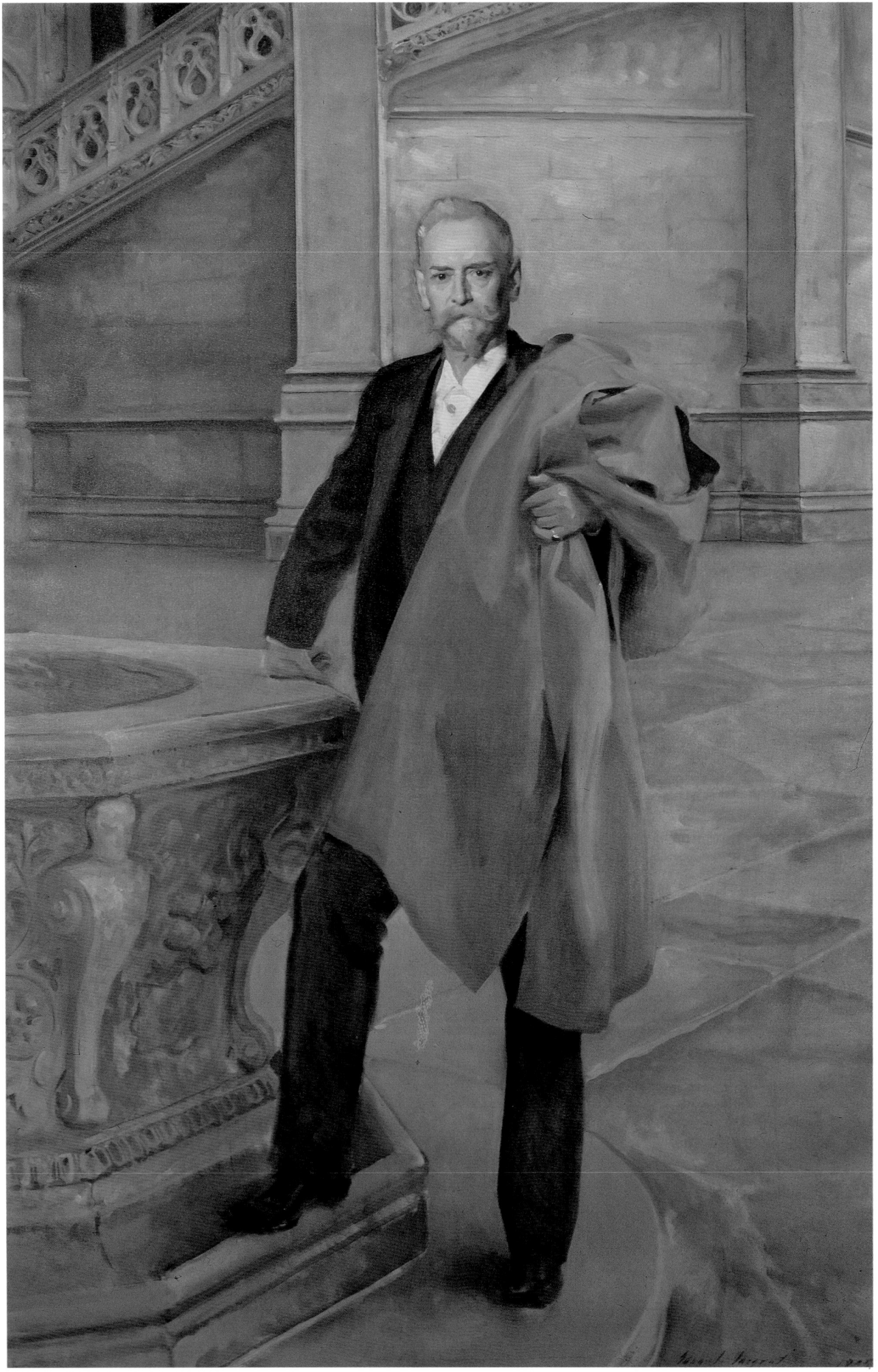

319

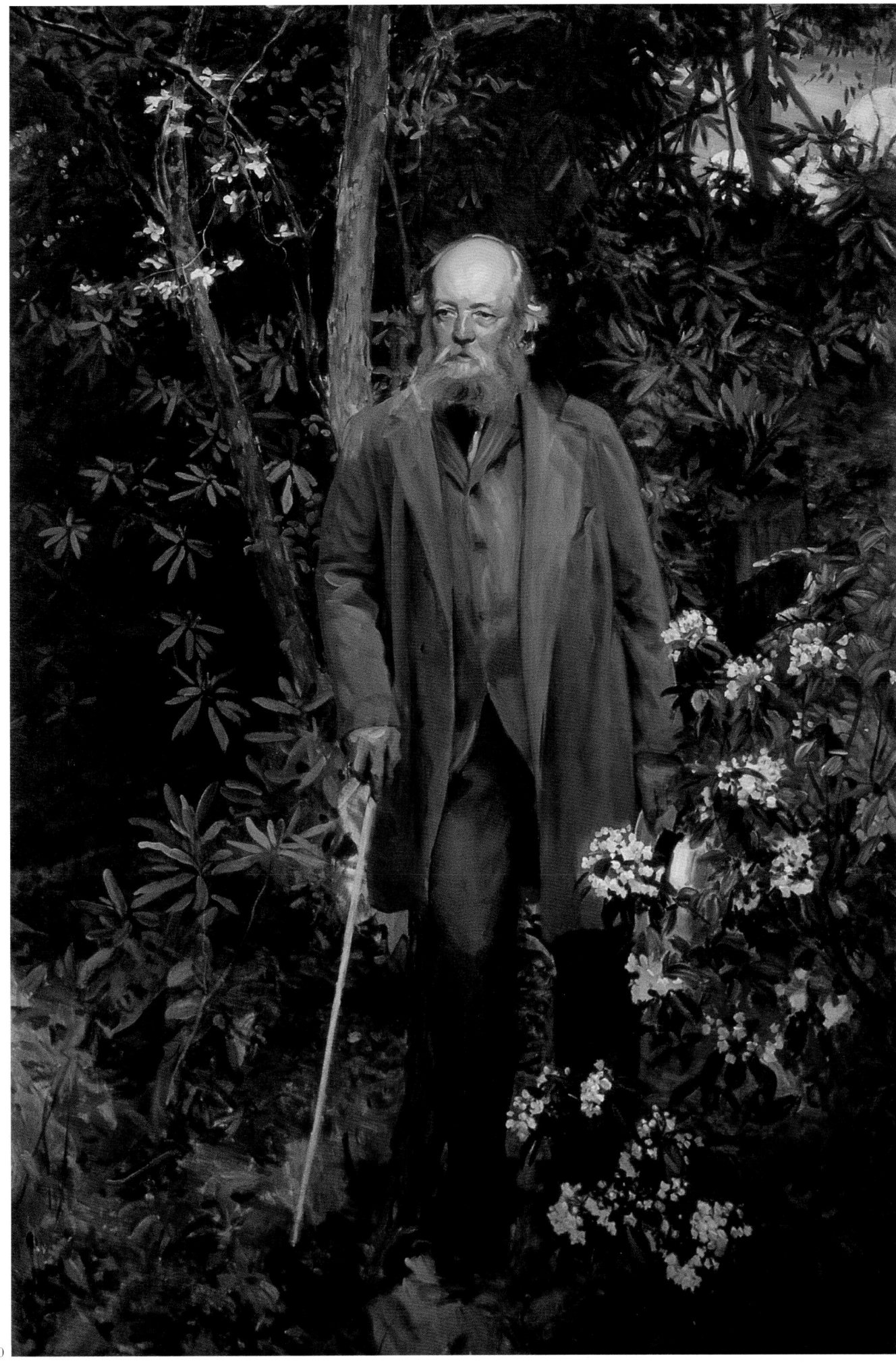

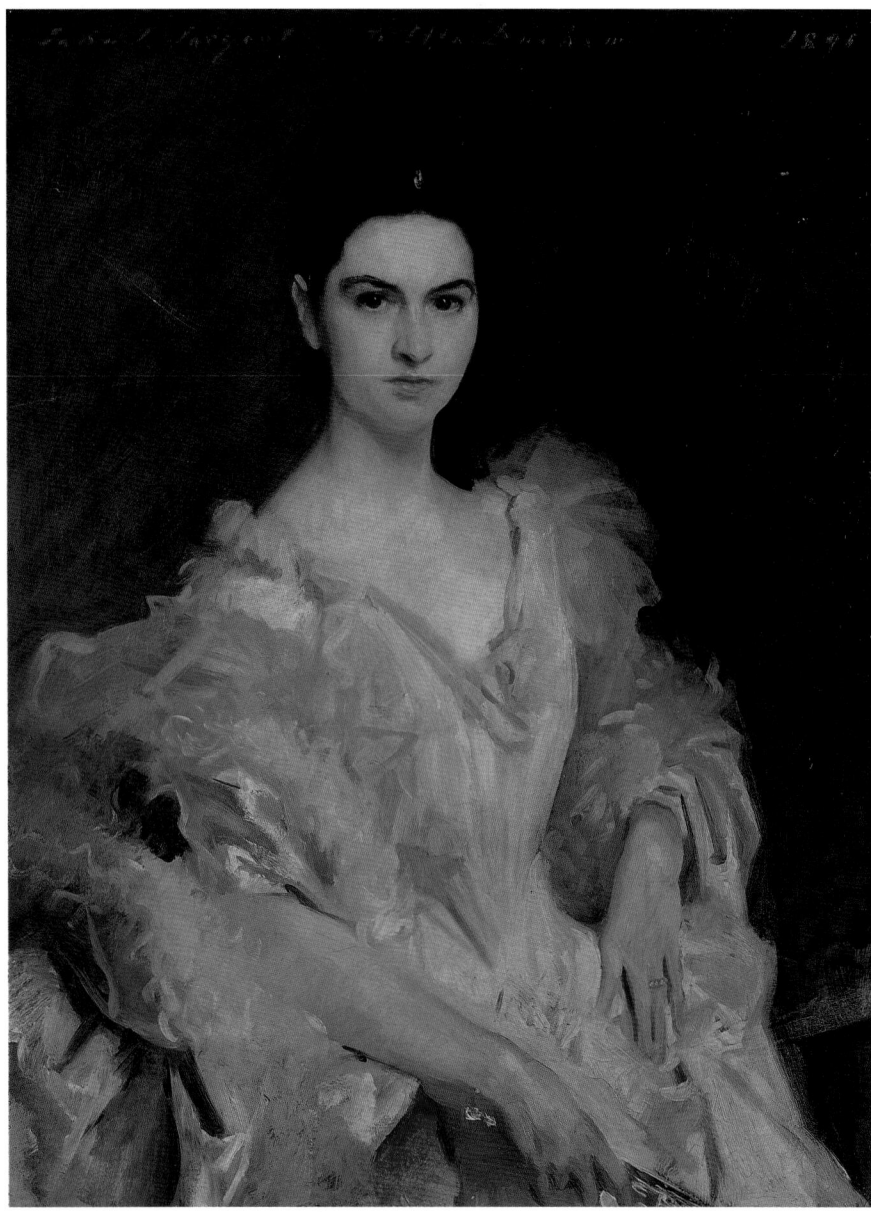

John Sargent is painting of father. It is a good likeness and a good portrait with no caricature about it as far as I can see. It is very interesting to see him work, he is so sure and firm. His drawing is certainly [illegible]. He stands off and takes a look and then gives a little lift to his shoulders and swing to his arms as though he were going to jump a fence or 'that sort of thing' – (a favorite expression of his) – and goes for the canvas. He puts his brush on the right place and works it rapidly with broad strokes'. (letter from Olmsted to Chester Aldrich, 13 June 1895, Frederick Law Olmsted Collection, Library of Congress, Washington, D.C.)

Writing to his mother, Frederick comments on the completed picture:

as to the look of the portraits they were quite successful. Mr Hunt's however seems to me much less successful as a picture. The background of father's was not spotty though there was nothing in the rest of it as good as the mass of Rhododendron leaves and shadows on the left. He lightened the blue of the sky in the upper right corner and introduced a good deal of white cloud with the effect of improving the picture considerably. (30 June 1895, copy book no. 5, pp. 115–20, Frederick Law Olmsted Collection, Library of Congress, Washington, D.C.)

A head of the young Frederick and a sketch of his father were both destroyed because Sargent was dissatisfied with them:

He painted a head of me the other day when it was too sunny to work outdoors. The lighting was rather peculiar and difficult and he said he was afraid you would be offended if you saw it. He destroyed it this morning and with it the sketch of father after offering the latter to us in a half hearted way. He was evidently not proud of them and would rather have them obliterated so I didn't enthuse much over the offer and let him blot them out. (letter from Frederick Law Olmsted Jr to his mother, 17 June 1895, Frederick Law Olmsted Collection, Library of Congress, Washington, D.C.)

321 *Etta Dunham*

1895
Oil on canvas, 39½ × 31½ inches (100 × 80 cm)
Inscribed, upper left: *John S. Sargent to Etta Dunham*; upper right: *189[5?]*
Fondazione Memmo, Rome

Harriet ('Etta') Lathrop Dunham (b. 1864) was the eldest of the six daughters of James H. Dunham of 29 Washington Square, New York. A renowned bluestocking, she married Marchese Antonio de Viti di Marco, financial director of Rome University in 1898, and they had three children,

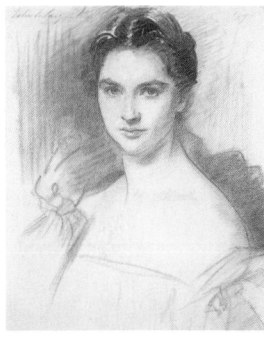

fig. 56 *Etta Dunham*, 1895. Pencil, 23 × 18 ½. Private Collection.

the lighting problems caused and, since he was impatient to be back at work elsewhere, he left his old clothes with his son, Frederick Law Olmsted Jr, so that the latter might pose in his stead while Sargent completed the picture. Young Frederick describes Sargent at work in several letters:

He would stand off, some twenty feet or so from his subject and the canvas, very deliberately but very alertly looking back and forth from one to the other and mixing a brush full of paint on his palette, then at last give a little lift of his shoulders and with a very springy motion for so heavy a man walk forward swiftly to the canvas and make a brush-stroke like an arrow going to the bullseye. (letter from Olmsted to Thomas A. Fox, 13 September 1933, quoted in Roper 1973, pp. 467–68)

A contemporary letter contains a vivid account of the sittings:

Just now I have to wait about writing or whatever till the day clouds over. Whenever it is gray I have to go and pose for the figure in the portrait

fig. 57 (facing page, bottom) *Etta Dunham*. Pencil. Private Collection.

Etta, Lucia and James. She lived in the Palazzo Orsini and later had the ancient villa Albani reconstructed. Theodore Robinson's diary (12 May 1895) records a notice that Etta is to marry the marchese (FARL).

In his reminiscences, Harrison Morris, director of the Pennsylvania Academy of Fine Arts, wrote:

> But one met most, in the beautiful house of the Marchesa Etta de Viti de Marco, the people of mark at that day in Rome. She was Miss Etta Dunham, of New York, the subject of one of Sargent's most notable portraits; accomplished, hospitable, attracting friends from everywhere, and at her parties the more intellectual side of Italian life – music, art, letters – were discussed in delightful exchanges of wit and wisdom. (Morris 1930, p. 284)

For further information on the Dunhams see the entry for Sargent's portrait of her sister Helen no. 279.

For two portrait drawings see figs 56, 57.

322 Léon Delafosse

c. 1895–8
Oil on canvas, 39¾ × 23⅜ (101 × 59.5)
Inscribed, upper left: *à M. Léon Delafosse souvenir amical*; upper right: *John S. Sargent*
Seattle Art Museum, Washington. Given in honor of Trevor Fairbrother

Léon Delafosse (1874–1955) was a brilliant, ambitious young pianist and composer, a sensitive interpreter of Chopin and Fauré, and a young man of quite angelic beauty. His virtuoso piano performances brought him to the attention of Proust, who probably drew on him for the character of the violinist Charles Morel in *A la recherche du temps perdu*. Proust introduced him to the poet Comte Robert de Montesquiou, whose protégé he was from 1894 to 1896: he set three of Montesquiou's poems to music and Montesquiou published verses on his piano playing in *Le Figaro* (10 April 1897). For an account of their association, see Philippe Juillian, *Robert de Montesquiou: A Fin de Siècle Prince*, London, 1967, pp. 164–9, 172–4 (a photograph of Delafosse is reproduced fig. 17).

It is uncertain whether Sargent and Delafosse knew each other when Sargent was living in Paris or whether they were introduced at a later date, but their enthusiasm for Fauré's music was a common bond. Percy Grainger, whose impressions of Sargent's contributions to music are included in Evan Charteris's biography, wrote: 'For many years . . . he [Sargent] had been the apostle of Gabriel Fauré in England, bringing over that great composer to London for public and private performances of his compositions, arranging performances of Fauré's work by the Cappe Quartet, Léon Delafosse, and other exquisite artists and the like' (Charteris 1927, p. 150).

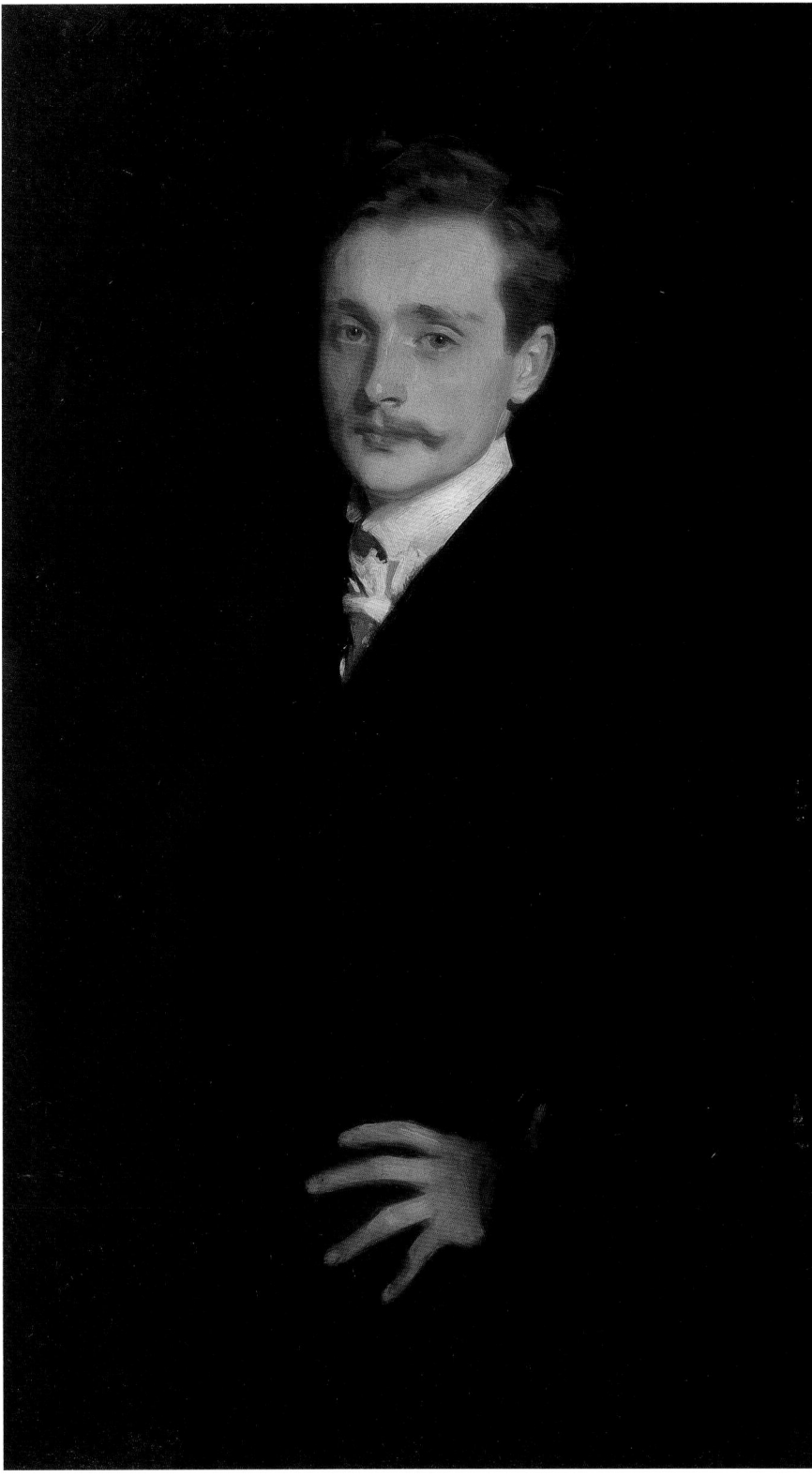

The portrait is undated, and it has not yet been established whether it was painted in Paris or London. It has been variously dated 1893, 1894 and 1899. The entry for the portrait in the 1899 Copley Hall exhibition catalogue notes 'Exhibited at the Royal Academy, London' and Downes specifies that it was exhibited at the Royal Academy in 1895. This is erroneous: the portrait was not shown at the Royal Academy until 1905. McKibbin records that the portrait was painted in Paris *c.*1893 and Mount that it was done in London in 1894, though neither gives justification

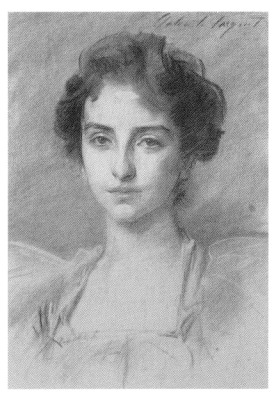

for his dating. Delafosse's physical appearance, the particular gesture of fingers outspread and held on the hip, and the overall *fin-de-siècle* mood recall the full-length portrait of another beautiful young aesthete, W. Graham Robertson (no. 306), which was certainly painted in 1894. Charteris dates the portrait of Delafosse to 1899, the year of its first exhibition at Copley Hall in Boston: the exhibition opened on 20 February, and it is just possible that the portrait was painted in the early weeks of the year.

Delafosse is mentioned in two letters from Sargent to Mrs Gardner, neither of which has a year date. One, dated 9 March, mentions the portrait specifically in the context of the Copley Hall show and must, therefore, be from 1899. Sargent wrote:

> Of course Delafosse is a decadent especially in the matter of neck-ties – but he is a very intelligent little Frenchman, and a composer and excellent pianist, who is probably going over to America in a year's time, so I sent his portrait over as a forerunner. I shall make bold to give him a note of introduction to you, and I am sure you will enjoy his playing and his French finesse. He is the only man who has taken the trouble to study certain difficult and beautiful piano compositions by Fauré. I am delighted that my show has found such favour in Boston – and that my later things are not pronounced to be a dégringolade [a collapse or falling off].

A second letter, dated 11 November, asks: 'Do you remember my request to introduce Monsieur Léon Delafosse to you? I take this opportunity as you are both in Paris, so that when he goes to Boston next year he will already be able to count you among his friends. Do make him play to you. I am sure you will have the greatest pleasure in his wonderful talent, both as a composer and a virtuoso' (ISGM archive).

When the portrait was shown at the Copley Hall exhibition, it was described as 'an admirable picture painted in half-length with subtle observation' (*Sun*, 21 February 1899, p. 6). Another critic wrote: 'The fragile tenderness, the subtle blend of depth and almost evanescent feeling, and the wistful earnestness of the face are wonderfully expressed' (*Artist*, March 1899, p. xlvi). The portrait was exhibited in 1902 at the Société nationale des beaux-arts in Paris, in 1903 at the Grosse Berliner Kunstausstellung, where it was awarded a Gold Medal, and in 1904 at the Brussels Salon. At the Royal Academy in 1905, A. C. R. Carter praised its 'quiet repose of method' (*Art Journal*, 1905, p. 166), and the critic for the *Spectator* described it as 'beautiful and subdued' (*Spectator*, 6 May 1905, p. 673).

The portrait appears to have been detained in London for a time after the Second World War. In a letter to McKibbin (16 June 1948), Marie-Louise Pailleron, whom Sargent had painted several times between 1879 and 1881 (see *Early Portraits* nos 18, 19, 37, 38, 39) writes: 'I have seen here in my appartment [*sic*] M. Delafosse the artist who has a painting of our painter. Unfortunately as M. Delafosse is French this beautiful portrait of him has been lent for an exposition [unidentified] in London before the late war . . . and he cannot have it back again it is *bloqué*' (McKibbin papers). In a second, undated letter, she writes: 'I know by M. Delafosse who lives in my house [99, rue de Verneuil, Paris] nothing has been done to deliver his portrait locked up now in London. I know he would have been happy to have it again' (McKibbin papers). The portrait seems to have been returned to Paris by September 1949. A letter to McKibbin (17 September 1949) from the Comtesse de Nélidoff, in which she suggests that McKibbin might visit Paris and see a number of Sargent's Paris paintings including the present work, implies that the portrait of Delafosse was physically in Paris by that date (McKibbin papers).

An undated water-colour of the Grand Canal, Venice, is inscribed 'à Léon Delafosse en toute admiration et amitié' (Fogg Art Museum, Cambridge, Massachusetts).

323 *The Honourable Laura Lister*

1896
Oil on canvas, 67½ × 45 (171.5 × 114.3)
Inscribed, upper right: *John S. Sargent 1896*
Fogg Art Museum, Cambridge, Massachusetts.
Bequest of Grenville L. Winthrop

Laura Lister (1892–1965) was the second daughter of the fourth Baron Ribblesdale, Master of the Queen's Buckhounds, and his wife, Charlotte Monkton ('Charty') Tennant, daughter of Sir Charles Tennant (see no. 406). She acted as hostess for her widowed father and in 1910 married a soldier, Simon, fourteenth Lord Lovat, who at the age of forty fell in love with her at first sight; they had two sons and two daughters. She entertained many fashionable and literary celebrities at Beaufort Castle, near Inverness; one of them, Sir Compton Mackenzie, remembered 'that tall and beautiful figure of fairyland's once upon a time' in an obituary notice for *The Times* (31 March 1965), p. 16.

Lord Ribblesdale was to be the subject of a memorable portrait by Sargent in 1902 (no. 421), but no details concerning this earlier portrait of his daughter have yet come to light. The seventeenth-century character of the dress and the appeal of the girl provoke obvious comparisons with the famous pictures of girls in historical costume by Sir John Everett Millais. She is painted in a gown of black satin with white or pale blue muslin sleeves, the gown is fitted at the waist with a full skirt reaching to the ground, and the yoke of white lace ends in rosettes. She is wearing a muslin mob cap, and her right hand is resting on wooden plinth, painted stone-colour; there is a pottery jardinière of classical design and an orange tree above. The formality of pose, gravity of characterization and the historical dress recall Sargent's portrait of Beatrice Goelet, painted in 1890 (no. 239). Both works are clearly indebted to Velázquez and his celebrated images of infantas.

The portrait was overshadowed by *Mrs Carl Meyer and her Children* (no. 324) at the Royal Academy, but it was warmly praised as 'the very essence of a child's archness and grace revealed on canvas' (*Art Journal*, 1897, p. 180). Writing to Mabel Hooper on 2 May 1897, Henry Adams expressed his admiration for the Meyer portrait at the Royal Academy, adding: 'Yet he has also a little girl in black – Laura Lister – which is in one respect even finer, at least to me, because it seems almost *felt*, a quality in painting and generally in art which not only has ceased to exist, but has ceased to be missed in the universal solvent of money valuations. These two works put Sargent quite by himself' (Adams 1988, vol. IV, p. 469).

324 *Mrs Carl Meyer and her Children*

1896
Oil on canvas, 79½ × 53½ (209.9 × 135.9)
Inscribed, lower left: *John S. Sargent*; lower right: *1896*
Private Collection

Mrs Carl Meyer, *née* Adèle Levis (*c.* 1861–1930), was the daughter of Julius Levis, a wealthy European rubber manufacturer. She married Carl Ferdinand Meyer, a Jewish banker, in 1883. He had been born in Hamburg but became a naturalized British subject in 1877. He was a foreign emissary for the London House of Rothschild, representing their interests in some of the major financial negotiations of the time, and was London chairman of the De Beers Company and director of the National Bank of Egypt. He was created Baronet of Shortgrove in 1910. A flamboyant hostess and leader of the artistic society of the day, Lady Meyer was passionately interested in music, theatre and opera. A fictionalized account of her and her family appears in Sylvia Thompson's *The Hounds of Spring* (1926). She is painted with her two children, Elsie Charlotte, later Mrs St John Lambert, secondly Mrs Harry Hulbert (1885–1954), and Frank Cecil (1886–1935).

In an unpublished memoir of her husband, 'A Sketch of the Life of Carl Ferdinand Meyer' (Private Collection), Lady Meyer recalls sitting to Sargent in the summer of 1896: 'Like so many artists he was extraordinarily many-sided, an ardent music lover, a marvellously well-read person and a great worker. That summer of sittings and talks with Sargent has ever been one of my most cherished memories.' (part IV, introduction) Lady Meyer quotes from several of Sargent's letters to her, all undated. He replies to invitations to be their weekend guest: 'There is nothing like time and absence, it has been noticed, for living down

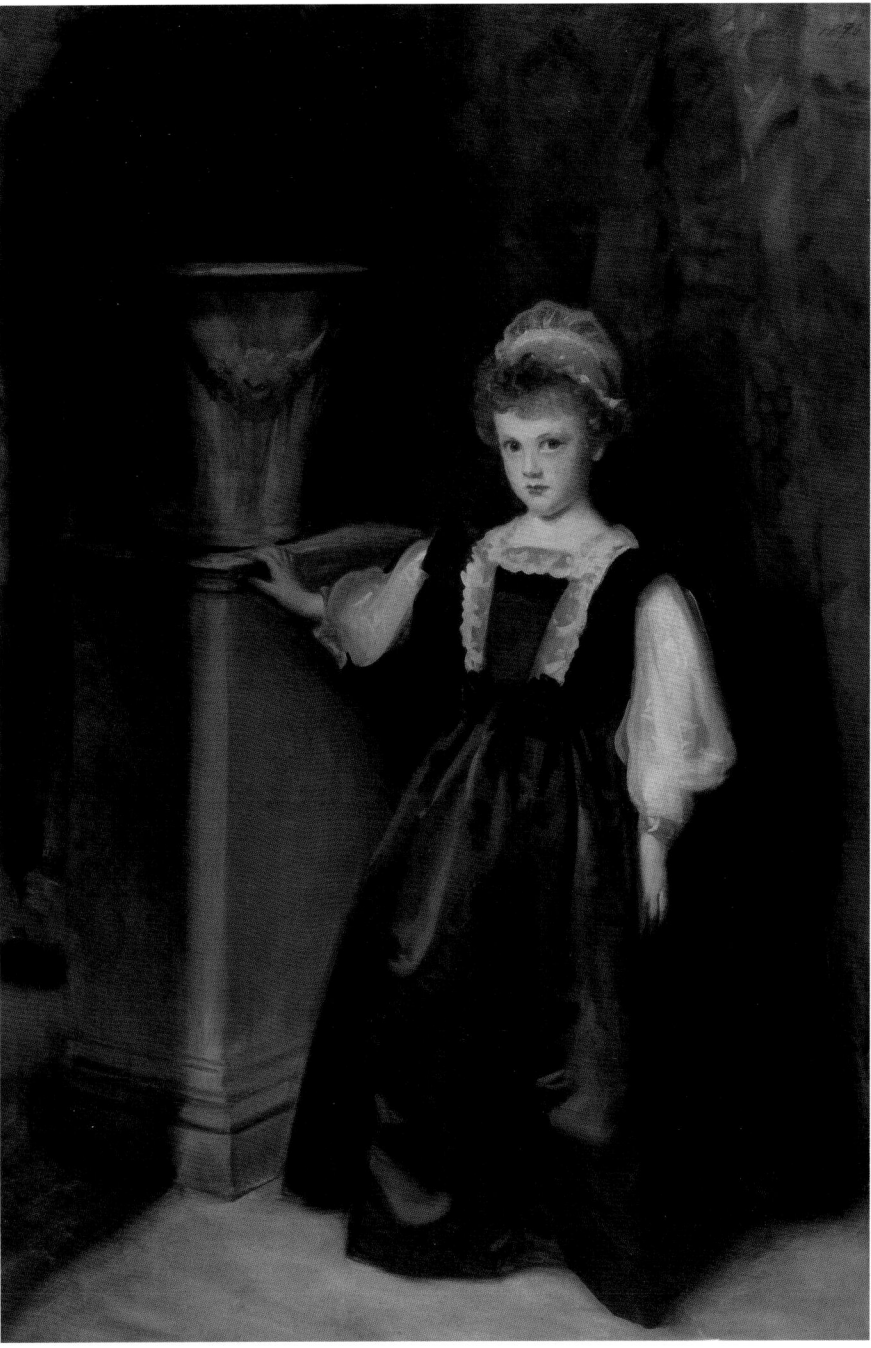

the instinctive and ungovernable repulsion from which I suffer, or at any rate to diminish the danger of explosions like those that pained you in the trying days when an inforced [*sic*] companionship brought out all that is devilish in our nature'; mentions her portrait's being exhibited in Paris: 'You know they have given Whistler and me the médaille d'honneur in Paris for the American section [Exposition universelle] – I have to thank you and your kindness in lending your picture'; and asks if she would 'consent to be the chief attraction' at the Copley Hall exhibition of 1899 (part IV, chapter I).

The characterization is a dazzling statement of the sitter's style and status. Her expansive personality dominates the picture; the perspective is acutely foreshortened, the figure leaning forward and the dazzling peach gown filling the foreground, while the children, withdrawn in a corner, peer shyly from the shadows. An elegant drawing-room is

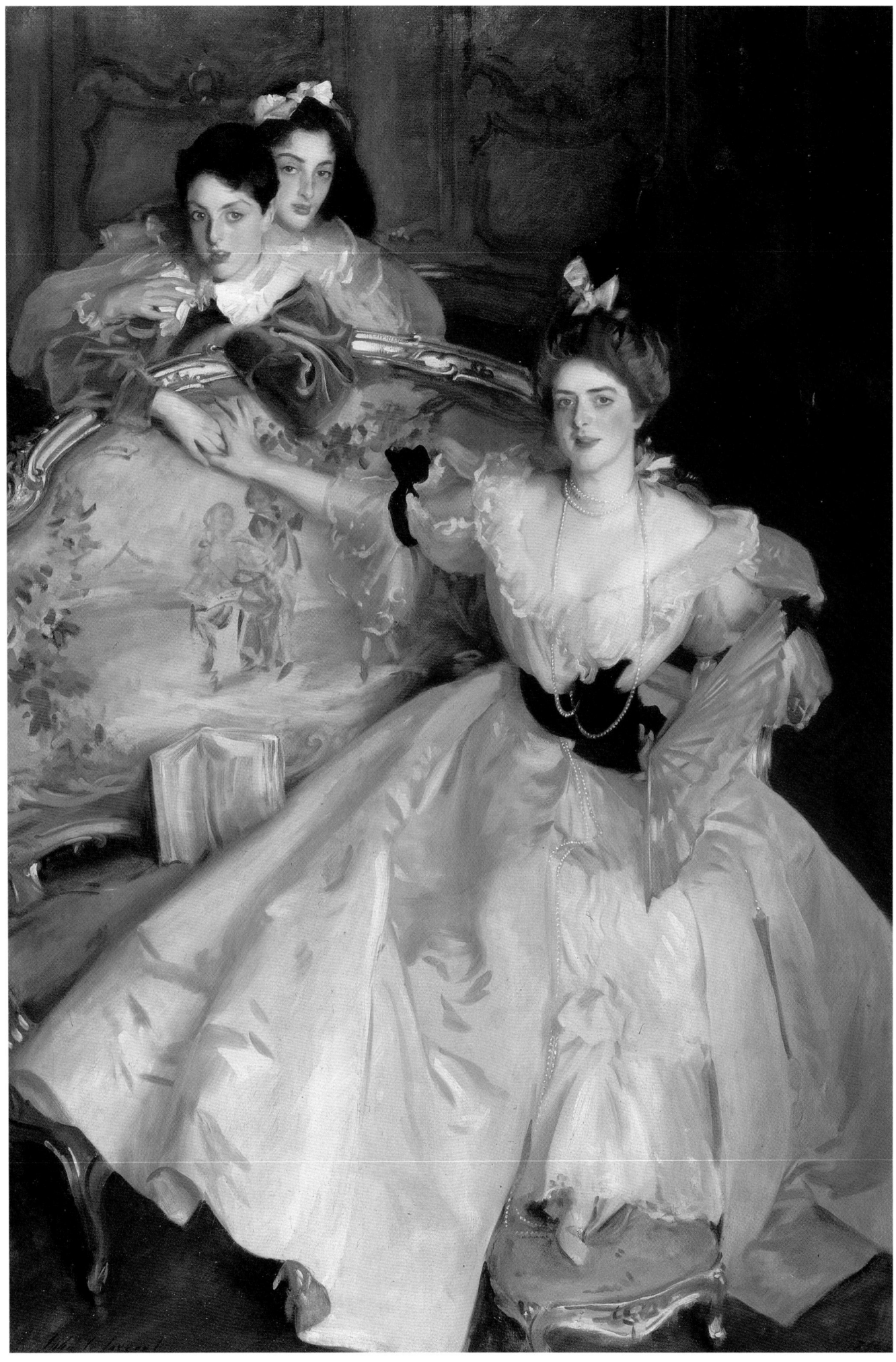

suggested by the Louis Quinze gilt sofa and matching stool with panels of Beauvais tapestry, and by the French rococo panelling in the background. The sofa seems to have been imported, for it does not appear in any other portrait, nor is it identifiable among the pieces of furniture in Sargent's studio. For the panelling, painted from a Louis Quinze-style door in Sargent's studio, see Accessories, p. xxiii, no. 17.

Mrs Meyer poses to theatrical effect, swathed in satins and velvets and surrounded by the sumptuous symbols of Edwardian affluence, absolutely assured and unashamed. Sargent creates a scene of profusion and elegant extravagance by piling up images of opulence: the voluminous skirt; the flounces, frills and ribbons; the extraordinarily long string of pearls; the lavish accessories – and of generous abandon: the book left open, the fan extended.

Mrs Carl Meyer and her Children represents the culmination of a number of portraits of seated women and owes a particular debt to *Mrs Hugh Hammersley* (no. 284) and the much earlier full-length of *Mrs Kate Moore* (see *Early Portraits*, no. 118). When it was exhibited at the Royal Academy in 1897, a few critics were troubled by the perspective, which was the subject of a caricature in *Punch* (see fig. 58), where the painting was described as 'on a sliding scale, a sort of drawing-room tobogganing exercise' (*Punch*, 8 May 1897, p. 227), and by the rarified atmosphere: 'We have, of course to admit certain conditions; it represents a highly artificial moment of civilization; it is of the world, worldly; we are in the midst of an atmosphere of silks and satins and old French furniture, and we have to do with what Lothair called "ropes of pearls"' (*The Times*, 1 May 1897, p. 16). The technical energy and pictorial mastery, the harmony of colour and the treatment of texture led to the expression of critical absolutes and to an overall sense that Sargent's reputation as the outstanding portrait painter of the day was being sanctioned. The *Times* reviewer wrote that Sargent 'seems to have reached a point in his art where certainty takes the place of experiment and assured possession that of revolt'; the *Academy*: 'Never was construction stronger, light purer, life keener, unity more absolute, or execution franker than in this astonishing work.' Henry James's passage on the painting in *Harper's Weekly* reads like a definitive statement:

Of these elements Mr Sargent has made a picture of a knock-down insolence of talent and truth of characterization, a wonderful rendering of life, of manners, of aspects, of types, of textures, of everything . . . he expresses himself as no one else scarce begins to do so in the language of the art he practices. The complete acquisition of this language seems to so few, as it happens, a needful precaution! Beside him, at any rate, his competitors appear to stammer; and his accent is not to be caught, his process, thank

heaven, not to be analyzed. (James 1956, p. 257)

The portrait was the subject of covert – and overt – anti-Semitic comment in contemporary writing. James described the children's faces as 'Jewish to a quaint orientalism, faces to peep out of the lattice or the curtains of closed seraglio or palanquin' (James 1956, p. 257). The *Spectator* wrote: 'Even Mr Sargent's skill has not succeeded in making attractive these over-civilised European Orientals. We feel that these people must go to bed in satin and live upon ices and wafer biscuits' (22 May 1897, p. 732). Henry Adams wrote in a letter to Mabel La Farge: 'The art of portraying Jewesses and their children may be varied but cannot be further perfected. Nothing better ever was done or can be done.' The portrait was one of the undoubted stars of Sargent's one-man show in Boston in 1899, but it continued to invite social as well as artistic comment, and one Boston newspaper was unambiguous, declaring that '$10,000 was not much for a multi-millionaire Israelite to pay to secure social recognition for his family' (unidentified clipping, dated Sunday, 5 March [1899], archives, the Copley Society of Boston, quoted in Fairbrother 1986, p. 195). For a discussion of Sargent's characterizations of his Jewish sitters, see Kathleen Adler, 'Sargent's Portraits of the Wertheimer Family', in Nochlin and Garb 1995, pp. 83–96.

In a letter of 28 October (no year date) to McKibbin, Mrs Meyer's daughter, Elsie mentions a drawing which Sargent did of her (Private Collection).

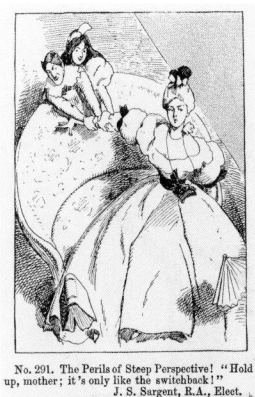

fig. 58 Caricature of *Mrs Carl Meyer and her Children*, *Punch*, CXII (8 May 1897), p. 227.

325 *Countess Clary Aldringen*

1896
Oil on canvas, 90 × 48 (228.5 × 122)
Inscribed, lower left: *John S. Sargent 1896*
Hirschl & Adler Galleries, Inc., New York

Countess Clary Aldringen (1867–1930), *née* Thérèse Kinsky, married Count Siegfried Clary Aldringen, an Austro-Hungarian diplomat, later sixth Prince of Clary and Aldringen, in 1885, and they had three children, Alfons, Elisalex, and a second daughter. From 1895 to 1897, Count Clary Aldringen was counsellor to the embassy in London.

The portrait was painted at the suggestion of the Duke and Duchess of Portland, who were close friends of the sitter. According to the duchess: 'My Duke and I insisted on her being painted and we were present most days at her sittings with Mr Sargent in London' (letter to McKibbin, 2 June 1947, McKibbin papers). According to the sitter's daughter, Countess Henri de Baillet Latour: 'She is extending her right arm, as if to invite some visitors to sit down. In reality she had a cigarette in her hand.' (letter to McKibbin, 22 September 1948, McKibbin papers)

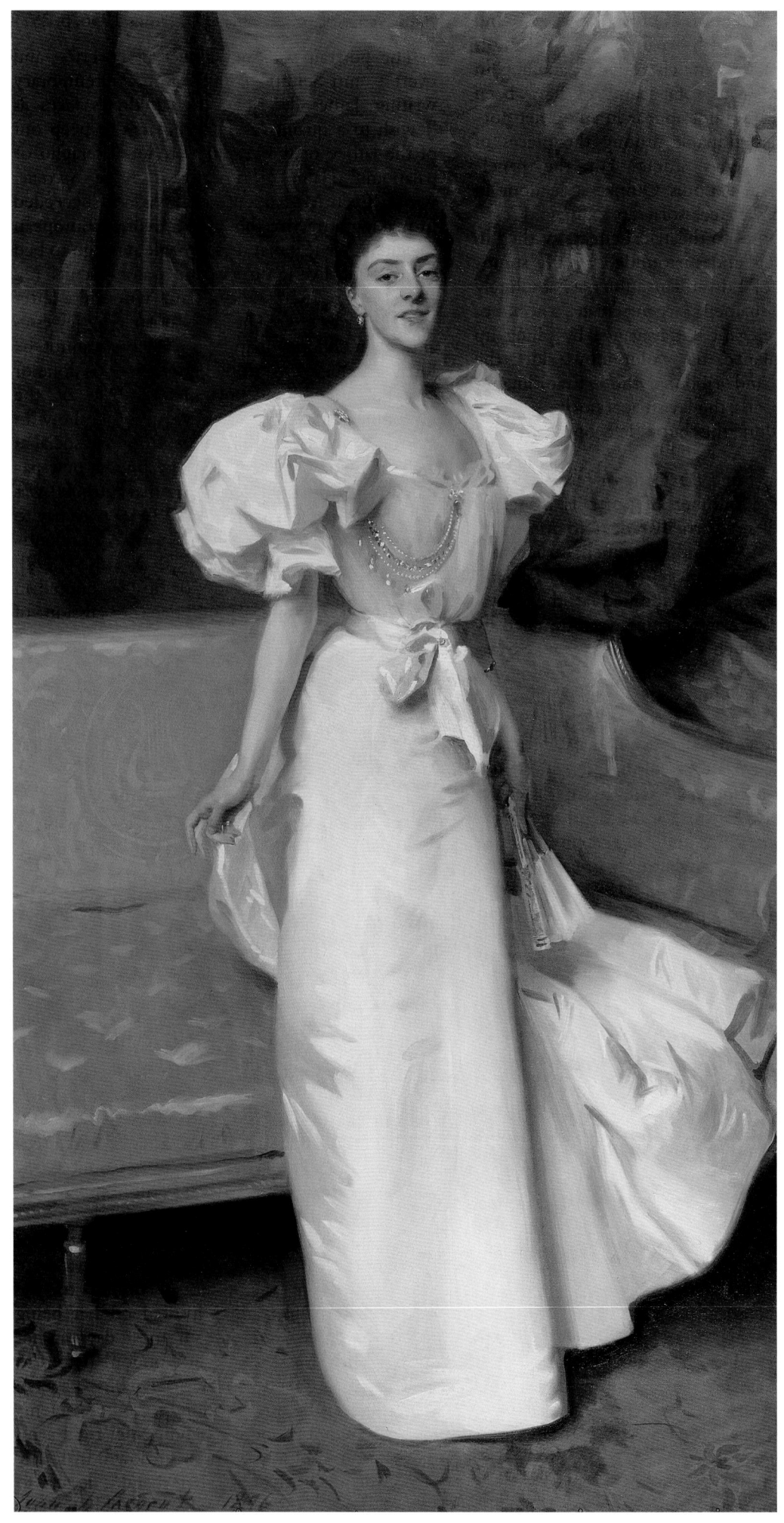

Notes prepared by Prince Clary, the sitter's son, record that the portrait used to hang in the Clary family's castle at Teplitz in Czechoslovakia (McKibbin papers). In her diary entry for 15 September 1945, Marie Vassiltchikov remembered seeing both the present work and an otherwise unrecorded portrait of the sitter's sister, Princess Löwenstein, there: 'I can remember Sargent's portrait of her [Princess Löwenstein] and her beautiful sister, Thérèse Clary, Alfy's mother, at Teplitz. What a contrast with their present plight [they were refugees] – the Edwardian Golden Age and now this!' (Vassiltchikov 1987, p. 302). Prince Clary and his family left Teplitz on 8 May 1945, taking valuables with them, including the portrait. These possessions were kept in a farmhouse near Žatec (Saaz) until the end of August 1945, when the Clarys were forced to flee, leaving their belongings behind in the hope that they would be able to send for them later. They were told that the Czechoslovakian state police arrived after their departure and took the valuables away. The portrait remained untraced until its reappearance in 1988.

The countess is dressed in a white satin evening gown with leg-of-mutton sleeves and a sash drawn round her small waist and tied in a bow at the front. She wears a diamond pendant chain looped across her front and pinned in the middle of her corsage and high on her right shoulders. Apart from earrings and a fan, she bears no other adornments. Her tall, slender figure is emphasized by the wide Louis Seize-style sofa behind her, a familiar Sargent prop (see Accessories, p. xxii, no. 1). The Flemish tapestry in the background also appears in the background of the portrait of Ada Rehan (no. 308), and the Aubusson carpet is one of several owned by the artist (see Accessories, p. xxiv, nos 33, 35).

The painting was admired when it was shown at the New Gallery in 1896. Claude Phillips wrote that nothing that Sargent exhibited at the Royal Academy quite equalled the present work 'in brilliancy and significance' (*Academy*, 9 May 1896, p. 389), and in the *Studio*, M. Aman Jean noted that it was a painting in Sargent's 'best manner. Broadly treated and full of life, this fine picture shows to perfection the artist's audacious methods. His subject seems just about to speak, her lips parted, as if to exchange a greeting, and her hand half open, as though bestowing alms' (*Studio*, 1896, p. 167). Sir Edward Burne-Jones's negative opinion of the portrait, which he saw at the New Gallery, was recorded by his studio assistant Thomas Rooke (see Lago 1982 p. 102).

326 *Mrs Walter Bacon*

1896
Oil on canvas, $81\frac{5}{8} \times 38\frac{1}{4}$ (207.3 × 97.2)
Inscribed, lower right: *John S. Sargent 1896*
The Biltmore Company, Biltmore House, Asheville, North Carolina

Mrs Walter Bacon, *née* Virginia Purdy Barker, was known as 'Jenny'. She was the daughter of Captain Smith Barker and Katherine Vanderbilt, the granddaughter of Commodore Cornelius Vanderbilt and sister of the musician Clarence Barker. She was educated in Bordeaux and, after her marriage to Walter Rathbone Bacon, divided her time between London, New York and Bordeaux. An accomplished musician and patron of the arts, she also devoted much of her time to philanthropic work. She died in 1919.

This was the last in a sequence of Vanderbilt portraits which Sargent had painted since 1888, several of them, like this, commissioned by George Vanderbilt (see no. 247). Sargent had stayed at Biltmore during the summer of 1895, where he painted portraits of Hunt and Olmsted. On 21 July 1895, he wrote to George Vanderbilt from Madrid: 'I saw the Bacons in New York and we were to correspond in view of doing her portrait in London. I expect to get a note here saying whether it is to come off this summer' (Biltmore House archive). In fact, the portrait was painted early in 1896. In a letter of 1 March 1896, in which he sent condolences on the death of Clarence Barker, Sargent wrote:

> I dare say you must have expected to get Mrs Bacon's portrait before this. I have been delayed principally by my want of success in finding a fine old frame for it. There is nothing to be found at all comparable to the one of Mr Hunt's or even of Mr Olmsted. I shall either get you the best one I can find, or else order you a new one made of a good pattern. Meanwhile will you write me instructions for shipping the portrait and frame . . . Mrs Bacon would have liked her portrait exhibited in New York before it went to Biltmore, but it is too late.

It was another six months before Sargent wrote to acknowledge receipt of Vanderbilt's cheque for £813 for portrait and frame: 'The frame is almost done and looks very nice and I expect to ship it to you soon.' Further delays occurred concerning the frame, and an additional £2 was required for alterations. Finally on 12 December, Sargent reported that the portrait was being packed at that moment: 'I have been working on it occasionally or you would have received it before. It is a picture that will I think improve in tone with time and if it is to be exhibited I should prefer it should not be for two or three years. I hope you will be pleased with the frame which is very nice to my thinking' (Biltmore House archive).

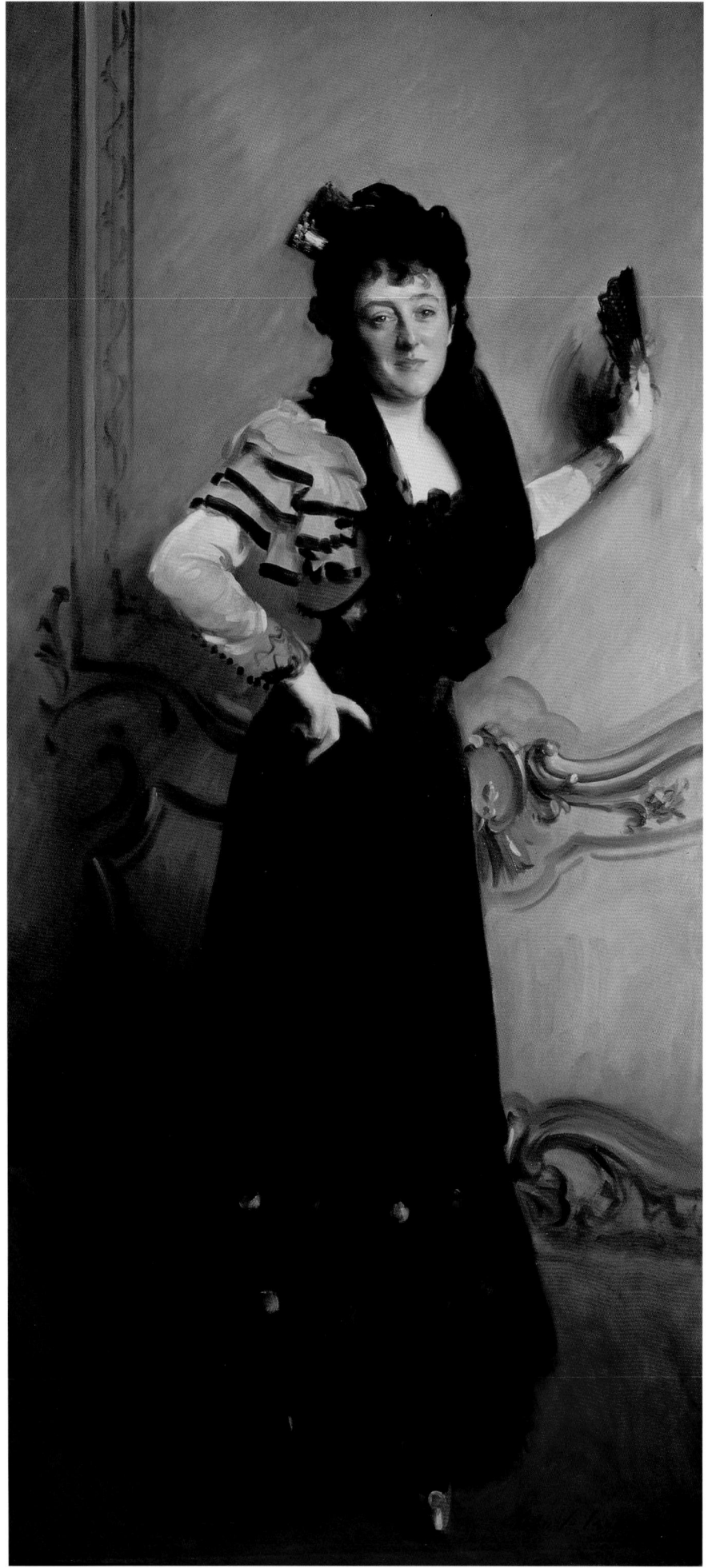

326

Mrs Bacon is portrayed in Spanish dress, a version of *maja* costume, with black lace mantilla, flounced skirts and fan.

327   *Mrs George Swinton*

1896–7
Oil on canvas, 90¾ × 48¾ (230.5 × 123.7)
Inscribed, lower left: *John S. Sargent*
Art Institute of Chicago. Wirt D. Walker Collection

Mrs George Swinton, *née* Elizabeth (Elsie) Ebsworth (1874–1966), was the daughter of Henry Ebsworth of Llandough Castle, Wales, and his wife, Zoë Miller. Her father ran the St Petersburg arm of William Miller & Co. of Leith, his father-in-law's business, and her childhood was spent in Russia. In 1895, she married Captain the Honourable George Swinton of Berwickshire; he was later Lyon King of Arms at the Royal College of Heralds and an influential member of the London County Council. They had three children – Alan, Mary and Elizabeth. Her husband's cousin, Sir Osbert Sitwell, described her as 'perhaps the most gifted of all English singers of her time, an artist of a remarkable kind', and recalled the 'incomparable warmth of her voice', her beauty of 'an unusual and moving kind', and her gaiety of spirit (Sitwell 1944, p. 215). She turned professional in 1906, giving her first professional performance at a private party held by her friend Lady Agnew (see Edinburgh 1997, p. 30), and later singing in English, French, Italian, German and Russian at private and public recitals. She was the friend and patron of many artists: Sir William Orpen painted a family group in 1901 (Private Collection); W. R. Sickert's *The Lady in a Gondola* (1905) and *Lady in Red* (*c.* 1906), both portraits of her, are in the Ashmolean Museum, Oxford, and the Fitzwilliam Museum, Cambridge, respectively; and a pastel of her by Charles Conder is in a private collection.

The portrait was commissioned as a wedding portrait by Mrs Ebsworth for her daughter and Captain Swinton. The history of the commission is recorded in a sequence of letters (many of them undated) from Sargent to Captain and Mrs Swinton (Private Collection). Early in 1895, Sargent was approached by Captain Swinton, on behalf of Mrs Ebsworth, to paint his fiancée, and on 26 March Sargent replied that he was delighted that 'it is to be a full-length which gives me more of a chance to do an interesting picture. I am leaving for America on the 6th of April and expect to be back in June – so that July would be the earliest time I can hope to begin.' There followed a series of delays; Sargent was telegraphed for from Spain because his mother, who was travelling there, was seriously ill with peritonitis (letter, headed Granada, July [1895]); he sailed to Gibraltar in June and remained in Spain for some weeks. When he returned to London, he was heavily involved with

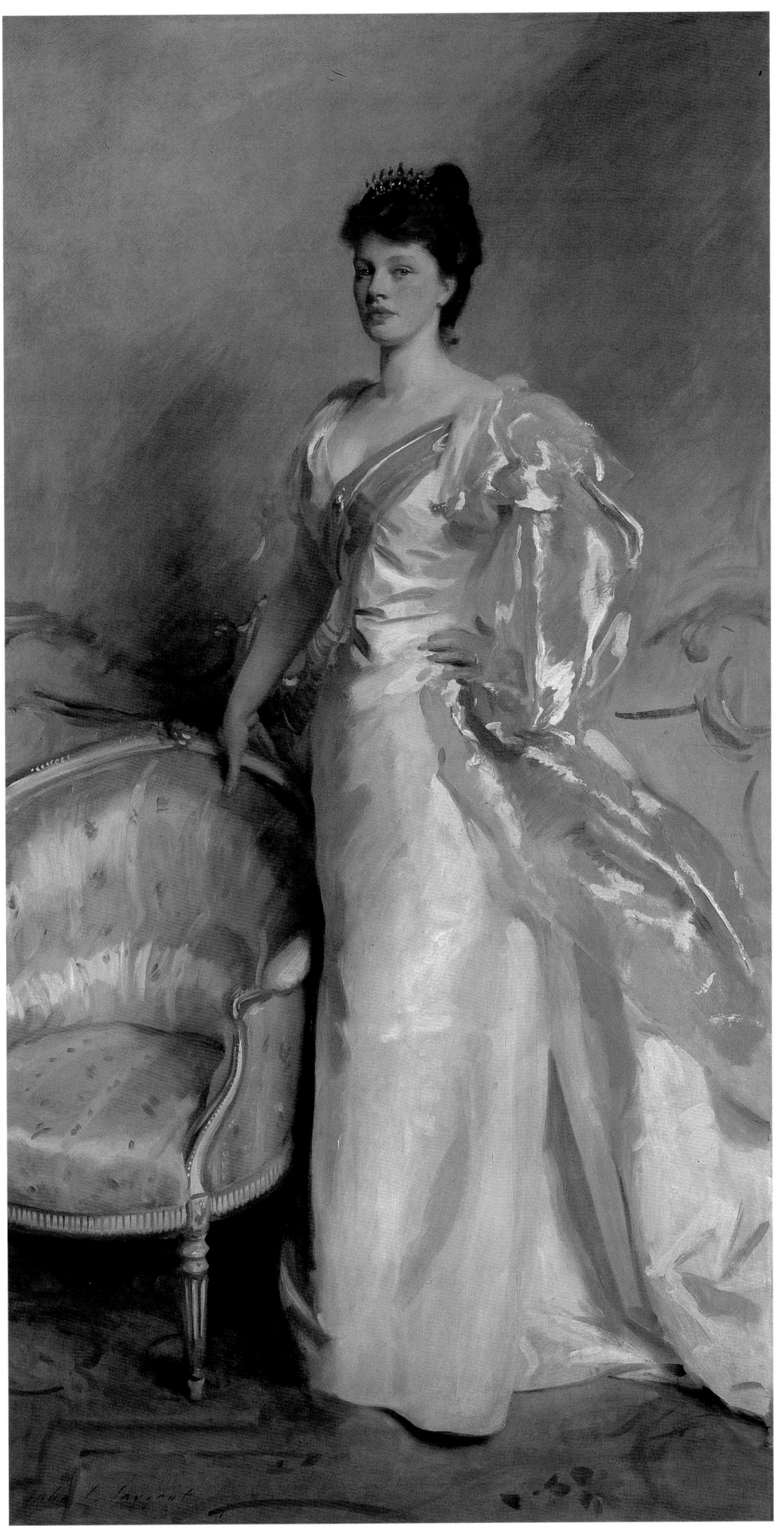

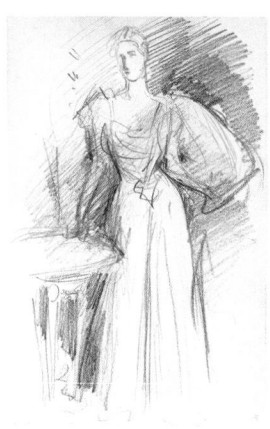

fig. 59 *Princess Demidoff.*
Pencil, 9 $\frac{7}{16}$ × 5 $\frac{15}{16}$
(24 × 15.1). Fogg Art
Museum, Harvard
University Art Museums,
1937.7.11 18 r.

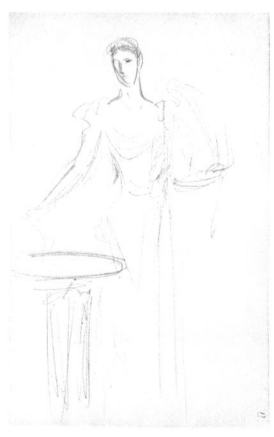

fig. 60 *Princess Demidoff.*
Pencil, 9 $\frac{7}{16}$ × 5 $\frac{15}{16}$
(24 × 15.1). Fogg Art
Museum, Harvard
University Art Museums,
1937.7.11 17 r.

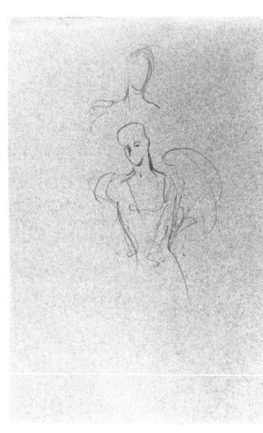

fig. 61 *Princess Demidoff.*
Pencil, 9 $\frac{7}{16}$ × 5 $\frac{15}{16}$
(24 × 15.1). Fogg Art
Museum, Harvard
University Art Museums,
1937.7.11 16 v.

the Boston mural decorations and was committed to teaching at the Royal Academy schools. Sittings were further postponed because Mrs Swinton was pregnant; her son was born in March 1896, and work eventually began on the portrait in April. Sargent wrote (letter postmarked 11 April 1896): 'I shall expect you on Tuesday morning between 11 and 1. The more dresses to choose from the better. I was sorry you could not come on picture Sunday, you would have seen things of different shapes and sizes. Mrs Ebsworth seemed in doubt as to whether it ought to be full-length or not.'

After the protracted start, progress was slow; in a letter written a number of years later, Mrs Swinton blamed their mutual love of music: 'It took a great many sittings, as we wasted a lot of time playing the piano and singing, instead of getting on with the picture' (cited by Downes 1925, p. 180). It is clear from a letter postmarked 9 January 1897, in which Sargent wrote that he was going to Sicily for six weeks, that the picture was still unfinished: 'I hope you will be inclined for another sitting then [on his return]. It has been too dark to paint for weeks.' He wrote from Florence (letter dated 26 February 1897), arranging a sitting for 2 March, and the picture was ready for exhibition at the New Gallery in May. Sargent received £525 in payment for the picture and wrote a letter to Mrs Ebsworth on 3 May 1897, thanking her for her cheque (Private Collection). Two further letters concern framing and photographing. The first is undated: 'I am horrified to think that I forgot all about the carpenter. I will tell him tomorrow morning to go to get the measurements of the picture during the day – His name is Neal and his address 68 Queen's Row Chelsea . . . Has the picture been photographed? If so I wish you would be so good as to let me have two proofs – one for myself & one for a maniac who collects all my things.' The second letter, postmarked 7 December 1897, recommends two photographers, Henry Dixon and J. Harold Roller, and continues: 'Personally I think that either of these would be better than any engraving company, for they do not retouch and the latter do. Besides the people who engraved Lady Agnew's portrait made it much too black, which is their tendency – & your picture is supposed to be light.'

Mrs Swinton is painted wearing a white satin evening gown with a diagonal sash across the bodice and a loose cape or train suspended from her left shoulder; her hair is done up in a chignon and held with a tiara of red stones. Her right hand is resting on a bergère chair covered in pink and grey striped material (see Accessories, p. xxii, no. 2 d). The French panelling behind her is a free interpretation of the Louis Quinze-style door in Sargent's studio (see Accessories, p. xxii, no. 17), and the artist's Aubusson carpet covers the floor (see Accessories, p. xxiv, no. 35).

The portrait is closely related to several full-lengths of the 1890s – for example, those of Ada

Rehan and Mrs Frederick Roller (nos 308, 311), and it represents Sargent's particular synthesis of impressionist technique and realistic portraiture. *Mrs Carl Meyer and her Children* (no. 324) at the Royal Academy was the more stunning critical success of 1897, but *Mrs George Swinton* at the New Gallery received considerable attention. The *Academy* praised its technical simplicity and discretion, noting that 'one difference between this shining work and something fine, but not so masterly, is that the greater achievement does not at all take you by surprise by its emphasis, whereas the lesser is sometimes overwhelming' (*Academy*, 1 May 1897, p. 479). The critic for the *Spectator* wrote:

> Even if there is nothing new in the arrangement of the figure and the accessories, still the fact that no one else can paint these things in a manner even approaching to Mr. Sargent makes one glad to see them again, when painted with such convincing mastery . . . One wonders if anyone else could have painted the left arm – or rather left it out – with such complete feeling of the solid structure beneath the loose scarf . . . nevertheless by the subtlety of the drawing of the folds of satin the presence of the limb is distinctly felt. It is by these resources of the art of suggestion that the painter has made his canvas seem alive . . . There is a great gap between this splendid piece of bravura and the attempt at a like style by Mr Shannon. (*Spectator*, 1 May 1897, p. 625)

Another critic declared: 'The brilliancy . . . is beyond dispute; the lady as she stands at her ease in a vivacious, almost defiant attitude, lives upon the canvas. The work is a triumph of dexterity, yet for all its *verve* and impressionism of the highest kind, it is, in appearance, little more summary in method than a Romney, and infinitely more skilful' (*Magazine of Art*, 1897, p. 136).

There was confusion in the catalogue for the Grosse Berliner Kunstausstellung exhibition in 1909. The portrait of Mrs Swinton was listed as no. 113 in the catalogue, and the portrait of Madame Pierre Gautreau was listed as no. 190 as 'Portrait' (see *Early Portraits*, no. 114); but the illustration of the portrait of Madame Gautreau was erroneously identified as 'Mrs Elsie Swinton'. Sargent wrote to Mrs Swinton from the Simpon-Kulm Hotel in Switzerland on 20 July [1909]: 'I will write to Berlin, but I am afraid if the stupid mistake is in the catalogue there is nothing to be done. The thrilling question is are you the nude Egyptian or Mme Gautreau?' (Private Collection).

When it was exhibited in Chicago in 1922, the portrait received the Potter Palmer Gold Medal and a prize of $1,000; as a result, it was purchased by the Art Institute of Chicago. A copy of the director's letter to Sargent (8 November 1922) announcing the award and purchase is in the institute's archives.

Sargent remained friendly with the Swintons, often attending their musical parties. He executed two charcoal drawings of Mrs Swinton in the context of her professional career (Private Collection). The first charcoal was done in connection with her debut as a professional singer on 22 May 1906 at the Aeolian Hall, London (for the drawing and associated letters, see Leeds 1979, no. 62, ill.). The second was executed in 1908, when she gave her first concert abroad (see Greer 1997, p. 89, ill., and Edinburgh 1997, no. 23, ill.). A charcoal of Captain Swinton of 1912 is in County Hall, London.

328 *Princess Demidoff*

c. 1896
Oil on canvas, 65¾ × 38³⁄₁₆ (167 × 97)
Inscribed, upper left: *John S. Sargent*
Toledo Museum of Art, Ohio. Gift of Florence Scott Libbey

Princess Demidoff, *née* Sophie Ilarinovna, Countess Woranzoff-Daschkoff (1871–1953), was the daughter of Count Woranzoff-Daschkoff, Minister of State at the courts of Czars Alexander III and Nicholas II, and Commander of the Russian southern front, 1914, and of his wife, Countess Elizabeth Schouvaloff. She married Prince Demidoff de San Donato, Russian diplomat and heir to a mining fortune, in 1893. He became ambassador to Greece in 1913 and he and his wife settled there after the Russian Revolution. She was a noted beauty, a leader of style, and a fine sportswoman.

The portrait was painted in London, where the princess was a prominent figure; her husband was then serving as first secretary at the Russian embassy. Her dress is a white satin evening gown with a sash and short, ruched sleeves. She is also wearing a red cape edged with fur and lined with pink; gold, diamond and emerald bracelets on both wrists; a double-string pearl necklace, and a diamond brooch with a drop pearl at her breast and another at her shoulder. She stands on one of the artist's Aubusson carpets before a Chinese lacquer screen (see Accessories, pp. xxiv, xxiii, nos 35, 25). Several pencil studies in a sketchbook are probably preliminary studies for the portrait (figs 59, 60, 61).

When the portrait was exhibited at the Royal Academy in 1896, Claude Phillips wrote: 'Its effect is something like that of a ringing trumpet tone in an orchestral passage of muted strings. The critic may protest on principal [*sic*], yet he will end by being subdued' (*Academy*, 9 May 1896, p. 389). Kit Anstruther-Thomson described the painting to Vernon Lee as 'a Russian Princess in a red cape. He has frankly let her go as a character . . . and has treated her as decoration (a bird from the tropics)' (undated letter, CC).

According to the sitter's nephew, Count Hilarion Woranzoff-Daschkoff, Sargent painted

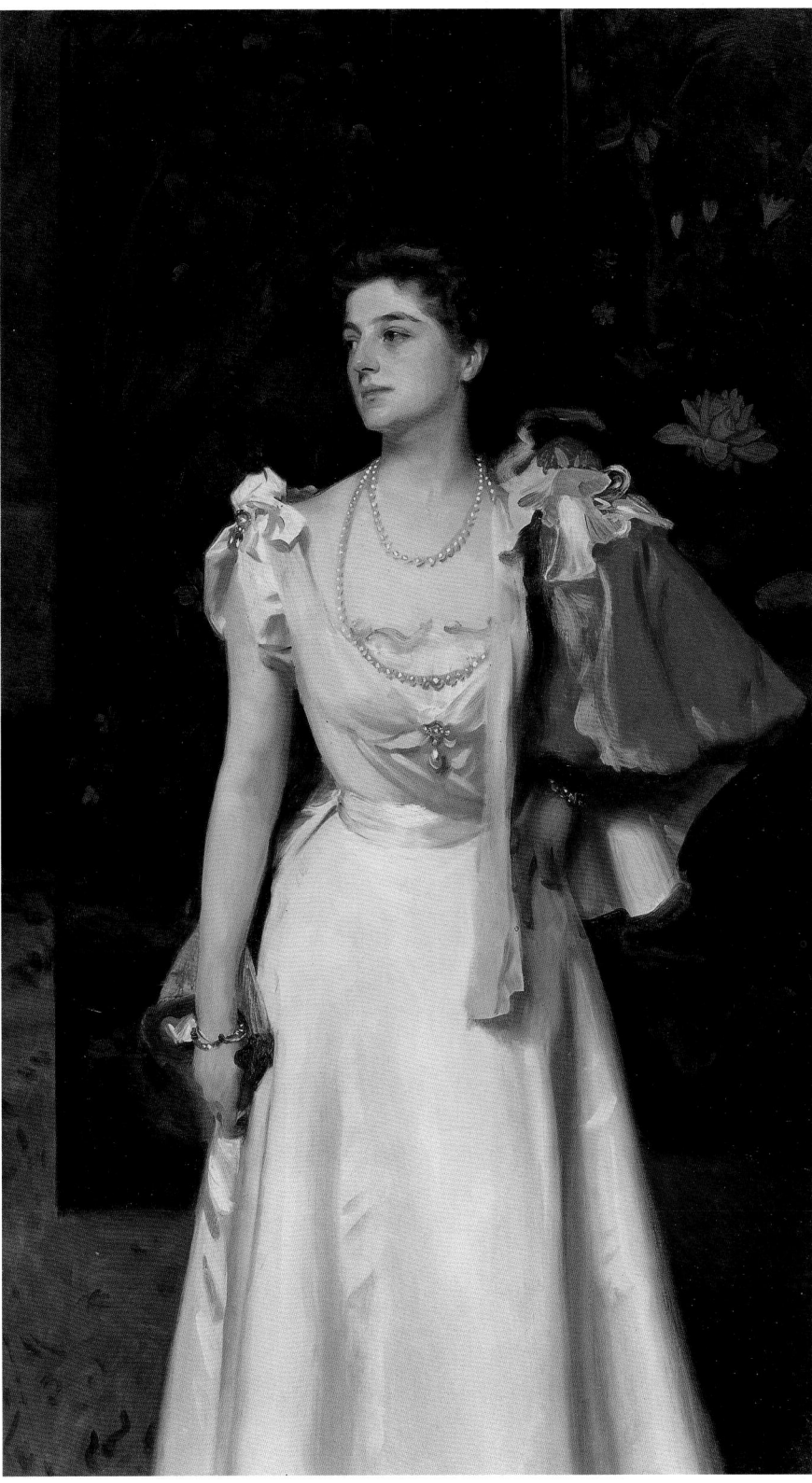

two further portraits of Princess Demidoff, one a small oval of her dressed in white (letter to the Toledo Museum of Art, 26 October 1978). These portraits are otherwise unrecorded.

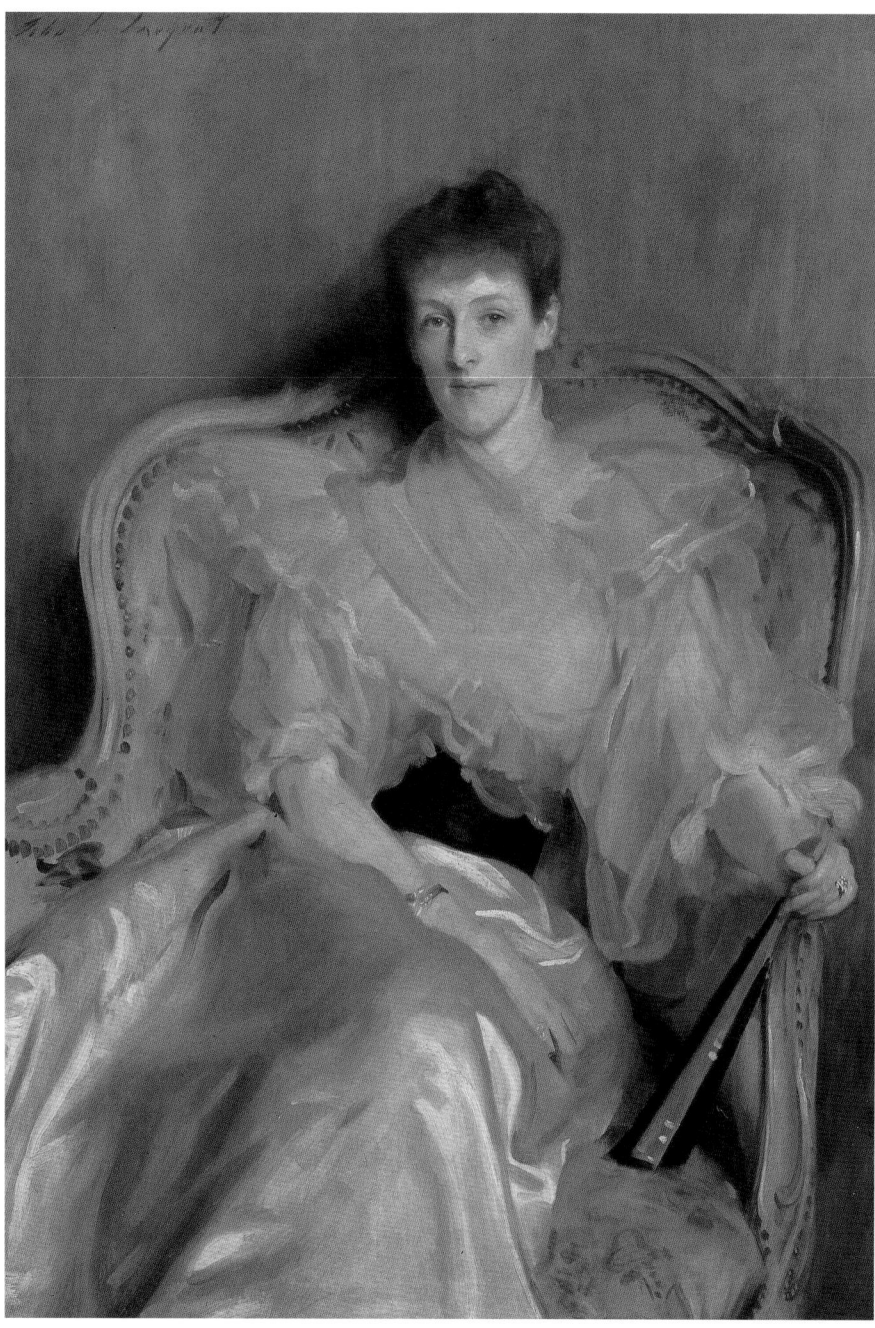

329 Mrs Ian Hamilton

c. 1896
Oil on canvas, 51¼ × 36¼ (130 × 92.5)
Inscribed, upper left: *John S. Sargent*
Tate Gallery, London. Gift of General Sir Ian
Hamilton

Mrs Ian Hamilton, *née* Jean Muir (d. 1941), was the eldest daughter of Sir John Muir, Bt of Deanston, Perthshire, Lord Provost of Glasgow from 1889 to 1892, and his wife, Margaret Morrison Kay. In 1887, she married Colonel, later General Sir Ian Hamilton, the distinguished soldier and art collector. She was herself a friend of Walter Sickert and a collector and patron of young artists. Hamilton's memoir *Jean*, written after his wife's death, reproduces a number of her poems and several of her pastel drawings. Portraits of her were also painted by Sir Charles Furse and Sir John Lavery. Colonel

Hamilton's brother, Vereker, was a friend of the artist, and the commission may have come through him. A companion portrait of Colonel Hamilton was painted in 1898 (no. 352).

Mrs Hamilton is dressed in a white satin evening gown; it has wide, flounced shoulders, and there is a gauzy scarf drawn tightly across her neck. She has a gold bracelet on her right arm and a diamond ring on the index finger of her left hand, and she holds a closed black fan. The chair in the portrait is identical with the one in which Lady Agnew (no. 286) sits (see Accessories, p. xxii, no. 2 a). A textured wall-hanging or drape of material fills the background. Colonel Hamilton wrote that 'the gleaming white satin [of her gown]. . . . was shown off by the jade green walls of her drawing room', where the picture hung (Hamilton 1942, p. 18).

In general composition and treatment, the portrait closely follows the pattern of *Lady Agnew of Lochnaw* (no. 286), the prototype for so many female portraits of the 1890s. Claude Phillips wrote that *Mrs Ian Hamilton* proved that Sargent could 'on occasion command the grateful quality of repose as well as that of momentariness and extreme vivacity' (*Academy*, 9 May 1896, p. 389). Contrasting its shimmering textures with the unpleasant and sticky surfaces of more academic work, the critic of the *Spectator* compared Sargent to an alchemist:

> What a beautiful substance mere paint has become. How it flows and changes its light and its colour, subservient to the artist's will, while remaining beautiful in itself. The solvent of an alchemist seems to have made some sea-shell plastic, and compelled it to take the billowy form and subtle colour of the dress in shadow where it flows in front of the warm flesh-tones of the arm . . . How many other painters could produce such solid and convincing modelling throughout a picture, using only these light tones? (*Spectator*, 16 May 1896, p. 706)

For a related drawing, see fig. 62.

For letters from Sargent to Harrison Morris (28 November [1904] and 10 December [1904]) about exhibiting the painting at the Pennsylvania Academy of Fine Arts in 1905, see Morris 1930, pp. 113–14. Sargent is mentioned in the private diaries of the sitter, Papers of Jean Miller Hamilton, Lady Hamilton, Liddell Hart Center for Military Archives, King's College, London

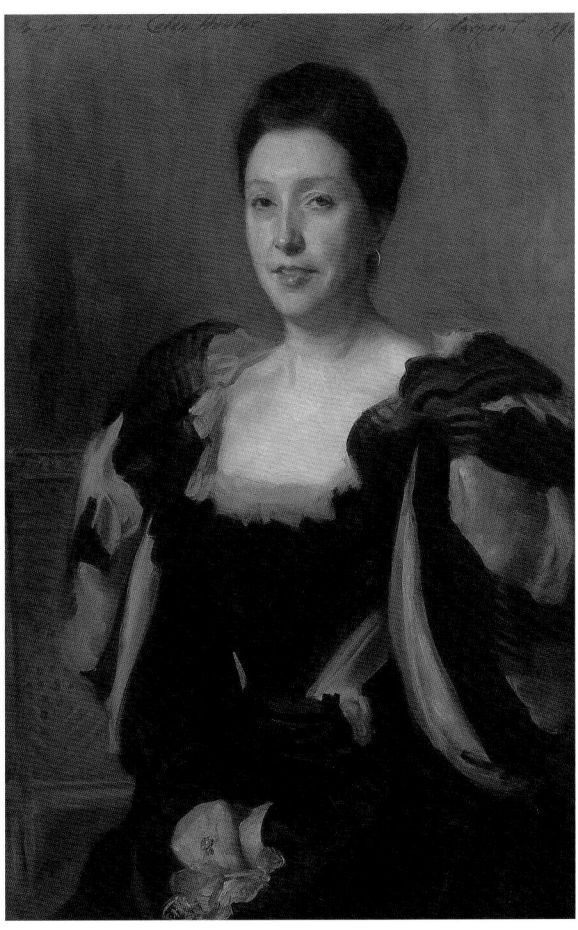

331 *Mrs William Shakespeare*

c. 1896
Oil on canvas, 29⅜ × 24½ (74.6 × 62.2)
Inscribed, upper left: *to my friend Shakespeare*;
upper right: *John S. Sargent*
Memorial Art Gallery of the University of
Rochester, New York. Marion Stratton Gould Fund

Mrs Shakespeare, *née* Louise Weiland (*c.* 1850–1911), was brought up at the court of Dresden and married the singer and teacher William Shakespeare in 1875. She was the hostess of a musical salon at which her daughter, Mimie, and husband performed. Brahms, the water-colour artist Hercules Brabazon, and Sargent were among her friends. Eva Ducat (a piano pupil of Mimie) describes her as a rather silent woman who 'hid brilliant gifts under a gentle, deprecating manner' (Ducat 1928, p. 75) and the portrait as 'one of the most tender, gentle, intimate things ever done in oils' (p. 77), and she relates that Sargent tried to capture Mrs Shakespeare's characteristic wistful expression by telling her sad tales as he painted.

 Mount dates the picture 1894, Charteris and McKibbin 1901; but the fullness of the leg-of-

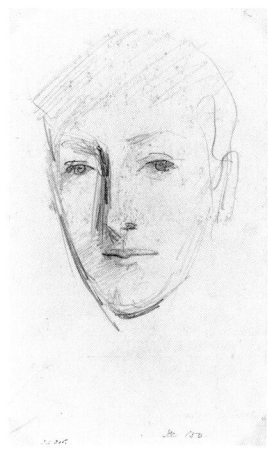

fig. 62 *Mrs Ian Hamilton.* Pencil, 6 ¹³⁄₁₆ × 4 ¹⁄₁₆ (17.4 × 10.3). Fogg Art Museum, Harvard University Art Museums. Gift of Miss Emily Sargent and Mrs Francis Ormond in memory of their brother, John Singer Sargent 1931.74 r.

330 *Mrs Colin Hunter*

1896
Oil on canvas, 37 × 24½ (94 × 62.2)
Inscribed, upper left: *to my friend Colin Hunter*; upper right: *John S. Sargent 1896*
Utah Museum of Fine Arts, Salt Lake City

Mrs Colin Hunter, *née* Isabella Rattray Young, was the daughter of John H. Young, a surgeon dentist. She married the well-known marine painter and Royal Academician Colin Hunter, in Glasgow in 1873, and they had two sons and two daughters. Hunter was a friend of the artist, who used to play duets with his wife.

 According to David McKibbin, the portrait was painted for Colin Hunter in exchange for a tapestry (unconfirmed source, McKibbin's index card for the picture, McKibbin papers).

 Mrs Hunter is painted in a black evening gown with flounced sleeves slashed with white in Renaissance style; she is seated in one of the cane-backed French *directoire* chairs which feature in Sargent's studio (see Accessories, p. xxii, no. 7).

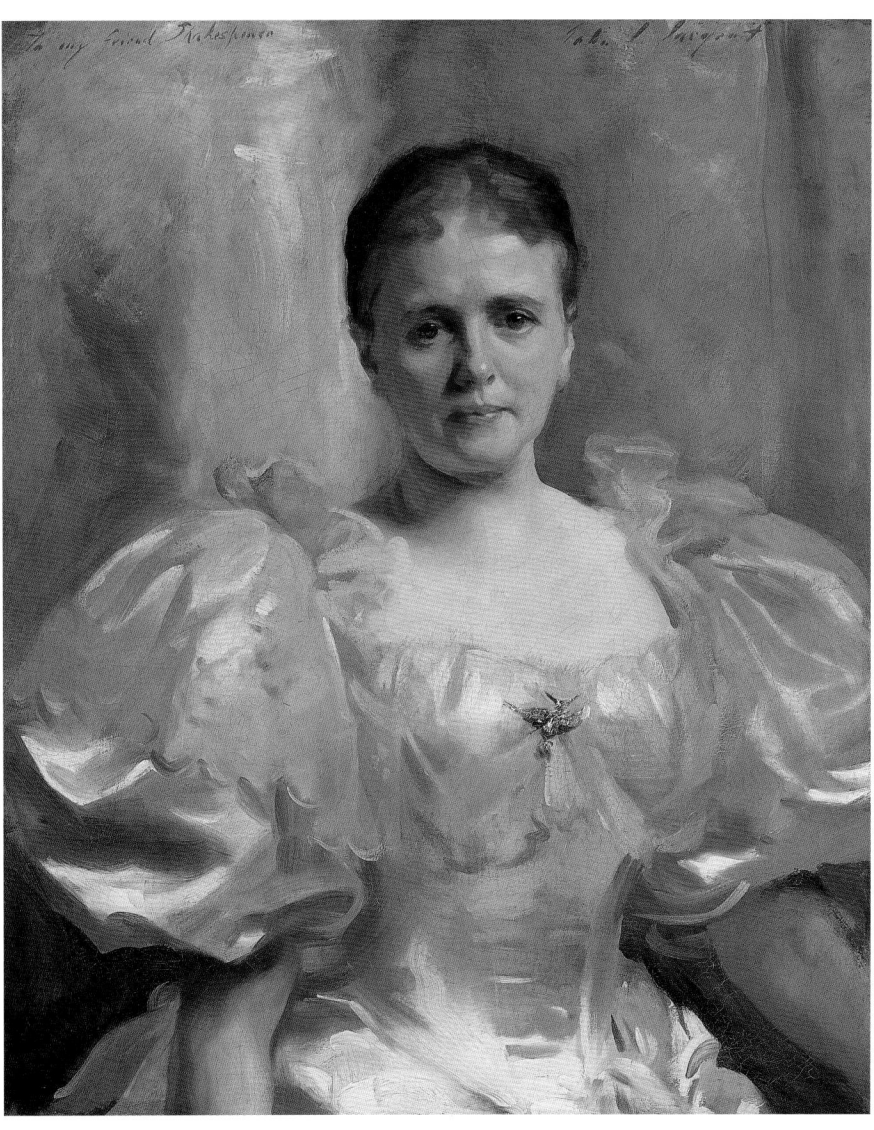

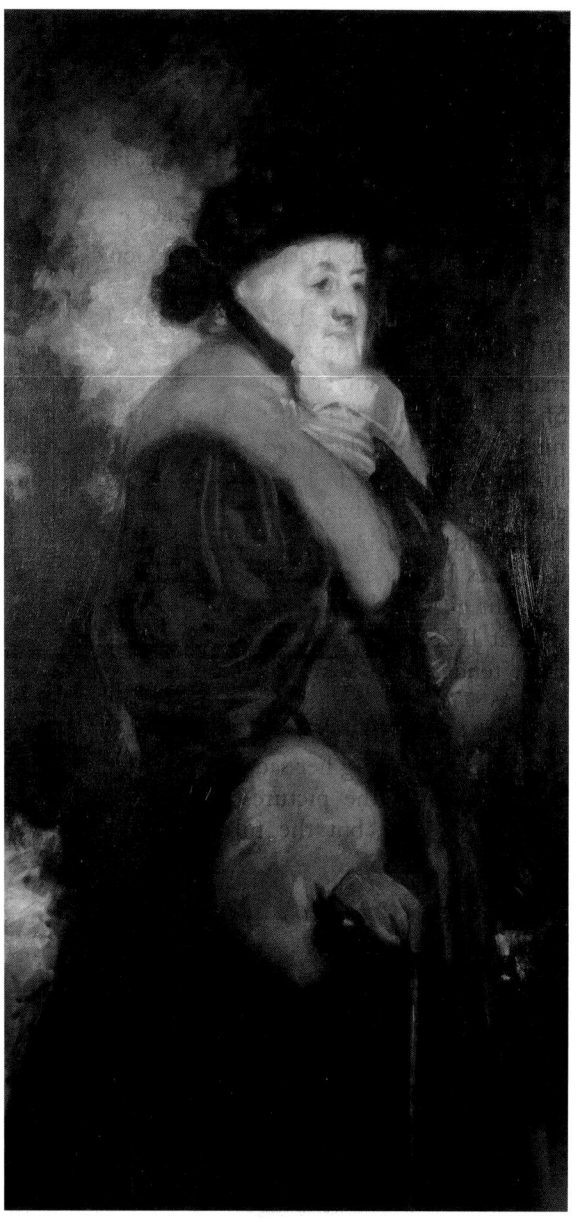

c. 1896
Oil on canvas, 54 × 27½ (137.2 × 70)
Inscribed, upper right: *John S. Sargent*
Josiah Wedgwood and Sons Ltd, Barlaston,
Staffordshire. Bequest of Ellinor Allen.

Mrs Robert Wedgwood, *née* Mary Halsey (1827–1905), was the second wife of the Reverend Robert Wedgwood, grandson of the famous eighteenth-century potter Josiah Wedgwood. They married in 1847. Their daughter, Eliza, was to become an intimate friend of Sargent and his sister Emily.

In 1894, Sargent painted another descendent of Josiah Wedgwood, Lancelot Allen (no. 309), and it was possibly this commission that led the Wedgwoods to select Sargent again. The story of the portrait is told by Eliza Wedgwood in a long typescript letter of 22 November 1925 to Evan Charteris (catalogue raisonné archive), which also recounts the story of her holidays with the Sargents. It was the artist Alfred Parsons who effected the introduction by writing to ask Sargent if he would paint Mrs Wedgwood. Sargent replied that he would be delighted, stating a fee of £250. Mrs Wedgwood sat twelve times for a first version, but Sargent felt unable to complete the portrait because 'the charm he tried to catch on canvas was so variable and fleeting'. Eliza Wedgwood called to see the 'beautiful but headless' portrait, but felt unable to disappoint her mother by telling her that it remained unfinished. Shortly afterwards, while on a visit to the Wedgwoods, Sargent was struck by a new possibility as he sat talking to Mrs Wedgwood in the garden, and asked her to sit again:

> She went up, knowing nothing of the failure, and was very much surprised when he took a new canvas and started a new pose. It was done in six sittings and I know John was satisfied with it, for one autumn when we were in Corfu [1909], and he had hurriedly to send in a work to the New Art Gallery [New English Art Club], he asked me to send up my mother's portrait. It had in those days no painted background, and when John saw it on his return to town, he had it sent to his studio when the exhibition closed, and painted in a delightful background, adding much to the beauty of the portrait.

This is an example of Sargent's use of a false landscape setting as a background in his portraits.

In a note to McKibbin, Ellinor Allen added a further footnote about the abandoned first version: 'I was told by my mother who used to go to the sittings that the first portrait of my grandmother was sitting, with on her lap a large muff made of a bearskin worn by Col. Wedgwood Guards, it had a crimson lining which shewed &

mutton sleeves of the pale silk celadon gown, which were quite out of fashion by 1897, would seem to confirm an earlier date. Mrs Shakespeare appears to be seated in a low chair, her only ornament an encrusted brooch in the form of a swallow. The background is covered by a richly textured curtain or hanging. In a letter to McKibbin (12 April 1949), Eva Ducat describes the portrait as 'extraordinarily expressive of her personality . . . the pathetic expression of the face. The whole picture speaks of her.' (McKibbin papers).

The sitter's son owned a copy of the portrait by R. G. Eves, but it has remained untraced since *c.* 1912. It is illustrated Ducat 1928, facing p. 76. Sargent painted Mrs Shakespeare's son, Wallace, in 1896, see no. 336.

one hand lay on the top, she had lovely hands like a Vandyck.' (loose sheet of *c.* 1947, now detached from the letter in which it was sent, catalogue raisonné archive).

333 *The Right Honourable Joseph Chamberlain*

1896
Oil on canvas, 65 × 37½ (165 × 95.2)
Inscribed, upper left: *John S. Sargent*; upper right: *1896*
National Portrait Gallery, London. Bequest of Mrs Mary Endicott Carnegie

The distinguished British statesman Joseph Chamberlain (1836–1914) was mayor of Birmingham from 1873 to 1875, and a Liberal MP in 1876, soon becoming one of the leading figures in his party. He was president of the Board of Trade in 1880, broke with Gladstone on the issue of Irish Home Rule in 1886, and, with Liberal Unionists, joined the Conservatives. He served under Salisbury as Secretary of State for the Colonies in 1895 and pursued imperialist policies. In 1903, he resigned from the government and championed tariff reform, advocating imperial preferences in place of free trade.

He is painted standing in a black frock-coat, starched wing collar, and dark silk necktie with gold pin. He is wearing the familiar monocle in his right eye and an orchid in his buttonhole, and his right hand is resting on a sheaf of papers concerning the recent Jameson Raid in South Africa, which lie on top of a kneehole desk. Chamberlain's pose is limp and the composition unremarkable. The circumstances in which the picture was painted may, in part, provide the reason. According to Sir Frank Swettenham, Sargent went to Chamberlain's home, Highbury, in Birmingham, to paint the picture because of the pressure under which the statesman was then working. When he did find time to give Sargent sittings, he was so exhausted that he lay listlessly on a sofa. Eventually, he cancelled all further sittings, and the portrait was completed with the help of the butler, who wore Chamberlain's clothes (see Swettenham 1942, p. 142).

For the *Academy*, Claude Phillips wrote that the portrait

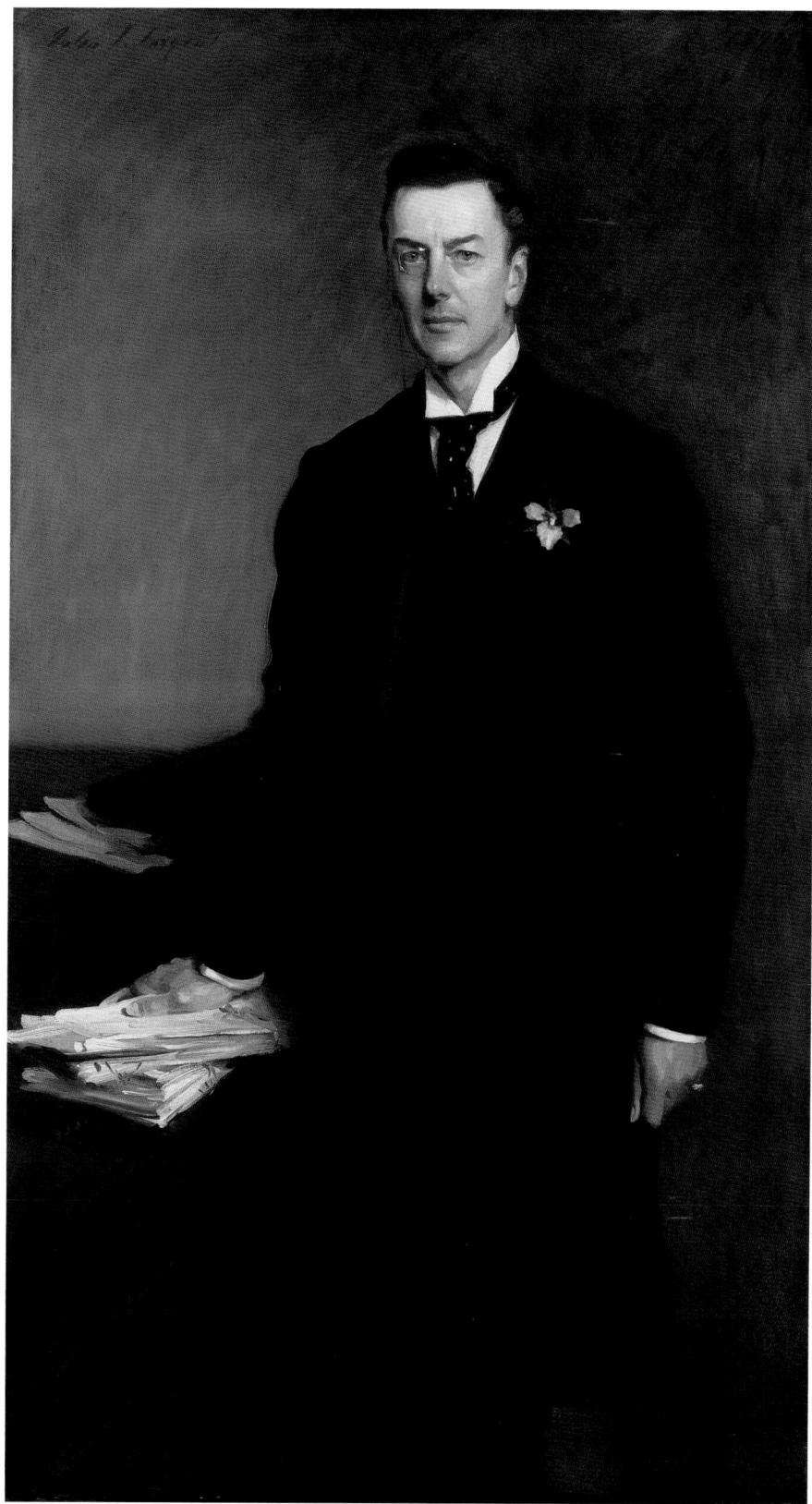

about exhausts the possibilities of a subject, not so interesting to the painter who seeks to bring to the surface the subtle complexities of a human individuality, as to him who should be in love with authority of mien, with swiftness and vitality. Notable points are especially the superb modelling of the mouth, the intensity of the questioning gaze, the Velazquez-like conciseness with which the hair is rendered, the eagerness expressed in an attitude of seeming quietude'. (*Academy*, 9 May 1896, p. 389)

Kit Anstruther-Thomson described it to Vernon Lee as 'fine enough for Velasquez' and remarked that there were now several Sargent imitators who painted 'school pictures', which were interesting in that they showed 'the difference between big fish and small fish' (undated letter, CC). Henry Adams wrote to Elizabeth Cameron, 29 May [1896]: 'I waltzed them [the daughters of Senator Calvin Brice; see nos 346, 533] through the Royal Academy too, where Sargent's portrait of

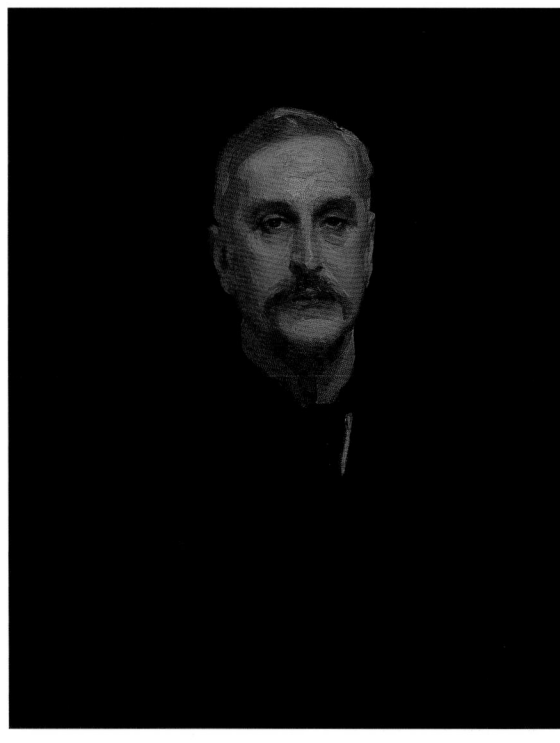

Chamberlain gave me acute delight' (Adams 1988, vol. IV, p. 384). The critic for the *Athenaeum*, however, considered it 'a striking example of the way in which an able and dashing painter can narrowly miss a considerable success' (*Athenaeum*, 27 June 1896, p. 849).

Sargent painted a portrait of Chamberlain's wife in 1902 (no. 417).

334 Colonel Thomas Edward Vickers

1896
Oil on canvas, 29 × 24 (73.8 × 61)
Inscribed, upper left: *John S. Sargent*
Private Collection

Colonel Thomas Edward Vickers (1833–1915) was the son of Edward Vickers of Tapton Hall, Sheffield. He was director and later chairman (1873–1909) of the Sheffield engineering and armaments firm Vickers, Sons & Co. Ltd, later Vickers, Sons & Maxim Ltd, now Vickers Ltd, which pioneered many new processes, and was Honorary Colonel of the Hallamshire Rifles. In 1860, he married Frances Douglas; they had six children: Douglas, Mabel, Clara, Florence, Ronald and Bertha.

Colonel Vickers was an old friend of Sargent as well as an important patron, commissioning the well-known picture of his three daughters as early as 1884. For detailed information about Sargent's relationship with the Vickers family, see *Early Portraits*, no. 129. The date of this portrait is given in the catalogue of the 1926 Royal Academy exhibition (London 1926, p. 61).

335 Sir George Lewis

c. 1896
Oil on canvas, 31½ × 23½ (80 × 59.6)
Inscribed, upper left: *John S. Sargent*
Private Collection

Sir George Henry Lewis (1833–1911) was the son of James Graham Lewis, a lawyer, and his wife, Harriet Davis. A Sephardic Jew by ancestry, whose religion barred him from Oxford University, he studied at University College, London, and became head of Lewis & Lewis, the law firm founded by his father and uncle. He was the leading London solicitor of his generation, specializing in sensitive and sensational divorce, libel and criminal cases, and he became the unofficial guardian of the secrets of the Victorian and Edwardian establishment. Oscar Wilde described him as 'the best in London. Brilliant. Formidable. A man of the world. Concerned in every great case in England. Oh, he knows all about us – and forgives us all' (quoted in Rupert Hart-Davis, ed., *The Letters of Oscar Wilde*, London, 1962, p. 92, n. 2). He acted in many of the most celebrated trials of the day: he advised

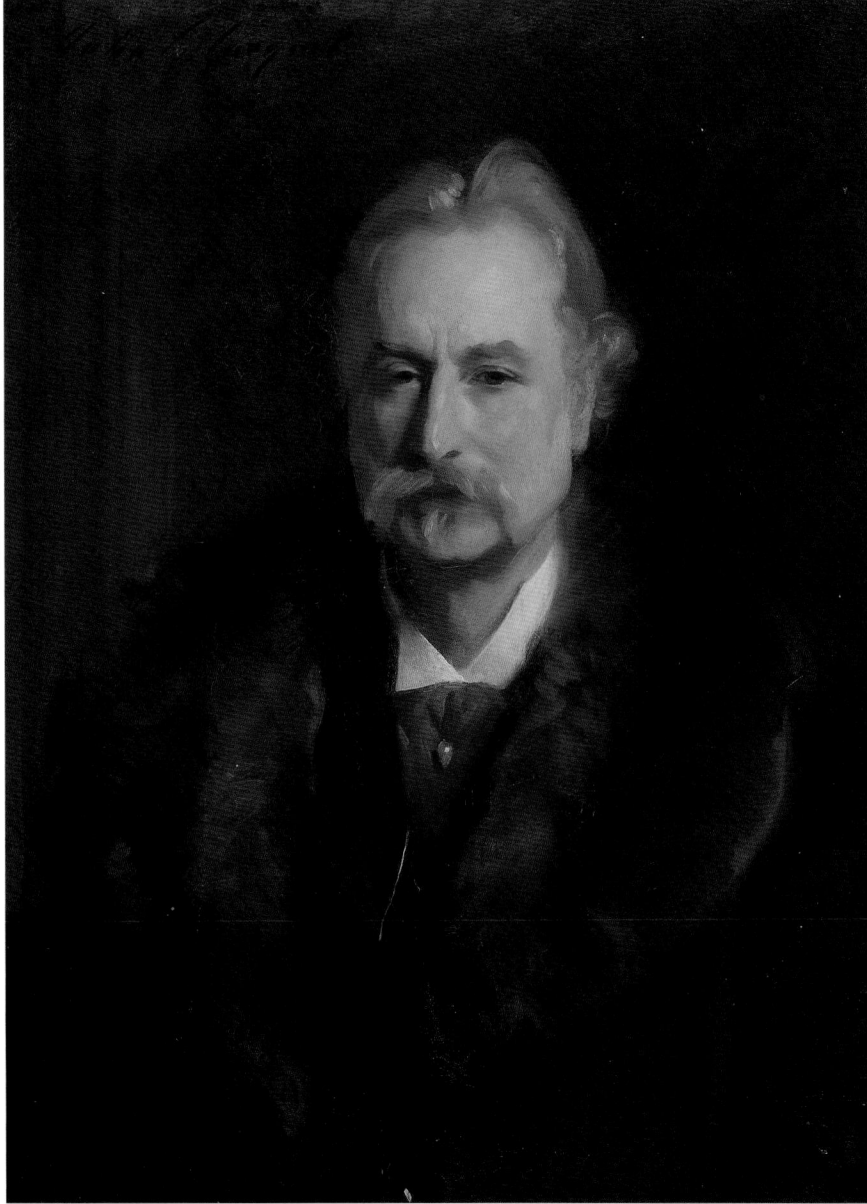

Whistler on his bankruptcy after the artist's libel battle with Ruskin in 1878; he was closely involved in the legal affairs of the Prince of Wales, extricating him from the embarrassing Tranby-Croft baccarat scandal; and he exposed the series of letters condoning the Phoenix Park murders, which were published as 'Parnellism and Crime' in *The Times* in 1887 as forgeries. He went on to represent the Irish nationalists for the Parnell Commission (1888–9) and, in recognition of his contribution, was knighted in 1892. In court, he combined a bold, intuitive approach with exhaustive preparation. He married, first, Victorine Kann in 1863 and, secondly, Elisabeth Eberstadt in 1867. He and his second wife entertained liberally and were the friends of many writers, artists and actors. In 1902, he was created a baronet by his friend and admirer Edward VII. For an early memoir, see 'Mr George Lewis at Ely Place', *Celebrities at Home* (reprinted from *The World*), London, 1878, pp. 267–78.

Sargent's characterization of Lewis presents him as a wealthy tycoon rather than a hard-working lawyer. The pearl tie-pin and the wide fur collar of the overcoat are symbols of power and opulence. Faintly visible in the background on the left are what appear to be the vertical lines of carved pilasters.

Sargent was a familiar figure in the Lewis household and a close friend. In 1892, he painted Lady Lewis (no. 280), probably to thank Sir George for helping to settle an unpleasant and irritating dispute with a farmer in Gloucestershire (see Charteris 1927, pp. 114–20 and Mount 1955, pp. 194–6 for an account of this episode). In 1906, he painted Sir George's daughter, Katherine (no. 519) and also executed a number of charcoal portraits of members of the family. In 1912, three copies of Sir George's portrait were produced for other members of the family by a protégé of Sargent, probably R. G. Eves. According to Katherine Lewis, the artist was dissatisfied with the heads and repainted them himself (letter from her to McKibbin, 14 August 1947, McKibbin papers). One of the copies, sold at Christie's, London, 4 November 1983, lot 23, was accompanied by a photostat copy from the 1912 diary of Mrs H. R. Lewis (niece by marriage of the sitter): 'In the spring of this year we went to Sargent's studio to see the copy of his portrait of H's uncle. He was most charming and took infinite pains to show us just the best light in which to hang the portrait. There were three copies made by a protégé of his and he told us that when the artist sent them to him he had not liked them and had repainted nearly the whole of the three heads.' The two other copies are in private collections.

Paintings from the collection of the Lewis family were sold Sotheby's, London, 7 June 1995. A water-colour sketch of Sir George Lewis by Jules Bastien-Lepage was lot 160 in the sale.

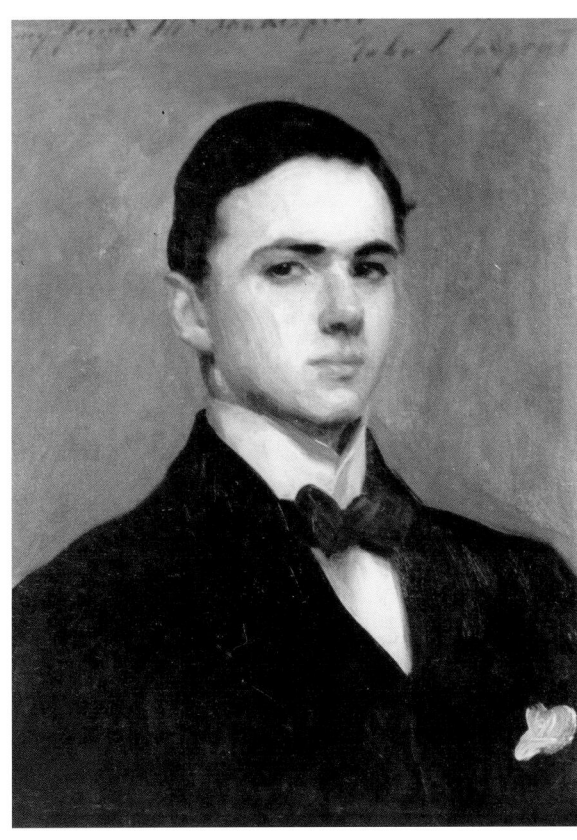

336 *Wallace Shakespeare*

1896
Oil on canvas, 24 × 18 (61 × 45.8)
Inscribed, across top: *to my friend Mrs Shakespeare Xmas 1896/John S. Sargent*
Untraced

Wallace Shakespeare (born *c.* 1876) was the son of Sargent's friend, the singer and teacher William Shakespeare, and his wife, Louise Weiland from Dresden (see no. 331). According to Eva Ducat,

the portrait was painted when he [Wallace] was about twenty and given as a surprise and present to Mrs Shakespeare by Sargent himself. It was a head only; & showed Wallace with rather full cheeks and chubby nose (which he had), brown hair, greyish-green eyes (not blue) and a sallowish complexion. It was like Wallace, but was not striking either as a portrait or as a painting, & was never considered one of Sargent's masterpieces. (letter to McKibbin, 12 April 1949, McKibbin papers)

The original line of the left shoulder is visible as a *pentimento*.

Eva Ducat, a piano pupil of William Shakespeare's daughter, Mimie, has left a charming picture of the Shakespeare household in her book of reminiscences (see Ducat 1928, pp. 74–7).

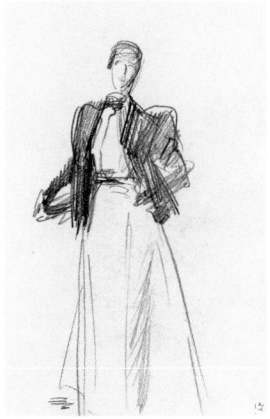

fig. 63 *Mrs Isaac Newton Phelps Stokes*. $9\,^7/_{16} \times 5\,^{15}/_{16}$ (24 × 15.1). Fogg Art Museum, Harvard University Art Museums. Gift of Mrs Francis Ormond, 1937.7.11. 24 r.

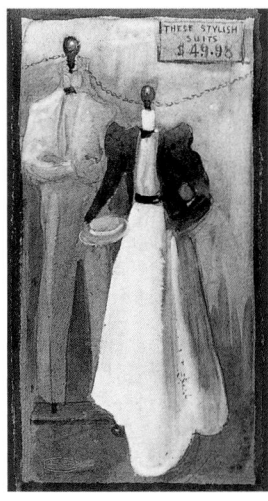

fig. 64 James Montgomery Flagg, Caricature of Sargent's portrait of Mr and Mrs I. N. Phelps Stokes. Watercolour, $12\,^1/_{16} \times 7\,^7/_8$ (30.6 × 20). Art Students League, New York.

337 *Mr and Mrs I. N. Phelps Stokes*

1897
Oil on canvas, $84\,^1/_4 \times 39\,^3/_4$ (214 × 101)
Inscribed, upper right: *John S. Sargent 1897*
Metropolitan Museum of Art, New York. Bequest of Edith Minturn Phelps Stokes

This double portrait is of Isaac Newton Phelps Stokes (1867–1944) and his wife, Edith Minturn Stokes (1867–1937). Stokes studied architecture at the atelier de Monclos-Chiflot in Paris and later practised in New York; his *Iconography of Manhattan Island* (1915–1928), in six volumes, remains a classic study. His parents, Mr and Mrs Anson Phelps Stokes, were painted by Cecilia Beaux in 1898 (Metropolitan Museum of Art, New York). Edith was the daughter of Robert Browne Minturn Jr, heir to a New York shipping fortune, and his wife, Susannah (*née* Shaw). She was involved in the education of young children and served as president of the New York Kindergarten Association from 1912 to 1933.

The couple were married on 25 August 1895; the portrait was intended as a wedding present from James A. Scrimser, a family friend. The finished picture differs in two ways from what was originally planned: a single portrait of Edith, and a more conventional composition. Stokes's memoir, *Random Recollections of a Happy Life* (1923), provides most of the information about the sittings, including entertaining anecdotes about Sargent's idiosyncratic manner of painting. The manuscript of Stokes's memoir is in the New-York Historical Society. Further information, including several letters from Stokes to the museum, is held in the archives of the Metropolitan Museum of Art (see Burke 1980, pp. 247–51).

In a letter headed '17th Feb [1896?]' and written from 33 Tite Street, Sargent wrote to Howard Cushing, brother of Mrs Edward Darley Boit (see *Early Portraits*, no. 205), who seems to have acted as an intermediary:

I am sure Mrs Stokes must be one of the two Misses Minturns whom I have met in America and here – It would be a great pleasure to paint her portrait. Tell Mrs Stokes that my price for a full length is five hundred guineas. I won't be over in Paris except for a flying visit to the exhibition and this spring and early summer I am afraid . . . that I am likely to be able to do – for I must get back to my decorative work later in the summer. I wonder if Mrs Stokes would feel inclined to wait a year? You oughtn't to have been deterred from coming to see me by rumours that I was busy. That is my normal condition, as also to be glad to see you' (Private Collection).

Sargent had intended to paint Edith in Venice in 1897 but had to remain in London, where sittings began in June. Edith modelled several dresses for the artist 'like a mannikin' (Stokes 1941, p. 116), and, after selecting a blue satin evening gown, he began to paint her seated next to one of his studio props – a round Empire table familiar from other portraits of the period (see Accessories, p. xxiii, no. 14) – which she was meant to be tapping with a fan. Sargent was dissatisfied with the progress of the painting after some four or five sittings and told the Stokeses that he would like to consider another pose.

On our next visit to the studio, a very warm morning, we had walked from our apartment. Edith had on a starched white piqué skirt, and a light shirt-waist under her blue serge, tailor-made jacket. As she came into the studio, full of energy, and her cheeks aglow from the brisk walk, Sargent exclaimed at once: 'I want to paint you just as you are.' We thought it wise to submit to his whim, although we had, even then, some apprehension lest our friends at home, and especially Mr Scrimser, might not altogether approve. However, within a few moments, the first portrait had been scraped off the canvas – the fate which later befell eight of the nine heads of the second portrait. A new pose was finally decided upon, in which Edith was to stand with one hand resting on the head of a tiger-striped Great Dane, which was to be selected from the kennels belonging to one of Sargent's friends. (Stokes 1941, p. 116)

Stokes also described Sargent's working method:

We were much amused in the studio by his eccentricities; for instance, his habit of standing before the canvas, with brush balanced like a poised dart – in perfect silence until the stroke had been successfully delivered – always accompanied by the exclamation: 'pish-tash; pish-tash!' He studied each stroke thoughtfully, and was not satisfied unless it was clearly defined, and of just the right form and consistency. He was particularly well satisfied with the 'spiral' stroke with which he produced the diamond in Edith's engagement ring, and cautioned me, if the picture were ever varnished, to be sure that the protruding wisp of paint was not injured. Alas! it has been. (Stokes 1941, p. 116)

Mrs Anson Stokes suggested a companion portrait of her son as an additional wedding gift to Edith. Sargent was, however, too pressed to accept a further commission and mentioned Whistler as an alternative; but Whistler's prices seemed prohibitively high, and the idea was given up.

A new development occurred when the Great Dane, who was to have featured as Mrs Stokes's 'accessory', could not be obtained. Mr Stokes had 'a sudden inspiration, and offered to assume the role of the Great Dane in the picture' (Stokes 1941, p. 117); his figure was painted in three sittings. Trevor Fairbrother has suggested that, as a compositional precedent, Sargent may have had in mind Van Dyck's portrait of James Stuart, fourth

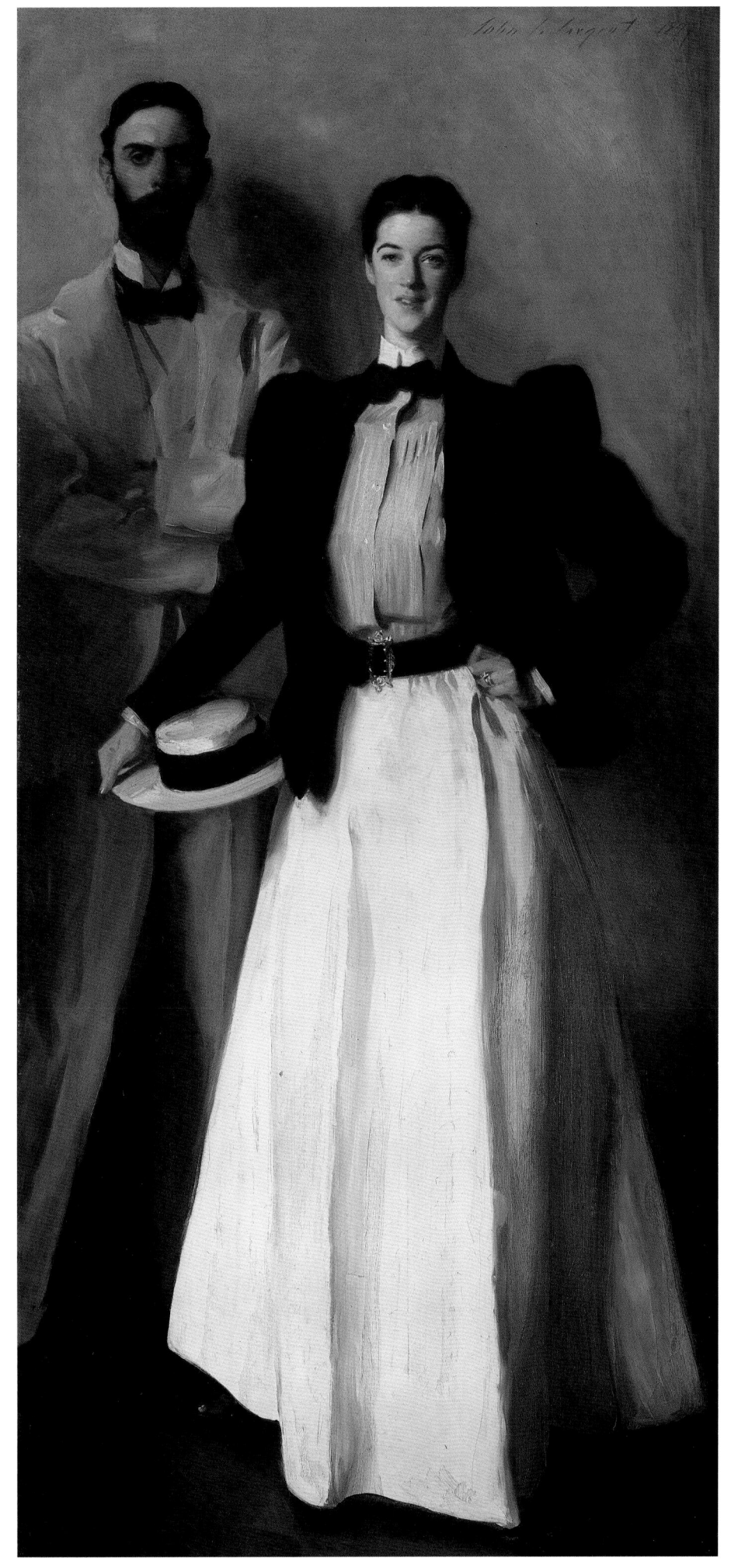

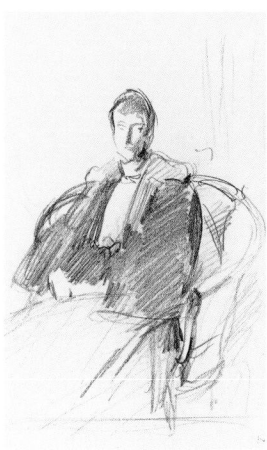

fig. 65 *Mrs Harold Wilson*. Pencil, 9 ⁷⁄₁₆ × 5 ¹⁵⁄₁₆ (24 × 15.1). Fogg Art Museum, Harvard University Art Museums. Gift of Mrs Francis Ormond, 1937. 7. 11 7 r.

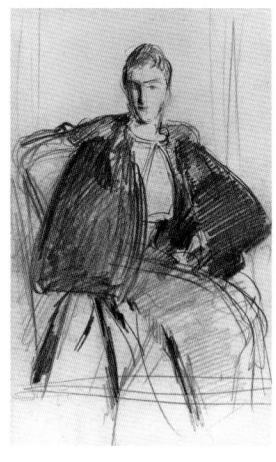

fig. 66 *Mrs Harold Wilson*. Pencil, 9 ⁷⁄₁₆ × 5 ¹⁵⁄₁₆ (24 × 15.1). Fogg Art Museum, Harvard University Art Museums. Gift of Mrs Francis Ormond, 1937. 7. 11 6 r.

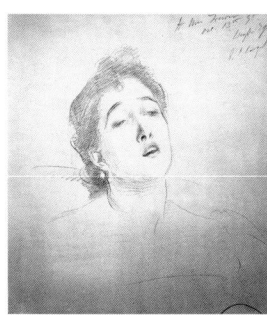

fig. 67 *Mrs George Batten Singing*. Pencil, 13 × 12 (33 × 30.5). Private Collection.

Duke of Lennox and first Duke of Richmond (*c.* 1633), which features a Great Dane nestling his head against his master's side; the portrait had been presented to the Metropolitan Museum of Art, New York, by Sargent's friend, the connoisseur Henry Gurdon Marquand (see no. 343), in 1889 (see Fairbrother 1986, pp. 370–1).

Mr and Mrs I. N. Phelps Stokes was shown at several contemporary exhibitions in America, and, while the emphasis on costume and the attenuated figures inspired reservations and criticisms about its 'cleverness' and 'superficiality', it was nevertheless regarded as a significant painting. Charles Caffin expressed an awareness of its technical strengths and weaknesses, describing it as

> a brilliant interpretation of the lady's white starched skirt, blue jacket, and gray shirt, and also of the impression of wholesome fragrance that such an apparition produces; but by the time that you have noted these qualities on many occasions the superficiality of the conception makes itself felt with a suggestion almost of annoyance that so much cleverness should have been expended to such trivial purpose. Perhaps, also, one is not wrong in feeling that in this case the cleverness is deliberately ostentatious, the white skirt being painted not so much with a Velasquez enjoyment of white as with a conscious desire to execute a tour de force. (*International Studio*, 14, 1901, p. xxi)

Reviewing the picture at the Society of American Artists a few years earlier, the critic writing for the *International Studio* was sensitive to a quality in the characterization that was particularly American, declaring that 'for a perspicuous bit of character rendering it is most eloquent. The young woman stands there smiling at her audience with all the confidence of American assurance. It is more than an individual portrait – it is "The American Girl" herself' (*International Studio*, 4, 1898, p. x). The accident of costume combined with an easy social assurance seemed to define Edith as a particular contemporary American type – the 'Gibson Girl' of Charles Dana Gibson's drawings.

There is a preliminary study for the finished version, showing her in the same pose and wearing a dark jacket and white skirt, and holding a boater hat in her right hand (see fig. 63).

The portrait was the subject of some thirteen caricatures by members of the Society of Fakirs in New York, and the first prize at the 1898 Fakirs show was awarded to Lewis Bundy for an ingenious pastiche, which used a convex sheet of zinc to mimic the extreme attenuation of the figures. Of these caricatures, apparently the only one to survive is a small water-colour by James Montgomery Flagg (1877–1960) depicting the couple as a pair of clothes-horses (fig. 64). Gustav Kobbé wrote that 'one fake [Flagg's] showed the costumes draped on headless lay figures, such as are sometimes seen in shop-windows, and bore the inscription, "These Stylish Suits $49.98"' (*Century*,

59, December 1899, p. 321, ill.). For details of Flagg's caricature, see Ronald G. Pisano and Bruce Weber, *Parodies of the American Masters: Rediscovering the Society of American Fakirs, 1891–1914*, New York, 1993 (exhibition catalogue), fig. 14A, and New York 1994, fig. 255.

338 *Mrs Harold Wilson*

1897
Oil on canvas, 60 × 38 (152.5 × 96.5)
Inscribed, upper left: *John S. Sargent*; upper right: *1897*
Private Collection

Mrs Harold Wilson, née Anna Margary (1866–1947), came from French Huguenot stock. She married Harold Wilson in 1888 and had six children. They had houses in Grosvenor Square in London, in Norfolk and later in St Andrews. Lady Penn, the sitter's granddaughter, to whom we are indebted for the biographical information above, recalls that the original receipt of payment (now lost) for the painting was for the improbably high sum of £2,000 (letter to authors, 8 September 1999, catalogue raisonné archive). No further details about the commission have yet come to light.

Mrs Wilson is dressed in a black satin gown, a black velvet jacket with a wide fur collar, and a white lace fichu. The frothy black materials at bottom left may represent her train or another garment. She is sitting in the chair end of a *duchesse brisé*, and behind is a piece of French panelling derived from the Louis Quinze-style door in Sargent's studio (see Accessories, p. xxii, nos 2 c, 17). There are two preliminary pencil sketches for the portrait in a sketchbook at the Fogg Art Museum, Cambridge, Massachusetts (figs 65, 66).

339 *Catherine Vlasto*

1897
Oil on canvas, 58½ × 33¾ (148.6 × 85.4)
Inscribed, upper right: *John S. Sargent 1897*
Hirshhorn Museum and Sculpture Garden, Smithsonian Institution, Washington, D.C.

Catherine or Caterina Vlasto (1875–1899) was the eighth child of Alexander Anthony Vlasto and his wife, Calliope Ralli. The family were of Greek descent. The sitter's father, Alexander Anthony Vlasto, was born in Trieste in 1833, but his father, Anthony A. Alexander Vlasto, was born on the Greek island of Chios in 1804; the family left the island in 1820, around the time of the Turkish massacres. Catherine died tragically young from acute appendicitis.

The portrait was unrecorded until its appearance on the art market in 1967. The sitter is dressed in a white silk evening gown with leg-of-

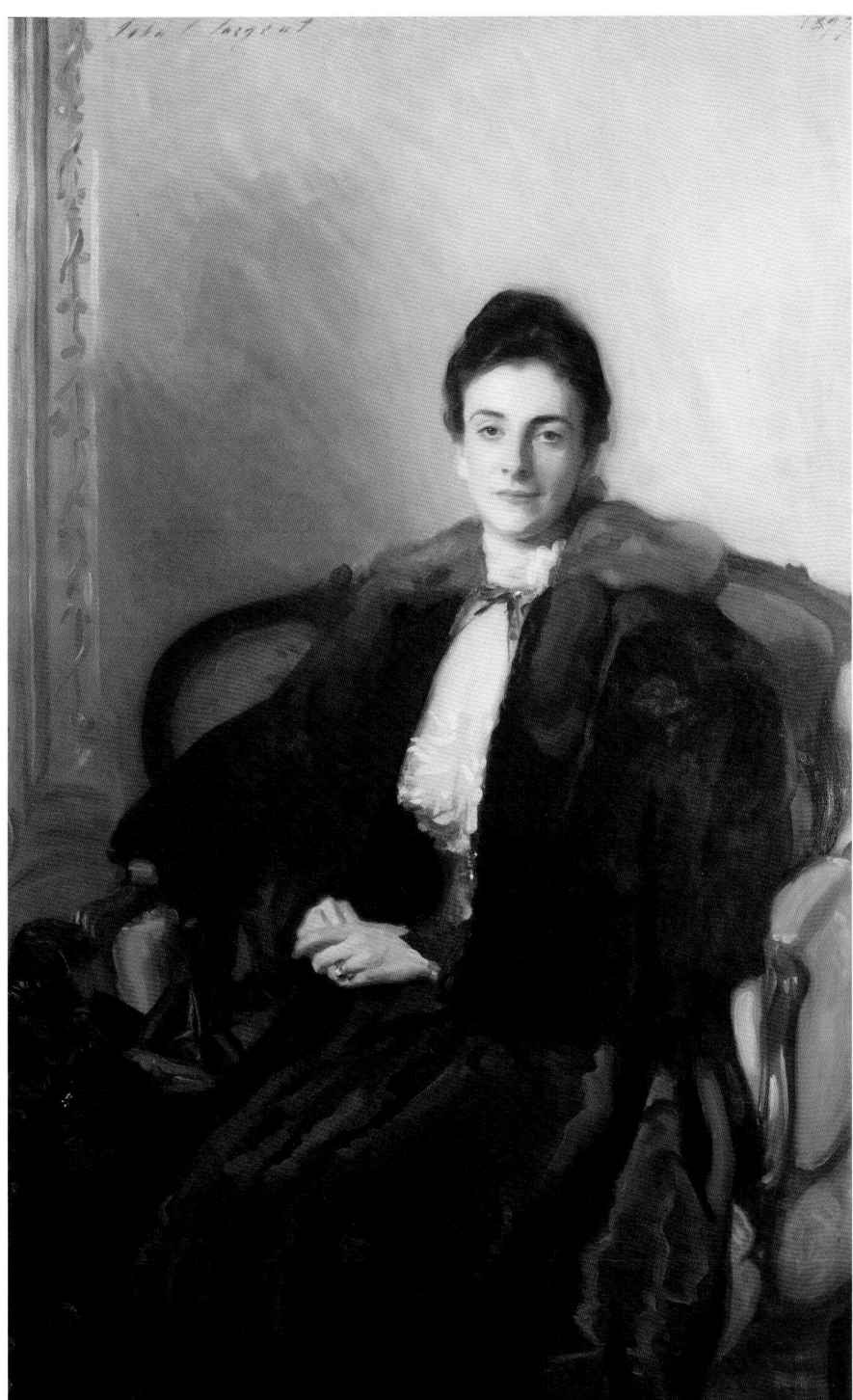

338

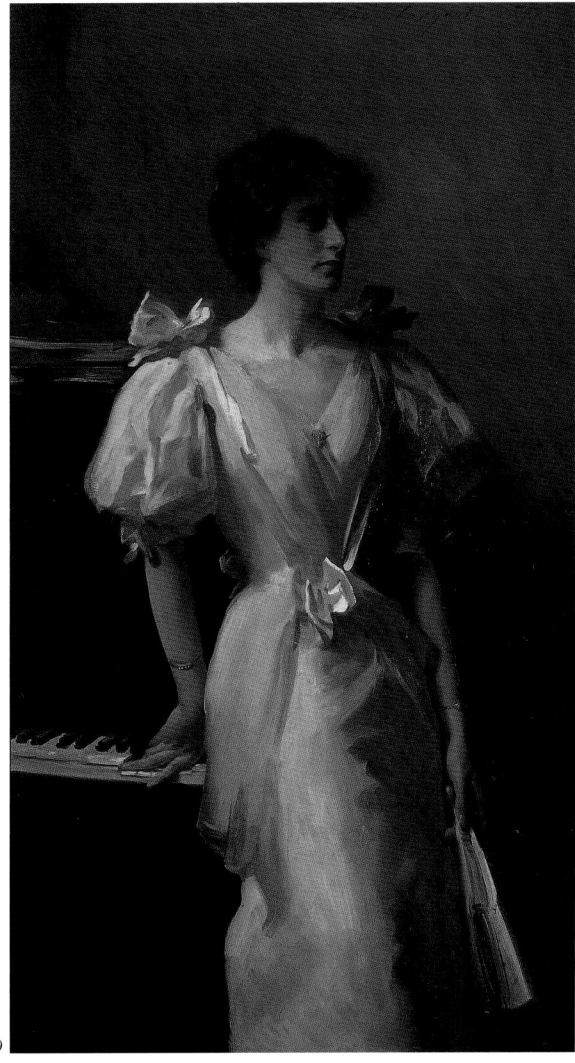

339

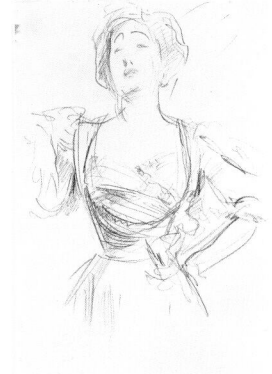

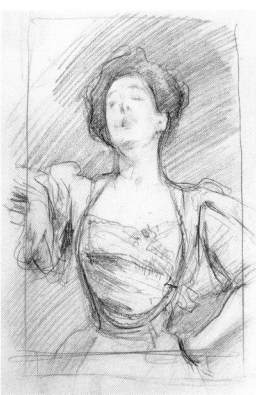

mutton sleeves decorated with bows at shoulders, elbows and waist. She wears no jewellery, apart from a brooch at the V of her bodice and a single bangle on each wrist, and holds a partially closed fan in her left hand, while with her right she is depressing several keys of Sargent's black upright Bechstein piano (see Accessories, p. xxiii, no. 16).

A portrait, *Miss Vlasto*, by Sir Hubert von Herkomer was exhibited at the Royal Academy in 1890.

340   *Mrs George Batten*

c. 1897
Oil on canvas, 35 × 17 (88.9 × 43.2)
Inscribed, across top: *to Mrs G. Batten John S. Sargent*
Glasgow Art Gallery and Museum, Kelvingrove

Mrs George Batten, *née* Mabel Veronica Hatch (*c.* 1857–1916), was the daughter of Major General George Hatch and his Indian wife. In India in 1875, she married George Henry Maxwell Batten, then private secretary to the British viceroy Lord Lytton. They returned to London, where she became a patron of music and the arts, and estab-lished a reputation as one of the leading amateur

fig. 68 (above, left)
Mrs George Batten.
Pencil, 14 ⁷⁄₁₆ × 9 ¹⁵⁄₁₆
(36.7 × 25.3). Fogg Art
Museum, Harvard
University Art
Museums, 1937. 7. 21.
23 v.

fig. 69 (above, right)
Mrs George Batten.
Pencil, 12 ¾ × 9 ¼
(32.4 × 23.5). Private
Collection.

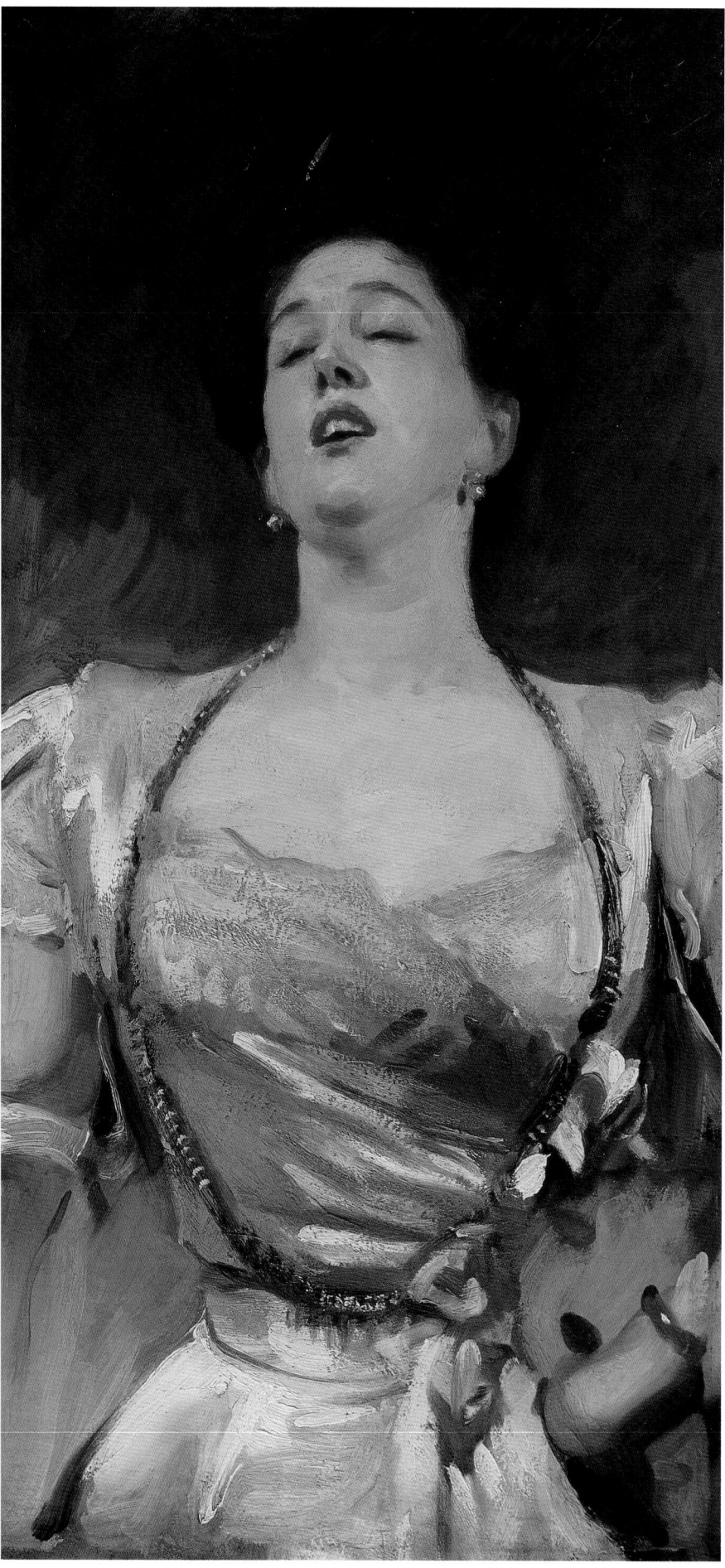

lieder singers of her day. She became the intimate friend and lover of the writer Marguerite Radclyffe Hall in 1907 (see Troubridge 1961, pp. 29–55), several of whose poems she set to music. Elsie Swinton (see no. 327) included at least one of Mrs Batten's songs in her own repertoire (see Greer, 1997, p. 134).

Sargent's expansive and intense study of Mrs Batten depicts her as having been carried away by the emotion of her song. In the 'Introductory Note' to her monograph *The Work of John S. Sargent, R.A.*, Alice Meynell wrote: 'An example of the portrait of a moment that is full of spirit and action is that of Mrs George Batten, which breathes the last note of a song – a song of Tosti's, one might guess' (Meynell 1903, n.p.). The Hamilton bequest catalogue notes that she is said to be singing the last note of Tosti's *Goodbye*, but this appears to be anecdotal (*The Hamilton Bequest: Paintings Presented to the Glasgow Art Gallery 1927–1977*, 1977, p. 16). The unusually narrow format of the portrait, the cropping of the shoulder and arms of the singer, emphasizes the lines of her opulent figure. This compositional compression appears to have been a deliberate, retrospective act on the artist's part: Miss Batten 'was not entirely happy with the portrait. She arrived at the studio one day to find that Sargent had cut away portions of her arms by reducing the width of the canvas' (Baker 1985, p. 35).

According to Radclyffe Hall's friend, Una, Lady Troubridge, the first inspiration for the portrait was a drawing executed at the home of Mrs Trower, a prominent music lover, at Weybridge on 13 October 1895 (letter to McKibbin, 7 October 1947, McKibbin papers). This drawing (see fig. 67), inscribed to Mrs Trower (ex Lady Troubridge, later collection Nicola Rossi-Lemeni, Rome; sold Sotheby's, 22 April 1970, lot 222), is a simple head-and-shoulders study of Mrs Batten singing and bears little relation to the oil. Mrs Trower owned several works by the artist: *Two Women Asleep in a Punt*, 1887 (Calouste Gulbenkian Museum, Lisbon), and four watercolours – *A Shadowed Stream* (Museum of Fine Arts, Boston) and three Venetian studies. Three further drawings are recorded: one in a private collection, a second is in the Fogg Art Museum, Cambridge, Massachusetts (fig. 68), and a third, one of several sketches given to sculptor Charles Sargeant Jagger by the artist's sister Emily, also in a private collection (fig. 69); the latter two are closely related in pose to the oil. Though Sargent may have had the idea of painting Mrs Batten in oils in 1895, it took him more than a year to arrange sittings. On 7 April 1897, he wrote to a friend, Miss Maxse (letter with Winifred A. Myers, 'Autographs', London, 1969), to say that Mrs Batten's portrait was 'hardly fit to be seen. Perhaps another sitting or two will pull it through'. He did 'pull it through' in time for the New Gallery exhibition, where it appeared in company with a portrait of another mezzo-soprano, Mrs George Swinton.

The critic writing for the *Athenaeum* described the picture as one of the artist's most effective *tours de force* (*Athenaeum*, 22 May 1897, p. 687) and the *Academy* noted its 'extraordinary spirit; the change and flicker of life are on the closed eyelids, the singing mouth, and the whole face lightly strained and mobile' (*Academy*, 1 May 1897, p. 479).

For a photograph of the portrait hanging *in situ* see fig. 70.

Mrs Batten bequeathed the portrait to Radclyffe Hall. Lady Troubridge makes several references to the portrait in her diaries (National Archive of Canada, Ottawa). On 26 January 1926, she notes, at a private view of the Sargent exhibition at the Royal Academy: 'Ladye's [Mabel Batten's nickname] portrait very well hung.' Lady Troubridge records that, in April 1926, both the oil portrait and a drawing were taken to the Tate, presumably for the opening exhibition of the Sargent Gallery in June of that year. By 1928, Radclyffe Hall was considering selling the portrait. She approached the Tate Gallery first: on 3 December 1928, Lady Troubridge records a visit made by Hall to the Tate, and the following day she visits the Tate again, with the portrait. The portrait was sold to Glasgow Art Gallery: the sale is recorded in Lady Troubridge's diary entry for 31 January 1929. Radclyffe Hall apparently donated the £1,000 to the Miners' Relief Fund: Miss Hall is reported as saying: 'I hope by parting with one of my most treasured possessions that I shall be able to inaugurate a sort of "gift in kind" movement to help the miners' (unidentified clipping, 31 January [1929], McKibbin papers).

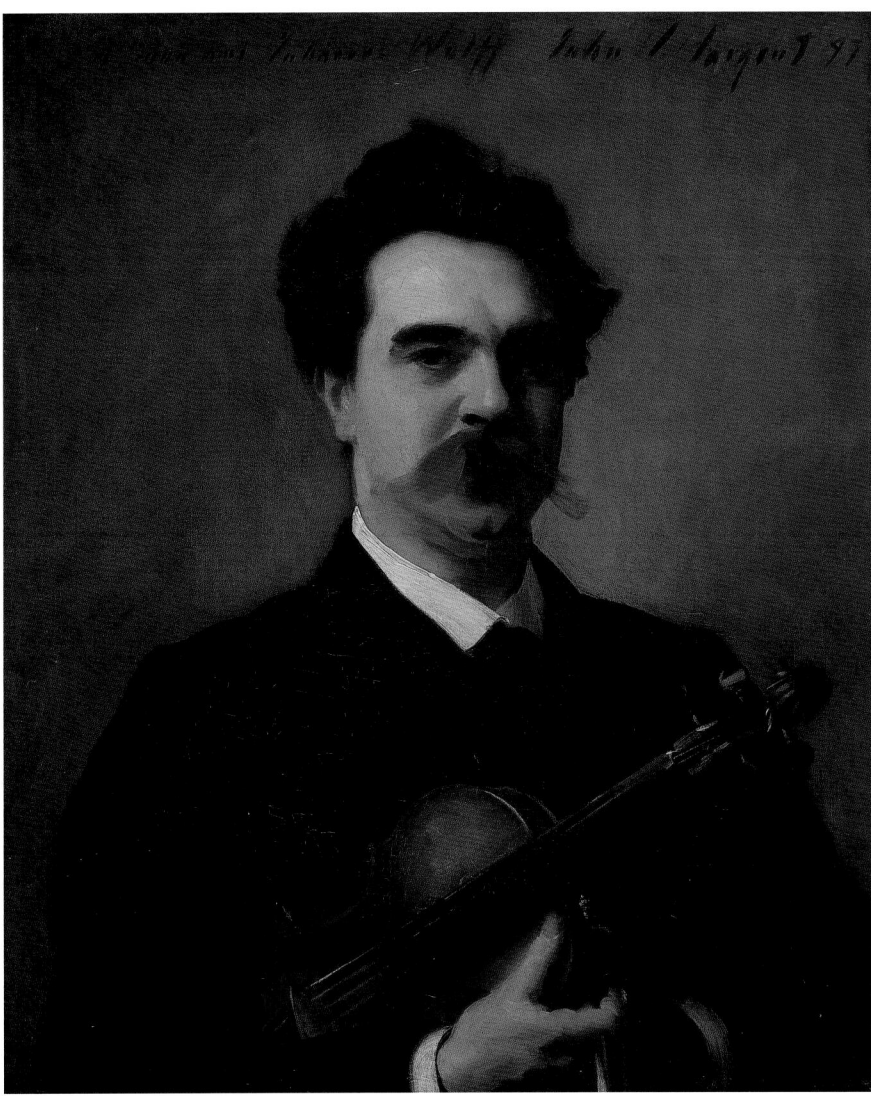

341   *Johannes Wolff*

1897
Oil on canvas, 30 × 25 (76.2 × 63.5)
Inscribed, across top: *à mon ami Johannes Wolff*
John S. Sargent '97
Fogg Art Museum, Cambridge, Massachusetts.
Bequest of Grenville L. Winthrop

The violinist Johannes Wolff was born in 1863 in The Hague, where his father was an official at the Dutch court. He studied under Rappoldi in Dresden and with Maurin at the Conservatoire in Paris, where he made his debut in the Pasdeloup concerts. He established a reputation as a fashionable society violinist in the 1890s, playing for Queen Victoria and other VIPs. He was a teacher at the Guildhall School of Music in London and professor of music at the University of Berlin. Much decorated at the time, he is now largely forgotten. He died in Nice in 1931.

Sargent was on close terms with many musicians, but nothing is known of his friendship with Wolff. The artist was living in Paris in the early 1880s when Wolff was playing at the Pasdeloup concerts: Sargent's two oil studies of rehearsals of the Pasdeloup orchestra at the Cirque d'Hiver

(private collection, on loan to the Art Institute of Chicago, and Museum of Fine Arts, Boston), probably predate Wolff's debut by a couple of years. Sargent would almost certainly have heard Wolff play in London, where the musician was a vital force in the 1890s: Wolff revived the 'Musical Union' in London around 1894, giving the first concert of the New Series at St James's Hall on 21 May 1894 and subsequent concerts in June, July and November. He also performed Fauré's Sonata, op. 13 at St James's Hall, on 19 December 1896, and it is possible that Sargent met Wolff through Fauré. For Sargent's friendship with Gabriel Fauré, see *Early Portraits*, no. 157.

The portrait must have been painted prior to 20 July 1897, when the artist wrote to the president and council of the Royal Academy expressing regret that he had been unable to fulfil the conditions of his recent election to full membership of the Academy by submitting a diploma work:

the portrait of Mr Bayard [see no. 342] which I did for the purpose not having turned out to my satisfaction or seeming worthy of having a place in the Diploma Gallery – It is my hope that within the next few months I will be able to offer a portrait of Mr. Alma Tadema who has kindly consented to sit. In the mean time, will

fig. 70 The writer Radclyffe Hall, with Lady Una Troubridge, portrait of Mrs George Batten visible to the left. Hulton Getty Picture Library, London.

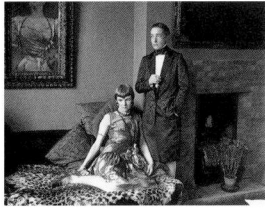

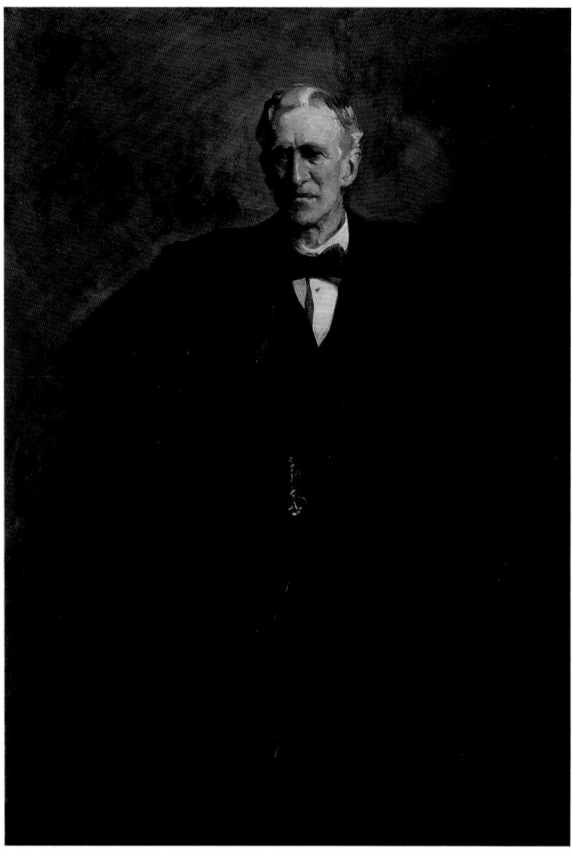

surviving record of the transaction. There is an entry in the account listing, which Winthrop kept of his framing expenses with M. Grieve & Co., which reads 'June 30, 1941 Wolff by Sargent 663'. It was Winthrop's custom to have paintings reframed soon after purchase (letter from Phoebe Peebles to compilers, 30 September 1985, catalogue raisonné archive).

Sargent paints Wolff holding his violin and bow, as he was later to paint another violinist, Charles Martin Loeffler (no. 444). Percy Colson writes of the portrait's showing a 'merciless ferocity. I knew Wolff well, and he was just like the portrait, both in character and appearance. Predatory, greedy and pushing his motto was "never refuse money". Wolff was the son of a Hamburg butcher. There were those who said he should have followed his father's profession' (Colson 1950, p. 117).

342   Thomas Francis Bayard

1897
Oil on canvas, 60 × 42 (152.4 × 106.7)
Inscribed, upper left: *offered to Mrs Bayard*; upper right: *John S. Sargent 1897*
Department of State, Washington, D.C. Gift of the estate of Alexis I. du Pont Bayard

Thomas Francis Bayard (1828–1898), the son of James Asheton Bayard, was born in Wilmington, Delaware, and began his law practice in Wilmington in 1851. He was a senator for Delaware from 1869 to 1885 and was an unsuccessful candidate for the Democratic presidential nomination in 1876, 1880 and 1884. He served as secretary of state for President Cleveland from 1885 to 1889 and was ambassador to Great Britain from 1893 to 1897. He married, first, Louise Lee (d. 1886) in 1856 and, secondly, Mary W. Clymer in 1889. During his ambassadorship in London, he is frequently mentioned in contemporary accounts of society events; Lady Gregory, for example, in her diary entry for 3 May 1895, numbers him among those at the Royal Academy private view (Pethica 1996, p. 71).

The portrait was painted in London in 1897, when Bayard was approaching the end of his term of office as ambassador at the Court of St James. Sargent apparently intended it as his Royal Academy diploma picture, but the finished work did not meet with his approval. He mentioned this in a letter of 20 July 1897 to the president and council of the Royal Academy: 'The portrait of Mr Bayard which I did for the purpose not having turned out to my satisfaction or seeming worthy of having a place in the Diploma Gallery – It is my hope that within the next few months I will be able to offer a portrait of Mr Alma Tadema who has kindly consented to sit' (Royal Academy Library, London, RAC/1/SA 6). No portrait of Alma-Tadema appears to have been painted; that of Johannes Wolff (no. 341) was deposited as a

the President and Council allow me to make a temporary deposit, and would the accompanying likeness of Mr Johannes Wolff be acceptable? (Royal Academy Library, London, RAC/1/SA 6)

This temporary arrangement was noted at the Royal Academy Council meeting of 27 July 1897, and is reported in the minutes (*Royal Academy Council Minutes*, XX, 1894–9, p. 319).

The portrait of Lawrence Alma-Tadema was apparently never painted. The secretary of the Royal Academy reminded Sargent about his failure to submit a diploma work, and, on 27 December 1899, he wrote offering *An Interior in Venice* (no. 367). This was accepted, and it is probable that the exchange took place shortly afterwards. The subsequent history of the Wolff portrait is uncertain until its appearance on the art market in the 1930s. A photograph of the painting in the Fogg Museum archives has the handwritten notation 'Durlacher Brothers', and it is possible that they were involved in its disposition or sale at some point. A search in the Durlacher archives, however, did not unearth any supporting documentation (E-mail communication from Mark Henderson, Reference Librarian, Special Collections and Visual Resources, Getty Research Library, Los Angeles, quoted in letter from Richard Finnegan to Elaine Kilmurray, 11 September 2000, catalogue raisonné archive). When it was exhibited at the Toledo Museum of Art, Ohio, in 1934 (*American Painters Memorial Exhibition*), it was listed as owned by John Levy Gallery [New York]. Grenville Winthrop had certainly acquired the painting by June 1941, though there is no temporary measure; and, finally, *A Venetian Interior* (no. 367) was submitted and accepted.

Sargent presumably offered the painting to Mrs Bayard after deciding against submitting it to the Royal Academy, which might explain the unusual inscription.

343 *Henry G. Marquand*

1897
Oil on canvas, 52 × 41¾ (132. × 106)
Inscribed, upper right: *John S. Sargent*
Metropolitan Museum of Art, New York. Gift of the trustees

Henry Gurdon Marquand (1819–1902), collector and philanthropist, made his fortune in real estate, banking and the St Louis, Iron Mountain & Southern Railroad, of which he was co-owner and vice-president. On its merger with the Missouri Pacific, he served on the new board as a director. His association with the Metropolitan Museum of Art began in 1881 and culminated in his gift of European paintings to the museum in 1889 and 1890. The Marquand gift comprised paintings by Hals, Rembrandt, Vermeer and other Dutch and Flemish artists; Van Dyck, Gainsborough, Turner and other British artists; and Italian masters. Marquand was, from 1889 until his death in 1902, the museum's president (see Ernest Knaufft, 'Henry G. Marquand as an American Art Patron', *Review of Reviews*, New York, February 1903).

A portrait was conceived as a gesture of recognition for his outstanding generosity and commitment to the museum; on 27 February 1896, a committee of three trustees – Cornelius Vanderbilt, William R. Ware and Charles Stewart Smith – was established to arrange the commission. While it is not known how the decision to approach Sargent was made and by whom, he was not a surprising choice. His relationship with Marquand went back as far as 1887, when he painted Mrs Marquand (see *Early Portraits*, no. 192), a commission which 'was a turning point in my fortunes for which I have most heartily to thank you' (Allan Marquand Papers, Firestone Library, Princeton University). Sargent also painted their daughter, Mabel, Mrs Henry Galbraith Ward (no. 278). Extensive correspondence concerning the commission is held in the archives of the Metropolitan Museum of Art and is listed in detail and quoted at length in Burke 1980, pp. 251–3.

Sargent wrote to Allan Marquand, teacher of art history at Princeton and son of the sitter, to explain that his commitments to the Boston Public Library mural work meant that he would be unable to come to America to paint his father but that he would be able to do the portrait in London in July or August (undated letter to [Allan] Marquand, Misc. MSS Sargent, AAA). A final decision was apparently made by May 1896,

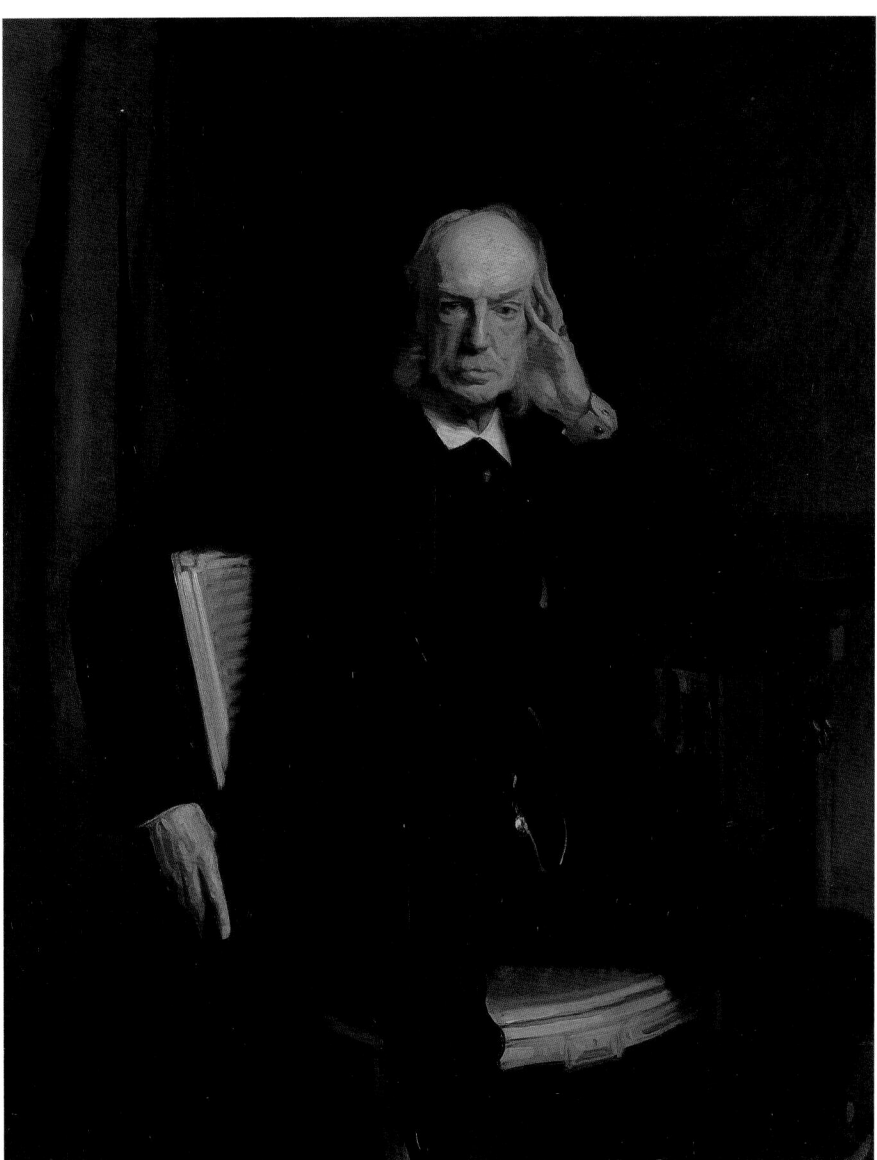

when Vanderbilt wrote to Marquand asking if he might telegram Sargent. He did so, received an affirmative reply, and the sittings were planned for July 1896 (MMA archives).

Marquand, who was suffering from ill health, apparently expressed some unease about the number and length of sittings which would be required. Writing from Paris, Sargent reassured him: 'It depends on how long you will be able to sit each time, especially as yours will not be the only portrait I will be doing' (letter to H. Marquand, 24 May [1896], AAA). In the event, Marquand was too ill to make the journey at all that summer but neglected to tell Sargent about the change of plan and the artist sent a reply, which did little to conceal his exasperation (letter to H. Marquand, 25 July [1896], AAA).

Sittings took place in the summer of the following year, ending on 31 July. Marquand wrote to the director of the Metropolitan Museum, Luigi P. di Cesnola, on 1 August: 'I have been sitting almost every day and resting when not sitting for the portrait' (MMA archives); and on 18 August, relaying Sargent's advice about the frame, explaining that he had written to Vanderbilt about the price and

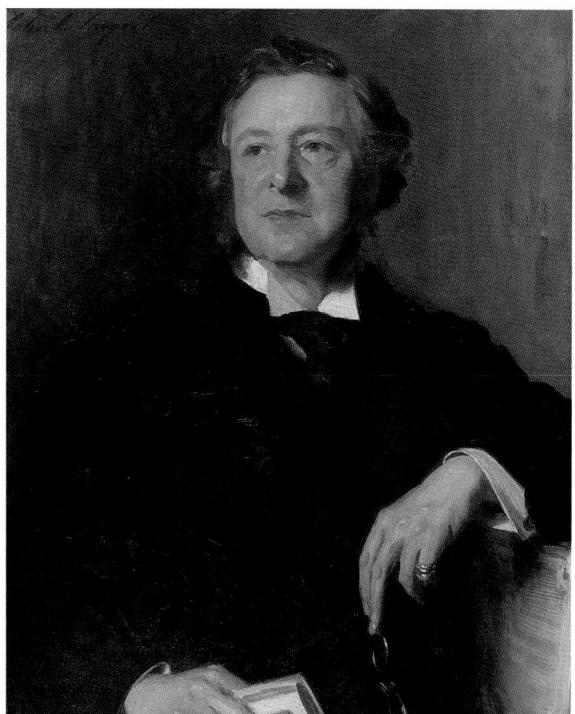

1897
Oil on canvas, 29½ × 25 (75 × 63.5)
Inscribed upper left: *John S. Sargent*
Private Collection

Arthur Cohen (1829–1914), the son of Benjamin Cohen and Justina Montefiore, became one of the most distinguished lawyers of his generation. He was educated at University College, London, and at Trinity College, Cambridge, where he was the first professing Jew to graduate. He was called to the bar in 1857, served as MP for Southwark from 1880 to 1887, was appointed standing counsel to the India Office in 1893, and was counsel for Great Britain in the Venezuela arbitration at The Hague in 1903. He married Emmeline Micholls of Manchester in 1860; they had eight children.

According to his daughter Lucy, the commission came about through the influence of Mrs George Lewis (see no. 280). In order to please his children and using some money that he had inherited, Cohen reluctantly consented to have his portrait painted. In her memoir of her father, Lucy Cohen records that the sittings took place during the Christmas holiday in 1897 and that, at the first sitting, Sargent, using pencil and notebook, drew a rapid preliminary sketch of his subject. The portrait was completed in nine relaxed sittings, each less than two hours' duration:

> He used to walk back several paces from the canvas, and then return and put on two rapid strokes of his brush, that had the effect of making the figure grow out of the background; then walk back again, look intently, and repeat the process, so that as much of his work seemed done away from the canvas as on it. He had just been painting Mr Chamberlain, the Countess of Essex, and Mr Wertheimer; this last picture was so intensely clever, and withal entertaining, that if my father looked dull, I would beg Sargent to bring forward his favourite picture, and his expression would at once relax. The portrait of my father went very easily; in many ways it is lifelike, but perhaps it fails to give the sweetness of expression of the mouth, and some of his admirers said that it did not nearly do him justice, but all agree that it is the one of the portraits of Sargent that presents no quality that one would wish not to be presented ([Lucy Cohen], *Arthur Cohen: A Memoir by His Daughter for His Descendants*, London, 1919, p. 149).

The sitter is dressed conventionally in a morning coat, wing collar and tie, and posed holding his place in a partially open book with the fingers of his right hand and dangling a pair of spectacles from the other, as if interrupted in reading. He rests his elbow on the edge of a plinth or tall piece of furniture.

The catalogue for the memorial exhibition held at the Royal Academy, London, in 1926 (see

that the portrait should not travel to America until the beginning of October because it was drying slowly in London (MMA archives).

Sargent's portrait of Marquand shows the sitter in contemplative mood, one arm resting on a round table and supporting his head, the other looped over the back of a cane chair. He is soberly dressed in a black morning coat, trousers and waistcoat, with a dark cravat and pin and a gold fob-chain. His angular physique is wittily painted. A curtain or hanging with deep folds defines the space behind and sets off the figure. For the chair and table, see Accessories, pp. xxii, xxiii, nos 7, 14).

There was correspondence between Sargent and Cesnola about the possibility of the portrait's being exhibited at the National Academy of Design (MMA archives). In three letters to Walter Clark of 9, 13 and 16 January [1924] about the proposed exhibition at the Grand Central Art Galleries, Sargent discussed what might be borrowed from the Metropolitan Museum, saying that, while the portrait of Marquand was not 'below the average . . . I think Mme X is worth ten of it' (GCAG archives).

It was the first of Sargent's paintings to enter the collection of the Metropolitan Museum of Art and was intended to be similar in size to the portraits of John Taylor Johnston (1880) by Léon Bonnat and William C. Prime (1892) by Daniel Huntington. Martin Birnbaum relates an anecdote told by the architect Welles Bosworth, who, when he was looking at the portrait hanging in the museum, spoke in its praise to Emily Sargent in the artist's hearing. Sargent was heard to respond: 'Chicken, – chicken! I can never think of anything else, when I look at this portrait, but plucked fowl in the markets!' (Birnbaum 1941, pp. 41–2).

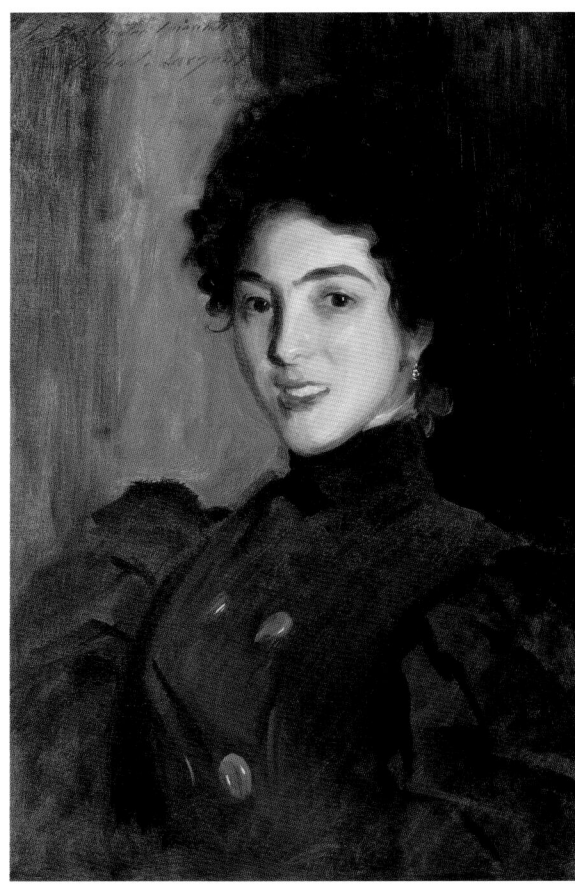

American museums. His success as a dealer/agent was underpinned by the 'vital contacts' he 'established with Italian aristocrats desperately in need of cash' (David Sox, *Bachelors of Art: Edward Perry Warren and the Lewes House Brotherhood*, London, 1991, p. 231), and it is possible that he acted for the contessa in the negotiations which saw the present portrait transferred from Italy to America.

According to Downes (Downes 1925 and 1926 eds, p. 265) and Charteris (Charteris 1927, p. 278), the portrait was with Ehrich Bros, New York, *c.* 1925–7; it was certainly with Newhouse Galleries, New York, by 1928 and was sold by them to Howard E. Green of Houston, Texas, the following year.

The contessa is dressed in a dark, high-necked day dress with puffed sleeves and large buttons.

346 *Senator Calvin Brice*

1898
Oil on canvas, $58\frac{1}{8} \times 36\frac{3}{4}$ (147.6 × 93.3)
Inscribed, upper right: *John S. Sargent 1898*; reverse (in another hand): *Painted London July 18ᵗʰ–28ᵗʰ 1898*
Allen County Historical Society, Lima, Ohio. Gift of Mrs W. M. Hobbs, Mrs F. M. Briggs and Mrs Eltham Allen

Calvin Brice (1845–1898) was the son of a minister from Morrow County, north-central Ohio. He served with the Union forces during the American Civil War, subsequently becoming a railroad tycoon and banker and serving as senator for Ohio from 1891 to 1897. He married Olivia Melly in 1870, by whom he had three sons and two daughters. He and his wife both liberally endowed the universities of which they were graduates, Miami University and Western College.

The Brices regularly visited London and Paris, and in 1894 Mrs Brice and her two daughters were painted by Carolus-Duran (Collection of Western College Alumnae Association). Sargent's portrait of Brice was painted in the artist's Tite Street studio over the course of ten days in July 1898. Within six months Brice was dead – from pneumonia caught after exposure to particularly bitter weather on a journey from Newport to New York.

Brice is shown in the Tite Street studio against a leaf of one of the artist's Chinese lacquer screens representing a peacock (see Accessories, p. xxiii, no. 25). He holds a pair of spectacles in one hand and a pair of gloves in the other and has a red flower, probably a carnation, in his buttonhole. The knob of what appears to be a cane is also visible near his left hand.

The portrait hangs in the Allen County Museum, Lima, Ohio. There is an etching after it by Robert Macbeth, probably commissioned for distribution to Brice's friends and admirers. For a later oil portrait of the sitter's daughter Helen Brice, see no. 533.

London 1926, p. 16) states, erroneously, that the portrait was exhibited at the New Gallery in 1907 (it was exhibited at the New Gallery in 1898). Mount mistakenly lists a portrait of Mrs Cohen (1955 ed., p. 435, no. 979; 1969 ed., p. 434, no. 979).

Frank Short's mezzotint after the portrait was sold Phillip's, London, 4–5 May 1982, lot 227.

345 *Contessa Chiericati*

c. 1897
Oil on canvas, 26 × 18 (66 × 45.7)
Inscribed, upper left: *to the Countess Chiercati / John S. Sargent*
Private Collection

The portrait represents the wife of Count Antonio Chiericati of Perugia, at one time prefect at Palermo, Sicily; the compilers have been unable to discover more about the sitter. According to McKibbin, the picture was painted in Palermo in January 1897, while Mount places it in London in 1894. The subsequent history of the portrait is uncertain. The indications are that it was still in the contessa's collection in late 1922; but it was in America (probably Boston) shortly afterwards and was exhibited in New York – at Macbeth Gallery – in January 1923.

McKibbin's index card for the painting lists Harold Parsons in the provenance without dates (McKibbin papers). This is almost certainly Harold Woodbury Parsons, the Bostonian dealer, who acted as European advisor to a number of

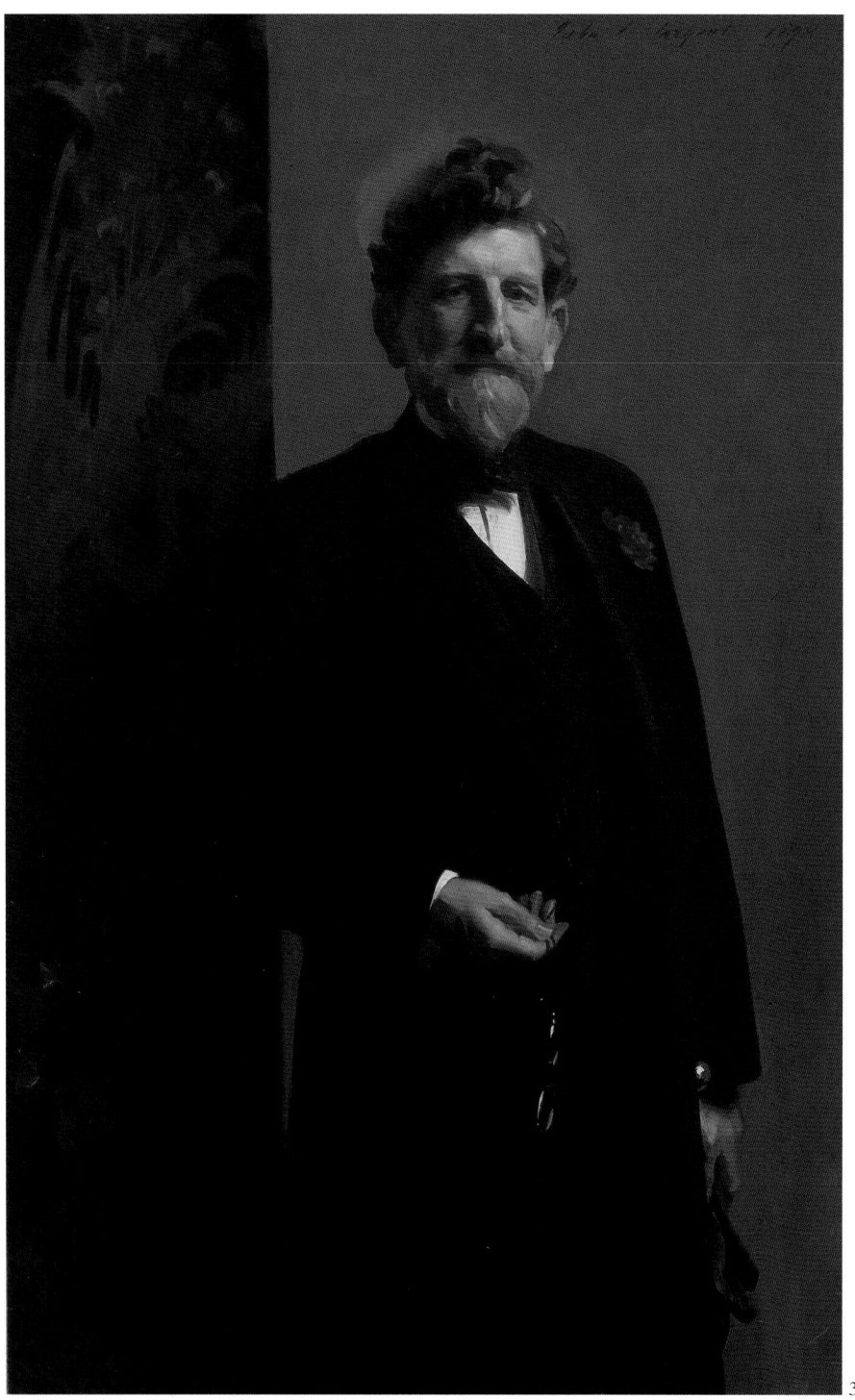

acting as a buyer for the Rothschild family. Asher and his brother Charles inherited both their father's instinct for fine art and his business acumen. Asher leased his father's premises at 158 New Bond Street and became a prominent dealer in his own right, specializing in French furniture, pictures, ceramics, silver and *objets d'art*, while Charles conducted his own business from his private residence. Asher's clients included Sir Richard Wallace, Frederick Spitzer and Baron Ferdinand de Rothschild, and his most outstanding transactions were the purchase in July 1898 of the Hope collection of Dutch and Flemish old masters (from Lord Francis Clinton-Hope for £121,550) and, with J. Seligman, the acquisition of the Chérèmèteff collection of Sèvres porcelain in Paris in 1906. His obituary in *The Times* noted that 'Mr Wertheimer was not only a fine judge of art, but a sound judge of human nature. In nearly all fine art disputes he was consulted and many were settled by his wise counsel.' ('Death of Mr Asher Wertheimer', *The Times*, 12 August 1918, p. 9). For a contemporary description of Wertheimer's gallery, see 'Mr Asher Wertheimer's New Gallery', *Athenaeum*, no. 3933 (14 March 1903, p. 345); and for an account of Wertheimer as dealer, including a list of the paintings that he handled and which are now in public collections, see Michelle Lapine, 'Mixing Business with Pleasure: Asher Wertheimer as Art Dealer and Patron', in New York 1999, pp. 43–53.

The companion portraits of Asher and his wife (no. 348) were painted to celebrate their silver wedding anniversary. Subsequently, artist and sitter became friends, and, in the ensuing ten years, the latter commissioned a celebrated sequence of twelve family portraits from Sargent, most of which Wertheimer left to the nation (ten are now in the Tate Gallery, London). The clutch of commissions led Sargent to complain to Lady Lewis (see no. 280) that he was in a state of 'chronic Wertheimerism' (Charteris 1927, p. 164). He was, in reality, at ease in the Wertheimers' company, visiting them at their country house, Temple, near Henley, and christening their dining-room, where eight of the portraits hung, 'Sargent's mess' (see Olson 1986, p. 209). Unfortunately, no correspondence between the two men survives, and there is a dearth of facts about their relationship. Correspondence concerning Wertheimer's bequest and the technicalities of his will is in the archives of the National Gallery, London.

The inscribed date on the canvas is 1898, but sittings must have taken place by the early summer of 1897: Isaac Phelps Stokes (see no. 337) saw the nearly completed canvas on an easel in Sargent's studio when he and his wife were sitting for their own portrait in June (see Stokes 1941, p. 118). It is possible that Sargent finished and inscribed the work at a later date.

The portrait of Wertheimer is the masterpiece of the set, a brilliant characterization of a complex character, shrewd, charming and confident. Thumb

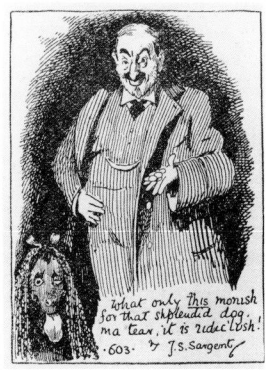

fig. 71 Caricature of Sargent's portrait of Asher Wertheimer, *Punch* (7 May 1898), p. 205.

347 *Asher Wertheimer*

1897–8
Oil on canvas, 58 × 38½ (147.5 × 98)
Inscribed, upper left: *John S. Sargent*; upper right: *1898*
Tate Gallery, London. Presented by the widow and family of Asher Wertheimer, in accordance with his wishes, 1922

Asher Wertheimer (1844–1918) was the son of Samuel Wertheimer, who had fled from religious persecution in Germany and settled in Britain in 1830. He created a highly successful business dealing in fine art, negotiating the dispersal of Russian aristocratic collections in the 1860s and in pocket, he holds open his overcoat in an expansive gesture, while in the other hand he balances a half-smoked cigar. The lolling tongue of his poodle, Noble, the brightest accent in the picture, is a witty foil to the equally dark figure of his master. Caught with a confiding smile on his face, Wertheimer is projected against the shadowy panels of what appears to be the Japanese lacquer screen in Sargent's studio.

The character of the man, caught with such subtle and penetrating force, amused the world without giving offence to its subject. It was one of the highlights of the Royal Academy exhibition in 1898. The *Athenaeum* reviewer described it as 'a masterpiece on which all artistic eyes have been fixed since the opening day', praising its 'profound and courageous sense of humour', its 'extraordinary simplicity of technique', and adding: 'Happy is the man whose portrait has been painted thus.' (*Athenaeum*, 11 June 1898, p. 762). The *Times* art critic admired the realism of the characterization, writing that Sargent was 'such a painter as Cromwell would have loved' (i.e. 'warts and all') and was sensitive to the fine line between caricature and intense realism that runs through much of Sargent's work:

He has sometimes been charged with a tendency, if not to caricature, at least to dwell upon some marked characteristic of a face, or some habitual attitude of his sitter, a little too exclusively . . . but [in the present work] . . . There is no dwelling upon any one feature at the expense of the rest, because everything here is characteristic and everything has been put in place by the painter with the most astonishing realism. It would be very hard to name any other modern painter that we could rank with this for sheer power of expression'. (*The Times*, 30 April 1898, p. 14)

The *Magazine of Art* wrote that the portrait 'best displays the painter's possibilities of reproducing his subject on canvas, with all those subtleties of insight and suggestion – *doublures*, as it were, of character or of personality' (*Magazine of Art*, 1898, p. 178).

There is a strain of social snobbery and racial typecasting underlying some contemporary comment. When Isaac Phelps Stokes saw the portrait in the artist's studio, he noted that the characteristic movement of Asher's thumb suggested that he was 'pleasantly engaged in counting golden shekels' (Stokes 1941, p. 118). A caricature in *Punch* showed Wertheimer with coins in his outstretched hand and a caption reading: 'What only *this* monish for that shplendid dog. Ma tear, it is ridic'lush!' (*Punch*, 7 May 1898, p. 205) (fig. 71). Henry Adams was explicit, writing to Charles Milnes Gaskell on 28 November [1897]: 'As for me I admire Dreifuss [Alfred Dreyfus, (1859–1935), Jewish army captain on the French general staff and the central figure in a celebrated legal case in France (1894–7), which polarized public opinion and exposed the extent of contemporary anti-Semitism]; but Sargent has painted another Jew, Wertheimer, a worse crucifixion than history tells off' (Adams 1988, vol. IV, p. 497). Seeing the portrait at the Royal Academy the following year, Adams wrote to Louisa Hooper (17 June 1898): 'Sargent's of Daisy Leiter [no. 358] is there, hung too high, so as to call out all that Sargent put into her. Also the Jew and dog. *Il ne manque que Joe*! But it is very much too too utterly expressive. Yet Sargent painted Daisy in absolute good faith! Poor Mary Curzon, between Daisy and Joe!'[1] (Adams 1988, vol. IV, p. 603).

In a later essay, Robert Ross eulogized the characterization as being: 'so instinct with life that no criticism was able to withstand the shock. Silence is even now the most discreet praise for what is surely one of the great portraits of the world, the only modern picture which challenges the Doria Velázquez [Innocent X] at Rome' (Ross 1911, p. 7). Roger Fry admired the paintings but wrote a cynical assessment of the social aspirations that underpinned Wertheimer's multiple commissions:

I see now that this marvellous group of portraits represents a social transaction quite analogous to the transaction between a man and his lawyer. A rich man has need of a lawyer's professional skill to ensure him to secure the transmission of his wealth to posterity, and a rich man, if he have the intelligence of Sir [*sic*] Asher Wertheimer and the luck to meet a Sargent, can, by the latter's professional skill, transmit this skill to posterity. (Fry 1926, p. 32)

The Wertheimer portraits have been the subject of recent conservation work at the Tate Gallery, London, begun by Anna Southall and continued by Jacqueline Ridge and Joyce Townsend (see Ridge and Townsend 1998); of critical reappraisal by Kathleen Adler (see Adler, in Nochlin and Garb 1995, pp. 83–96, and New York 1999, pp. 21–33); and of an exhibition, *John Singer Sargent: Portraits of the Wertheimer Family*, held in New York in 1999. Adler presents a penetrating analysis of the portraits against the background of contemporary attitudes towards Jewishness and in the context of contemporary racial stereotypes.

There is a preliminary pencil study for the picture in a sketchbook in the Fogg Art Museum, Cambridge, Massachusetts (fig 72). Leopold Goetze executed a mezzotint after the oil portrait. A pencil study of Wertheimer's head is in a private collection (fig. 73).

Mrs Charles Wertheimer was painted by Sir John Everett Millais in 1891 (see Mordaunt Crook 1999, pl. XIV), and there are portraits of both Charles and his wife by the then young and relatively untried William Orpen (see Bruce Arnold, *Orpen: Mirror to an Age*, London, 1981, pp. 219, 220).

The museum's old accession number for the picture is 3705.

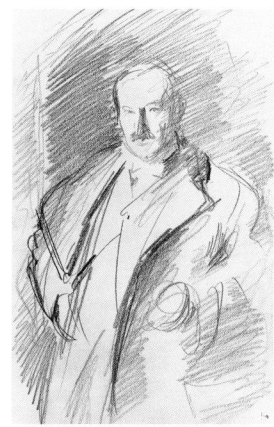

fig. 72 *Asher Wertheimer*. Pencil, 9 $^{7}/_{16}$ × 5 $^{15}/_{16}$ (24 × 15.1). Fogg Art Museum, Harvard University Art Museums, 1937.7.11 9 r.

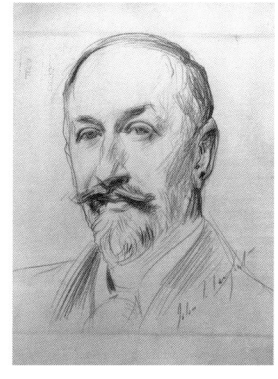

fig. 73 *Asher Wertheimer*. Pencil sketch. Private Collection.

1. *Il ne manque que Joe!* appears to refer to Joseph Leiter, the brother of Daisy Leiter and Mary Curzon. Henry Adams assumes that Daisy Leiter's father, Levi Zeigler Leiter is Jewish (he was of Swiss Mennonite descent), and seeing the portrait of Asher Wertheimer and his dog, comments that only Joe is missing.

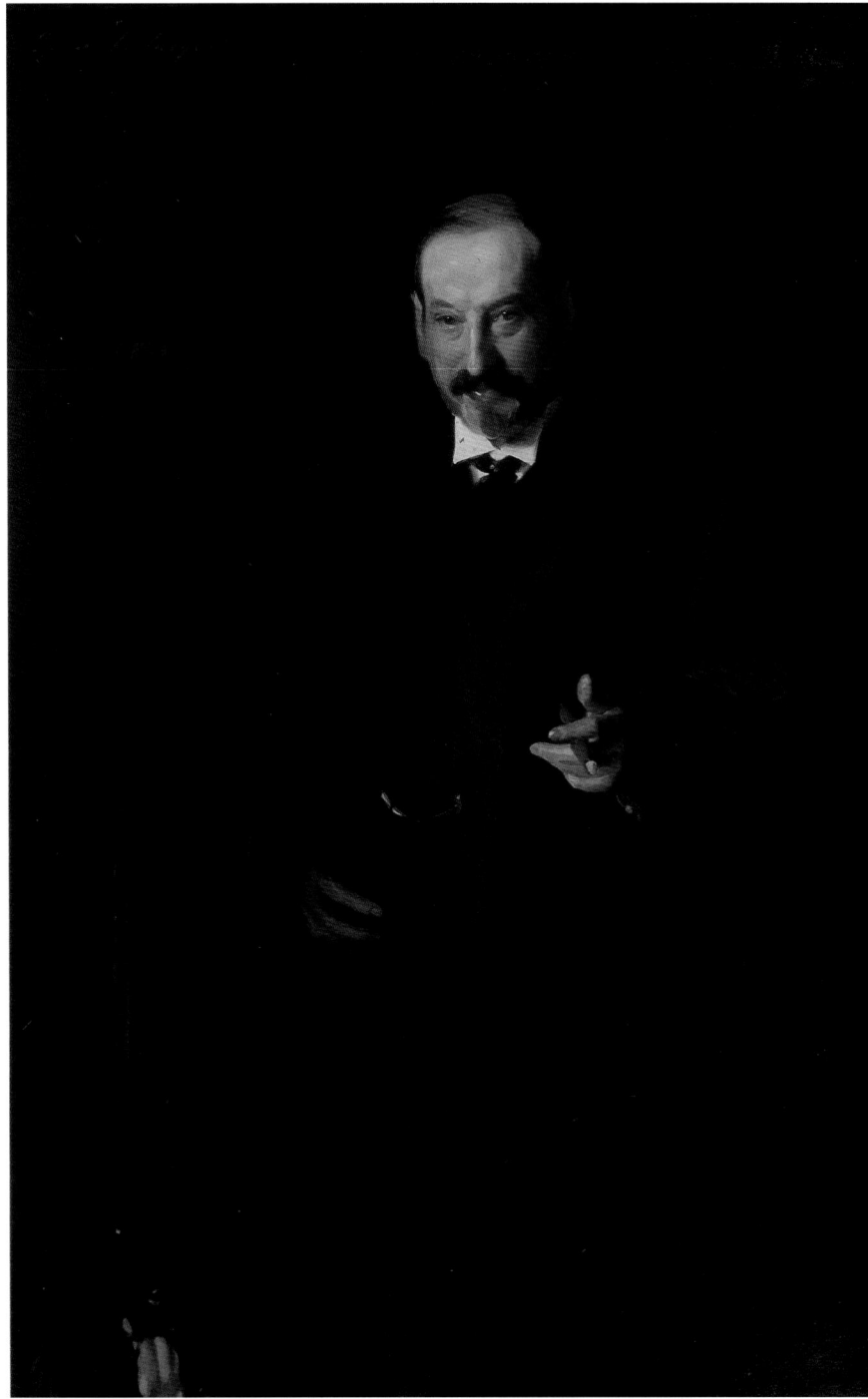

347

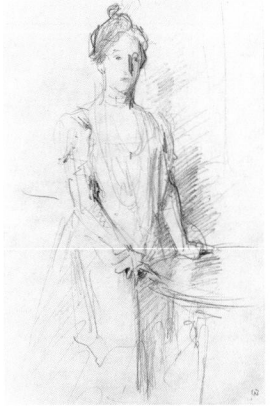 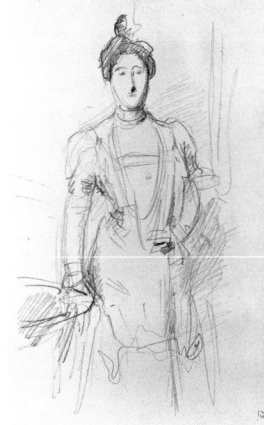

c. 1898
Oil on canvas, 58 × 37½ (147.3 × 95.2)
Inscribed, upper left: *John S. Sargent*
New Orleans Museum of Art. Museum purchase in
memory of William H. Henderson

Flora Joseph (d. 1922) married the prominent
Bond Street art dealer Asher Wertheimer *c.* 1873.
With their ten children, they lived in a grand and
sociable manner in their house in Connaught
Place, London. This and the companion portrait of
her husband (no. 347) were painted to commemorate their silver wedding anniversary, and were the
first in the great series of Wertheimer portraits.

In 1904, Sargent painted a second portrait of
Mrs Wertheimer because the first was not considered satisfactory, and it was this second picture that
was given with the family series to the National
Gallery.

Mrs Wertheimer is shown in an ivory satin
evening gown trimmed with lace and with lace
sleeves. She wears a pearl choker and a loop of
pearls with the two ends hanging loose, one end of
which is wrapped around her left hand. Other
pieces of jewellery include a pearl and diamond
brooch in the centre of her corsage, a pair of
silvered diamond bracelets, diamond drop earrings,
a ruby and diamond ring on her right hand,
and a diamond aigrette in her hair. She leans her
right hand against a French-style rosewood Louis
Quinze bureau with ormolu mounts, almost
certainly a piece supplied by Wertheimer. The panelling behind is a loose adaptation of one of the
Louis Quinze-style doors in the artist's studio (see
Accessories, p. xxiii, no. 17).

Two preliminary pencil studies show her standing just behind a small, circular, neoclassical table
in a pose different to that in the finished oil (figs
75, 76).

fig. 74 (far left)
Mrs Asher Wertheimer.
Pencil, 9 ⁷⁄₁₆ × 5 ¹⁵⁄₁₆
(24 × 15.1). Fogg Art
Museum, Harvard
University Art
Museums. Gift of Mrs
Francis Ormond,
1937.7.11, 12 r.

fig. 75 (left) *Mrs Asher
Wertheimer*. Pencil,
9 ⁷⁄₁₆ × 5 ¹⁵⁄₁₆ (24 × 15.1).
Fogg Art Museum,
Harvard University Art
Museums. Gift of Mrs
Francis Ormond,
1937.7.11, 13 r.

349 *Thomas Sutherland*

1898
Oil on canvas, 56½ × 44½ (143.5 × 113)
Inscribed upper left: *John S. Sargent*; upper right:
1898
Peninsular & Oriental Steam Navigation Company,
London

Thomas (later Sir Thomas) Sutherland (1834–
1922), rose from the position of a junior clerk to
managing director and, later, chairman of the
famous shipping company, Peninsular & Oriental
Steam Navigation Company (P. & O.). Under his
chairmanship (1881–1914), the company went
through a period of unprecedented expansion and
prosperity. Sutherland was frequently consulted by
government and served as an MP for twenty years.
He was a friend of Whistler and a noted collector

of paintings, and the selection of Sargent as the artist of his portrait may well have originated with Whistler. According to the minutes of the director's meeting for 19 January 1897 (P. & O. archives), a motion was unanimously passed asking if the chairman was prepared to sit for his portrait, to which he agreed; Sargent's name was then proposed for the commission. The artist probably painted the portrait the following winter or sometime before the spring of 1898, when the painting was exhibited at the Royal Academy. In the *Punch* review of the Academy show, the portrait was caricatured with the title 'Peninsular & Oriental "Pines, Prunes & Prisms"' (fig. 77).

Sutherland is represented in dark morning suit, with wing collar, silk tie, pearl tie-pin, and watch and chain; he has his left hand in his pocket and holds a document in his right. A large globe, vaguely indicated rather than fully realized, is to the right. The globe is visible in two preliminary pencil studies (figs 78, 79).

A portrait of Lady Sutherland by Edwin Arthur Ward is in a private collection.

350 *Francis Cranmer Penrose*

c. 1898
Oil on canvas, 56½ × 37½ (143.5 × 95.2)
Inscribed upper left: 1898; upper right: *John S. Sargent*
Royal Institute of British Architects, London

Distinguished architect, archaeologist and astronomer, Francis Cranmer Penrose (1817–1903) was surveyor of St Paul's Cathedral from 1852. He observed eclipses, made researches into the orientation of Greek temples, designed the British School in Athens, and was president of the Royal Institute of British Architects (RIBA) from 1894 to 1896. His early book *Principles of Greek Architecture* (1851) remains a classic.

On his retirement, it was decided to commission a portrait of him for the collection of presidents' portraits. A special committee of the RIBA, including Sargent's friend, the artist Lawrence Alma-Tadema, was appointed for this task on 14 December 1896 (RIBA Council Minutes, vol. 16). Sargent was selected as the artist, presumably on Alma-Tadema's recommendation, and the portrait begun by 21 February 1898, when the secretary of the RIBA reported that only £109 had been subscribed for the portrait and that the artist's fee alone was £150 (RIBA Council Minutes, vol. 16). It was resolved that the council would draw a cheque for the full amount when the payment became due.

The portrait shows Penrose seated in an Italian seventeenth-century-style armchair (see Accessories, p. xxii, no. 10), with a leather folder of drawings or plans beside him. His knees are crossed, and his hands are clasped on his lap. His raised head, reinforced by his full, Dundeary whiskers, gives him an amusing and quizzical look. The portrait was

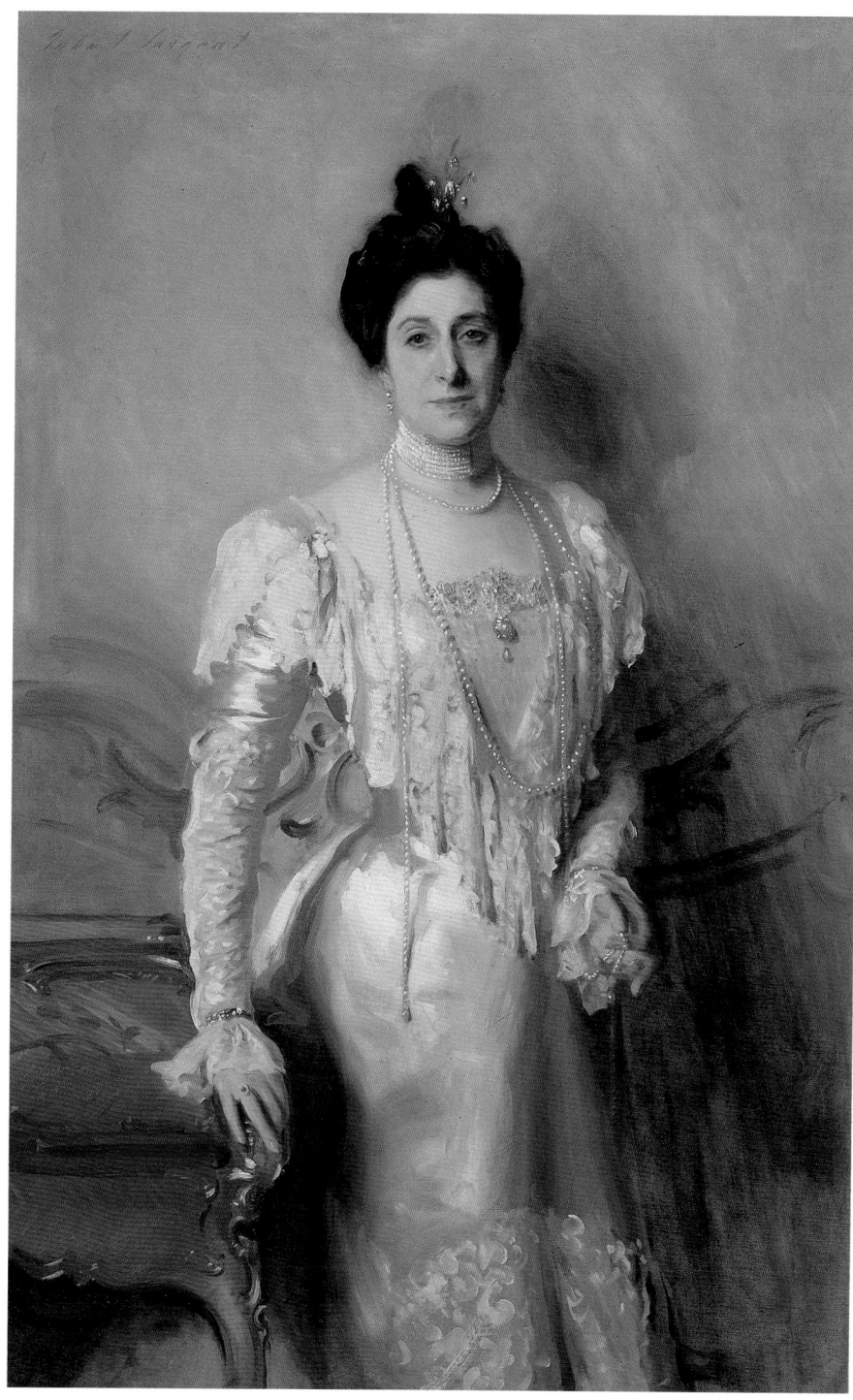

348

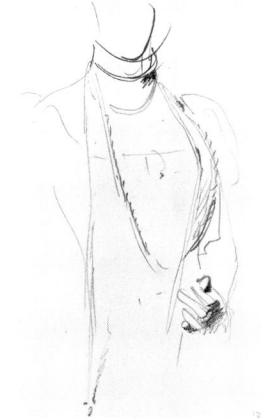

fig. 76 *Mrs Asher Wertheimer*. Pencil on paper, 9 ⁷⁄₁₆ × 5 ¹⁵⁄₁₆ (24 × 15.1). Fogg Art Museum, Harvard University Art Museums. Gift of Mrs Francis Ormond, 1937.7.11, 14 r.

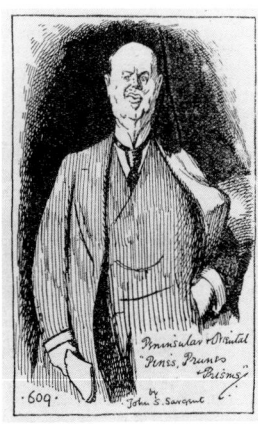

fig. 77 Caricature Sargent's portrait of Sir Thomas Sutherland, *Punch* (7 May 1898), p. 205.

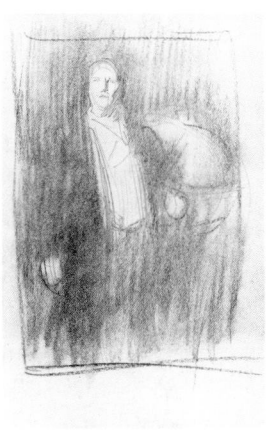

fig. 78 *Sir Thomas Sutherland*. Pencil, 9 ⁷⁄₁₆ × 5 ¹⁵⁄₁₆ (24 × 15.1). Fogg Art Museum, Harvard University Art Museums. Gift of Mrs Francis Ormond. 1937.7.11. 25 v.

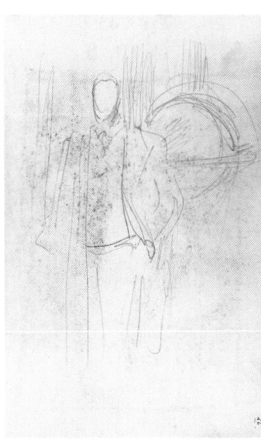

fig. 79 *Sir Thomas Sutherland*. Pencil, 9 ⁷⁄₁₆ × 5 ¹⁵⁄₁₆ (24 × 15.1). Fogg Art Museum, Harvard

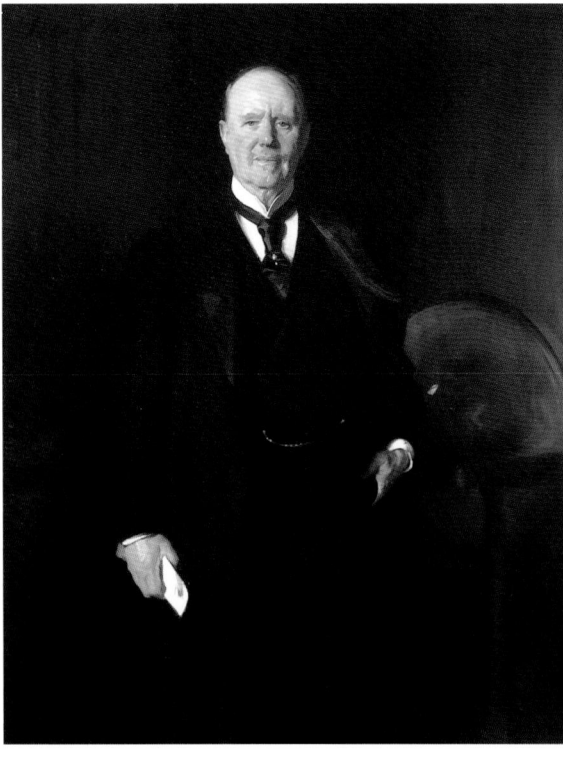

349

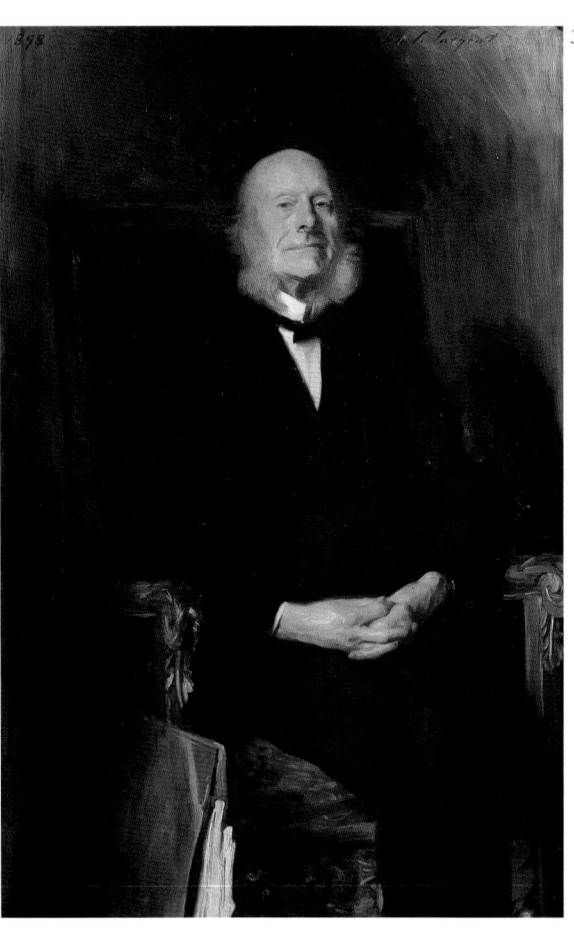

350

University Art Museums. Gift of Mrs Francis Ormond, 1937. 7.11. 26 r.

unveiled by Alma-Tadema, with much ceremony and speechifying, on 21 March in the presence of artist, sitter and a numerous gathering (see *Journal of the Royal Institute of British Architects*, 1898, pp. 277–8). When the work was exhibited at the Royal Academy in 1898, the critic of the *Athenaeum* noted that it was quite admirable 'in its vigorous characterization, powerful and harmonious painting and admirable breadth and force' (*Athenaeum*, 11 June 1898, p. 762). For a *Punch* caricature, see fig. 80

A copy of the portrait by R. G. Eves was in Eves's studio sale, Phillips, London, 30 October 1974, lot P54.

351   *Lord Watson*

c. 1898
Oil on canvas, 92 × 48 (233.7 × 121.9)
Faculty of Advocates, Parliament Hall, Edinburgh

William Watson (1827–1899), son of Reverend Thomas Watson of Covington, Lanarkshire, and his wife, Eleonora McHaffie, became the most distinguished judge of his generation. He was solicitor-general for Scotland from 1874 to 1876, Lord Advocate from 1876 to 1880, dean of the Faculty of Advocates and Conservative MP for Glasgow and Aberdeen Universities. He was created a life peer as Baron Watson of Thankerton, County Lanark, 1880. In 1868, he married Margaret Bannatyne, by whom he had four sons and one daughter.

It has not been possible to trace papers concerning this important commission, but it is likely that it was paid for by subscription, raised by a group of Advocates. Lord Watson is posed before what could be the panelling of a room similar to that shown in Sargent's portrait of Mrs Huntington (no. 361), but it is more likely to be the early eighteenth-century style armoire from Sargent's studio, positioned side-on, see Accessories, p. xxii, no. 13. In an undated letter (the envelope is postmarked 2 February 1898) to Mrs George Swinton (see no. 327) written from Tite Street, Sargent mentions one of Watson's sittings: 'I find on coming home that my Thursday afternoon sitting is an old Scotch judge instead of Mrs Hunter [*Mrs Charles Hunter*, no. 363]' (Private Collection).

The portrait was one of thirty-six pictures listed by the *Academy* (14 May 1898, pp. 530–1) as hung too high for proper viewing at the Royal Academy in 1898 (ironically, Sargent served on the hanging committee that year). Those listed were regarded as 'particularly fine' works 'to which the Academy visitor ought to turn, and which will well reward him for his pains – in the neck'.

Two preliminary pencil drawings are in a sketchbook at the Fogg Art Museum, Cambridge, Massachusetts (figs 81, 82).

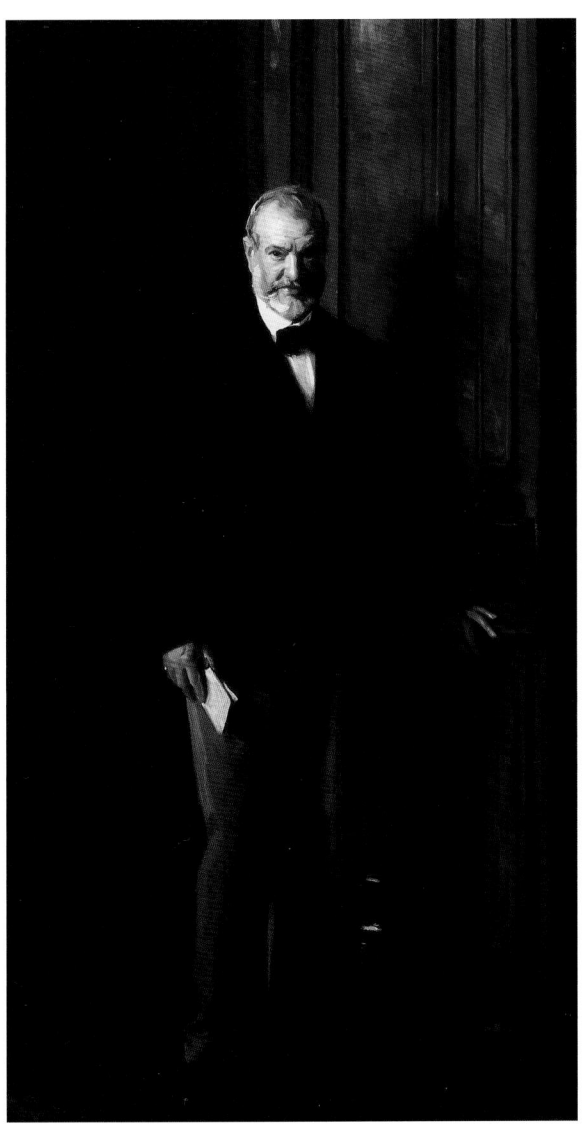

351

352   *Colonel Ian Hamilton*

c. 1898
Oil on canvas, 54½ × 31 (138.5 × 79)
Inscribed, upper left: *John S. Sargent*
Tate Gallery, London. Gift of General Sir
Ian Hamilton

Colonel (later General Sir) Ian Standish Monteith Hamilton (1853–1947), a leading military figure, served with distinction in South Africa against the Boers, becoming chief of staff to Lord Kitchener. He joined the army in 1873, was colonel of the Queen's Own Cameron Highlanders and Gordon Highlanders. He was knighted in 1910. In 1915, he led the ill-fated expedition to Gallipoli, which he described in *Gallipoli Diary* (2 vols, London 1920), an exemplary record of its kind. He married Jean Muir, daughter of Sir John Muir, in 1887.

Hamilton, who was interested in contemporary painting, had commissioned Sargent to paint his wife (no. 329) in 1896, and his own portrait was a sequel, painted to commemorate the storming of the Dargai Heights on the north-western frontier of India by the Third Brigade of the Tirah Expeditionary Force. Hamilton is shown as

Commander of the Third Brigade, in full regimental dress uniform, with red frogged jacket, campaign medals, and dark blue army greatcoat. He was, in reality, unable to command his brigade in battle at Dargai owing to a recently broken leg.

This was Sargent's first portrait of an officer in uniform and it is undeniably heroic. The critic of the *Art Journal* wrote: 'The pose is essentially dramatic, and the picture might be labelled "Imperialism". Hot reds are splashed upon the muscular jaw and throat, and the chin shoots out in challenging disdain. The open cloak reveals the medalled chest, and the sinewy hands – right over left – that clutch the sword hilt, are even more suggestive of the man than the almost anatomical neck.' (*Art Journal*, 1899, p. 187). In a long passage devoted to the portrait in the *Academy*, R. A. M. Stevenson wrote that Sargent had 'again held us spellbound with his clear, well cut, nervously drawn portrait, "Colonel Ian Hamilton". . . . the visitor [to the New Gallery] . . . will find so much explained to him by so clear, so direct a method that he cannot cease to admire the delightful disproportion between the simplicity of means used and the completeness of illusion attained.' (*Academy*, 6 May 1899, p. 510.) D. S. MacColl wrote of it as

> a masterpiece in its kind . . . Mr Sargent strikes me often as coldly hostile to his subjects, particularly when they are women. He declaims the tirades of their toilettes with a haughty half-angry brush. But here the declamation of his magnificent drawing finds a fit subject in the tense sinewy figure of the soldier. A man meets his match, and the tussle is superb. The portrait stands up on the canvas as if painted from a single challenging gesture of the whole form, the hands set down on the sword-hilt with the same movement that swung the chin up and turned the profile. . . . With a mind free from many aesthetic problems Mr Sargent develops his own specific quality of concise eloquent drawing'. (*Saturday Review*, 29 April 1899, p. 523)

When the portrait was exhibited at the Pennsylvania Academy of Fine Arts in 1901, it hung in the place of honour in the main gallery. It commanded attention, but more than one critic expressed reservations, for example, 'despite the brilliant technique displayed by the artist, and the pathetic force of the gaunt, sickly subject, the painting is inferior to some other portraits in the exhibition. Zorn's portrait of Halsey Ives has a pictorial strength, and Thomas Eakins's portrait of Louis Kenton has a simplicity and vigor one misses in the Hamilton portrait' (*Brush and Pencil*, February 1901, p. 264).

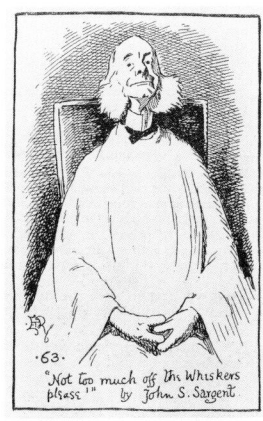

fig. 80 Caricature of Sargent's portrait of Francis Cranmer Penrose, *Punch* (7 May 1898), p. 205.

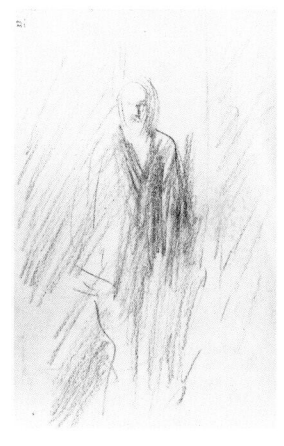

fig. 81 *Lord Watson.* Pencil, 9 $^7/_{16}$ × 5 $^{15}/_{16}$ (24 × 15.1). Fogg Art Museum, Harvard University Art Museums, 1937.7.11 33 r.

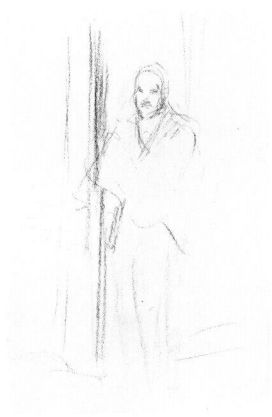

fig. 82 *Lord Watson.* pencil, 9 $^7/_{16}$ × 5 $^{15}/_{16}$ (24 × 15.1). Fogg Art Museum, Harvard University Art Museums, 1937.7.11 33 v.

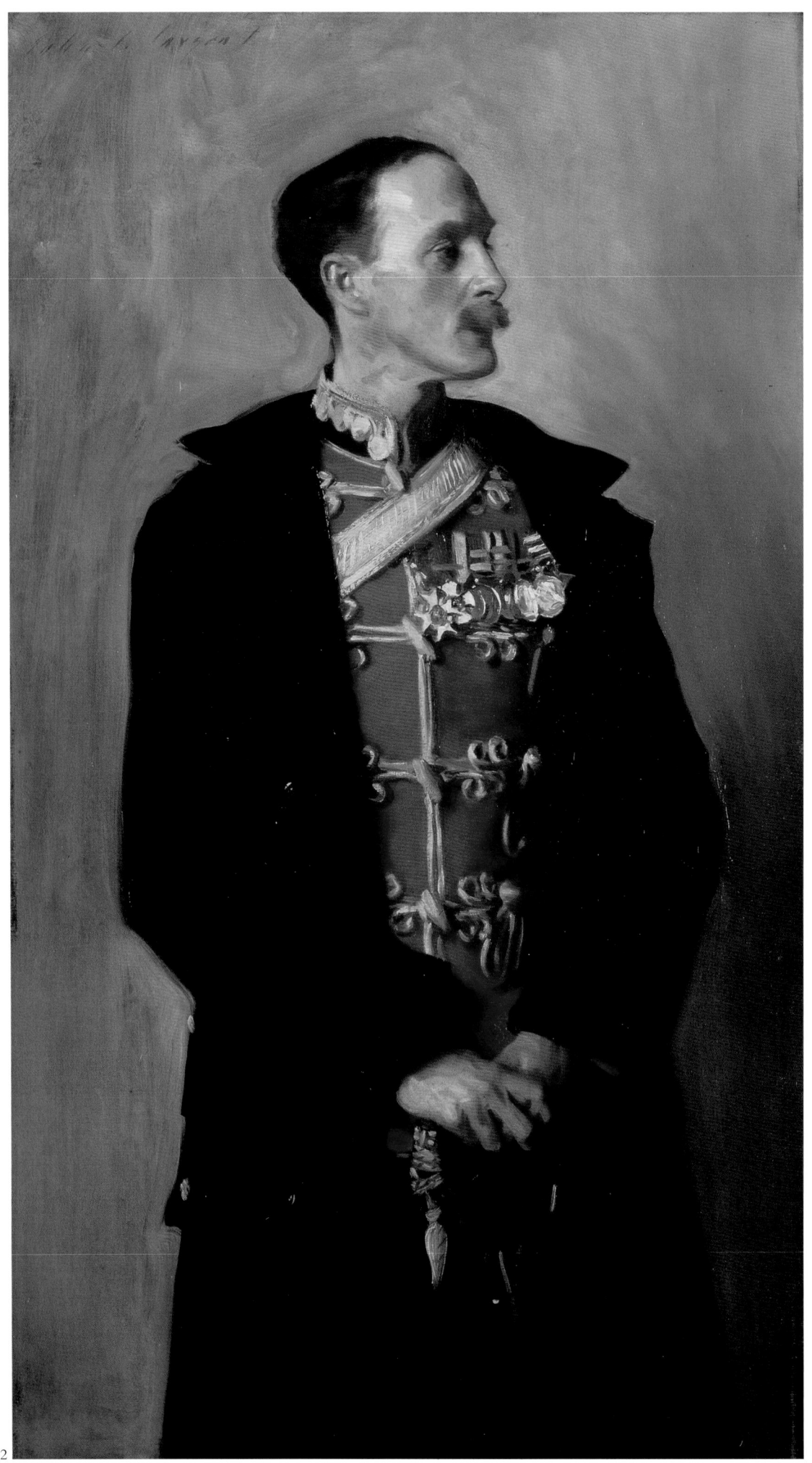

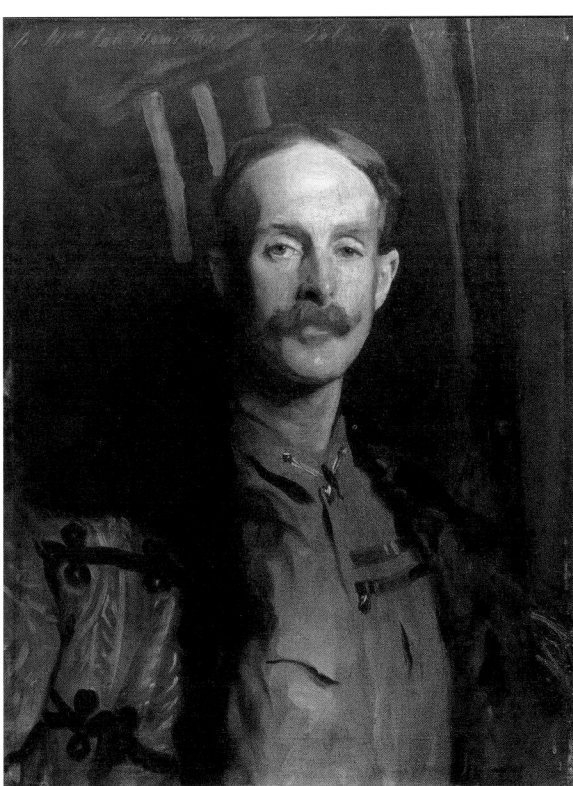

353 Colonel Ian Hamilton

c. 1898
Oil on canvas, 28¼ × 21¼ (71.8 × 54)
Inscribed, upper left: *to Mrs Ian Hamilton*; upper right: *John S. Sargent*
Scottish National Portrait Gallery, Edinburgh. Gift of Lady Hamilton

A more relaxed presentation sketch of Hamilton, painted at the same period as the formal three-quarter length (no. 352). Hamilton is painted wearing plain khaki drill uniform and an Afghan coat (he served in the Afghan War from 1878 to 1880). Hamilton wrote to Sir Hew Dalrymple (chairman of the trustees of the National Galleries of Scotland) on Christmas Day 1940: 'But the most beautiful Sargent we possess, in our opinion and that of most of our friends . . . was a present from Sargent to my wife and represents me as Commander of the Third Brigade just before the Battle of Dargai. The banner is made decorative use of, also the picturesque sheepskin coat embroidered with yellow silk which many officers wore out there' (Scottish National Portrait Gallery archives, Edinburgh).

The formal portraits of Colonel Hamilton and his wife (nos 329, 352) were offered to the Scottish National Portrait Gallery in 1940. The ethos of the Portrait Gallery, which places primary emphasis on the national significance of the individuals represented rather than on the aesthetic quality of the works of art representing them, prevented its director, Stanley Cursiter, from guaranteeing that the portrait of Lady Hamilton might not be moved to the National Gallery of Scotland, and both portraits were subsequently

offered to the Tate Gallery, London (see Edinburgh 1997, p. 76). The present work was presented to the Scottish National Portrait Gallery by Lady Hamilton in January 1941.

354 Antonio Mancini

c. 1898
Oil on canvas, 26½ × 19¾ (67 × 50.5)
Inscribed, lower left: *John S. Sargent*
Original inscription (below the artist's signature) in Mancini's hand, lost when the picture was cut down: *Mancini ringrazia / devotamente Mr Sargent / che e così buono / con il pittore cattivo Manciney / Londra*[1] (date illegible)
Galleria Nazionale d'Arte Moderna, Rome. Gift of the artist

The Italian painter Antonio Mancini (1852–1930) noted for his genre scenes and portraits. His technique, involving densely impasted surfaces, expressive brushwork and a Post-Impressionist palette, is powerful in effect and quite individual. Sargent, an admirer of his work and a firm friend, encouraged him to come to London, where he helped to find him patrons, including Asher Wertheimer, Mrs Charles Hunter, Mrs Leopold Hirsch and Hugh Lane (see nos 347, 363, 418, 525).

Four paintings by Mancini were in Sargent's estate sale of 1925, lots 298–300, and another was given by him to the Municipal Gallery, Dublin. A man of furious energy and mental instability, Mancini was not easy to handle, and his uninhibited behaviour often caused complications.

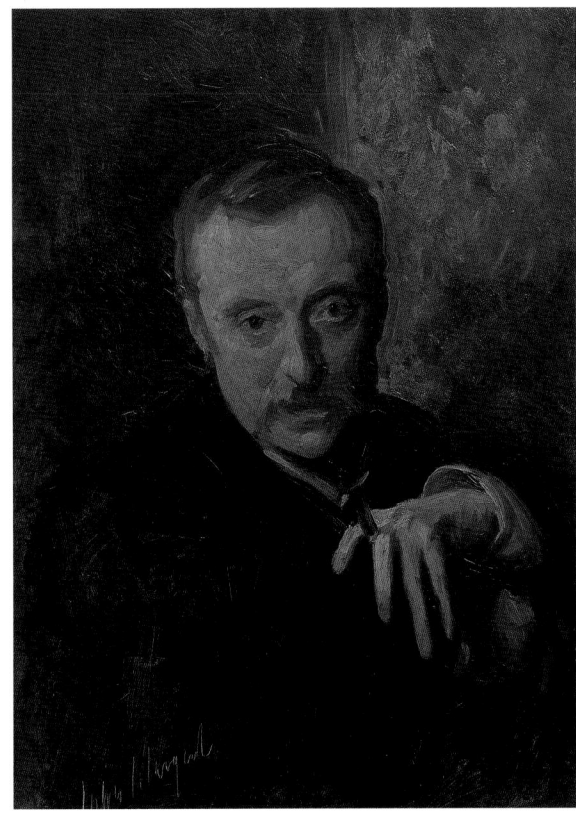

1. Mancini greatly thanks Mr Sargent / who is so good / to Manciney the bad painter / London.

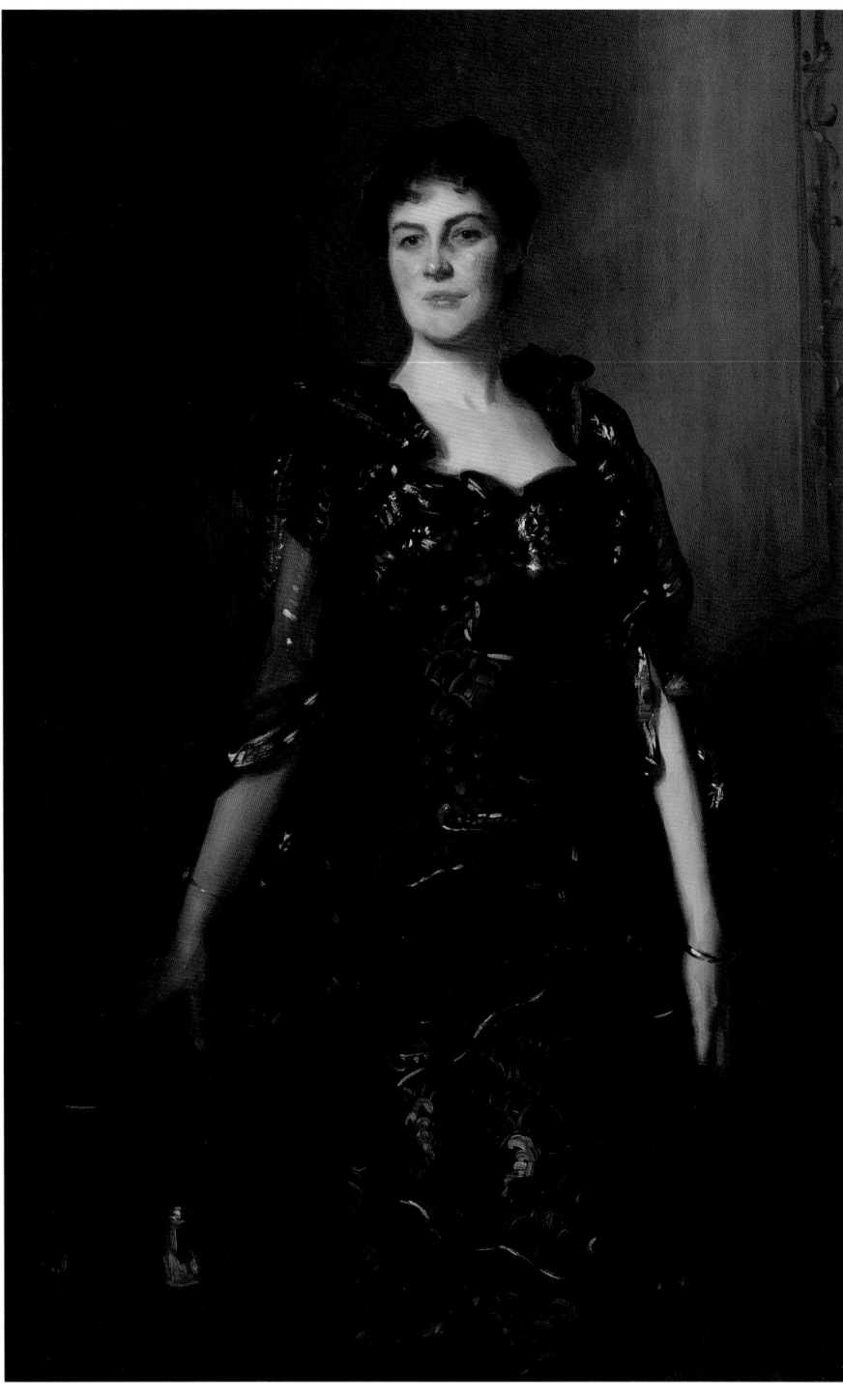

etc. It seems Sargent now considers Rossetti the greatest modern artist. He also recommends to his sitters the abominable work of an Italian, Mancini, who plasters his paint on by the inch and has the taste of a *commis-voyageur*. Sargent gave this protaganist in paint a sketch by himself. This Mancini gave it to a really great artist, Wertheimer's French cook; the cook in turn gave it to young Wertheimer, who gave it to his father, who in turn gave it back to Sargent. (Lewis 1939 p. 74)

There is a photograph of Sargent's studio at 33 Tite Street (fig. 20), showing the sketch of Mancini resting against the fireplace. The illustration in Meynell (1903) and Meynell Manson (1927) shows the original inscription. It must have been cut down sometime after 1903, probably by the artist.

For a later water-colour sketch of Mancini with Ena Wertheimer see no. 479.

355   *Mrs Charles Anstruther-Thomson*

c. 1898
Oil on canvas, 58½ × 38½ (148.6 × 97.8)
Inscribed, upper left: *John S. Sargent*
Private Collection

Mrs Charles Anstruther-Thomson, *née* Agnes Dorothy Guthrie (d. 1941), was the daughter of James Alexander Guthrie of Craigie, a director of the Bank of England, and of his wife, Eleanor Stirling. In 1882, she married Charles Anstruther-Thomson of Charlton, another prominent Scottish landowner. A noted socialite, she held salons at their London house in Rutland Gate, and also undertook philanthropic work, looking after a settlement in Lambeth. Her sister-in-law, the artist and writer Clementina (Kit) Anstruther-Thomson, was an old friend and protégé of Sargent, who had painted her picture in 1889 (see *Early Portraits*, nos 216, 217).

Mrs Anstruther-Thomson is dressed in a magnificent evening gown of oriental black silk spangled with flower motifs. The silk gauze sleeves appear to be part of the dress rather than a separate shawl. She wears a diamond brooch with pendant pearl at her breast and plain bracelets on both arms. Her right hand rests on one of two turquoise-coloured pieces of glass or ceramic in a gesture reminiscent of that in the portrait of Madame Pierre Gautreau (see *Early Portraits*, no. 114). The round table and panelling behind are familiar Sargent studio props (see Accessories, p. xxiii, nos 14, 17).

Kit Anstruther-Thomson saw the portrait at the New Gallery in 1898 and wrote to Vernon Lee: 'My sister-in-law's portrait is there, such splendid painting but he wasn't interested in *her* I see' (CC).

According to Downes, the sketch was painted in a little more than an hour (Downes 1925 and 1926 eds, p. 171), and according to Rebecca Insley, it was executed at the Wertheimer villa in Rome in 1894 (quoted Downes 1925 and 1926 eds, pp. 171–2). There is no evidence that Sargent knew Wertheimer well before he painted his portrait in 1898, and the inscription (now lost and extremely difficult to decipher from an old photograph) on the Mancini sketch was written in London, though this could have been added later. The early provenance of the sketch is given by Charles Ricketts in a diary entry for 6 March [1902]:

Rothenstein and his wife to dinner, full of amusing and malicious gossip about Sargent,

356 *Mrs Ernest Franklin*

c. 1898
Oil on canvas, 48 × 42½ (121.9 × 107.9)
Inscribed, upper left: *John S. Sargent*
Private Collection

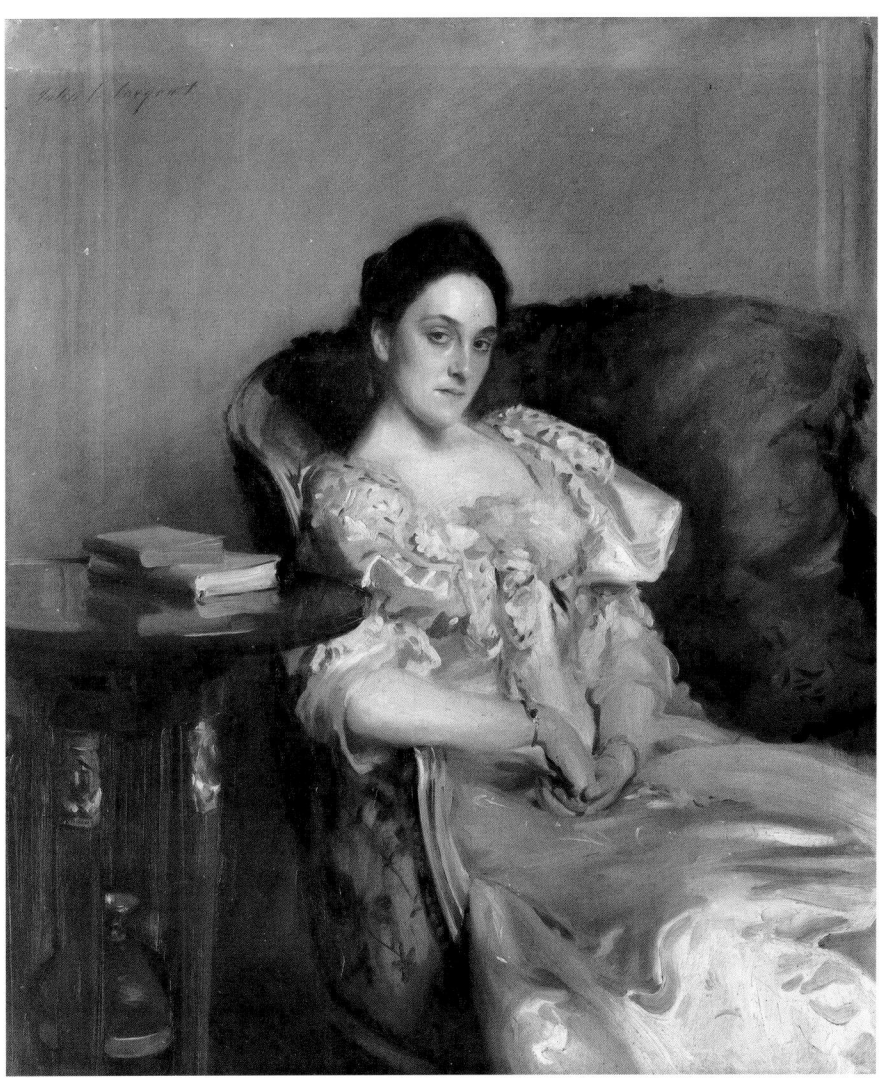

Henrietta (Netta) Samuel Montagu (1866–1964) was the daughter of Samuel Montagu, later first Baron Swaythling, founder of the bank of Samuel Montagu & Co., and of his wife, Ellen Cohen. In 1885, she married Ernest Louis Franklin, a senior partner in Samuel Montagu. Apart from bringing up a family of six children, she immersed herself in public work, playing a leading role in the Parents' National Education Union, the movement for liberal Judaism, the National Council of Women, and numerous other progressive causes; she was awarded a CBE in 1950. Both Franklin houses – at 50 Porchester Terrace, London, and Glenalla in Donegal, Ireland – were famous for liberal hospitality.

Ernest Franklin was interested in contemporary painting, collecting works by French and English artists, and it was he who selected Sargent to paint his wife's portrait; he later commissioned Glyn Philpot to paint two of his sons. According to Mrs Franklin's biographer, Monk Gibbon, she found the artist 'very shy, smoking cigarettes incessantly and sometimes, during a rest interval, sitting down and playing movingly on the piano. His efforts to make conversation were anything but successful. Presently he suggested that someone should come and read aloud during the sittings, an arrangement which worked very satisfactorily' (Gibbon 1960, p. 55). The portrait was considered far too restful by her friends, but her husband approved it.

Mrs Franklin is dressed in a white satin evening gown trimmed with lace. Apart from two simple bracelets, she wears no other jewellery. She is sitting in the armchair made famous by *Lady Agnew of Lochnaw* (no. 286). While she is squashed to one side, the other half of the chair is occupied by a large cushion covered in Chinese silk picked out with delicate calligraphy. Beside her are two books on the round table, another of the artist's familiar props (see Accessories, pp. xxii, xxiii, nos 2 a, 14). There are several preliminary studies for the portrait, showing the sitter in seated and standing poses (figs 83–9). In two of the studies, the chair is different from that in the finished portrait.

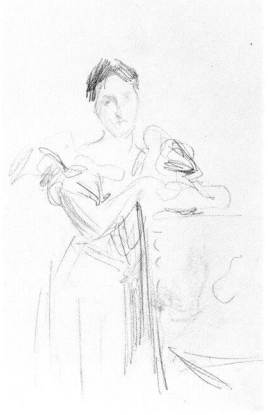

fig. 83 *Mrs Ernest Franklin*. Pencil, 9 ⁷⁄₁₆ × 5 ⁵⁄₁₆ (24 × 15.1). Fogg Art Museum, Harvard University Art Museums. Gift of Mrs Francis Ormond, 1937.7.11.2 v.

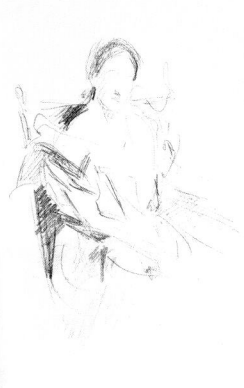

fig. 84 *Mrs Ernest Franklin*. Pencil, 9 ⁷⁄₁₆ × 5 ⁵⁄₁₆ (24 × 15.1). Fogg Art Museum, Harvard University Art Museums. Gift of Mrs Francis Ormond, 1937. 7. 11. 2 r.

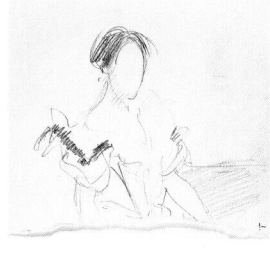

fig. 85 *Mrs Ernest Franklin*. Pencil, 9 ⁷⁄₁₆ × 5 ¹⁵⁄₁₆ (24 × 15.1). Fogg Art Museum, Harvard University Art Museums. Gift of Mrs Francis Ormond 1937.7.11.1 r.

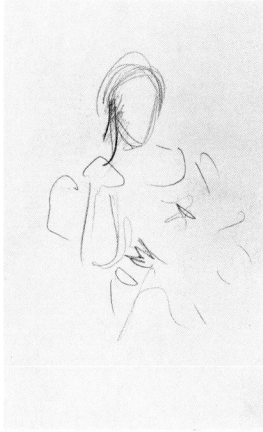

fig. 86 *Mrs Ernest Franklin*. Pencil, 9 ⁷⁄₁₆ × 5 ⁵⁄₁₆ (24 × 15.1). Fogg Art Museum, Harvard University Art Museums. Gift of Mrs Francis Ormond, 1937. 7. 11. 4 v.

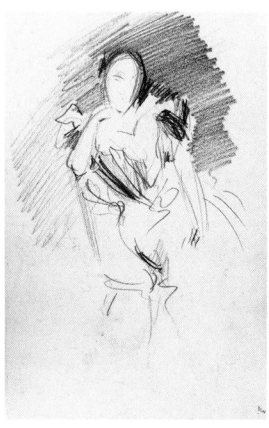

fig. 87 *Mrs Ernest Franklin*. Pencil, 9 ⁷⁄₁₆ × 5 ⁵⁄₁₆ (24 × 15.1). Fogg Art Museum, Harvard University Art Museums. Gift of Mrs Francis Ormond, 1937. 7. 11. 3 r.

357 *The Honourable Pauline Astor*

1898–9
Oil on canvas, 98 × 50 (248.9 × 127)
Inscribed, lower left: *John S. Sargent*
Private Collection

Pauline Astor (1880–1970) was born in New York, the daughter of the American financier William Waldorf Astor and Mary Dahlgreen Paul of Philadelphia, known as Mamie. Her father had suffered political disappointments, and, probably partly as a result of this and in an attempt to escape the persecution of the American press, he moved to England in 1891. He established his family there, buying two grand houses – Cliveden in Berkshire and Hever Castle in Kent. He became a British subject in 1899, a baronet in 1916 and a viscount in 1917. When Pauline's mother died in 1894, Pauline assumed the role of hostess and later nursed her younger sister Gwendolyn, who died in 1902. She lived briefly in Romania with Crown Prince Ferdinand and his wife, Princess Marie. She married Lieutenant Colonel Herbert Spender-Clay (d. 1937), a soldier in the Life Guards and later a Conservative MP for Tunbridge Wells, in 1904, and they had two daughters, Rachel, later Lady Bowes-Lyon and Phyllis, later Lady Nichols. They lived at Ford Manor in Surrey, and life at Ford is remembered by the actress Joyce Grenfell, who spent part of her childhood there (*Joyce Grenfell Requests the Pleasure*, London, 1976, pp. 82–5). Francis Nichols provided biographical information about his grandmother in a letter to compilers (20 March 1986, catalogue raisonné archive).

According to a letter from the sitter to McKibbin of 1 July 1948, the picture was begun in the autumn of 1898 but not finished until the beginning of 1899 (McKibbin papers). In a later letter to McKibbin (23 August 1964), Mrs Spender-Clay recalled that the King Charles spaniel in the picture was called 'Mossie' (McKibbin papers).

Pauline Astor is dressed in a white silk evening gown with a corsage of gauze. A lilac silk shawl edged with fur is wrapped around her arms, and she holds a fur muff in both hands. There are flowers at her breast and a diamond aigrette in her hair. The setting recalls the landscape at Cliveden, where the grounds stretch down to a curve in the River Thames, through a wooded hillside. The autumnal foliage in the picture creates a lyrical and wistful mood.

Like *Daisy Leiter* (no. 358), to which it is closely related, it is one of the earliest works in which Sargent adopts the landscape setting associated with the tradition of eighteenth-century English portraiture and with Gainsborough in particular.

Sargent painted the sitter's sister-in-law, Nancy Astor, in 1908 (no. 554).

358 *Daisy Leiter*

1898
Oil on canvas, 90 × 47 (228.6 × 119.4)
Inscribed, lower left: *John S. Sargent*; lower right: *1898*
Kenwood, London (English Heritage), The Iveagh Bequest.

Marguerite ('Daisy') Hyde Leiter (*c.* 1879–1968) was the younger daughter of the American multimillionaire Levi Ziegler Leiter, whose family, of Swiss Mennonite descent, had founded the village of Leitersburg in Maryland in 1811. Levi Leiter left Leitersburg for Chicago in 1854 and joined forces with another young merchant, Marshall Field; in 1865 they created the store which bore Field's name and which made both men wealthy. The Leiters moved from Chicago to Washington, where Daisy and her sister, Mary Victoria, American dollar princesses *par excellence*, were educated, groomed and introduced into society in considerable style. Both Leiter daughters married into the English aristocracy. Mary married George Nathaniel Curzon (see no. 569), the eldest son of the first Earl of Scarsdale, in 1895, and when he was appointed Viceroy of India and created Baron Curzon of Kedleston in 1898, she became Baroness Curzon and Vicereine of India (this remained for many years the highest political rank held by an American woman). In 1904, Daisy married Henry Molyneux Paget Howard, nineteenth Earl of Suffolk and twelfth Earl of Berkshire, and became Countess of Suffolk and Berkshire. She was widowed in 1917, after which she returned to America, living in Tucson, Arizona, and re-adopting American citizenship.

Sargent's portrait of this young American heiress is one of the first to show the influence of earlier British portraitists in its pastoral setting and mood of elegant grandeur and artifice. Trevor Fairbrother has pointed specifically to the windswept figure in Sir Joshua Reynolds's *Lady Jane Halliday* of 1778–9 (see Fairbrother 1986, p. 373), a painting bought by Baron Ferdinand de Rothschild from Asher Wertheimer in 1888 and now in the Rothschild Collection, Waddesdon Manor, Berkshire. For the painting's history see Waterhouse 1967, p. 76, ill.

Henry James was equivocal about the world of romantic portraiture evoked in the portrait, writing wryly to Isabella Stewart Gardner from London (3 April 1898) that Sargent had painted Miss Leiter 'in a very brilliant Gainsborough way. But there is also a slight Watteau element in the thing against which the six feet of stature and the little intensely modern Fifth Avenue face of the young woman rather militates' (ISGM archive).

The portrait was one of eight works – the maximum permitted – exhibited by Sargent at the Royal Academy in 1898. A. C. R. Carter noted 'a concession to the early British School in the adoption of a low landscape background . . . much enigmatical brushwork [and] the bravura, inseparable from Mr Sargent's portraits of women, [which] is directly supplied by the streamers which flaunt from the lady's shoulders' (*Art Journal*, 1898, p. 178). Another critic praised 'its tonality and . . . comprehensive grasp of natural character', but found the 'extreme length of the figure' difficult to account for: 'Mr Sargent has often puzzled us before with problematical ladies, but by hiding these feet in voluminous skirts and twisting these bodies he has prevented us from studying their structures strictly. In this case he has not attempted any such disguise' (*Athenaeum*, 11 June 1898, p. 762). For Henry Adams's comments on the portrait, see no. 347.

Sir Edgar Vincent saw the portrait hanging in the Leiter house in Washington in January 1908. Writing to his wife, he described the house as 'a dream of vulgarity & tawdry splendour', adding that 'this awful place contains the best Bonnat of Leiter père the best Sargent of Daisy the best Carolus-Durand [*sic*] of Mary [Mary Leiter, later Lady Curzon]' (BL Add. MS 48935 no. 197). Two pencil drawings in the Fogg Art Museum may be preliminary sketches for the portrait (figs 90, 91).

A portrait of Daisy Leiter as a child by Eastman Johnson (1884) was sold Sotheby's, New York, 17 March 1994, lot 54A.

359 *Mrs Ralph Curtis*

1898
Oil on canvas, 86⅜ × 41¼ (219.3 × 104.8)
Inscribed, upper left: *to Ralph and Lisa Curtis / John S. Sargent 1898*
Cleveland Museum of Art,
Ohio. Leonard C. Hanna Jr Fund

Eliza (Lisa or Lise) De Wolfe Colt (1871–1933), heiress to the Colt firearms fortune, came from Providence, Rhode Island. She married the Boston architect Arthur Rotch, a friend of Sargent's from the latter's Paris days, in 1892; Rotch died in 1894, and she married Sargent's cousin Ralph Wormeley Curtis in 1898. Edith Wharton's story 'The Verdict', which portrays a failed artist and his rich, vacuous wife, was widely seen to be modelled on the young Curtises (see Edith Wharton, *The Hermit and the Wild Woman*, 1908). Henry Adams, however, wrote to Elizabeth Cameron (18 September 1899): 'Mrs Ralph is charming when she says she knows she's a fool. I've learned to mistrust women who know they're fools. It has taken me sixty years to learn what a fool is, and a woman who knows it before thirty is dangerous' (Adams 1988, vol. V, p. 40).

Sargent depicts Mrs Curtis in a close-fitting ball gown of light grey satin with pink lights and a train spreading out behind her, the silhouette of the dress emphasizing her tall and slender figure.

Her hair is gathered into a tight bun on top of her head, and there is a notable absence of jewellery. Behind her is a round eighteenth-century side-table with triangular foot, and on it a shawl or stole. A billowy French hanging or drape, picked out with a gold floral motif, falls behind the table, and there is a flowered Aubusson carpet on the floor.

Sargent has posed his sitter against the table, supporting herself with both arms, with the result that she is thrown provocatively forward and appears to pirouette on one leg (her left foot seems barely to touch the ground). The steep pitch of the floor emphasizes this unsettling airborne effect.

The Curtises were married in November 1898, and the portrait was probably a wedding gift from the artist. Henry James saw this painting and *An Interior in Venice* (no. 366) in Sargent's studio in January 1899 and wrote to Ralph's mother, Mrs Daniel Sargent Curtis, with his impressions (16 March 1899):

I ought long ago to have reported on my visit to Sargent's (in January) studio & my vision, there, of the 2 pictures. *But* – it's difficult. Frankly, candidly, crudely – I didn't like the portrait of Mrs Ralph *at all*! and don't take it as worthy of anyone concerned. I don't understand, among other things, why and how artist and husband conspired to dress her so – for, I think the dress (and I'm not speaking in the least of the *décolletage* in particular), [neither] agreeable [n]or distinguished: indeed it seems to me that her certainly very striking beauty is of an order to rejoice in clothes the least fustian possible. (Henry James to Mr and Mrs Daniel Curtis, 16 March 1899, DCL)

He saw the young couple a few days later and wrote a postscript to his letter: 'She is singularly handsome, to my vision, and harmonious and sympathetic – every way gentle and gracious and charming: miles beyond the infelicitous picture. It does her poor justice' (DCL). The portrait was in Boston in February, and was included in Sargent's one man show at the Copley Gallery.

The portrait is shown *in situ* in the salon of the Curtis house, Villa Sylvia, at Saint-Jean-sur-Mer, near Beaulieu (*Country Life*, LXI, 15 January 1927, p. 91).

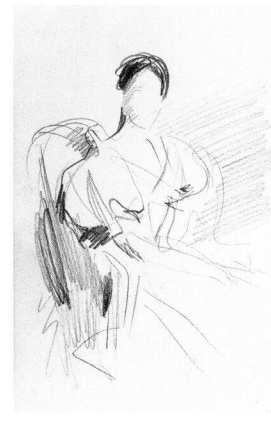

fig. 88 *Mrs Ernest Franklin*. Pencil, 9 ⁷⁄₁₆ × 5 ⁵⁄₁₆ (24 × 15.1), Fogg Art Museum, Harvard University Art Museums. Gift of Mrs Francis Ormond, 1937. 7. 11. 5 r.

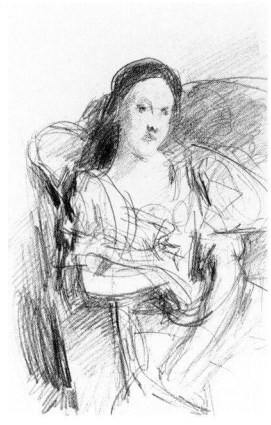

fig. 89 *Mrs Ernest Franklin*. Pencil, 9 ⁷⁄₁₆ × 5 ⁵⁄₁₆ (24 × 15.1), Fogg Art Museum, Harvard University Art Museums. Gift of Mrs Francis Ormond, 1937. 7. 11. 3 v.

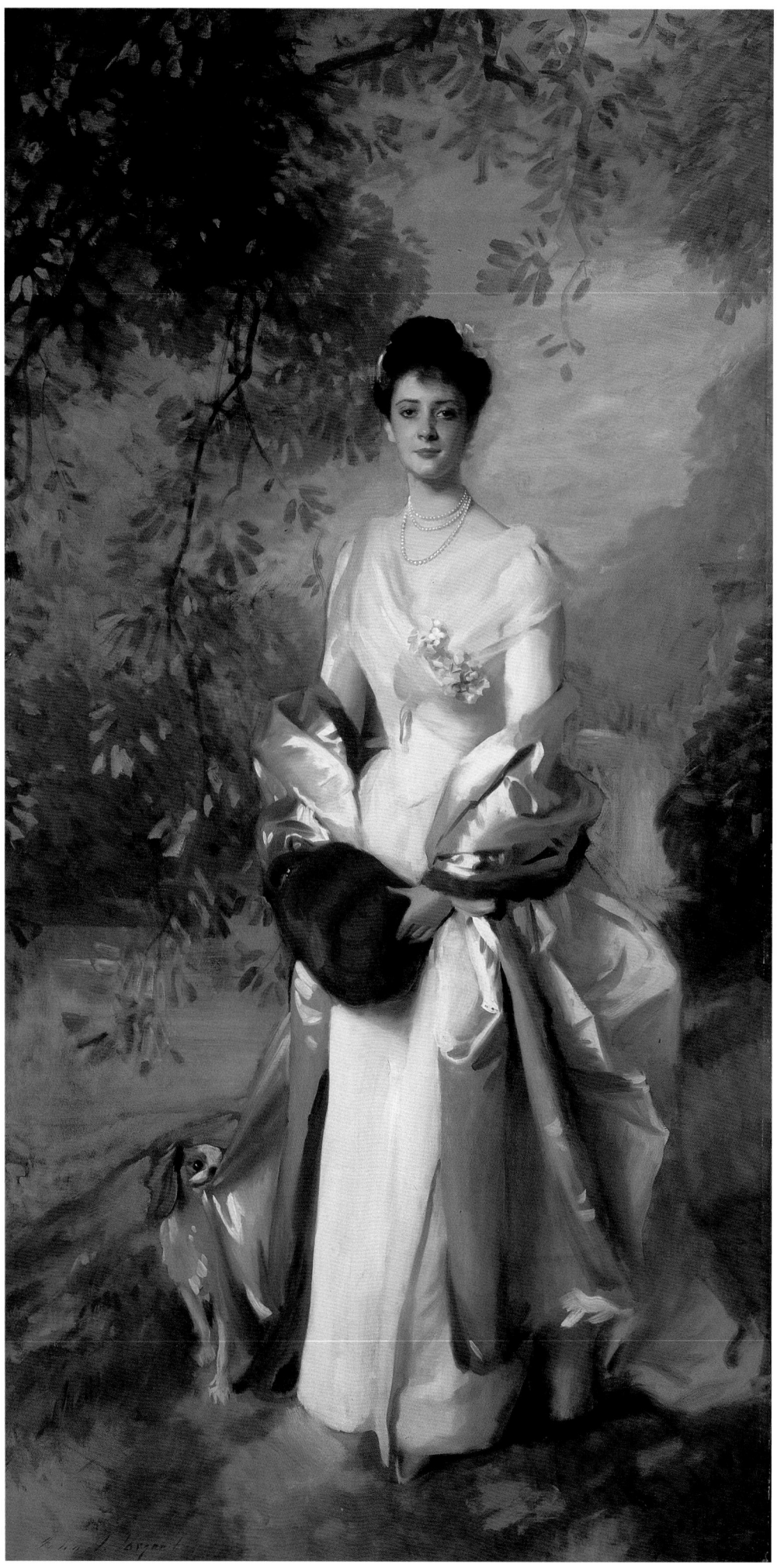

357

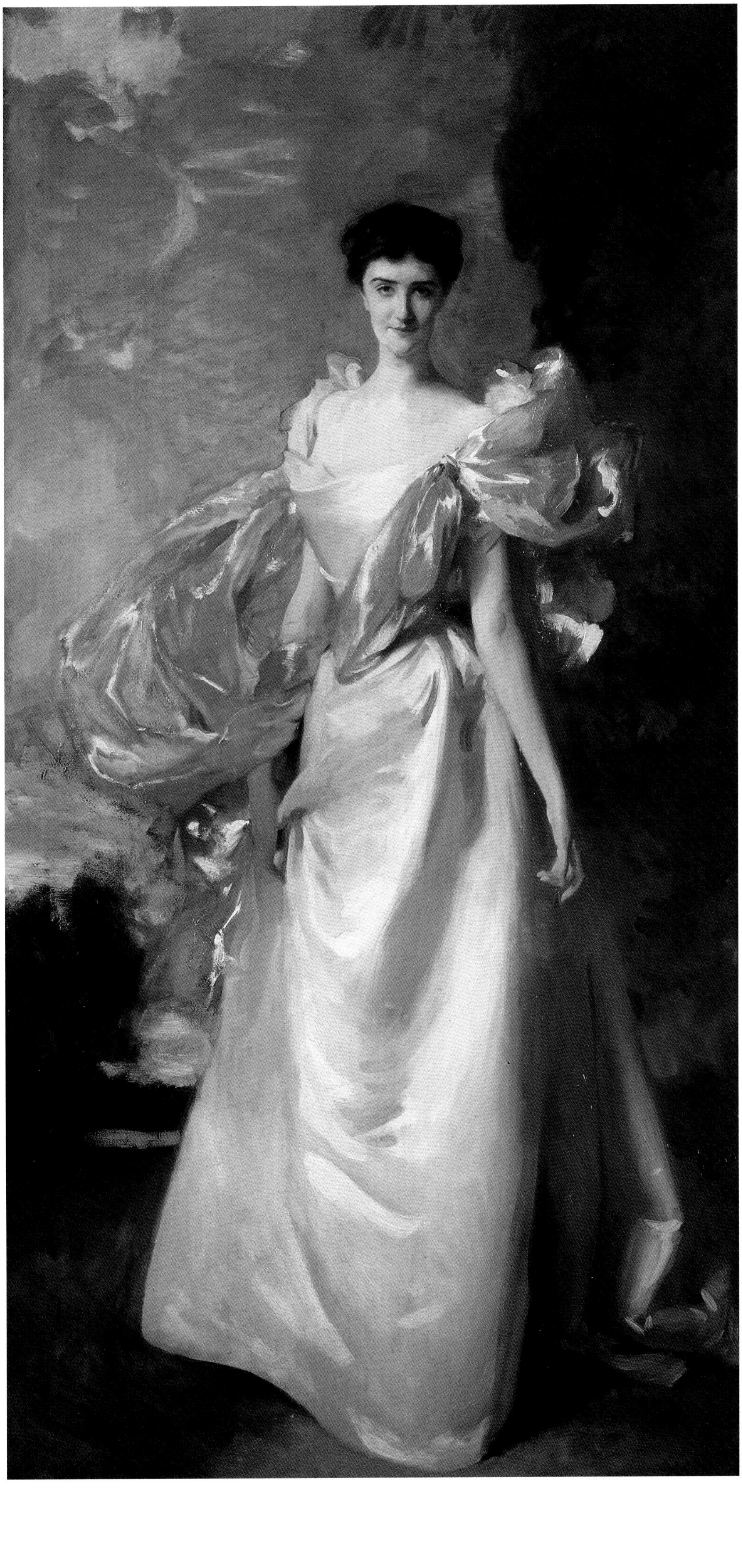

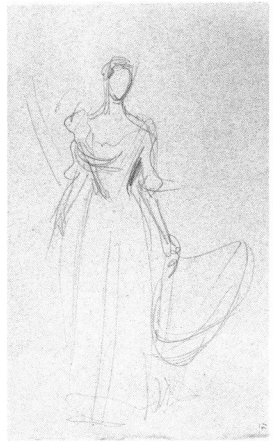

fig. 90 Possibly a study
for *Daisy Leiter*. Pencil,
9 $\frac{7}{16}$ × 5 $\frac{5}{16}$ (24 × 15.1).
Fogg Art Museum,
Harvard University Art
Museums. Gift of Mrs
Francis Ormond 1937 7.
11 16 r.

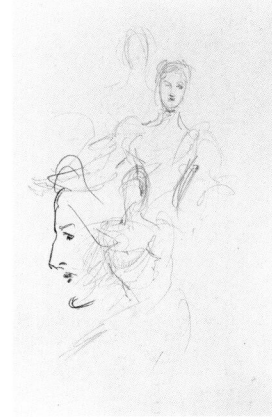

fig. 91 Possibly a study
for *Daisy Leiter*. Pencil,
9 $\frac{7}{16}$ × 5 $\frac{5}{16}$ (24 × 15.1).
Fogg Art Museum,
Harvard University Art
Museums. Gift of Mrs
Francis Ormond 1937 7.
11 15 v.

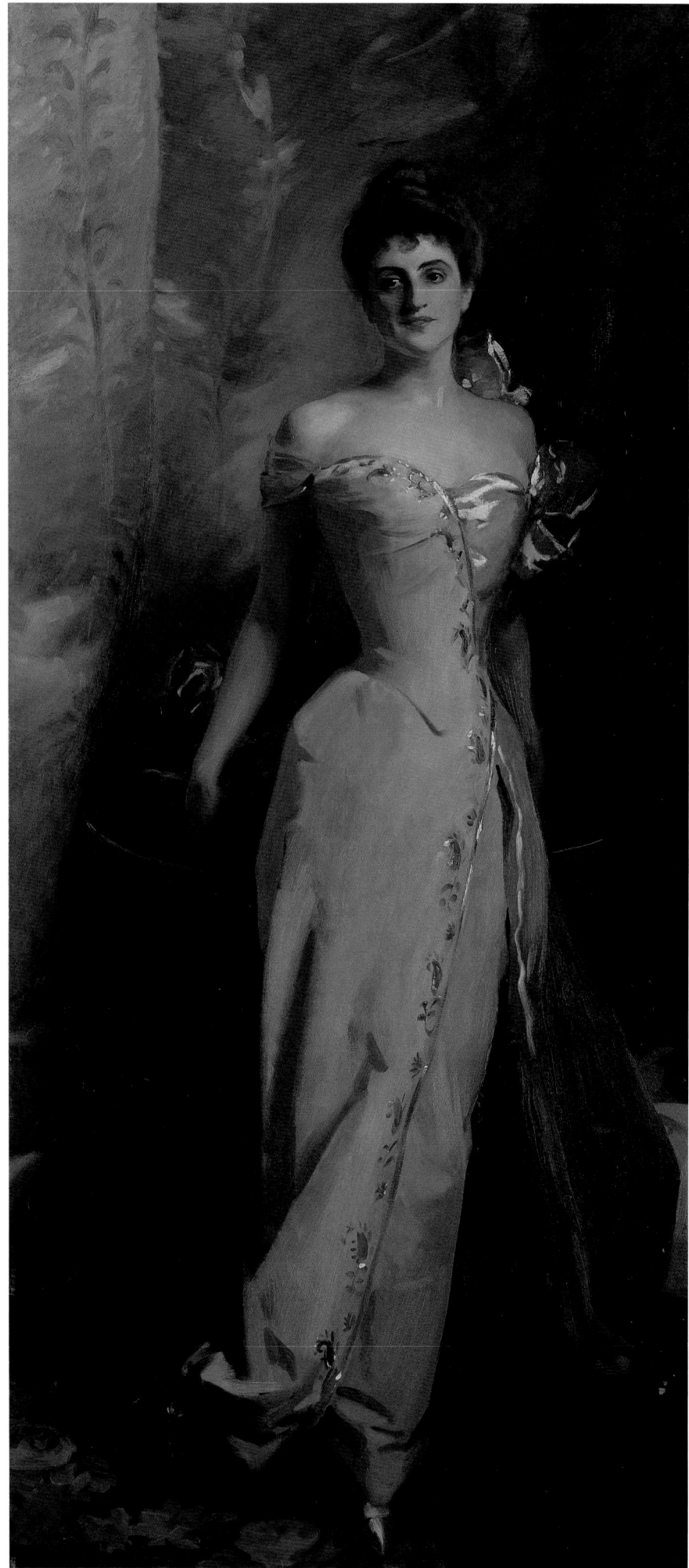

359

360 *Mrs Charles Thursby*

c. 1898
Oil on canvas, 78 × 39¾ (198.1 × 101)
Inscribed upper left: *John S. Sargent*
Newark Museum, New Jersey

Mrs Charles Thursby, *née* Alice Brisbane (1856–1953), was the eldest daughter of Albert Brisbane, a New York socialist philosopher and author, and his wife, Sarah White, and the sister of Arthur Brisbane, editor and correspondent of the *New York Times*. She was brought up in Paris and studied painting there in the 1870s. In 1888, she married Charles Radcliffe Thursby, an English engineer and member of a landed family with estates near Abington. Due to the nature of Thursby's work, the couple divided their time between London and Argentina until his death in 1903. After his death, she lived in Williamstown, Massachusetts, and Charleston, South Carolina.

Mrs Thursby is shown in an unusual costume, probably intended for day wear, with a voluminous mauve skirt, a black frogged jacket over a high-necked white shirt, a black and lilac bow at her breast, and a long silver chain suspended from her neck. She perches energetically on the edge of the familiar bergère armchair, with a footstool at her feet, a Chinese turquoise silk hanging behind, and an Aubusson carpet on the floor (see Accessories, pp. xxii, xxiv, nos 2 b, 34, 35).

Clementina Anstruther-Thomson called the picture 'simply a masterpiece. She looks like an 18th century coachman very dainty, her chair, and she seem[s] to be flying along' (undated letter to Vernon Lee, CC). The same point was made by Fernand Khnopff in the *Magazine of Art*: 'Though the placing of a touch may sometimes seem a little forced, a little too artificially instantaneous, and though the attitude of his figures very often is one of unstable equilibrium, we cannot, on the other hand, too highly praise certain "condensed effects" if I may say so, which are really quite marvellous' (*Magazine of Art*, 1898, p. 430).

A preliminary pencil study for the portrait shows the pose reversed (fig. 92). For a partial study of the sitter's skirt and feet, see fig. 93.

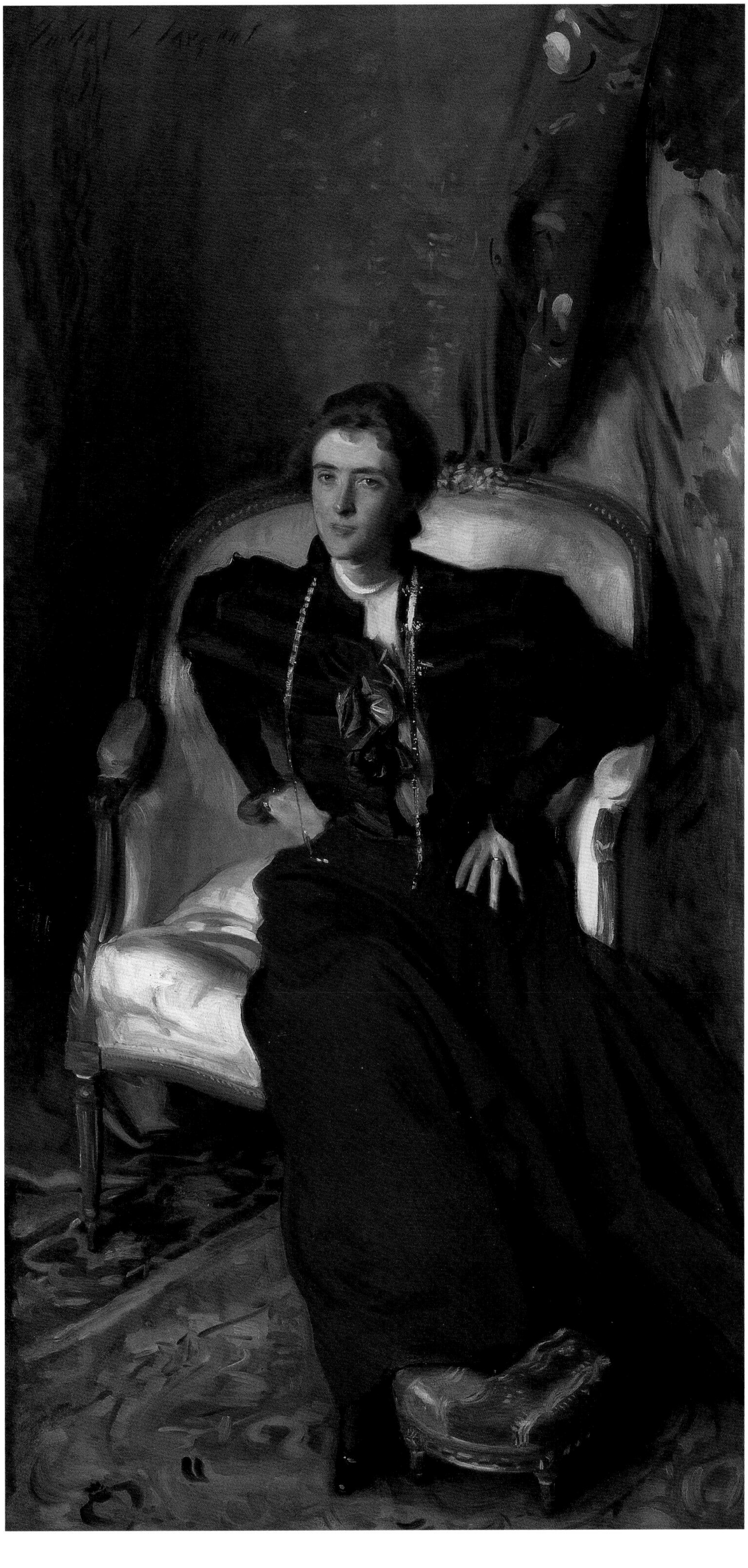

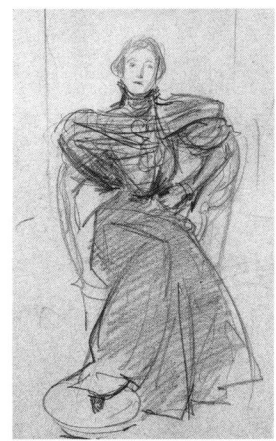

fig. 92 *Mrs Charles Thursby*. Pencil, dimensions unknown. Untraced.

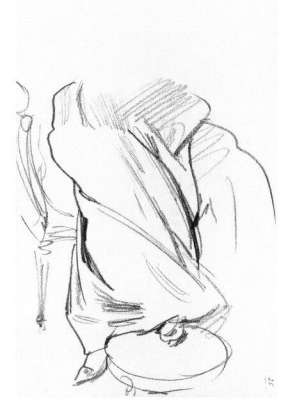

fig. 93 *Mrs Charles Thursby*. Pencil, 9 $\frac{7}{16}$ × 5 $\frac{5}{16}$ (24 × 15.1). Fogg Art Museum, Harvard University Art Museums. Gift of Mrs Francis Ormond, 1937.7.11 25 r.

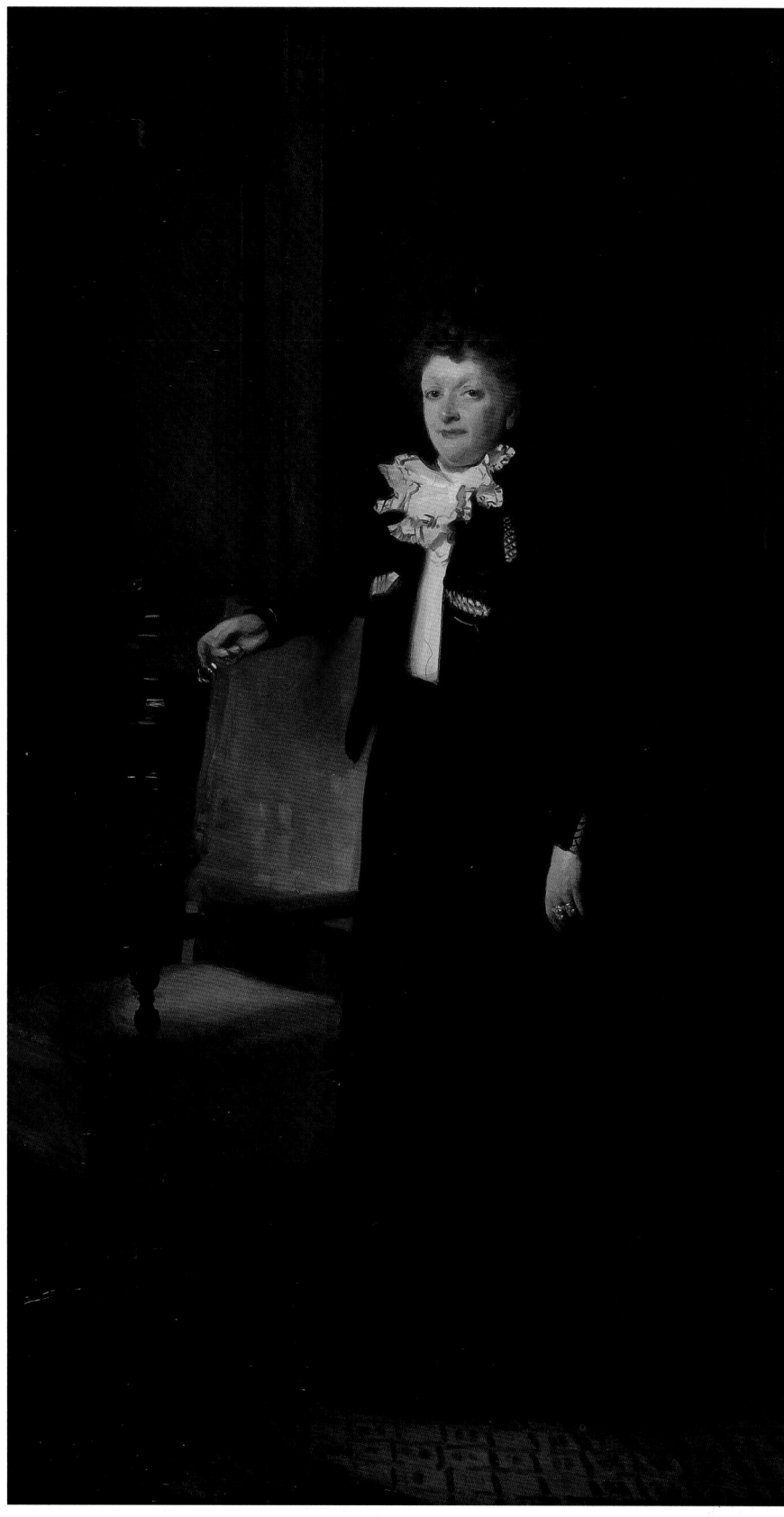

361 Mrs Charles Huntington

c. 1898
Oil on canvas, 93¼ × 51¼ (237 × 130.2)
Inscribed, upper left: *John S. Sargent*
Brooklyn Museum of Art, New York.
A. Augustus Healy Fund

Mrs Charles Huntington, *née* Jane Hudson Sparkes
(d. 1911), was the daughter of Walter Sparkes of
Merton, Surrey. She married Charles Huntington,
a wealthy Lancashire wallpaper manufacturer and
an MP, in 1876. He was created a baronet in 1906,
the year of his death. They had five sons and three
daughters. Of their sons, three died in infancy, the
last in 1928.

The date of the portrait, given in the Royal
Academy 1926 catalogue, was confirmed in an
undated letter from Amy Huntington to
McKibbin (McKibbin papers). The sitter's grandson, Lord Rathcreedan, recounts various family
anecdotes about the portrait (letter to compilers,
July 1984, catalogue raisonné archive). When Mrs
Huntington first visited the artist's studio, she went
with her youngest daughter, Marguerite, then aged
about sixteen. Sargent offered to paint the daughter for nothing if Huntington would release him
from the contract to paint his wife, which the latter declined to do. Mrs Huntington appeared at
the studio in a variety of fine dresses, none of them
to the artist's liking. Then one day she went in an
ordinary black dress to remonstrate ' "I see you! I
see you!", said Sargent and insisted on painting her
as she was. During the sittings Mrs Huntington
remarked to the artist: "You are quite a good portrait painter but you are not good at painting
hands. I have very good [hands] so now you have
your opportunity." I think it is agreed that the
painting of the hands in the portrait is exceptionally fine and the best part of the portrait.'

Mrs Huntington is dressed in a plain black skirt,
a black jacket with wide collar and lapels and inset
panels of lacing, and a black and white, frilly-
edged jabot. She has rings on her left hand and
holds a pair of spectacles in her right. Her arm
rests on the back of an Italian seventeenth-century
arm-chair; the background is a richly panelled
interior, and on the wooden floor is one of the
artist's Aubusson carpets (see Accessories, pp. xxii,
xxiv, nos 9, 13, 35).

362 *Lady Faudel-Phillips*

1898
Oil on canvas, 57 × 37 (144.8 × 94)
Inscribed, upper left: *John S. Sargent*; upper right:
1898
Private Collection

Lady Faudel-Phillips, *née* Helen Levy (d. 1916), was the daughter of J. M. Levy, founder of the *Daily Telegraph*, and the sister of the first Baron Burnham. In 1867, she married George Faudel-Phillips, a wealthy banker, bibliophile and sportsman. He became Lord Mayor of London in 1896 and a baronet the following year; his father, Sir Benjamin Faudel-Phillips, had been Lord Mayor from 1865 to 1866. They lived at 52 Grosvenor Gardens in London and at Balls Park, Hertford; they had two sons and three daughters.

Lady Faudel-Phillips is dressed in a black satin evening gown, trimmed square at the neck to reveal a rectangle of flesh and edged with a black and grey flounce. She wears a fantastic hairpiece, a black ribbon and diamond aigrette. Other items of jewellery include a diamond and emerald necklace tightly fastened at the neck by a silver medal secured with a blue ribbon at her shoulder, a cartouche-shaped brooch at her breast, gold bracelets, rings and earrings. She is seated in a seventeenth-century-style Italian armchair covered in red figured velvet or damask (see Accessories, p. xxii, no. 9), resting her right elbow on a large red cushion. The effect of opulence and extravagance is further enhanced by the rich red hanging or drape which fills the background.

Seated with her Pomeranian dog Teufel, she is a flamboyant creation, a characterization touching the edge of satire. The *Spectator* critic wrote: 'bravura is used with the power of a satire of [Alexander] Pope. Hard, merciless wit, without caricature, is the general impression produced by this picture' (*Spectator*, 6 May 1899, p. 641); to the *Athenaeum*, the painting bore 'numerous traces of [Sargent's] fine sense of humour' (*Athenaeum*, 3 June 1899, p. 693); and the *Art Journal* described it as 'the legitimate successor to the "Asher Wertheimer" [see no. 347] of last year, in which there was so much subtle suggestion that the borderline of caricature was shaved all along it' (*Art Journal*, 1899, p. 177). For a caricature published in *Punch*, see fig. 94

Sir George Faudel-Phillips was Mayor of London in the year of Queen Victoria's Diamond Jubilee and Sargent's portrait of Lady Faudel-Phillips was presented to mark the end of his mayoralty.

Sir George was painted by Solomon J. Solomon in 1897 (Private Collection).

Lady Faudel-Phillips may be one of the figures represented in Max Beerbohm's cartoon of ladies queuing up outside Sargent's studio to be painted (Charteris 1927, ill. facing p. 160).

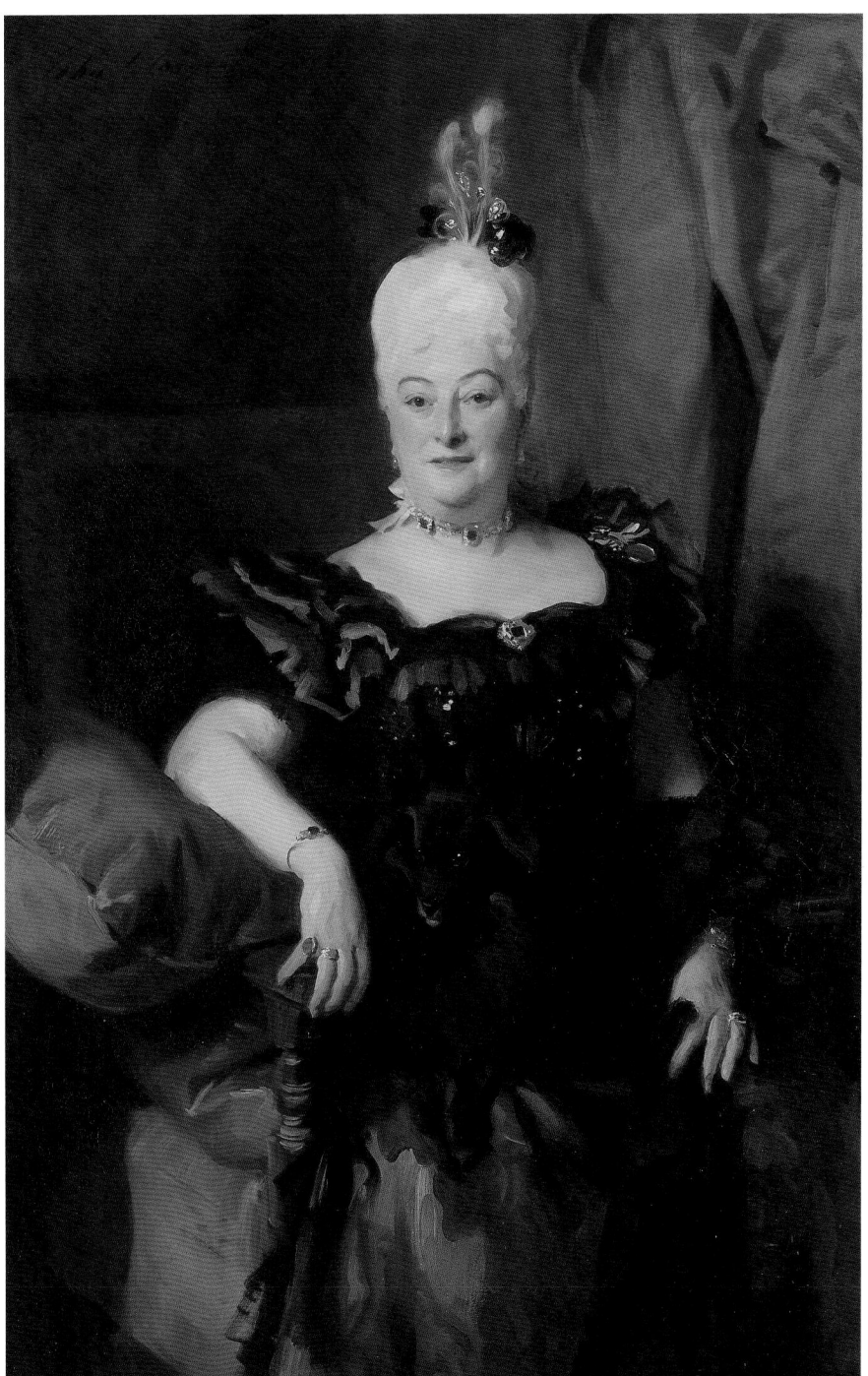

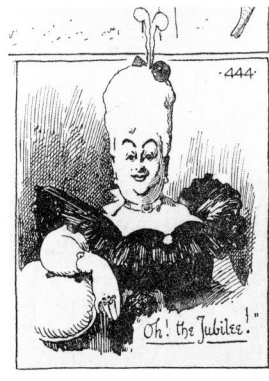

fig. 94 Caricature of Sargent's portrait of Lady Faudel-Phillips, *Punch* (3 May 1899), p. 214.

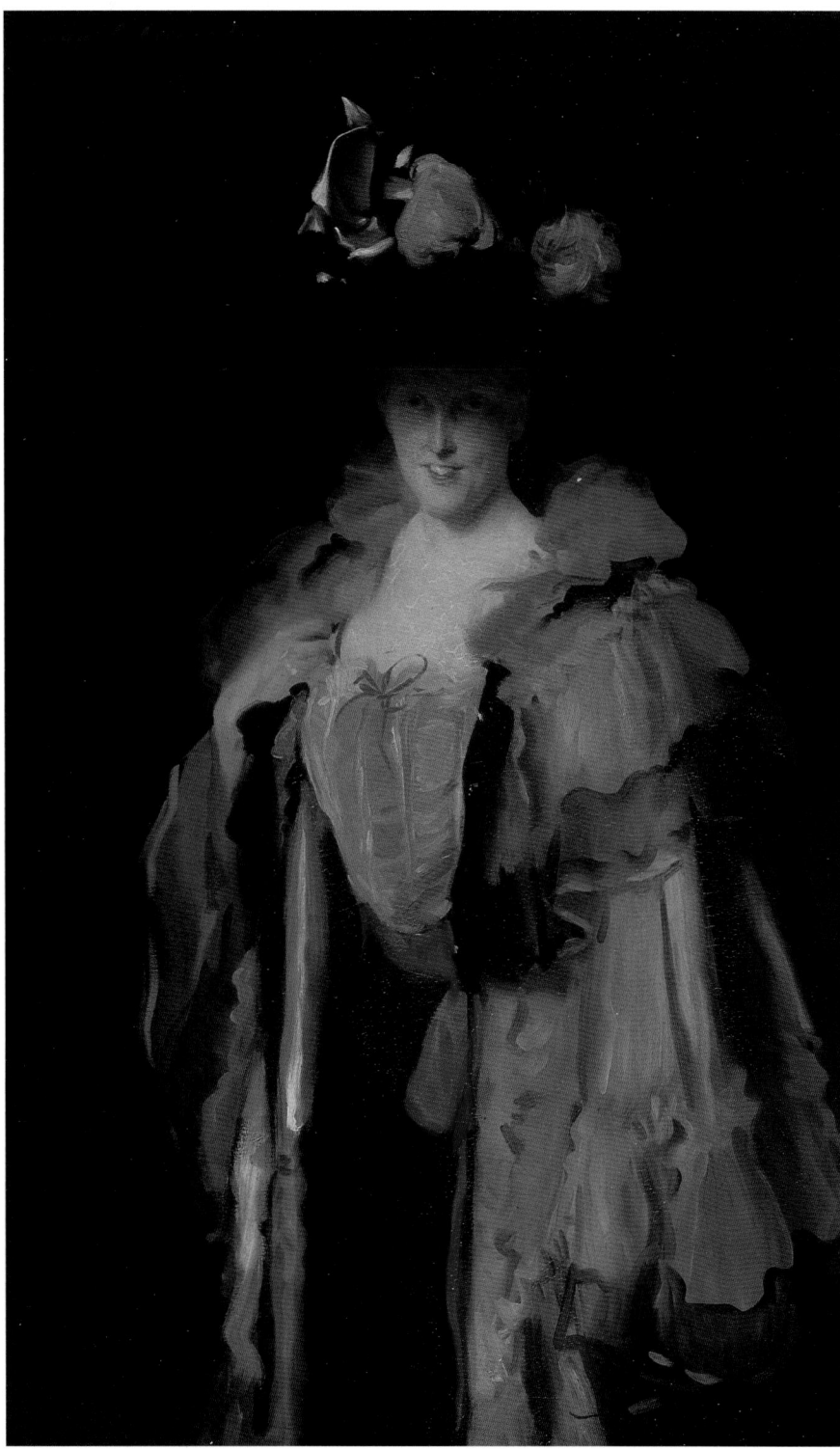

1898
Oil on canvas, 58¼ × 35¼ (148 × 89.5)
Inscribed upper left: *John S. Sargent*; upper right:
1898
Tate Gallery, London. Gift of the sitter, via the
National Art Collections Fund

Mrs Charles Hunter, *née* Mary Smyth (1857–
1933), was the second of six daughters of Major-
General John Hall Smyth and his wife, Emma
Strutt. She married a wealthy coalmine owner
Charles Edward Hunter, by whom she had three
daughters. She was famous for her salons in
London and her house parties in Hill Hall, Epping.
Extravagant, impulsive, generous and warm-
hearted, Mrs Hunter became Sargent's devoted
friend and confidante, some whispered his mistress, though this seems unlikely. They are said to
have met around 1895, and there can be no doubt
of the pleasure the artist took in her company or
of the important place she occupied in his personal life. He was a frequent visitor to Hill Hall,
which he helped to decorate, and he was responsi-
ble for introducing many of his artist friends to her
as a patron. She commissioned portraits of herself
by Auguste Rodin (marble bust, 1906, Tate Gallery,
London, no. N 04116) and Antonio Mancini, and
owned works by Paul Helleu and Claude Monet.
Sargent's surviving letters to her are in the
Archives of American Art, Smithsonian Institution,
Washington, D.C. After a life of great wealth and
splendour, she spent her later years in genteel
poverty.

The portrait was clearly begun early in 1898. In
an undated letter (the envelope is postmarked 2
February 1898) to Mrs George Swinton (see
no. 327), Sargent mentions Mrs Hunter's coming
to the studio to sit: 'I find on coming home that
my Thursday afternoon sitting is an old Scotch
judge [Lord Watson, see no. 351] instead of Mrs
Hunter. She comes Friday afternoon' (Private
Collection).

D. S. MacColl commented in the *Saturday
Review* that 'some afterthought – admiration, per-
haps, or the idea of a picture – has clouded his ter-
rible eye' (*Saturday Review*, 6 May 1899, p. 556). In
Punch, Mrs Hunter was lampooned as 'La Belle
Chiffonière. "Oh, I'll put on any rags to sit in; what
do I care as long as my likeness is painted by
JOHN S. SARGENT, R. A." ' (*Punch*, 3 May 1899,
p. 209), The *Art Journal* was specific about the portrait's antecedents, comparing it to Rubens's
Chapeau de Paille (National Gallery, London) (*Art
Journal*, 1899, p. 177). A contemporary portrait in
the same idiom is that of Mrs J. W. Crombie (no.
364).

Two preliminary pencil studies for this oil are in
a sketch-book in the Fogg Art Museum,
Cambridge, Massachusetts (figs 95, 96); one of the
studies shows both hands coming up to clasp the

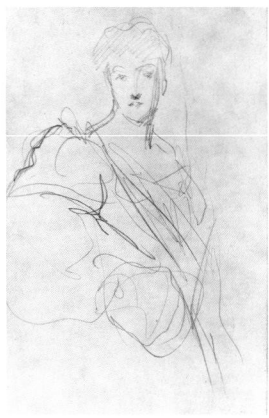

fig. 95 *Mrs Charles
Hunter*. Pencil,
9 ⁷⁄₁₆ × 5 ⁵⁄₁₆ (24 × 15.1).
Fogg Art Museum,
Harvard University Art
Museums. Gift of Mrs
Francis Ormond 1937.
7. 11 27 v.

cape. A water-colour of her seated in a gondola is dated 'Venice Sept. 1902' (no. 437). A charcoal drawing of her in a large feathered hat (Memorial Art Gallery of the University of Rochester, New York) is illustrated in Hills *et al.* 1986, fig. 245.

Sargent was also a friend of Mrs Hunter's sister, Ethel Smyth, composer and feminist, and a drawing of her of 1901 is inscribed to Mrs Hunter (National Portrait Gallery, London, no. 3243). Sargent painted Mrs Hunter's daughters in 1902 (no. 410).

364 *Mrs John William Crombie*

1898
Oil on canvas, 38 × 29 (96.5 × 73.6)
Inscribed, upper left: *John S. Sargent*; upper right: *1898*
Aberdeen City Art Gallery. Gift of the sitter

Mrs John William Crombie, *née* Minna Watson (1872–1951), was the daughter of Eugene Watson, a prominent Scottish lawyer and Liberal MP, and his wife, Eleanor Williams of Dolgelly, Wales. In 1895, she married another Liberal MP, J. W. Crombie, a director of the woollen manufacturers J. & J. Crombie Ltd, and had one son and one daughter. The Crombies lived at 91 Onslow Square, London, and Balgownie Lodge, Aberdeen. She was widowed in 1907, and her beloved son, Eugene, died in action in 1917. After his death, she took up Braille and would spend hours transcribing popular books on a special six-key typewriter. Her grandson, David Paton, remembers her as 'a very warm and generous person with a considerable sense of humour' (letter to compilers, 9 April 1984, catalogue raisonné archive). Sargent's introduction to the Crombies was probably effected through Robert Farquharson, another Scottish MP, whom Sargent had painted in 1880 (see *Early Portraits*, no. 65).

As with the contemporary portrait of Mrs Charles Hunter (no. 363) in which the sitter's extravagant accessories match the personality of the sitter, Sargent plays on the theme of Rubens's *Chapeau de Paille* (National Gallery, London) and the tradition of Van Dyck dress.

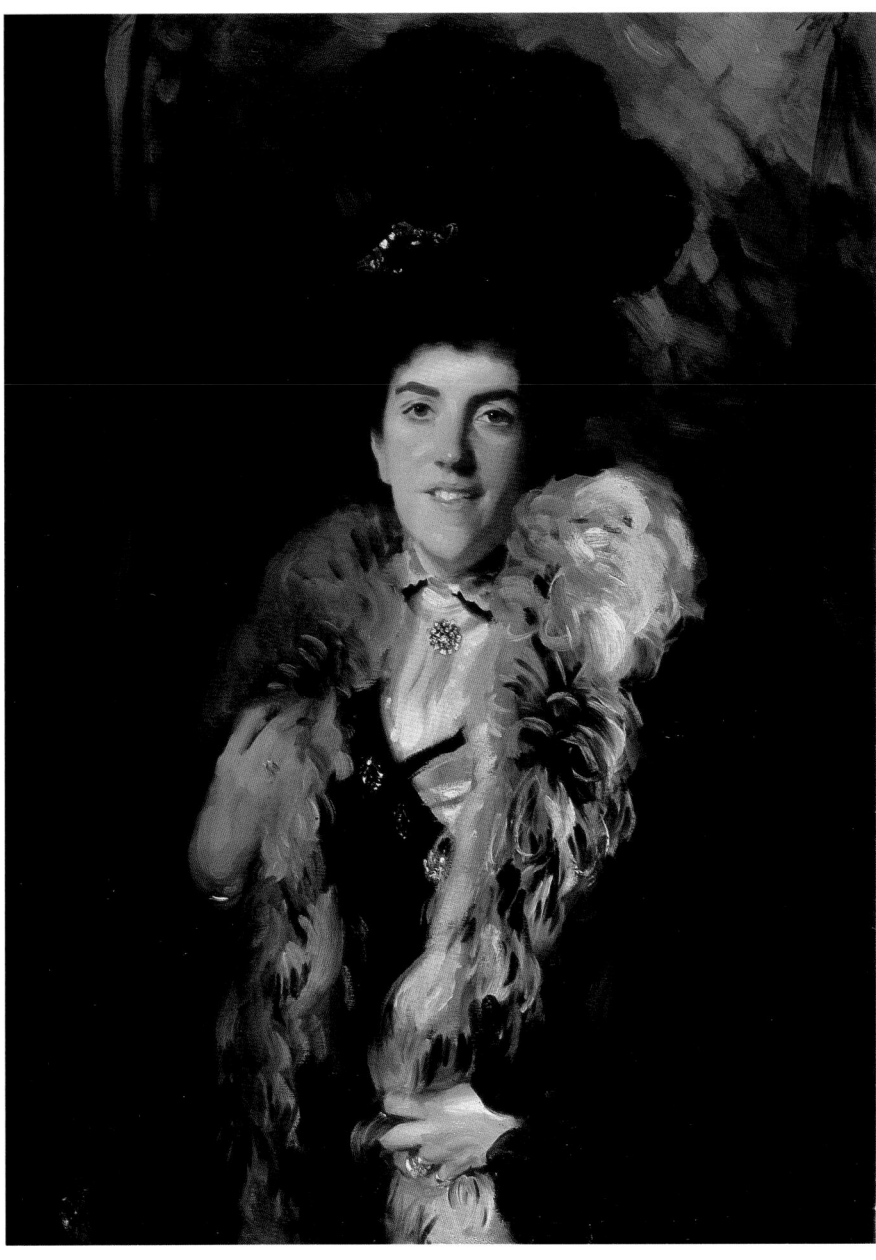

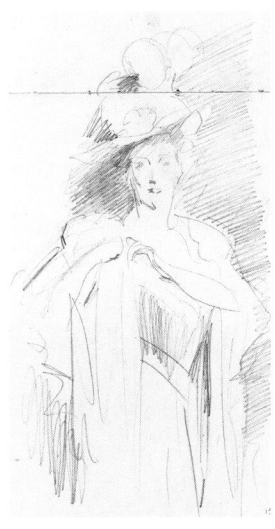

fig. 96 *Mrs Charles Hunter*. Pencil 9 $\frac{7}{16}$ × 5 $\frac{5}{16}$, (24 × 15.1). Fogg Art Museum, Harvard University Art Museums. Gift of Mrs Francis Ormond, 1937.7. 11 26 r and v.

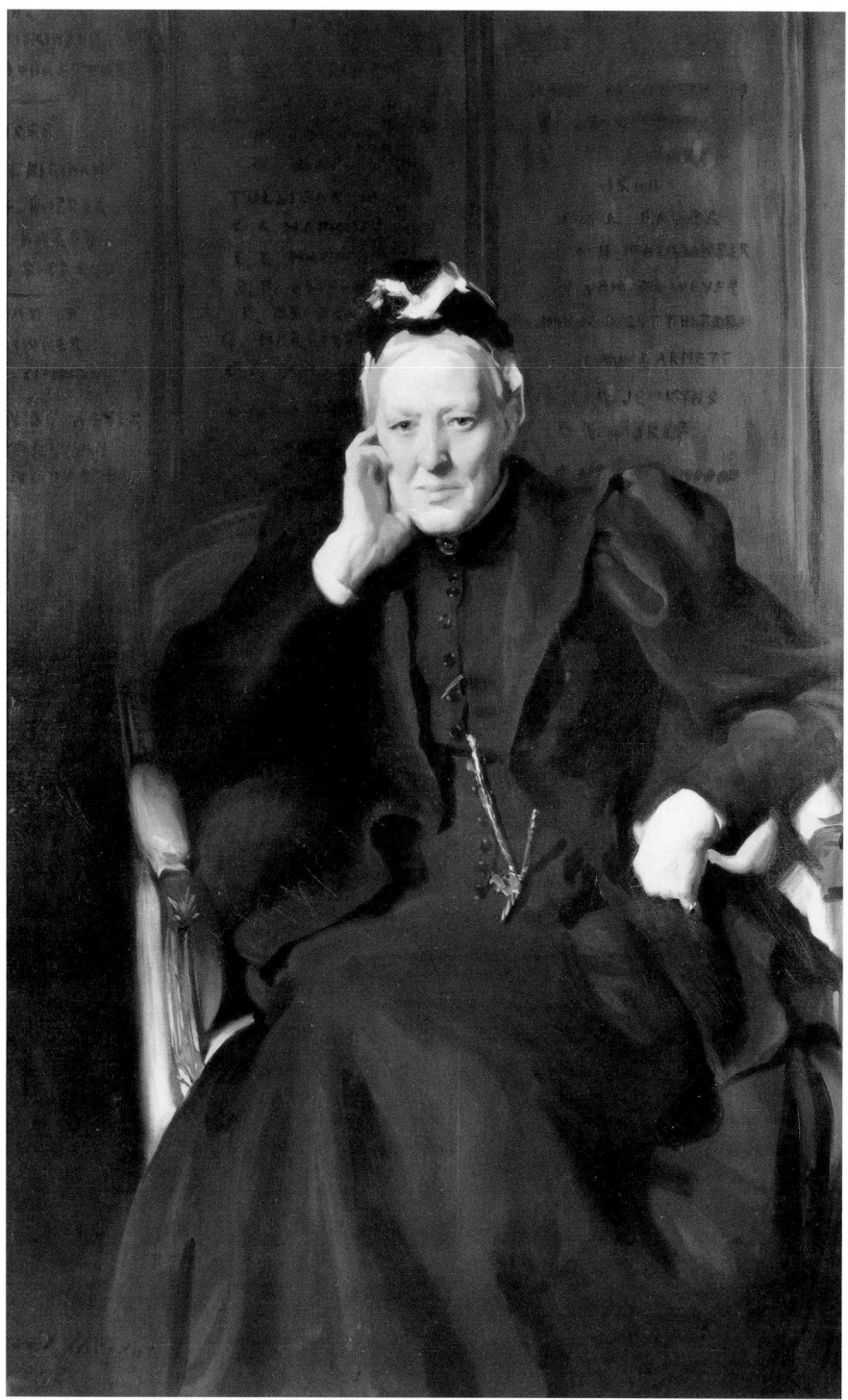

365 *Miss Jane Evans*

1898
Oil on canvas, 56¾ × 36½ (144 × 93)
Inscribed, lower left: *John S. Sargent / 1898*
Provost and Fellows of Eton College, Berkshire

Jane Evans (1826–1906) is often described as the last of the Eton Dames, but her status was somewhat different from that of the formidable group of women, originally simply landladies, who ran independent lodging houses for the Oppidan boys of Eton College, the last of whom retired in 1873. She was the third child and second daughter of William Evans ('Evans of Eton'), who had succeeded his father, Samuel, as drawing master at

Eton in 1823, and of his wife, Jane Jackson. William Evans had bought one of the Dames' houses from Mrs Vallancey in 1839. When ill health forced him to retire from its active management in 1863, it was run in his name by his daughter Annie with Jane's assistance.

Upon Annie's death in 1871, Jane assumed sole responsibility (still in the name of William Evans), though she had moral support from her brother, Sam (S. T. Evans), the third of his family in succession as drawing master. When William Evans died in 1877, the house became known as 'Miss Evans's' for the first time.

A woman of great character and moral force, Jane Evans earned the devotion of her boys by her exceptional powers of sympathy and insight: 'She could see through a boy as if he were a pane of glass, and to stand up to her was assuredly to go to the wall . . . She said what she had to say in a few, quiet, strong sentences, and with an inclination of the head and a deep, serious, almost distressed look in the eyes that one has never forgotten, and then she would go away leaving one ashamed' (Gambier Parry 1907, p. 187).

The idea of commissioning a portrait of her was a spontaneous expression of admiration and affection on the part of her Old Boys. First suggested by Bishop John Selwyn and Mrs Ralph Bond (whose six brothers had been in the House), the proposal quickly gained ground, a committee was appointed, and Miss Evans's reluctance was overcome. The choice of Sargent seems to have been made on the recommendation of the writer Howard Sturgis, who arranged a preliminary lunch for artist and sitter at Windsor on 17 October 1897. Sargent was to write how impressed he had been by 'the honesty, directness and power of her personality' (Gambier Parry 1907, p. 385). The first of ten sittings took place the following March. According to Miss Evans's diary, Sargent 'got quite excited about making a picture of me, and made a sort of outline, which pleased Sturgis, but which I don't think is quite natural' (Gambier Parry 1907, p. 385). She records the last sitting on 4 July with sadness, for she and Sargent had grown fond of one another.

The portrait was formally presented to Miss Evans on 26 July 1898 at a large gathering and was hung in a place of honour in the hall of her house. She remained as Dame of Evans's until her death on 27 January 1906, when the boys in her house were distributed, as was then the custom, among other housemaster's houses. Two petitions (one from her Old Boys, the other from boys in the school) asking that her nephew Sidney Evans (W. S. V. Evans, then drawing master) be allowed to take over the house were ineffective. The headmaster, Dr Warre, had indeed earlier made it clear to Sidney Evans that he would not succeed to the house upon his aunt's death.

The ownership of the portrait reverted to her Old Boys, who presented it to the college to be hung on the panelling, which they also gave, at the east end of the school hall (opened by Edward VII in November 1908 but not completed until the end of 1909).

Sargent's picture is a powerful study of character. Miss Evans is depicted in the black dress and coat of her calling, a matching bonnet with white ribbons, and a fob-chain, symbol of her office, suspended from a button on her dress front. Hunched up in the French bergère chair (see Accessories, p. xxii, no. 2b), her large form dominating its fragile shape, she belongs to a different world from Sargent's fashionable clients. One hand on her hip in a gesture of authority, the other supporting her head in the pose of a thinker, she enshrines generations of moral certainty. Behind her are three of the famous boards with the carved names of over 750 members of her house, those visible covering the years 1857 to 1860, beginning with E. H. Ward, upper left, and ending with R. H. Jelf.

At the Royal Academy, R. A. M. Stevenson applauded the 'studied, dignified calm' of the characterization (*Academy*, 6 May 1899, p. 509).

Four pencil sketches, indicating variant poses for the portrait, are in a sketchbook in the Fogg Art Museum, Cambridge, Massachusetts (figs 97–100).

366 *Octavia Hill*

1898
Oil on canvas, 39¾ × 30½ (101 × 77.5)
Inscribed upper left: *John S. Sargent*
National Portrait Gallery, London.
Bequest of the sitter

Octavia Hill (1838–1912), the daughter of James Hill and his wife, Caroline Southwood Smith, and granddaughter of the famous sanitary reformer, Thomas Southwood Smith, was herself an eminent philanthropist and reformer. In 1864, John Ruskin financed the purchase of three houses for the poor in London, which enabled her to put her social theories into practice, and she became a leading protagonist of housing reform. She was a passionate advocate of open spaces for public use and was a co-founder of the National Trust.

A group of Octavia Hill's friends, led by Lady Frederick Pollock and C. S. Loch, whom Sargent was to paint in 1900 (nos 387, 388), persuaded her to sit for her portrait and raised the necessary funds. The portrait was formally presented to her on 1 December 1898 at Grosvenor House in the presence of her friends and admirers; she replied to the tributes to her achievements in what was regarded as a memorable and moving speech.

Her kinsman, William Thomson Hill, summarizes the quality of the portrait:

The black sleeves and the mass of white lace round the face and neck were perhaps old fashioned even then. Yet beneath the wide brow, silvered with parted hair, the eyes glow with a

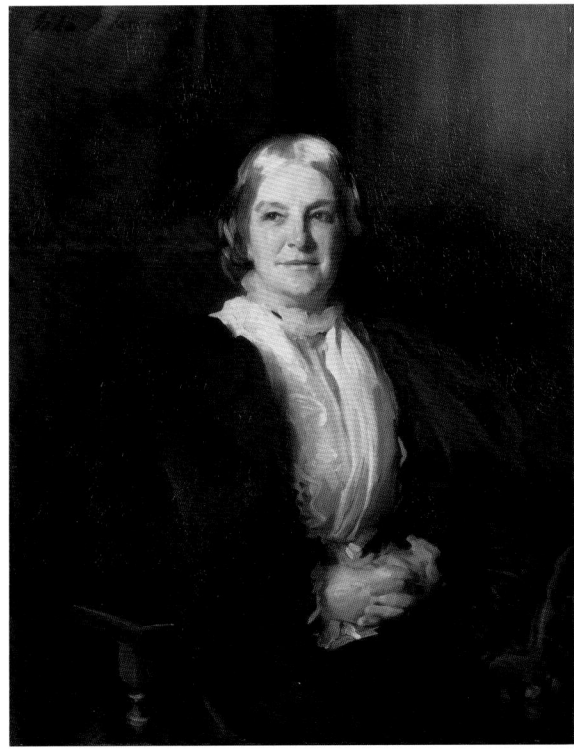

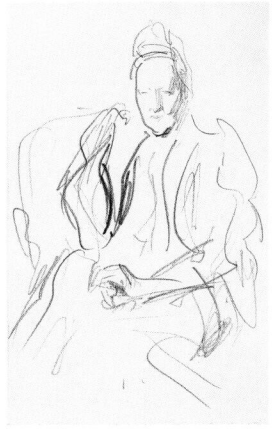

fig. 97 *Miss Jane Evans*. Pencil, 9 ⁷⁄₁₆ × 5 ⁵⁄₁₆ (24 × 15.1). Fogg Art Museum, Harvard University Art Museums. Gift of Mrs Francis Ormond, 1937.7.11 28 v.

fire which has nothing of old age in it. They express ardour and something more. These are very sane eyes, shrewd, serene and kindly, but eyes which you feel nothing could escape. The large mouth and chin are those of a very determined person – but for the suggestion of a humorous twist at the corners, beyond question a capable face – capable also of righteous indignation. Sargent's portrait betrays a man's sense of her power. But we miss some of the sympathy which lives within those eyes; the enthusiasm which could kindle others. (Hill 1956, p. 21)

The Italian seventeenth-century-style chair in which Octavia Hill sits appears in other portraits of the period (see Accessories, p. xxii, no. 9).

When the portrait was exhibited at the Royal Academy in 1899, it inspired conflicting responses. The *Spectator* reviewer wrote that Sargent's characteristic bravura was here used to good effect: 'One cannot but pity the numbers of people who in their search for what they call "honest work" will overlook this picture to fix on some tiresome accumulation of petty details miscalled "finish"' (*Spectator*, 6 May 1899, p. 641); while the *Magazine of Art* critic was questioning:

Mr Sargent's amazing work does not seem entirely free from the suggestion of the conjuror. Vivacity in portraiture has probably never been so completely obtained in modern times, and to match the 'Miss Jane Evans' [no. 365], the 'Lady Faudel Phillips' [no. 362], or even the 'Miss Octavia Hill', the mind wanders to Vandyck's 'Cornelius van der Geest' (the Gevartius of more ignorant days). The veracity is startling and the handling brilliant amongst the most dashing bravura passages ever executed; and yet there is a lack of repose in these faces and figures which

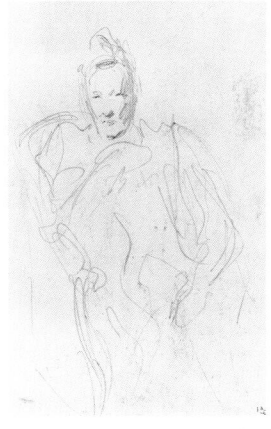

fig. 98 *Miss Jane Evans*. Pencil, 9 ⁷⁄₁₆ × 5 ⁵⁄₁₆ (24 × 15.1). Fogg Art Museum, Harvard University Art Museums. Gift of Mrs Francis Ormond, 1937.7.11 29 r.

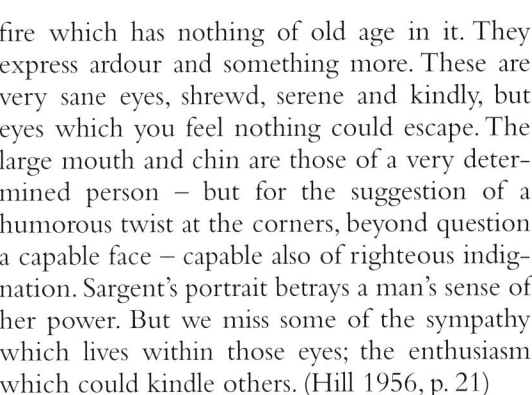

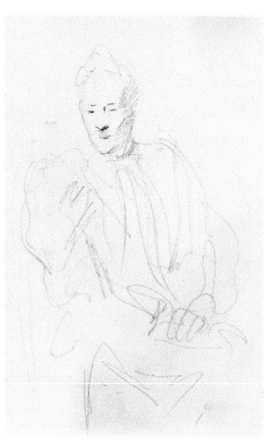

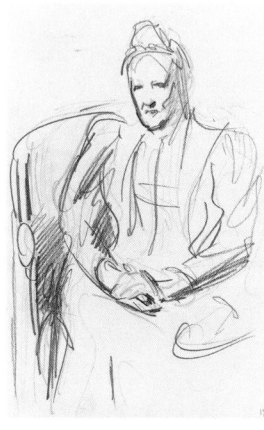

alone makes a picture delightful to live with, just as there is a lack of that repose in the painting which alone makes the execution a continuous delight to study. Have we not here, one feels after a while, a somewhat perverted mastery? That the portraits are masterpieces in their way there is no sort of doubt; but are they masterpieces for all time? Is *premier coup* painting the highest, truest kind, after all? And will the name of Sargent in the future rank as high as Franz Hals, to say nothing of Velasquez? Such are the questions that start to the mind in the presence of these astonishing performances, and an uncomfortable doubt seems to answer back no reassuring response. (*Magazine of Art*, 1899, p. 340)

In a letter of 23 February [1915] to Mr Holmes of the National Portrait Gallery, which is principally concerned with photographic copyright, Sargent wrote: 'I am glad to hear that Miss Octavia Hill is received into Valhalla' (Registered Packet, Registry, National Portrait Gallery, London).

For information about the frame, see Simon 1996, p. 182.

367   *An Interior in Venice*

1898
Oil on canvas, 26 × 33 (66 × 83.5)
Inscribed, lower left: *John S. Sargent 1899*
Royal Academy of Arts, London

The painting depicts, from left to right, Ralph Wormeley Curtis (1854–1922) (see *Early Portraits*, no. 82), his wife, Lisa De Wolfe Colt Curtis (1871–1933) (see no. 359), and his parents, Ariana Wormeley Curtis (1833–1922) (see *Early Portraits*, no. 50), and Daniel Sargent Curtis (1825–1908) taking tea in the salon of the Palazzo Barbaro in Venice. Daniel Sargent Curtis, a Bostonian and a distant cousin of Sargent's father, had brought his family to Europe in 1879, where they lived a civilized and leisured expatriate life. They rented the upper apartments of the Palazzo Barbaro on the Grand Canal in 1881 and bought them in 1885. The Curtises' hospitality and the romantic atmosphere of the Barbaro attracted and captivated artists and writers: Robert Browning visited and read his poetry there; Henry James was a frequent guest, re-creating it as Palazzo Leporelli in *The Wings of the Dove* (1902); F. Hopkinson Smith wrote of 'the Barbaro with its exquisite salon, by far the most beautiful in Europe' (Smith 1902, p. 157); and, in a letter to Mrs Curtis (27 May 1898), Sargent described its unique charm: 'The Barbaro is a sort of Fontaine de Jouvence, for it sends one back twenty years, besides making the present seem remarkably all right' (Boston Athenaeum, Sargent Papers, box 1, folder 4). Isabella Stewart Gardner tried to realize its magic in America; it was the inspiration for Fenway Court, her Venetian palazzo in Boston.

This conversation piece was painted in the *salone*, the principal room of the palazzo, in the early summer of 1898 and was intended as a gift to Mrs Curtis. According to Charteris, she declined to accept it because she felt that it represented her as too old and because her son's casual pose offended her sense of propriety. Letters from her granddaughter, Sylvia Curtis Owen (14 August 1947, McKibbin papers), and grandson, Ralph Curtis II (10 February 1953, McKibbin papers), to McKibbin confirm the story with some minor variations. Mrs Owen remembered that Sargent's portrayal of Mrs Curtis did not gratify the latter's vanity and that she wanted him to make changes, while Ralph Curtis thought that she disliked the smallness of her figure in the large picture space. Henry James saw the picture in Sargent's London studio in January and wrote to Mrs Curtis on 16 March 1899: 'The *Barbaro Saloon* [*sic*] thing . . . I absolutely & unreservedly *adored*. I can't help thinking you have a slightly fallacious impression of the effect of your (*your*, dear Mrs Curtis) indicated head & face. It is an indication so *sommaire* that I think it speaks entirely for itself – as a simple sketchy hint – & it didn't displease me . . . I've seen few things of S's that I've ever craved more to possess! I hope you haven't altogether let it go' (Baker Library, DCL). In 1900, Sargent gave Mrs Curtis a bronze cast of the small version of the crucifix he had made for the Boston Public Library, in a second attempt to thank her for her hospitality.

Sargent had temporarily deposited his portrait of Johannes Wolff (no. 341) at the Royal Academy in 1897 as his diploma work (letter from Sargent to the president and council of the Royal Academy, 20 July 1897, Royal Academy Library, London, RAC/1/SA 6), but on Mrs Curtis's refusing *An Interior in Venice*, he substituted it for *Johannes Wolff*. He wrote: 'I have the honour of submitting to you the picture which I propose to offer as my diploma work – a "Venetian Interior" – and hope that it will meet with your approval and acceptance' (letter from Sargent to the president and council of the Royal Academy, 29 December 1899, Royal Academy Library, London, RAC/1/SA 7). It is recorded in the Royal Academy Annual Report (*Annual Report from the Council of the Royal Academy to the General Assembly of Academicians for the Year 1900*, London, 1901, Appendix no. 10, p. 54).

When it was exhibited at the Royal Academy in the summer of 1900, the painting met with considerable critical praise. Whistler's was a rare dissenting voice: he called it 'the little picture' and compared it unfavourably with the tradition of Dutch interior painting: 'smudge everywhere. Think of the finish, the delicacy, the elegance, the repose of a little Terborgh or Metsu – these were masters who could paint chandeliers and the rest, and what a difference' (Pennell 1921, p. 39). Roger Fry was similarly unimpressed: 'Sargent is too fond of the sparkle and glitter of life to

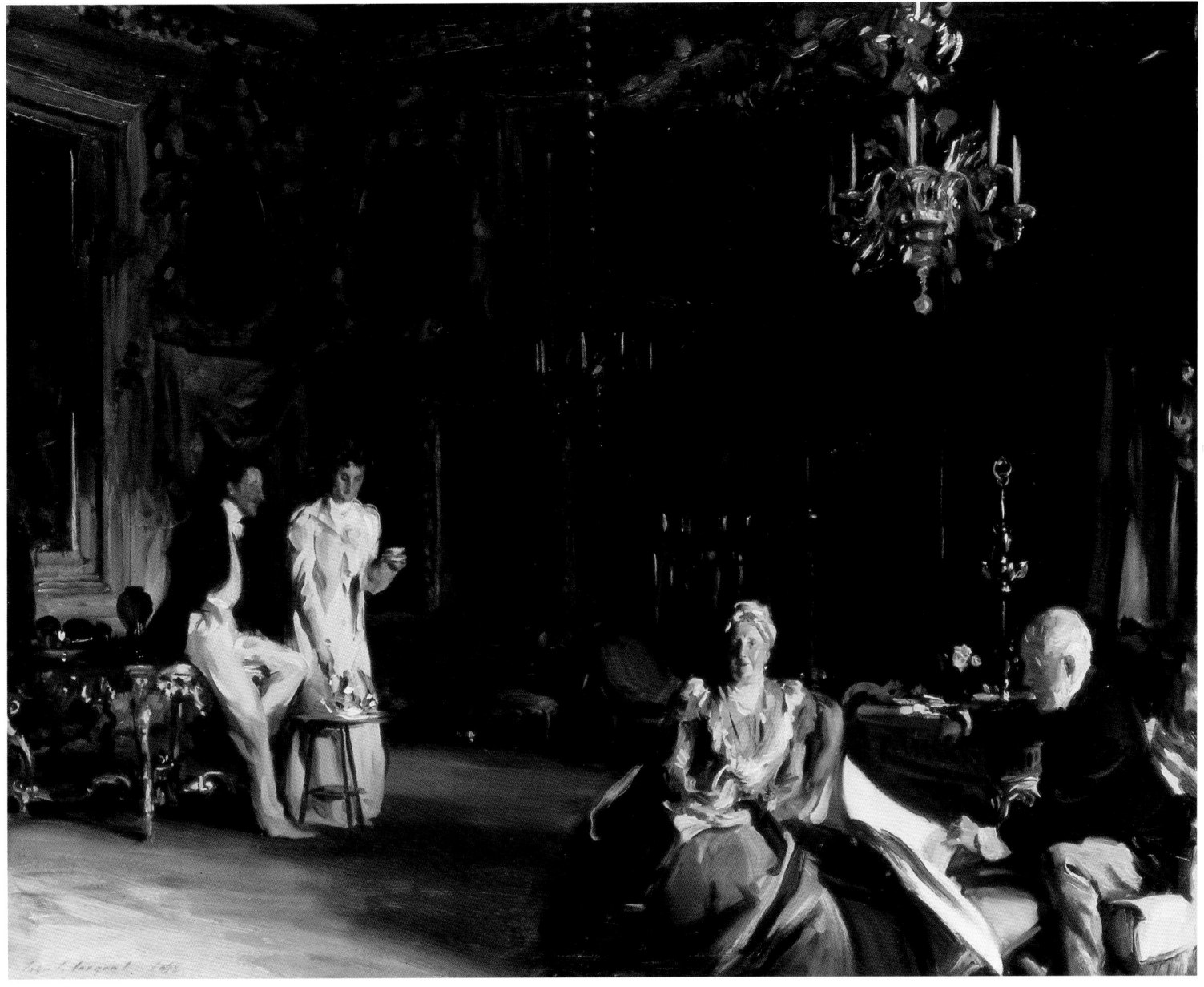

give us any sense of the dreamy gloom of a seventeenth-century palace. He appears to harbour no imagination that he could not easily avow at the afternoon tea he so brilliantly depicts' (*Pilot*, 12 May 1900, p. 121).

The American artist Walter Gay, who specialized in painting interiors, painted the salon of the Barbaro in 1902 and 1910. When he and his wife saw Sargent's painting in London in 1910, she wrote in her diary:

> The interior of Palazzo Barbaro interested us very much, as W. G. has done such a brilliant one of that beautiful salon. Sargent has given the impression of a dark background, in fact has hardly done the room at all, in order to throw out the figures of the Curtis family. The latter, with the exception of Lisa, are admirable. The old gentleman, so naturally turning over the leaves of a portfolio, the old lady, with her stone face . . . Ralph, a graceful *flâneur* attitude, so typical of him (Rieder 2000, p. 107).

Gay's *Interior of Palazzo Barbaro, Venice* (1902) is in the Museum of Fine Arts, Boston.

368 Lady Elcho, Mrs Adeane and Mrs Tennant or The Wyndham Sisters

1899
Oil on canvas, 115 × 84⅛ (292.1 × 213.7)
Inscribed, lower right: *John S. Sargent*
Metropolitan Museum of Art, New York. Wolfe Fund, Catharine Lorillard Wolfe Collection

The portrait represents the three beautiful and talented daughters of the Honourable Percy Scawen Wyndham and his wife, Madeline; from left to right: Madeline, Pamela and Mary. The Wyndhams as a family were central to the group known as 'the Souls' who frequently gathered at the Wyndham country house, Clouds, in Wiltshire.

Mary Constance (1862–1937) married Hugo Richard Wemyss Charteris Douglas, Lord Elcho, in 1883, and as hostess, their home, Stanway House in

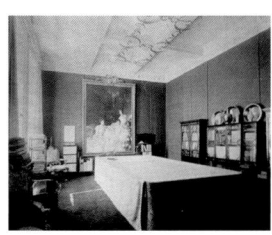

fig. 101 Photograph of *Lady Elcho, Mrs Tennant and Mrs Adeane* in the dining room at Clouds. Private Collection.

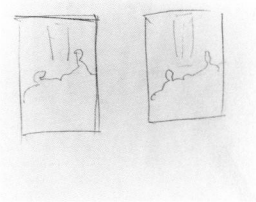

fig. 102 Two compositional studies for *Lady Elcho, Mrs Tennant and Mrs Adeane*. Pencil, 9 × 11 ¹¹/₁₆ (22.9 × 29.7). Fogg Art Museum, Harvard University Art Museums. Gift of Mrs Francis Ormond, 1937.7.20. 10 v.

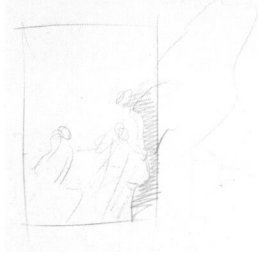

fig. 103 Compositional study for *Lady Elcho, Mrs Tennant and Mrs Adeane*. Pencil, 9 × 11 ¹¹/₁₆ (22.9 × 29.7). Fogg Art Museum, Harvard University Art Museums, 1937. 7. 20, 11 r.

Gloucestershire, became legendary for its house parties. She had remarkable gifts of sympathy, was the confidante of Arthur Balfour (see no. 550) and perhaps the leading female figure in the Souls. Sargent had known her since 1886, when she was sometimes of the company at Broadway; he was a visitor at Stanway, and his letters to her are in a private collection. Her brother-in-law, the Honourable Evan Charteris, became Sargent's first biographer. Lord Elcho became the eleventh Earl of Wemyss and March on his father's death in 1914.

Madeline (1869–1941) married Charles R. W. Adeane in 1889; he was the Lord Lieutenant of Cambridgeshire, and they lived at Babraham in Cambridgeshire, somewhat removed from the circles in which her family moved.

Pamela (1871–1928), vivacious and strong-minded, married Edward Tennant in 1895 and became Lady Glenconner on her husband's accession to the title in 1911. She wrote spirited and witty letters and anecdotes, and published several books. Her husband died in 1920, and she married Viscount Grey of Fallodon in 1922.

Percy Wyndham commissioned Sargent to paint a group portrait of his three daughters in 1898 for £2,000. Sargent wrote to Wyndham on 20 December [1898]: 'I have received your letter, and assure you that I am looking forward with the greatest interest to painting your three daughters, and that I shall allow nothing to interfere with it on my part. Will you please let me know when you arrive [in London] in March or, at any rate when my three sitters will get together' (Clouds Papers, the executors of the estate of the late Geoffrey Houghton-Brown).

The portrait was not painted in Sargent's studio, but in the drawing-room of the Wyndham's London house, 44 Belgrave Square. The writer Wilfrid Scawen Blunt (Percy Wyndham's cousin), wrote in his diary entry for 16 February 1899: 'Mary, Pamela and Madeline are sitting for their portraits in a group to Sargent. It is being painted in the drawing-room. In the background there will be their mother's portrait by Watts' (Blunt 1932, p. 313). Blunt is referring to the full-length portrait of the sitters' mother, Mrs Percy Wyndham (*née* Madeline Caroline Frances Eden Campbell), painted by George Frederic Watts in 1877, which is visible behind the figures in the background of the picture. Work on the portrait had begun the previous day. An entry by Madeline Wyndham in the Clouds visitors' book reads: 'The Great Picture Portrait of Mary, Madeline & Pamela was begun in London at 44 Belgrave Square by Mr Sargent on Feb 15th 1899' (Private Collection).

A number of abbreviated, occasionally cryptic, entries in Mary Elcho's journal chart the progress of the sittings. The entry for 15 February 1899 reads:

Put on white gown with roses & went to 44 . . . found Papa Mamma Sargent & Madeline –

the latter looking very nice in a pink gown, Pamela came later everyone in a great state of excitement. We were to be in the drawing room on a big sofa which we sat on Stumbled over & twisted this way & that until it was supposed that we were all properly grouped. This lasted til about 1.30 when we all lunched (Lady Elcho's journal, Private Collection).

On 17 February: 'Went to 44 & sat all the morning . . . Pamela came late not realized the sitting was settled for that day'; and 20 February: 'No sitting Sargents mother ill, acute bronchitis.' There were sittings on the next three consecutive days – 21 February: 'He painted me all the morning – Madeline sat in Pamela's place the latter has a cold . . . Left off once he had to go'; 22 February: 'Went to 44, he painted Madeline and I did nothing much – Its very nice being there in the nice room with Papa Mamma George popping in etc – & Papa likes Sargent as a man very much – sat in sun'; 23 February: 'Went to 44 – lay on sofa most of time Madeline's gown painted – at the end Dorothy [her cousin Dorothy Carleton] sat in Pamela's place & I posed for attitude arms etc & we settled [illegible owing to ink blots] position. Her face will come more profile.' The following week Sargent again worked for three days, from Wednesday to Friday. On 7 March: 'Got to 44 before 10.30 & saw Minnie [*née* Brooke, the first wife of her brother Guy] off – the 3 sisters & Sargent assembled & we settled the grouping of Pamela & me, I went home to change & returned to lunch'; 8 March: 'Went to 44 & he painted my neck & shoulders – home to change'; and 9 March: '44 at 10.30 Pamela was painted & seems going to be very like.' It was at this point that Wilfrid Blunt, who was a frequent visitor to the house, saw the picture in progress. On 9 March, he wrote:

Saw the first sketching in of Pamela's head which Sargent had just done in a couple of hours' work. It is wonderful as a likeness and as a bit of rapid execution, giving just her playful prettiness and the peculiar wave of her hair, a sketch in the manner of Velasquez, with exactly his strong touches, unintelligible when looked close into, but alive when seen at a distance. Mary, too, has been sketched in not unsuccessfully, and Madeline less well. It should be a remarkable picture, probably Sargent's best. He is to be allowed no license with the magentas and mauves he loves'. (Blunt 1932, p. 314)

Working on such a huge canvas was physically onerous. When Blunt encountered Sargent on the Wyndham's doorstep after the morning's sitting, he described him as 'a rather good looking fellow in a pot hat, whom at my first sight I took to be a superior mechanic' (Blunt 1932, pp. 314–15). On 10 March, Mary Elcho continued: 'Sat for picture 44 as usual 10.30 – he painted my neck & shoulders' (Lady Elcho's journal, Private

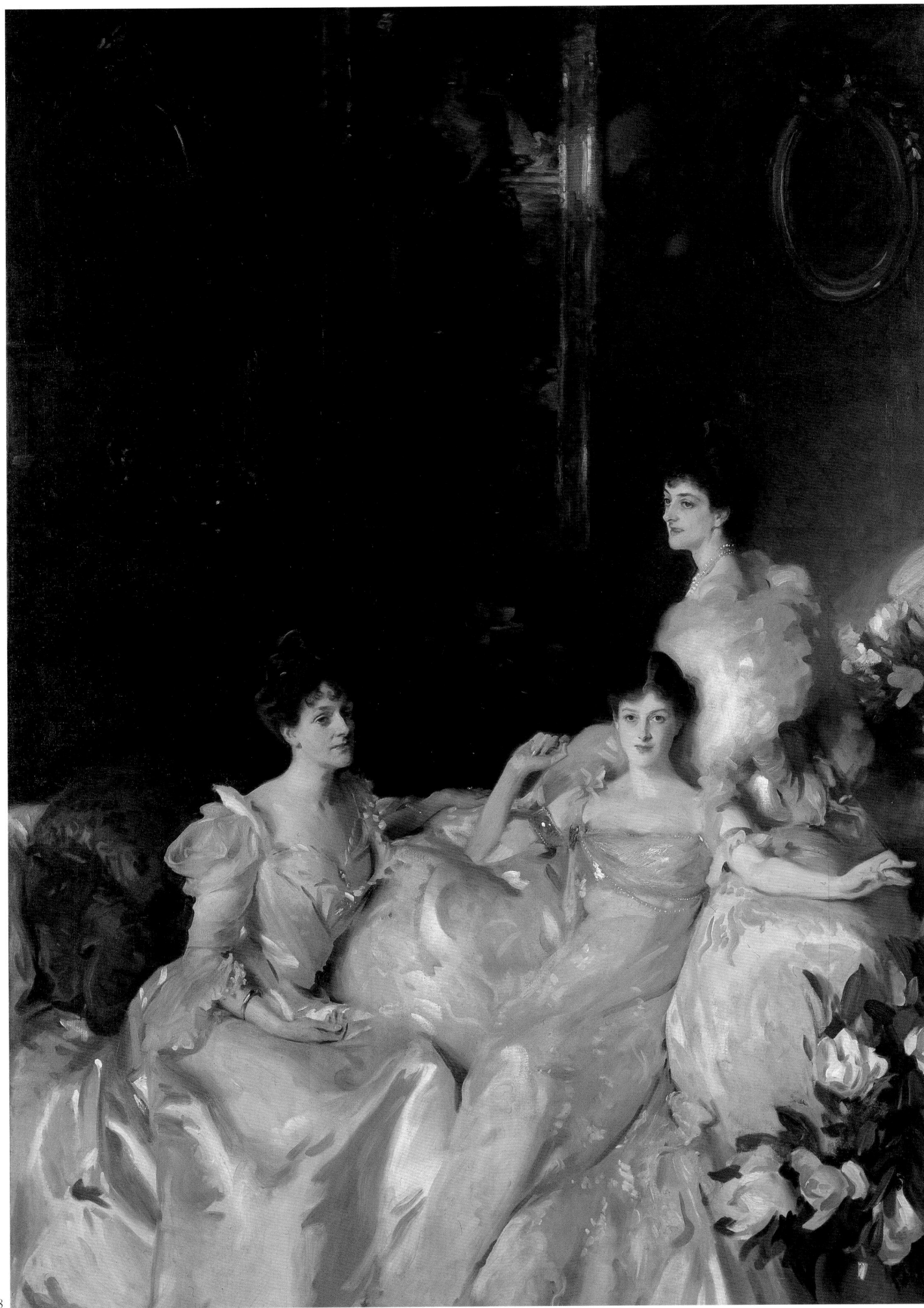

Collection). The sittings continued to be intensive. On 13 March: 'Went to Paddington [from Gloucestershire by train] in white satin gown – to Belgrave Square in thick fog, painting impossible came home to dress'; 14 March: 'Went to 44 but again it was too foggy – & Mr Sargent made some pencil drawings of my face'; 15 March: 'Had a sitting – great discussion as to who was to hold a fan'; and 17 March 'Not necessary for me to sit & Mad and Pam's knees were to be done & the weather being foggy nothing got on well.' On Saturday 18, she was 'let off' sitting, but on Tuesday 21: 'Went 44 10.30 to 1.' On 22 March: 'Went to 44, Sargent painted Pamela's face, it is very like and both Papa and Mamma are very pleased with it'; 23 March: 'Grey day I felt tired & cross Sargent tried to do me & I tried to sit, we both failed & the light was hideous – gave up about 12 or so'; and 24 March: 'Had a more satisfactory sitting, but it its not supposed to be like me yet.'

Mary Elcho does not record any sittings in April. On 16 May, she notes: 'Sat for my picture 10 to 1', and 18 May: 'Went to 44 – Sargent worked at my face – He gave Papa an awful shock by saying he must have Pamela's head off – Papa likes it so much & thinks it so good that he would never recover if it were to be altered. I tried to tell Mr Sargent what a fearful risk it would be – Papa said to me after that even if it were yet done he should never get over the dreadful feeling of insecurity'. On 19 May, she writes: 'Went again to Belgrave Square, my face is supposed to be finished'; and 5 and 6 June, there are two further mentions: 'Hugo [her husband] came with me to 44. We were rather late, I sat for my face eyes altered' and 'Went again to 44', respectively. On 20 June: 'Mamma . . . had a birthday dinner party & all the people who came saw the picture.'

Sargent's concerns about Pamela's head did not abate. Early in 1900, when he found himself seated next to her at the Ribblesdales', he pressed for further sittings. She wrote to her father on 8 February 1900:

I sat beside Mr Sargent last night at the Ribblesdales. He is very anxious for some more sittings from me, and & enquired my plans most pertinaciously. I said I was quite ready to sit but that I should have to write & tell you – & he acquiesced saying he . . . felt sure you would not mean it to be as it is. Mrs Adeane in particular he said must be changed. Then in parenthesis 'and now I see you oh it must be worked on' – squirming & writhing in his evening suit – at present your face is a sketch – waving his hand – 'no finish – no finish' – he got quite excited. So at present it stands (as I am up in London till Thursday or Friday & he thinks the weather will hold good) that I am to turn up at his studio (where it seems he has had the picture removed to) on Sat at 2.30 *unless I hear from you to the contrary*. (Clouds Papers)

In a letter to her father of 13 February 1900, she gave a full account of her sittings:

My sittings are over now – and he has not repainted the face. He worked on little corners of it and has much improved it I think. He has done the modelling of my nose, and taken a little of the colour out of my cheeks, this improves it – and has strengthened the lines of my hair. That is, where it was all fluffy and rather trivial looking before in the picture he has put in the sweep of hair turned back. This has strengthened it, and made it *more* like my head really. Then he has found out that the straight line of my blue 'plastron' was disturbing to the *scheme*. And much as I regret my pretty blue front I *quite* see it was rather proclusive of other things in the picture as a whole. For instance both sisters seem to *gain* by its removal – one's eye is not checked & held by it. It was too distinct a feature in itself to compose well with other parts. He has not eliminated it wholly – but he has disguised it as if I had drawn the lace veil of my dress across it. My face also seems to gain significance by its removal. He is very keen that Madeline shd. sit to him again – and I hope you will use your influence if Charlie [Adeane] is against it – that she should give him a week. It is a very short time – and *then* he says he could get it done for the Acad. [Royal Academy] this year. It seems a pity if it is so near it shouldn't be managed; as we shall all be old and haggard before the public sees it! . . . About Mary says he wishes to get a more 'dreamy' expression in her eyes. He asked me if I liked it first & I *could* say honestly I liked it, but did not think it 'contemplative' enough in expression for her (it seemed to me too 'sweet' & trivial in expression for her). No sooner had I said the word 'contemplative' than he caught at it. 'Dreamy – I must make it a *little* more dreamy!' and this he says he can do by touching the *lids*. As Mary's eyelids are a most characteristic feature of her face, I think he is right, but of course he will not do it till she sits to him (Clouds Papers).

The figures, in white evening gowns, are highlighted against an evocatively dim, green-walled interior, a ray of light catching the gilt of picture frames and touching the light in fabric, jewellery and flowers. Madeline and Pamela are seated on a large sofa, covered in figured ivory damask, while Mary is posed in semi-profile, perching on the back of the sofa. Madeline and Pamela wear evening gowns in neo-eighteenth-century style. Madeline's dress has a fitted bodice with sleeves tight to the elbow and trimmed with ruffles, and a full skirt and train; she has a gold bangle on her right arm and a silver brooch at her breast. Pamela is dressed in a white silk Empire-style gown or *robe de chemise*, the bodice lightly splashed with pale blue and the skirt spangled with gold; she wears a long chain of pearls, held by a brooch, across her breast and a wide bangle adorned with pearls on her upper arm. Mary wears a white dress with long fitted sleeves, a three-strand pearl necklace and a frothy wrap. Watts's full-length portrait of the girls' mother, Madeline Wyndham, hangs in the centre background, and there is a sideboard on which stand several silver objects and above which and to the left hangs a rectangular painting in a deep gilded frame. A portrait with a barely decipherable subject, possibly a female head and shoulders, in an eighteenth-century French curved oval frame with a cartouche and swags, is on the wall to the right, with a similar portrait, barely visible to the left. There are two vases of flowers, possibly magnolia, or magnolia and roses, at the lower right and a third under the large portrait.

When the portrait was exhibited at the Royal Academy in 1900, it was hailed as a masterpiece. The *Art Journal* critic wrote that he would 'hazard the opinion that as a vital and brilliant work in this kind it will be accounted in the future as one of the noteworthy products of the last quarter of a century' (*Art Journal*, 1900, p. 164), while *The Times* described the portrait as 'the greatest performance from the point of view of pure art . . . and . . . in spite of certain obvious faults . . . the greatest picture which has appeared for many years on the walls of the Royal Academy' (*The Times*, 15 May 1900, p. 3). D. S. MacColl noted the possible influence of Sargent's mural work on his sense of design and management of space in such a large canvas: 'Perhaps Mr Sargent's recent work on large schemes of formal design [his decorative schemes for the Boston Public Library] has strengthened his building power and grasp of a large harmony' (*Saturday Review*, 12 May 1900, p. 583). MacColl went on to praise the colour as 'a continuum that is varied and that yet holds all through, one ever-changing light' and its 'organic, as opposed to mechanical finish'. The *Athenaeum* reviewer wrote:

It is beyond a doubt the finest of Mr Sargent's portraits [in this particular exhibition], for it illustrates most happily his peculiar methods, which have not yet become mannered nor lost the charm of freshness, and it betrays less than his former works of his not less characteristic shortcomings – we might almost say perversities. A development of a portion of the art of Gainsborough, it is not inferior to Gainsborough in the painting of the faces, nor in veracity and brilliance, and that homogeneity of the whole which distinguishes it and adds to its effect upon the spectator (*Athenaeum*, 9 June 1900, p. 726).

He went on to praise its 'breadth and force and the extreme limpidity of its shadows' and its 'technical beauty', while criticizing 'a little queer and illogical drawing, the insufficiency of the composition and the awkward pose of at least two of the ladies'. Roger Fry, in his first season as an art critic, wrote: 'Since Sir Thomas Lawrence's time, no one has been able thus to seize the exact *cachet* of fashion-

able life, or to render it in paint with a smartness and piquancy which so exactly correspond to the social atmosphere itself. Such works must have an enduring interest to posterity simply as perfect records of the style and manners of a particular period' (*Pilot*, 12 May 1900, p. 321). Henry James wrote to John Hay (3 April 1900) that he had seen the 'vast & dazzling portrait of the 3 Percy Wyndham sisters – with Watts's portrait of their mother looming up behind – & felt quite weak & foolish after my first stare at it. I mean as one feels when the lady is shot from the cannon . . . I came away biting my thumb . . . & with my ears burning from the sense of how it's not the age of *my* dim trade' (Monteiro 1965, p. 124). At the Royal Academy banquet in 1903, the Prince of Wales dubbed the picture 'The Three Graces' (see *Art Journal*, 1903, pp. 62–3), a title which has remained associated with it.

The portrait was destined to hang at Clouds, in Wiltshire, which had been designed by the architect Philip Webb. The walls of the billiard room were painted dark blue to complement the predominantly white tonalities of the painting. Madeline Wyndham wrote to her daughter Mary about a visit from Webb's pupil Detmar Blow in November 1901, describing the decorative scheme they devised to accommodate the painting: 'Detmar Blow arrived vy last train & we have been arranging the Billiard Room all day – & I think it will look vy well – the picture looks 100 times better than it did & the room looks *larger* & the Picture *smaller*. We have put dark blue all over the walls & the Morris tapestry opposite the window & all the curtains white' (quoted in Dakers 1993, p. 97).

The portrait left Clouds twice in 1908 to be shown in exhibitions in London. Madeline Wyndham's entry in the Clouds visitors' book for 10 October 1908 reads:

Sargent's picture returned today unhurt save two slight injuries to the frame. What it has seen and heard if it could only speak! What variety of nations, of people, what private conversation, and what comments on itself and the Exhibition generally! The picture left Clouds on February 18th to go to the Exhibition of Fair Women at the New Gallery [an International Society exhibition]. There was a considerable interval of time between the closing of this exhibition and the reception of pictures at the Franco British. It was out of the question to have it down here, and its size precludes its being taken in at 44 Belgrave Square. Eventually it was housed in Mr Sargent's studio at Fulham Road till the Franco British was sufficiently finished to receive it (Private Collection).

For a photograph of the portrait hanging at Clouds, see fig. 101.

Three compositional studies for the portrait are in a sketchbook at the Fogg Art Museum, Cambridge, Massachusetts (figs 102, 103).

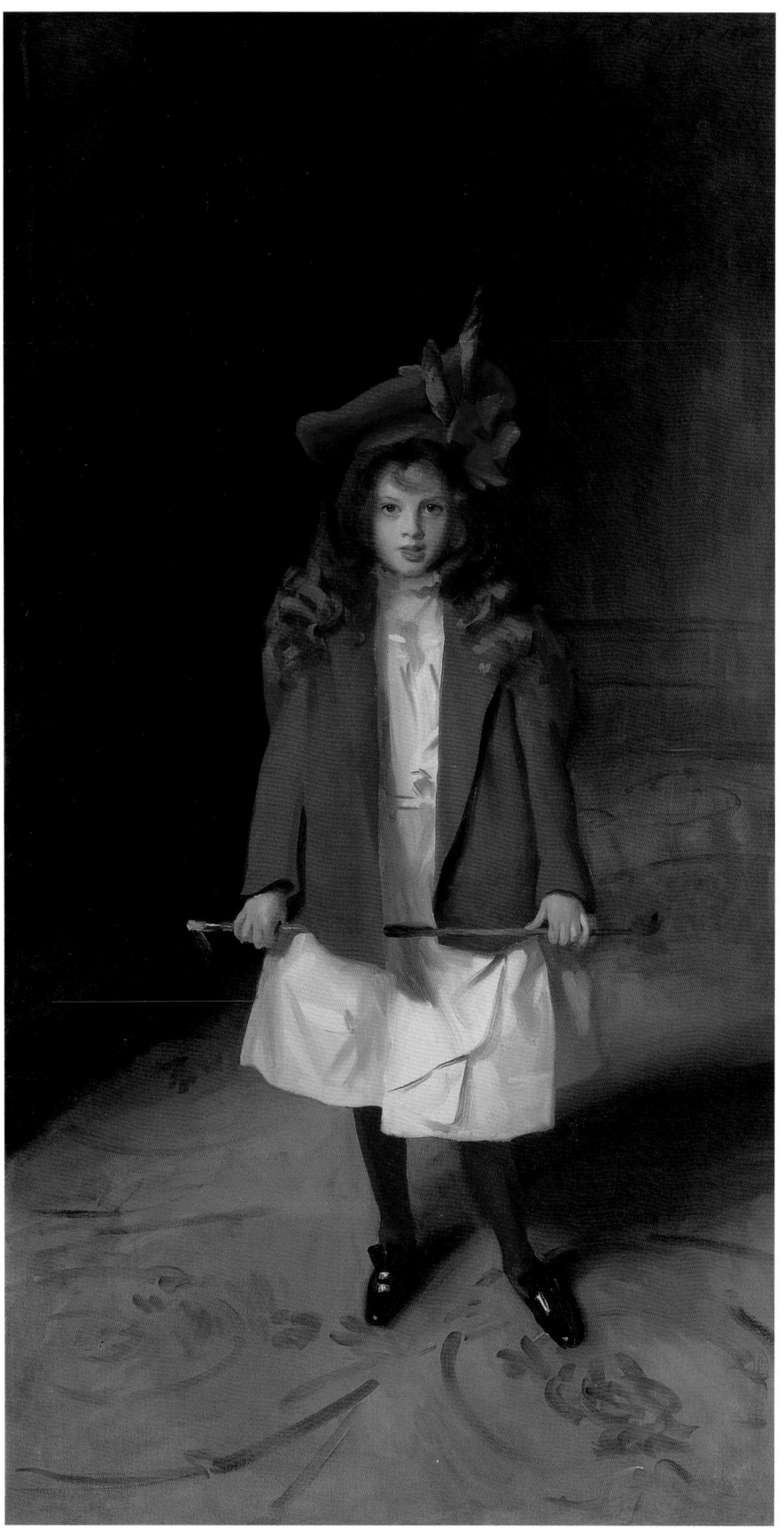

369 *The Honourable Victoria Stanley*

1899
Oil on canvas, 77½ × 44½ (196.8 × 105.4)
Inscribed, upper right: *John S. Sargent 1899*
Private Collection

Victoria Stanley (1892–1927) was the daughter of Edward George Villiers Stanley, later seventeenth Earl of Derby, and his wife, Lady Alice Maud Olivia Montagu. She married, first, the Honourable Neil Primrose, the son of the fifth Earl of Rosebery (d. 1917), in 1915, and, secondly, Captain Sir Malcolm Bullock, Bt, in 1919. She had two daughters, Ruth and Priscilla, one from each marriage. She died as a result of a hunting accident.

Victoria is wearing a high-necked white dress, a red coat and a matching bonnet with bow and feathers, red stockings and black shoes. She is holding a hunting crop and, rather than wearing full traditional hunting costume, is dressed to suggest hunting. She is standing in a shadowy interior on one of the artist's Aubusson carpets (see Accessories, p. xxiv, no. 35). Like Van Dyck, Sargent could capture the essence of children in even the grandest of compositions, which imitate the conventions of adult portraiture. Victoria Stanley presents a delightfully confident and carefree figure, and Sargent has matched her youth with all his powers of bravura. The portrait was exhibited at the New Gallery, London, in 1900. 'The simplicity of the portrait is half its charm', wrote the critic of *The Times*. 'The other half lies in the colour of the whole composition, in the alertness of the little figure, and in the bonny freshness of the child's face. Seldom has Mr Sargent given us so much positive colour – red without a hint of decadence, set over against a cream white, that is dazzling in its brilliancy. The eyes, too, sparkle with life and are brimming with laughter' (*The Times*, 23 April 1900, p. 8). Writing for the *Saturday Review*, D. S. MacColl did not succumb to its charm, describing it as 'a rather savage Sargent. Imagine a portrait of Little Red Riding Hood by the Wolf' (*Saturday Review*, 5 May 1900, p. 555).

370 *Mrs Joshua Montgomery Sears*

1899
Oil on canvas, 58¼ × 38¼ (148.0 × 97.2)
Inscribed, upper right: *John S. Sargent 1899*
Museum of Fine Arts, Houston. George R. Brown funds given in honor of his wife, Alice Pratt Brown

Mrs Joshua Montgomery Sears, *née* Sarah Carlisle Choate (1858–1935), was born in Cambridge, Massachusetts, the daughter of Charles Francis Choate. She was an artist, painting portraits and floral still lifes in water-colour and pastel. She studied with Sargent's friend, Dennis Miller

Sargent went on to paint several figures connected to the Wyndhams and their circle: Sir Charles Tennant (no. 406) in 1901, Lord Ribblesdale (no. 421) in 1902 and Lord Wemyss (no. 556) in 1909.

Bunker at the Cowles Art School in Boston (see *Early Portraits*, no. 204) and at the School of the Museum of Fine Arts, Boston, with Edmund Tarbell, Abbott Thayer and George de Forest Brush. She later exhibited her work extensively and was awarded several medals: the William T. Evans Prize of the American Watercolor Society (1892) and medals at exhibitions in Chicago (1893), Paris (1900), Buffalo (1901) and St Louis (1904). She married Joshua Montgomery Sears, Boston's leading real estate owner, in 1877 and had a son and a daughter, Helen, whom Sargent painted in 1895 (no. 318). In the 1890s, she became interested in photography, and her work in this medium was highly regarded: she was a member of the pioneering photographic groups such as the Photo-Secession and the Linked Ring. Among the rare photographs of Sargent at work are those she took at Fenway Court in 1903. Although she had homes at 12 Arlington Street, Boston, in Southborough, Massachusetts, and in Maine, she had a European outlook and was a frequent traveller to Paris, living there for periods of time following the death of her husband and then their son. An adventurous art collector, acquiring works by Degas, Manet, Matisse, Cézanne and Cassatt, she sought Mary Cassatt's advice on purchases but was frequently more avant-garde in her tastes (see Erica E. Hirshler, 'Helping "Fine Things Across the Atlantic": Mary Cassatt and Art Collecting in the United States', in *Mary Cassatt: Modern Woman*, exhibition catalogue, Art Institute of Chicago, 1998, pp. 193–5). She was a generous patron of artists, playing a primary role as artistic hostess in Boston, second only to that of the more flamboyant Isabella Stewart Gardner. For an introductory account, see Stephanie Mary Buck, 'Sarah Choate Sears: Artist, Photographer, and Art Patron' (Master's thesis, Syracuse University, 1985).

It seems that Sargent was approached to paint Mrs Sears as early as 1890 but declined to do so, pleading pressure of work: 'A letter had come asking him to paint Mrs Sears; and at about this time he [word crossed out] said again that he didn't think he could do it – He didn't think he could undertake anything more' (diary of Lucia Fairchild, 2 October 1890, DCL). The portrait was apparently painted in London in 1899.

Mrs Sears is painted seated in one of Sargent's bergère chairs (see Accessories, p. xxii, no. 2b). She is wearing a white satin dress with a train, which falls over the side of the chair; around her neck is a necklace with a gold and enamel brooch and pendant pearl; and she is holding a bouquet of pink roses. The table, which is barely distinguishable, may be Sargent's round Empire table (see Accesssories, p. xxii, no. 14); there are a couple of silver objects on the table, which are difficult to read.

Mrs Sears owned several works by the artist: two oils – *Glacier Streams–The Simplon* (Museum of Fine Arts, Springfield, Massachusetts) and *Femme en barque* (Private Collection), and several water-colours – *At Aranjuez, Marble Vase* (Charles and Emma Frye Art Museum, Seattle), *Vianna do Castello, Portugal* (Museum of Fine Arts, Boston), *Woods in Maine* (Private Collection), and *Fresh Snow* (Unlocated).

371 *Cicely Horner*

1899
Oil on canvas, 24½ × 16¼ (62.2 × 41.2)
Inscribed, upper left: *to Mrs Horner / Mells 99*;
upper right: *John S. Sargent*
Denver Art Museum Collection. Centennial gift of the Edward D. Pierson Family

Cicely, or Cecily, Horner (1883–1972) was the daughter of Sir John Horner of Mells Park, Somerset, and his wife, Frances (*née* Graham). Frances was the daughter of William Graham, a prosperous India merchant, a Liberal MP for Glasgow, and an enthusiastic collector and patron. She became a leading light among the Souls, several of whom Sargent painted. The artist Edward Burne-Jones was infatuated by her; he drew a series of exquisite profile drawings of her, and their relationship remained an inspiration to him throughout the last twenty years of his life. Cicely married the Honourable George Lambton, son of the Earl of Durham, in 1908.

Sargent visited Mells in May 1896, when the Asquiths (Herbert Asquith, later first Earl of Oxford and Asquith and Prime Minister, and his wife, Margot, *née* Tennant) were also of the party. Frances Horner wrote to Burne-Jones on 20 May 1896: 'I liked Mr Sargent: he was very nice and simple, & he was very shy & not the least like an American & he wasn't very like an artist either! – He was very frightened of Margot [Asquith] . . . he hated discussing all his great friends, & having his coat collar stroked, & talking about his pictures' (Mells Papers, the Earl of Oxford and Asquith). There appears to have been some discussion about Sargent's being commissioned to paint portraits of the Horner children. In an undated letter, Burne-Jones, who was antagonistic to Sargent's work and possessive about his own relationship with the Horners, wrote to Frances: 'Of course I felt a bitter pang when you told me Sargent was going to paint from Cicely – who is mine – who was made to fulfil a dream of mine – I suffered a great pang – and then I rather hate criticizing the living . . . but the dabs are all that I hate in execution – and the colour is often hideous – & not one faintest glimmer of imagination has he – the world is growing sick of what is beautiful' (Mells Papers, the Earl of Oxford and Asquith).

Cicely is painted wearing a white dress with puffed sleeves and a pink sash. In her book of reminiscences, Lady Horner recalls a visit by Sargent to Mells in June 1899, where he 'did two pictures of Cicely, not very successful ones' (Horner 1933, p. 97). She also quotes an undated letter, which seems to refer to the earlier visit:

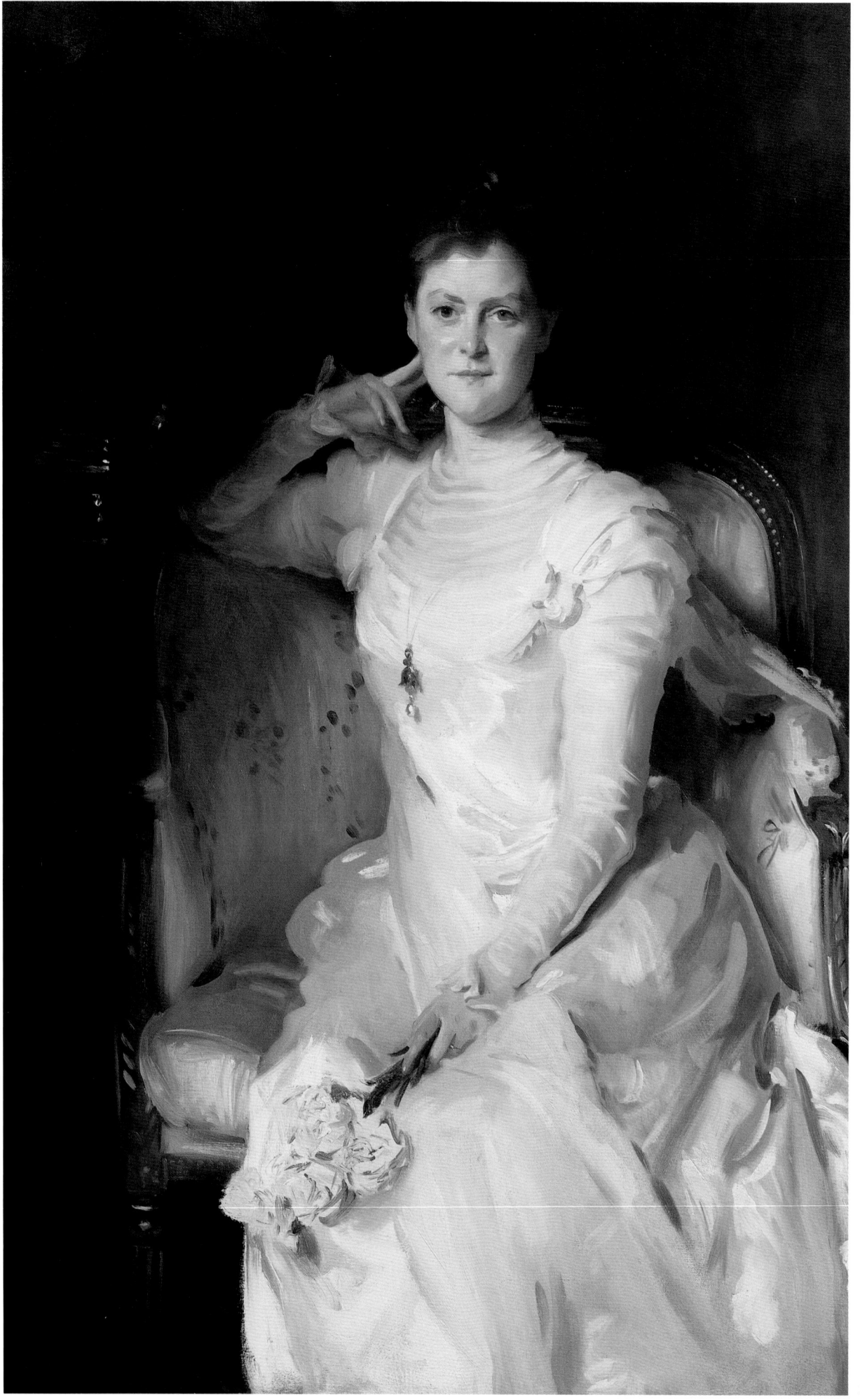

Many thanks for your very kind letter, which mentions the word *friendship*, which makes me proud and sensible of great good fortune – thus granted. I have been thinking ever since those pleasant days at Mells of those four beautiful faces that I mean to do – and of how to do them. If it were not for other pictures I should propose posting straight back, and starting in at once. As it is I suppose next spring and in my studio – if that suits everyone (Mells Papers, the Earl of Oxford and Asquith).

Apart from a charcoal drawing of Cicely's sister, Katherine, later Mrs Raymond Asquith, no other portraits of members of the Horner family are known. In a letter to McKibbin of 29 June 1947, Cicely herself recalled sitting to Sargent in the schoolroom at Mells: 'Sargent was staying with my mother & gave both portraits to her. Actually we never liked them very much which was I think why my mother eventually sold them!' (McKibbin papers). It is not certain when or how Lady Horner disposed of the portraits, but the second one seems to have been with Grand Central Art Galleries, New York, by 1924. According to the American Art Association sale catalogue of 1927, the present portrait was 'sold to close an account', presumably by Knoedler, who had the painting from the dealer John Levy in April 1925.

Cicely's husband, the Honourable George Lambton, was painted by Sir William Orpen (Private Collection).

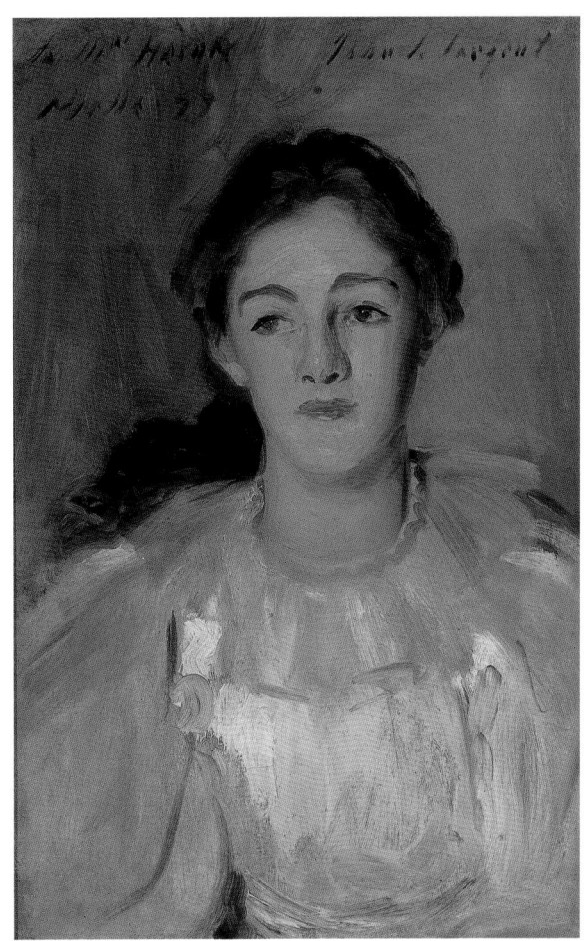

371

372 *Cicely Horner*

c. 1899
Oil on canvas, 24 × 16 (61 × 40.7)
Inscribed, upper left: *John S. Sargent*; upper right: *1910*
Untraced

Clearly painted in the same frock and on the same occasion as no. 371, Cicely is shown here in semi-profile. The inscribed date on the photograph, taken by Grand Central Art Galleries, New York, in 1924, appears to read 1910, which is clearly erroneous. Another early negative, by Peter Juley, from the 1920s (Smithsonian Collection, Washington, D.C.) shows the picture in its frame. Though photographed in the year of Sargent's one-man show at the Grand Central Art Galleries, the sketch of Cicely Horner was not included in the exhibition catalogue. It is, however, probable that its sale was handled by the firm. The portrait has since remained untraced.

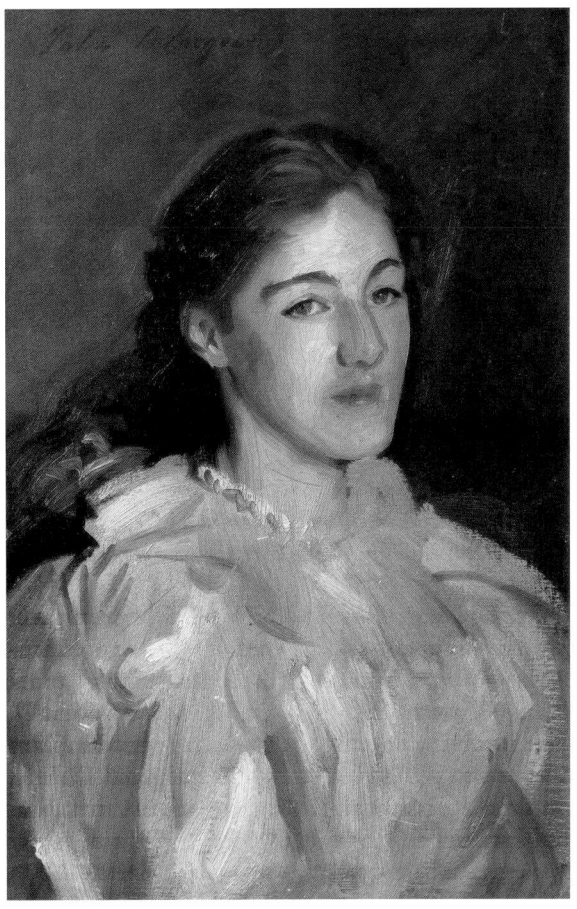

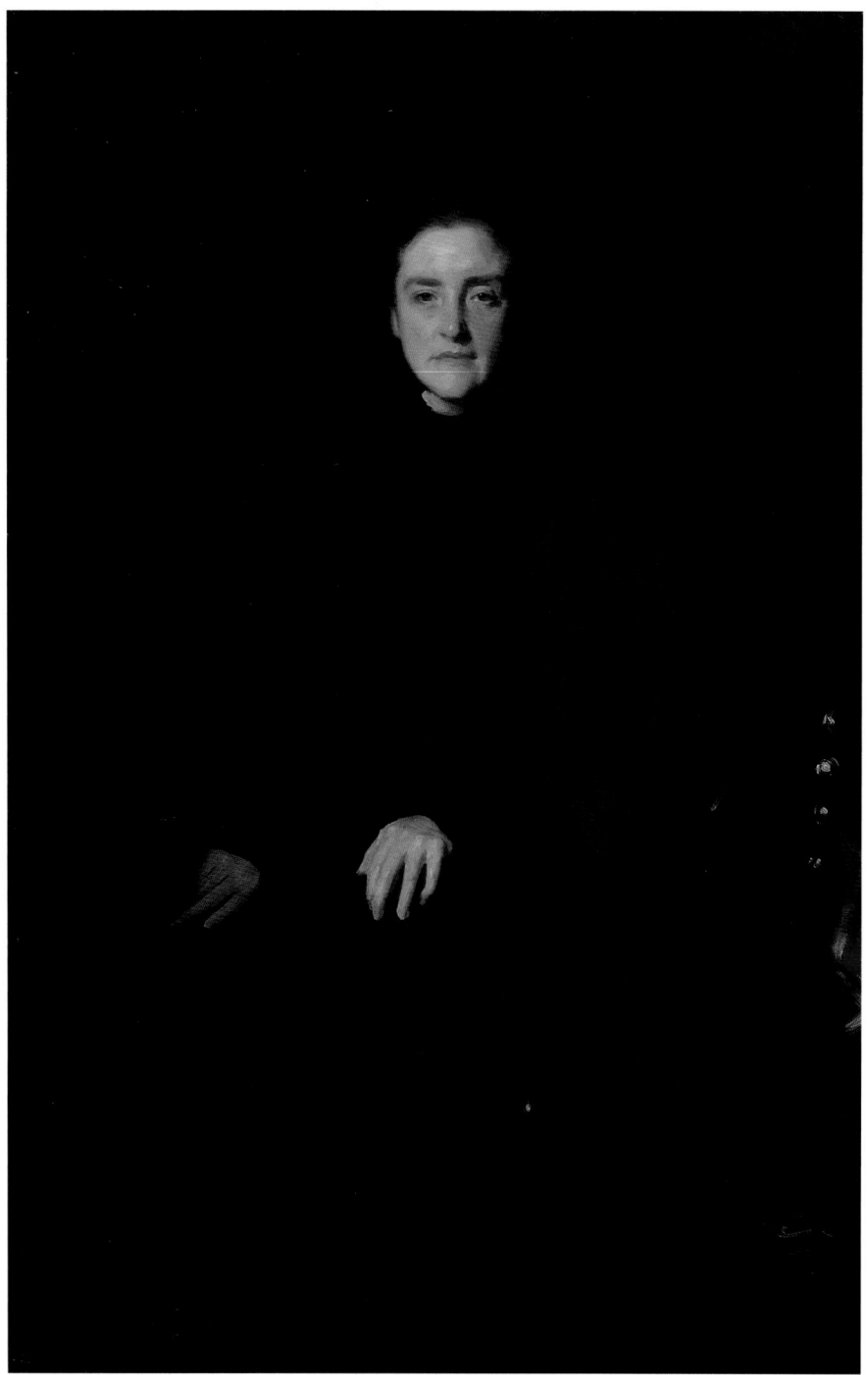

373 *M. Carey Thomas*

1899
Oil on canvas, 58 × 38 (147.3 × 96.5)
Inscribed, upper left: *John S. Sargent*
Bryn Mawr College, Bryn Mawr, Pennsylvania

M[artha] Carey Thomas (1857–1935), a prominent woman suffragist and pioneer in women's education, was born in Baltimore, the daughter of James Carey Thomas and his wife, Mary (*née* Whitall). She studied at Quaker schools, at Johns Hopkins University, the universities of Leipzig and Zurich, and the Sorbonne in Paris. She was the first dean and professor of English (1885) of Bryn Mawr College and its second president (1894–1922). With Mary Elizabeth Garrett (see no. 469), she

was associated with founding the Bryn Mawr School for Girls in Baltimore.

The portrait was commissioned in 1898 by a committee of alumnae and students of the college; Sargent wrote to accept the commission on 14 April [1898] (letter from Sargent to a person unknown, 14 April 1898, M. Carey Thomas Papers, reel no. 56, Bryn Mawr College, Bryn Mawr, Pennsylvania). The following summer, Carey Thomas travelled to Europe with Mary Elizabeth Garrett and sat to Sargent over six days in July in his London studio. She wrote several letters to her companion Mamie Gwinn (Mary Mackle Gwinn, who was also a member of the faculty at Bryn Mawr) On 14 July, she wrote that Sargent had chosen the position in which she would be painted 'sitting *full* face' (Alfred and Mary Gwinn Hodder Collection, box 51, folder 14, Princeton University Libraries); on 20 July, she noted that Sargent admired her face and would not change anything, and on 26 July, that Sargent thought the portrait was 'like a [Agnolo] Bronzino'. She is painted seated in her black academic robes, which are edged with dark blue velvet Ph.D. stripes, and dark blue hood.

By October, the painting had been framed under Sargent's supervision and at Mary Elizabeth Garrett's expense, and had arrived at the college. Carey Thomas gave Mamie's verdict on the portrait in a letter to Mary Elizabeth Garrett, who had stayed on in Europe (31 October 1899, M. Carey Thomas Papers, Bryn Mawr College, reel 22, frame 623): 'Mamie is delighted with it & thinks it one of the very nicest Sargents she has ever seen, a new era in his style. She thinks it very stately & full of the detachment of a great work of art, very melancholy, not at all "all there" as she considers I am, a youthful knight like St George conception of me, more like the im werden Minnie [a girlhood nickname] in 1877 – all of wh she thinks shows his high artistic conception'. The portrait was moved to Carey Thomas's own residence, the Deanery, a few days later. She described its impact in a letter to Mary Elizabeth Garrett: 'the other day I was in my bedroom by the bay window & looked up to see a perfect presentation of myself sitting at the window of your room. It was the portrait through the window. It really looked alive. Mamie & I pay it frequent visits. All the color has come back – that had faded during the voyage & even Mamie admits it looks less contemplative & more energetic daily' (Carey Thomas to Mary Elizabeth Garrett, 13 November 1899, M. Carey Thomas Papers, Bryn Mawr College, reel 22).

On 18 November 1899, the portrait was unveiled at a formal presentation, at which trustees and alumnae of the college spoke in tribute to Carey Thomas. For Carey Thomas's account of the occasion, see her letter to Mary Elizabeth Garrett (20 November 1899, M. Carey Thomas Papers, Bryn Mawr College, reel 22, frame 691), in which she notes: 'Miss Martha Thomas then unveiled the portrait. I took off my cap & assumed the attitude [in the portrait] & the applause was of course tremendous & unending'.

In 1900, the portrait was exhibited at the Pennsylvania Academy of Fine Arts and at the Paris Exposition. In a letter to Mary Elizabeth Garrett, Carey Thomas notes that the portrait is to be shown in these exhibitions (Carey Thomas to Mary Elizabeth Garrett, 7 December 1899, reel 22 frame 756, M. Carey Thomas Papers, Bryn Mawr College). In subsequent years, it was shown in exhibitions in Boston, Washington and Rome. When the portrait was shown in Philadelphia, the critic Francis J. Ziegler noted that Carey Thomas had been 'made to look too young' (*Brush and Pencil*, March 1900, p. 262).

374 *Lawrence Harrison*

c. 1899
Oil on canvas, 22 × 19 (56 × 48.2)
Inscribed, upper left: *John S. Sargent*
Private Collection

Lawrence Harrison (1834–1899), son of Frederick Harrison and Jane Brice, was a stockbroker, succeeding his father as chairman of the stockbrokers Hichens and Harrison. He was a brother of the distinguished historian and philosopher Frederic Harrison, and of the musical connoisseur Robert Harrison, whose wife and son Sargent painted (see *Early Portraits*, nos 142, 178). He married Mary Anna Clarke in 1865; his sons Lawrence ('Peter') and Leonard ('Ginx') were intimate friends of the artist.

The date of this portrait is uncertain, and some features suggest that it might have been painted posthumously.

375 *Lord Russell of Killowen*

1899
Oil on canvas, 64½ × 43½ (163.8 × 110.5)
Inscribed, upper left: *John S. Sargent*; upper right: *1899*
Lincoln's Inn, London. Gift of his son, second Lord Russell of Killowen

Charles Russell (1832–1900) was the son of Arthur Russell of Newry, County Down, Ireland, and Margaret Mullin. He married Ellen Mulholland of Belfast in 1858; they had five sons and four daughters. He enjoyed a brilliant legal career as a Liberal MP from 1880, supporting Irish causes, serving twice as Attorney-General, and acting as leading counsel for Charles Stewart Parnell in the Parnell Commission. He was created a life peer as Baron Russell of Killowen and was appointed Lord Chief Justice in 1894.

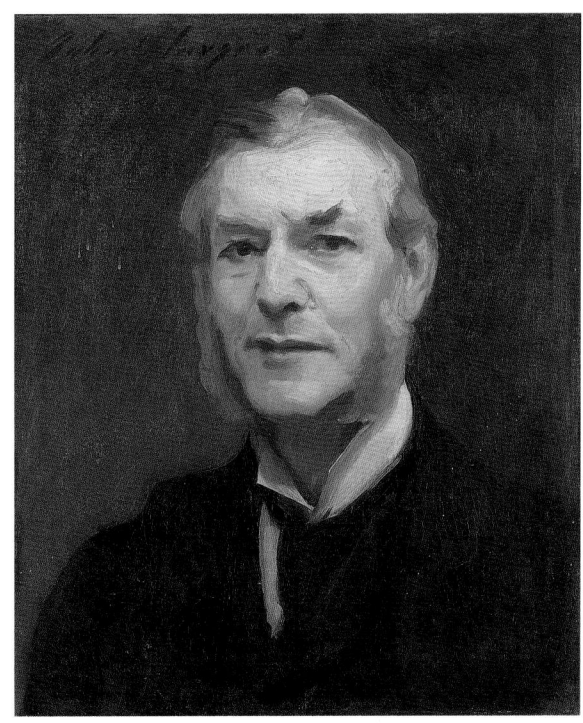
374

Lord Russell sat to Sargent twice in 1899. Here he is painted in the black and red ermine-lined robes of the Lord Chief Justice, with a full-buttoned wig and collar of S's. The political journalist Henry Lucy (see no. 477) saw the portrait hanging on the staircase of Russell's house in Cromwell Road: 'It was painted in broad-bottomed wig, and the picturesque robes of the Lord Chief Justice. Sitting by the host in the drawing-room after dinner, I was struck afresh with the rare beauty of the shape of his head. Remarking that it seemed a pity that in a portrait it should be covered by a wig, I ask if he would sit for my collection of portraits of contemporaries' (Lucy 1909, p. 285).

In 1900, Sargent painted Russell's daughter-in-law, Adah (who had married his son Charles in 1889) (no. 382).

376 *Lord Russell of Killowen*

c. 1899
Oil on canvas, 37½ × 27½ (95.2 × 70)
Inscribed, upper left: *John S. Sargent*
Sir Charles Russell, fourth Baronet

This portrait was commissioned by the sitter at the same time as he was sitting for the more formal work now at Lincoln's Inn (no. 375). His daughter, the Honourable Mrs Henry Drummond, confirmed that the Lincoln's Inn portrait was painted first in a letter to David McKibbin of 18 February 1948 (McKibbin papers). Russell's family and friends much preferred this more lively and informal portrait. A replica was painted for the Russell Memorial Committee (no. 377), and a copy by R. G. Eves was in the sale of works from

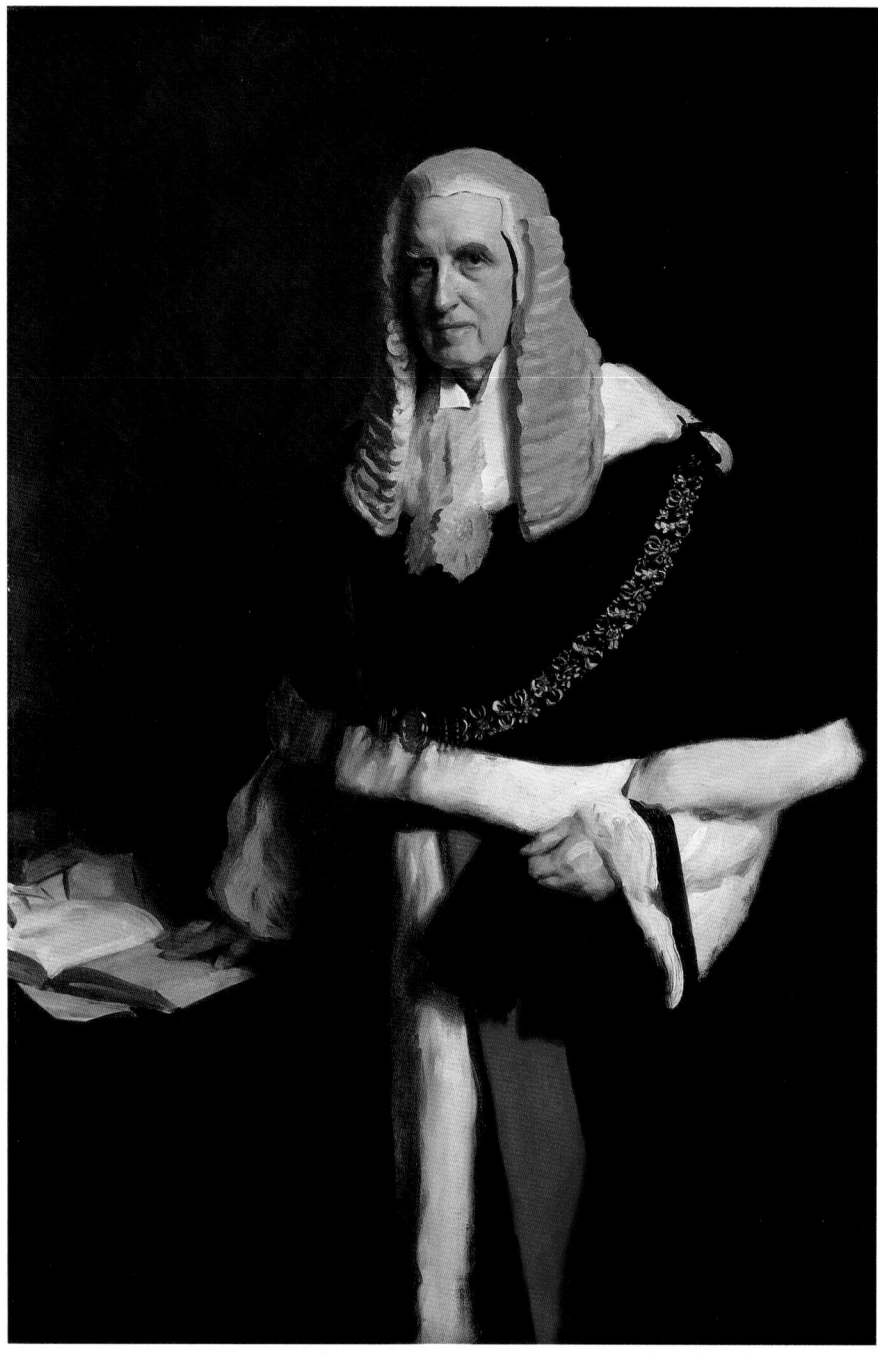

375

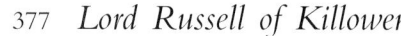

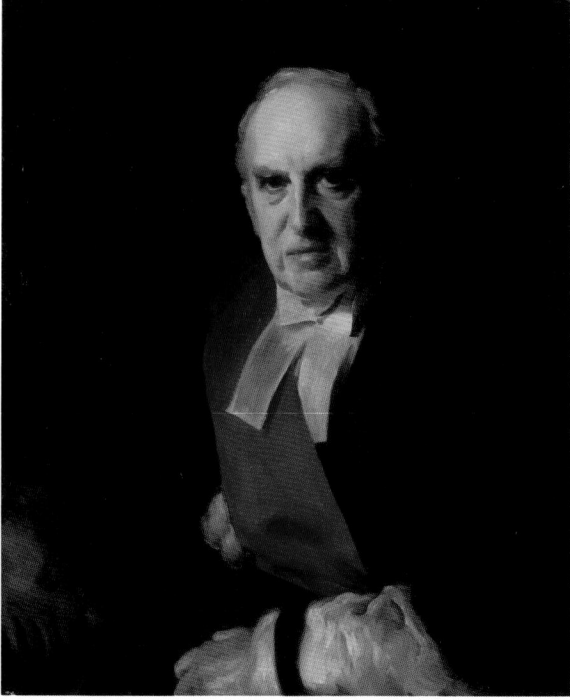

377 *Lord Russell of Killowen*

c. 1902
Oil on canvas, 33½ × 28 (85.1 × 71.1)
National Portrait Gallery, London. Gift of the Lord
Russell of Killowen Memorial Committee Fund

In December 1900, a committee was formed for the purpose of 'erecting a fitting memorial to the late lamented Lord Russell of Killowen' (circular, National Portrait Gallery, London, archives). It was determined that the memorial should take the form of a statue to be placed in the Law Courts and a replica of one of Sargent's two portraits of Russell, which had recently been exhibited at the

his studio, Phillips, London, 30 October 1973, lot P55. Another copy hangs in the offices of Russell & Russell, London.

Lord Russell is painted seated in his ordinary black and ermine-lined *nisi prius* robe with white bands and red sash. Family tradition records that when Sargent had finished painting Russell in the robes of the Lord Chief Justice, Russell pulled off his wig and threw it into a corner of the room; Sargent then asked him to remain where he was because he was going to paint another portrait (letter from the sitter's great-grandson, Sir Charles Russell, third Bt to the compilers, 6 October 1985, catalogue raisonné archive).

Royal Academy (no. 376). Sargent accepted the commission and produced a replica, apparently painted wholly by his hand, in January 1902. The committee offered the portrait to the trustees of the National Portrait Gallery in a letter of 21 January 1902 (National Portrait Gallery, London, Registered Packet), but owing to the rule normally excluding sitters dead for less than ten years, the portrait was not finally accepted until 1921. It hung at Lincoln's Inn in the interval. The marble statue of Russell, commissioned from Sir Thomas Brock, is in the Law Courts, London.

378 Sir David Richmond

1899
Oil on canvas, 96 × 53 (243.8 × 134.6)
Inscribed, lower left: *John S. Sargent*
Glasgow Museums. Art Gallery and Museum, Kelvingrove.

David Richmond (1843–1908) was the Lord Provost of Glasgow and managing director of David Richmond & Co, manufacturers of iron tubes. He was elected to Glasgow Town Council in 1879 and was associated with reforms and improvements to the city for over twenty years. He was Lord Provost from 1896 to 1899, when he was knighted. In the portrait, he is wearing the red uniform of a deputy lieutenant with the black and ermine robes of the Lord Provost, a red and gold sash and his chain and badge of office; he carries a red-plumed hat in his right hand.

In the late nineteenth century, Glasgow was one of the most advanced cities in Britain as far as the arts were concerned; the Corporation of Glasgow bought Whistler's celebrated portrait of Thomas Carlyle (*Arrangement in Grey and Black, No. 2: Thomas Carlyle*) amidst much controversy in 1891. The decision to select Sargent for a prestigious city commission was in this progressive tradition. On 16 December 1898, a subcommittee of the finance committee was appointed to carry out the decision of the council to commission a portrait of Richmond for the corporation 'to mark their sense of the valuable services rendered by Lord Provost Richmond to the city by asking him to give sittings for his portrait for the Corporation'. The portrait was to hang with the portraits of former Lord Provosts, and a replica of it was to be presented to his wife (no. 379). On 25 August 1899, the subcommittee reported that they had given the commission for both portraits to Sargent at a fee of 1,000 guineas. A cheque (£1,050 10s 7d, incorporating bank charges) was sent to Sargent on 17 November 1899, and the large portrait was formally unveiled at the City Chambers on 6 November (information from entries in the Glasgow Corporation minutes, Strathclyde Regional Council Archives, Glasgow). Sargent painted relatively few official portraits of this type.

379 Sir David Richmond

1899
Oil on canvas, 58 × 38 (147.3 × 96.5)
Inscribed, upper left: *John S. Sargent*
Glasgow Museums. Art Gallery and Museum, Kelvingrove. Bequest of Mrs A. J. Fairley

This picture was commissioned with the official presentation portrait of Richmond (see no. 378) in August 1899, at an inclusive fee of 1,000 guineas, and finished by November. The city had a tradition of presenting a second portrait to the wife of the retiring Lord Provost. Sargent's picture, clearly done from fresh sittings and quite different in pose and character to the whole length, is couched in less formal and grandiloquent terms. Richmond is dressed in black morning coat and in the red, black and ermine robes of the Lord Provost.

380 James Coolidge Carter

1899
Oil on canvas, 58 × 38 (147.3 × 96.5)
Inscribed, upper left: *John S. Sargent*
Harvard Club of New York City

James Coolidge Carter (1827–1905), son of Solomon and Elizabeth Carter of Lancaster, Massachusetts, was an eminent lawyer. He was called to the New York bar in 1853, and established a reputation as one of the most formidable advocates of his time. He fought strenuously against the codification of civil law, was concerned with municipal reform and wrote widely on legal issues. He was president of the American Law Association from 1894 to 1895 and president of the Harvard Club from 1870 to 1872 and 1895 to 1899.

The commission for the portrait followed that for Joseph Hodges Choate (no. 381) and was paid for from subscriptions collected by a special committee of members of the Harvard Club, led by Evert Jansen Wendell. A letter to members of the club (20 September 1899) from Wendell, William G. Peckham and Francis C. Huntington records:

A number of the members of the Club have expressed a desire to have also a companion portrait of Mr James C. Carter, by the same eminent artist. At the request of the Committee, Mr Carter has kindly consented to sit to Mr Sargent, and arrangements have been made to have the portrait painted, to hang, together with that of Mr Choate, on the walls of our Club house. The portrait is probably now in process of completion; and the two will be sent to us together within a very short time'. (Harvard Club of New York archive)

The letter also details the financial arrangements: the price of the portraits and the sum still to be raised.

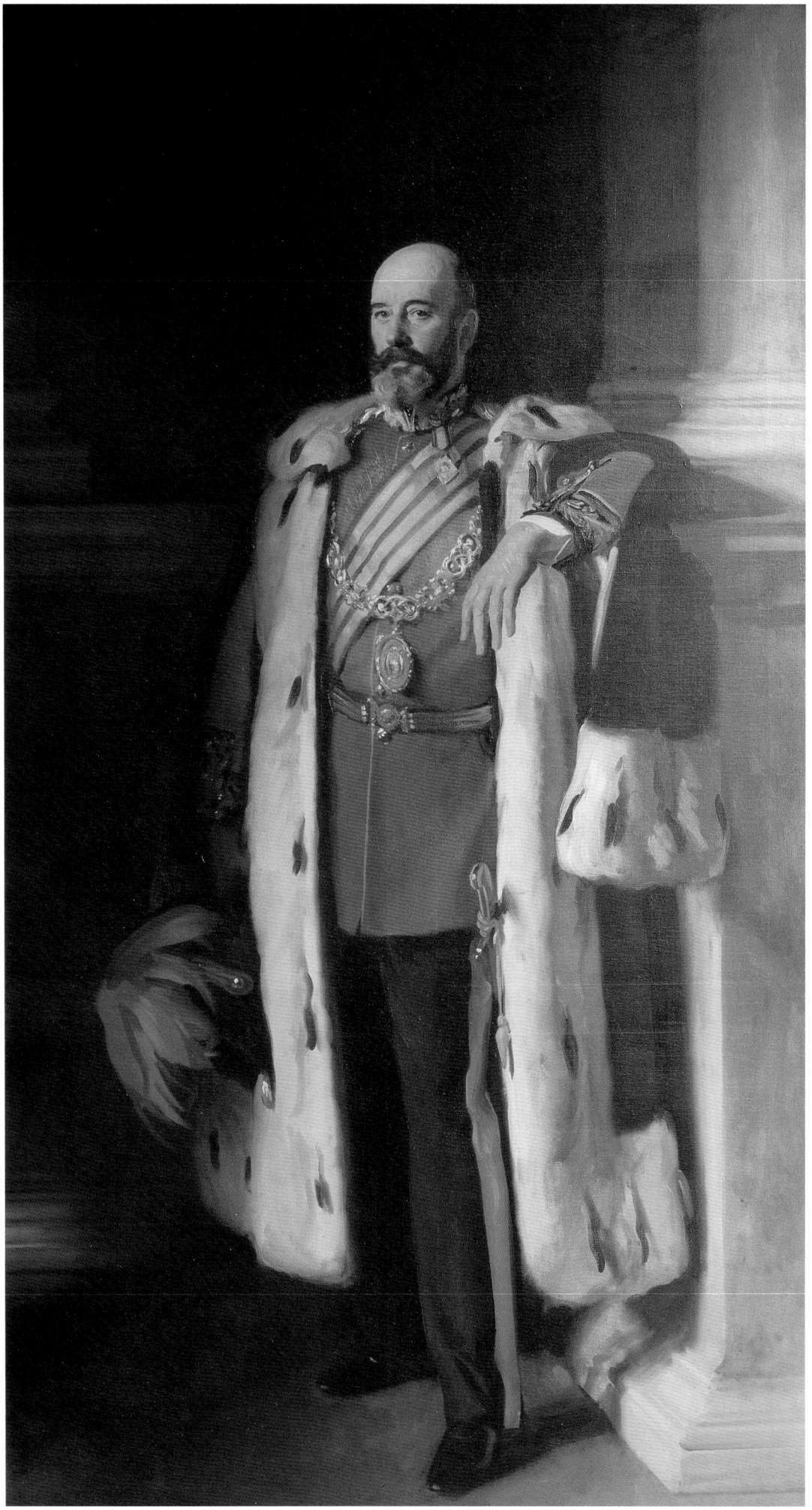

378

The portraits were painted in Sargent's Tite Street studio and were accepted as gifts by the club in late 1899 or early 1900. At a meeting of 10 December 1900 (Harvard Club minutes) a surplus was noted and a vote taken to devote it to the purchase of a portrait of James Russell Lowell by Dora Wheeler Keith.

381 *Joseph Hodges Choate*

1899
Oil on canvas, 58 × 38 (147.3 × 96.5)
Inscribed, upper left: *John S. Sargent*
Harvard Club of New York City

Joseph Hodges Choate (1832–1917), the son of Dr George Choate and Margaret Hodges of Salem, Massachusetts, was an eminent lawyer and diplomat. He was called to the Massachusetts Bar in 1855 and practised law for sixty two years, during which time he persuaded the Supreme Court to find the income tax unconstitutional, organized the demise of Boss Tweed and the Tammany Ring in New York, and established the New York Bar Association. He married Caroline Sterling in 1861, by whom he had four children. He was a trustee of the American Museum of National History and the Metropolitan Museum of Art, New York, and was a famous club man. He was a popular and successful ambassador to Great Britain from 1899 to 1905, headed the American delegation to the second Hague conference of 1907, and was president of the Harvard Club from 1874 to 1878, and from 1906 to 1908.

The genesis of the commission appears to date from 1896. In a letter to J. G. Peckham of 11 May 1896, Sargent wrote:

> I have received your letter with respect to a portrait to be painted for the Harvard Club. In the first place I must state that I shall probably not be in America before about two years from now, and that I shall be exclusively engaged upon my library decorating until next Spring, when I shall do some portraits here in London. My prices are 2,000, 3,000 and 4,000 dollars for head and shoulders, ¾ length and full-length respectively. If, as you intimate, the Harvard Club has difficulty in making those figures, I would make a reduction of five hundred dollars on each of them. (Harvard Club of New York archive)

Both this and the portrait of James Coolidge Carter (no. 380) were paid for by subscriptions collected by a special committee of club members led by Evert Jansen Wendell. A letter to members of the Harvard Club of 20 September 1899 detailing the background of and financial arrangements for the commission notes that 'the portrait has now been finished and is pronounced excellent by your Chairman' (Harvard Club of New York

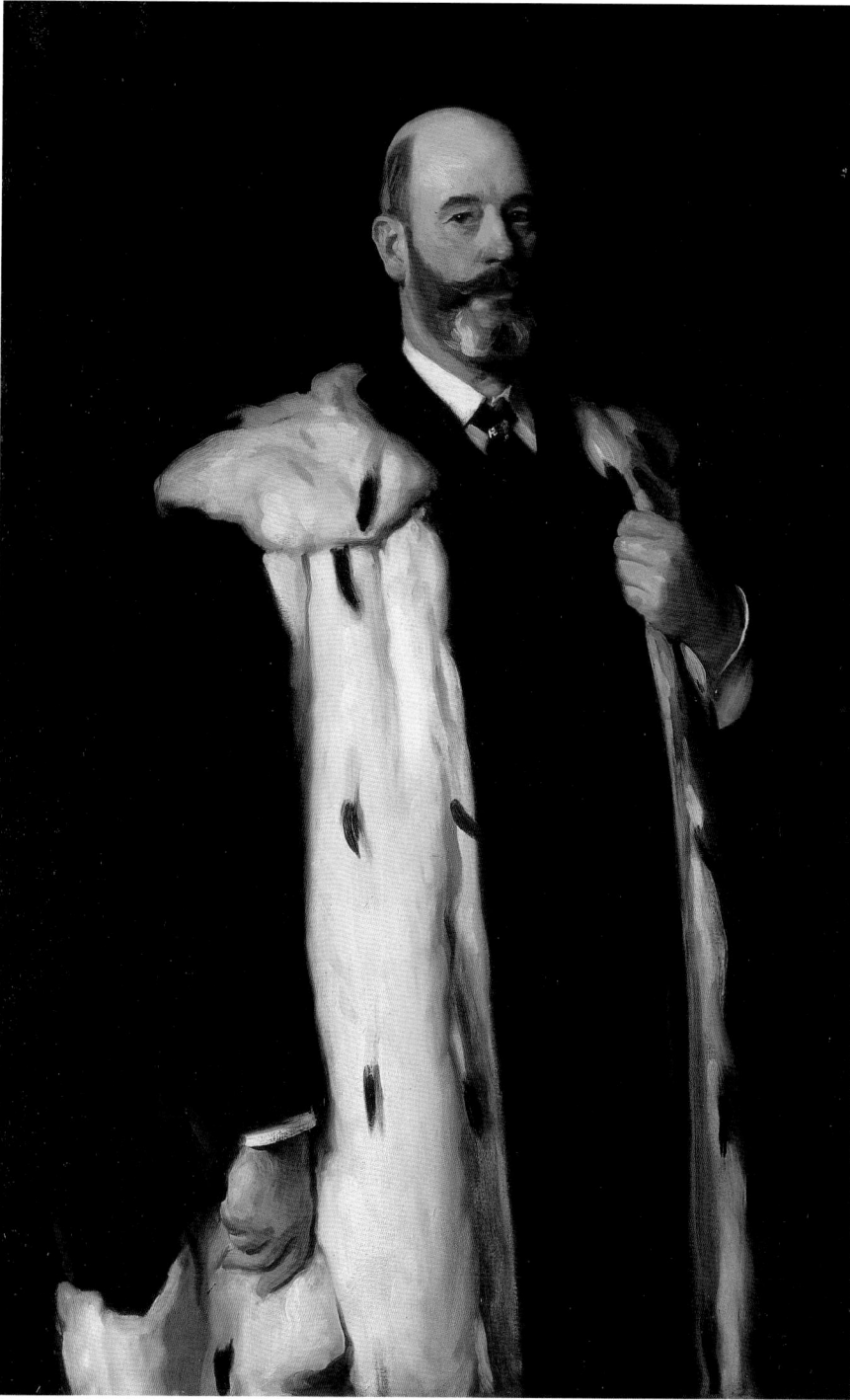

379

archive). Both portraits were accepted as gifts by the club in late 1899 or early 1900 (Harvard Club minutes, 10 December 1900). A surplus was devoted to the purchase of a portrait of James Russell Lowell by Dora Wheeler Keith. The portrait of Choate was painted in Sargent's Tite Street studio following Choate's appointment as US ambassador to London.

Edward S. Martin's *Life of Joseph Hodges Choate* (2 vols New York, 1920), based chiefly on Choate's letters, records his seeing Sargent's portrait of the Honourable Pauline Astor (no. 357) at the Guildhall exhibition in London in 1900 (vol. 2, p. 135); his sitting opposite Sargent's 'fine portrait' of the Wyndham sisters (no. 368) at the Royal Academy dinner of 1900 (vol. 2, p. 139); and his

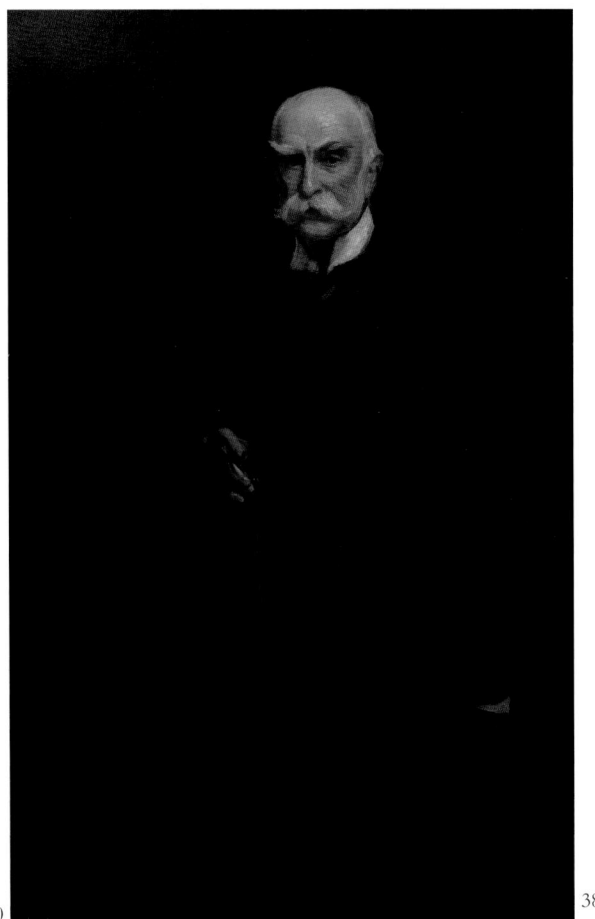

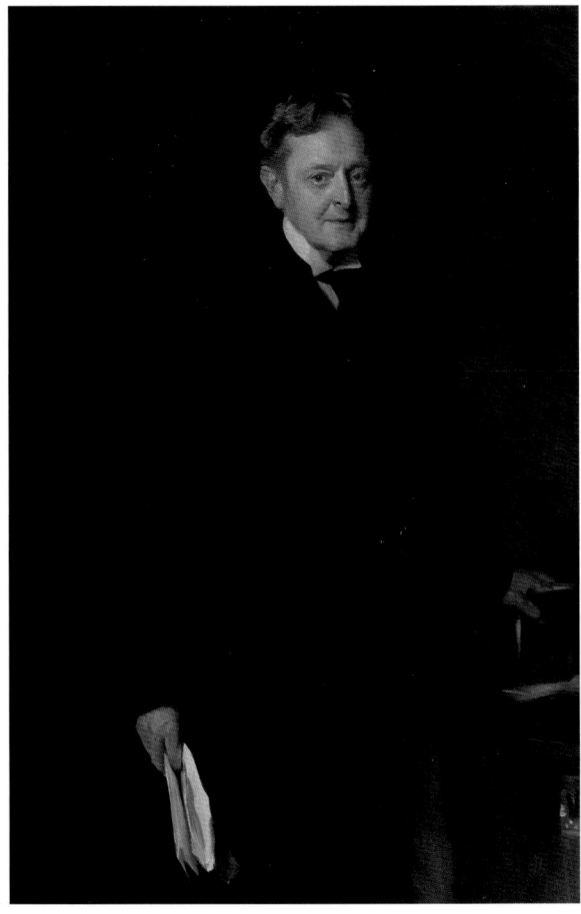

380

381

letter to his wife of 30 December 1901 from Biltmore, describes the house as a living monument to its architect, Richard Morris Hunt, whom Sargent had painted in 1895 (no. 319) (vol. 2, p. 206).

A 1905 drawing of Choate by Sargent hangs in the Choate residence, Naumkeag, Stockbridge, Massachusetts, the house designed for Choate by McKim, Mead & White, 1885–6.

The principal archival sources for this volume, other than those held in private or family collections, are as follows:

American Architectural Archives: Diary of Catharine Clinton Howland Hunt.

Archives of American Art, Smithsonian Institution, Washington, D.C.: Dwight Blaney Papers; Dennis M. Bunker letters; Ferargil Galleries records; letters from Sargent to Mrs Hunter; Macbeth Gallery Papers; Milch Gallery Papers; Francis Davis Millet and Millet family papers; Charles Jackson Paine Papers; Dora Wheeler Keith Papers; John Singer Sargent Collection; Misc. MSS Sargent.
   Where material is available on microfilm, the relevant roll and frame numbers have been cited. Unmicrofilmed material is in the Archives of American Art, Washington, D.C.

Archives Nationale, Paris: letter from Sargent to directeur des beaux-arts, Musée du Luxembourg.

Archivos del Prado, Museo del Prado, Madrid: Libros de Registro: Los copistas (1887–95) and (1903).

Bancroft Library, University of California, Los Angeles: Julie H. Heyneman Papers.

Biblioteca Marucelliana, Florence: letters from Sargent to Carlo Placci.

Biltmore House archive, Asheville, North Carolina: letters from Sargent to George Washington Vanderbilt.

Bodelian Library, Oxford, Department of Western Manuscripts: Lewis Family Papers

Boston Athenaeum, Boston, Massachusetts: Sargent Papers: correspondence between Sargent and members of the Curtis and Fairchild families, Thomas A. Fox Papers and miscellaneous correspondence.

British Library, London, Department of Manuscripts: letters from Sargent to Sir Edgar Vincent. Letters from Sir Edgar Vincent to Lady Vincent.

Boston Public Library: correspondence relating to the Boston Public Library mural contracts and commission.

Bryn Mawr College, Bryn Mawr, Pennsylvania: M. Carey Thomas Papers.

Carnegie Institute archives, Pittsburgh: letter from Sargent to Augusta Saint-Gaudens.

Dartmouth College Library, Hanover, New Hampshire: Lucia Fairchild Fuller Papers; Henry James Letters; letters from Sargent to Augustus Saint-Gaudens.

Folger Shakespeare Library, Washington, D.C.: letters from Sargent to Ada Rehan and one letter from Sargent to Catharine Lasell Whitin.

Frick Art Reference Library, New York: diaries of Theodore Robinson. Photographic archive.

Glasgow University Library: letters from Sargent to James McNeill Whistler, Whistler collection.

Grand Central Art Galleries archives, New York: letters from Sargent to Walter Clark.

Harvard Club of New York City: Harvard Club Minutes.

Houghton Library, Harvard University, Cambridge, Massachusetts: letter from Sargent to Henry James; Henry James Papers.

Huntington Library, Art Collections and Botanical Gardens, San Marino, California: letters from Sargent to Mrs J. T. Fields and to W. Graham Robertson.

Isabella Stewart Gardner Museum archives, Boston: letters from Sargent, Dennis Miller Bunker, Ralph Wormeley Curtis and Henry James to Isabella Stewart Gardner.

Knoedler archives, New York: stockbooks and files of M. Knoedler & Co., New York.

Library of Congress, Washington, D. C.: Asher Hind diary; Frederick Law Olmsted Collection.

Massachusetts Historical Society, Boston: diary of Marian Lawrence (Mrs Harold Peabody); Henry Cabot

Lodge Papers; letter from Sargent to Mrs Peter Chardon Brooks; letter from Sargent to Mrs Morton Prince.

Metropolitan Museum of Art, Department of American Painting and Sculpture: letters from Sargent to Mrs Hugh Hammersley, Henry Gurdon Marquand, the Metropolitan Museum of Art.

Millar Library, Colby College, Waterville, Maine: Special Collections, letters from Clementina Anstruther-Thomson to Vernon Lee.

National Academy (formerly National Academy of Design), New York: James Carroll Beckwith Papers.

National Archives of Canada, Ottawa: Lady Troubridge's diary.

National Gallery of Scotland archives, Edinburgh: letters from Lady Agnew and General Ian Hamilton.

Peninsular & Oriental Steam Navigation Company archives, London: Peninsular & Oriental Steam Navigation Company Minutes.

University Archives, University of Pennsylvania: Dr James William White Papers.

Princeton University Library, Princeton, New Jersey (Firestone Library): Marquand Papers.

Royal Academy Library, London: letters from Sargent to the President and Council of the Royal Academy.

Royal Institute of British Architects, London: Royal Institute of British Architects Minutes.

Scottish Record Office, Edinburgh: Agnew of Lochnaw archives.

Strathclyde Regional Council Archives, Glasgow: Glasgow Corporation Minutes.

Tate Gallery archives, London: letter from Sargent to Edwin Russell.

Witt Library, London: photographic archive.

Worcester Art Museum archives: letters from Sargent to Francis Henshaw Dewey.

AAA   Archives of American Art, Smithsonian Institution, Washington, D.C.

CC   Special Collections, The Millar Library, Colby College, Waterville, Maine.

DCL   Dartmouth College Library, Hanover, New Hampshire.

ES   Emily Sargent.

FARL   Frick Art Reference Library, New York.

GCAG   Grand Central Art Galleries, New York.

ISGM   Isabella Stewart Gardner Museum, Boston

JSS   John Singer Sargent

McKibbin Papers   David McKibbin's index cards for each painting, his correspondence with sitters, collectors, dealers and institutions, Sargent catalogue raisonné archive.

MFA   Museum of Fine Arts, Boston.

MHS   Massachusetts Historical Society, Boston.

MMA   Metropolitan Museum of Art, New York.

ND   National Academy (formerly National Academy of Design, New York).

NPG   London National Portrait Gallery, London.

NYHS   New-York Historical Society.

VL   Vernon Lee.

232 *Edwin Booth*

PROVENANCE: Commissioned for The Players, New York; The Players, New York to 2002; Private Collection.

EXHIBITIONS: New York, MMA, 1926, no. 25.

LITERATURE: *Boston Evening Transcript* (27 January 1890), p. 6; Aldrich 1891, pp. 328–9; William Winter, *Life and Art of Edwin Booth*, London, 1893, p. 265, ill. frontis.; Grossman 1894, pp. 103–4, 110–11; Dixon 1899, p. 118; Meynell 1903, n.p. ill.; Van Dyke 1903, p. 36; Harper 1912, pp. 466–7; Van Dyke 1919, p. 259; Mrs Thomas Bailey Aldrich, *Crowding Memories*, London, 1921, pp. 265–7; Downes 1925, pp. 31–2, 156; Downes 1926, pp. 31–2, 156; New York 1926, p. 5, ill.; Charteris 1927, pp. 109, 262; Meynell Manson 1927, n.p. ill.; Morris 1930, pp. 231–2; Eleanor Ruggles, *Prince of Players: Edwin Booth*, London, 1953, pp. 284–5; Mount 1955, pp. 161–3, 175, 178, 414–15, 432 (907); 1957 ed., pp. 136–8, 150, 341 (907); 1969 ed., pp. 161–3, 175, 178, 414–15, 432 (907); McKibbin 1956, p. 84; Fairbrother 1986, pp. 157, 158, fig. 37; Olson 1986, pp. 161, 167, 185; David Garrard Lowe, *Stanford White's New York*, New York, 1992, pp. 93, 153, and p. 152, ill.; Boston 1994, p. 73.

233 *Edwin Booth*

PROVENANCE: Given by the artist to Sally Fairchild; her friend, Dorothy Elmhirst; Elmhirst sale, Kende Gallery, New York, 1942; Guy Ayrault; Mrs Milton Rose; M. Schweitzer & Co., New York, 1973; Private Collection.

EXHIBITIONS: Boston 1896, no. 207; Philadelphia 1905, no. 442; Boston, MFA, 1916.

LITERATURE: *Boston Evening Transcript* (27 January 1890), p. 6; Caffin 1903, ill. p. 4107; Van Dyck 1903, ill. p. 34; Downes 1925, pp. 31–2, 156; Downes 1926, pp. 31–2, 156; Charteris 1927, p. 262; Mount 1955, pp. 162, 432 (906); 1957 ed., pp. 138, 341 (906); 1969 ed., pp. 162, 432 (906); McKibbin 1956, p. 84; Fairbrother 1986, pp. 157–8.

234 *La Carmencita*

PROVENANCE: Purchased from the artist by the French state for the Musée du Luxembourg, 1892; Musée du Jeu de Paume, 1922; Musée national d'art moderne, 1946; Musée du Louvre, 1973; Musée d'Orsay, 1982 (R.F. 746).

EXHIBITIONS: New York, SAA, 1890, no. 153, Chicago 1890, no. 151; London, RA, 1891, no. 544; Paris, Salon du Champs de Mars, 1892, no. 926; Paris 1919, no. 46; London, RA, 1926, no. 277; Paris 1963, no. 18; Ostend, *Europa 1900*, 1964, no. 60; Washington 1964, no. 52; Leeds 1979, no. 35; Edinburgh 1997, no. 8.

LITERATURE: 'My Note Book', *Art Amateur*, 22 (May 1890), p. 112; 'The Society of American Artists Exhibition', *Art Amateur*, 23 (June 1890), p. 3; 'American and European Art Notes', *Art Interchange*, XXIV (24 May 1890), p. 176; 'Art Notes', *Art Interchange*, XXV (16 August 1890), p. 61; 'The Fine Arts, The Society of American Artists', *Critic*, 13 (3 May 1890), p. 225; 'Some Portraits in the Exhibition of the Society of American Artists', *Studio*, 5 (24 May 1890), pp. 245–6; 'The Saunterer' *Town Topics*, 23 (3 April 1890), p. 2; 'Fine Art. The Royal Academy. II', *Academy*, XXXIX (16 May 1891), p. 471; 'My Note Book', *Art Amateur*, 25 (July 1891), p. 24; Claude Phillips, 'The Royal Academy and the New Gallery', *Art Journal* (1891), p. 198; 'The Royal Academy', *Athenaeum*, no. 3314 (2 May 1891), p. 577; *Black and White*, 1 (1891), p. 461; 'The Royal Academy III', *Graphic*, XLIII (23 May 1891), p. 590; Lionel G. Robinson, 'The Royal Academy Exhibition', *Illustrated London News*, XCVIII (2 May 1891), p. 573; M. H. Spielmann, 'Current Art. The Royal Academy, 1891. – II', *Magazine of Art*, (1891), p. 254; 'The Royal Academy', *Pall Mall Gazette*, LII (2 May 1891), p. 3; 'The Picture Galleries', *Saturday Review*, LXXI (23 May 1891), p. 621; 'Art. The Royal Academy. [First Notice]', *Spectator*, 66 (2 May 1891), pp. 625–6; 'The Royal Academy. (First Notice)', *The Times* (2 May 1891), p. 14; 'Art Gossip', *Art Interchange*, XXVI (6 June 1891), p. 179; 'Illustrations in the Magazines', *Art Interchange*, XXVII (July 1891), p. 7; Theodore Child, 'The Salon of the Champ de Mars', *Art Amateur*, 27 (July 1892), p. 27; 'Infallibility in Art', *Art Amateur*, 28 (December 1892), p. 3; *Art Journal* (1892), p. 273; Gustave Geffroy, *La Vie Artistique*, Paris 1893, pp. 313–14; 'Paris Letter', *Art Interchange*, XXXI (August 1893), p. 35; Fowler 1894, p. 688; 'The London Letter', *Art Amateur*, 38 (January 1898), p. 31; Baldry 1900, I, pp. 21; Baldry 1900, II, ill. p. 115; Léonce Bénédite, *Le Musée nationale du Luxembourg, Catalogue raisonné et illustré des peintures, sculptures, dessins, gravures en médailles et sur pierre fines et objets d'art divers des écoles contemporaines*, Paris 1900, p. 96; Caffin 1903, ill. p. 4112; Cortissoz 1903, pp. 515, 528, 532; Meynell 1903, n.p. ill.; Van Dyke 1903, p. 36 *L'Art et la couleur: Les Maîtres contemporains*, Paris, 1907, no. 12; McSpadden 1907, p. 291, ill. facing p. 290; Brinton 1908, p. 164; Fiske 1908, ill. p. 70; Wood 1909, pl. II; *Letters of George Meredith*, vol. 2, 1912, p. 455; Roof 1917, pp. 156–8; Van Dyke 1919, p. 261, ill. facing p. 262; Cortissoz 1924, pp. 345–6; Starkweather 1924, pp. 6–7, ill. p. 6; Downes 1925, pp. 31–2, 160–1, ill.; Jacomb-Hood 1925, p. 313; Blanche 1926, p. 560; Downes 1926, pp. 31–2, 160–1, ill.; London

1926, p. 42; *RA Ill. 1926*, p. 1; *Revue de L'Art*, 49 (1926), p. 15, ill.; Charteris 1927, pp. 109–13, 116, 263; Meynell Manson 1927, n.p. ill.; Rilla Evelyn Jackman, *American Arts*, Chicago, 1928, pl. XCVII; Robertson 1931, pp. 244–6; Mount 1955, pp. 150, 164–74, 204–5, 433 (9019); 1957 ed., pp. 127, 139–48, 168, 341 (9019); 1969 ed., pp. 150, 164–74, 204–5, 433 (9019); Denys Sutton, 'The Luminous Point', *Apollo* (March 1967), p. 221; Cline 1970, vol. II, p. 1104; Ormond 1970, pp. 43, 246–7, pl. 63; Burke 1980, pp. 87–9; Fairbrother 1982, pp. 30–2, ill. fig. 4; Ratcliff 1982, pp. 121, 122, 124, 157, 175–6, 183, pl. 173 (colour); Fairbrother 1986, pp. 161–5, 168, 170, 172, 176, 185, 324, fig. 41; Olson 1986, pp. 73, 162–3 and n., 177–8, 184; Reynolds in Hills *et al.* 1986, p. 159, fig. 106; Robert Rosenblum, *Paintings in the Musée d'Orsay*, New York, 1989, p. 62, ill. p. 622 (colour); Isabelle Compin, Geneviève Lacambre and Anne Roquebert, *Catalogue sommaire illustré des peintures du Musée d'Orsay*, vol. 2, Paris, 1990, p. 415, ill.; Susan Grant, 'Les achats de tableaux américains pour les collections publiques françaises (1879–1900)', *Le Commerce de l'art sous la direction de Laurence Bertrand Dorleac*, Bordeaux, 1992, pp. 179, 192–3, 196; Fairbrother 1994, pp. 76–7, 79, ill. p. 77; Edinburgh 1997, pp. 71–2, pl. 4 (colour); London 1998, pp. 32, 71, 136, 139, 141, fig. 33; Prettejohn 1998, p. 37; Fairbrother 2000, p. 29; Herdrick and Weinberg 2000, pp. 124–5, 207.

235 *La Carmencita*

PROVENANCE: Presented by the artist to the Musée du Luxembourg, 1892; entered the Musée du Jeu de Paume, 1930; then the Musée national d'art moderne; transferred to the Louvre, 1977; Musée du Louvre, Paris, Département des arts graphiques (R.F. 40.110).

EXHIBITIONS: Paris, Musée du Louvre, Cabinet des dessins, *De Burne-Jones à Bonnard, Dessins provenant du musée national d'art moderne*, 28 March–29 May 1977, no. 87; Blérancourt, Musée de la Coopération Franco-Américaine, Château de Blérancourt, *Dessins Américains des collections nationals de 1760 à 1945*, 15 June–30 September 1991, no. 15.

LITERATURE: McKibbin 1956, p. 87.

236 *La Carmencita*

PROVENANCE: The artist (possibly in the sitter's possession for a period of time); the artist's sale, Christie's, London, 24 July 1925, lot 119, as 'A Sketch of Carmencita singing, in white dress, with red rose in her hair', bt in by Mrs Thayer for the artist's sisters; Violet Ormond to 1955; her son, Jean-Louis Ormond to 1986; Coe Kerr

Gallery, New York, 1987; Mr and Mrs Harry Spiro.

EXHIBITIONS: Boston 1899, no. 69, as 'Sketch of *Carmencita* Singing'; London, Carfax, 1903, no. 29, as 'Carmencita'; Edinburgh 1928, no. 207; New York 1989, no. 39, ill.

LITERATURE: Boston 1899, p. 17; Christie's 1925, p. 17; Downes 1925, p. 161; Downes 1926, p. 161; Charteris 1927, pp. 109, 262; *Sargent Trust List* [1927], p. 32. Hartrick 1939, p. 127; Mount 1955, p. 432 (909); 1957 ed., p. 341 (909); 1969 ed., p. 433 (909); McKibbin 1956, p. 87.

237   *La Carmencita*

PROVENANCE: Early history unknown at present; Salvatore D'Amico; Mark Borghi, New York, 1996; Adelson Galleries, Inc., New York, 1998; Private Collection.

EXHIBITIONS: Chicago 1911, no. 324, as 'Sketch of Carmencita dancing'.

238   *Dr Carroll Dunham*

PROVENANCE: Commissioned by Louis Butler McCagg; apparently destroyed.

EXHIBITIONS: New York, SAA, 1898, no. 74, as 'Portrait of Dr C. D.'; Boston 1899, no. 29, as 'Portrait of Dr C. D.'; Philadelphia 1899, no. 70.

LITERATURE: Boston 1899, p. 8; Downes 1925, p. 154; Downes 1926, p. 154; Charteris 1927, p. 266; Mount 1955, p. 433 (9037); 1957 ed., p. 342 (9037); 1969 ed., p. 437 (9037); McKibbin 1956, p. 86.

239   *Beatrice Goelet*

PROVENANCE: Mr and Mrs Robert Goelet; their son, Robert Walton Goelet, to 1941; Private Collection.

EXHIBITIONS: New York, SAA, 1891, no. 199, as 'Portrait of Miss Beatrice Goelet'; New York, NAD, 1895, no. 267, as 'Beatrice'; Cambridge, Massachusetts, Fogg Art Museum, 1946; San Francisco 1959, no. 9, ill.

LITERATURE: Malcolm Bell, 'My Note Book. The Society of American Artists', *Art Amateur*, 25 (June 1891), p. 5; G[leason] W[hite], 'Art in New York' *Artist*, 12 (August 1891), p. 229; 'Art Gossip', *Art Interchange*, XXVI (9 May 1891), p. 145; *Boston Evening Transcript* (4 June 1891), p. 6; 'What the Artists Think of Sargent's "Beatrice"', *Harper's Weekly*, 35 (9 May 1891), pp. 346–7; M. G. van Rensselaer, 'Open letters. American Artist Series', *Century Magazine*, 43 (1892), p. 798, ill. p. 772; *New York Times* (26 April 1891), p. 6; 'Paris Letter', *Art Interchange*, 31 (August 1893), p. 35; Fowler 1894, p. 688; 'New York Portrait Loan Exhibition', *Art Amateur*, 34 (December 1895), p. 3; *New York Times* (30 October 1895), p. 4; 'Pittsburgh's Picture Exhibition', *Art Amateur*, 35 (December 1896), p. 137; Coffin 1896, p. 178, ill. p. 174; Dixon 1899, p. 118; Downes 1900, p. 172; Harrison S. Morris, 'American Portraiture of Children', *Scribner's Magazine*, XXX (1901), pp. 650–1; Caffin 1903a, p. 443, as 'Beatrix'; Cortissoz 1903, pp. 515, 522, 528; Van Dyke 1903, p. 39; Fiske 1908, p. 85; 'Cost and Value of "Sargents"',

Literary Digest, 45 (7 December 1912), p. 1065; Van Dyke 1919, p. 262; Mechlin 1924, pp. 177, 185, 188; Starkweather 1924, ill. p. 4; Downes 1925, pp. 36, 161–3, ill. facing p. 140; Downes 1926, pp. 36, 161–3, ill. facing p. 140; Charteris 1927, pp. 109–10, 262; Meynell Manson 1927, n.p. ill.; Mount 1955, pp. 167, 433 (9013); 1957 ed., pp. 142, 341 (9013); 1969 ed., pp. 167, 440 (9013); McKibbin 1956, p. 98; Ratcliff 1982, p. 125; Fairbrother 1986, pp. 170, 171–4, 185, 190, 205 nn. 46, 53, fig. 47; Reynolds in Hills *et al.* 1986, pp. 148, 151, 159; London 1998, p. 32, fig. 34 (colour); Fairbrother 2000, p. 220 n. 11.

240   *Richard Aldrich McCurdy*

PROVENANCE: By family descent to Dr Thaddeus Hoyt Ames; Elizabeth Marsh Ames (the chronology of descent has not been definitively established); Mr and Mrs Richard McCurdy Ames; Sotheby's, New York, 30 April–3 May 1980, lot 368B; Hirschl & Adler, New York to 1981; Private Collection; Charles Hosmer Morse Museum of American Art, Winter Park, Florida.

LITERATURE: Mount 1955, pp. 160–1, 433 (9038); 1957 ed., pp. 136–7, 342 (9038); 1969 ed., pp. 160–1, 446 (9038); McKibbin 1956, p. 107; Fairbrother 1986, pp. 154–5, 295, fig. 36; Olson 1986, p. 137 n.

241   *Mrs Thomas Lincoln Manson Jr*

PROVENANCE: Mr and Mrs Thomas Lincoln Manson Jr; their daughter, Mrs Kiliaen Van Rensselaer; sold American Art Association, Anderson Art Galleries, New York, 14 December 1933, lot 67; Julius Weitzner by 1934; Minneapolis Institute of Arts, Minnesota, 1938; Huntington Hartford; sold 1968 Hirschl & Adler, New York; bt Honolulu Academy of Arts, 1969 (3584.1).

EXHIBITIONS: London, RA, 1891, no. 1097; New York, NAD, 1894, no. 258; Boston 1899, no. 30; Buffalo 1901, no. 31, as 'Portrait'; New York, GCAG, 1924, no. 50; College Art Association, *Figure Painting from American Ancestors to Our Day*, 1934, no. 20; Palm Beach 1959, no. 9; New York, Hirschl & Adler, *Twenty-five American Masterpieces*, 23 April–11 May 1968, no. 20.

LITERATURE: 'Fine Art. The Royal Academy. II', *Academy*, XXXIX (16 May 1891), p. 471; 'Portraits', *Art Journal* (1891), p. 198; 'The Royal Academy', *Pall Mall Gazette*, LII (2 May 1891), p. 3; 'Portraits at the Royal Academy', *Saturday Review*, LXXI (13 June 1891), p. 715; 'Art. The Royal Academy. [First Notice.]', *Spectator*, 66 (2 May 1891), pp. 625–6; 'The Royal Academy. (First Notice)', *The Times* (2 May 1891), p. 14; 'Art Notes and News', *Art Amateur*, 31 (November 1894), p. 141; Coffin 1896, p. 178; Dixon 1899, pp. 118, 119; *Art and Progress*, 4 (June 1913), pp. 984, 988; Mechlin 1924, p. 177; New York 1924, p. 14, ill. p. 30; Downes 1925, pp. 36, 163; Downes 1926, pp. 36, 163; Charteris 1927, pp. 116, 264; *Art Digest*, 13 (1939), p. 21; *Bulletin of the Minneapolis Institute of Arts*, 28 (7 January 1939), pp. 2–4, ill.; Mount 1955, p. 186, 433 (9033); 1957 ed., p. 342

(9033); 1969 ed., pp. 186, 445 (9033); McKibbin 1956, p. 108; *Gazette des beaux-arts* (February 1970), p. 388, ill. no. 381; Honolulu Academy of Arts, *Calendar News* (September 1969), ill. cover; *Apollo*, CIX (February 1979), ill. p. 70; New York 1980, Checklist; Fairbrother 1986, pp. 169–70, 188, fig. 45; Honolulu Academy of Arts, *Selected Works*, 1990, p. 223, ill. (colour).

242   *Mrs Thomas Lincoln Manson Jr*

PROVENANCE: Cronyn and Lowndes Gallery, New York, 1933; J. J. Haverty and Mary E. Haverty; presented by them to the Atlanta Art Association and High Museum of Art, Atlanta, Georgia, 1949 (49.30).

LITERATURE: 'In all Mediums: Paintings, Concrete and Abstract', *New York Herald Tribune* (24 December 1933), p. 10, ill.; McKibbin 1956, p. 108; Mount 1957, p. 342 (9044) dated 1890; 1969 ed., p. 445 (9044), dated 1890; New York 1980, Checklist.

243   *Homer Saint-Gaudens and his Mother*

PROVENANCE: Augustus Saint-Gaudens to 1907; his widow, Augusta Saint-Gaudens, to 1926; her son, Homer Saint-Gaudens, to 1932; purchased by the Carnegie Institute, Pittsburgh, 1932 (32.1).

EXHIBITIONS: Philadelphia, Art Club, 1890, no. 65, as 'Portrait – Son of Mr Saint-Gaudens'; Paris, Salon du Champs de Mars, 1891, no. 850 as 'Portrait de jeune garçon'; New York, SAA, 1892, no. 191, as 'Portrait of a Lady and Boy'; Chicago 1893, no. 881 (revised catalogue no. 686); Pittsburgh 1897–8, no. 198; Boston 1899, no. 38; Buffalo 1901, no. 26, as 'Portrait of a Boy'; New York 1903, no. 214; Buffalo 1924, no. 185; New York, GCAG, 1924, no. 45; Boston, MFA, 1925, no. 44 (revised catalogue no. 46); San Francisco 1926–7, no. 165, as 'Portrait of a Boy'; Cleveland 1936, no. 369; New York, NAD, 1939, Special Exhibition, no. 249, as 'Portrait of a Boy', ill.; Pittsburgh, Carnegie Institute, *The Patrons Art Fund Paintings*, 1940, no. 9; San Francisco, Palace of Fine Arts, Golden Gate International Exposition, *Art-Official Catalogue*, 1940, no. 1217; New York, Portraits, Inc., 1947, *The Family, 1847–1947*, no cat.; Columbus Gallery of Fine Arts, Ohio, *Paintings from the Pittsburgh Collection*, 1952, no cat.; Grand Rapids 1955, no. 25; Pittsburgh 1957, no. 105; Pittsburgh, Carnegie Institute, *Retrospective Exhibition of Paintings from Previous Internationals*, 1958–9, no. 8; Palm Beach 1959, no. 6; Art Gallery of Toronto, *American Paintings, 1865–1905*, 1961 (travelling exhibition), p. 383, no. 61; Bonn, Rheinisches Landesmuseum (organized by the Baltimore Museum of Art), *Two Hundred Years of American Art, 1776–1976*, 1976–7, no. 29.

LITERATURE: 'The Philadelphia Art Club Exhibition', *Art Amateur*, 24 (December 1890), p. 4; 'Art Notes', *Art Interchange*, 25 (20 December 1890), p. 203; Cecil Nicholson, 'The French Salons – III', *Academy*, 39 (16 May

1891), p. 472; 'The Salons', *Art Journal*, (1891), p. 248; 'The New Salon', *Black & White*, 1 (1891), p. 574; *Revue des deux mondes*, 106 (1891), p. 201; 'The Society of American Artists', *Art Amateur*, 27 (June 1892), p. 3; 'The Fourteenth Exhibition of the Society of American Artists', *Harper's Weekly* (14 May 1892), p. 469, ill.; Walton 1893–5, p. 17; J. Fairman, *Essays on Art*, Pittsburgh, 1898, p. 45; *Art Amateur*, 40 (April 1899), p. 95; 'The Sargent Exhibition at Copley Hall, Boston', *Artist*, 24 (March 1899), p. xlv; Harrison S. Morris, 'American Portraiture of Children', *Scribner's Magazine*, XXX (1901), p. 651; Caffin 1902, p. 64; Caffin 1903, ill. p. 4103; Caffin 1903a, p. 446; Cortissoz 1903, p. 528; McSpadden 1907, pp. 288–9; Fiske 1908, p. 85; Cortissoz 1913, p. 232; Saint-Gaudens 1913, pp. 348, 351; Bryant 1923, pp. 4–5; Berry 1924, pp. 103, 106, ill. p. 105; Mechlin 1924, pp. 177, 185; New York 1924, p. 14, ill. p. 43; Boston 1925, p. 6; Boston 1925a, p. 6; Downes 1925, p. 171; Downes 1926, p. 171; F. J. Mather Jr, *Estimates in Art: Series 2*, 1931, pp. 240–1; J. O'Connor Jr, 'Sargent's Portrait of a Boy – Patrons Art Fund Purchase', *Carnegie Magazine*, 6 (April 1932), pp. 8–9; 'Carnegie Buys Famous Sargent', *Art News*, 30 (7 May 1932), pp. 194–5; 'An Artist's Document Bought for Carnegie', *Art Digest*, 6 (15 May 1932), p. 12; Saint-Gaudens 1941, p. 40; Mount 1955, pp. 175–6, 180–1, 287, 433 (9028); 1957 ed., pp. 235, 341 (9028); 1969 ed., pp. 175–6, 180–1, 287, 451 (9028); McKibbin 1956, p. 121; Homer Saint-Gaudens, 'Looking Backward', *American Artist*, 21 (December 1957), pp. 54, 69–72; F. A. Myers, 'Portrait of a Boy', *Carnegie Magazine*, 41 (March 1967), p. 105; Louise Hall Tharp, *Augustus Saint-Gaudens and the Gilded Era*, Boston, 1968, pp. 241, 243; Donald Miller, 'Inspired Friendship: Sargent and Saint-Gaudens', *Carnegie Magazine*, 53 (April 1979), pp. 4–11; New York 1980, Checklist; Fairbrother 1986, pp. 170–1, 185, 204 nn. 43 and 44, 214, fig. 46; Gerdts in Hills *et al.* 1986, p. 144 n. 50; Miller 1986, p. 7; Olson 1986, p. 168; Reynolds in Hills *et al.* 1986, p. 159, fig. 108; Diana Strazdes, *American Paintings and Sculpture to 1945 in the Carnegie Museum of Art*, New York, 1991, pp. 419–20.

244   Benjamin P. Kissam

PROVENANCE: The sitter; Mrs Arthur C. Train to 1945; her daughter, Mrs Boris Samsonoff; sold to the Reverend Thomas Barry, 1982; Barridoff Galleries, Portland, Maine, 4 August 1999, lot 229; Private Collection.

EXHIBITIONS: Boston 1899, no. 40, as 'The Late Benjamin P. Kissam'; Boston, MFA, 1925, no. 2 (revised catalogue no. 54).

LITERATURE: Boston 1899, p. 10; Boston 1925, p. 3, dated 1875; Boston 1925a, p. 7, dated 1890; Downes 1925, p. 156; Downes 1926, p. 156; Charteris 1927, pp. 39, 257, dated 1875; Arthur Train, 'The Portrait That Sargent Forgot', *Atlantic Monthly*, 129 (1929), pp. 663–4; Mount 1955, p. 433 (9039); 1957 ed., p. 342 (9039); 1969 ed., p. 443 (9039); McKibbin 1956, p. 104; Fairbrother 1986, pp. 113, 138 n. 40.

245   Mrs Hamilton McKown Twombly

PROVENANCE: The sitter; her daughter, Mrs W. A. M. Burden; presented by her to Columbia University, New York (Twombly-Burden Room), 1964.

EXHIBITIONS: New York, SAA Retrospective, 1892, no. 275, as 'Portrait'; New York, NAD, 1894, no. 264, as 'Mrs Hamilton McK. Twombly'; Boston, MFA, 1925, no. 50 (revised catalogue no. 52); New York 1943, no. 37; New York, NYHS, 1945, ill. frontis.

LITERATURE: *New York Times* (3 December 1892), p. 4; 'The Society of American Artists: Retrospective Exhibition', *Art Amateur*, 28 (January 1893), p. 44; 'Art Gossip', *Art Interchange*, XXX (February 1893), p. 39; Baldry 1900, I, ill. p. 12; Boston 1925, p. 7; Boston 1925a, p. 7; Downes 1925, p. 169; Downes 1926, p. 169; Charteris 1927, p. 263; Mount 1955, pp. 167, 433 (9029); 1957 ed., pp. 142, 341 (9029); 1969 ed., pp. 167, 454 (9029); McKibbin 1956, p. 127 (dated 1889); Fairbrother 1986, pp. 168–70.

246   Cornelius Vanderbilt

PROVENANCE: The sitter to 1899; his daughter, Gladys (Countess Széchényi), to 1965; her daughter, Gladys (first, Countess of Winchilsea and Nottingham; secondly Mrs Arthur Talbot Peterson), to 1978; untraced.

EXHIBITIONS: New York, NAD (Annual), 1891, no. 388 as 'Portrait'.

LITERATURE: '"The Academy" Exhibition', *Art Amateur*, 24 (May 1891), p. 142; McKibbin 1956, p. 127, dated 1895; Mount 1957, p. 344 (9512), dated 1895; 1969 ed., p. 454 (9512), dated 1895; Duveneck 1970, p. 147; Fairbrother 1986, p. 138 n. 40; Auchincloss 1989, p. 38.

247   George Washington Vanderbilt

PROVENANCE: The sitter to 1914; his widow, Mrs Edith Stuyvesant Vanderbilt, later Mrs Peter Goelet Gerry, to 1958; the Biltmore Company, Biltmore House, Asheville, North Carolina.

EXHIBITIONS: New York, SAA, 1890, no. 154 or 155, both listed as 'Portrait'; Washington 1916–17, no. 214, as 'The Late George Vanderbilt'; Philadelphia 1917, no. 275.

LITERATURE: *New York Daily Tribune* (26 April 1890), p. 7; 'Society of American Artists', *New York Times* (28 April 1890), p. 4; 'The Society of American Artists', *Critic*, 16 (3 May 1890), p. 225; 'American and European Art Notes', *Art Interchange*, 24 (24 May 1890), p. 176; 'The Society of American Artists Exhibition', *Art Amateur*, 23 (June 1890), p. 3; Downes 1925, pp. 39, 176; Downes 1926, pp. 39, 176; Mount 1955, pp. 212, 435 (957), dated 1895; 1957 ed., pp. 176, 343 (957); 1969 ed., pp. 212, 454 (957); McKibbin 1956, p. 127, dated 1895; New York 1980, Checklist; Ratcliff 1982, p. 141; Fairbrother 1986, pp. 159, 160–1, fig. 40; Dorment and MacDonald 1994, p. 280; Fairbrother 2000, p. 161.

248   Julian Alden Weir

PROVENANCE: The sitter; Mrs G. Page Ely (*née* Caroline Weir); untraced.

LITERATURE: McKibbin 1956, p. 129; Mount 1957 ed., p. 342 (9045); 1969 ed., p. 455 (9045); Dorothy Weir Young, *The Life and Letters of J. Alden Weir*, New Haven, 1960, pl. 36.

249   Grace Woodhouse

PROVENANCE: The sitter's father, Lorenzo Guernsey Woodhouse; possibly his nephew, Lorenzo E. Woodhouse; the sitter's daughter, Olga, Mrs Sidney C. Graves by 1956; presented by her to the National Gallery of Art, Washington, D.C., 1962 (1962. 6.1).

EXHIBITIONS: New York, NAD (Annual), 1891, no. 30, as 'Portrait'; Museum of the Brooklyn Institute of Arts and Sciences, 1909–13 (on loan).

LITERATURE: '"The Academy" Exhibition', *Art Amateur*, 24 (May 1891), pp. 142, 145; Mount 1955, p. 433 (9020); 1957 ed., p. 341 (9020); 1969 ed., p. 450 (9020); McKibbin 1956, p. 120; Washington, National Gallery of Art, *American Paintings: An Illustrated Catalogue*, 1980, p. 220, ill.; Douglas Greenwood, *Art in Embassies; 25 Years at the U.S. Department of State 1964–1989*, Washington, D.C., 1989, p. 16, ill (colour); New York 1980, Checklist; Torchia 1998, pp. 111, 113, ill. p. 112 (colour).

250   Mrs Edward Davis and her Son, Livingston

PROVENANCE: Mr and Mrs Edward Livingston Davis to 1916; their daughter, Mrs A. Winsor Weld, to 1918; Livingston Davis, to 1932; his widow, Mrs Livingston Davis, to 1969; sold Sotheby Parke-Bernet, New York, 19–20 March, 1969, lot 74; Schweitzer Gallery, New York, 1969; James Graham and Sons, New York, 1969; bt Los Angeles Museum of Art (Frances and Armand Hammer Purchase Fund), 1969 (M.69.18).

EXHIBITIONS: New York, NAD (Autumn), 1890, no. 252; Philadelphia 1891, no. 257, as 'Portrait Group'; Boston, SAA, 1891, no. 169; Worcester 1891, no. 119; Chicago 1893, no. 875 (no. 809 revised catalogue) as 'Mother and Child'; Boston 1895, no. 257; Worcester 1898, no. 76 as 'Portrait'; Boston 1899, no. 5; Worcester 1909, no. 17 as 'Portrait'; on deposit at the Museum of Fine Arts, Boston, on several occasions: 1913, no. 757; 1916, no. 573; 1918, no. 480; 1919, no. 413; 1920, no. 340; 1921, no. 420; 1922, no. 273; Boston, MFA, 1916; New York, GCAG, 1924, no. 20; Boston, MFA, 1925, no. 53 (no. 56 in revised catalogue); New York, MMA, 1926, no. 26; Boston 1956, no. 20; Memphis, Brooks Memorial Art Gallery, *The Armand Hammer Collection*, 1969, no. 57; Washington, D.C., Smithsonian Institution, Museum of Natural History, and San Francisco, California Palace of the Legion of Honor, *The Armand Hammer Collection*, 1970–1, no. 63; Los Angeles County Museum of Art (travelling exhibition), *The Armand Hammer Collection*, 1972–3, no. 54;

Caracas, Venezuela, Museo de Belles Artes, and Lima, Peru, Museo de Arte Italiano, *La Colección de Armand Hammer*, 1975, no. 52; Mexico City, Palacio de Bellas Artes (travelling exhibition), *La Collección de Armand Hammer*, 1977, no. 52; Oslo, Norway, National Gallery of Norway, and Stockholm, Sweden, National Museum, *The Armand Hammer Collection*, 1978–9, no. 57; Houston, Museum of Fine Arts, *The Armand Hammer Collection: Four Centuries of Masterpieces*, 1979–80, no. 60; Los Angeles County Museum of Art, *Selections from the Armand Hammer Collection*, 1980, no. 58; Washington, D.C., Corcoran Gallery of Art (travelling exhibition), *The Armand Hammer Collection: Five Centuries of Masterpieces*, 1980–1, no. 58; Los Angeles 1981, no. 53; Huntington, West Virginia, Huntington Galleries, *The Armand Hammer Collection: Five Centuries of Masterpieces*, 1982, no. 58; Washington, D.C., National Gallery of Art, *American Paintings from the Armand Hammer Collection: An Inaugural Celebration*, 1985, unnumbered; New York and Chicago 1986; London 1998, no. 49.

LITERATURE: 'Art Notes', *Art Interchange*, XXV, New York (20 December 1890), pp. 201, 202; 'A Distinguished Artist: Mr John S. Sargent at the Worcester Club', *Worcester Evening Gazette* (4 June 1890), p. 4; 'Personal', *Worcester Daily Spy* (5 June 1890), p. 8; *Worcester Daily Spy* (21 June 1890), p. 8; 'The National Academy of Design', *Art Amateur*, 24 (January 1891), p. 31; Mariana Griswold van Rensselaer, 'Another Portrait by Sargent', *Harper's Weekly*, 35 (19 December 1891), p. 1012; 'The Pennsylvania Academy Exhibition', *Independent* (26 February 1891), cutting in the Pennsylvania Academy of the Fine Arts archives; 'A Fine Collection', *Worcester Evening Gazette* (30 March 1891), p. 4; 'The Loan Exhibition', *Worcester Daily Spy* (1 April 1891), p. 1; *Worcester Daily Spy* (27 April 1891), p. 8; 'American Painting. IV – Whistler, Dannat, Sargent', *Art Amateur*, 29 (November 1893), p. 134; William A. Coffin, 'The Columbian Exposition. – II. The Fine Arts: The United States Section', *Nation*, 57 (10 August 1893), p. 97; 'Portraiture at the Fair by a Portrait Painter', *Art Interchange*, XXXI, New York (October 1893), p. 87; Boston 1899, p. 2; Downes 1900, p. 172; Leila Mechlin, 'A Museum with a Fortune', *Art & Progress*, 1 (1909), p. 17, ill. p. 2; 'John Doe', 'Boston', *American Art News*, XIV (20 May 1916), p. 3; Berry 1924, ill. p. 100; Mechlin 1924, p. 177, ill. p. 184; New York 1924, p. 13, ill. p. 45; Pousette-Dart 1924, p. viii; J. B. Manson, 'Notes on the Works of J. S. Sargent', *Studio*, 90 (1925), p. 81, ill.; Boston 1925, p. 7 (erroneously dated 1891); Boston 1925a, p. 7 (erroneously dated 1891); Downes 1925, pp. 33, 157–8, ill. facing p. 128; Downes 1926, pp. 33, 157–8, ill. facing p. 128; New York 1926, p. 6 (erroneously dated 1891), ill.; Charteris 1927, pp. 109–10, 137, 263; Mount 1955, pp. 183, 433 (9024); 1957 ed., pp. 153, 341 (9024); 1969 ed., pp. 183, 436 (9024); Boston 1956, p. 43, fig. 23; McKibbin 1956, pp. 43, 68, 91, ill. p. 41; *Los Angeles County Museum of Art Annual Report* (1968–9), pp. 17–18, ill.;

Ormond 1970, pp. 43, 246, pl. 61; New York 1980, Checklist; Ratcliff 1982, pp. 124–5, 127, pl. 178; Strickler 1982–3, pp. 22–3; Fairbrother 1986, pp. 166–7, 168, 172, 182, 183, 185, 202–3 n. 33; 205 n. 53, 308; Reynolds in Hills *et al.* 1986, p. 159, ill. facing p. 147; Fairbrother 1994, p. 79, ill. p. 78 (colour); London 1998, p. 141, ill. p. 142 (colour); Prettejohn 1998, p. 56, fig. 32 (colour).

251 *Mrs Francis Henshaw Dewey*

PROVENANCE: The sitter; her daughter, Elizabeth, later Mrs Rochwood Bullock; her daughter, Mary, later Mrs Alden P. Johnson; presented by her to the Worcester Art Museum, 1981 (289).

EXHIBITIONS: Worcester 1891, no. 121; Worcester 1895–6, no. 67 or no. 61, as 'Portrait' (no. 67 in second edition of catalogue; no. 61 in third edition; unlisted in first edition) Worcester 1898, no. 77; Washington 1912, no. 32, as 'Picture of a Lady'; probably Pittsburgh 1913, no. 250, as 'Picture of a Lady'; Worcester 1914, no. 37; Boston, MFA, 1925, no. 51 (revised catalogue no. 53); Stockholm and Copenhagen 1930, no. 85.

LITERATURE: Boston 1925, p. 7; Boston 1925a, p. 7; Downes 1925, p. 159; Downes 1926, p. 159; Charteris 1927, pp. 109, 262; Mount 1955, p. 432 (9010); 1957 ed., p. 341 (9010); 1969 ed., p. 436 (9010); McKibbin 1956, p. 92; Strickler 1982–3, pp. 22–3, fig. 5; Olson 1986, p. 137 n.

252 *Mrs Alexander Hamilton Bullock*

PROVENANCE: The sitter's son, A. G. Bullock; his son, Chandler Bullock; his daughter, Mrs George S. McElroy; Candace McElroy Bahrenburg; presented by the grandchildren of the sitter to the Worcester Art Museum, 1995.

EXHIBITIONS: Worcester 1891, no. 120.

LITERATURE: Mount 1955, p. 433 (9036); 1957 ed., p. 342 (9036); 1969 ed., p. 432 (9036); Boston 1956, p. 43; McKibbin 1956, p. 86; Strickler 1982–3, pp. 22–3, fig. 4.

253 *Katharine Pratt*

PROVENANCE: Presented by the artist to Frederick S. Pratt, 1891; his daughter, Elizabeth, Mrs W. Irving Clark; her son, William I. Clark; presented by him to the Worcester Art Museum, 1983 (36).

EXHIBITIONS: Probably Worcester 1891, no. 123, as 'Out-door portrait sketch'; probably Philadelphia 1896–7, no. 287, as 'Sketch'; probably Worcester 1914, no. 39, as 'Portrait Sketch'.

LITERATURE: Downes 1925, p. 158, as 'Portrait Sketch'; Downes 1926, p. 158, as 'Portrait Sketch'; Mount 1955, p. 433 (9041); 1957 ed., p. 342 (9041); 1969 ed., p. 448 (9041); McKibbin 1956, p. 117; Strickler 1982–3, pp. 24–5, ill.; Fairbrother 1986, p. 179.

254 *Katharine Pratt*

PROVENANCE: Frederick Sumner Pratt to 1924; the sitter, his daughter (d. 1942); purchased from her estate by Vincent Morgan, 1963; given to his wife, the sitter's niece, Mrs Vincent

Morgan; Coe Kerr Gallery, New York, 1987; Peters Corporation, Santa Fe, New Mexico.

EXHIBITIONS: Probably Chicago 1893, no. 880, as 'Portrait' (revised catalogue no. 509); probably Philadelphia 1894–5, no. 5, as 'Portrait'; probably Boston 1895, no. 258; probably Boston 1899, no. 45; probably New York, SAA, 1899, no. 134, as 'Portrait'; probably Washington 1910, as 'Portrait of a Girl'; Boston, MFA, 1916; probably New York, GCAG, 1924, no. 54; probably Boston, MFA, 1925, no. 49 (revised catalogue no. 51).

LITERATURE: Probably Boston 1899, p. 12; W. H. Downes, 'Mr Sargent's Paintings', *Boston Evening Transcript* (10 May 1916), Part Two, p. 12; probably New York 1924, p. 14; probably Boston 1925, p. 7; probably Boston 1925a, p. 7; Downes 1925, pp. 36, 158; Downes 1926, pp. 36, 158; Charteris 1927, pp. 109, 137, 263; Mount, 1955, p. 433 (9025); 1957 ed., p. 341 (9025); 1969 ed., pp. 183, 448 (9025); McKibbin 1956, p. 117; Strickler 1982–3, pp. 24–5, fig. 9; Fairbrother 1986, pp. 181, 185.

255 *Florence Addicks*

PROVENANCE: The sitter or her parents; Pennsylvania Academy of Fine Arts, March 1926; M. Knoedler & Co., New York, March 1926 (16414); Tolley & Allender Biays of Baltimore, October 1928; Bryn Mawr Trust Company; Arthur J. Secor, Toledo; presented by him to the Toledo Museum of Art, Ohio, 1933 (33.36).

EXHIBITIONS: Philadelphia 1926, no. 217; Cincinnati 1926, no. 33; Dallas 1927, no. 119; New York, Knoedler, 1927, no. 12; Utica 1953, no. 31; Grand Rapids 1955, no. 24.

LITERATURE: Mount 1955, p. 433 (9035); 1957 ed., p. 342 (9035); 1969 ed., p. 430 (9035); McKibbin 1956, p. 81; Toledo Museum of Art, *American Paintings*, 1979, p. 97, pl. 96; New York 1980, Checklist.

256 *Peter Chardon Brooks*

PROVENANCE: The sitter; his daughter, Eleanor, later Mrs Richard M. Saltonstall; her daughter, Muriel, later Mrs George Lewis; Private Collection.

EXHIBITIONS: Boston, St Botolph Club, 1890, no. 22, as 'Portrait'; probably Boston 1898, no. 76 as 'Portrait'; Boston 1899, no. 2; New York, GCAG, 1924, no. 56; Boston, MFA, 1925, no. 47 (revised catalogue no. 49).

LITERATURE: Boston 1899, p. 1; New York 1924, p. 14; Boston 1925, p. 7; Boston 1925a, p. 7; Downes 1925, pp. 159–60; Downes 1926, pp. 159–60; Charteris 1927, pp. 109, 262; Mount 1955, pp. 183, 432 (904); 1957 ed., pp. 153, 341 (904); 1969 ed., pp. 183, 432 (904); McKibbin 1956, p. 86; Fairbrother 1986, p. 267 n. 13; Eric Zafran, 'Monet in Boston' *Monet and His Contemporaries: Masterpieces from the Museum of Fine Arts*, Tokyo, Bunkamura Museum of Art, 1992, fig. 7.

257   Mrs Peter Chardon Brooks

PROVENANCE: The sitter; her daughter, Eleanor, later Mrs Richard M. Saltonstall; her daughter, Muriel, later Mrs George Lewis; on deposit since 1963 at the Peabody Museum, Salem (M11, 509).

EXHIBITIONS: Boston 1895, no. 253; Possibly Boston 1899, no. 21 or 25; Boston 1915; Boston, MFA, 1925, no. 48 (revised catalogue no. 50).

LITERATURE: Possibly Boston 1899, p. 6 or 7; Boston 1925, p. 7, ill.; Boston 1925a, p. 7, ill.; Downes 1925, p. 160; Downes 1926, p. 160; Charteris 1927, pp. 109, 262; Mount 1955, pp. 183, 432 (905); 1957 ed., pp. 153, 341 (905); 1969 ed., pp. 183, 432 (905); McKibbin 1956, p. 86; Fairbrother 1986, p. 267 n. 13.

258   Eleanor Brooks

PROVENANCE: Mr and Mrs Brooks; the sitter, Mrs R. Saltonstall, to 1961; her daughter, Muriel, later Mrs George Lewis; Berry-Hill Galleries, New York, 1999; Private Collection.

EXHIBITIONS: Boston 1895, no. 251 or 252; possibly Boston 1899, no. 21 or 25; Boston, MFA, 1925, no. 45 (revised catalogue no. 47); Boston 1956, no. 18; Boston 1986, no. 2.

LITERATURE: Possibly Boston 1899, p. 6 or p. 7; Boston 1925, p. 6; Boston 1925a, p. 7; Downes 1925, p. 160; Downes 1926, p. 160; Charteris 1927, pp. 262–3; Mount 1955, pp. 183, 432 (903); 1957 ed., pp. 153, 341 (903); 1969 ed., pp. 183, 432 (903); McKibbin 1956, p. 86: Boston 1986, pp. 45, 94, ill. (colour); Fairbrother 1986, p. 267 n. 13.

259   Eleanor Brooks

PROVENANCE: The sitter, later Mrs R. M. Saltonstall, to 1961; her daughter, Muriel, later Mrs George Lewis; presented by Mrs Leverett Saltonstall to the Peabody Essex Museum, Salem, 1991 (M23, 411).

EXHIBITIONS: Boston 1895, no. 251 or 252; possibly Boston 1899, no. 21 or 25; Boston, MFA, 1925, no. 46 (revised catalogue no. 48).

LITERATURE: Possibly Boston 1899, p. 6 or p. 7; Boston 1925, p. 6; Boston 1925a, p. 7; Charteris 1927, p. 262; Mount 1955 p. 432 (902); 1957 ed., p. 341 (902); 1969 ed., p. 432 (902); McKibbin 1956, p. 86; Fairbrother 1986, p. 267 n. 13.

260   Gordon Fairchild

PROVENANCE: Mrs Charles Fairchild to 1924; her daughter, Sally Fairchild, to 1960; her niece, Mrs Warner Taylor; her daughter, Mrs Harry J. Miller; sold, Sotheby Parke-Bernet, New York, 4 December 1980, lot 22; Private Collection.

EXHIBITIONS: Probably Boston 1896, no. 208; Boston, Copley Gallery, 1917, no. 10; Boston, MFA, 1925, no. 38 (no. 40 in revised catalogue), as 'Boy in Chair'; Boston 1956, no. 21; Washington 1964, no. 53.

LITERATURE: Boston 1925, p. 6; Boston 1925a, p. 6; Downes 1925, pp. 147–8; Downes 1926, pp. 147–8, 337; Charteris 1927, p. 262; Mount

1955, p. 433 (9011); 1957 ed., p. 341 (9011); 1969 ed., p. 438 (9011); Boston 1956, fig. 10; McKibbin 1956, p. 95; Olson 1986, p. 139; Reynolds in Hills *et al.* 1986, p. 159.

261   Lady with a Blue Veil (Sally Fairchild)

PROVENANCE: The artist's sale, Christie's, 24 July 1925, lot 149A; bt David Croal Thomson, London; M. Knoedler & Co., 1925 (16309); to Charles S. Carstairs, December 1925; Charles Carstairs, to 1929; M. Knoedler & Co., New York, May 1930 (A 1162); to Mr and Mrs J. Duncan Pitney, October 1955; presented by him to the Newark Museum, New Jersey, 1957, no. 57.19; deaccessioned by the Newark Museum, 1985; Terra Museum of American Art, Chicago (Daniel J. Terra Collection), 1986–9, via Hirschl & Adler, New York; Christie's, New York, 25 May 1989, lot 248; Private Collection.

EXHIBITIONS: New York, Knoedler, 1925, no. 12, as 'Lady with a Blue Veil'; Newport 1935, no. 7, as 'Lady with Blue Veil'; Sarasota, Florida, John and Mabel Ringling Museum of Art, *American Painting, Three Centuries*, 1949, no. 28; Boston 1956, no. 22; American Federation of Fine Arts, *American Impressionists: Two Generations*, 1963–5, travelling exhibition, no. 32; New York, M. Knoedler & Co., *Aspects of a Collection: 18th and 19th Century American Painting from The Newark Museum*, April 1977.

LITERATURE: Mount 1955, pp. 182, 433 (9034); 1957 ed., p. 342 (9034); 1969 ed., pp. 182, 438 (9034); Boston 1956, fig. 12; McKibbin 1956, p. 95; Mount, *Art Quarterly* 1957, p. 318; New York 1980, Checklist; Fairbrother 1986, p. 179; Gerdts in Hills *et al.* 1986, p. 132, fig. 95; Olson 1986, p. 139.

262   Mrs James Thomas Fields

PROVENANCE: The sitter; her nephew, Boylston Adams Beal; his son, the Reverend Holland Beal; the sitter's niece, Mrs E. Sturgis Hinds; presented by her to the Boston Athenaeum, 1973 (BA URB).

EXHIBITIONS: Boston, MFA, 1925, no. 34 (revised catalogue no. 36).

LITERATURE: Boston 1925, p. 5; Boston 1925a, p. 6; Downes 1925, p. 261; Downes 1926, p. 261; Charteris 1927, p. 262; Mount 1955, p. 433 (9012); 1957 ed., p. 341 (9012); 1969 ed., p. 438 (9012); McKibbin 1956, p. 96; New York 1980, Checklist.

263   Mrs Augustus Hemenway

PROVENANCE: The sitter to 1960; her daughter, Hetty, Mrs Auguste Richard; her daughter, Elvine, Mrs Paul Scott Rankine to 1980; Coe Kerr Gallery, New York, 1981; Richard Manoogian, Coe Kerr Gallery, New York, 1984; Mrs Charles W. Ireland, 1984; Adelson Galleries, New York, 1993; Private Collection.

EXHIBITIONS: Boston 1895, no. 254; Boston 1899, no. 12, as 'Portrait'; Boston 1915, unnumbered; Boston MFA 1916; New York, GCAG, 1924, no. 22; Boston, MFA, 1925, no. 33 (revised

catalogue no. 35); Boston 1956, no. 22; Japan 1989, no. 28.

LITERATURE: Boston 1899, p. 4; John Doe [sic], 'Boston', *American Art News*, XIV (20 May 1916), p. 3; W. H. Downes, 'Mr Sargent's Paintings', *Boston Evening Transcript* (10 May 1916), Part Two, p. 12; 'Sargent in Retrospect', *Boston Herald* (14 May 1916); Mechlin 1924, ill. p. 181; New York 1924, p. 13, ill. p. 31; Starkweather 1924, ill. p. 14; Boston 1925, p. 5, ill.; Boston 1925a, p. 6, ill.; Downes 1925, pp. 36, 163–4, ill. facing p. 144; Downes 1926, pp. 36, 163–4, ill. facing p. 144; Charteris 1927, pp. 138, 174, 262; Mount 1955, pp. 182, 433 (9015); 1957 ed., pp. 153, 341 (9015); 1969 ed., pp. 182, 441 (9015); Boston 1956, fig. 22; McKibbin, 1956, p. 101; Adelson in Adelson *et al.* 1986, p. 58, fig. 33; Japan 1989, p. 141, ill. p. 70 (colour).

264   Henry Cabot Lodge

PROVENANCE: The sitter; his grandson, Henry Cabot Lodge; presented by him to the National Portrait Gallery, Washington, D.C. (1967.67.58).

EXHIBITIONS: New York, SAA, 1897, no. 271, as 'Portrait'; Philadelphia 1898, no. 398; Boston 1899, no. 14; Washington 1908, no. 116; Washington 1998, unnumbered.

LITERATURE: 'The Pennsylvania Academy of Fine Arts Exhibition', *Art Amateur*, 38 (February 1898), p. 60; Boston 1899, p. 4; Downes 1925, p. 157; Downes 1926, p. 157; Charteris 1927, pp. 109, 263; Mount 1955, p. 182, 433 (9023); 1957 ed., pp. 152, 341 (9023); 1969 ed., pp. 182, 444 (9023); McKibbin 1956, p. 106; M. Christman, *Fifty American Faces*, 1978, pp. 182–7; New York 1980, Checklist; Strickler 1982–3, p. 25; Fairbrother 1986, pp. 158–9, fig. 39; Barber 1998, p. 24, ill. p. 25 (colour); Fairbrother 2000, p. 30.

265   Mrs Augustus Peabody Loring

PROVENANCE: Augustus Peabody Loring to 1938; his son, Caleb Loring; apparently destroyed by fire.

EXHIBITIONS: Boston, SAA, 1891, no. 168, as 'Portrait'; Boston 1899, no. 48, as 'Mrs L. . . .'; Boston, MFA, 1916; New York, GCAG, 1924, no. 21, as 'Portrait of a Lady'; Boston, MFA, 1925, no. 52 (revised catalogue no. 55), as 'Portrait of a Lady'; New York, MMA, 1926, no. 24, as 'Portrait of a Lady'.

LITERATURE: *Boston Evening Transcript* (4 June 1891), p. 6; Boston 1899, p. 12; W. H. Downes, 'Mr Sargent's Paintings', *Boston Evening Transcript* (10 May 1916), Part Two, p. 12; Marian P. Waitt, 'Loan Exhibit of Sargent Art at Museum', *Boston Journal* (11 May 1916); New York 1924, p. 13; Boston 1925, p. 7, ill.; Boston 1925a, p. 7, ill.; Downes 1925, p. 159; Downes 1926, p. 159; New York 1926, p. 5, ill.; Charteris 1927, pp. 109, 263; Mount 1955, p. 433 (9022); 1957 ed., p. 341 (9022); 1969 ed., p. 444 (9022); McKibbin 1956, p. 106; Fairbrother 1986, pp. 181–2, 205 n. 53.

266 *Louisa Loring*

PROVENANCE: The sitter to 1924; her sister, Katherine Peabody Loring, to 1943; Charles G. Loring; Private Collection.

EXHIBITIONS: Boston, MFA, 1925, no. 42 (revised catalogue no. 44); Boston 1956, no. 56, where it is erroneously listed as a water-colour.

LITERATURE: Boston 1925, p. 6; Boston 1925a, p. 6; Downes 1925 and 1926 eds, p. 285; Charteris 1927, p. 263; Mount 1955, p. 433 (9021); 1957 ed., p. 341 (9021); 1969 ed., p. 444 (9021); McKibbin 1956, p. 106; Fairbrother 1986, p. 179.

267 *George Peabody*

PROVENANCE: The sitter to 1892; George Peabody Gardner; George Peabody Gardner II.

EXHIBITIONS: Boston 1898, no. 77a; Boston 1899, no. 46; Boston, MFA, 1925, no. 43 (revised catalogue no. 45).

LITERATURE: Boston 1899, p. 12; Boston 1925, p. 6; Boston 1925a, p. 6; Downes 1925, p. 159; Downes 1926, p. 159; Charteris 1927, pp. 109, 263; Mount 1955, pp. 182–3, 433 (9026); 1957 ed., pp. 153, 341 (9026); 1969 ed., pp. 182–3, 448 (9026).

268 *Royal Elisha Robbins*

PROVENANCE: The sitter to 1902; his daughter, Mrs John Caswell, to 1951; Mrs Robert B. Coate; Phyllis Robbins; sold Weiner's Antique Shop, Boston, 1966; James R. Bakker; Dr Robert P. Coggins; Christie's, New York, 24 October 1979, lot 155 (unsold); Robert P. Coggins; Berry-Hill Galleries, New York; Vose Galleries, Boston, 1988–90; Private Collection.

EXHIBITIONS: Boston, MFA, 1925, no. 138 (revised catalogue no. 26); Atlanta, the High Museum of Art, *Selections from the Robert P. Coggins Collection of American Paintings*, 1976–7, ill.

LITERATURE: Boston 1925, p. 14, dated 1887; Boston 1925a, p. 5; Downes 1926, p. 336; Charteris 1927, p. 260, dated 1887; Mount 1955, p. 431 (877), dated 1887; 1957 ed., p. 340 (877), dated 1887; 1969 ed., p. 450 (877), dated 1890; McKibbin 1956, p. 119.

269 *Violet Sargent*

PROVENANCE: Lucia Fairchild (Mrs Henry Brown Fuller); bought by Isabella Stewart Gardner, *c.* 1895; Isabella Stewart Gardner Museum, Boston (P3w35).

EXHIBITIONS: Boston 1995, no. 23.

LITERATURE: Charteris 1927, p. 278; Mount 1955, p. 433 (9032); 1957 ed., p. 342 (9032); 1969 ed., p. 451 (9032); Boston 1956, fig. 21; McKibbin 1956, p. 113, fig. 21; Hendy 1974, p. 224, ill.; New York 1980, Checklist.; Fairbrother 1986, p. 179, fig. 49; Boston 1995, p. 44, ill. p. 45 (colour).

270 *Violet Sargent*

PROVENANCE: The sitter to 1955; her son Jean-Louis Ormond, to 1986; Private Collection.

271 *Self-Portrait*

PROVENANCE: Louisa Putnam Loring to 1924; Augustus P. Loring; William Caleb Loring; Private Collection.

EXHIBITIONS: Boston 1956, no. 26.

LITERATURE: McKibbin 1956, p. 122; Mount 1955, p. 433 (9042); 1957 ed., p. 342 (9042); 1969 ed., p. 451 (9042).

272 *Lawrence Barrett*

PROVENANCE: Commissioned by Edwin Booth for presentation to The Players, New York.

EXHIBITIONS: New York, NAD (Autumn), 1890, no. 83.

LITERATURE: 'Art Notes', *Art Interchange*, 25 (1890), p. 201; Downes 1925, p. 156; Downes 1926, p. 156; Charteris 1927, pp. 109, 262; Walter Leighton Clark, *Leaves from an Artist's Memory*, Camden, N. J., 1937, p. 228; Mount 1955, pp. 178, 180, 432 (908); 1957 ed., pp. 150, 341 (908); 1969 ed., pp. 178, 180, 431 (908); McKibbin 1956, p. 83.

273 *Joseph Jefferson*

PROVENANCE: Commissioned by Edwin Booth and Lawrence Barrett for The Players, New York.

EXHIBITIONS: New York, NAD, 1890 (Autumn), no. 92; New York, MMA, 1926, no. 22; Washington, D.C., National Portrait Gallery, *Portraits of the American Stage*, 1971, no. 26, ill.

LITERATURE: 'Art Notes', *Art Interchange*, 25 (20 December 1890), p. 201; 'The Academy of Design', *Art Amateur*, 24 (January 1891), p. 31; Coffin 1896, p. 162, ill.; Downes 1925, p. 157; Downes 1926, p. 157; New York 1926, p. 5, ill.; Charteris 1927, pp. 109, 262; Mount 1955, pp. 180, 433 (9016); 1957 ed., pp. 341 (9016); 1969 ed., pp. 180, 443 (9016); McKibbin 1956, p. 103; Fairbrother 1986, pp. 166, 203 n. 34; Fairbrother 2000, p. 216 n. 34.

274 *Joseph Jefferson*

PROVENANCE: The artist to 1925; his sister Violet Ormond to 1955; her daughter Reine, Mrs Hugo Pitman, to 1971; Private Collection.

EXHIBITIONS: Boston, MFA, 1890; London, NEAC, 1893, no. 49; Boston 1899, no. 57, as 'Sketch of *Joseph Jefferson*, Esq.'; London, Carfax, 1903, no 14, as 'Sketch of Jefferson'; London, SPP, 1909, no. 95; San Francisco 1915, no. 3632; Washington 1916–17, no. 219; Boston 1922, no. 6; New York, GCAG, 1924, no. 17; London, Tate, 1926; New York, MMA, 1926, no. 23; Washington 1964, no. 51; Leeds 1979, no. 36.

LITERATURE: 'Exhibitions', *Magazine of Art* (1893), p. xxx; D. S. M[acColl], 'The New English Art Club and the Meissonier Exhibition', *Spectator*, 70 (22 April 1893), p. 523; 'Art Exhibitions', *The Times*, (10 April 1893), p. 7; Caffin 1903, ill. p. 4101; Meynell 1903, n.p., ill.; McSpadden 1907, p. 290; Berry 1924, p. 110, ill. p. 108; New York 1924, p. 13, ill. p. 36; Starkweather 1924, ill. p. 15; Downes 1925, p. 157; Downes 1926, p. 157; New York 1926, p. 5, ill.; Charteris 1927, p. 262;

Meynell Manson 1927, n.p., ill.; Birnbaum 1941, p. 33; Mount 1955, pp. 180, 433 (9017); 1957 ed., p. 341 (9017); 1969 ed., pp. 180, 443 (9017); McKibbin 1956, p. 103; Ormond 1970, pp. 43, 249, pl. 74; Leeds 1979, p. 52, ill.; Ratcliff 1982, p. 124, fig. 176.

275 *Mrs Leslie Cotton*

PROVENANCE: The sitter; M. Knoedler, & Co., New York, December 1910 (C3809); taken into stock (12262), January 1911; bt James Deering, January 1911; untraced.

EXHIBITIONS: Philadelphia 1901, no. 636, as 'Portrait'.

LITERATURE: McKibbin 1956, p. 90.

276 *Dr Morton Prince*

PROVENANCE: The sitter to 1929; presented at an unknown date in the mid-1940s by Prince's daughter Mrs Clara Wolcott Hanks to Tufts University, Medford, Massachusetts (AI 41500).

EXHIBITIONS: Medford, Massachusetts, Aidekman Arts Center, Tufts University Gallery, *Collection Selections*, 22 February–1 April 2001.

277 *Honorable Thomas Brackett Reed*

PROVENANCE: Commissioned by twenty-one members of the Fifty-first US Congress, for presentation to the US House of Representatives, Washington, D.C.

EXHIBITIONS: New York, Schaus Gallery, 1891; Boston 1899, no. 31; Philadelphia 1899, no. 69, ill.; Boston, MFA, 1925, no. 54 (revised catalogue no. 57).

LITERATURE: 'Various Exhibitions', *Art Amateur*, 25 (November 1891) [page number illegible]; Mariana Griswold van Rensselaer, 'Another Portrait by Sargent', *Harper's Weekly*, 35 (19 December 1891), p. 1012; Boston 1899, p. 8; 'Pennsylvania Academy of Fine Arts Exhibition as Seen and Heard', *Art Collector* (1 February 1899), p. 102; Glenn Brown, *History of the United States Capitol*, vol. 2, Washington, D.C., 1903, p. 189; Van Dyke 1903, p. 36; Samuel W. McCall, *The Life of Thomas Brackett Reed*, Boston and New York, 1914, p. 183; Van Dyke 1919, p. 258; Edward P. Mitchell, *Memoirs of an Editor*, New York, 1924, p. 429; Boston 1925, p. 7; Boston 1925a, p. 7; Downes 1925, p. 186; Downes 1926, p. 186; Belleroche 1926, p. 44; Charteris 1927, p. 264; Robinson 1930, pp. 295–6; Mount 1955, pp. 191–2, 345, 415, 433 (911); 1957 ed., pp. 158, 283, 342 (911); 1969 ed., pp. 191–2, 345, 415, 449 (911); Barbara Tuchman, *The Proud Tower. A Portrait of the World Before the War, 1890–1914*, New York, 1966, pp. 117, 129; New York 1980, Checklist; Ratcliff 1982, p. 125.

278 *Mabel Marquand, Mrs Henry Galbraith Ward*

PROVENANCE: Henry Galbraith Ward; presented by him to the Metropolitan Museum of Art, New York, 1930 (30.26).

EXHIBITIONS: New York, NAD, 1894, no. 262; Philadelphia 1894, no. 271; Pittsburgh 1898, no. 142.

LITERATURE: *Critic*, 25 (10 November 1894), p. 317; Charles H. Caffin, 'Art In Pittsburg', *Harper's Weekly*, XLII (12 November 1898), p. 1102; Downes 1925, p. 264, erroneously printed as H. Galbraith Ward; Downes 1926, p. 264, erroneously printed as H. Galbraith Ward; Mount 1955, p. 431 (879), dated 1887; 1957 ed., p. 340 (879); 1969 ed., p. 455 (879); McKibbin 1956, p. 108, as Mabel Marquand, dated 1890; Burke 1980, p. 239, ill.; New York 1980, Checklist; Fairbrother 1986, p. 188; Olson 1986, p. 137.

279   *Helen Dunham*

PROVENANCE: James H. Dunham; his daughter (the sitter) Mrs Holmes Spicer; sold to John F. Braun, Philadelphia, 1931; Grand Central Art Galleries, New York, 1931; Farish Collection, Houston; Grand Central Art Galleries, New York, by 1934; Coe Kerr Gallery, New York; sold to Richard Manoogian 1984; David H. Koch.

EXHIBITIONS: London, NEAC, 1892, no. 99, as 'Miss Duncomb'; Chicago 1893, no. 882 (revised catalogue no. 513); New York, NAD, 1895, no. 270; New York, SAA, 1897, no. 278, as 'Portrait of a Lady'; Boston 1899, no. 6; London, RA, 1926, no. 10; Glasgow 1929, no. 474; Grand Central Art Galleries, New York, 1931; New York, the Forum, Rockefeller Center, *The First Annual Fine Arts Exposition*, 1 November–11 December 1934; Detroit 1983, no. 62; Chicago 1986; Washington, San Francisco, New York, Detroit, *American Paintings from the Manoogian Collection*, 1989–90, no. 48; Edinburgh 1997, no. 9.

LITERATURE: D. S. M[acColl], 'Art: The New English Art Club', *Spectator*, 69 (26 November 1892), p. 770; Walton 1893–5, p. 17; probably 'New York Portrait Loan Exhibition', *Art Amateur*, 34 (December 1895), p. 3; 'The Exhibition of the Society of American Artists', *Art Amateur*, 36 (May 1897), p. 108; Coffin 1896, p. 178; Boston 1899, p. 2; Downes 1925, pp. 36, 167–8, and p. 260 as 'Miss Helen Daub'; Downes 1926 eds, pp. 36, 167–8, and p. 260 as 'Miss Helen Daub'; London 1926, p. 8; *RA Ill. 1926*, p. 95; Charteris 1927, pp. 137, 138, 264; 'Braun Collection Acquires a Fine Sargent', *Art Digest*, 5 , no. 17 (1 June 1931), p. 9; Jane Schwartz, 'Contemporary Art', *Art News* XXXIII, no. 6 (10 November 1934), p. 15, ill. inside front cover; Mount 1955, pp. 199, 433 (921); 1957 ed., pp. 164, 342 (921); 1969 ed., pp. 199, 437 (921); McKibbin 1956, p. 93; Ormond 1970, p. 247, ill. pl. 66; Fairbrother 1986, p. 136, n. 28; Olson 1986, p. 184; Reynolds in Hills *et al.* 1986, p. 174, ill. fig. 109 (colour); *American Paintings from the Manoogian Collection*, Washington, D.C., 1989, p. 134, ill.; Edinburgh 1997, p. 72, ill. p. 16 (colour).

280   *Mrs George Lewis*

PROVENANCE: Sir George and Lady Lewis; their daughter Katherine Lewis to 1961; her nephew, Anthony Burney, to 1989; Private Collection.

EXHIBITIONS: London, New Gallery, 1893, no. 177; London, RA, 1926, no. 382.

LITERATURE: 'Fine Arts The New Gallery. (First Notice.)', *Athenaeum*, no. 3419 (6 May 1893), p. 578; Frederick Wedmore, 'The New Gallery', *Magazine of Art* (1893), p. 290; 'The New Gallery. *Second Notice*', *Saturday Review*, LXXV (10 June 1893), p. 627; Downes 1925, p. 169; Downes 1926, pp. 169, 360; London 1926, p. 57; Charteris 1927, pp. 137, 264; Mount 1955, p. 434 (925); 1957 ed., p. 342 (925); 1969 ed., p. 444 (925); McKibbin 1956, p. 105; Olson 1986, p. 211 n.; Herdrich and Weinberg 2000, p. 207

281   *Self-Portrait*

PROVENANCE: Painted for the National Academy of Design, New York, 1892; National Academy, New York (1122).

EXHIBITIONS: Boston, MFA, 1925, no. 55 (revised catalogue no. 58); New York, MMA, 1926, no. 27; New York, NAD, 1926, no. 21; Boston 1956, no. 24; Washington 1964, no. 57, ill. frontis.; New York, NAD, 1983, unnumbered, ill. (colour); Milan, Pinacoteca Ambrosiana, and Florence, Galleria della Uffizi, *Da Pittore a Pittore*, 1987–8, no. 20, ill.

LITERATURE: Boston 1925, p. 7; Boston 1925a, p. 7; Downes 1925, p. 168; Downes 1926, p. 168; New York 1926, p. 6, ill.; Charteris 1927, p. 264; Mount 1955, p. 434 (924); 1957 ed., p. 342 (924); 1969 ed., p. 451 (924), ill. frontis.; McKibbin 1956, p. 122; New York 1980, Checklist; Fairbrother 1986, pp. 325, 357 n. 59.

282   *Master Skene Keith*

PROVENANCE: Thomas Skene Keith, and thence by family descent; Christie's, New York, 4 December 1997, lot 30; Adelson Galleries, New York, 1997; Private Collection.

EXHIBITIONS: London, RA, 1926, no. 367.

LITERATURE: Downes 1926, p. 359; London 1926, p. 55; *RA Ill. 1926*, p. 14; Charteris 1927, p. 264; Mount 1955, p. 434 (922); 1957 ed., p. 342 (922); 1969 ed., p. 443 (922); McKibbin 1956, p. 104.

283   *John Alfred Parsons Millet*

PROVENANCE: Lily, Mrs Frank Millet to 1932; the sitter to 1976; sold by his heirs to Hirschl & Adler, New York, 1980; Richard Manoogian.

EXHIBITIONS: London, RA, 1926, no. 327; Washington 1989, no. 47, ill.

LITERATURE: Downes 1926, p. 337; London 1926, p. 49; *RA Ill. 1926*, p. 24; Charteris 1927, p. 264; Mount 1955, p. 434 (923); 1957 ed., p. 342 (923); 1969 ed., p. 446 (923); McKibbin 1956, p. 110.

284   *Mrs Hugh Hammersley*

PROVENANCE: Mr and Mrs Hugh Hammersley; bt from Hugh Hammersley by Charles Deering, 1923; Charles Deering, 1923–7; his daughter, Mrs Richard Danielson, 1927–c.1962; her daughter, Mrs Douglass Campbell, c.1962–98; presented by Mr and Mrs Douglass Campbell to the Metropolitan Museum of Art, New York, 1998 (1998.365).

EXHIBITIONS: London, New Gallery, 1893, no. 128; Paris, Salon du Champs de Mars, 1894, no. 1036; Berlin 1895, no. 1483, as 'Damenbildniss'; London, Corporation of London Art Gallery, *Loan Collection of Pictures, By Painters of the British School who have Flourished During Her Majesty's Reign*, 1897; Boston 1899, no. 11; Dublin, Irish International, 1907, no. 113; Pittsburgh 1923, no. 45; Chicago 1954, no. 59.

LITERATURE: 'Fine Art. The Royal Academy. II', *Academy*, XLIII (13 May 1893), pp. 420–1; 'The New Gallery', *Athenaeum*, no. 3419 (6 May 1893), p. 578; 'The Society of Portrait Painters', *Black and White*, V (20 May 1893), p. 601; 'The New Gallery', *Graphic*, XLVII (6 May 1893), p. 495; Frederick Wedmore, 'The New Gallery', *Magazine of Art* (1893), p. 290; 'The New Gallery', *Saturday Review*, LXXV (13 May 1893), p. 510; 'The New Gallery. *Second Notice*.', *Saturday Review*, LXXV (10 June 1893), p. 627; D. S. M[acColl], 'Art. The New Gallery', *Spectator*, 70 (6 May 1893), p. 606; G[eorge] M[oore], 'A Portrait in the New Gallery', *Speaker* (6 May 1893), pp. 512–13; 'Art Notes', *New York Times* (2 July 1893), p. 20; 'The New Gallery', *Pall Mall Gazette*, LVI (1 May 1893), p. 2; 'The New Gallery', *The Times* (1 May 1893), p. 10; Walter Armstrong, 'Notes on British Painting in 1893', *Art Journal* (January 1894), p. 2; Pierre Véron, 'Les Salons de 1894 au Champ-de-Mars', *Le Charivari* (26 Avril 1894), n.p.; 'Portrait of Mrs Hugh Hammersley', *Graphic* XLIX (2 June 1894), ill. p. 664; Claude Phillips, 'The Salons. Salon of the Champ de Mars', *Magazine of Art*, 17 (1894), p. 381; 'Art and Artists', *Sunday Times* (14 January 1894), p. 8; 'Current News of the Fine Arts', *New York Times* (18 May 1894), p. 43; 'The Salons', *Saturday Review*, LXXVII (19 May 1894), p. 525; 'The Royal Academy. First Notice', *The Times* (5 May 1894), p. 16; Boston 1899, p. 3; Dixon 1899, p. 119; Baldry 1900 I, p. 21; 'Carnegie Sells Two Sargents for $60,000', *Art News*, XXII (10 November 1923), p. 1; Forbes Watson, 'The International Exhibition at Pittsburgh', *Arts*, III (May 1923), pp. 354, 356; Downes 1925, pp. 36, 37, 168–9; Downes 1926, pp. 36, 37, 168–9; Ernest Thesiger, *Practically True: Reminiscences with Portraits*, London, 1927, pp. 9–10; Charteris 1927, pp. 137, 184, 265; Chicago 1954, p. 61, ill. p. 60; Mount 1955, p. 434 (933); 1957 ed., p. 343 (933); 1969 ed., p. 440 (933); McKibbin 1956, p. 100; Ormond 1970, pp. 51, 57; New York 1980, Checklist; Fairbrother 1986, pp. 191, 362–3 n. 99; Reynolds in Hills *et al.* 1986, p. 177, fig. 127; Olson 1986, pp. 185 and n., 193, 211 n.; Adams 1988, vol. IV, pp. 134–5; Japan 1989, pp. 18, 27; Fairbrother 1994, pp. 80, 82–3, ill. p. 80 (colour); Edinburgh 1997, pp. 22–8, 37; London 1998, pp. 34, 35, 144, fig. 35; Prettejohn 1998, pp. 44–5, 55, fig. 32 (colour); Herdrich and Weinberg 2000, pp. 13, 123, 207–8, fig. 74.

285 Mrs Hugh Hammersley

PROVENANCE: Henry Tonks; bequeathed to Sir Francis D'Arcy Osborne, later twelfth Duke of Leeds, a nephew of Hugh Hammersley, 1937; his cousin, Robin Campbell; sold by him, Christie's, London, 12 November 1976, lot 56; Newhouse Galleries, New York; Hirschl & Adler Galleries, New York; Mr and Mrs C. Buchanan, 1977; bequeathed by Mrs C. Buchanan to the New Britain Museum of American Art, the Charles and Elizabeth Buchanan Collection (1989.41).

EXHIBITIONS: Liverpool 1925, no. 147; London, RA, 1926, no. 393; London, Tate, 1926; Birmingham 1964, no. 22; New York, Hirschl & Adler Galleries, *A Gallery Collects*, 1977, no. 46, ill.

LITERATURE: London 1926, p. 59; *RA Ill. 1926*, p. 74; Charteris 1927, pp. 137, 264; Mount 1955, p. 434 (932); 1957 ed., p. 343 (932); 1969 ed., p. 440 (932); McKibbin 1956, p. 100; New Britain Museum of American Art, *The Charles and Elizabeth Buchanan Collection*, 1990, n.p., ill.

286 Lady Agnew of Lochnaw

PROVENANCE: Sir Andrew Noel Agnew, Bt, to 1925; bt National Gallery of Scotland, Edinburgh, 1925 (with funds from the Cowan Smith Bequest) (NG1656).

EXHIBITONS: London, RA, 1893, no. 30; London, *Fair Women*, 1894, no. 132; Boston 1899, no. 1; London, National Portrait Society, 1911, no. 51; Pittsburgh 1924, no. 73; London, RA, 1926, no. 25; Leeds 1979, no. 37; New York and Chicago 1986; Edinburgh, Scottish National Portrait Gallery, *The Art of Jewellery in Scotland*, 1991, no. 66; Japan, *Masterpieces from the National Gallery of Scotland*, 1993–4, no. 49; Washington, D.C., National Gallery of Art, *The Victorians: British Painting 1837–1901*, 1997, no. 62; Edinburgh 1997, no. 10; London 1998, no. 50.

LITERATURE: 'Fine Art. The Royal Academy. II', *Academy*, XLIII (13 May 1893), p. 420; R. A. M. Stevenson, 'General Impressions of the Royal Academy of 1893', *Art Journal* (1893), pp. 242–3; 'Fine Arts The Royal Academy. (Fourth Notice. – The Portraits.)' *Athenaeum*, no. 3423 (3 June 1893), p. 704; [M. H. Spielmann] 'The Royal Academy. – II', *Magazine of Art* (1893), p. 258; L.R., 'The Royal Academy – The Pictures and the People. The Pictures – First Notice', *Black and White*, V (6 May 1893), p. 536; 'The New Gallery. *Second Notice.*', *Saturday Review*, LXXV (10 June 1893), p. 627; D. S. M[acColl], 'Art. The Royal Academy', *Spectator*, 70 (29 April 1893), p. 573; D. S. M[acColl], 'Art. The New Gallery', *Spectator*, 70 (6 May 1893), p. 606; 'The Royal Academy. I', *Saturday Review*, LXXV (6 May 1893), p. 487; 'The Royal Academy. (First Article.) *The Times* (29 April 1893), p. 13; 'The Royal Academy', *Illustrated London News*, CII (29 April 1893), p. 514; 'London Letter', *Art Interchange*, 31 (July 1893), p. 10; *Pall Mall Gazette* (1 May 1893); *Pall Mall Gazette* (24 April 1893), p. 1; Walton 1893–5, pp. 17–18; 'Art and Artists', *Sunday Times* (14 January 1894), p. 8; 'The Royal Academy. First

Notice', *The Times* (5 May 1894), p. 16; 'The Grafton Galleries', *The Times* (3 October 1894), p. 8; *The Times* (4 January 1895); F. Harcourt Williamson, *The Book of Beauty*, (*Late Victorian Era*), 1896, p. 53, ill.; Boston 1899, p. 1; Dixon 1899, p. 119; *New York Sun* (21 February 1899) ill. in *Boston Evening Transcript* (21 February 1899), p. 7; Baldry 1900, I, p. 21; Cortissoz 1903, p. 529; Meynell 1903, n.p., ill.; Van Dyke 1903, pp. 37, 38; Brinton 1906, ill. p. 270; 'The National Portrait Society', *Athenaeum*, no. 4344 (28 January 1911), p. 104; Van Dyke 1919, p. 260; Cortissoz 1924, p. 348, ill.; 'Some Recent Additions to the National Gallery of Scotland', *Studio*, XC (September 1925), p. 164, ill. p. 162; Downes 1925, pp. 36, 170–1; Downes 1926, pp. 36, 170–1; London 1926, p. 25; Charteris 1927, pp. 136, 264; Meynell Manson 1927, n.p. ill.; *Vernon Lee's Letters* 1937, p. 352; *Studio*, 130 (October 1945), p. 104, ill; Mount 1955, p. 434 (931); 1957 ed., p. 343 (931); 1969 ed., p. 430 (931); McKibbin 1956, p. 81; Ormond 1970, pp. 46, 51, 54, 247, pls 67, 69; Robin Gibson, *British Portraits*, London, 1970, ill.; Leeds 1979, pp. 55–6, ill. and cover (colour); Fairbrother 1986, pp. 6, 153, 183, 186, 191, 192–3, 305, fig. 52; Olson 1986, pp. 184, 185, 189, 193; Reynolds 1986, p. 982, pl. VI (colour); Reynolds in Hills 1986 *et al.*, pp. 154, 162, fig. 110 (colour); Linda Nochlin, 'Issues of Gender in Cassatt and Eakins', in Stephen F. Eisenman, *Nineteenth Century Art: A Critical History*, London, 1994, pp. 260, 262, fig. 256; Fairbrother 1994, pp. 79, 82, ill. p. 82; Edinburgh 1997, pp. 17–32, 35, 36–7, 38, 47, 55, 72–3, ill. frontis. and cover (colour), between pp. 25–8, detail (colour); London 1998, pp. 34, 35, 36, 144, ill. p. 145 (colour); Prettejohn 1998, p. 31, fig. 23 (colour); Fairbrother 2000, pp. 28, 29, 30, fig. 1.11; Herdrich and Weinberg 2000, pp. 208–9, fig. 75.

287 Elizabeth Chanler

PROVENANCE: The sitter's sister Margaret, later Mrs Richard Aldrich, to 1963; the sitter's son, Chanler A. Chapman, to 1980; presented by him to the National Museum of American Art, Washington, D.C. (1980.71).

EXHIBITIONS: London, RA, 1894, no. 61; New York, NAD, 1894, no. 263; Philadelphia 1896–7, no. 288; Boston 1899, no. 47, as 'Mrs J. J. Chapman'; Charleston 1901, no. 147, as 'Portrait of Miss C.'; New York 1903, no. 216a; Washington 1916–17, no. 221, as 'Portrait of Miss C.'; Pittsburgh 1921, no. 303, as 'Portrait of Miss C.'; New York, GCAG, 1924, no. 43; National Museum of American Art, Washington, D.C., travelling exhibition, *Treasures from the National Museum of American Art*, 1986–7; Washington 1997.

LITERATURE: Claude Phillips, 'Fine Art. The Royal Academy. III', *Academy* 45 (2 June 1894), p. 460; 'Fine Arts. The Royal Academy. (Fourth Notice. – Portraits and Landscapes.)', *Athenaeum* no. 3476 (9 June 1894), p. 746; 'Portraits of Women', *Critic*, 25 (10 November 1894), p. 317; 'The Royal Academy III.', *Graphic* (19 May 1894), p. 583; [M.H. Spielmann] 'The Royal Academy, 1894. – III', *Magazine of Art*, 17

(1894), p. 291; 'Portraits at the Royal Academy', *Saturday Review*, LXXVII (16 June 1894), p. 639; D. S. M[acColl], 'Art. The Academy. – I', *Spectator*, 72 (12 May 1894), p. 652; 'The Royal Academy. First Notice', *The Times* (5 May 1894), p. 16; 'Portraits of Women', *Art Amateur*, 32 (January 1895), p. 45; Coffin 1896, p. 178, ill. p. 176; *Art Amateur* 36 (1897), p. 55; Boston 1899, p. 12; Baldry 1900, I, p. 21; New York 1924, p. 14, ill. p. 46; Downes 1925, pp. 36–7, 169–70; Downes 1926, pp. 36–7, 169–70; Charteris 1927, p. 264; Mount 1955, pp. 199, 434 (927); 1957 ed., pp. 164, 342 (927); 1969 ed., pp. 199, 434 (927); McKibbin 1956, p. 88; Richard B. Hovey, *John Jay Chapman – An American Mind*, New York, 1959, p. 79; Fairbrother 1986, p. 188; Fairbrother 1994, p. 80, ill. p. 81 (colour).

288 Elsie Wagg

PROVENANCE: The sitter to 1949; her brother, Alfred Wagg; his daughter, Mrs Muriel Gore; Agnew's, London, by 1969; Private Collection.

EXHIBITIONS: London, RA, 1926, no. 36; Japan 1989, no. 33.

LITERATURE: Downes 1926, p. 342; London 1926, p. 12; Charteris 1927, p. 264; Mount 1955, p. 434 (936); 1957 ed., p. 343 (936); 1969 ed., p. 455 (936); McKibbin 1956, p. 128; T. Venison, 'Thank you, Miss Wagg', *Country Life* (26 March 1987), p. 134, fig. 6; Japan 1989, pp. 142–3, ill. p. 75 (colour).

289 Mrs Mahlon Day Sands

PROVENANCE: The sitter; her son Morton Harcourt Sands; his son, M. C. Sands; Private Collection.

EXHIBITIONS: London, RA, 1926, no. 358.

LITERATURE: Downes 1926, p. 358; London 1926, p. 54; Charteris 1927, p. 279; McKibbin 1956, p. 121 (dated 1884); Mount 1969, p. 451 (0114), dated 1901; Wendy Baron, *Miss Ethel Sands and Her Circle*, London, 1977, pp. 24–7; Edel 1980, p. 456; Olson 1986, pp. 187, 188–9.

290 Mrs Mahlon Day Sands

PROVENANCE: The sitter's daughter Miss Ethel Sands; sold by her executors, Christie's, London, 12 June 1970, lot 20; bt M. Schweitzer & Co., New York; Bernard Osher.

LITERATURE: McKibbin 1956, p. 121, dated 1884; Mount 1957, p. 339 (8422).

291 Louis Alexander Fagan

PROVENANCE: The sitter; apparently presented by the artist to an institution, possibly a London club, *c.* 1894 or 1897 (the dates Sargent was elected ARA and RA respectively); Sotheby's, London, 20 July 1966, lot 14; bt Julius Weitzner; David David, Philadelphia; Sloan & Roman, 1968; bt Hirschl & Adler, New York, 1968; bt International Business Machines, New York; Sotheby's, New York, 25 May 1995, lot 61; Private Collection.

LITERATURE: 'Chronicle of Art–April', *Magazine of Art*, 1, new series (1903), p. 311, ill.;

Charteris 1927, p. 278; Mount 1955, p. 434 (9410), dated 1894; 1957 ed., p. 343 (9410); 1969 ed., p. 438 (9410); McKibbin 1956, p. 95, dated 1894; *Art News* (January 1967), advertisement.

292 *Henry Augustus Cram*

PROVENANCE: The sitter to 1894; his widow, Mrs Henry A. Cram; their son, Henry Spencer Cram, to 1936; Private Collection.

EXHIBITIONS: New York, NAD (Annual), 1908, no. 29; New York, MMA, 1926, ex catalogue.

LITERATURE: Mount 1955, p. 434 (939); 1957 ed., p. 343 (939); 1969 ed., p. 435 (939); McKibbin 1956, p. 90.

293 *Mrs Frederick Mead*

PROVENANCE: The sitter to 1897; her daughter, Mrs E. A. Abbey, to 1931; Edwin Austin Abbey; Yale University Art Gallery, New Haven, Edwin Austin Abbey Memorial Collection (1937.4001).

EXHIBITIONS: London, RA, 1926, no. 360.

LITERATURE: Downes 1926, p. 358; London 1926, p. 54; Charteris 1927, p. 264; Mount 1955, p. 434 (935); 1957 ed. p. 343 (935); 1969 ed. p. 445 (935); McKibbin 1956, p. 10; New York 1980, Checklist; Theodore E. Stebbins, Jr and Galina Gorokhoff, *A Checklist of American Paintings at Yale University*, New Haven, 1982, p. 121, ill.

294 *Mrs Frederick Mead*

PROVENANCE: The sitter to 1897; her daughter, Mrs E. A. Abbey, to 1931; Edwin Austin Abbey; Yale University Art Gallery, New Haven, Edwin Austin Abbey Memorial Collection (1937.4002).

LITERATURE: Mount 1955, p. 434 (9310); 1957 ed., p. 343 (9310); 1969 ed., p. 445 (9310); McKibbin 1956, p. 109; New York 1980, Checklist; Theodore E. Stebbins Jr and Galina Gorokhoff, *A Checklist of American Paintings at Yale University*, New Haven, 1982, p. 121, ill.

295 *Mrs Frederick Mead*

PROVENANCE: The sitter to 1897; her daughter, Mrs E. A. Abbey, to 1931; Edwin Austin Abbey; Yale University Art Gallery, New Haven, Edwin Austin Abbey Memorial Collection (1937.4190).

296 *Hercules Brabazon Brabazon*

PROVENANCE: The sitter to 1906; sold by his family at the time of the dispersal of his studio, *c.* 1925, through Croal Thomson of Barbizon House, London; Charles Deering; in store at Museum of Fine Arts, Boston, during the Second World War period; sold from estate of Deering's daughter, Barbara Deering Danielson, Sotheby's, New York, 8 December 1983, lot 200; bt National Portrait Gallery, London (5706).

EXHIBITIONS: London, Barbizon House, 1925, no. 11, ill.

LITERATURE: Charteris 1927, p. 268; Mount

1955, p. 434 (938); 1957 ed., p. 343 (938); 1969 ed., p. 432 (938); McKibbin 1956, pp. 85–6; Fairbrother 1986, p. 362–3 n. 99; Herdrich and Weinberg 2000, p. 224.

297 *Hercules Brabazon Brabazon*

PROVENANCE: The artist's sale, Christie's, 24 July 1925, lot 149, as 'Portrait Sketch of H. B. Brabazon, Esq., in dark coat'; bt the Misses Davies, through Hugh Blaker; bequeathed by Miss Margaret Davies to the National Museum of Wales, Cardiff, 1963 (N.M.W.A. 179).

EXHIBITIONS: London, NEAC, 1925, no. 84, as 'Portrait sketch of Hercules B. Brabazon'; London, RA, 1926, no. 587; London, Tate, 1926; London, Fine Art Society, *Hercules Brabazon Brabazon 1821–1906*, unnumbered; Hastings, Museum and Art Gallery, *The Wide World of Hercules Brabazon Brabazon*, 1976, unnumbered; London, Christie's, *The New English Art Club Centenary Exhibition*, 27 August–17 September 1986, no. 28.

LITERATURE: Christies 1925, p. 22; Downes 1926, p. 328; London 1926, p. 84; Charteris 1927, p. 268; Ducat 1928, ill. facing p. 80; Mount 1955, pp. 434 (937), and see pp. 375, 376, 377; 1957 ed., p. 343 (937), and see pp. 309–10; 1969 ed., p. 432 (937), and see pp. 375, 376, 377; McKibbin 1956, pp. 85–6; Herdrich and Weinberg 2000, p. 224, ill.

298 *Eleonora Duse*

PROVENANCE: The artist's sale, Christie's, 24 July 1925, lot 137, as 'Head of Mme. Eleanor Duse, in dark dress with white front'; bt Scott and Fowles; Mrs Stevenson Scott; Harold Hecht; Coe Kerr Gallery, New York; Wildenstein & Co.; Private Collection.

EXHIBITIONS: London, Carfax, 1903, no. 5 as 'A Portrait of a Lady'; London, Tate 1926; Venice 1934, no. 24; New York 1948; Washington 1964, no. 59; Leeds 1979, no. 38.

LITERATURE: *Art Journal* (1903), p. 221; Meynell 1903, n.p., ill., as 'Lady with White Waistcoat'; Mauclair 1906–7, p. 376; Starkweather 1924, p. 9; Christie's 1925, p. 20; Downes 1925, p. 259; Downes 1926, pp. 259, 393; Meynell Manson 1927, n.p., ill., as 'Lady with White Waistcoat'; Charteris 1927, pp. 158, 278; Birnbaum 1941, pp. 23–4, pl. 2; Mount 1955, p. 435 (9510), dated 1895; 1957 ed., p. 343 (9510); 1969 ed., p. 437 (9510); McKibbin 1956, p. 93 (dated 1893); Ormond 1970, p. 248, pl. 68; Leeds 1979, p. 57, ill. p. 56; Ratcliff 1982, pp. 164, 167, pl. 241.

299 *William Frederick Hewer*

PROVENANCE: The sitter to 1947; his widow, Mrs W. F. Hewer; their son, Thomas Hewer; his widow, Mrs T. Hewer, to 1990; Private Collection.

LITERATURE: Charteris 1927, p. 264; Mount 1955, p. 434 (934); 1957 ed., p. 343 (934); 1969 ed., p. 441 (934); McKibbin 1956, p. 102.

300 *William Frederick Hewer*

PROVENANCE: Edwin Austin Abbey; Yale

University Art Gallery, New Haven, Edwin Austin Abbey Memorial Collection (1937.2497).

301 *J. P. Wolff*

PROVENANCE: Early history unknown; possibly sold by the auctioneers, Frederich Muller, Amsterdam, *c.* 1940; Roelandt, from whom purchased by Goudstikker Galleries, Amsterdam; Private Collection, Amsterdam; Kende Galleries, New York, 1951; bt Mr and Mrs Frank S. Kent, 1951; presented by them to the Stamford Museum and Nature Center, Stamford, Connecticut (1956 56.1).

LITERATURE: McKibbin 1956, p. 132, dated *c.* 1890; Mount 1969, p. 457 (9111), dated 1897.

302 *Coventry Patmore*

PROVENANCE: The sitter; presented by his widow to the National Portrait Gallery, London, 1897 (1079).

EXHIBITIONS: London, RA, 1895, no. 172; London, RA, 1926, no. 58; Paris, Bibliothèque Nationale, *Le Livre Anglais*, 1951–2, ex catalogue; London, Royal Academy, *Bicentenary Exhibition*, 1968–9, no. 410; London, National Portrait Gallery, *Faces as Art*, 1977; Leeds 1979, no. 39; London 1996, no. 106.

LITERATURE: Claude Phillips, 'Fine Art. The Royal Academy. I', *Academy*, 47 (11 May 1895), p. 407; R. Jope Slade, 'The Royal Academy of Arts, 1895', *Art Journal* (1895), p. 179; 'The Royal Academy (Fourth Notice)', *Athenaeum*, no. 3530 (22 June 1895), p. 811; 'The Royal Academy Exhibition. – II', *Magazine of Art* (1895), pp. 281–2; 'The Salon and the Royal Academy', *Saturday Review*, LXXIX (11 May 1895), pp. 617–18; 'The Royal Academy (First Article)', *The Times* (4 May 1895), p. 12; Coventry Patmore, *Pathos and Delight*, London, 1895, selected A. Meynell, ill. frontis.; 'First Impressions of the Royal Academy', *Punch*, CVIII (11 May 1895), ill. p. 220 (caricature); Dixon 1899, p. 118; Baldry 1900, I, ill. p. 3; Champneys 1900, vol. 1, pp. 342, 389–90, vol. 2, p. 260, ill. frontis.; Cortissoz 1903, p. 526; Meynell 1903, n. p. ill.; Cournos 1915, p. 234; Brinton 1906, ill. p. 277; Mauclair 1906–7, p. 378; Mechlin 1924, p. 188; Downes 1925, pp. 173–4, ill. facing p. 152; Downes 1926, pp. 173–4, ill. facing p. 152; London 1926, p. 16; Charteris 1927, pp. 140, 153–4, 174, 265; Meynell Manson 1927, n.p. ill.; Shane Leslie, *Sublime Failures*, London, 1932, pp. 115–16, pp. 177–8; F. J. Patmore, 'Coventry Patmore; A Son's Recollections', *English Review* (February 1932), p. 138; Patmore 1949, pp. 5–6, 208–10, 226; Mount 1955, pp. 209, 434 (945); 1957 ed., pp. 173–4, 343 (945); 1969 ed., pp. 209, 447 (945); McKibbin 1956, p. 115; Ormond 1970, pp. 52, 56, 249–50, fig. 22 (detail); Leeds 1979, pp. 57–8, ill. and pl. VI (colour); Yung 1981, p. 437, ill.; Ratcliff 1982, pp. 163, 174, pl. 238; Thwaite 1984, ill. between pp. 216–17; Fairbrother 1986, p. 325; Olson 1986, pp. 184, 190, 193; Pethica 1996, p. 71; Simon 1996, p. 182, fig. 80; Fairbrother 2000, p. 29, fig. 1. 12.

303 Coventry Patmore

PROVENANCE: Presented by the artist to Mrs Patmore; Barbizon House Gallery, London, 1921; Kojiro Matsukata, Kobe, Japan; untraced.

EXHIBITIONS: London, RA, 1895, no. 737; Edinburgh 1922, no. 195.

LITERATURE: Claude Phillips, 'Fine Art. The Royal Academy. I', *Academy*, 47 (11 May 1895), p. 407; R. Jope Slade, 'The Royal Academy of Arts, 1895', *Art Journal* (1895), p. 179; 'The Royal Academy (Fourth Notice)', *Athenaeum* no. 3530 (22 June 1895), p. 811; 'The Salon and the Royal Academy', *Saturday Review*, LXXIX (11 May 1895), pp. 617–18; *International Studio* 75 (1922), p. 465, ill.; Downes 1925 and 1926 eds, p. 174; Charteris 1927, p. 265; Mount 1955, p. 434 (944); 1957 ed., p. 343 (944); 1969 ed., p. 447 (944); McKibbin 1956, p. 115; Ormond 1970, p. 249; Pethica 1996, p. 71.

304 Coventry Patmore

PROVENANCE: The artist's sale, Christie's, London, 24 July 1925, lot 150, as 'Portrait Sketch of Coventry Patmore, Esq., for a prophet'; bt in; Mrs Francis Ormond to 1955; Guillaume Ormond to 1971; Private Collection.

EXHIBITIONS: Boston 1899, no. 62; London, RA, 1926, no. 442; York 1926, no. 16; London, Tate, 1926; Falmouth 1962, no. 51; Birmingham 1964, no. 24; Leeds 1979, no. 40.

LITERATURE: Boston 1899, p. 15; Champneys 1900, vol. 2, ill. facing p. 58; Christies 1925, p. 23; London 1926, p. 66; Charteris 1927, pp. 154, 265; *Sargent Trust List* [1927], p. 35; D. Patmore, *Coventry Patmore*, London, 1949, p. 209, ill. facing p. 208; Mount 1955, pp. 209, 210, 434 (943); 1957 ed., pp. 173, 174 (943); 1969 ed., pp. 209, 210, 447 (943); McKibbin 1956, p. 115; Ormond 1970, pp. 90, 249–50, pl. 80; Leeds 1979, p. 58, ill.; Ratcliff 1982, p. 163, pl. 237; Olson 1986, p. 184; Herdrich and Weinberg 2000, p. 212 (where it is confused with no. 302).

305 Mrs Graham Moore Robertson

PROVENANCE: Graham Robertson; bequeathed by him to Kerrison Preston; sold by him, Christie's, London, 22 July 1949, lot 152, bt in; purchased from Preston by the Watts Gallery, Compton, Surrey, 1951.

EXHIBITIONS: Birmingham 1964, no. 23.

LITERATURE: Robertson 1931, pp. 233–4; Mount 1955, pp. 199–200, 434 (947); 1957 ed., pp. 165, 343; 1969 ed., pp. 199–200, 450; McKibbin 1956, p. 119; Olson 1986, p. 189.

306 W. Graham Robertson

PROVENANCE: The sitter; presented by him to the Tate Gallery, London, 1940 (N05066).

EXHIBITIONS: London, RA, 1895, no. 503; Paris, Salon du Champs de Mars, 1896, no. 1134; Venice 1901, no. 16; London, SPP, 1907, no. 61; Toronto, Canadian National Exhibition, *Paintings by British Artists*, 1908, no. 26, ill. p. 6; Berlin 1910, no. 60, ill. supplement; London, RA, 1926, no. 417; London, Tate, 1926;

London, Tate, 1946; London 1992, no. 66; London 1998, no. 51.

LITERATURE: Claude Phillips, 'Fine Art. The Royal Academy. I', *Academy*, 47 (11 May 1895), p. 407; S. Haras, 'The Royal Academy, London', *American Architect and Building News*, 48 (22 June 1895), p. 122; R. Jope Slade, 'The Royal Academy of Arts, 1895', *Art Journal* (1895), p. 179; Claude Phillips, 'Pictures of the Year. The Royal Academy and the New Gallery', *Fortnightly Review*, 63 (June 1895), p. 936; 'The Royal Academy Exhibition. – II', *Magazine of Art* (1895), pp. 281–2; 'The Royal Academy', *Manchester Guardian* (4 May 1895), p. 9; N.N. 'The Royal Academy', *Nation*, 60 (30 May 1895), p. 419; 'The Royal Academy', *Observer* (5 May 1895), p. 7; 'The Royal Academy', *Observer* (12 May 1895), p. 6; 'First Impressions of the Royal Academy', *Punch*, CVIII (11 May 1895), p. 220 (caricature); *Royal Academy of Art* (1895), p. 179; 'The Salon and the Royal Academy', *Saturday Review*, LXXIX (11 May 1895), p. 618; 'The Royal Academy' *Sketch* (15 May 1895), p. 138; D. S. MacColl, 'The Academy – IV', *Spectator* (1 June 1895), p. 753; Frederick Wedmore, 'Some Portraits Seen This Season', *Studio* 5 (July 1895), p. 120; 'The Royal Academy', *Daily Telegraph* (20 May 1895), p. 4; 'The Royal Academy (First Article)', *The Times* (4 May 1895), p. 12; 'The Royal Academy – Third Article', *The Times* (1 June 1895), p. 14; 'My Note Book', *Art Amateur*, 35 (June 1896), p. 3; André Michel, 'The Paris Salons III', *Athenaeum* (13 June 1896), p. 784; Pierre Véron, 'Le Salon du Champ de Mars', *Le Charivari* (24 April 1896), p. 2; Edouard Conte, 'Salon du Champ de Mars, Troisième Article', *L'Echo de Paris* (27 April 1896), p. 2; Agnes Farley Millar, 'Fine Arts: The Salon of the Champ de Mars', *Independent* (9 July 1896), p. 931; A. Dalligny, 'L'Exposition de la Société nationale', *Journal des arts* (25 April 1896), p. 1; André Michel, Les Salons de 1896', *Journal des Débats* (23 May 1896), p. 2; Olivier Merson, 'Les Salons de 1896 au Champ-de-Mars', *Le Monde illustré* (25 July 1896), p. 54; M. Rochefort, 'M. Rochefort on the Champ de Mars Salon', *New York Herald* (25 April 1896), p. 9; E. Pattee, 'Thoughts on the Salons', *Quartier Latin*, 1 (1896), p. 10; Charles Frémine, 'Le Salon du Champs de Mars', *Le Rappel* (25 April 1896), p. 2; Edouard Hubert, 'Le Salon du Champ-de-Mars, III', *La République française* (1 May 1896), p. 3; Charles Frémine, 'Le Salon de Champs de Mars', *XIXe Siècle* (25 April 1896), p. 2; Thiébault-Sisson, 'Le Salon du Champs-de-Mars', *Le Temps* (24 April 1896), p. 3; Roger Marx, 'Les Salons de 1896 – Au Champs-de-Mars', *Le Voltaire* (25 April 1896), p. 2; Dixon 1899, p. 118; Baldry 1900, I, p. 21, ill. p. 4; M. H. Spielmann, 'Our Rising Artists: Mr W. Robertson', *Magazine of Art*, 24 (1900), ill. p. 74; P. G. Konody, 'John Singer Sargent und Seine Kunst', *Kunst und Kunsthandwerk*, 8 (1905), p. 105; Mauclair 1906–7, p. 377; 'London Exhibitions', *Art Journal* (1908), p. 29; Wood 1909, pl. IV; Downes 1925, pp. 39, 173; Downes 1926, pp. 39, 173; London 1926, p. 63; *RA Ill. 1926*, p. 21;

Charteris 1927, pp. 140, 154, 174, 177, 265, ill. facing p. 154; Meynell Manson 1927, n.p. ill.; Robertson 1931, pp. 133–8, 241, ill. frontis.; Preston 1953, pp. xiv, 162, 268, 367, 455, 488, ill. frontis. (detail of head); Mount 1955, pp. 201–2 (946); 1957 ed., pp. 166, 343 (946); 1969 ed., pp. 201–2, 450 (946); McKibbin 1956, p. 119; *Tate Gallery Catalogue*, 1964, vol. 2, pp. 604–5, pl. 34; Ormond 1970, p. 52, 248, pl. 70; Ratcliff 1982, p. 174, pl. 159; Boime in Hills *et al.* 1986, p. 104, fig. 69; Fairbrother 1986, pp. 354 n. 26, 379 n. 3; Olson 1986, pp. 184, 189–90, 193; Reynolds 1986, p. 982; Tate 1992, p. 194, ill. (colour); Fairbrother 1994, p. 83, ill. p. 84; Edgar Munhall, *Whistler and Montesquiou: The Butterfly and the Bat*, New York and Paris, 1995 (exhibition catalogue), pp. 90–1, fig. 68 (colour); Egerton 1998, p. 237, fig. 2; London 1998, pp. 36, 144–5, 162, ill. p. 143 (colour); Prettejohn 1998, p. 47, fig. 35 (colour); Jacqueline Ridge, 'Preparing for the Sargent Exhibition', *Tate: The Art Magazine* (Summer 1998), pp. v–vi; Ridge and Townsend 1998, p. 26; New York 1999, pp. 38–9, 41, fig. 19; Fairbrother 2000, pp. 161, 163, fig. 6. 8 (colour); Aileen Ribeiro, *The Gallery of Fashion*, London, 2000, p. 203, fig. 79.1 (colour).

307 W. Graham Robertson

PROVENANCE: Discovered during cleaning *c.* 1960, on the same stretcher as the portrait of Mrs Russell Cooke (no. 314); sold by Professor O. A. Harker via Ware Gallery, London, to John Levy; anon. sale, Christie's, London, 3 March 1978, lot 105; bt Hirschl & Adler Galleries, New York; Spanierman Galleries, New York.

EXHIBITIONS: Birmingham, 1964, no. 98 (hors catalogue); Arts Council, UK, *Decade 1890–1900*, 1967, no. 21; Hirschl & Adler Galleries, New York, *Recent Acquisitions of American Art*, 1979, no. 36.

LITERATURE: *Saturday Book*, 25 (1965), ill. p. 21; Mount 1969, p. 450, unnumbered; Ormond 1970, pp. 52, 248, fig. 49.

308 Ada Rehan

PROVENANCE: Commissioned by Mrs G. M. Whitin; bequeathed by her to the Metropolitan Museum of Art, New York, in memory of Ada Rehan, 1940 (40.146).

EXHIBITIONS: London, New Gallery, 1895, no. 199; New York, NAD, 1895, no. 271; Philadelphia 1895–6, no. 298; Boston 1896, no. 206; New York, Daly's Theatre, 1896; Worcester 1898, no. 75; Washington 1898; Boston 1899, no. 18; Boston 1906, no. 206; Worcester 1914, no. 36; Washington 1914–15, no. 108; Boston 1915; New York, GCAG, 1924, no. 30; Boston, MFA, 1925, no. 58 (revised catalogue no. 61).

LITERATURE: 'The New Gallery. (First Notice.)', *Athenaeum*, no. 3523 (4 May 1895), p. 579; 'The New Gallery', *Magazine of Art* (1895), p. 288; R. Jope Slade, 'The Royal Academy of Arts, 1895', *Art Journal* (1895), p. 179; 'New York Portrait Loan Exhibition', *Art Amateur*, 34 (December 1895), p. 3; 'Pennsylvania Academy Exhibition', *Art Amateur*, 34 (February 1896), p. 58; *Collector*, 8 (1 December 1896), p. 35; E. A. Dithmar,

Memories of Daly's Theatres, 1897, ill. frontis.; 'Art News and Notes', *Art Amateur*, 39 (June 1898), p. 20; G. P. Lathrop, *Century Magazine*, 34 (June 1898) ill. p. 269; W. Winter, *Ada Rehan*, London and New York, 1898, ill. p. 23; *Artist*, 24 (March 1899), p. xiv; Caffin 1903, ill. p. 4113; Van Dyke 1903, ill. p. 34; *Museum of Fine Arts Bulletin*, supplement to vol. 13 (February 1915); New York 1924, p. 13, ill. p. 27; Pousette-Dart 1924, n.p.; P. B[oswell], *American Art News*, 22 (23 February 1924), ill. p. 2; *American Art Student and Commercial Artist*, 7 (March 1924), p. 17; Berry 1924, p. 89, ill.; Starkweather 1924, p. 8, ill. p. 27; Boston 1925, p. 7, ill.; Boston 1925a, p. 8, ill.; Downes 1925, pp. 39, 172–3; Downes 1926, pp. 39, 172–3; Charteris 1927, pp. 154, 265; Martha A. S. Shannon, 'The Isabella Stewart Gardner Museum, Fenway Court', *American Magazine of Art*, XVIII (April 1927), p. 181; Robertson 1931, pp. 234–5; H. W. W[illiams], Jr, 'Ada Rehan by Sargent', *Metropolitan Museum of Art Bulletin*, 36 (January 1941), p. 19, ill.; *Theatre Arts*, 25 (March 1941), ill. p. 251; *Art Digest*, 15 (1 March 1941), ill. p. 22; H. W. Williams, 'Four Letters by J. S. Sargent Concerning His Portrait of Ada Rehan', *Art in America*, 29 (July 1941), pp. 173–4; Mount 1955, pp. 199–201, 203–4, 210, 212–13, 434 (951); 1957 ed., pp. 164–6, 168, 343 (951); 1969 ed., pp. 199–201, 203–4, 210, 212–13, 449 (951); McKibbin 1956, p. 118; Ormond 1970, pp. 51, 63; Burke 1980, pp. 245–7, ill. p. 245; New York 1980, Checklist; Ratcliff 1982, pp. 164–7, pl. 240; Fairbrother 1986, pp. 184, 206 n. 62, 319, 357 n. 51; Olson 1986, pp. 184, 188, 189, 190, 211 n.; Reynolds in Hills *et al.* 1986, pp. 148, 154; Herdrich and Weinberg 2000, pp. 9, 10, fig. 18; Fairbrother 2001, p. 320.

309   *Lancelot Allen*

PROVENANCE: The sitter's aunt, Kate Allen; her sister, Rachel Allen, *c.* 1949; their cousin, Bertram Allen; his widow, Mrs Bertram Allen; her son Lieutenant Colonel J. R. C. Allen; sold Sotheby's, New York, 30 May 1984, lot 45; Alfred A. Taubman.

EXHIBITIONS: London, RA, 1926, no. 35, as 'Lancelot, son of the late Judge Wilfred Allen'.

LITERATURE: Downes 1926, p. 342; *My Magazine* (1926), ill. p. 299 (colour); London 1926, p. 12; Charteris 1927, p. 265; Mount 1955, p. 434 (941); 1957 ed., p. 343 (941); 1969 ed., p. 430 (941); McKibbin 1956, p. 81.

310   *Don Rafael del Castillo*

PROVENANCE: The sitter; his son, Ben del Castillo; his son, Marchese Raffaele Núñez del Castillo, 1948; his sister's collection, whence it was stolen; untraced.

LITERATURE: Mount 1955, p. 430 (849) 1957 ed., p. 338 (849); McKibbin 1956, p. 113.

311   *Mrs Frederick Roller*

PROVENANCE: The sitter to 1898; her son Major George C. Roller, to 1941; his widow, Emily Roller, to 1949; on loan to Bristol Art Gallery, *c.* 1947–54; M. Knoedler & Co., New York, 1954;

Walter P. Chrysler Jr, 1958; M. Knoedler & Co., New York, 1973; Hammer Galleries, New York 1980; Charles and Emma Frye, 1981; Charles and Emma Frye Art Museum, Seattle.

EXHIBITIONS: London, RSPP, 1924, no. 8; Glasgow 1925, no. 404; London, RA, 1926, no. 296.

LITERATURE: *Morning Post* (23 January 1924), n.p.; Jacomb-Hood 1925, p. 284; Downes 1926, p. 355; London 1926, p. 45; Charteris 1927, p. 265; Mount 1955, p. 434 (952); 1957 ed., p. 343 (952); 1969 ed., p. 450 (952); McKibbin 1956, p. 120; Ormond 1970, p. 51; *The Charles and Emma Frye Art Museum. A Handbook of the Collection*, Seattle, 1989, p. 108, ill. p. 109 (colour).

312   *Mrs Ernest Hills*

PROVENANCE: The sitter to 1932; bequeathed by her to the National Gallery of Scotland, Edinburgh, 1932 (1787).

EXHIBITIONS: London, RA, 1895, no. 31.

LITERATURE: 'The Royal Academy (Fourth Notice)', *Athenaeum*, no. 3530 (22 June 1895), p. 811; R. Jope Slade, 'The Royal Academy of Arts, 1895', *Art Journal* (1895), p. 179; Downes 1925, p. 175; Downes 1926, p. 175; Charteris 1927, pp. 154, 265; Mount 1955, pp. 200, 434 (949); 1957 ed., pp. 165, 343 (949); 1969 ed., pp. 200, 441 (949); McKibbin 1956, p. 102; Mordaunt Crook 1999, fig. XV, as 'Mrs Frank Hills'.

313   *Mrs William Lionel Wyllie*

PROVENANCE: The sitter's husband to 1931; destroyed during the Second World War.

EXHIBITIONS: London, RA, 1926, no. 390; York 1926, no. 38.

LITERATURE: Downes 1926, p. 360; London 1926, p. 58; *RA Ill. 1926*, p. 56; Charteris 1927, p. 279; 457; McKibbin 1956, p. 132; Mount 1969, p. 457.

314   *Mrs William Russell Cooke*

PROVENANCE: The sitter to 1914; her daughter, Mrs O. A. Harker, to 1947; her widower, O. A. Harker, to 1967/8; the sitter's grandson, Sir John Dilke, Bt; Sotheby's, New York, 25 September 1968, lot 32; bt Spanierman Gallery, New York; Bernard Danenberg Galleries, Inc., New York, 1975; Meredith Long & Company, Houston, Texas; Private Collection.

EXHIBITIONS: London, RA, 1895, no. 647; London, RA, 1926, no. 398.

LITERATURE: Claude Phillips, 'Fine Art. The Royal Academy. I', *Academy*, XLVII (11 May 1895), p. 408; Baldry 1900, I, p. 21, ill. p. 16; Downes 1925, p. 175; Downes 1926, p. 175; London 1926, p. 60; Charteris 1927, pp. 154, 265; Mount 1955, p. 434 (953); 1957 ed., p. 343 (953); 1969 ed., p. 435 (953); McKibbin 1956, p. 90; Mount 1963, p. 389.

315   *Madame Flora Reyntiens*

PROVENANCE: The sitter; her grandson, Patrick Reyntiens; James Kirkman Ltd, London, 1989; Private Collection.

316   *Frances Winifred Hill or Expectancy*

PROVENANCE: John Maddocks; his sale, Christie's, London, 30 April 1910, lot 87; bt P. D. Colnaghi & Co., London; Alexander Teixeira de Mattos, to 1921; his son, Jonkheer E. L. Teixeira de Mattos; bt from him by J. William Middendorf; Sotheby Parke-Bernet, New York, April 19–20, 1972, lot 55A; bt M. Schweitzer & Co., New York; Private Collection; Sotheby's, New York, 5 December 1991, lot 77; Private Collection.

LITERATURE: Mount 1969, p. 479.

317   *Gardiner Greene Hammond Jr*

PROVENANCE: The sitter (d. 1921); his daughter, Frances, Mrs MacKinley Helm; her nephew, Gardiner Greene Hammond IV; Private Collection.

EXHIBITIONS: Boston 1896, no. 211; New York, NAD (Annual), 1896, no. 241; Boston 1898, no. 77; Boston 1899, no. 44; Boston, MFA, 1925, no. 60 (revised catalogue no. 63); San Francisco 1959, no. 12.

LITERATURE: 'The National Academy of Design', *Art Amateur*, 34 (May 1896), p. 129; 'The Spring Academy', *New York Times* (27 March 1896), p. 5; Boston 1899, p. 11; Boston 1925, p. 8; Boston 1925a, p. 8; Downes 1925, p. 175; Downes 1926, p. 175; Charteris 1927, p. 265; Mount 1955, p. 435 (958); 1957 ed., p. 343 (958); 1969 ed., p. 440 (958); McKibbin 1956, p. 100; Sweet 1966, p. 150; Ormond 1970, p. 249, pl. 78; Fairbrother 1986, pp. 184, 205 n. 55; Mathews 1994, p. 247.

318   *Helen Sears*

PROVENANCE: The sitter; presented by her to the Museum of Fine Arts, Boston, 1955 (55.1116).

EXHIBITIONS: New York, SAA, 1896, no. 163; Boston 1897, no. 84, as 'Portrait of a Child'; Boston 1899, no. 35, as 'Portrait of a Child'; either this portrait or no. 370, Boston 1900, no. 109; Boston 1905; either this portrait or no. 370, Boston 1914, no. 17, as 'Portrait'; Boston, MFA, 1916; Boston, MFA, 1925, no. 59 (revised catalogue no. 62), ill.; New York, MMA, 1926, no. 28, ill.; Boston 1956, no. 30; Palm Beach 1959, no. 12; San Francisco 1959, no. 11; New York, Portraits Inc., *Portraits of Children, 1860–1960*, 18 April–9 May 1960, no. 53; Tokyo, National Museum of Western Art, travelling exhibition, *Human Figures in Fine Arts*, 1978, no. 44, ill. (colour); New Haven, Yale University Art Gallery, *Emblem for an Era: Selected Images of American Victorian Womanhood from the Yale Collections, 1837–1911*, 1982.

LITERATURE: 'The Society of American Artists', *Art Amateur*, 34 (May 1896) p. 130; 'The Society of American Artists', *New York Times* (28 March 1896), p. 5; 'My Note Book', *Art Amateur*, 36 (April 1897), p. 82; Boston 1899, p. 9; 'The Sargent Portrait Show', *Sun*, LXVI (21 February 1899), p. 6; W. H. Downes, 'Mr Sargent's Paintings', *Boston Evening Transcript* (10 May 1916), Part Two, p. 12; 'Loan Exhibit of

Sargent Art at Museum', *Boston Journal* (11 May 1916), n.p.; Boston 1925, p. 8, ill.; Boston 1925a, p. 8, ill.; Downes 1925, pp. 174–5; Downes 1926, pp. 174–5; New York 1926, p. 6, ill.; Charteris 1927, p. 265; Mount 1955, p. 435 (959); 1957 ed., p. 343 (959); 1969 ed., p. 451 (959); McKibbin 1956, p. 122; Boston MFA 1969, vol. 1, p. 228, fig. 456; New York 1980, Checklist; Ratcliff 1982, pl. 236; New York 1980, Checklist; Fairbrother 1986, p. 184, 205 n. 55; Burns 1992, p. 48, fig. 11; Troyen *et al.* 1997, p. 245, ill.; Hirshler 2001, p. 59, fig. 32.

319 *Richard Morris Hunt*

PROVENANCE: George Vanderbilt to 1914; his daughter, Cornelia Amherst Cecil, to 1978; the Biltmore Company, Biltmore House, Asheville, North Carolina.

LITERATURE: Coffin 1896, p. 173, ill. p. 177; Van Dyke 1903, p. 36; Van Dyke 1919, p. 259; Martin 1920, vol. 2, p. 206; Downes 1925, p. 175; Downes 1926, p. 175; Charteris 1927, p. 265; Mount 1955, pp. 212, 435 (955); 1957 ed., pp. 176, 343 (955); 1969 ed., pp. 212, 442 (955); McKibbin 1956, p. 102; Paul R. Baker, *Richard Morris Hunt*, Cambridge, Mass., 1980, pp. 428, 431, 452, ill. facing p. 431, fig. 121; New York 1980, Checklist; Ratcliff 1982, p. 141; Fairbrother 1986, pp. 183, 205 n. 55; Olson 1986, p. 192.

320 *Frederick Law Olmsted*

PROVENANCE: George Vanderbilt to 1914; his daughter, Cornelia Amherst Cecil, to 1978; the Biltmore Company, Biltmore House, Asheville, North Carolina.

EXHIBITIONS: London 1998, no. 52 (exhibited in Washington, D.C., only).

LITERATURE: Downes 1925, pp. 175–6; Downes 1926, pp. 175–6; Charteris 1927, p. 278; Mount 1955, pp. 212, 435 (956); 1957 ed., pp. 176, 343 (956); 1969 ed., pp. 212, 447 (956); Roper 1973, pp. 467–8; New York 1980, Checklist; Ratcliff 1982, p. 141, ill. p. 128, fig. 181; Fairbrother 1986, pp. 183, 205 n. 55; Olson 1986, p. 192; London 1998, pp. 34, 146, ill. p. 147 (colour).

321 *Etta Dunham*

PROVENANCE: The sitter; history uncertain until acquired by Roberto Memmo *c.* 1947; Fondazione Memmo, Rome.

LITERATURE: Downes 1925, p. 260 as 'Miss Etta Daub'; Downes 1926, p. 260 as 'Miss Etta Daub'; Morris 1930, p. 284.

322 *Léon Delafosse*

PROVENANCE: The sitter, probably to 1955; subsequent history uncertain (probably the sitter's family) until Galerie Schmit, Paris, 1989; bt Seattle Art Museum, 2001.

EXHIBITIONS: Boston 1899, no. 7; Paris, Salon du Champs de Mars, 1902, no. 1044; Berlin 1903, no. 790; Brussels, Salon, 1904, no. 134, ill.; London, RA, 1905, no. 553.

LITERATURE: Boston 1899, p. 2; 'The Sargent Exhibition at Copley Hall, Boston', *Artist*, 24 (March 1899), p. xlvi; 'The Sargent Portrait Show', *Sun*, LXVI (21 February 1899), p. 6; Baldry 1900, I, ill. p. 6; Henri Frantz, 'The Salons of 1902. La Société Nationale des Beaux-Arts', *Magazine of Art*, 26 (1902), p. 447; Meynell 1903, n.p., ill.; A. C. R. Carter, 'The Royal Academy', *Art Journal* (1905), pp. 166–7; 'The Royal Academy – I', *Graphic* (29 April 1905), p. 494; H.S., 'Art. The Academy. – I', *Spectator* (6 May 1905), p. 673; 'The Royal Academy. (First Article.)', *The Times* (29 April 1905), p. 14; Downes 1925, p. 174; Downes 1926, p. 174; Charteris 1927, pp. 175, 267 (dated 1899); Meynell Manson 1927, n.p. ill.; Mount 1955, p. 434 (9412); 1957 ed., p. 343 (9412); 1969 ed., p. 436 (9412); McKibbin 1956, p. 92; Fairbrother 2000, pp. 30, 161, 164 fig. 6.7 (colour); Jean-yves Tadié, *Marcel Proust, A Life*, New York, 2001, p. 181, n.

323 *The Honourable Laura Lister*

PROVENANCE: The sitter; Dawson-Bennet sale, American Art Association, New York, 16 November 1933, lot 20; bt Scott and Fowles; bt Grenville L. Winthrop, 1933; bequeathed with his collection to the Fogg Art Museum, Cambridge, Massachusetts, 1943 (1943.156).

EXHIBITIONS: London, RA, 1897, no. 605; Boston 1899, no. 13; Edinburgh 1928, no. 373; M. Knoedler & Co., New York, *Loan Exhibition in Honour of Royal Cortissoz*, 1941, no. 33; Fogg Art Museum, *Grenville L. Winthrop: Retrospective for a Collector*, 23 January–31 March 1969, no. 88, ill.

LITERATURE: 'Art. The Royal Academy', *Academy*, 51 (8 May 1897), p. 502; A. C. R. Carter, 'The Royal Academy, 1897', *Art Journal* (1897), pp. 180, 181; 'Fine Arts. The Royal Academy. (First Notice)', *Athenaeum*, no. 3627 (1 May 1897), p. 581; 'The Royal Academy. (Fifth Notice)', *Athenaeum* no. 3635 (26 June 1897), p. 846; M. H. Spielmann, 'The Royal Academy. – I', *Graphic*, LV (1 May 1897), p. 530; 'The Royal Academy. First Notice', *Illustrated London News*, CX (8 May 1897), p. 645; 'The Exhibition of the Royal Academy. – I', *Magazine of Art*, 21 (1897), pp. 60–1; H.S. 'Art: The Academy. II', *Spectator* 78 (22 May 1897), p. 732; 'The Royal Academy. (First Article)', *The Times* (1 May 1897), p. 16; Boston 1899, p. 4; 'The Sargent Portrait Show', *Sun*, LXVI (21 February 1899), p. 6; Baldry 1900, I, p. 21, ill. p. 10; Downes 1900, p. 172; Cortissoz 1903, p. 528; Meynell 1903, n.p. ill.; Brinton 1906, ill. p. 273; Mauclair 1906–7, p. 376; Mechlin 1924, pp. 177, 185, 188; Downes 1925, p. 179, ill. facing p. 152; Downes 1926 p. 179, ill. facing p. 152; Charteris 1927, pp. 109, 226; Meynell Manson 1927, n.p. ill.; Portland 1937, ill. facing p. 224; *Fogg Art Museum Bulletin* (November 1943), ill.; Mount 1955, p. 435 (967); 1957 ed., p. 344 (967); 1969 ed., p. 444 (967); McKibbin 1956, p. 106; New York 1980, Checklist; Fairbrother 1986, p. 191; Adams 1988, vol. IV, p. 469.

324 *Mrs Carl Meyer and her Children*

PROVENANCE: Sir Carl Meyer, first Bt, to 1922; his widow, Lady Meyer, to 1930; their son, Sir Frank Meyer, second Bt, to 1935; Private Collection.

EXHIBITIONS: London, RA, 1897, no. 291; Liverpool 1897, no. 1096; Boston 1899, no. 15; Paris 1900, no. 60; London, RSPP, 1921, no. 179; London, RA, 1926, no. 331; London, Tate, 1926; Birmingham 1964, no. 25, ill.; Tokyo, National Museum of Western Art, *English Portraits*, 1975, no. 63; Leeds 1979, no. 41; London 1985, no. 38; New York and Chicago 1986; London 1992, no. 67; London 1998, no. 53; London 2000, no. 99.

LITERATURE: A.M. 'Art. The Royal Academy', *Academy*, LI (8 May 1897), p. 502; A. C. R. Carter, 'The Royal Academy, 1897', *Art Journal* (1897), p. 180; 'Fine Arts. The Royal Academy. (First Notice)', *Athenaeum*, no. 3627 (1 May 1897), p. 581; *Black and White*, 13 (8 May 1897), p. 579; M. H. Spielmann, 'The Royal Academy. – I', *Graphic*, LV (1 May 1897), p. 530; 'The Royal Academy. First Notice', *Illustrated London News*, CX (8 May 1897), p. 645; 'The Exhibition of the Royal Academy. – I', *Magazine of Art* (1897), p. 58; Henri Frantz, 'A French View of the English Art of 1897', *Magazine of Art* (1897), p. 169; 'At Burlington House', *Punch*, CXII (8 May 1897), p. 227, ill. p. 226 (caricature); D. S. M[acColl], 'Painting at the Academy', *Saturday Review*, LXXXIII (1897), p. 572; H.S., 'Art: The Academy. II', *Spectator* 78 (22 May 1897), p. 732; 'The Royal Academy. (First Notice)', *The Times* (1 May 1897), p. 16; Boston 1899, p. 4; Frederick P. Vinton, 'Letter to the Editor', *Boston Evening Transcript* (18 February 1899), p. 5; Dixon 1899, p. 119; Baldry 1900, I, p. 21, ill. p. 1; Downes 1900, pp. 169, 172; Caffin 1903a, p. 443; Meynell 1903, n.p. ill.; Cortissoz 1903, p. 529; Mauclair 1906–7, p. 376; Brinton 1908, p. 165; Fiske 1908, p. 84, ill. p. 76; 'Cost and Value of "Sargents"', *Literary Digest*, 45 (7 December 1912), p. 1065, ill.; Cortissoz 1924, p. 348; Emil Fuchs, *With Pencil, Brush and Chisel: The Life of an Artist*, New York and London, 1925, p. 32; Downes 1925, pp. 41, 49, 178; Downes 1926, pp. 41, 49, 178; London 1926, p. 50; *RA Ill. 1926*, p. 49; Charteris 1927, pp. 174, 266; Meynell Manson 1927, n.p. ill.; H. D. Cater, ed., *Henry Adams and his Friends*, Boston, 1947, p. 404; Mount 1955, pp. 222, 435 (968); 1957 ed., pp. 185, 344 (968); 1969 ed., pp. 222, 446 (968); James 1956, pp. 254, 256, 257; McKibbin 1956, p. 109; Ormond 1970, pp. 51, 249, pl. 77; Tintner 1975, pp. 129, 131, ill.; John Sunderland, *Painting in Britain 1525 to 1975*, Oxford, 1976, p. 241, pl. 179; Leeds 1979, pp. 58–9, ill. and pl. VII (colour); Ratcliff 1982, pp. 80, 168, 170, 171, 172, pl. 245 (colour); London 1985, p. 92, ill. p. 93; Fairbrother 1986, pp. 191, 194–5, 204 n. 39, 319, 357 n. 51, 375, fig. 53; Olson 1986, pp. 206–8, 223; Reynolds in Hills *et al.* 1986, pp. 167, 174, 177, fig. 114 (colour) and ill. cover (colour); Adams 1988, vol. V, pp. 122–3; Burns 1992, pp. 40–1, fig. 7; Tate 1992, p. 196, ill. (colour); Fairbrother 1994, pp. 91, 94; Adler in Nochlin and Garb 1995, p. 86, ill. p. 87; Sarah Burns, *Inventing the Modern Artist: Art and Culture in Gilded Age America*, New Haven and London, 1996, pp. 1, 175, 180–1, fig. 73; Edinburgh 1997, pp. 62, 66, 74, ill. facing p. 62 (colour); London 1998, pp. 35, 148, ill. p. 149 (colour); Mordaunt Crook 1999, p. 10, ill. cover (colour); Prettejohn 1998, pp. 42, 45, 56, fig. 31 (colour); Fischer *et al*. 1999, p. 23, fig. 30 (colour); New York 1999, p. 25, fig. 14; Fairbrother 2000, pp. 29, 30, 32, fig. 1.16; London 2000, pp. 51, 156, 439, ill. p. 172 (colour) and p. 157 detail (colour).

325   Countess Clary Aldringen

PROVENANCE: The sitter to 1930; her daughters Countess Henri de Baillet Latour and her sister, 1930–45; Private Collection, 1945; acquired by *c*. 1960 by unknown collector and sold by his heir; Sotheby's, New York, 22 November 1988, lot 56; Hirschl & Adler, New York.

EXHIBITIONS: London, New Gallery, 1896, no. 240; Paris, Salon du Champs de Mars, 1898, no. 1115 as 'Portrait de Mme La Comtesse C.A.'; Brussels, Salon, 1904, no. 133; Liège 1905, no. 63, as 'Portrait de Mme La Comtesse C.A.'; New York, Hirschl & Adler Galleries, Inc., *Another Perspective*, 1990; New York, Hirschl & Adler Galleries, Inc., *Elegant Lives: European and American Art, 1875–1910*, 1991; London, Mallet Gallery, *Predominantly People: Paintings and Drawings at the Mallet Gallery*, 1996 (listed in catalogue, but not included in the exhibition).

LITERATURE: Claude Phillips, 'Fine Art. The Royal Academy', *Academy*, XLIX (9 May 1896), p. 389; M. Aman Jean, 'Some Pictures at the New Gallery. Criticized by a French Painter', *Studio*, VIII (1896), p. 167; 'The Paris Salons. The New Salon', *Magazine of Art*, 22 (1898), pp. 535–6; H.S., 'Art. The New Gallery', *Spectator*, 76 (2 May 1896), p. 632; Baldry 1900, I, p. 21; Abel Letalle, 'Etats-Unis d'Amérique', *La Peinture à l'Exposition internationale de Liège, 1905*, Liège, 1907, pp. 124–5; Downes 1925, listed twice, p. 148, as 'Countess Clary Aldringen' (erroneously said to have been exhibited New Gallery, London, 1888), and p. 181, as 'Countess'; Downes 1926, listed twice, p. 148 as 'Countess Clary Aldringen' (erroneously said to have been exhibited New Gallery, London, 1888), and p. 181, as 'Countess'; Charteris 1927, p. 265; Portland 1937, ill. facing p. 221; Mount 1955, p. 435 (961); 1957 ed., p. 344 (961); 1969 ed., p. 434 (961); McKibbin 1956, p. 89; Lago 1982, p. 102; Vassiltchikov 1987, p. 302.

326   Mrs Walter Bacon

PROVENANCE: George Vanderbilt to 1914; his daughter the Honourable Mrs J. F. A. Cecil; the Biltmore Company, Biltmore House, Asheville, North Carolina.

EXHIBITIONS: Boston, MFA, 1925, no. 41 (revised catalogue no. 43).

LITERATURE: Boston 1925, p. 6; Boston 1925a, p. 6; Downes 1925, p. 260; Downes 1926, p. 260; Charteris 1927, p. 261, dated 1890; Mount 1955, p. 432 (901), dated 1890; 1957 ed., p. 341; 1969 ed., p. 431; McKibbin 1956, p. 82, dated 1890; New York 1980, Checklist.

327   Mrs George Swinton

PROVENANCE: Commissioned as a wedding portrait by Mrs Ebsworth (the sitter's mother) for Captain and Mrs George Swinton; their collection to 1921; M. Knoedler & Co., New York, 1921 (F 670); bt Art Institute of Chicago, Wirt D. Walker Collection (1922.4450).

EXHIBITIONS: London, New Gallery, 1897, no. 245; Berlin 1909, no. 113; Edinburgh 1917, no. 142; Pittsburgh 1921, no. 304; New York 1922, no. 25; Cincinnati 1922, no. 38; Chicago 1922, no. 202; Chicago 1924 (no catalogue); Boston, MFA, 1925, no. 95 (revised catalogue no. 97); New York, MMA, 1926, no. 29; Leeds 1979, no. 42; New York and Chicago 1986; Edinburgh 1997, no. 12.

LITERATURE: A.M., 'The New Gallery. Summer Exhibition', *Academy*, LI (1 May 1897), p. 479; 'The New Gallery and Other Exhibitions', *Art Journal* (1897), p. 189; 'My Note Book', *Art Amateur*, 37 (June 1897), p. 126 (where it is misidentified as *Mrs Van Rensslaer Cruger*); 'Fine Arts. The New Gallery. (Second and Concluding Notice.)', *Athenaeum*, no. 3630 (22 May 1897), p. 687; 'Art Notes', *Illustrated London News*, CX (1 May 1897), p. 608; 'Current Art. The New Gallery', *Magazine of Art*, 21 (1897), p. 136; H.S., 'Art. The New Gallery', *Spectator*, 78 (1 May 1897), p. 625; 'The New Gallery (First Article)', *The Times* (24 April 1897), p. 10; Baldry 1900, I, p. 21; *Art Institute of Chicago Bulletin*, X, no. 2 (February 1916), ill. p. 141; *Arts and Decoration*, XVII, no. 2 (June 1922), p. 118, ill.; *Art Institute of Chicago Annual Report*, 1922, p. 40, ill. p. 32; *Art Institute of Chicago Bulletin*, XVI, no. 7 (December 1922), p. 92 (dated 1906–7), ill. p. 89; *International Studio*, LXXVI, no. 307 (December 1922), ill. p. 211; *American Magazine of Art*, XIV (January 1923), p. 6; Berry 1924, pp. 89, 92, ill. p. 191; Starkweather 1924, ill. p. 29; Boston 1925, p. 11; Boston 1925a, p. 11; Downes 1925, pp. 41, 179–80, ill. facing p. 160; Downes 1926, pp. 41, 179–80, ill. facing p. 160; H. B. Wehle, 'The Sargent Exhibition', *Bulletin of the Metropolitan Museum of Art*, 22, no. 1 (January 1926), p. 4, ill. p. 5; Helen Gardner, *Art Through the Ages*, New York, 1926, pl. 155b, ill. facing p. 388; New York 1926, p. 6, ill.; Charteris 1927, p. 266; *Art Institute of Chicago Catalogue*, 1932, p. 123, ill.; Sitwell 1944, pp. 215–17; *Art Institute of Chicago Catalogue*, 1961, p. 41; Mount 1955, pp. 267, 278, 435 (969); 1957 ed., 219, 227, 344 (969); 1969 ed., pp. 267, 278, 435 (969); John Maxon, *The Art Institute of Chicago*, New York, 1970, pp. 269, 285, ill.; Ormond 1970, pp. 51–2; David A. Hanks, 'American Paintings at the Art Institute of Chicago', *Magazine Antiques*, I, no. 104 (November 1973), pp. 895–905, ill. p. 903; Leeds 1979, pp. 59–60, colour pl. VIII; New York 1980, Checklist; Ratcliff 1982, pp. 172, 174, pl. 246 (colour); Olson 1986, pp. 206–7, 211 n.; Reynolds in Hills *et al*. 1986, p. 167, ill. fig. 118 (colour); Art Institute of Chicago, *Brushstrokes*,

Fall 1988, ill.; Burns 1992, pp. 38–9, fig. 5; Raitt 1992, pp. 23–9; Sarah Burns, *Inventing the Modern Artist: Art and Culture in Gilded Age America*, New Haven and London, 1996, pp. 173–4, fig. 71; Greer 1997, pp. 55–9, 98, 146–7, ill. frontis. (colour); Edinburgh 1997, pp. 62, 66, 74, ill. facing p. 62 (colour); Barter *et al*. 1998, pp. 282–4, ill. p. 283 (colour); Fairbrother 2000, p. 30.

328   Princess Demidoff

PROVENANCE: Prince Demidoff to 1925; Spink & Son, London; John Levy Galleries, New York; Henry Reinhardt Gallery, New York; Florence Scott Libbey; presented by her to the Toledo Museum of Art, Ohio, 1925 (25.109).

EXHIBITIONS: London, RA, 1896, no. 402 as 'Portrait of a Lady'.

LITERATURE: Claude Phillips, 'Fine Art. The Royal Academy. I', *Academy*, 49 (9 May 1896), p. 389; 'The Royal Academy, 1896', *Art Journal* (1896), p. 181; 'The Royal Academy (Fifth Notice)', *Athenaeum*, no. 3583 (27 June 1896), p. 849; Mrs C. W. Earle, *Pot-Pourri from a Surrey Garden*, New York, 1897, p. 292; Downes 1925, p. 177, as 'Portrait of a Lady'; Downes 1926, p. 177, as 'Portrait of a Lady'; Charteris 1927, p. 266, as 'Portrait of a Lady'; Mount 1955, p. 435 (962); 1957 ed., p. 344 (962); 1969 ed., p. 436 (962); McKibbin 1956, p. 92; Susan E. Strickler, *American Paintings. The Toledo Museum of Art*, University Park, Pa., 1979, p. 97; New York 1980, Checklist.

329   Mrs Ian Hamilton

PROVENANCE: Sir Ian Hamilton; presented by him to the Tate Gallery, London, 1940 (5247).

EXHIBITIONS: London, RA, 1896, no. 129; Boston 1899, no. 23; Brussels 1900, no. 149; Philadelphia 1905, no. 433, ill.; London, International Society, 1910, no. 27; Liverpool 1910, no. 1034; London, RA, 1926, no. 328; York 1926, no. 28; Edinburgh 1928, no. 226.

LITERATURE: Claude Phillips, 'Fine Art. The Royal Academy. I', *Academy* 49 (9 May 1896), p. 389; H.S. 'Art. The Academy.- II. The Portraits.', *Spectator*, 76 (16 May 1896), p. 706; 'The Royal Academy. (Fifth Notice)', *Athenaeum* no. 3583 (27 June 1896), p. 849; Baldry 1900, I, p. 21, ill. facing p. 12; Mauclair 1906–7, p. 377; Layard 1907–8, ill. p. 27; Cournos 1915, p. 236; Van Dyke 1919, p. 262; Downes 1925 and 1926 eds, p. 164; Meynell Manson 1927, n.p. ill.; Charteris 1927, p. 266; Morris 1930, pp. 113–14; Hamilton 1942, p. 18; Mount 1955, p. 435 (965); 1957 ed., p. 344 (965); 1969 ed., p. 440 (965); McKibbin 1956, p. 100; *Tate Gallery Catalogue*, 1964, vol. 2, p. 606; Ormond 1970, p. 51; Fairbrother 1986, p. 191.

330   Mrs Colin Hunter

PROVENANCE: Colin Hunter; Milch Galleries, New York; Detroit Institute of Arts, Laura H. Murphy Fund, 1927 (27.581); Sotheby's, New York, 27 May 1993, lot 34; Adelson Galleries, Inc., New York, 1993; Utah Museum of Fine Arts, Salt Lake City, 1996.

EXHIBITIONS: London, RA, 1896, no. 591; London, RA, 1926, no. 551; San Francisco 1959, no. 13, ill.; Big Rapids, Michigan, Ferris State College, Sixth Annual Festival of Arts, 1964; Roslyn Harbor, New York, Nassau County Museum of Art, *La Belle Epoque*, 24 September – 11 June 1995, ill.

LITERATURE: Baldry 1900, I, p. 21; Downes 1925, p. 178; Downes 1926, p. 178; London 1926, p. 551; Charteris 1927, p. 265; *Detroit Institute of Arts Bulletin*, 9 (1927), p. 18, ill.; 'Art Notes', *Milch Gallery Art Notes* (1928–9), p. 11, ill. p. 8; *Detroit Catalogue of Paintings*, 1943, p. 199; Mount 1955, p. 435 (964); 1957 ed., p. 344 (964); 1969 ed., p. 442; (964) McKibbin 1956, p. 102; New York 1980, Checklist; Ratcliff 1982, pl. 9.

331   Mrs William Shakespeare

PROVENANCE: William Shakespeare; sold by him, Christie's, London, 24 June 1927, lot 81; Mr. Moore, London; Ferargil Galleries, New York, by 1928; bt from them by Memorial Art Gallery of the University of Rochester, New York, 1957 (Marion Stratton Gould Fund 57.1).

EXHIBITIONS: New York, Ferargil Galleries, 1928; New York, Anderson Galleries, *All American Exhibition*, 1928, no. 107; Newark, New Jersey, 1930–1; Memphis, Tennessee, Brooks Memorial Art Gallery, *One Hundred and Fifty Years of American Painting*, 30 September – 30 October 1934, no. 31; Utica 1953, no. 39; Rochester, New York, Memorial Art Gallery of the University of Rochester, *In Focus: A Look at Realism in Art*, 1965, no. 67; New York, Wildenstein & Co., *Treasures from Rochester*, 1977, ill.; Roslyn Harbor, New York, Nassau County Museum of Fine Art, *American Artists Abroad: The European Experience in the Nineteenth Century*, 1985, no. 98, ill.

LITERATURE: Charteris 1927, p. 268; Ducat 1928, pp. 76, 77; 'The Art Market', *Parnassus*, 6 (November 1932), p. 12, ill.; Mount 1955, p. 434 (9411); 1957 ed., p. 343 (9411); 1969 ed., p. 452 (9411); McKibbin 1956, p. 123; Memorial Art Gallery, *Handbook*, Rochester, New York, 1961, p. 110, ill.; M. S. Young, 'Treasures from Rochester', *Apollo* (April 1977), p. 304, ill., reprinted *Rochester Review*, Fall 1977, p. 13, ill.; New York 1980, Checklist.

332   Mrs Robert Wedgwood

PROVENANCE: The sitter to 1905; her daughter, Eliza Wedgwood, to 1947; her niece, Ellinor Allen; bequeathed by her to Josiah Wedgwood & Sons, 1960.

EXHIBITIONS: London, NEAC (Winter) 1909, no. 55; London, RA, 1926, no. 378.

LITERATURE: Downes 1925, p. 233; Downes 1926, p. 233; London 1926, p. 57; *RA Ill. 1926*, p. 26; Charteris 1927, p. 185; Mount 1955, p. 435 (9612); 1957 ed., p. 344 (9612); 1969 ed., p. 455 (9612); McKibbin 1956, p. 129.

333   The Right Honourable Joseph Chamberlain

PROVENANCE: The sitter; his widow, Mrs Mary Endicott Carnegie; bequeathed by her to the National Portrait Gallery, London, 1957 (4030).

EXHIBITIONS: London, RA, 1896, no. 64; Birmingham 1896, no. 274; Wembley, Palace of Arts, *British Empire Exhibition*, 1925, no. 29, ill.; London, RA, 1926, no. 332; Brussels, Académie Royale de Belgique, *De Ingre à Paul Delvaux – du deuxième centenaire*, 1973, no. 38.

LITERATURE: Claude Phillips, 'Fine Art. The Royal Academy. I', *Academy*, XLIX (9 May 1896), p. 389; 'The Royal Academy (Fifth Notice)', *Athenaeum*, no. 3583 (27 June 1896), p. 849; 'The Royal Academy, 1896', *Art Journal* (1896), p. 191; M. P. J., 'The Royal Academy. – III', *Magazine of Art* (1896), p. 358; 'The Royal Academy. (First Notice.)', *Saturday Review*, 81 (9 May 1896), p. 471; H.S., 'Art. The Academy. – II. The Portraits.', *Spectator*, 76 (16 May 1896), p. 706; Baldry 1900, I, p. 21; Van Dyke 1903, p. 36; Van Dyke 1919, p. 258; *RA Ill. 1926*, p. 98; Lucy 1922, p. 103; Downes 1925, p. 177; Downes 1926, p. 177; Charteris 1927, pp. 140, 204, 265; Swettenham 1942, p. 142; Mount 1955, p. 435 (963); 1957 ed., p. 344 (963); 1969 ed., p. 434 (963); McKibbin 1956, p. 88; *National Portrait Gallery 1957–58. One Hundred and First Annual Report of the Trustees*, 1959; Ormond 1970, p. 56; Yung 1981, p. 103, ill.; Adams 1988, vol. IV, p. 384; Aileen Ribeiro, *The Gallery of Fashion*, London, 2000, pp. 191–2, fig. 75.1 (colour).

334   Colonel Thomas Edward Vickers

PROVENANCE: The sitter to 1915; his son Douglas Vickers to 1935; Angus Vickers; Sotheby's, New York, 1 December 1994, lot 18; Private Collection.

EXHIBITIONS: London, RA, 1926, no. 405.

LITERATURE: Downes 1926, p. 361; London 1926, p. 61; Charteris 1927, p. 266; Mount 1955, p. 435 (9610); 1957 ed., p. 344 (9610); 1969 ed., p. 455 (9610); McKibbin 1956, p. 128.

335   Sir George Lewis

PROVENANCE: The sitter to 1911; his son, Sir George Lewis, second Bt, to 1945; his daughter, Mrs George Wansborough; Sotheby's, New York, 22 May 1996, lot 20; Private Collection.

EXHIBITIONS: London, RA, 1896, no. 473; London, RA, 1926, no. 408; Birmingham 1964, no. 26.

LITERATURE: 'Fine Art. The Royal Academy. I.', *Academy*, XLIX (9 May 1896), p. 389; 'The Royal Academy. (Fifth Notice)', *Athenaeum*, no. 3583 (27 June 1896), p. 849; Baldry 1900, I, p. 21; *Dictionary of National Biography*, 2nd supplement, vol. 2, London, 1912, p. 461; Downes 1925, p. 178; Downes 1926, p. 178; Charteris 1927, p. 266, and see pp. 116 and 119–20; Mount 1955, p. 435 (966); 1957 ed., p. 344 (966); 1969 ed., p. 444 (966); McKibbin 1956, p. 105; John Juxon, *Lewis and Lewis: The Life and Times of a Victorian Solicitor*, London, 1983, p. 289, ill.

336   Wallace Shakespeare

PROVENANCE: Mrs William Shakespeare to 1911; Carl Anderson of Carson, Pirie & Scott, Chicago; purchased, *c.* 1933–4, by T. E. Hanley; James H. Welch; anonymous sale, Parke-Bernet, New York, 16 October 1974, lot 36; untraced.

LITERATURE: Ducat 1928, p. 76; McKibbin 1956, p. 123.

337   Mr and Mrs I. N. Phelps Stokes

PROVENANCE: Mr and Mrs I. N. Phelps Stokes; bequeathed by Edith Minturn Phelps Stokes to the Metropolitan Museum of Art, New York, 1938 (38.104).

EXHIBITIONS: New York, SAA, 1898, no. 284; Pittsburgh 1898, no. 52; Philadelphia 1899, no. 9; Boston 1899, no. 34; Buffalo 1901, no. 28; Charleston 1901, no. 127, as 'Portraits'; New York, GCAG, 1924, no. 58; New York, MMA, 1926, no. 30; New York, Metropolitan Museum of Art, *Life in America*, 1939, no. 262; New York 1943, no. 34; Toronto, Canadian National Exhibition, 1949; Chicago 1954, no. 60; Indianapolis Museum of Art, *Treasures from the Metropolitan*, 1970–1, no. 1; New York 1994, no. 64.

LITERATURE: 'The Society of American Artists', *Art Amateur*, 38 (May 1898), p. 132; 'American Artists' Annual Exhibition', *Saturday Review of Books and Art, New York Times* (19 March 1898), p. 191; 'The Week in the Art World', *Saturday Review of Books and Art, New York Times* (26 March 1898), p. 197; 'The Society of American Artists Exhibition', *Critic*, 29 (26 March 1898), p. 220; C. H. Caffin, 'Art in Pittsburg', *Harper's Weekly*, XLII (12 November 1898), p. 1102; 'American Fakirs' Exhibit', *New York Times* (19 April 1898), p. 7; 'American Studio Talk', *International Studio*, 4 (1898), p. x; 'The American Survey: Sixty-Eighth Annual Exhibition of the Pennsylvania Academy', *Artist* 24 (February 1899), p. xxix; F. J. Zeigler, 'Sixty-eighth Annual Exhibition of the Pennsylvania Academy of the Fine Arts', *Brush and Pencil*, 3 (February 1899), pp. 292–3; Gustav Kobbé, 'Fakes and Fakirs', *Century*, 59 (December 1899), p. 321, ill. (caricature); Charles H. Caffin, 'The Picture Exhibition at the Pan-American Exposition, Continued', *International Studio*, 14 (1901), p. xxi; J. W. Pattison, *Painters since Leonardo*, New York and London, 1904, pp. 252–4; H. McBride, 'Modern Art', *Dial* 76 (April 1924), pp. 386–7; Mechlin 1924, ill. p. 186; Watson 1924, p. 144; Downes 1925, pp. 41, 180–1; Downes 1926, pp. 41, 180–1; New York 1926, p. 6, ill.; H. B. Wehle, *Metropolitan Museum of Art Bulletin*, 21 (January 1926), p. 4; Charteris 1927, p. 266; *Metropolitan Museum of Art Bulletin*, 33 (September 1938), p. 210, ill.; 'Seven Feet of Sargent', *Art Digest*, 13 (1 October 1938), p. 17; Stokes 1941, pp. 115–18, ill. facing p. 115; Jerome Mellquist, 'The Man Who Reconstructed Manhattan', *American Collector*, 15 (June 1946), p. 8, ill.; Andrew Bell, 'Pot-Pourri on the Toronto Waterfront', *Canadian Art*, VII (Christmas – New Year, 1949–50), p. 71, ill. p. 70; Mount 1955, p. 448 (972); 1957 ed., p.

344 (972); 1969 ed., p. 448 (972); Chicago 1954, p. 61, ill.; McKibbin 1956, p. 124; Albert Ten Eyck Gardner, 'American Art at the Metropolitan', *Antiques*, 87 (April 1965), p. 438, ill.; Ormond 1970, pp. 52, 248, pl. 71; Burke 1980, pp. 247–51, ill. p. 249; New York 1980, Checklist; Ratcliff 1982, pp. 167–8, pl. 242 (colour); Fairbrother 1986, pp. 368–71, 373, fig. 104; Olson 1986, p. 206; Reynolds in Hills *et al.* 1986, p. 174, p. 166, fig. 115; J. L. Greaves 'Portrait of Mr. and Mrs. Isaac Newton Phelps Stokes by John Singer Sargent (1856–1925)', unpublished paper (copy in MMA archives); New York 1994, pp. 258, 260, 261, ill. p. 259 (colour); Fairbrother 1994, pp. 92, 94, ill. p. 92 (colour); London 1998, p. 35, fig. 36; Prettejohn 1998, pp. 56, 58, fig. 43 (colour), and detail ill. p. 54; Herdrich and Weinberg 2000, pp. 10, 123, 209–11, fig. 77.

338   Mrs Harold Wilson

PROVENANCE: The sitter; her daughter, Mrs Aubyn Wilson; her son, Ralph Stewart-Wilson; sold by him, Christie's, New York, 9 December 1983, lot 210; bt William Wiltshire; Western Heritage sale, Shamrock Hilton Hotel, Houston, Texas, 1985; Sotheby's, London, 23 June 1987, lot 73; Pyms Gallery, London; Private Collection.

EXHIBITIONS: London, RA, 1898, no. 69; Edinburgh 1902, no. 161; London, Pyms Gallery, *Orpen and the Edwardian Era*, 1987, no. 7, ill.

LITERATURE: 'Art. The Hundred Best Academy Pictures', *Academy* (7 May 1898), p. 504; 'The Royal Academy. First Notice', *Illustrated London News*, CXII (7 May 1898), p. 673; 'The Royal Academy. (First Notice)', *The Times* (30 April 1898), p. 14; Downes 1925, p. 184; Downes 1926, p. 184; Charteris 1927, p. 266; Mount 1955, p. 435 (975); 1957 ed., p. 344 (975); 1969 ed., p. 456 (975); McKibbin 1956, p. 131; *Western Heritage Newsletter*, 10 (January 1985), p. 1.

339   Catherine Vlasto

PROVENANCE: Alexander Anthony Vlasto, the sitter's father, to 1899; his son, Anthony Alexander Vlasto, to 1932; his widow, Erato Vlasto, to 1966; her grandson, R. A. Vlasto; sold by him, Christie's, London, 10 March 1967, lot 51, ill.; Gimpel Fils, London, 3 April 1967; bt Joseph Hirshhorn, 1967; transferred with his collection to the Hirshhorn Museum and Sculpture Garden, Smithsonian Institution, Washington, D.C. (72.256).

EXHIBITIONS: Hirshhorn Museum and Sculpture Garden, Washington, D.C., *Inaugural Exhibition*, 1 October 1974–15 September 1975; New York and Chicago 1986; Washington, D.C., Smithsonian Institution Travelling Exhibition Service, *New Horizons: American Painting*, 1987–8; Montclair 1999.

LITERATURE: Abram Lerner, ed., *The Hirshhorn Museum and Sculpture Garden*, New York, 1974, p. 744, fig. 77; New York 1980, Checklist; Edwards Park, *Treasures of the Smithsonian*,

Washington, D.C., 1983, ill.; Robert Atkins, 'Saluting Sargent', *Horizon* (October 1986), p. 12, ill.; Reynolds in Hills *et al.* 1986, p. 174, fig. 113 (colour).

340   Mrs George Batten

PROVENANCE: The sitter to 1916; bequeathed by her to Radclyffe Hall; purchased from her with funds from the Hamilton bequest for the Glasgow Art Gallery and Museum, 1929 (1769).

EXHIBITIONS: London, New Gallery, 1897, no. 175; Paris, Salon du Champs de Mars, 1902, no. 1043; London, RA, 1926, no. 43, as *étude*; London, Tate, 1926; Glasgow Art Gallery, *The Hamilton Bequest: Paintings Presented to the Glasgow Art Gallery 1927–1977*, 14 September–30 October 1977, no. 9; Edinburgh 1997, no. 13.

LITERATURE: A.M., 'The New Gallery. Summer Exhibition', *Academy*, LI (1 May 1897), p. 479; 'Fine Arts. The New Gallery (Second and Continuing Notice)', *Athenaeum*, no. 3630 (22 May 1897), p. 687; 'Art Notes', *Illustrated London News*, CX (1 May 1897), p. 608; 'Current Art. The New Gallery', *Magazine of Art*, 21 (1897), p. 136; Henri Frantz, 'The Salons of 1902. La Société Nationale des Beaux-Arts', *Magazine of Art*, 26 (1902), p. 447; Meynell 1903, n.p.; Mauclair 1906–7, p. 376, ill. p. 374; Downes 1925, p. 180; Downes 1926, p. 180; London 1926, p. 13; *RA Ill. 1926*, p. 22; Charteris 1927, p. 265; Meynell Manson 1927, n.p.; Mount 1955, p. 435 (954); 1957 ed., p. 343 (954); 1969 ed., p. 431 (954); McKibbin 1956, pp. 83–4; Glasgow Art Gallery and Museum, *Summary Catalogue of British Oil Paintings*, 1971, p. 81; Glasgow Art Gallery and Museum, *The Hamilton Bequest: Paintings Presented to the Glasgow Art Gallery 1927–1977*, 1977, p. 16, ill.; Baker 1985, p. 35; Raitt 1992, p. 24; Edinburgh 1997, pp. 65–6, 74–5, ill. p. 56 (colour); Fairbrother 2000, p. 30, fig. 1.13.

341   Johannes Wolff

PROVENANCE: Temporarily deposited as diploma work, Royal Academy, London, 1897–1900; presumably the sitter; possibly a French dealer or auction house; John Levy Galleries, New York, by 1934; Private Collection; Parke-Bernet, New York, 4 November 1938, lot 61; bt J. N. Gattle; purchased by Grenville Winthrop from an unknown source by 1941; bequeathed with his collection to the Fogg Art Museum, Cambridge, Massachusetts (1943.151).

EXHIBITIONS: London, RA, 1898, no. 250; New York 1935, no. 34, ill.

LITERATURE: *Royal Academy Council Minutes*, XX, 1894–9, p. 319; 'Art. The Hundred Best Academy Pictures', *Academy* (7 May 1898), p. 504; Cortissoz 1903, p. 521; Meynell 1903, n.p. ill.; Downes 1925, p. 183; Downes 1926, p. 183; Charteris 1927, pp. 163, 266; Meynell Manson 1927, n.p. ill.; Colson 1950, p. 117; Mount 1955, p. 435 (974); 1957 ed., p. 344 (974); 1969 ed., p. 457 (974); McKibbin 1956, p. 132; New York 1980, Checklist; Fairbrother 1986, p. 325; Fairbrother 1994, p. 101; Fairbrother 2000, p. 30.

342   Thomas Francis Bayard

PROVENANCE: Mrs Thomas Francis Bayard; her son, Thomas Francis Bayard Jr; presented by the estate of his son, Alexis I. du Pont Bayard, to the US Department of State, Washington, D.C., 1986 (86.7).

LITERATURE: Mount 1969, p. 431.

343   Henry G. Marquand

PROVENANCE: Commissioned by the trustees of the Metropolitan Museum of Art, New York, 1897 (97.43).

EXHIBITIONS: Boston, MFA, 1925, no. 63 (revised catalogue no. 66); New York, MMA, 1926, no. 31.

LITERATURE: *Art Interchange*, 39 (December 1897), ill. p. 121; 'Mr Sargent's Portrait of Mr Marquand', *Critic*, 31 (13 November 1897), p. 286; *International Studio*, 3 (January 1898), pp. x–xi; Arthur Hoeber, *The Treasures of the Metropolitan Museum of Art of New York*, New York, 1899, pp. 118, 120; Caffin 1902, pp. 62, 64, ill. facing p. 62; Caffin 1903, p. 4115, ill. p. 4105; Caffin 1903a, p. 445; Van Dyke 1903, pp. 36, 38, ill. p. 37; Meynell 1903, n.p., ill.; Isham 1905, ill. p. 435; *Metropolitan Museum of Art Bulletin*, 1 (November 1905), p. 10; Brinton 1906, ill. p. 274; C. H. Caffin, *The Story of American Painting*, London and Garden City, N.J., 1907, 1937, ill. p. 248; McSpadden 1907, ill. facing p. 296; W. A. Coffin, *Palette and Bench*, 3 (October 1910), p. 9, ill.; *Arts and Decoration*, 6 (July 1916), pp. 6, 396; Van Dyke 1919, pp. 257, 258; Mechlin 1924, p. 188; Starkweather 1924, ill. p. 23; Boston 1925, p. 8, ill.; Boston 1925a, p. 8, ill.; Blashfield 1925, p. 649; Downes 1925, pp. 41–2, 181; Downes 1926, pp. 41–2, 181; New York 1926, p. 6, ill.; A. D. Patterson, 'Sargent: A Memory', *Canadian Magazine*, 65 (March 1926) p. 31; Charteris 1927, p. 266; Meynell Manson 1927, n.p., ill.; Birnbaum 1941, pp. 41–2; F. J. Mather Jr, *Magazine of Art*, 39 (November 1946), p. 304, ill.; J. P. Leeper, *Magazine of Art*, 44 (January 1951), p. 15, ill. p. 13; Mount 1955, pp. 367, 435 (971); 1957 ed. pp. 303, 344 (971); 1969 ed., pp. 367, 445 (971); McKibbin 1956, p. 108,: Ormond 1970, pp. 52, 250, pl. 84; W. D. Garrett, *Metropolitan Museum of Art Journal*, 3 (1970), p. 311, ill.; Burke 1980, pp. 251–3, ill.; New York 1980, Checklist; Ratcliff 1982, p. 185; Fairbrother 1986, pp. 184, 325; Olson 1986, pp. 137, 206; Herdrich and Weinberg 2000, p. 1, fig. 2.

344   Arthur Cohen

PROVENANCE: The sitter to 1914; his daughter, Lucy Cohen, to 1951; her nephew, Judge Arthur Cohen to 1995; Private Collection.

EXHIBITIONS: London, New Gallery, 1898, no. 182; London, RA, 1926, no. 62; Victoria and Albert Museum, London, *Anglo-Jewish Art and History Exhibition*, 19656.

LITERATURE: 'Art. At the New Gallery', *Academy* (30 April 1898), p. 479; Fernand Khnopff, 'The New Gallery', *Magazine of Art*, 22 (1898), p. 430, where it is mistakenly called 'Mrs Cohen'; D. S. M[acColl], 'The New Gallery and Old Water Colour Society', *Saturday Review*, LXXXV (30 April 1898), pp. 590, 591; [Lucy Cohen], *Arthur Cohen: A Memoir by His Daughter for His Descendants*, London, 1919, pp. 120, 148–9, ill. frontis.; London 1926, p. 16; *RA Ill. 1926*, p. 30; *Dictionary of National Biography 1912–1921*, 1927, p. 122; Mount 1955, p. 439 (0614), dated 1906; 1957 ed., p. 348 (0614); 1969 ed., p. 434 (0614); McKibbin 1956, p. 90.

345   *Contessa Chiericati*

PROVENANCE: The sitter; probably via Harold Parsons to Ehrich Bros, New York, by 1925; bt Wharton Sinkler; Newhouse Galleries, New York, by 1928; bt Howard E. Green, 1929; John E. Greene Jr; his widow, Mrs John E. Greene Jr; by family descent to Richard D. Sheldom, 1958; Private Collection.

EXHIBITION: New York, Macbeth Gallery, 1923, no. 31; City Art Museum of St Louis, *American Art in St Louis*, 22 October–30 November 1969.

LITERATURE: Downes 1925, p. 265; Downes 1926, p. 265; Charteris 1927, p. 278; 'Notes of the Month', *International Studio* (August 1928), ill. p. 65; 'Picture Galleries', *New York Times* (2 June 1929), VI, ill. [p. 6]; Mount 1955, p. 434 (948); 1957 ed., p. 343 (948); 1969 ed., p. 434 (948); McKibbin 1956, p. 89.

346   *Senator Calvin Brice*

PROVENANCE: The sitter; his daughter Helen Olivia Brice (d. *c.* 1950 or 1951); her nieces, Monica (Mrs W. M. Hobbs), Kate (Mrs F. M. Briggs), and Jean (Mrs Eltham Allen); presented by them to the Allen County Historical Society, Lima, Ohio, 1950 (878.1).

EXHIBITIONS: New York, NAD, 1898–9, no. 218; New York, Schaus Gallery, 1899; Boston 1899, no. 20; Philadelphia 1900, no. 18; Boston, MFA, 1925, no. 64 (revised catalogue no. 67); New York, MMA, 1926, no. 33; Oxford, Ohio, Miami University Art Museum, *An Exhibition for the Western College Alumnae and Friends*, 1979.

LITERATURE: Boston 1899, p. 6; 'The Collector', *Art Amateur*, 40 (January 1899), p. 33; 'The Portrait Show', *Art Amateur*, 40 (January 1899), p. 33; W. P. Lockington, 'The Pennsylvania Academy's Annual Exhibition', *Collector and Art Critic*, II (1 February 1900), p. 121; 'Academy's Exhibition', *Philadelphia Inquirer* (1 January 1900), p. 10; Boston 1925, p. 8, ill.; Boston 1925a, p. 8, ill.; Downes 1925, p. 184; Downes 1926, p. 184; New York 1926, p. 6; Charteris 1927, p. 266; Mount 1955, p. 435 (983); 1957 ed., p. 344 (983); 1969 ed., p. 432 (983); McKibbin 1956, p. 86; New York 1980, Checklist; *Western College Alumnae Association*, 55 (1981), no. 1; Fairbrother 1986, p. 184.

347   *Asher Wertheimer*

PROVENANCE: The sitter to 1918; presented by the widow and family of Asher Wertheimer, in accordance with his wishes, to the National Gallery, London, 1922; transferred to the Tate Gallery, London, 1926 (N03705).

EXHIBITIONS: London, RA, 1898, no. 603; New York, NAD, 1898–9, no. 220; Boston 1899, no. 19; Paris 1900, no. 5; Berlin 1907–8, no. 23; London, Tate, 1946; New York and Chicago 1986; London 1998, no. 54; New York 1999, no. 1.

LITERATURE: 'Art. The Hundred Best Academy Pictures', *Academy* (7 May 1898), p. 505; A. C. R. Carter, 'The Royal Academy, 1898', *Art Journal* (1898), pp. 177–8; 'Fine Arts The Royal Academy. (Fourth Notice)', *Athenaeum*, no. 3685 (11 June 1898), p. 762; 'The Royal Academy. First Notice', *Illustrated London News*, CXII (7 May 1898), p. 673; 'The Royal Academy Exhibition – I', *Magazine of Art* (1898), p. 422; 'The Pick of the Pictures', *Punch* (7 May 1898), p. 207; 'Unconscious Humour at the Royal Academy!', *Punch* (7 May 1898), p. 205, ill. (caricature); H.S. 'Art. The Academy. – I', *Spectator*, 80 (7 May 1898), p. 655; 'The Royal Academy. (First Notice)', *The Times* (30 April 1898), p. 14; 'The Portrait Show', *Art Amateur*, 40 (January 1899), p. 33; Dixon 1899, p. 119, ill. p. 117; Baldry 1900, I, p. 21; Downes 1900, p. 170; Gustave Geffroy, *La Vie Artistique*, Paris, 1901, p. 199; Cortissoz 1903, p. 515; Van Dyke 1903, p. 36; Brinton 1906, ill. p. 279; Mauclair 1906–7, p. 377; Brinton 1908, p. 165; Ross 1911, pp. 7–8, ill, p. 2; Cournos 1915, pp. 233, 234; 'A Sargent Year', 'Letters and Art', *Literary Digest*, LIII (9 September 1916), p. 608, ill. p. 609; Pousette-Dart 1924, n.p., ill.; Starkweather 1924, p. 10; Watson 1924, p. 149; Downes 1925, pp. 43–6, 182, ill. facing p. 168; Minchin 1925, p. 742; Downes 1926, pp. 43–6, 182, ill. facing p. 168; Fry 1926, p. 32; Charteris 1927, pp. 140, 164–5, 177, 267; Shane Leslie, *The Passing Chapter*, London, 1934, pp. 152–3; W. C. Ford, ed., *Letters of Henry Adams*, 2 vols, Boston, 1938, vol. 2, p. 137; Meynell Manson 1927, n.p. ill.; Blanche 1937, p. 158; Stokes 1941 p. 118; Mount 1955, pp. 223–5, 229, 398–9, 435 (981); 1957 ed., 186–8, 191, 330–1, 344 (981); 1969 ed., pp. 223–5, 229, 398–9, 456 (981); McKibbin 1956, p. 130; *Tate Gallery Catalogue*, 1964, vol. 2, pp. 594–5; Ormond 1970, pp. 53, 248, pls 72, 75 (detail); Ratcliff 1982, p. 174, 177, ill. pl. 257; Olson 1986, p. 269; Reynolds 1986, p. 982, fig. 1; Reynolds in Hills *et al.* 1986, pp. 148, 174, fig. 116; Adams 1988, vol. IV, pp. 497, 603; Adler in Nochlin and Garb 1995, pp. 83, 84, 88–91, ill. p. 89; Fairbrother 1994, p. 94, ill. p. 95; London 1998, pp. 38, 129, 148, 151, ill. p. 150 (colour); Prettejohn 1998, pp. 40, 42, fig. 29 (colour); Ridge and Townsend 1998, pp. 23, 24, 26, fig. 2 (colour); New York 1999, pp. 16–19, 22, 26–7, 41, pl. 1; Fairbrother 2000, pp. 30, 82–3, 84, 85, 87, fig. 3. 12.

348   *Mrs Asher Wertheimer*

PROVENANCE: Mr and Mrs Asher Wertheimer; their daughter Hylda, Mrs H. Wilson-Young; her son, Ian Wilson-Young; his widow; her son, Conway Wilson-Young; Julius Weitzner; M. Knoedler & Co., New York, 1976 (JA 10221);

Hammer Galleries, 23 February 1978; purchased by the New Orleans Museum of Art, 1978 (78.3).

EXHIBITIONS: London, RA, 1898, no. 936; either this or no. 468, Glasgow 1913, no. 340; New York 1999, no. 2.

LITERATURE: 'Art. The Sky-Line at the Royal Academy', *Academy* (14 May 1898), p. 530; *Magazine of Art* (1899), p. 116, ill.; Ross 1911, p. 8; 'A Sargent Year', 'Letters and Art', *Literary Digest*, LIII (9 September 1916), p. 609; Downes 1925, p. 183; Downes 1926, p. 183; Charteris 1927, pp. 164, 267; Mount 1955, pp. 225, 435 (982); 1957 ed., pp. 187, 344 (982); 1969 ed., pp. 225, 456 (982); McKibbin 1956, p. 130; Ormond 1970, p. 248; Joan Caldwell, *Handbook of the Collection, New Orleans Museum of Art*, New Orleans, 1980, p. 139, ill. p. 24 and cover; New York 1980, Checklist; 'The Eternal Masterpieces: Portrait of Mrs Asher B. Wertheimer', *Franklin Mint Almanac*, 12 (November–December 1981), p. 15; Adler in Nochlin and Garb 1995, p. 84; New York 1999, p. 22, pl. 12 (colour); Fairbrother 2000, pp. 87–8, fig. 3.14 (colour).

349   *Thomas Sutherland*

PROVENANCE: Commissioned by the Peninsular & Oriental Steam Navigation Company, 1897–8; P. & O., London.

EXHIBITIONS: London, RA, 1898, no. 609; Venice 1903, no. 33; London, RA, 1926, no. 285.

LITERATURE: 'Art. The Hundred Best Academy Pictures', *Academy*, (7 May 1898), p. 505; 'The Royal Academy. First Notice', *Illustrated London News*, CXII (7 May 1898), p. 673; 'The Pick of the Pictures' *Punch* (7 May 1898), p. 207; 'Unconscious Humour at the Royal Academy!', *Punch* (7 May 1898), p. 205, ill. (caricature); 'The Royal Academy. (First Notice)', *The Times* (30 April 1898), p. 14; Baldry 1900 I, p. 21; Meynell 1903, n.p. ill.; Mauclair 1906–7, p. 378; Downes 1925 and 1926 eds, p. 183; London 1926 p. 43; Charteris 1927, p. 267; Meynell Manson 1927, n.p. ill.; Boyd Cable, *A Hundred Year History of the P. & O. 1837–1937*, London, 1937, ill. facing. p. 176; Mount 1955, p. 436 (9814); 1957 ed., p. 345 (9814); 1969 ed., p. 453 (814); McKibbin 1956, p. 125.

350   *Francis Cranmer Penrose*

PROVENANCE: Commissioned by the Royal Institute of British Architects, London, 1898.

EXHIBITIONS: London, RA, 1898, no. 63; Boston 1899, no. 17; Venice 1907, no. 27; Berlin 1907–8, no. 12; London, RA, 1926, no. 45; York 1926, no. 25.

LITERATURE: 'Art. The Hundred Best Academy Pictures', *Academy* (7 May 1898), p. 504; 'Fine Arts The Royal Academy. (Fourth Notice)', *Athenaeum*, no. 3685 (11 June 1898), p. 762; 'The Royal Academy. First Notice', *Illustrated London News*, CXII (7 May 1898), p. 673; 'Unconscious Humour at the Royal Academy!', *Punch* (7 May 1898), p. 205, ill. (caricature); H.S., 'Art. The Academy. – I', *Spectator*, 80 (7 May 1898), p. 655;

Journal of the Royal Institute of British Architects, vol. (1898), pp. 277–8; Boston 1899, p. 17; Baldry 1900, I, p. 21, ill. p. 5; Downes 1900, p. 170; Caffin 1903a, p. 446; Downes 1925, pp. 181–2; Downes 1926, pp. 181–2; London 1926, p. 14; *RA Ill. 1926*, p. 90; Charteris 1927, p. 267; Mount 1955, p. 436 (9812); 1957 ed., p. 345 (9812); 1969 ed., p. 448 (9812); McKibbin 1956, p. 116.

351 *Lord Watson*

PROVENANCE: Commissioned by members of the legal profession in Scotland; Faculty of Advocates, Parliament Hall, Edinburgh.

EXHIBITIONS: London, RA, 1898, no. 906; London, RA, 1926, no. 359.

LITERATURE: 'Art. The Sky-Line at the Royal Academy', *Academy* (14 May 1898), p. 530; A. A. Grainger Taylor, *Portraits in the Hall of the Parliament House in Edinburgh*, Edinburgh, 1907, no. 10, ill.; Downes 1925, p. 182; Downes 1926, p. 182; *RA Ill. 1926*, p. 28; Charteris 1927, p. 266; Mount 1955, p. 435 (973); 1957 ed., p. 344 (973); 1969 ed., p. 455 (973); McKibbin 1956, p. 129; Colin Sutherland and Sheriff Roger Craik eds, *Parliament House Portraits*, Edinburgh, 2000, no. 98, ill. (colour).

352 *Colonel Ian Hamilton*

PROVENANCE: The sitter; presented by him to the Tate Gallery, London, 1940 (5246).

EXHIBITIONS: London, New Gallery, 1899, no. 149; Brussels 1900, no. 148; Philadelphia 1901, no. 28; either this or no. 353, Liverpool 1901, no. 999; either this or no. 353, Glasgow 1902, no. 384; Venice 1907, no. 26; Berlin 1907–8, no. 10; London, Guildhall Art Gallery, *Naval and Military Works*, 1915, no. 38; Sheffield, Mappin Art Gallery, 1915, no catalogue; London, RA, 1926, no. 21; York 1926, no. 10.

LITERATURE: R. A. M. Stevenson, 'The Art Season. Mr Sargent and Others', *Academy* (6 May 1899), p. 510; 'The New Gallery Summer Exhibition, 1899', *Art Journal* (1899), p. 187, ill.; J. C. Robinson, 'Fine Arts. The New Gallery', *Athenaeum*, no. 3732 (6 May 1899), p. 568; 'Current Art. The Royal Academy. The New Gallery', *Magazine of Art*, 23 (1899), p. 343; D. S. M[acColl], 'The Miracle of the Sacred Fire', *Saturday Review* (29 April 1899), p. 523; Baldry 1900, I, p. 21, ill. p. 2; 'Philadelphia Art Exhibition', *Brush and Pencil*, VII (February 1901), p. 264; 'Wealth of Paintings to be Exhibited at the Academy of Fine Arts', *Evening Bulletin* (12 January 1901), p. 9; *Philadelphia Evening Telegraph* (12 January 1901), n.p.; 'The Academy's Annual Exhibition', *Philadelphia Inquirer* (13 January 1901), p. 11; 'Seventieth Annual Salon at the Academy of the Fine Arts', *Philadelphia Press* (13 January 1901), n.p.; Brinton 1906, ill. p. 272; Mauclair 1906–7, p. 377, ill. p. 378; Layard 1907–8, ill. p. 26; Downes 1925, pp. 185–6, ill. facing p. 184; Downes 1926, pp. 185–6, ill. facing p. 184; London 1926, p. 10; *RA Ill. 1926*, p. 60; Charteris 1927, p. 267; Meynell Manson, 1927, n.p., ill.; Mount 1955, p. 436 (9810); 1957 ed., p. 345 (9810); 1969 ed., p.

440 (9810); McKibbin 1956, p. 100; *Tate Gallery Catalogue*, 1964, vol. 2, pp. 605–6; Ormond 1970, p. 52; Olson 1986, p. 235; Fairbrother 1994, pp. 126–7; Edinburgh 1997, pp. 75–6, fig. 4; Fairbrother 2000, ill. p. 33; John Lee, *A Soldier's Life. General Sir Ian Hamilton 1853–1947*, London, 2000, ill. cover (colour).

353 *Colonel Ian Hamilton*

PROVENANCE: Mrs Ian Hamilton, later Lady Hamilton; presented by her to the Scottish National Portrait Gallery, Edinburgh 1941 (PG 1406).

EXHIBITIONS: London, New Gallery, 1900, no. 124; either this or no. 352, Liverpool 1901, no. 999; either this, or no. 352, Glasgow 1902, no. 384; London, RA, 1926, no. 53; York 1926, no. 3; Edinburgh 1997, no. 16.

LITERATURE: W. St Chad Boscawen, 'Fine Arts. The New Gallery', *Athenaeum*, no. 3783 (28 April 1900), p. 534; 'The New Gallery', *Illustrated London News*, 116 (5 May 1900), p. 597; 'The New Gallery', *Magazine of Art*, 24 (1900), p. 392; 'The New Gallery', *The Times* (23 April 1900), p. 8; 'Philadelphia Art Exhibition', *Brush and Pencil*, VII (February 1901), p. 264; Meynell 1903, n.p. ill.; Downes 1925, p. 192; Downes 1926, p. 192; London 1926, p. 53; Charteris 1927, p. 267; Meynell Manson 1927, n.p. ill.; Mount 1955, p. 436 (989); 1957 ed., p. 345 (989); 1969 ed., p. 440 (989); McKibbin 1956, p. 100; Smailes 1990, p. 136, ill. p. 137; Fairbrother 1994, ill. p. 32; Edinburgh 1997, pp. 75–6, ill.

354 *Antonio Mancini*

PROVENANCE: The sitter; returned to the artist at an unknown date; presented by him to the Galleria Nazionale d'Arte Moderna, Rome, 1925 (2666).

EXHIBITIONS: Rome 1923–4.

LITERATURE: Meynell 1903, n.p., ill.; Helen Gerard, 'The Roman International', *American Magazine of Art*, XV (July 1924), p. 347, ill. p. 346; Downes 1925, pp. 171–2, dated 1894; Downes 1926, pp. 171–2, dated 1894; Charteris 1927, p. 265, dated 1894; Meynell Manson 1927, n.p., ill.; Lewis 1939, p. 74; Mount 1955, p. 434 (942), dated 1894; 1957 ed., p. 343 (942); 1969 ed., p. 445 (942); McKibbin 1956, p. 108; Ormond 1970, p. 21.

355 *Mrs Charles Anstruther-Thomson*

PROVENANCE: The sitter; her daughter, Grizel, Baroness Knut Bonde; her son, Baron John Bonde; anonymous sale, Sotheby's, New York, 25 April 1980, lot 7; Sotheby's, New York, 29 May 1981, lot 52; Private Collection; Ira Spanierman, New York, 1989; Private Collection.

EXHIBITIONS: London, New Gallery, 1898, no. 223.

LITERATURE: 'Art. At the New Gallery', *Academy* (30 April 1898), p. 479; 'The New Gallery', *Illustrated London News*, 112 (21 May 1898), p. 741; Fernand Khnopff, 'The New Gallery',

Magazine of Art, 22 (1898), p. 430; 'The New Gallery', *Punch* (14 May 1898), p. 220; Baldry 1900, p. 21; Downes 1925 and 1926 eds, p. 184; Charteris 1927, p. 267; Mount 1955 (9817); 1957 ed., p. 345 (9817); 1969 ed., p. 430 (9817); McKibbin 1956, p. 126.

356 *Mrs Ernest Franklin*

PROVENANCE: Ernest Franklin; the sitter; on loan to the Walker Art Gallery, Liverpool, 1953–64; Private Collection.

EXHIBITIONS: London, New Gallery, 1898, no. 234; London, RA, 1926, no. 356.

LITERATURE: 'Art. At the New Gallery', *Academy* (30 April 1898), p. 479; 'The New Gallery', *Illustrated London News*, 112 (21 May 1898), p. 741; Fernand Khnopff, 'The New Gallery', *Magazine of Art*, 22 (1898), p. 430, ill., p. 429; Baldry 1900 I, p. 21; Downes 1925, p. 184; Downes 1926, p. 184; London 1926, p. 54; Charteris 1927, p. 266; Mount 1955, pp. 268, 435 (986); 1957 ed., pp. 219, 344 (986); 1969 ed., pp. 268, 439 (986); McKibbin 1956, p. 96; Gibbon 1960, pp. 31, 55, 237, ill. frontis.

357 *The Honourable Pauline Astor*

PROVENANCE: The sitter to 1972; her grandson, Francis Nichols; Sotheby's, New York, 3 December 1997, lot 13; Private Collection.

EXHIBITIONS: London, Guildhall, 1900, no. 47; London, RA, 1926, no. 283; Bradford Museum and Art Gallery, Cartwright Hall, *Jubilee Exhibition*, 1954, no. 825.

LITERATURE: Edward S. Martin, *The Life of Joseph Hodges Choate*, 2 vols, London, 1920, vol. 2, p. 135; *RA Ill. 1926*, p. 45; Charteris 1927, p. 270, dated 1903; Mount 1955, p. 437 (0227), dated 1902; 1957 ed., p. 346 (0227), dated 1902; 1969 ed., p. 430 (0227), dated 1902; McKibbin 1956, p. 82; Ormond 1970, p. 58.

358 *Daisy Leiter*

PROVENANCE: The sitter to 1968; bequeathed to English Heritage with the Suffolk Collection by the sitter's daughter-in-law, Mrs Greville Howard, 1994; the Iveagh Bequest, Kenwood, London.

EXHIBITIONS: London, RA, 1898, no. 272 as 'Portrait of a Lady'; London, RA, 1926, no. 271; Edinburgh 1928, no. 188.

LITERATURE: 'Art. The Hundred Best Academy Pictures', *Academy* (7 May 1898), p. 505; Montague Marks, 'The London Letter', *Art Amateur*, 39 (June 1898), p. 3; A. C. R. Carter, 'The Royal Academy, 1898', *Art Journal* (June 1898), pp. 177–8; 'Fine Arts. The Royal Academy (Fourth Notice)', *Athenaeum*, no. 3685 (11 June 1898), p. 762; Meynell 1903, n.p., ill.; Cox 1908, p. 258; Downes 1925, p. 151; Downes 1926, p. 151; London 1926, p. 41; *RA Ill. 1926*, p. 61; Charteris 1927, p. 267; Meynell Manson 1927, n.p., ill.; Mount 1955, p. 436 (9813); 1957 ed., p. 345 (9813); 1969 ed., p. 453 (9813); McKibbin 1956, p. 105; Ormond 1970, pp. 57, 65; Fairbrother 1986, pp. 355–6 n. 40, pp. 372–5, fig. 105; Adams 1988, vol. IV, p. 603;

Adams 1988, vol.V, p. 655; Fairbrother 2000, fig. 1.21.

359 Mrs Ralph Curtis

PROVENANCE: Painted as a wedding present for Ralph Curtis and his wife; the sitter to 1933; her son, Ralph Curtis Jr; Cleveland Museum of Art, Ohio, 1998.168.

EXHIBITIONS: Boston 1899, no. 4.

LITERATURE: Boston 1899, p. 2; Downes 1925, p. 183; Downes 1926, p. 183; Charteris 1927, p. 267; 'Houses & Gardens of the Riviera: Villa Sylvia, Cap Ferrat. The Home of Mrs Lisa Curtis', *Country Life*, LXI (15 January 1927), p. 91; Mount 1955, p. 436 (9816); 1957 ed., p. 345 (9816); 1969 ed., p. 435 (9816); McKibbin 1956, p. 91.

360 Mrs Charles Thursby

PROVENANCE: The sitter to 1953; her niece, Mrs William T. Tooker Jr; sold by the executors of her estate, Christie's, New York, 9 December 1983, lot 189a; bt Hirschl & Adler Galleries, New York; Newark Museum, New Jersey.

EXHIBITIONS: London, New Gallery, 1898, no. 200; Dublin, Royal Hibernian Academy, *Proposed City of Dublin Gallery: Pictures Presented and Lent to Form a Nucleus of Modern Art*, 1904–5; New York, Hirschl & Adler Galleries, *The Art of Collecting*, 1984, no. 27; New York and Chicago 1986; Edinburgh 1997, no. 14.

LITERATURE: 'Fine Arts. The New Gallery', *Athenaeum*, no. 3680 (7 May 1898), p. 604; 'The New Gallery', *Illustrated London News*, CXII (21 May 1898), p. 741; Fernand Khnopff, 'The New Gallery', *Magazine of Art*, 22 (1898), p. 430; 'The New Gallery', *Punch* (14 May 1898), p. 220; D. S. M[acColl], 'The New Gallery and Old Water Colour Society', *Saturday Review*, LXXXV (30 April 1898), pp. 590, 591; H.S., 'Art. The New Gallery', *Spectator*, 80 (30 April 1898), p. 625; Baldry 1900, I, p. 21; Downes 1925, pp. 51, 184–5; Downes 1926, pp. 51, 184–5; Charteris 1927, p. 267; Mount 1955, p. 435 (9615), dated 1896; 1957 ed., p. 344 (9615), dated 1896; 1969 ed., p. 453 (9615), dated 1896, with incorrect dimensions; McKibbin 1956, p. 126; Reynolds 1986, p. 982, pl. IV (colour); Reynolds in Hills *et al.* 1986, pp. 154, 170, 174, fig. 119 (colour); Edinburgh 1997, pp. 24, 75, pl. 20 (colour).

361 Mrs Charles Huntington

PROVENANCE: The sitter; her daughter Miss Amy Huntington to 1960; her nephew, Lord Rathcreedan; sold by him, Sotheby's, London, 17 March 1965, lot 33; bt Weitzner; M. Knoedler & Co., New York, May 1965 (A 8886); purchased by the Brooklyn Museum, 1968 (68.24).

EXHIBITIONS: London, RA, 1926, no. 392.

LITERATURE: Downes 1926, p. 361; London 1926, p. 59; Charteris 1927, p. 267; Mount 1955, p. 436 (988); 1957 ed., p. 344; 1969 ed., p. 442; McKibbin 1956, p. 102; Ormond 1970, pp. 27, 52; New York 1980, Checklist.

362 Lady Faudel-Phillips

PROVENANCE: Sir George Faudel-Phillips, first Bt, to 1922; his son, Sir Lionel Faudel-Phillips, second Bt, to 1941; his daughter, Miss Jean Faudel-Phillips, to 1988; Private Collection.

EXHIBITIONS: London, RA, 1899, no. 444; Edinburgh 1902, no. 149; London, RSPP, 1912, no. 39; London, RA, 1926, no. 350.

LITERATURE: R. A. M. Stevenson, 'The Art Season. Mr Sargent and Others', *Academy* (6 May 1899), p. 509; A. C. R. Carter, 'The Royal Academy of 1899', *Art Journal* (1899), pp. 177–8; André Michel, 'Fine Arts The Royal Academy. (Third Notice)', *Athenaeum*, no. 3736 (3 June 1899), p. 693; 'The Royal Academy –I', *Magazine of Art*, 23 (1899), p. 340; 'Pearls without Price at the Royal Academy', *Punch* (3 May 1899), p. 214, ill. (caricature); H.S., 'Art. The Academy. – I', *Spectator* (6 May 1899), p. 641; Baldry 1900, I, p. 21; Meynell 1903, n.p., ill.; Downes 1925, p. 187; Downes 1926, p. 187; London 1926, p. 52; Charteris 1927, pp. 140, 156, 174, 266; Meynell Manson 1927, n.p., ill.; Mount 1955, p. 435 (987); 1957 ed., p. 344 (987); 1969 ed., p. 438 (987); McKibbin 1956, p. 116; Fairbrother 2000, fig. 1.26.

363 Mrs Charles Hunter

PROVENANCE: The sitter; presented by her to the Tate Gallery, London, 1929, via the National Art Collections Fund (4469).

EXHIBITIONS: Boston 1899, no. 9; London, RA, 1899, no. 18; Newcastle-upon-Tyne, Laing Art Gallery, *Special Inaugural Exhibition*, 1904, no. 178; Venice 1907, no. 27; Liverpool 1925, no. 144; London, RA, 1926, no. 303; York 1926, no. 30; London, Tate, 1926; Washington 1964, no. 62; Japan 1989, no. 34.

LITERATURE: Boston 1899, p. 3; R. A. M. Stevenson, 'The Art Season. Mr Sargent and Others', *Academy* (6 May 1899), p. 509; A. C. R. Carter, 'The Royal Academy of 1899', *Art Journal* (1899), p. 177; André Michel, 'Fine Arts The Royal Academy. (Third Notice)', *Athenaeum*, no. 3736 (3 June 1899), p. 693; 'At the Royal Academy', *Punch*, 116 (3 May 1899), p. 209; D. S. M[acColl], 'The Academy', *Saturday Review*, LXXXVII (6 May 1899), p. 556; H.S., 'Art. The Academy. I', *Spectator*, 82 (6 May 1899), p. 641; Baldry 1900, I, p. 21; possibly Mauclair 1906–7, p. 376; *Country Life* (19 May 1917), ill. frontis.; Downes 1925, pp. 52, 186–7; Downes 1926, pp. 52, 186–7; London 1926, p. 46; Charteris 1927, pp. 168, 267; Meynell Manson 1927, n.p., ill. (detail); *Tate Gallery Review of Acquisitions 1927–29*, 1930, p. 45; *N.A.C.F. Report, 1929*, 1930, p. 44, ill.; Edith Wharton, *A Backward Glance*, New York and London, 1934, p. 297; Mount 1955, pp. 214–15, 436 (9811); 1957 ed., pp. 177–8, 345; 1969 ed., pp. 214–15, 442; McKibbin 1956, p. 102; *Tate Gallery Catalogue*, 1964, vol. 2, pp. 601–2; Olson 1986, p. 214, pl. XXVII; Japan 1989, p. 143, ill. p. 76 (colour); Fairbrother 2000, fig. 1.18 (detail).

364 Mrs John William Crombie

PROVENANCE: The sitter; presented by her to Aberdeen Art Gallery, 1946 (46.4.3).

EXHIBITIONS: Aberdeen 1910, no. 268; London, RA, 1926, no. 415; Edinburgh 1947, no. 194; Glasgow 1953, no. 434; Boston, Boston Athenaeum, 1970.

LITERATURE: London 1926, p. 62; Charteris 1927, p. 266; Mount 1955, p. 435 (984); 1957 ed., p. 344 (984); 1969 ed., p. 435 (984); McKibbin 1956, p. 95; *Aberdeen Art Gallery Permanent Collection Catalogue*, 1968, p. 87.

365 Miss Jane Evans

PROVENANCE: Commissioned by the Old Boys of Evans's and presented to the sitter; Eton College, Berkshire.

EXHIBITIONS: London, RA, 1899, no. 237; Brussels 1900, no. 147; London, International Society, 1908, no. 343; London, RA, 1926, no. 339; Birmingham 1964, no. 28.

LITERATURE: R. A. M. Stevenson, 'The Art Season. Mr Sargent and Others', *Academy*, LVI (6 May 1899), p. 509; André Michel, 'Fine Arts The Royal Academy. (Third Notice)', *Athenaeum*, no. 3736 (3 June 1899), p. 693; A. C. R. Carter, 'The Royal Academy of 1899', *Art Journal* (1899), p. 177; 'The Royal Academy –I', *Magazine of Art*, 23 (1899), p. 340; 'At the Royal Academy', *Punch*, 116 (3 May 1899), p. 209; D. S. M[acColl], 'The Academy', *Saturday Review*, LXXXVII (6 May 1899), p. 556; Baldry 1900, I, p. 21; Gambier Parry 1907, pp. 231, 381–90, ill. facing p. 390; 'London Exhibitions', *Art Journal* (1908), p. 121; Laurence Binyon, 'Fair Women and Other Pictures', *Saturday Review*, CV (28 March 1908), p. 399; Downes 1925, p. 187; Downes 1926, p. 187; London 1926, p. 51; *RA Ill. 1926*, p. 27; Charteris 1927, pp. 174, 266; Mount 1955, p. 435 (985); 1957 ed., p. 344 (985); 1969 ed., p. 438 (985); McKibbin 1956, p. 95; Shane Leslie, *Long Shadows*, London, 1966, pp. 62–3; J. McConnell, ed., *Treasures of Eton*, London, 1976, pp. 90–1, pl. 13 (colour).

366 Octavia Hill

PROVENANCE: The sitter; bequeathed by her to the National Portrait Gallery, London, 1915 (1746).

EXHIBITIONS: London, RA, 1899, no. 122; London, RA, 1926, no. 27; London 1996, no. 107.

LITERATURE: A. C. R. Carter, 'The Royal Academy of 1899', *Art Journal* (1899), p. 177; André Michel, 'Fine Arts The Royal Academy. (Third Notice)', *Athenaeum*, no. 3736 (3 June 1899), p. 693; 'The Royal Academy –I', *Magazine of Art*, 23 (1899), p. 340; H.S., 'Art. The Academy. –I', *Spectator* (6 May 1899), p. 641; Baldry 1900, I, p. 21; Brinton 1906, p. 282; Brinton 1908, p. 162; C. Edmund Maurice, ed., *Life of Octavia Hill as Told in her Letters*, London, 1913, p. 506, ill.; Downes 1925, p. 185; Downes 1926, p. 185; London 1926, p. 11; *RA Ill. 1926*, p. 83; Charteris 1927, p. 267; E. Moberly Bell,

Octavia Hill, London, 1942, pp. 241–2, ill.; Mount 1955, p. 436 (993); 1957 ed., p. 345 (993); 1969 ed., p. 441 (993); Hill 1956, pp. 21, 161; McKibbin 1956, p. 102; Evelyne White, *Women of Devotion and Courage*, London, 1957, ill. facing p. 8; Yung 1981, p. 276, ill.; Simon 1996, p. 182, fig. 115.

367   *An Interior in Venice*

PROVENANCE: Offered to Mrs Curtis and refused by her; presented by the artist to the Royal Academy of Arts, London, as his diploma work, 1899.

EXHIBITIONS: London, RA, 1899, no. 729; London, RA, 1926, no. 14; Bournemouth, Russell Cotes Art Gallery and Museum, *Loan Exhibition from the Royal Academy*, 1957, no. 840; London, RSPP, *Works by Past Members*, 1960, no. 22; Washington 1964, no. 63; London, Royal Academy, *Bicentenary Exhibition*, 1968, no. 414; Columbus Gallery of Fine Arts, *British Art 1890–1928*, 1971, no. 91; London, Wildenstein & Co., *Venice Rediscovered*, 1972, no. 37; London, South London Art Gallery, *Edwardian Artists*, 1973, no. 90; London, Wildenstein & Co., and Liverpool, Walker Art Gallery, *American Artists in Europe 1800–1900*, 1976, no. 62; Edinburgh, Royal Scottish Academy, *150th Anniversary Exhibition*, 1976, no. 16; Milton Keynes, Great Linford Art Centre, *Royal Academy Retrospective*, 1982, no. 43; International Exhibitions Foundation, Washington, D.C., *Paintings from the Royal Academy: Two Centuries of British Art*, 1983–4, no. 41; Swansea, Glynn Vivian Art Gallery and Museum, *Fine Art: A Selection of Paintings, Sculptures and Drawings by Royal Academicians 1770–1980*, 1985, no. 19; San Francisco 1985, no. 60; New York and Chicago 1986; US touring exhibition, *The Edwardians and After: The Royal Academy 1900–1950*, 1988–9; Boston 1992, no. 116; London 1998, no. 55.

LITERATURE: *Annual Report from the Council of the Royal Academy to the General Assembly of Academicians for the Year 1900*, London, 1901, Appendix no. 10, p. 54; *Art Journal* (1900), p. 183; 'The Royal Academy. (Third Notice)', *Athenaeum*, no. 3787 (26 May 1900), p. 662; 'The Royal Academy', *Graphic*, 61 (5 May 1900), p. 647; 'The Royal Academy. – II', *Magazine of Art*, 24 (1900), p. 385; Roger Fry, 'Royal Academy', *Pilot* (12 May 1900), p. 321; 'Our Own "Private View"', *Punch* (9 May 1900), p. 338; D. S. M[acColl], 'The Academy. I. – "Rude Things."', *Saturday Review*, 89 (12 May 1900), p. 584; D. S. [MacColl], 'The Academy. II. – "The Poor Man's Tea"', *Saturday Review*, 89 (19 May 1900), pp. 614–15; H.S., 'The Academy. – III', *Spectator*, 84 (26 May 1900), p. 742; Cortissoz 1903, p. 527; Pennell 1921, p. 39; Pousette-Dart 1924; Downes 1925, pp. 189–90, as 'Interior of a Palazzo in Venice', ill. facing p. 192; Minchin 1925, p. 743; Downes 1926, pp. 189–90, ill. facing p. 192; *RA Ill. 1926*, p. 101; Charteris 1927, pp. 163, 285; Mount 1955, p. 448 (K991); 1957 ed., p. 357; 1969 ed., p. 470; Sidney C. Hutchison, *The History of the Royal Academy 1768–1968*, London, 1968, pl. 45, colour;

Jeremy Maas, *Victorian Painters*, London, 1969, p. 222; Richard Ormond, 'The Diploma Paintings from 1840 Onwards', *Apollo*, 89 (January 1969), pp. 60–1, fig. 6; Ormond 1970, pp. 54, 63, 70, 251, pl. 90 (colour); Lovell 1984, pp. 107–9, ill. p. 107; Ayres in Hills *et al.* 1986, fig. 44 (colour); Fairbrother 1986, p. 325; Olson 1986, p. 218; Mary Anne Stevens, ed., *The Edwardians and After: The Royal Academy 1900–1950*, London, 1988, p. 141, ill., pl. 54 (colour); Boston 1992, pp. 404, 406, ill. p. 405 (colour); Fairbrother 1994, pp. 99, 101, ill. p. 98 (colour); Adelson et al. 1997, pp. 184–6, plate 180 (colour); London 1998, pp. 151–2, ill. p. 151 (colour); Fairbrother 2000, pp. 144, 145, 171, fig. 5.22 (colour); Rieder 2000, p. 107, ill. p. 96 (colour).

368   *Lady Elcho, Mrs Adeane and Mrs Tennant* or *The Wyndham Sisters*

PROVENANCE: Hon. Percy Wyndham to 1911; his son, Rt Hon. George Wyndham to 1913; Captain Guy Richard Charles Wyndham to 1927; M. Knoedler & Co. London, 1926–7 (L.C. 239); acquired directly from Captain Wyndham by the Metropolitan Museum of Art, New York (Wolfe Fund, Catharine Lorillard Wolfe Collection), 1927 (27.67).

EXHIBITIONS: London, RA, 1900, no. 213, as 'Lady Elcho, Mrs Adeane, and Mrs Tennant'; London, International Society, 1908, no. 341; London, Franco-British Exhibition, 1908, no. 168; Edinburgh 1911, no. 67; Glasgow 1920, no. 437; London, RA, 1926, no. 292.

LITERATURE: Frank Rinder, 'The Royal Academy of 1900', *Art Journal* (1900), pp. 164–8; 'The Royal Academy', *Athenaeum*, no. 3787 (26 May 1900), p. 726; 'Fine Arts. The Royal Academy. (Fourth Notice)', *Athenaeum*, no. 3789 (9 June 1900), p. 726; W. Walton, *Exposition Universelle, 1900: The Chefs-d'Oeuvre*, 5 vols, Philadelphia, vol. [?], 1900, p. 21; 'The Royal Academy', *Graphic*, 61 (5 May 1900), p. 647; 'The Royal Academy', *Illustrated London News*, CXVI (5 May 1900), p. 597; 'The Royal Academy', *Magazine of Art*, 24 (1900), p. 340; 'The Royal Academy. – II', *Magazine of Art*, 24 (1900), p. 385; Roger Fry, 'Royal Academy', *Pilot*, 1 (12 May 1900), p. 321; D. S. M[acColl], 'The Academy. I. – "Rude Things."', *Saturday Review*, LXXXIX (12 May 1900), pp. 583–4; H.S., 'Art. The Academy. – I', *Spectator* (5 May 1900), p. 631; 'The Royal Academy. First Notice', *The Times* (5 May 1900), p. 14; 'The Royal Academy. Second Notice', *The Times* (15 May 1900), p. 3; N.N. [E. Pennell], *Nation*, 70 (31 May 1900), p. 413; *Pearson's Magazine* 11 (April 1901), p. 570, ill.; Caffin 1902, p. 59; *Living Age*, 233 (12 April 1902), pp. 83–4; 'Passing Events', *Art Journal* (1903), pp. 62–3; Caffin 1903a, p. 443; Cortissoz 1903, p. 530; Meynell 1903, n.p.; 'A Gallery of Sargents', *Saturday Review*, XCVII (19 March 1904), p. 365; Brinton 1906, p. 281, ill. p. 280; Mauclair 1906–7, pp. 375, 378; '"Fair Women" at the New Gallery', *Athenaeum*, no. 4193 (7 March 1908), p. 296; 'London Exhibitions', *Art Journal* (1908), pp. 120, 121; Brinton 1908, p. 162; Burlington Fine Arts Club, London, *Illustrated Memoir of Charles*

Wellington Furse, A.R.A. (exhibition catalogue), London, 1908, pp. 28–9; Cox 1908, pp. 257–8; M. H. Spielmann, *Figaro illustré*, no. 221 (August 1908), n.p.; Wood 1909, pl. VI; 'A Sargent Year', 'Letters and Art', *Literary Digest*, LIII (9 September 1916), p. 608; Blunt 1919, vol. 1, pp. 386, 387–8; Pennell 1921, pp. 39, 154; Cortissoz 1924, p. 350; Mechlin 1924, p. 188; Starkweather 1924, p. 9, ill. p. 2; Downes 1925, pp. 54–5, 188–9; Downes 1926, pp. 54–5, 188–9; M. Feuillet, *Le Figaro artistique*, 3 (15 October 1925), p. 11; J. W. Mackail and Guy Wyndham, *Life and Letters of George Wyndham*, 2 vols., London, 1925, vol. 1, ill. facing p. 219; R. Mortimer, *New Statesman*, 26 (23 January 1926), p. 447; H.S., 'Sargent Memorial at Burlington House', *Connoisseur*, 74 (March 1926), pp. 185–6; 'Sargent Portrait Group to be Sold', *Art News*, 25 (9 October 1926), p. 3; L.G.S., 'Famous Sargent May Come Here', *Art News*, 25 (16 October 1926), p. 2, ill.; 'Our Colour Plates', *Apollo*, IV (December 1926), p. 278, ill. facing p. 262 (colour); *New York American* (8 December 1926), ill. p. 5; London 1926, p. 44; *RA Ill. 1926*, p. 2; Charteris 1927, pp. 68–9, 174–5, 268; Meynell Manson 1927, n.p. ill.; 'Metropolitan May Have Bought the "Wyndham Sisters"', *Art News*, 25 (12 March 1927), pp. 1, 2, and 'Hearn, Sargent and the Metropolitan', *Art News*, 25 (12 March 1927), p. 8; 'Fears Art Museum Misuses Hearn Fund', *New York Times* (12 March 1927), p. 14; 'Metropolitan Buys Sargent's "Graces"', *New York Times* (13 March 1927), p. 19; Shane Leslie, *The Passing Chapter*, London, 1934, pp. 152–3; Sitwell 1944, pp. 224–5; Balsan 1953, p. 157; Mount 1955, pp. 228–9, 284–5, 457 (997); McKibbin 1956, p. 132; Monteiro 1965, p. 124; Ormond 1970, pp. 54, 63, 97, 252, pls xiii (detail), 92; Tintner 1975, p. 129; Burke 1980, pp. 253–7, ill. p. 254; New York 1980, Checklist; Ratcliff 1982, pp. 172, 179, pl. 253 (colour); Abdy and Gere 1984, pp. 99, 108, 111, 123, ill. p. 100; Fairbrother 1986, pp. 281–2, 317; Olson 1986, pp. 133, 218–19, 235, 265; Reynolds in Hills *et al.* 1986, 170, 174, fig. 112; Philip Hoare, *Serious Pleasures: The Life of Stephen Tennant*, London, 1990, pp. 2, 324; Dakers 1993, pp. 96–7, 163–5, 218–20, 224, pl. XIX (colour): Fairbrother 1994, pp. 94, 97, ill. p. 96, p. 138 (colour), and cover (colour); London 1998, pp. 38, 154, fig. 38 (colour); Prettejohn 1998, pp. 32, 39, 61, fig. 24; Fairbrother 2000, pp. 32, 33, fig. 1.22; Herdrich and Weinberg 2000, pp. 8, 208, 209–11, 212, fig. 76.

369   *The Honourable Victoria Stanley*

PROVENANCE: The seventeenth Earl of Derby to 1948; his son-in-law, the sitter's widower, Sir Malcolm Bullock to 1966; Private Collection.

EXHIBITIONS: London, New Gallery, 1900, no. 248; Liverpool 1900, no. 68; London, RA, 1926, no. 421; Birmingham 1964, no. 30; Leeds 1979, no. 43.

LITERATURE: 'Fine Arts. The New Gallery', *Athenaeum*, no. 3783 (28 April 1900), p. 534; 'The New Gallery', *Art Journal* (1900), p. 186; 'The New Gallery', *Illustrated London News*, CXVI (5 May 1900), p. 597; 'The New Gallery',

Magazine of Art, 24 (1900), p. 392; H. Hamilton Fyfe, 'Mr Sargent at the Royal Academy', *Nineteenth Century*, 292 (June 1901), p. 1023; D. S. M[acColl], 'The New Gallery and Two Others', *Saturday Review*, 89 (5 May 1900), p. 555; H.S., 'Art. The New Gallery', *Spectator*, 85 (28 April 1900), p. 599; 'The New Gallery', *The Times* (23 April 1900), p. 8; Meynell 1903, n.p. ill.; Mechlin 1924, p. 177; Downes 1925, pp. 191–2; Downes 1926, pp. 191–2; London 1926, p. 421; Charteris 1927, p. 268; Meynell Manson 1927, n.p. ill.; Mount 1955, p. 436 (996); 1957 ed., p. 345 (996); 1969 ed., p. 452 (996); McKibbin 1956, p. 124; Leeds 1979, pp. 60–1, pl. IX (colour); Fairbrother 2000, fig. 1.23.

370 Mrs Joshua Montgomery Sears

PROVENANCE: The sitter to 1935; her daughter, Mrs James D. Cameron Bradley, 1939; Charles D. Childs Gallery, Boston; Benjamin Sonnenberg, New York, 1950–79; his sale, Sotheby Parke-Bernet, New York, 7 June 1979, lot 685; Hirschl & Adler Galleries, New York; George R. Brown; presented by him to the Museum of Fine Arts, Houston, 1981.

EXHIBITIONS: Either this portrait or no. 318, Boston 1900, no. 109, as 'Portrait'; Boston 1905; either this portrait or no. 318, Boston 1914, no. 17, as 'Portrait'; Boston, Copley Society, *Exhibition of Portraits by Living Artists*, 1919; Boston, MFA, 1925, no. 61 (revised catalogue no. 64), dated 1898; New York, MMA, 1926, no. 34; Boston 1956, no. 31; New York 1980, no. 34; Houston 1998, no. 68, ill.

LITERATURE: *Collector and Art Critic*, IV (November 1905), p. 24; Boston 1925, p. 8; Boston 1925a, p. 8; Downes 1925 and 1926 eds, p. 188; 'The Sargent Memorial Exhibition', *Arts*, IX (January 1926), p. 43, ill.; New York 1926, p. 34, ill.; 'The World of Art/John Singer Sargent's Portrait of Mrs J. Montgomery Sears', *Vanity Fair*, XXV (January 1926), p. 59, ill., dated 1898; Charteris 1927, p. 266; Meynell Manson 1927, n.p.; Mount 1955, p. 452 (9611), dated 1896; Mount 1957 ed., p. 344; 1969 ed., p. 452; McKibbin 1956, p. 122, fig. 50; Ormond 1970, p. 57; Weston Naef, *The Collection of Alfred Stieglitz: Fifty Pioneers of Modern Photography*, New York, 1978, pp. 428–9, ill.; Hirshler 2001, fig. 28.

371 Cicely Horner

PROVENANCE: Mrs (later Lady) Horner; John Levy, New York, by 1925; M. Knoedler & Co., New York, April 1925 (16133); American Art Association, American Art Galleries, New York, *XVIII–XIX Century Oil Paintings*, 5–6 January 1927, lot 148; bt A. W. Newton; Newhouse Galleries, New York, by 1931; Parke-Bernet, New York, 18 April 1940, lot 45; Charles Bolles Rogers, Minneapolis to 1977; Edward D. Pierson; presented by his family to the Denver Art Museum, 1991.839.

EXHIBITIONS: Cincinnati 1925, no. 49; Portland, Oregon, Portland Art Association, *Survey of American Painting Arranged by the College Art Association*, 1931, no. 14; New London, Connecticut, Lyman Allyn Museum, *American Painting of the Last Fifty Years*, 1934, no. 68; Denver, Colorado, 1985.

LITERATURE: Downes 1925, pp. 187–8; Downes 1926, pp. 187–8; Charteris 1927, p. 269; Horner 1933, p. 97; Mount 1955, p. 435 (976); 1957 ed., p. 344 (976); 1969 ed., p. 443 (976); McKibbin 1956, p. 102.

372 Cicely Horner

PROVENANCE: Mrs (later Lady) Horner; probably Grand Central Art Galleries, New York, 1924; untraced.

LITERATURE: Mount 1955, p. 435 (977); 1957 ed., p. 344 (977); 1969 ed., p. 442 (977); McKibbin 1956, p. 102.

373 M. Carey Thomas

PROVENANCE: Commissioned by a committee of alumnae and students of Bryn Mawr College, 1898.

EXHIBITIONS: Philadelphia 1900, no. 32; Paris 1900, no. 14; Boston, *Fair Women*, 1902, no. 79; Washington 1907, no. 48; Rome 1911, no. 96; Boston, MFA, 1925, no. 65 (revised catalogue no. 68); New York, MMA, 1926, no. 32; Tallahassee, Florida State University Gallery, 1970; Philadelphia, Penn Mutual Bicentennial Exhibition, 1976; Montclair 1999.

LITERATURE: 'Alumnae Notes', *Fortnightly Philistine*, 6 (10 November 1899), p. 11; 'the Presentation of Miss Thomas' Portrait', *Fortnightly Philistine*, 6 (24 November 1899), pp. 6–8; W. P. Lockington, 'The Pennsylvania Academy's Annual Exhibition', *Collector and Art Critic*, II (1 February 1900), p. 121; 'Academy's Exhibition', *Philadelphia Inquirer* (1 January 1900), p. 10; Meynell 1903, n.p., ill.; Victor D. Hecht, 'The Rome Exposition', *American Art News*, IX (13 May 1911), p. 3; 'Leading Articles of the Month – The American Painters' Exhibit at Rome: An Italian Appreciation', *Review of Reviews*, 44 (August 1911), p. 225; S[elwyn] B[rinton], 'Studio-Talk: Rome', *Studio*, LIV (October 1911), p. 80; Giuseppe Antonelli, *La Pittura a Valle Giulia: Esposizione internazionale di Roma del 1911*, Rome, 1912, pp. 99–100; Mechlin 1924, p. 188; Starkweather 1924, ill. p. 24; Boston 1925, p. 8, ill.; Boston 1925a, p. 8, ill.; Downes 1925, p. 192; Downes 1926, p. 192; New York 1926, p. 6, ill.; Charteris 1927, p. 267; Meynell Manson 1927, n.p. ill.; Margaret Emerson Bailey, *Goodbye, Proud World*, New York, 1945, p. 263; Edith Finch, *Carey Thomas of Bryn Mawr*, New York and London, 1947, p. 244, ill. facing p. 150; Mount 1955, p. 436 (9815); 1957 ed., p. 345; 1969 ed., p. 453 (9815); McKibbin 1956, p. 126; New York 1980, Checklist; Fairbrother 1986, pp. 305, 355 n. 35; Helen Lefkowitz Horowitz, *The Power and Passion of M. Carey Thomas*, New York, 1994, pp. 315–16, 354, ill.; Fischer *et al.* 1999, p. 23, fig. 29 (colour).

374 Lawrence Harrison

PROVENANCE: The sitter to 1899; his son Leonard Harrison to 1939; his son, Michael Harrison to 1965; his widow, Mrs Michael Harrison to *c.* 1970; Private Collection.

EXHIBITIONS: Birmingham 1964, no. 32.

LITERATURE: Mount 1957, p. 351; 1969 ed., p. 441; McKibbin 1956, p. 100.

375 Lord Russell of Killowen

PROVENANCE: The sitter; his widow to 1918; their son, second Lord Russell of Killowen; presented by him to Lincoln's Inn, London.

EXHIBITIONS: London, RA, 1900, no. 190; either this or no. 376, Liverpool 1900, no. 1027; either this or no. 376, Cork 1902, no. 152; either this or no. 376 Dublin 1903, no. 21; Liverpool 1925, no. 133 or 148; London, RA, 1926, no. 284.

LITERATURE: Frank Rinder, 'The Royal Academy of 1900', *Art Journal* (1900), p. 166; 'The Royal Academy. (Fourth Notice)', *Athenaeum*, no. 3789 (9 June 1900), p. 726; 'The Late Lord Chief Justice', *Illustrated London News*, CXVII (18 August 1900), p. 222, ill. p. 235; 'The Royal Academy', *Magazine of Art*, 24 (1900), p. 340; 'The Royal Academy. – II', *Magazine of Art*, 24 (1900), p. 385; 'Our Own "Private View", R.A.', *Punch* (9 May 1900), p. 337; Lucy 1909, pp. 284–5; Lucy 1922, p. 116; Starkweather 1924, p. 8; Downes 1925, p. 191; Downes 1926, p. 191; London 1926, p. 43; Charteris 1927, p. 267; Mount 1955, p. 436 (994); 1957 ed., p. 345; 1969 ed., p. 451; McKibbin 1956, p. 121.

376 Lord Russell of Killowen

PROVENANCE: The sitter to 1900; his son, Sir Charles Russell, first Bt to 1928; his daughter, Monica, who married her first cousin, Sir Alec Russell, second Bt to 1977; her son, Sir Charles Russell, third Bt to 1997; his son, Sir Charles Russell, fourth Bt

EXHIBITIONS: London, RA, 1900, no. 630; either this or no. 375, Liverpool 1900, no. 1027; Dublin 1901, no. 18; either this or no. 375, Cork 1902, no. 152; either this or no. 375, Dublin 1903, no. 21; London, RSPP, 1925, no. 39; Liverpool 1925, no. 133 or 148; London, RA, 1926, no. 12; Birmingham 1964, no. 31.

LITERATURE: Frank Rinder, 'The Royal Academy', *Art Journal* (1900), p. 166; 'The Royal Academy. (Fourth Notice.)', *Athenaeum*, no. 3789 (9 June 1900), p. 726; 'The Royal Academy', *Magazine of Art*, 24 (1900), p. 340; 'The Royal Academy. – II', *Magazine of Art*, 24 (1900), p. 385; 'Our Own "Private View", R.A.', *Punch* (9 May 1900), p. 337; Meynell 1903, n.p. ill.; *Dictionary of National Biography*, Supplement, vol. III, London 1901, p. 332; Lucy 1922, p. 116; Starkweather 1924, p. 8; Downes 1925, p. 191; Downes 1926, p. 191; London 1926, p. 8; *RA. Ill. 1926*, p. 89; Charteris 1927, p. 268; Meynell Manson 1927, n.p. ill.; Mount 1955, p. 436 (995); 1957 ed., p. 345 (995); 1969 ed., p. 451 (995); McKibbin 1956, p. 121; Fairbrother 2000, fig. 1.24 (detail).

377   *Lord Russell of Killowen*

PROVENANCE: Commissioned by the Lord Russell of Killowen Memorial Committee Fund, 1900, and presented by them to the National Portrait Gallery, London, 1921 (1907).

LITERATURE: 'Two Portraits for the Nation', *The Times* (1 July 1921), p. 13 ill. (detail); McKibbin 1956, p. 121; Yung 1981, p. 493, ill.

378   *Sir David Richmond*

PROVENANCE: Commissioned by the Corporation of Glasgow, 1899; Glasgow Art Gallery and Museum, 1899 (899).

EXHIBITIONS: London, RA, 1900, no. 625; either this or no. 379 Aberdeen 1900, no. 275; Glasgow 1900, no. 107; London, RA, 1926, no. 597.

LITERATURE: 'The Royal Scottish Academy and Glasgow Institute Exhibitions', *Magazine of Art*, 24 (1900), p. 329, ill.; 'The Royal Academy. – II', *Magazine of Art*, 24 (1900), p. 385; Downes 1925, p. 191; Downes 1926, p. 191; London 1926, p. 86; Charteris 1927, p. 268; Mount 1955, p. 436 (003), dated 1900; 1957 ed., p. 345 (003); 1969 ed., p. 449 (003); McKibbin 1956, p. 118; *Glasgow Art Gallery and Museum: Summary Catalogue of British Oil Paintings*, Glasgow 1971, p. 81.

379   *Sir David Richmond*

PROVENANCE: Presented to Lady Richmond by the Corporation of Glasgow, 1899; her daughter, Mrs A. J. Fairley; bequeathed by her to the Glasgow Art Gallery and Museum, 1946 (2567).

EXHIBITIONS: Either this or no 378 Aberdeen 1900, no. 275.

LITERATURE: Mount 1955, p. 436 (004), dated 1900; 1957 ed., p. 345 (004); 1969 ed., p. 449 (004); McKibbin 1956, p. 119; *Glasgow Art Gallery and Museum: Summary Catalogue of British Oil Paintings*, Glasgow, 1971, p. 81.

380   *James Coolidge Carter*

PROVENANCE: Commissioned by a group of members of the Harvard Club, New York, 1899.

EXHIBITIONS: Pittsburgh 1900, no. 212; New York 1925; Boston, MFA, 1925, no. 67 (revised catalogue no. 70); New York, MMA, 1926, no. 35; Washington, D.C., National Portrait Gallery, *Portraits of American Law*, 1 September 1989–30 January 1990.

LITERATURE: Austin E. Howland, 'The Pittsburg [sic] Art Exhibition', *Brush and Pencil*, VII (December 1900), p. 139; Henry E. Howard, 'The Practice of the Law in New York', *Century Magazine*, LXII (October 1901) p. 817, ill. (woodcut by Henry Wolf); Boston 1925, p. 8; Boston 1925a, p. 8; Downes 1925, pp. 204–5; Downes 1926, pp. 204–5; New York 1926, p. 7, ill.; Charteris 1927, p. 267; Mount 1955, p. 436 (991); 1957 ed., p. 345 (991); 1969 ed., p. 433 (991); McKibbin 1956, p. 88.

381   *Joseph Hodges Choate*

PROVENANCE: Commissioned by a group of members of the Harvard Club, New York, 1899.

EXHIBITIONS: Pittsburgh 1900, no. 211; New York 1925; Boston, MFA, 1925, no. 66 (revised catalogue no. 69); New York, MMA, 1926, no. 36; Washington, D.C., National Portrait Gallery, *Portraits of American Law*, 1 September 1989–30 January 1990.

LITERATURE: Starkweather 1924, p. 8; Boston 1925, p. 8, ill.; Boston 1925a, p. 8, ill.; Downes 1925, p. 260; Downes 1926, p. 260; New York 1926, p. 7, ill.; Charteris 1927, pp. 138, 267; Mount 1955, p. 436 (992); 1957 ed. 345 (992); 1969 ed. p. 424 (992); McKibbin 1956, p. 89.

References are given here for all exhibitions cited in abbreviated form in the individual catalogue entries. Abbreviations indicate the first location in which the exhibition took place and the date. As there are frequently a number of exhibitions in any one year in major cities, a further abbreviation may be included to differentiate one institution/exhibition from another. The list is organized chronologically; where specific dates within a particular year are not known, the list proceeds alphabetically by city.

NEW YORK, SAA, 1890 Society of American Artists, New York, Fifth Avenue Art Galleries, *Twelfth Exhibition*, 28 April–24 May 1890.

CHICAGO, 1890 The Art Institute of Chicago, *Third Annual Exhibition of American Oil Paintings*, 9 June–30 July 1890.

PHILADELPHIA, ART CLUB, 1890 The Art Club of Philadelphia, *Second Special Exhibition*, 3 November–7 December 1890.

NEW YORK, NAD (AUTUMN), 1890 National Academy of Design, New York, *Ninth Annual Autumn Exhibition*, 24 November–20 December 1890.

BOSTON, ST BOTOLPH CLUB, 1890 St Botolph Club, Boston, *Exhibition*, 29 December 1890–17 January 1891.

PHILADELPHIA, 1891 Pennsylvania Academy of the Fine Arts, Philadelphia, *Sixty-First Annual Exhibition*, 29 January–6 March 1891.

WORCESTER, 1891 Worcester Art Society, *Loan Collection of Portraits Exhibited by the Worcester Art Society in the New Public Library Building*, 31 March–30 April 1891.

NEW YORK, NAD, 1891 National Academy of Design, New York, *Sixty-sixth Annual Exhibition*, 6 April–16 May 1891.

NEW YORK, SAA, 1891 Society of American Artists, New York, *Thirteenth Exhibition*, 27 April–23 May 1891.

LONDON, RA, 1891 Royal Academy, London, *The One Hundred and Twenty-third Summer Exhibition*, 4 May–3 August 1891.

PARIS, SALON DU CHAMPS DE MARS, 1891 Société nationale des beaux-arts, Champs de Mars, Paris, May 1891.

BOSTON, SAA, 1891 Boston, Museum of Fine Arts, *Thirteenth Exhibition of the Society of American Artists*, 4 June–2 July 1891.

PHILADELPHIA, ART CLUB, 1891 The Art Club of Philadelphia, *Third Annual Exhibition of Oil Paintings and Sculpture*, 16 November–13 December 1891.

NEW YORK, SCHAUS GALLERY, 1891 Schaus Gallery, New York, 1891.

NEW YORK, SAA, 1892 Society of American Artists, New York, *Fourteenth Exhibition*, 2–28 May 1892.

PARIS, SALON DU CHAMPS DE MARS, 1892 Société nationale des beaux-arts, Champs de Mars, Paris, 1892.

LONDON, NEAC, 1892 New English Art Club, London, *Winter Exhibition*, November 1892.

NEW YORK, SAA, RETROSPECTIVE, 1892 Society of American Artists, New York, *Retrospective Exhibition*, 5–25 December 1892.

LONDON, RA, 1893 Royal Academy, London, *The One Hundred and Twenty-fifth Exhibition*, 1 May–7 August 1893.

LONDON, NEW GALLERY, 1893 New Gallery, London, *Sixth Summer Exhibition*, May 1893.

LONDON, NEAC, 1893 New English Art Club, London, *Tenth Exhibition*, 1893.

CHICAGO, 1893 Art Institute of Chicago, *World's Columbian Exhibition*, 1893.

PHILADELPHIA, 1893–4 Pennsylvania Academy of the Fine Arts, Philadelphia, *Sixty-third Annual Exhibition*, 18 December 1893–24 February 1894.

LONDON, RA, 1894 Royal Academy, London, *The One Hundred and Twenty-sixth Exhibition*, 7 May–6 August 1894.

PARIS, SALON DU CHAMPS DE MARS, 1894 Société nationale des beaux-arts, Champs de Mars, Paris, 1894.

NEW YORK, NAD, 1894 National Academy of Design, New York, *Loan Exhibition of Portraits of Women for the Benefit of St John's Guild and the Orthopaedic Hospital*, 1–21 November 1894.

PHILADELPHIA, 1894–5 Pennsylvania Academy of the Fine Arts, Philadelphia, *Sixty-fourth Annual Exhibition*, 17 December 1894–23 February 1895.

LONDON, FAIR WOMEN, 1894 London, Grafton Gallery, *Fair Women*, October–December 1894.

PHILADELPHIA, 1894–5 Pennsylvania Academy of the Fine Arts, Philadelphia, *Sixty-Fourth Annual Exhibition*, 17 December 1894–23 February 1895.

BOSTON, 1895 Copley Hall, Boston, *Loan Collection of Portraits of Women for the Benefit of the Boston Children's Aid Society and the Sunnyside Day Nursery*, 11–31 March 1895.

LONDON, RA, 1895 Royal Academy, London, *The One Hundred and Twenty-seventh Exhibition*, 6 May–5 August 1895.

LONDON, NEW GALLERY, 1895 New Gallery, London, *Eighth Exhibition*, summer 1895.

NEW YORK, NAD, 1895 National Academy of Design, New York, *Loan Exhibition of Portraits for the Benefit of St John's Guild and the Orthopaedic Hospital*, 30 October–7 December 1895.

BERLIN, 1895 Grosse Berliner Kunstausstellung, 1895.

PHILADELPHIA, 1895–6 Pennsylvania Academy of the Fine Arts, Philadelphia, *Sixty-fifth Annual Exhibition*, 23 December 1895–22 February 1896.

WORCESTER, 1895–6 Worcester Art Society, *Winter Exhibition*, 1895–6.

BOSTON, 1896 Copley Society, Boston, *Loan Collection of Portraits for the Benefit of the Associated Charities and the North End Union*, 2–23 March 1896.

NEW YORK, SAA, 1896 Society of American Artists, New York, *Eighteenth Annual Exhibition*, 28 March–2 May 1896 (held at the galleries of the American Fine Arts Society, 215 West Fifty-seventh Street).

NEW YORK, NAD (ANNUAL), 1896 National Academy of Design, New York, *Seventy-first Annual Exhibition*, 30 March–16 May 1896.

LONDON, RA, 1896 Royal Academy, London, *The One Hundred and Twenty-eighth Exhibition*, 4 May–3 August 1896.

PARIS, SALON DU CHAMPS DE MARS, 1896 Société Nationale des Beaux-Arts, Champs de Mars, Paris, May 1896.

LONDON, NEW GALLERY, 1896 New Gallery, London, *Ninth Exhibition*, Summer 1896.

BIRMINGHAM, 1896 Royal Birmingham Society of Artists, *Seventieth Autumn Exhibition*, 1896.

PHILADELPHIA, 1896–7 Pennsylvania Academy of the Fine Arts, Philadelphia, *Sixty-sixth Annual Exhibition*, 21 December 1896–22 February 1897.

NEW YORK, SAA, 1897 Society of American Artists, New York, *Nineteenth Annual Exhibition*, 28 March–1 May 1897 (held at the galleries of the American Fine Arts Society, 215 West Fifty-seventh Street).

LONDON, RA, 1897 Royal Academy, London, *The One Hundred and Twenty-ninth Exhibition*, 3 May–2 August 1897.

LONDON, NEW GALLERY, 1897 New Gallery, London, *Tenth Exhibition*, Summer 1897.

LIVERPOOL, 1897 Walker Art Gallery, Liverpool, *Twenty-Seventh Autumn Exhibition of Modern Pictures in Oil and Water-Colours*, 30 August–11 December 1897.

PITTSBURGH, 1897 Carnegie Institute, Pittsburgh, *The Second Annual Exhibition*, 4 November 1897–1 January 1898.

BOSTON, 1897 Copley Hall, Boston, *Loan Exhibition of One Hundred Masterpieces*, 1897.

BRUSSELS, 1897 *Exposition Internationale de Bruxelles*, Section Grande Bretagne, 1897.

PHILADELPHIA, 1898 Pennsylvania Academy of the Fine Arts, Philadelphia, *Sixty-seventh Annual Exhibition*, 10 January–22 February 1898.

BOSTON, 1898 Copley Hall, Boston, Copley Society of Boston, *Loan Exhibition of One Hundred Masterpieces*, 5–28 March 1898.

NEW YORK, SAA, 1898 Society of American Artists, New York, *Twentieth Annual Exhibition*, 19 March–23 April 1898 (held at the galleries of the American Fine Arts Society, 215 West Fifty-seventh Street).

LONDON, RA, 1898 Royal Academy, London, *The One Hundred and Thirtieth Exhibition*, 2 May–1 August 1898.

PARIS, SALON DU CHAMPS DE MARS, 1898 Société nationale des beaux-arts, Champs de Mars, Paris, 1898.

LONDON, NEW GALLERY, 1898 New Gallery, London, *Eleventh Exhibition*, Summer 1898.

WORCESTER, 1898 Worcester Art Society, *First Exhibition of the Worcester Art Museum with the Cooperation of the Worcester Art Society*, June 1898.

PITTSBURGH, 1898 Carnegie Institute, Pittsburgh, *The Third Annual Exhibition*, 3 November 1898– 1 January 1899.

WASHINGTON, 1898 Corcoran Gallery of Art, Washington, D.C. *Loan Exhibition*, 1898.

NEW YORK, NAD, 1898–9 National Academy of Design, New York, *Loan Exhibition of Portraits for the Benefit of the Orthopaedic Hospital*, 14 December 1898–14 January 1899.

PHILADELPHIA, 1899 Pennsylvania Academy of the Fine Arts, Philadelphia, *Sixty-eighth Annual Winter Exhibition*, 16 January–25 February 1899.

BOSTON, 1899 Copley Hall, Boston, *Paintings and Sketches by John S. Sargent*, 20 February–13 March l899.

NEW YORK, SAA, 1899 Society of American Artists, New York, *Twenty-first Annual Exhibition*, 25 March–29 April 1899 (held at the galleries of the American Fine Arts Society, 215 West Fifty-seventh Street).

LONDON, RA, 1899 Royal Academy, London, *The One Hundred and Thirty-first Exhibition*, 1 May–7 August 1899.

LONDON, NEW GALLERY, 1899 New Gallery, London, *Twelfth Exhibition*, Summer 1899.

PHILADELPHIA, 1900 Pennsylvania Academy of the Fine Arts, Philadelphia, *Sixty-ninth Annual Exhibition*, 15 January–24 February 1900.

LONDON, RA, 1900 Royal Academy, London, *The One Hundred and Thirty-second Exhibition*, 7 May–6 August 1900.

LONDON, NEW GALLERY, 1900 New Gallery, London, *Thirteenth Summer Exhibition*, 1900.

LIVERPOOL, 1900 Walker Art Gallery, Liverpool, *Thirtieth Autumn Exhibition of Modern Pictures in Oil and Water-Colours*, 17 September 1900–5 January 1901.

ABERDEEN, 1900 Aberdeen Artists' Society, Aberdeen Art Gallery, *Tenth Exhibition of Works by Modern Masters*, October–December 1900.

PITTSBURGH, 1900 Carnegie Institute, Pittsburgh, *The Fifth Annual Exhibition*, 1 November 1900– 1 January 1901.

BOSTON, 1900 Boston Art Students' Association, Copley Hall, *First Annual New Gallery Exhibition of Contemporary Art*, 1900.

BRUSSELS, 1900 Septième Exposition [de la] Société des Beaux-Arts, Brussels, 1900.

GLASGOW, 1900 The Royal Glasgow Institute of the Fine Arts, 1900.

LONDON, GUILDHALL, 1900 London, Guildhall, Corporation of the City of London, *Loan Exhibition*, 1900.

PARIS, 1900 Exposition Universelle, American Pavilion, Paris, 1900.

PHILADELPHIA, 1901 Pennsylvania Academy of the Fine Arts, Philadelphia, *Seventieth Annual Exhibition*, 14 January–23 February 1901.

VENICE, 1901 *IVa Esposizione Internazionale d'Arte della Città di Venezia*, 22 April–31 October 1901.

BUFFALO, 1901 Albright Gallery, Buffalo, *Pan-American Exhibition*, 1 May–1 November 1901.

LIVERPOOL, 1901 Walker Art Gallery, Liverpool, *Thirty-first Autumn Exhibition of Modern Pictures in Oil and Water-Colours*, 16 September 1901–4 January 1902.

CHARLESTON, 1901 The South Carolina Inter-State and West Indian Exposition, Charleston, South Carolina, *Exhibition of Fine Arts*, 1901–2.

DUBLIN, 1901 Royal Hibernian Academy of Arts, Dublin, 1901.

GLASGOW, 1901 The Royal Glasgow Institute of the Fine Arts, 1901.

NEW YORK, SAA, 1902 Society of American Artists, *Twenty-fourth Annual Exhibition*, 28 March–4 May 1902.

PARIS, SALON DU CHAMPS DE MARS, 1902 Société nationale des beaux-arts, Champs de Mars, Paris, May 1902.

BERLIN, 1902 Berlin Secession, 1902 (Unidentified Portrait, no 230).

BOSTON, *FAIR WOMEN*, 1902 Copley Hall, Boston, *Loan Collection Portraits and Pictures of Fair Women*, 1902.

CORK, 1902 Cork, Republic of Ireland, *Cork International Exhibition*, 1902.

EDINBURGH, 1902 Royal Scottish Academy, Edinburgh, 1902.

GLASGOW, 1902 The Royal Glasgow Institute of the Fine Arts, 1902.

VENICE, 1903 *Quinta Esposizione Internazionale d'Arte*, Venice, 22 April–31 October 1903.

LONDON, CARFAX, 1903 *Loan Exhibition of Sketches and Studies by J. S. Sargent R.A. Carfax & Co., Ltd, 17 Ryder Street, St. James*, London (May–June 1903).

NEW YORK, 1903 The American Art Association, American Art Galleries, New York, *Loan Exhibition of Portraits for the Benefit of the Orthopaedic Dispensary and Hospital*, opened 18 November 1903.

BERLIN, 1903 Grosse Berliner Kunstausstellung, 1903.

DUBLIN, 1903 Royal Hibernian Academy of Arts, Dublin, 1903.

BIRMINGHAM, 1904 Royal Birmingham Society of Artists, *The Seventy-eighth Autumn Exhibition*, 1904.

BRUSSELS, SALON, 1904 Le Salon, Brussels, 1904.

DUBLIN, 1904 Gallery of Modern Art (Abbey Street), Dublin, 1904.

DÜSSELDORF, 1904 Stadtischen Kunstpalast, Düsseldorf, *Internationale Kunstausstellung*, 1904.

GLASGOW, 1904 The Royal Glasgow Institute of the Fine Arts, 1904 [no. 645, unidentified Wertheimer portrait].

CHICAGO, 1905 Art Institute of Chicago and Exhibition Committee of the Municipal Art League of Chicago, *Loan Exhibition of Portraits*, 2–22 January 1905.

PHILADELPHIA, 1905 Pennsylvania Academy of the Fine Arts, Philadelphia, *One Hundredth Anniversary Exhibition*, 23 January–4 March 1905.

LONDON, RA, 1905 Royal Academy, London, *The One Hundred and Thirty-seventh Exhibition*, 1 May–7 August 1905.

BOSTON, 1905 Boston Museum of Fine Arts, *Pictures from Mrs Sears's Collection*.

LIÈGE, 1905 Liège, Belgium, *Exposition universelle et internationale*, 1905.

LONDON, SPP, 1906 Society of Portrait Painters, London, 1906.

BELFAST, 1906 Corporation of Belfast, *Art Loan Exhibition*, 1906.

BOSTON, 1906 Copley Hall, Boston, *Loan Exhibition of Portraits*, 1906.

WASHINGTON, 1907 Corcoran Gallery of Art, Washington, D.C., *First Annual Exhibition, Oil Paintings by Contemporary American Artists*, 7 February–9 March 1907.

VENICE, 1907 *Settina Esposizione Internazionale d'Arte della Città di Venezia*, 22 April–31 October 1907.

LONDON, SPP, 1907 Society of Portrait Painters, New Gallery, London [November?] 1907.

BRUSSELS, 1907 Le Salon, Brussels, 1907.

DUBLIN, IRISH INTERNATIONAL, 1907 *Irish International Exhibition*, Dublin, 1907.

BERLIN, 1907–8 Königliche Akademie der Kunstausstellung, *Zweite Ausstellung der Königlichen Akademie der Künste*, 1907–8.

LONDON, INTERNATIONAL SOCIETY, 1908 International Society of Sculptors, Painters and Gravers, New Gallery, London, *Exhibition of Fair Women*, February and March 1908.

NEW YORK, NAD (ANNUAL), 1908 National Academy of Design, New York, *Eighty-third Annual Exhibition*, 14 March–18 April 1908.

LONDON, FRANCO–BRITISH EXHIBITION, 1908 *Franco-British Exhibition*, London, August 1908.

WASHINGTON, 1908 Corcoran Gallery of Art, Washington, D.C., *Second Annual Exhibition, Oil Paintings by Contemporary American Artists*, 8 December 1908–17 January 1909.

NEW YORK, NAD (WINTER), 1908 National Academy of Design, New York, *Winter Exhibition*, 12 December 1908–9 January 1909.

LONDON, SPP, 1908 Society of Portrait Painters, New Gallery, London, *Eighteenth Exhibition*, 1908.

LONDON, INTERNATIONAL SOCIETY, 1909 International Society, London, *Exhibition of Fair Women*, 1909.

WORCESTER, 1909 Worcester Art Museum, *Summer Exhibition*, 1909.

LONDON, SPP, 1909 Society of Portrait Painters, New Gallery, London (November?) 1909.

LONDON, NEAC (WINTER), 1909 New English Art Club, London, *Winter Exhibition*, 1909.

EDINBURGH, 1909 Royal Scottish Academy, Edinburgh, 1909.

BERLIN, 1909 Grosse Berliner Kunstausstellung, 1909.

LONDON, INTERNATIONAL SOCIETY, 1910 International Society of Sculptors, Painters and Gravers, Grafton Gallery, London, *Exhibition of Fair Women*, 26 May–31 July 1910.

LIVERPOOL, 1910 Walker Art Gallery, Liverpool, *Autumn Exhibition of Modern Art*, 1910.

WASHINGTON, 1910 Corcoran Gallery of Art, Washington, D.C., *Third Exhibition of Oil Paintings by Contemporary American Artists*, 13 December 1910–22 January 1911.

ABERDEEN, 1910 Aberdeen Artists' Society, Aberdeen Art Gallery, *Fourteenth Exhibition of Works by Modern Masters*, November 1910–January 1911.

BERLIN, 1910 Königliche Akademie der Kunst zu Berlin, *Ausstellung Amerikanischer Kunst*, 1910.

LONDON, NATIONAL PORTRAIT SOCIETY, 1911 National Portrait Society, London, 1911.

BUFFALO, 1911 Buffalo Fine Arts Academy, Albright Art Gallery, *Sixth Annual Exhibition of Selected Paintings by American Artists*, 12 May–28 August 1911 (unidentified 'Portrait of a Lady').

CHICAGO, 1911 Art Institute of Chicago, *Twenty-fourth Annual Exhibition of American Oil Paintings and Sculpture*, 14 November–27 December 1911.

EDINBURGH, 1911 Royal Scottish Academy, Edinburgh, 1911.

ROME, 1911 Roman Art Exhibition, Rome, Pavilion of the United States of America, 1911.

LONDON, RSPP, 1912 London, Royal Society of Portrait Painters, 1912.

WASHINGTON, 1912 Corcoran Gallery of Art, Washington, D.C., *Fourth Exhibition of Oil Paintings by Contemporary American Artists*, 17 December 1912–26 January 1913.

PITTSBURGH, 1913 Carnegie Institute, Pittsburgh, *The Seventeenth Annual International Exhibition of Paintings*, 24 April–30 June 1913.

PHILADELPHIA, 1913 Pennsylvania Academy of the Fine Arts, Philadelphia Water Color Club, Pennsylvania Society of Miniature Painters, *Eleventh Annual Philadelphia Water Color Exhibition and Twelfth Annual Exhibition of Miniatures*, 9 November–14 December 1913.

BELFAST, 1913 Belfast, *Loan Exhibition of Modern Paintings* (Autumn) 1913.

GLASGOW, 1913 The Royal Glasgow Institute of the Fine Arts, Glasgow, 1913.

NEW YORK, 1914 M. Knoedler & Co., New York, *Exhibition of the National Association of Portrait Painters Inc*, 2–14 February 1914.

WASHINGTON, 1914 United States National Museum, Washington, D.C., *National Association of Portrait Painters: Third Annual Circuit Exhibition*, 14 March–12 April 1914.

BOSTON, 1914 The Copley Society, Copley Hall, Boston, *Portraits of Living Painters*, loan collection, March 1914.

WORCESTER, 1914 Worcester Art Museum, *Exhibition of Contemporary American Paintings Owned in Worcester County*, 5 April–10 May, 1914.

WASHINGTON, 1914–15 Corcoran Gallery of Art, Washington, D.C., *Fifth Exhibition of Oil Paintings by Contemporary American Artists*, 15 December 1914–24 January 1915.

BOSTON, 1915 Museum of Fine Arts, Boston, *Opening Exhibition, Robert Dawson Evans Memorial Galleries for Paintings*, 1915 (opened February).

SAN FRANCISCO, 1915 Panama-Pacific International Exposition, San Francisco, Spring 1915.

BOSTON, MFA, 1916 Museum of Fine Arts, Boston, *Paintings by John Singer Sargent: Bostonian Paintings*, 10 May–1 November 1916.

WASHINGTON, 1916–17 Corcoran Gallery of Art, Washington, D.C., *Sixth Exhibition of Oil Paintings by Contemporary American Artists*, 17 December 1916–21 January 1917.

BOSTON, COPLEY GALLERY, 1917 Copley Gallery, Boston, *Exhibition of Paintings and Drawings by John Singer Sargent for the Benefit of the American Ambulance Hospital in Paris*, 22 January–3 February 1917.

PHILADELPHIA, 1917 Pennsylvania Academy of the Fine Arts, Philadelphia, *One Hundred and Twelfth Annual Exhibition*, 4 February–25 March 1917.

DUBLIN, 1917 Royal Hibernian Academy of Arts, Dublin, 1917.

EDINBURGH, 1917 Royal Scottish Academy, Edinburgh, 1917.

WORCESTER, 1918 Worcester Art Museum, *Exhibition of Paintings by Contemporary American Artists*, 10 November–24 November 1918.

PARIS, 1919 Musée du Luxembourg, Paris, *Exposition d'artistes de l'école américaine*, October–November 1919.

GLASGOW, 1920 The Royal Glasgow Institute of the Fine Arts, Glasgow, 1920.

PITTSBURGH, 1921 Carnegie Institute, Pittsburgh, *Twentieth Annual International Exhibition of Paintings*, 28 April–30 June 1921.

LONDON, RSPP, 1921 Royal Academy of Arts, London, *Exhibition of the Royal Society of Portrait Painters*, 12 November–17 December 1921.

LONDON, NATIONAL PORTRAIT SOCIETY, 1921 Grafton Gallery, London, National Portrait Society Exhibition, 1921.

NEW YORK, 1922 National Association of Portrait Painters, New York, *Tenth Annual Exhibition*, 1–13 May 1922.

CINCINNATI, 1922 Cincinnati Art Museum, *Twenty-Ninth Annual Exhibition of American Art*, 27 May–31 July 1922.

CHICAGO, 1922 Art Institute of Chicago, *Thirty-fifth Annual Exhibition of American Paintings and Sculpture*, 2 November–10 December 1922.

BOSTON, 1922 St Botolph Club, Boston, *Exhibition of Paintings and Drawings by John S. Sargent*, 20 November–2 December 1922.

EDINURGH, 1922 Royal Scottish Academy, Edinburgh.

NEW YORK, MACBETH GALLERY, 1923 Macbeth Gallery, New York, *Thirteenth Annual Exhibition: Thirty Paintings by Thirty Artists*, 23 January–12 February 1923.

PITTSBURGH, 1923 Carnegie Institute, Pittsburgh, *Twenty-second Annual International Exhibition of Paintings*, 26 April–17 June 1923.

ROME, 1923–4 Palazzo delle Belle Arti, Rome, *Second Biennale Romana, Mostra Internazionale di Belle Arti*, 23 November 1923–April 1924 (extended to May).

LONDON, RSPP, 1924 Royal Society of Portrait Painters, London, *Thirty-fourth Annual Exhibition*, 19 January–9 February 1924.

NEW YORK, GCAG, 1924 Grand Central Art Galleries, New York, *Retrospective Exhibition of Important Works by John Singer Sargent*, 23 February–22 March 1924.

CHICAGO, 1924 Chicago, The Art Institute of Chicago, *Paintings by John Singer Sargent*, 14 April–1 July 1924.

BUFFALO, 1924 The Buffalo Fine Arts Academy, Albright Art Gallery, Buffalo, *Eighteenth Annual Exhibition of Selected Paintings and Small Bronzes by American Artists*, 20 April–30 June 1924.

PITTSBURGH, 1924 Carnegie Institute, Pittsburgh, *Twenty-third Annual International Exhibition of Paintings*, 24 April–15 June 1924.

CLEVELAND, 1924 Cleveland Museum of Art, Ohio, *The Fourth Exhibition of Contemporary American Painting*, 1924 (opened 13 June).

LONDON, NEAC, 1925 New English Art Club, London, 5 January–14 February 1925.

NEW YORK, 1925 National Association of Portrait Painters, New York, *Twelfth Annual Exhibition*, 15–31 January 1925.

LONDON, RSPP, 1925 Royal Academy of Arts, London, *Royal Society of Portrait Painters Exhibition*, 24 January–21 February 1925.

LONDON, 1925 Barbizon House, London.

CINCINNATI, 1925 Cincinnati Art Museum, *Thirty-second Annual Exhibition of American Art*, 23 May–31 July 1925.

LIVERPOOL, 1925 Walker Art Gallery, Liverpool, *Fifty-third Autumn Exhibition*, including a collective exhibit of works by the late John S. Sargent, R.A., 19 September–12 December 1925.

WASHINGTON, 1925 Corcoran Gallery of Art, Washington, D.C., *Commemorative Exhibition by Members of the National Academy of Design 1825–1925,* 17 October–15 November 1925, and the Grand Central Art Galleries, New York, 1 December 1925–3 January 1926 (organized by National Academy of Design).

NEW YORK, KNOEDLER, 1925 M. Knoedler & Co., New York, *An Exhibition of Paintings by the Late John Singer Sargent, R.A.,* 2–14 November 1925.

BOSTON, MFA, 1925 Museum of Fine Arts, Boston, *Memorial Exhibition of the Works of the Late John Singer Sargent,* 3 November–27 December 1925. The second edition of the catalogue, published in January 1926, incorporates some late additions to the exhibition into its chronological listing of works shown, which results in differences in numeration. We give the number of the work exhibited as it appears in the first edition and place the revised number in brackets afterwards.

GLASGOW, 1925 The Royal Glasgow Institute of the Fine Arts, 1925.

NEW YORK, MMA, 1926 The Metropolitan Museum of Art, New York, *Memorial Exhibition of the Work of John Singer Sargent,* 4 January–14 February 1926.

LONDON, RA, 1926 *Exhibition of Works by the Late John S. Sargent, R.A.,* Winter Exhibition, 14 January–13 March 1926.

PHILADELPHIA, 1926 Pennsylvania Academy of the Fine Arts, Philadelphia, *One Hundred and Twenty-first Annual Exhibition of American Paintings and Sculpture,* 31 January–21 March 1926.

YORK, 1926 York City Art Gallery, *Spring Exhibition: Loan Exhibition of Works by the Late John S. Sargent, R.A.,* 31 March–May 1926.

NEW YORK, NAD, 1926 The Union League Club of New York, *Exhibition of Paintings from the Collection of the National Academy of Design,* 7–11 April 1926.

CINCINNATI, 1926 Cincinnati Art Museum, *Thirty-third Annual Exhibition of American Art,* 29 May–31 July 1926.

LONDON, TATE, 1926 National Gallery (Millbank), London, *Opening of Sargent Gallery,* June– October 1926.

SAN FRANCISCO, 1926–7 California Palace of the Legion of Honor, San Francisco, *First Exhibition of Selected Paintings by American Artists,* 15 November 1926–30 January 1927.

DALLAS, 1927 Dallas Art Association (sixth exhibition), *Exhibition of Paintings and Sculpture by Leading Living American Artists, under Auspices of Dallas Art Association . . .* From Grand Central Art Galleries, New York, 5–25 February 1927.

BUFFALO, 1927 The Buffalo Fine Arts Academy, Albright Art Gallery, Buffalo, *Twenty-first Annual Exhibition of Selected Paintings by American Artists,* 24 April–19 June 1927.

NEW YORK, KNOEDLER, 1927 M. Knoedler & Co., New York, *Nineteenth Annual Summer Exhibition of American Paintings,* 1927.

EDINBURGH, 1928 Royal Scottish Academy, Edinburgh, *One Hundred and Second Annual Exhibition of the Royal Scottish Academy,* 21 April–25 August 1928.

GLASGOW, 1929 The Royal Glasgow Institute of the Fine Arts, 1929.

STOCKHOLM AND COPENHAGEN, 1930 Kungl. Akademien för de fria Konstnerna, Stockholm, *Utställning av Amerikansk Konst,* 15 March–7 April 1930; shown at Ny Calsberg Glyptothek, Copenhagen, 3–22 May 1930.

LIVERPOOL, 1933 Walker Art Gallery, Liverpool, *Fifty-ninth Autumn Exhibition,* 1933.

VENICE, 1934 *XIX Biennale Internazionale d'Arte,* Venice, May–October, 1934

NEW YORK, 1935 College Art Association, New York, *Memorial Exhibition: American Painters since 1900* (touring exhibition: Guild Hall, East Hampton, New York; Toledo Museum of Art, Ohio; Springfield Museum of Fine Arts, Massachusetts; Louisville Art Association, Kentucky; Currier Gallery of Art, Manchester, New Hampshire; Buffalo Fine Arts Academy, New York; Memorial Art Gallery, Rochester, New York (September 1934–June 1935).

NEWPORT, 1935 M. Knoedler and Co., 206 Bellevue Avenue, Newport, Rhode Island, *Paintings and Water-colours by John Singer Sargent, R..A.,* 19 August–3 September 1935.

CLEVELAND, 1936 Cleveland Museum of Art, *Twentieth Anniversary Exhibition of the Cleveland Museum of Art: The Official Art Exhibit of the Great Lakes Exposition,* 1936.

NEW YORK, NAD, 1939, Special Exhibition National Academy of Design, New York, *Special Exhibition,* 8 May–25 July 1939.

NEW YORK, 1943 Grand Central Art Galleries, New York, *Portraits of Yesterday and Today,* 'A loan exhibition showing Distinguished Personalities of the New York Scene in The Golden Nineties . . . For the Benefit of The American Red Cross, Grand Central Art Galleries, Gotham Hotel, New York', 5–19 May 1943.

NEW YORK, NYHS, 1945 New-York Historical Society, National Society of Portrait Painters, *Portraits of Americans by Americans,* 1 April–5 May 1945.

EDINBURGH, 1947 Royal Scottish Academy, Edinburgh, 1947.

LONDON, TATE, 1946 Tate Gallery, London, *American Paintings from the Eighteenth Century to the Present,* 1946.

NEW YORK, 1948 Scott and Fowles, New York, *Ten Sargents from Sargent's Own Collection,* 24 February–24 March 1948.

NEW YORK, NAD, 1951 National Academy of Design, New York, *The American Tradition, Exhibition of Paintings,* 3 December–16 December 1951.

GLASGOW, 1953 The Royal Glasgow Institute of the Fine Arts, 1953.

UTICA, 1953 Munson-Williams-Proctor Institute, Utica, New York, *Expatriates: Whistler, Cassatt, Sargent,* 4–25 January 1953.

CHICAGO, 1954 The Art Institute of Chicago, *Sargent, Whistler and Mary Cassatt,* 14 January–25 February 1954 (touring exhibition).

GRAND RAPIDS, 1955 Grand Rapids Art Gallery, Michigan, *Cassatt, Whistler and Sargent Exhibition,* 15 September–15 October 1955.

BOSTON, 1956 Museum of Fine Arts, Boston, *A Centennial Exhibition: Sargent's Boston,* 3 January–7 February 1956.

CINCINNATI, 1957 Cincinnati Art Museum, *An American Viewpoint: Realism in Twentieth Century American Painting,* 12 October–17 November 1957.

PITTSBURGH, 1957 Carnegie Institute, Pittsburgh, *American Classics of the Nineteenth Century,* 17 October–1 December 1957.

PALM BEACH, 1959 The Society of the Four Arts, Palm Beach, Florida, *Loan Exhibition of Works by John Singer Sargent (1856–1925) and Mary Cassatt (1845–1926),* 7 March–5 April 1959.

SAN FRANCISCO, 1959 California Palace of the Legion of Honor, San Francisco, *Sargent and Boldini,* 24 October–29 November 1959.

FALMOUTH, 1962 The Polytechnic Arts Committee, Falmouth, Cornwall, *John Singer Sargent,* 1962.

PARIS, 1963 Centre Culturel Americain, Paris, *John S. Sargent 1856–1925,* 15 February–30 March 1963.

BIRMINGHAM, 1964 Museum and Art Gallery, Birmingham, England, *Exhibition of Works by John Singer Sargent, R.A. 1856–1925,* 25 September–18 October 1964.

WASHINGTON, 1964 Corcoran Gallery of Art, Washington, D.C., *The Private World of John Singer Sargent,* 18 April–14 June 1964, (touring exhibition).

WORCESTER, 1969 Worcester Art Museum, Massachusetts, *Art in America, 1830–1950,* 9 January–23 February 1969.

BUFFALO, 1974 Albright-Knox Art Gallery, Buffalo, *American Art In Upstate New York,* 12 July–25 August 1974 (touring exhibition).

Leeds, 1979 Leeds Art Galleries (Lotherton Hall), England, *John Singer Sargent and the Edwardian Age,* 5 April–10 June 1979; National Portrait Gallery, London, 6 July–9 September 1979; Detroit Institute of Arts, 17 October–9 December 1979.

NEW YORK, 1980 Hirschl & Adler Galleries, New York, *American Art from the Galleries Collection,* 4–25 October 1980.

LOS ANGELES, 1981 Los Angeles County Museum of Art, *American Portraiture in the Grand Manner 1720–1920,* 1981.

DETROIT, 1983 The Detroit Institute of Arts, *The Quest for Unity: American Art between Worlds Fairs, 1876–1893,* 1983.

NEW YORK, NAD, 1983 National Academy of Design, New York, *Artists by Themselves: Artists' Portraits from the National Academy of Design,* 3 November 1983–1 January 1984 (touring exhibition).

LONDON, 1985 Colnaghi and the Clarendon Gallery, London, *Society Portraits 1850–1939*, 30 October–14 December 1985.

SAN FRANCISCO, 1985 California Palace of the Legion of Honor, San Francisco, and the Cleveland Museum of Art, *Venice: The American View 1860–1920*, 20 October 1984–20 January 1985 and 27 February 1985–21 April 1985, respectively.

BOSTON, 1986 Museum of Fine Arts, Boston, *The Bostonians: Painters of an Elegant Age, 1870–1930*, 11 June–14 September 1986 (touring exhibition; Denver Art Museum, 25 October 1986–18 January 1987; Terra Museum of American Art, Chicago, 13 March–10 May 1987).

NEW YORK AND CHICAGO, 1986 Whitney Museum of American Art, New York, and Art Institute of Chicago, *John Singer Sargent*, 7 October 1986–4 January 1987 and 7 February–19 April 1987, respectively.

JAPAN, 1989 Isetan Museum of Art, Tokyo, *John Singer Sargent: Sargent Exhibition in Japan*, 26 January–23 February 1989, (touring exhibition: Yamaguchi Prefectural Museum of Art, 2 March–2 April 1989; Kumamoto Prefectural Museum of Art, 8 April–7 May 1989; Museum of Modern Art, Shiga, 13 May–11 June 1989).

NEW YORK, 1989 Coe Kerr Gallery, New York, *American Impressionism II*, 19 May–23 June 1989.

WASHINGTON, 1989 National Gallery of Art, Washington, D.C., *American Paintings from the Manoogian Collection*, 4 June 1989–4 September 1989; Fine Arts Museum of San Francisco, 23 September 1989–26 November 1989; the Metropolitan Museum of Art, New York, 18 December 1989–25 February 1990; Detroit Institute of Arts, 27 March 1990–27 May 1990.

NEW YORK, 1990 Adelson Galleries, New York, *Inaugural Exhibition: One Hundred Years of American and European Art*, 1 November–15 December 1990.

BOSTON, 1992 Musem of Fine Arts, Boston, *The Lure of Italy: American Artists and the Italian Experience* 16 September 1992–13 December 1992; Cleveland Museum of Art, 3 February –11 April 1993; Msuem of Fine Arts, Houston, 23 May–8 August 1993.

LONDON, 1992 Tate Gallery, London, *The Swagger Portrait*, 14 October 1992–10 January 1993.

NEW YORK, 1994 Metropolitan Museum of Art, New York, *American Impressionism and Realism: The Painting of Modern Life 1885–1915*, 10 May–24 July 1994; Amon Carter Museum, Fort Worth, 21 August–30 October 1994; Denver Art Museum, Colorado, 3 December 1994– 5 February 1995; Los Angeles County Museum of Art, 12 March–14 May 1995.

BOSTON, 1994 Museum of Fine Arts, Boston, *Dennis Miller Bunker: American Impressionist*, 13 January–4 June 1995; Terra Museum of American Art, Chicago, 1 July–24 September 1995; Denver Art Museum, 14 October–31 December 1995.

BOSTON, 1995 Isabella Stewart Gardner Mseum, Boston, *Dennis Miller Bunker and his Circle*, 13 January–4 June 1995.

LONDON, 1996 National Portrait Gallery, London, *The Art of the Picture Frame: Artists, Patrons and the Framing of Portraits in Britain*, 8 November 1996–9 February 1997.

EDINBURGH, 1997 National Gallery of Scotland, Edinburgh, *The Portrait of a Lady: Sargent and Lady Agnew*, 8 August–19 October 1997.

WASHINGTON, 1997 National Portrait Gallery, Washington, D.C., *Edith Wharton's World: Portraits of People and Places*, 26 September 1997–25 January 1998.

HOUSTON, 1998 Museum of Fine Arts, Houston, *John Singer Sargent in Houston Collections*, 11 October–9 November 1998.

LONDON, 1998 Tate Gallery, London, *Sargent*, 15 October 1998–17 January 1999; National Gallery of Art, Washington, D.C., 21 February 1999–31 May 1999; Museum of Fine Arts, Boston, 23 June–26 September 1999.

MONTCLAIR, 1999 Montclair Museum of Art, New Jersey, *Paris 1900: The 'American School' at the Universal Exposition*, 18 September 1999– 16 January 2000; Pennsylvania Academy of Fine Arts, Philadelphia, 11 February–16 April 2000; Columbus Museum of Art, Ohio, 18 May– 13 August 2000; Elvehjem Museum of Art, University of Wisconsin at Madison, 16 September–3 December 2000; Musée Carnavalet, Paris, 2 February–15 May 2001.

NEW YORK, 1999 Jewish Museum, New York, *John Singer Sargent: Portraits of the Wertheimer Family*, 17 October 1999–6 February 2000; New Orleans Museum of Art, 4 March–21 May 2000; Virginia Museum of Fine Arts, Richmond, 11 July–29 October 2000; Seattle Art Museum, 14 December 2000–18 March 2001.

LONDON, 2000 Royal Academy of Arts, London, *1900: Art at the Crossroads*, 16 January–3 April 2000; Solomon R. Guggenheim Museum, New York, 18 May–13 September 2000.

SEATTLE, 2000 Seattle Art Museum, *John Singer Sargent*, 14 December 2000–18 March 2001 (incorporating *John Singer Sargent: Portraits of the Wertheimer Family* [see New York 1999]).

ABDY AND GERE 1984 Jane Abdy and Charlotte Gere, *The Souls*, London, 1984.

ADAMS 1988 J. C. Levenson, Ernest Samuels, Charles Vandersee and Viola Hopkins Winner, eds. *The Letters of Henry Adams*, Cambridge, 1988 (vols IV, V and VI).

ADELSON *et al.* 1986 Warren Adelson, *Sargent at Broadway: The Impressionist Years*, New York and London, 1986. Essays by Warren Adelson, Stanley Olson and Richard Ormond.

ADELSON *et al.* 1997 Warren Adelson, Donna Seldin Janis, Elaine Kilmurray, Richard Ormond and Elizabeth Oustinoff, *Sargent Abroad: Figures and Landscapes*, New York, 1997.

ADELSON AND OUSTINOFF 1992 Warren Adelson and Elizabeth Oustinoff, 'Sargent's Spanish Dancer – A Discovery', *Magazine Antiques*, 141 (March 1992), pp. 460–71.

ALDRICH 1891 Thomas Bailey Aldrich, 'Sargent's Portrait of Edwin Booth at "The Players"', *Harper's New Monthly Magazine*, 82 (February 1891).

AUCHINCLOSS 1989 Louis Auchincloss, *The Vanderbilt Era*, New York, 1989.

BAKER 1985 Michael Baker, *Our Three Selves: A Life of Radclyffe Hall*, London, 1985.

BALDRY 1900, I A. Lys Baldry, 'The Art of J. S. Sargent, R.A.: Part I', *International Studio*, 10 (March 1900), pp. 3–21.

BALDRY 1900, II A. Lys Baldry, 'The Art of John S. Sargent, R.A.: Part II', *International Studio*, 10 (April 1900), pp. 107–19.

BALSAN 1953 Consuelo Vanderbilt Balsan, *The Glitter and the Gold*, London, 1953.

BARBER 1998 James Barber, *Theodore Roosevelt: Icon of the American Century*, foreword by John Allen Gable, and essay by Amy Verone, Washington, D.C., 1998 (exhibition catalogue).

BARTER *et al.* 1998 Judith A. Barter, Kimberley Rhodes, and Seth A. Thayer (with contributions by Andrew Walker), *American Arts at The Art Institute of Chicago: From Colonial Times to World War I*, the Art Institute of Chicago, 1998.

BELLEROCHE 1926 Albert de Belleroche, 'The Lithographs of Sargent', *The Print Collectors Quarterly*, XIII (February 1926), pp. 30–45.

BERRY 1924 Rose V. S. Berry, 'John Singer Sargent: Some of His American Work', *Art and Archaeology*, 18 (September 1924), pp. 83–112.

BIDDLE 1926 George Biddle, 'Some Memories of Mary Cassatt', *Arts*, X (August 1926), pp. 107–11.

BIRNBAUM 1941 Martin Birnbaum, *John Singer Sargent, January 12, 1856–April 15, 1925: A Conversation Piece*, New York, 1941.

BLANCHE 1926 Jacques-Émile Blanche, 'Un Grand Américain: L'Exposition John Sargent à Londres', *Revue de Paris* (1 April 1926), pp. 570–1.

BLANCHE 1937 Jacques-Émile Blanche, *Portraits of a Lifetime: The Late Victorian Era, the Edwardian Pageant, 1870–1914*, trans. and ed. Walter Clement, London, 1937; New York, 1938.

BLANCHE 1939 Jacques-Émile Blanche, *More Portraits of a Lifetime*, trans. and ed. Walter Clement, London, 1939.

BLASHFIELD 1925 Edwin H. Blashfield, 'John Singer Sargent – Recollections', *North American Review*, no. 221 (June–August 1925), pp. 641–53.

BLUNT 1932 Wilfrid Scawen Blunt, *My Diaries: Being a Personal Narrative of Events, 1888–1914*, foreword by Lady Gregory, London, 1932 (first published in two volumes 1919 and 1920).

BORGLUM 1923 Gutzon Borglum, 'John Singer Sargent – Artist: The Greatest of American Portrait-Painters', *Delineator*, CII (February 1923), pp. 15, 106.

BOSTON 1899 *Catalogue of Paintings and Sketches by John S. Sargent, R.A.*, Copley Hall, Boston, 1899 (exhibition catalogue).

BOSTON 1925 *Catalogue of the Memorial Exhibition of the Works of the Late John Singer Sargent*, Museum of Fine Arts, Boston, 1925, foreword by J. Templeman Coolidge (exhibition catalogue).

BOSTON 1925a *Catalogue of the Memorial Exhibition of the Works of the Late John Singer Sargent, Museum of Fine Arts, Boston*, 1925, foreword by J. Templeman Coolidge (second edition of exhibition catalogue with revised numeration).

BOSTON 1956 David McKibbin, *Sargent's Boston: With an Essay & a Biographical Summary & a Complete Check List of Sargent's Portraits*, Boston, Museum of Fine Arts, 1956 (exhibition catalogue). The checklist of portraits is listed separately as 'McKibbin 1956'.

BOSTON MFA 1969 *American Paintings in the Museum of Fine Arts, Boston*, 2 vols, Boston, Museum of Fine Arts, 1969.

BOSTON 1986 Trevor J. Fairbrother, *The Bostonians: Painters of an Elegant Age 1870–1930*, contributions by Theodore E. Stebbins Jr, William L. Vance and Erica E. Hirshler, Boston 1986 (exhibition catalogue).

BOSTON 1992 Theodore E. Stebbins, Jr, *The Lure of Italy: American Artists and the Italian Experience*, with essays by William H. Gerdts, Erica E Hirshler, Fred S. Licht and William L. Vance, New York 1992 (exhibition catalogue).

BOSTON 1994 Erica E. Hirshler, *Dennis Miller Bunker: American Impressionist*, Boston, Museum of Fine Arts, 1994, with an essay by David Park Curry, introduction by Theodore E. Stebbins Jr and contributions by Efrat Adler Porat and Deanna M. Griffin (exhibition catalogue).

BOSTON 1995 James T. Boulton, ed., *Lawrence in Love: Letters to Louie Burrows*, Nottingham, University of Nottingham, 1968.

BRINTON 1906 Erica E. Hirshler, *Dennis Miller Bunker and his Circles*, Boston 1995 (exhibition catalogue).

BRINTON 1908 Christian Brinton, *Modern Artists*, New York, 1908.

BRYANT 1923 L. M. Bryant, 'Our Great Painter John Sargent, and Some of His Child-Portraits', *Saint Nicholas*, 51 (November 1923), pp. 4–5.

BURKE 1980 Doreen Bolger Burke, *American Paintings in the Metropolitan Museum of Art: A Catalogue of Works by Artists Born between 1846 and 1864*, vol. 3, New York, 1980.

BURNS 1992 Sarah Burns, 'The "Earnest, Untiring Worker" and the Magician of the Brush: Gender Politics in the Criticism of Cecilia Beaux and John Singer Sargent', *Oxford Art Journal*, vol. 15 (1992), pp. 36–53.

CAFFIN 1902 C. H. Caffin, *American Masters of Painting*, New York, 1902, pp. 55–67.

CAFFIN 1903 Charles H. Caffin, 'John S. Sargent: The Greatest Contemporary Portrait Painter', *World's Work*, 7 (November 1903), pp. 4099–116.

CAFFIN 1903a Charles H. Caffin, 'The Art of John Singer Sargent', *Current Literature*, XXIV (April 1903), pp. 443–8 (extracted from Charles H. Caffin, *American Masters of Painting*, New York, 1902).

CARGHER 1980 John Cargher, ed., *Melodies and Memories: The Autobiography of Nellie Melba*, London, 1980.

CARTER 1947 H. D. Carter, ed. *Henry Adams and his Friends*, 1947.

CHAMPNEYS 1900 Basil Champneys, *Memoirs and Correspondence of Coventry Patmore*, London, 2 vols, 1900.

CHARTERIS 1927 Evan Charteris, *John Sargent*, London, 1927.

CHARTERIS 1931 Evan Charteris, *The Life and Letters of Sir Edmund Gosse*, London, 1931.

CHICAGO 1954 Frederick A. Sweet, *Sargent, Whistler and Mary Cassatt*, Chicago, 1954 (exhibition catalogue).

CHRISTIE'S 1925 *Catalogue of Pictures and Water Colour Drawings by J. S. Sargent, R.A. and Works by other Artists, the property of the late John Singer Sargent, R.A., D.C.L., LLD . . . which . . . will be sold by auction by Messrs. Christie, Manson & Woods . . . on Friday July 24, and Monday, July 27, 1925*, London, 1925 (with 19 illustrations).

CLINE 1970 C. L. Cline, ed., *The Letters of George Meredith*, Oxford, 1970, 2 vols.

COFFIN 1896 William A. Coffin, 'Sargent and His Painting, With Special Reference to His Decorations in the Boston Public Library', *Century Magazine*, 52 (June 1896), pp. 163–78.

COLSON 1950 Percy Colson, *A Story of Christie's*, London, 1950.

CORTISSOZ 1903 Royal Cortissoz, 'John S. Sargent', *Scribner's Magazine*, XXIV, (November 1903), pp. 514–32. repr. as *Art and Common Sense*, New York, 1913.

CORTISSOZ 1913 Royal Cortissoz, *Art and Common Sense*, New York, 1913 (see above).

CORTISSOZ 1924 Royal Cortissoz, 'Sargent: The Painter of Modern Tenseness, the Nature of His Genius', *Scribner's Magazine*, LXXV (March 1924), pp. 345–52.

COURNOS 1915 John Cournos, 'John S. Sargent', *Forum*, 54 (August 1915), pp. 232–6.

COX 1908 Kenyon Cox, 'Sargent', *Old Masters and New: Essays in Art Criticism*, New York, 1908, pp. 255–65.

CUSHING 1925 Harvey Cushing, *The Life of Sir William Osler*, 2 vols, Oxford, 1925.

DAKERS 1993 Caroline Dakers, *Clouds: The Biography of a Country House*, New Haven and London, 1993.

DE WOLFE HOWE 1937 M. A. De Wolfe Howe, *John Jay Chapman and His Letters*, New York, 1937.

DIXON 1899 Marion Hepworth Dixon, 'Mr John S. Sargent as a Portrait-Painter', *Magazine of Art*, 23 (1899), pp. 112–19.

DORMENT AND MACDONALD 1994 Richard Dorment and Margaret MacDonald, *Whistler*, London, 1994 (exhibition catalogue).

DOWNES 1900 William Howe Downes, 'John Sargent's Portraits', *Twelve Great Artists*, Boston, 1900, pp. 165–72.

DOWNES 1925 William Howe Downes, *John S. Sargent: His Life and Work*, Boston, 1925.

DOWNES 1926 William Howe Downes, *John S. Sargent: His Life and Work*, London, 1926.

DUCAT 1928 Eva Ducat, *Another Way of Music*, London, 1928.

DUVENECK 1970 Josephine W. Duveneck, *Frank Duveneck. Painter-Teacher*, San Francisco, 1970.

EARLY PORTRAITS Richard Ormond and Elaine Kilmurray, *John Singer Sargent: The Early Portraits (Complete Paintings, vol. I)*, New Haven and London, 1998.

EDEL 1963 Leon Edel, *Henry James: The Middle Years*, Philadelphia, 1963.

EDEL 1972 Leon Edel, *Henry James: The Master*, London, 1972.

EDEL 1980 Leon Edel, ed., *Henry James Letters*, vol. III (1883–1895), London, 1980.

EDEL 1984 Leon Edel, ed., *Henry James Letters*, vol. IV (1895–1916), Cambridge, Massachusetts, 1984.

EDEL 1985 Leon Edel, *Henry James: A Life*, London, 1985.

EDINBURGH 1997 Julia Rayer Rolfe, *The Portrait of a Lady: Sargent and Lady Agnew*, essays by David Cannadine, Kenneth McConkey and Wilfrid Mellers, Edinburgh, 1997.

EGERTON 1998 Judy Egerton, *The British School* (National Gallery Catalogues), New Haven and London, 1998.

FAIRBROTHER 1982 Trevor J. Fairbrother, 'Notes on John Singer Sargent in New York, 1888–1890', *Archives of American Art Journal*, 22 (1982), pp. 27–32.

FAIRBROTHER 1986 Trevor Fairbrother, *John Singer Sargent and America*, New York, 1986.

FAIRBROTHER 1994 Trevor Fairbrother, *John Singer Sargent*, New York, 1994.

FAIRBROTHER 2000 Trevor Fairbrother, *John Singer Sargent: The Sensualist*, New Haven and London, 2000 (published in conjunction with the exhibition *John Singer Sargent* at the Seattle Art Museum). See 'Exhibitions Cited in Abbreviated Form', Seattle 2000.

FAIRBROTHER 2001 Trevor Fairbrother, 'Possessions and Props: The Collection of John Singer Sargent', *Magazine Antiques*, CLIX (February 2001), pp. 314–23.

FINCH 1947 Edith Finch, *Carey Thomas of Bryn Mawr*, New York and London, 1947.

FISCHER *et al.* 1999 Diane P. Fischer, ed., *Paris 1900: The 'American School' at the Universal Exposition*, essays by Linda J. Docherty, Robert W. Rydell, Gail Stavitsky and Gabriel P. Weisberg, New Brunswick, New Jersey and London, 1999 (exhibition catalogue).

FISKE 1908 Charles Henry Fiske, 'The Story of American Painting: VI. Modern Portrait Painting', *Chautauquan*, 50 (March 1908), pp. 56–88.

FOWLER 1894 Frank Fowler, 'An American in the Royal Academy, a Sketch of John S. Sargent', *Review of Reviews*, IX (June 1894), pp. 685–8.

FRY 1926 Roger Fry, 'J. S. Sargent as Seen at the Royal Academy Exhibition of His Works, 1926, and in the National Gallery', *Nation* (1926); repr. in *Transformations*, New York, 1956, pp. 169–82.

GAMBIER PARRY 1907 E. Gambier Parry, *Annals of an Eton House*, London, 1907.

GETSCHER AND MARKS 1986 Robert H. Getscher and Paul G. Marks, *James McNeill Whistler and John Singer Sargent: Two Annotated Bibliographies*, New York, 1986.

GIBBON 1960 Monk Gibbon, *Netta*, London, 1960.

GREER 1997 David Greer, *A Numerous and Fashionable Audience: The Story of Elsie Swinton*, London, 1997.

GROSSMAN 1894 Edwina Booth Grossman, *Edwin Booth: Recollections by His Daughter*, New York, 1894.

HAMILTON 1942 Ian Hamilton, *Jean. A Memoir*, London, 1942.

HARPER 1912 J. Henry Harper, *The House of Harper*, New York and London, 1912, pp. 466–7.

HART-DAVIS 1962 Rupert Hart-Davis, ed., *The Letters of Oscar Wilde*, London, 1962.

HARTRICK 1939 A. S. Hartrick, *A Painter's Pilgrimage through Fifty Years*, Cambridge, 1939.

HENDY 1974 Philip Hendy, *European and American Paintings in the Isabella Stewart Gardner Museum*, Boston, 1974.

HERDRICH AND WEINBERG 2000 Stephanie L. Herdrich and H. Barbara Weinberg, *American Drawings and Watercolors in the Metropolitan Museum of Art: John Singer Sargent*, with an essay by Marjorie Shelley, New York, 2000.

HILL 1956 William Thomson Hill, *Octavia Hill: Pioneer of the National Trust and Housing Reformer*, London, 1956.

HILLS *et al.* 1986 *John Singer Sargent*, essays by Linda Ayres, Annette Blaugrund, Albert Boime, William H. Gerdts, Patricia Hills, Stanley Olson and Gary A. Reynolds, New York, 1986 (exhibition catalogue).

HIRSHLER 2001 Erica E. Hirshler, *A Studio of Her Own: Women Artists in Boston 1870–1940*, Boston, 2001 (exhibition catalogue).

HORNE 1999 Philip Horne, ed., *Henry James: A Life in Letters*, London, 1999.

HORNER 1933 Frances Horner, *Time Remembered*, London, 1933.

IRWIN 1930 Grace Irwin, *Trail-Blazers of American Art*, New York, 1930.

ISHAM 1905 Samuel Isham, *The History of American Art*, New York, 1905.

JACOMB-HOOD 1925 G. P. Jacomb-Hood, 'John Sargent', *Cornhill Magazine*, 59 (September 1925), pp. 280–90.

JAMES 1887 Henry James, 'John S. Sargent', *Harper's New Monthly Magazine*, 75 (October 1887), pp. 683–91.

JAMES 1893 Henry James, *Picture and Text*, New York, 1893.

JAMES 1907 Henry James, *The American Scene* (1907), Bloomington, Indiana, and London, 1968.

JAMES 1920 Percy Lubbock, ed., *The Letters of Henry James*, vol. II, London, 1920.

JAMES 1947 F. O. Matthiessen and Kenneth B. Murdoch, *The Notebooks of Henry James*, New York, 1947.

JAMES 1956 Henry James, *The Painter's Eye: Notes and Essays on the Pictorial Arts*, London, 1956.

JAPAN 1989 Denys Sutton, ed., *Sargent*, essay by Denys Sutton, Japan, 1989, (exhibition catalogue).

LAGO 1982 Mary Lago, ed., *Burne-Jones Talking: His Conversations 1895–1898*, London, 1982.

LAYARD 1907–8 Arthur Layard, 'John Singer Sargent', *Die Kunst für Alle*, 23 (1907–8), pp. 25–33.

LEEDS 1979 James Lomax and Richard Ormond, *John Singer Sargent and the Edwardian Age*, Leeds Art Galleries and National Portrait Gallery, London, 1979 (exhibition catalogue).

LEWIS 1939 Cecil Lewis, ed., *Self-Portrait: Taken from the Letters & Journals of Charles Ricketts, R.A.*, London, 1939.

LEWIS HIND 1926 C. Lewis Hind, 'John Sargent', *Fortnightly Review*, CXIX (1926), pp. 403–12.

LONDON 1926 *Exhibition of Works by the Late John S. Sargent, R.A.*, London, 1926 (exhibition catalogue).

LONDON 1985 Christopher Newall, *Society Portraits 1850–1939*, London, 1985 (exhibition catalogue).

LONDON 1998 Elaine Kilmurray and Richard Ormond, eds, *Sargent*, essays by Richard Ormond and Mary Crawford Volk, contributions by Erica Hirshler, Theodore E. Stebbins Jr and Carol Troyen, London, 1998 (exhibition catalogue).

LONDON 2000 Robert Rosenblum, Maryanne Stevens and Ann Dumas, *1900: Art at the Crossroads*, New York, 2000 (exhibition catalogue).

LOVELL 1984 Margarette M. Lovell, *Venice: The American View 1860–1920*, San Francisco, the Fine Arts Museums, 1984 (exhibition catalogue).

LUCAS 1921 E.V. Lucas, *Edwin Austin Abbey, Royal Academician: The Record of His Life and Work*, 2 vols, London, 1921.

LUCY 1909 Henry W. Lucy, *Sixty Years in the Wilderness: Some Passages by the Way*, London, 1909.

LUCY 1920 Sir Henry Lucy, *The Diary of a Journalist*, London, 1920.

LUCY 1922 Sir Henry Lucy, *The Diary of a Journalist: Later Entries*, London, 1922.

LUTYENS 1985 Clayre Percy and Jane Ridley, eds, *The Letters of Edwin Lutyens to His Wife Lady Emily*, London, 1985.

MCKIBBIN 1956 A complete checklist of Sargent's portraits. See Boston, 1956.

MCLAREN et al. 1980 Andrew McLaren Young, Margaret F. MacDonald and Robin Spencer, with the assistance of Hamish Miles, *The Paintings of James McNeill Whistler*, New Haven and London, 1980.

MCSPADDEN 1907 Joseph Walker McSpadden, 'John Singer Sargent: The Painter of Portraits', in *Famous Painters of America*, New York, 1907.

MARTIN 1920 Edward Sanford Martin, *The Life of Joseph Hodges Choate*, 2 vols, London, 1920.

MATHEWS 1994 Nancy Mowll Mathews, *Mary Cassatt: A Life*, New York, 1994.

MAUCLAIR 1906–7 Camille Mauclair, 'John Sargent', *L'Art et les Artistes*, 4 (December 1906), pp. 368–79.

MECHLIN 1924 Leila Mechlin, 'The Sargent Exhibition: Grand Central Art Galleries, New York', *American Magazine of Art*, XV (April 1924), pp. 169–90.

MEYNELL 1903 Alice Christiana Meynell, *The Work of John S. Sargent, R.A.*, London and New York, 1903.

MEYNELL MANSON 1927 *The Work of John S. Sargent, R.A.*, intro. by J. B. Manson and A. C. Meynell, London and New York, 1927.

MILLER 1986 Lucia Miller, 'John Singer Sargent in the Diaries of Lucia Fairchild, 1890–1891', *Archives of American Art Journal*, 26, no. 4 (1987), pp. 2–16.

MINCHIN 1925 Hamilton Minchin, 'Some Early Recollections of Sargent', *Contemporary Review*, CXXVII (1925), pp. 735–43.

MONKSWELL 1944 E. Collier, ed., *A Victorian Diarist: Extracts from the Journals of Mary, Lady Monkswell, 1873–1895*, London, 1944.

MONTEIRO 1965 George Monteiro, *Henry James and John Hay: The Record of a Friendship*, Providence, Rhode Island, 1965.

MONTESQUIOU 1905 Comte Robert de Montesquiou, 'Le Pavé Rouge, Quelques Refléxions sur "l'Oeuvre" de M. Sargent', *Les Arts de la Vie*, 3 (June 1905), pp. 329–48.

MOORE 1929 Charles Moore, *The Life and Times of Charles Follen McKim*, Boston and New York, 1929.

MOORE 1988 Rayburn S. Moore, ed., *Selected Letters of Henry James to Edmund Gosse: A Literary Friendship*, Baton Rouge and London, Louisiana State University Press, 1988.

MORDAUNT CROOK 1999 J. Mordaunt Crook, *The Rise of the Nouveaux Riches*, London, 1999.

MORRIS 1930 H. S. Morris, *Confessions in Art*, New York, 1930.

MOUNT 1955 Charles Merrill Mount, *John Singer Sargent: A Biography*, New York, 1955.

MOUNT 1957 Charles Merrill Mount, *John Singer Sargent: A Biography*, London, 1957.

MOUNT 1963 Charles Merrill Mount, 'Carolus-Duran and the Development of Sargent', *Art Quarterly*, XXVI (Winter 1963), pp. 384–417.

MOUNT 1969 Charles Merrill Mount, *John Singer Sargent: A Biography*, New York, 1969 (Kraus reprint).

MUTHER 1896 Richard Muther, *The History of Modern Painting*, London, 1896.

NEWTON 1941 Lord Newton, *Retrospection*, London, 1941.

NEW YORK 1924 *Retrospective Exhibition of Important Works of John Singer Sargent*, New York, Grand Central Art Galleries, 1924 (exhibition catalogue).

NEW YORK 1926 *Memorial Exhibition of the Work of John Singer Sargent*, intro. Mariana Griswold Van Rensselaer, New York, Metropolitan Museum of Art, 1926 (exhibition catalogue).

NEW YORK 1980 *John Singer Sargent: His Own Work*, intro. by Warren Adelson, checklist by Meg Robertson, New York, 1980 (exhibition catalogue).

NEW YORK 1994 H. Barbara Weinberg, Doreen Bolger and David Park Curry, with the assistance of N. Mishoe Brennecke, *American Impressionism and Realism: The Painting of Modern Life, 1885–1915*, New York, Metropolitan Museum of Art, 1994 (exhibition catalogue).

NEW YORK 1999 Norman Kleeblatt, ed., *John Singer Sargent: Portraits of the Wertheimer Family*, essays by Kathleen Adler, Trevor Fairbrother, Alan Gurganus, Norman L. Kleeblatt and Michelle Lapine, New York 1999 (exhibition catalogue).

NOCHLIN AND GARB 1995 Kathleen Adler, 'Sargent's Portraits of the Wertheimer Family', in Linda Nochlin and Tamar Garb, eds, *The Jew in the Text: Modernity and the Construction of Identity*, London, 1995, pp. 83–96.

OLSON 1986 Stanley Olson, *John Singer Sargent: His Portrait*, London, 1986.

ORMOND 1970 Richard Ormond, *John Singer Sargent: Paintings, Drawings, Watercolours*, London, 1970.

PATMORE 1949 D. Patmore, *Coventry Patmore*, London, 1949.

PENNELL 1921 Elisabeth Robins Pennell and Joseph Pennell, eds, *The Whistler Journal*, Philadelphia, 1921.

PETHICA 1996 James Pethica, ed., *Lady Gregory's Diaries, 1892–1902*, New York, 1996.

PISANO AND WEBER 1993 Ronald G. Pisano and Bruce Weber, *Parodies of the American Masters: Rediscovering the Society of American Fakirs, 1891–1914*, New York, 1993 (exhibition catalogue).

PORTLAND 1937 The Duke of Portland, *Men, Women and Things: Memories of the Duke of Portland*, London, 1937.

POUSETTE-DART 1924 Nathaniel Pousette-Dart, *John Singer Sargent*, New York, 1924, with an introduction by Lee Woodward Zeigler.

PRESTON 1953 Kerrison Preston, ed., *Letters from Graham Robertson*, 1953.

PRETTEJOHN 1998 Elizabeth Prettejohn, *Interpreting Sargent*, London, 1998.

PROMEY 1999 Sally M. Promey, *Painting Religion in Public: John Singer Sargent's 'Triumph of Religion' at the Boston Public Library*, Princeton, 1999.

QUICK 1981 Michael Quick, *American Portraiture in the Grand Manner 1720–1920*, essays by William H. Gerdts, Michael Quick and Marvin Sadik, Los Angeles County Museum of Art, Los Angeles, 1981 (exhibition catalogue).

RA ILL. 1926 *Illustrations of the Sargent Exhibition Royal Academy 1926*, London, 1926.

RAITT 1992 Suzanne Raitt, 'The Singers of Sargent: Mabel Batten, Elsie Swinton, Ethel Smyth', *Women: A Cultural Review*, 3 (1992), pp. 23–9.

RATCLIFF 1982 Carter Ratcliff, *John Singer Sargent*, New York, 1982.

REYNOLDS 1986 gary A. Reynolds, 'Sargetn and the Grand Manner Portrait', *Magazine Antiques*, cxxx (Novmeber 1986), pp. 980–3.

RIDGE AND TOWNSEND 1998 Jacqueline Ridge and Joyce Townsend, 'John Singer Sargent's Later Portraits: The Artist's Technique and Materials', *Apollo*, CXLVIII (September 1998), pp. 23–30.

RIEDER 2000 William Rieder, *A Charmed Couple: The Art and Life of Walter and Matilda Gay*, New York, 2000.

ROBERTSON 1931 W. Graham Robertson, *Life Was Worth Living*, New York and London, 1931.

ROBINSON 1930 William A. Robinson, *Thomas B. Reed, Parliamentarian*, New York, 1930.

ROOF 1917 Katharine Metcalf Roof, *The Life and Art of William Merritt Chase*, New York, 1917.

ROPER 1973 Laura Wood Roper, *F.L.O: A Biography of Frederick Law Olmsted*, Baltimore, 1973.

ROSS 1911 Robert Ross, 'The Wertheimer Sargents', *Art Journal*, 73 (1911), pp. 1–10.

ROTH 1983 Leland M. Roth, *McKim, Mead & White Architects*, New York, 1983.

ROTHENSTEIN 1978 William Rothenstein, *Men and Memories: Recollections 1972–1938 of William Rothenstein*, abr. Mary Lago, London, 1978.

SAINT-GAUDENS 1913 Homer Saint-Gaudens, ed., *The Reminiscences of Augustus Saint-Gaudens*, New York, 1913.

SAINT-GAUDENS 1941 Homer Saint-Gaudens, *The American Artist and His Times*, New York, 1941.

SARGENT TRUST LIST [1927] *The Sargent Trust List of Pictures and Drawings* [London, 1927].

SHAND-TUCCI 1997 Douglass Shand-Tucci, *The Art of Scandal: The Life and Times of Isabella Stewart Gardner*, New York, 1997.

SIMON 1987 Robin Simon, *The Portrait in Britain and America*, with a biographical dictionary of portrait painters 1680–1914, Oxford, 1987.

SIMON 1996 Jacob Simon, *The Art of the Picture Frame: Artists, Patrons and the Framing of Portraits in Britain*, London, 1996 (exhibition catalogue).

SIMPSON 1998 Marc Simpson, 'Sargent, Velázquez, and the critics. "Velasquez come to life again"', *Apollo*, CXLVIII (September 1998), pp. 3–12.

SITWELL 1944 Osbert Sitwell, *Left Hand Right Hand!*, London, 1944.

SMAILES 1990 Helen Smailes, *The Concise Catalogue of the Scottish National Portrait Gallery*, Edinburgh 1990.

SMITH 1902 F. Hopkinson Smith, *Gondola Days*, Boston, 1902.

STARKWEATHER 1924 William Starkweather, 'The Art of John S. Sargent', *Mentor*, 12 (October 1924), pp. 3–29.

STOKES 1941 I. N. P. Stokes, *Random Recollections of a Happy Life*, New York, 1923; rev. ed., 1941.

STRICKLER 1982–3, Susan E. Strickler, 'John Singer Sargent and Worcester', *Worcester Art Museum Journal*, 6 (1982–3), pp. 19–39.

SUTTON 1964 Denys Sutton, 'A Bouquet for Sargent', *Apollo*, LXXIX (May 1964), pp. 395–400.

SWEET 1966 Frederick A. Sweet, *Miss Mary Cassatt: Impressionist from Pennsylvania*, Norman, Oklahoma, 1966.

SWETTENHAM 1942 Sir Frank Swettenham, *Footprints in Malaya*, London, 1942.

TATE GALLERY CATALOGUE 1964 *Tate Gallery Catalogues: The Modern British Paintings, Drawings and Sculpture*, 2 vols, London, Tate Gallery, 1964.

TATE 1992 Andrew Wilton, *The Swagger Portrait: Grand Manner Portraiture in Britain from Van Dyck to Augustus John 1630–1930*, London, 1992 (exhibition catalogue).

THWAITE 1984 Ann Thwaite, *Edmund Gosse: A Literary Landscape 1849–1928*, London, 1984.

TINTNER 1975 Adeline R. Tintner, 'Sargent in the Fiction of Henry James', *Apollo*, CII (August 1975), pp. 128–32.

TORCHIA 1998 Robert Wilson Torchia, *American Paintings of the Nineteenth Century: The Collections of the National Gallery of Art Systematic Catalogue*, New York and Oxford, 1998.

TROUBRIDGE 1961 Una, Lady Troubridge, *The Life and Death of Radclyffe Hall*, London, 1961.

TROYEN *et al.* 1997 Carol Troyen, Charlotte Emans Moore and Priscilla Kate Diamond, *American Paintings in the Museum of Fine Arts, Boston: An Illustrated Summary Catalogue*, intro. by Theodore E. Stebbins, Jr, Boston, 1997.

VAN DYKE 1903 John C. Van Dyke, 'Sargent the Portrait Painter', *Outlook*, 74 (2 May 1903), pp. 31–9.

VAN DYKE 1919 John C. Van Dyke, 'John S. Sargent', *American Painting and its Tradition*, New York, 1919, pp. 245–70.

VASSILTCHIKOV 1987 Marie Vassiltchikov, *Berlin Diaries, 1940–1945*, New York, 1987, p. 302.

VERNON LEE'S LETTERS 1937 *Vernon Lee's Letters*, preface by I. Cooper Willis, London, 1937, privately printed.

WALTON 1893–5 William Walton, *World's Columbian Exposition: The Art and Architecture*, Philadelphia, vol. 10, 1893–5.

WASHINGTON 1992 Mary Crawford Volk, *John Singer Sargent's 'El Jaleo'*, essay by Warren Adelson and Elizabeth Oustinoff, Washington, D.C., 1992 (exhibition catalogue).

WATERHOUSE 1967 Ellis Waterhouse, *The James A. De Rothschild Collection at Waddesdon Manor: Paintings*, Fribourg, Office du Livre, 1967.

WATSON 1924 Forbes Watson, 'John Singer Sargent', *Arts*, V (March 1924), pp. 145–50.

WEINBERG 1980 H. Barbara Weinberg, 'John Singer Sargent. Reputation Redivivus', *Arts Magazine*, 54 (March 1980), pp. 104–9.

WEIR YOUNG 1960 Dorothy Weir Young, *The Life & Letters of J. Alden Weir*, New Haven and London, 1960.

WILDENSTEIN III Daniel Wildenstein, *Claude Monet: Biographie et catalogue raisonné*, vol. III: 1887–98, Lausanne, 1979.

WOOD 1909 T. Martin Wood, *Sargent*, Masterpieces in Colour series, London, 1909.

YUNG 1981 K. K. Yung, *National Portrait Gallery: Complete Illustrated Catalogue 1856–1979*, London, 1981.

ZORZI 1998 Rosella Mamoli Zorzi, *Henry James: Letters from the Palazzo Barbaro*, London, 1998.

Dunham, Etta, 56; drawings of, figs 56, 57; portrait of, **no. 321**

Dunham, Grace, *see* Luling, Mrs Theodore

Dunham, Helen, xiii, 19, 66, 75; drawing of, fig. 48; portrait of, **no. 279**

Dunham. James, 56

Durand-Ruel, 41

Durlacher Brothers, 128

Duse, Eleonora, 56; portrait of, **no. 298**

Duveneck, Frank, 31

Eakins, Thomas, portrait of Louis Kenton, 137

Ebsworth, Mrs Henry, 112

Ehrich Brothers, 131

Elcho, Lady (Mary), *see Lady Elcho, Mrs Adeane and Mrs Tennant*, **no. 368**

Essex, The Countess of, 130

Evans, Jane, preliminary drawings of, figs 97–100, portrait of, **no. 365**

Eves, R.G., 118, 121, 136, 164–5

Fagan, Louis Alexander, portrait of, **no. 291**

Fairchild, Charles, xi, xii, xiii, 19, 41, 44, 45, 51, 55, 68

Fairchild, Mrs Charles, xi, xii, xiii, 19, 41, 42, 44, 45

Fairchild, Gordon, portrait of, **no. 260**

Fairchild, Lucia, xiii, diary, xii, 21, 41, 42, 45, 49, 50, 161

Fairchild, Sally, 21, 45, 50; *see Lady with a Blue Veil*, **no. 261**

Farquharson, Robert, 151

Faudel-Phillips, Lady, portrait of, **no. 362**

Fauré, Gabriel, 105, 106, 127

Ferrara, Rosina, 21

Fields, Mrs James Thomas, xii; portrait of, **no. 262**

Fildes, Sir Luke, 2

Flagg, James Montgomery, 124, fig. 122

Flaubert, Gustave, 16 n. 23; *Un Coeur Simple*, 25

Foinet, Paul, 76

Fortuny, Mariano, xvii n. 45, 46

Fowke, Sir George, 95

Fowke, Lady, 95

Fox, Thomas A., 93, 104

Franklin, Mrs Ernest, preliminary drawings of, figs 83–9, **no. 356**

Freer, Charles L., xviii n. 48

Frick, Henry, 6

Frith, W.P., 1; *The Derby Day*, 1

Fry, Roger, 133, 154

Furse, Charles Wellington, 2, 61, 116

Gage, Mabel, 24

Gainsborough, Thomas, 1, 2, 83 n. 12, 129, 142, 159

Gardner, Isabella Stewart, xi, xiii, xv, xvii n. 18, 21, 27, 45, 50, 54, 56, 58, 92, 106, 142, 154

Garrett, Mary Elizabeth, 164, 165

Gay, Walter, xxi, *Interior of Palazzo Barbaro, Venice*, 155

Gérôme, Jean-Louis, 34

Gibson, Charles Dana, 124

Giorgione, xiii

Giraudon, Auguste, 95

Giron, Charles, 71

Gladstone, William Ewart, 2, 69

Goelet, Beatrice, xi, xii; portrait of, **no. 239**

Goelet, Robert, 25

Goering, Hermann, 77

Goodrich, Caspar, xii

Gosse, Sir Edmund, 15 n. 1, 84

Goudstikker, Jacques, 76

Goya y Lucientes, Francisco, 12, 13, 16 n. 24; Sargent compared to, 81, 83 n. 6; Sargent copy after, 83 n. 6, *Don Manuel Osorio Manrique de Zuñiga*, fig. 32; *Portrait of Xavier Goya*, 81, 83 n. 7, fig. 52

Graham Robertson, see Robertson

Grainger, Percy, 105

Grand Central Art Galleries, New York, 163; exhibition of Sargent's work at (1924), 30, 37, 40, 53, 56, 92, 99, 130

Grant, Sir Francis, 1

Graves, [Henry?], portrait of Mrs Graham Robertson, 87

Gray, Ronald, 61

Greco, El, studies works by at the Prado, xv

Greene, Howard E., 131

Gregory, Lady, 85, 128

Grenfell, Joyce, 142

Grieve & Co., M., 128

Gunn, Peter, xi

Guthrie, Sir James, 2, 16 n. 30

Gwinn, Mary Mackle 'Mamie', 164

Hale, Mary, 44, 50

Hall, Radclyffe (Marguerite Radclyffe-Hall), 126, 127

Hals, Franz, 12, 68, 84, 129, 154

Hamilton, Colonel Ian, portraits of, **nos 352, 353**

Hamilton, Mrs (later Lady) Ian, 139; preliminary drawing of, fig. 62; portrait of, **no. 329**

Hammersley, Hugh, xiii, 64

Hammersley, Mrs Hugh, xiii, xiv; portraits of, **nos 284, 285**

Hammond, Gardiner Greene, Jr, portrait of, **no. 317**

Hammond family, 6

Hardy, Eleanor, *see* Platt, Eleanor

Harper, Henry, 17

Harrison, Lawrence, portrait of, **no. 374**

Harrison, Robert, 165

Harrison, Mrs Robert, xiii, 96

Hartrick, A.S., 24

Hassam, Childe, 46

Hay, John, xv, xviii n. 49, 63, 159

Helleu, Paul, xii, xv, 21, 61, 150

Hemenway, Augustus, 46

Hemenway, Mrs Augustus, portrait of, **no. 263**

Henner, Jean, 53

Henschel, Sir George (or Georg), xii, xiii, 75

Herkomer, Sir Hubert von, 2; *Kitchener of Khartoum, Field Marshal*, 2; *Miss Vlasto*, 125

Hewer, William Frederick, portraits of, **nos 299, 300**

Heyneman, Julie, 22, 63

Hichens, Robert, 81, 83 n. 5

Hill, Frances Winifred, portrait of, **no. 316**

Hill, Octavia, portrait of, **no. 366**

Hills, Mrs Ernest, portrait of, **no. 312**

Hind, Asher, 55

Hirsch, Mrs Leopold, 139

Holl, Frank, 2, 33; *Newgate – Committed for Trial*, 2; *Sir W.S. Gilbert*, fig. 26

Holmes-Spicer, Mrs Theodore, *see* Dunham, Helen,

Homer, Winslow, 46

Hoppner, John, 40

Horner, Cicely, portraits of, **nos 371, 372**

Horner, Sir John, xv

Horner, Katherine, *see* Asquith, Mrs Raymond

Horner, Lady (Frances Graham), xv

Hunt, Catharine Clinton Howland, 99, 101

Hunt, Richard Morris, 33, 170, portrait of, **no. 319**

Hunt, William Morris, 42, 99

Hunter, Mrs Charles, 139, watercolour and charcoal drawings of, 151; preliminary drawings of, figs 95, 96; portrait of, **no. 363**

Hunter, Mrs Colin, portrait of, **no. 330**

Huntington, Mrs Charles, portrait of, **no. 361**

Hutton, Lawrence, 17

Ingres, Jean-Auguste-Dominique, *Odalisque*, xiii, 38

An Interior in Venice, **no. 367**

Irving, Sir Henry, 11, 93

Jacomb-Hood, G.P., 93

James, Henry, 13, 46, 61, 69, 89, 93, 109; on Sargent's work: *La Carmencita*, 22; *Mrs Carl Meyer and her Children*, 82; *Daisy Leiter*, 142; *Mrs Ralph Curtis*, 143; *An Interior in Venice*, 154; *Lady Elcho, Mrs Adeane and Mrs Tennant*, 159

James, William, 45

Jean. M. Aman, 111

Jefferson, Joseph, xi, xii, portraits of, **nos 273, 274**

Jensen, Robert, 4

John, Augustus, 61

Johnson, Eastman, portrait of Daisy Leiter as a child, 143

Joseph, Flora, *see Mrs Asher Wertheimer*, **no. 348**

Keith, Dora Wheeler, Sargent works in her studio xi, 25, portrait of James Russell Lowell, 169

Keith, Master Skene, portrait of, **no. 282**

Khnopff, Fernand, 146

Kissam, Benjamin P., portrait of, **no. 244**

Kissam, Mrs Benjamin, xii

Knoedler & Co., M, 163

Kobbé, Gustav, 124

La Farge, John, 99

La Thangue, H.H., 97

Lambton, Mrs George, *see Cicely Horner*, **nos 371, 372**

Lane, Sir Hugh, 139

Lavery, Sir John, 2, 16 n. 30, 116

Lawrence, Sarah, *see* Brooks, Mrs Peter Chardon

Lawrence, Sir Thomas, 1, 40, 83 n. 12, 159

Lee, Eugene, 71

Lee, Vernon, xi, xiii, 56, 63, 75, 82, 119, 140, 146; comments on Sargent's work, xiv, 12; *Lady Agnew of Lochnaw*, 66; on the nervous quality of Sargent's style, 82, 83 n. 11

Leighton, Frederic, 1, 63; *Cimabue's Celebrated Madonna is Carried in Procession through the Streets of Florence*, 1; *May Sartoris*, 1, fig. 23

Leiter, Daisy, preliminary drawings of, figs 90, 91; portrait of, **no. 358**

Leiter, Joseph, 133 n. 1

Lely, Sir Peter, 2

Lenbach, Franz von, *Portrait of Peggy Guggenheim*, 15–16 n. 20; portrait of Eleonora Duse in character, 75

Leonardo da Vinci, xiii

Levy, John, 128, 163

Lewis, Sir George, acts for Sargent in a legal dispute, xiii; 59; portrait of, **no. 335**

Lewis, Mrs George, xiv, 130, 132; portrait of, **no. 280**

Lewis, Katherine, 59, 121

Leyland, F. R., xv

Liebermann, Max, 4

Lister, Charles, xvi

Lister, the Honourable Laura, portrait of, **no. 323**

Loch, C.S., 153

Lodge, Henry Cabot, xii, 19, 55; portrait of, **no. 264**

Loeffler, Charles Martin, xii, 128

Loring, Mrs Augustus Peabody, xii; portrait of, **no. 265**

Loring, Katharine, 48

Loring, Louisa, 21, 50; portrait of, **no. 266**

Loring family, 6

Lowell, James Russell, 169

Lucy, Henry, 165

Luling, Mrs Theodore, 31

Macbeth Gallery, 131

Macbeth, Robert, 131

McCagg, Louis, 24

MacColl, D.S., 16 n. 30, 58, 61, 137, 150, 159

McCulloch, Alexander, *see On his Holidays*

McCulloch, George, 82

McCurdy, Richard, xi; portrait of **no. 240**

Mackenzie, Sir Compton, 106

McKim, Charles Follen, xi, xiii, 25

McKim, Mead & White, xi, xiv, 25, 28, 170

MacMonnies, Frederick, xiv

Maddocks, John, 97

Madrazo y Garetta, Raimundo de, 92

Mancini, Antonio, 150, water-colour portrait of (with Ena Wertheimer), 140; portrait of, **no. 354**

Manet, Edouard, 12, 13, 15 n. 19, 16 n. 22, 161; *Woman with a Parrot*, 13, 16 n. 22, fig. 31, 25; *Lola de Valence*, 21

Manson, Thomas Lincoln, Jr, xi

Manson, Mrs Thomas Lincoln, Jr, xi, xii, portraits of **nos 241, 242**

In most cases the illustrations have been made from the photographs or transparencies provided by the owners or by the custodians of their works. Those for which further credit is due are:

Aberdeen Art Galleries & Museums, 364; Ali Elai, Camerarts, New York/Courtesy Adelson Galleries, Inc., New York, fig. 14; The Trustees of the Allendale Settled Estates, fig. 22; Photograph © 1994, The Art Institute of Chicago. All Rights Reserved; Artothek, Weilheim, Germany, fig. 53; Visitors of the Ashmolean Museum, Oxford, fig. 46; Courtesy Berry-Hill Galleries, New York, 258; Courtesy of the Biltmore Estate, Asheville, North Carolina, 247, 319, 320, 326; Courtesy Museum of Fine Arts, Boston, 318; Bridgeman Art Library, London, 324; Christopher Burke, Quesada Burke, NY/Courtesy Adelson Galleries, Inc., New York, 239, 245, 272, 273; Christopher Burke, Quesada Burke, NY/Courtesy Coe Kerr Gallery, New York, 236, 254, 263, 298, 315; A.C. Cooper/ Courtesy Royal Institute of British Architects, London, 350; © Denver Art Museum, 371; © English Heritage/Jonathan Bailey, 358; Courtesy of Faculty of Advocates, Edinburgh, 351; Courtesy Frick Collection, New York, fig. 51; Glasgow Museums. Art Gallery& Museum, Kelvingrove, 340, 378, 379, figs 24, 36; Courtesy Harvard University Art Museums, 323, figs 35, 43, 44, 59, 60, 61, 62, 63, 65, 66, 68, 72, 74, 75, 76, 78, 79, 81, 82, 83, 84, 85, 86, 87, 88, 89, 90, 91, 93, 95, 96, 97, 100, 102, 103; © President and Fellows of Harvard College, Harvard University/Katya Kallsen, 341; Courtesy Hirschl & Adler Galleries, New York, 325; Hirshhorn Museum and Sculpture Garden, Smithsonian Institution/Lee Stalsworth and John Tennant, 339; Hulton Getty Picture Library, London, fig. 70; Isabella Stewart Gardner Museum, Boston, 269, figs 39, 40, 41, 42; Jean-Claude Bloch, Paris, fig. 8; Joseph Painter/ Courtesy Bryn Mawr College, Pennsylvania, 373; Julius Lowy, Inc., New York/Courtesy Adelson Galleries Inc., New York, 232; The Honourable Society of Lincoln's Inn/Photograph Courtauld Institute of Art, London, 375; Los Angeles County Museum of Art, 250; Melville McLean/Portland Museum of Art, Maine, 274; Meredith Long & Co., Houston, Texas, 314; Metropolitan Museum of Art, New York, 278, 284, 308, 337, 343, 368, figs 31, 32, 50; National Galleries of Scotland, Edinburgh, 286, 312; Courtesy National Museums and Galleries of Wales, Cardiff, 297; Courtesy National Portrait Gallery, London, 296, 302, 333, 366, 377; National Portrait Gallery, Smithsonian Institution, Washington, D.C., 264; © Board of Trustees, National Gallery of Art, Washington, D.C., 249, figs 27, 28; The Newark Museum/Art Resource, New York, 360; New Britain Museum of American Art/E. Irving Blomstrann, 285; Courtesy Peninsular and Orientation Steam Company, London, 349; Peter A. Juley & Son Collection, Smithsonian American Art Museum, Washington, D.C., fig. 37; Philip Starling, 289; Pollitzer, Strong & Meyer/Courtesy Harvard Club of New York City, 380, 381; Prudence Cuming Associates, Ltd/Courtesy Adelson Galleries, Inc., New York 232, 270, 280, 299, 304, 305, 335, 344, 362, 369, 374, figs 5, 6, 9, 10, 11, 12, 13, 29; Pyms Gallery, London, 338; Réunion des Musées Nationaux, 234, 235; Royal Academy of Arts, London, 367; Mark Sexton/Courtesy the Peabody Essex Museum, Salem, 257, 259; Smithsonian American Art Museum, Washington, D.C., 287; Courtesy Sotheby's, New York, 260, 316, 334; Courtesy Spanierman Gallery, New York, 307, 355; Tate Gallery, London, 306, 329, 347, 352, 363; Thomas Powel Photography /Courtesy Adelson Galleries, Inc., New York, 237, 282, 330; Courtesy Vose Galleries, Boston, 268; Worcester Art Museum, 251, 252, 253; Yale University Art Gallery, 293, 294, 295, 300, fig. 38